Studies in the History of Linguistics

TRADITIONS AND PARADIGMS

Studies

IN THE

History of Linguistics

TRADITIONS AND PARADIGMS

Edited by Dell Hymes

P
61
.H9

Indiana University Press

BLOOMINGTON LONDON

Publication of this book was assisted by the American Council of
Learned Societies under a grant from the Andrew W. Mellon Foundation.

Published in Canada by
Fitzhenry & Whiteside Limited, Don Mills, Ontario
Library of Congress catalog card number: 72-88630
ISBN: 0-253-35559-1

Manufactured in the United States of America

CONTENTS

Introduction: Traditions and Paradigms   1
    Dell Hymes

I Contrastive Beginnings

1   Very Ancient Linguistics: Babylonian Grammatical Texts   41
    Thorkild Jacobsen

2   The Origin and Development of Linguistics in India   63
    J. F. Staal

II Traditions: The Nature of Language and of Grammar

3   Toward a History of Linguistics in the Middle Ages, 1100–1450   77
    G. L. Bursill-Hall

4   The Tradition of Condillac: The Problem of the Origin of Language   93
in the Eighteenth Century and the Debate in the Berlin Academy
before Herder
    Hans Aarsleff

5   The Dithyramb to the Verb in Eighteenth and Nineteenth   157
Century Linguistics
    Edward Stankiewicz

6   Vicissitudes of Paradigms   191
    Pieter A. Verburg

III First Paradigm (?): Comparison and Explanation of Change

7   The Indo-European Hypothesis in the Sixteenth and Seventeenth   233
Centuries
    George J. Metcalf

8   Some Eighteenth Century Antecedents of Nineteenth Century   258
Linguistics: The Discovery of Finno-Ugrian
    János Gulya

9   The Foundation of Comparative Linguistics: Revolution or Con-   277
tinuation?
    Paul Diderichsen

10 Rask's View of Linguistic Development and Phonetic Correspond- 307
ences
W. Keith Percival

11 Friedrich Diez's Debt to pre-1800 Linguistics 315
Yakov Malkiel

12 From Paleogrammarians to Neogrammarians 331
Paul Kiparsky

13 Fallacies in the History of Linguistics: Notes on the Appraisal 346
of the Nineteenth Century
Henry M. Hoenigswald

IV The Slow Growth of Grammatical Adequacy

14 Sixteenth and Seventeenth Century Grammars 361
John Howland Rowe

15 Humboldt's Description of the Javanese Verb 380
W. Keith Percival

16 On Bonaparte and the Neogrammarians as Field Workers 390
Eric P. Hamp

17 Phonemics in the Nineteenth Century, 1876–1900 434
Rulon Wells

18 The Boas Plan for the Study of American Indian Languages 454
George W. Stocking, Jr.

V Complementary Perspectives

19 The History of Science and the History of Linguistics 487
John C. Greene

20 Notes on the Sociology of Knowledge and Linguistics 502
Kurt H. Wolff and Barrie Thorne

21 Some Comments on History as a Moral Discipline: "Transcending 511
'Textbook' Chronicles and Apologetics"
George W. Stocking, Jr.

PREFACE

The very possiblility of such a book as this indicates the growth in activity and maturity of the study of the history of linguistics in the last decade or so. Not only have two general studies, more penetrating than any predecessors, appeared (Mounin 1967, Robins 1967), as well as two very useful anthologies (Arens 1955, 1969, Sebeok 1966), but also an increasing number of able scholars have been attracted to the subject. Received versions of the past have been reassessed, new topics taken up, and familiar themes freshly explored.

Linguists, considering the history of their subject, have been far less prone than members of other disciplines, perhaps, to define their history narrowly or to truncate it in time. Perhaps this reflects the impact at a critical formative stage of the discovery of Sanskrit, the recognition as a marvel (and still today as an inspiration) of a grammar more than two millennia old, and the continued relevance for several generations of training in classical Greek and Latin. Be that as it may, serious linguists, whatever their evaluation and emphasis, have tended to embrace as part of their history any analytic study or even reflection on the structure and nature of language.

This book reflects this openness, ranging as Roman Jakobson has observed over four millennia of linguistic research. The book reflects an attempt to open the context for such study as well, by introducing the perspectives of the history of science, the sociology of knowledge, and the history of anthropology and other social sciences, together with reflections on methodology motivated from within linguistics itself.

The actuality of this book has depended very much on the openness to the subject of the Wenner-Gren Foundation for Anthropological Research, and its Director of Research, Lita Osmundsen. The Foundation supported a conference on the history of anthropology, organized through the Social Science Research Council, in 1962, from which came the germ of the idea for subsequent conferences on the history of linguistics. In 1964 a symposium focused on the relevance to the history of linguistics of Thomas Kuhn's notions of paradigm and scientific relevance was held at the Foundation's summer headquarters, Burg Wartenstein bei Gloggnitz, Austria. In 1968 the

Foundation enabled the Newberry Library to hold a successor conference in Chicago. We are much indebted to the Newberry Library too, whose important linguistic holdings, particularly in its Louis-Lucien Bonaparte and Edward E. Ayer Collections, have given it an important role and interest in the study of the history of linguistics.

I should like to thank all the participants in the two conferences, and to thank particularly the contributors to this volume for their cooperation and patience.

The Newberry Conference was illuminated by the knowledge and zest for the subject of Roman Jakobson. It is a source of profound regret to all of us that it has not been possible to have the written contribution hoped for from him, as concluding essay. Let me thank Dr. Florence M. Voegelin and Dr. Regna Darnell for their help at the Burg Wartenstein and Newberry Library conferences, respectively; John Van Sickle and Henry Hoenigswald for help with the translation of some Greek and Latin passages; and Mrs. Susan Thomas Brown for help with the preparation of the manuscript.

Philadelphia, Pennsylvania   Dell Hymes

INTRODUCTION
Traditions and Paradigms

Dell Hymes

Linguistics is a discipline and a science, and its history is part of the general history of disciplines and sciences. Nevertheless, this book is written mostly by linguists and will be read mostly by linguists. Analogous situations seem to prevail in the historiography of the various human sciences. Efforts toward adequate history may borrow a notion and a term, such as 'paradigm', from general writings on the history of science, but writers on the general history of science do not much notice the efforts. This situation must change, but the basis for change must be laid principally by work to establish the relevant facts and to discern the intrinsic relationships in the particular field. We still have far to go to achieve the historiographic equivalents of what Chomsky once labeled 'observational' and 'descriptive' adequacy.

In this introduction I shall say something about the contributions its contents make to the achievement of such adequacy. The book is, I think, a timely one, that speaks very much to our present condition. In the course of the introduction I shall say something about our present condition and lines of work that are needed. In particular, I shall discuss the use and abuse of the notion of 'paradigm', when the topic of the history of general linguistics has been reached.[1]

Let me say something about each section of the book in turn, then, considering general questions as they arise. And let me stress that the sections *are* conceived as groups of papers, whose parts should be read in mutual relationship. So much may seem obvious. The papers do come in groups. Reviewers and readers, nevertheless, tend to take papers in isolation, evaluating them in relation to almost anything except their partners and the plan embracing them. Of course, that is their right, and I cannot pretend that the present papers are as integrated, say, as a sonata movement. That lack reflects, not on the abilities of the contributors, but the state of the art. Each section does have a point, and so does the order of the whole, as I shall try to bring out.

Contrastive Beginnings

We tend to take linguistics for granted, since its florescence since the Second World War. It is sobering and healthy to consider the possibility that it might not exist, even though it is one of the oldest intellectual activities to become codified and distinct. Were present linguistics to disappear, one would conjecture, surely practical needs and curiosity would bring it into being, as they did before. Such needs and curiosity, however, are not everywhere or always the same. Cultural values (explicit and latent), matrices of institutions, individual personalities and abilities, and the nature of materials at hand, all shape the needs that are felt and the directions that curiosity takes. (Cf. the delineation of factors in Malkiel 1964.) There is also the stage to which prior configurations of such factors will have brought matters; given a fresh start, without prior configuration as a determinant, the outcome might be quite different. It is a useful thought-experiment to imagine what the outcome might be.

In effect, the question of beginnings is always with us. As generations change, so do the 'beginnings' of linguistics in the contexts and motives (partly unconscious) of those who enter linguistics and renew it. And the complex history of linguistics, closely considered, resolves into an overlapping series of local scenes, specific 'structures of feeling' (Williams 1965: 64-66), approachable through biographies (as in Sebeok 1966—cf. Austerlitz 1972) and lesser writings, more than through isolated classics. There is a certain logic in the course of ideas, yes, but the pace and places of its working out, and whether a particular logic is worked out at all, is invisible in the 'great works'. Isolated works may suffice, if our interest in the past is only to praise or condemn. If our interest is to know what happened, we must enter into the contexts of personal and institutional origins. Our history must become a history, not only of great men, but also of circles, and not only of circles, but also of institutions, governments, rulers, wars and the ways in which these have shaped the renewed origins of linguistics in successive generations.

Folk Linguistics

Such a perspective gives reason to consider the nature and sources of reflection on language in all conditions of community. Scholarly studies have begun with the point at which reflection on language, and analysis of it, has left written trace. There is something to be gained, however, from inquiry into the conceptions of language held by societies without institutionalized linguistics. Comparative study of such information can shed light on the range of interests and motives for reflection on language. Given due caution, such study can suggest something of the earliest matrices of interest in language, out of which what we know as linguistics has grown. It can suggest something of the matrices of interest in language in which linguistics takes root (or fails to take root) in the world today. (For while linguistics aspires to be the science of language as a whole, in subject, it is the science of but part of the world, in participants. On this problem, see Hale 1972.)

The best difinition of the temporal scope of the history of linguistics thus is probably the widest. Following Hallowell (1960) in his depiction of anthropology as an emergent out of folk-anthropology, as having continuity with man's earliest efforts to obtain reliable knowledge about himself and his place in the universe, we can begin with 'folk linguistics'. (Cf. Hoenigswald 1966 for a valuable discussion of the scope of the topic.)

The motives most frequently cited for emergence of attention to linguistic features can be generalized as recognition of difference or discrepancy. What sort of difference is recognized may vary. Most often cited are differences between social varieties or levels of speech within a single community; between distinct communities; and between the current state of a language and retained knowledge of an earlier stage. (The types are not mutually exclusive, and may merge.) It is this last kind of recognition that figures in the historically known rise of linguistic study in the classical societies of India, China, Greece, and Rome, and that figures again in the positive interest of many American Indian communities today in the services of linguists. It seems likely, however, that in any community at any time, differential individual competence, including that between adults and children, as well as between neighbors, may have sufficed to give rise to some overt linguistic consciousness.

Sapir (1915) remains the fullest study of conscious exploitation of phonological features, followed by few others (cf. Frachtenberg 1917). Gudschinsky (1959) has reported a Soyaltepec Mazatec conception of phonemic tones as 'thick' vs. 'thin' and J. D. Sapir (1973) another use of the 'thick':'thin' contrast among the Diola of Senegal. Elmendorf and Suttles (1960) have put into social context what amounts to virtual recognition of the distinctive feature of nasality among the Halkomelem Sälish. Lowie (1935) has documented normative consciousness of linguistic features among the Crow, and Bloomfield devoted an article to his unexpected discovery of its pervasiveness among the Menominee (1927). Ferguson (1971) has brought to the fore the kind of implicit analysis involved in simplification for talk to those outside the normal adult community, foreigners and babies. Generally, elaboration of folk analysis of speech, as codified in vocabulary, appears to be in regard to speech styles and speech acts. Communities with little more than a general word for 'language, speech, word(s)', may have quite precise and interesting terminology for talking like X, Y, or Z or talk to accomplish A, B, or C. Gossen (1972, 1974) and Stross (1974) provide rich accounts of this from Mayan communities.

It remains true that we lack systematization and comparative study of such systems of terminology and conception as to speech. The concerns of the 'prehistory' of linguistics and of the ethnography of speaking here coincide, so that it can be hoped that the lack will be made good, given the surge of activity in the latter field.

Sometimes scholars have perpetuated notions of the discontinuity between 'primitive' and 'civilized' societies, on scientific grounds, by ignoring, and even denying, the presence of reflection on speech, among the non-Western communities in which they have worked. Such notions have been held to be the product of rationalization, probably of misguided school traditions, and a source of interference with one's task. Certainly notions about language cannot override or replace realistic analysis (as some linguists are today again discovering), but to ignore them is to miss one aspect of reality. Indeed, the very interaction of linguist with native speaker (another or himself) is subject to the influence of terminology, even if ad hoc terminology, and hence the validity of the resulting data, is very much subject to conceptions acquired from the linguist (whether fieldworker or self-consulting). One might think that the self-consciousness about sources of social knowledge so widespread today would rear its head in linguistics; but the only mention of the emergence of terminology in linguistic investigation that I know is reported from his Nootka work by Swadesh (1960).

When we investigate a language, another's or our own, we cannot avoid in some degree terms and notions already locally extant; if we ignore them, they may influence the outcome of our work nonetheless. Thus the interests of validity in linguistics, and the curiosities of ethnographers, folklorists, and historians, come into contact here. If demonstration is needed that notions about language show continuity from the earliest known societies to modern times, White's chapter on philology (1896) and Borst (1957-63) are excellent.

The origin and spread of writing systems plays a part here. Invention or adaptation of such systems is prima facie evidence of analysis of language on the part of the inventors or adaptors. Kroeber (1940) has called attention to cases of 'stimulus diffusion' in this regard, and indeed, our interest here is not satisfied by restriction to one or a few cases of wholly unmediated invention of writing from scratch (no pun intended). Evidence of analysis is given, as has just been said, in diffusion as well as in pristine invention. The role of knowledge of the alphabet as stimulus to Sequoyah's invention of a Cherokee syllabary is of much less interest than what Sequoyah did with Cherokee. Similarly with the question of possible stimuli to the Korean Hangul system. The present century offers rich opportunity for understanding writing systems as manifestations of pre- or para-disciplinary linguistic analysis, where literacy has not been imposed by fiat, but introduced to a language in collaboration with its users.

National Philologies

For the most part, it is true, writing systems involve a second stage of conscious attention to linguistic features, one that may be called the stage of *national philologies*. It is not that there is a necessary relationship between the two; at least it would be rash to take one for granted. The Greek tradition, insofar as it was a matter of rhetorical education, might have carried on with oral means; and the Indic tradition, centering around maintenance of sacred texts, was so carried on in the first instance, continuing to focus on oral memorization and recitation after writing was introduced into the society. Only in the cases of the Babylonian and Chinese traditions, and those much later in which a national philology is begun by foreigners, can one say that writing is intrinsic. The stage of national philology represents a focussing and cultivation of consciousness of language which might arise repeatedly, requiring, not special means (graphic), but only special interest.

The ancient Mesopotamian attempts at analysis of language, described here by THORKILD JACOBSEN, are earlier than any other known attempt, dating from about 1600 B.C. They are also very little known. (I am indebted to Roman Jakobson for bringing the possibility of including this work in the volume to my attention.) Professor Jacobsen brings out the nature of analysis in terms of paradigms in the first period known to us (Old Babylonian) and the analysis of elements in the later period (Neo-Babylonian). He concludes that efforts to consider and order in isolation elements which had no independent existence seem to have taken place.

The circumstances of the Babylonian work seem to have been similar to those of other classical civilizations: concern to preserve a literature embodied in a language becoming obsolete. In the Old Babylonian period, Sumerian (in which the major part of Ancient Mesopotamian literature was written) was rapidly dying out as a living language, being replaced by Akkadian. It would seem that consciousness of imminent loss is what counts, and that it does not matter whether the linguistic varieties involved are separate languages, or related dialects, or styles.

In India, as STAAL brings out, the primary aim was to preserve a Vedic heritage required for recitation in ritual. The earliest evidence of great activity, word for word recitation, may be from between the tenth and seventh centuries B.C., some centuries later than the origins of the Babylonian tradition (although the Babylonian manuscripts are from roughly the sixth and fifth centuries B.C.). Explicit analysis went much further, as is generally known, and as Staal succintly shows. It is in India, indeed, that one can earliest identify distinct authors and schools, in developments over time, and in controversies. In particular, although the tradition stemming from Pāṇini became central to linguistics in India, it is important to remember that it was not the beginning nor did it become the only tradition. The richness of the Indian history of linguistics goes further, in that its work was applied to other languages, in India (e.g., Tamil) and in other countries (e.g., Tibet). We have here an invaluable contrastive case for the comparative study of the relation between linguistic models and languages of structure different from those in connection with which they were developed. We have, too, an instructive contrast to the situation in the West, in which linguistics has often aspired to the prestige of mathematics or a natural science (with results of mixed value). In India it was linguistics that was considered the norm of a science, a status to which other traditional subjects aspired.

Most accounts of the history of linguistics begin, whether insightfully or patronizingly, with the Greeks and Romans (sometimes missing the significance of the Romans [Romeo and Tiberio 1971]). Conceptions of the history of linguistics so limited to the standard conception of the 'march of civilization', are prone to error. The essays by Jacobsen and Staal, together with the discussion of 'folk linguistics' in this introduction, hopefully may help to correct the situation. The history of linguistics, like linguistics itself, must aim for univerality of scope and explanation.

For the general study of the development of classical traditions of national philology, Kroeber (1944) has a chapter on philology which may serve as an introduction. The material for the several lines—Indian, Chinese, Japanese, Korean, Arabic, Greek, Roman, and others—is unfortunately difficult of access for any but the specialist in each. Dispassionate case studies, conceived so as to facilitate comparative study, are greatly to be desired. In some cases a particular scholar might be able to provide comparison (Japanese: Korean, Indo Aryan: Dravidian, etc.). Ultimately the roles played by type of linguistic study could be assessed.

In this last respect, our present recognition of linguistics as an independent discipline can do us a disservice. (Nor does calling it a branch of some other recent discipline, such as cognitive psychology, help.) The treatment of linguistic structure has been closely linked to other interests, such as logic, rhetoric, poetics, philosophy, theology—in short, with the uses of language recognized and valued by the societies in which lines of national philology have emerged, or to which they have spread. Some modern histories do treat together two such foci: Steinthal (1863) joins classical linguistics with logic, Sandys (1921) joins classical linguistics and literature). Mostly today we get treatment of one contemporary focus of interest—linguistics, logic, literary criticism, philosophy, rhetoric—by itself. We do not get treatment of the study of language, or the field of linguistics, as conceived and conducted in history itself. The separateness is understandable, and difficult to surmount, but it is unfortunate for our understanding of the development of the subject, cutting off essential aspects of generalization and explanation. (It is also unfortunate for the contribution that comprehensive historical studies could make to a general theory of the use of language. From one standpoint, the history of linguistics, if it seeks explanation, is an aspect of sociolinguistics.)

The traditions of national philology of course persist past the emergence of general linguistics, and the interactions between the two are of special interest. One such interaction is the emergence of new traditions of 'national philology', initially motivated by general linguistic concerns, as when the work recorded and published by an anthropologist or missionary comes to be the baseline for later activity in a traditionally nonliterate community. It is a distinctive trait of the period of general linguistics indeed, that many 'national' philologies are begun by strangers to the people and language studied (e.g., Eskimo philology by the Danes). This fact of provenience may reflect normative attitudes, as when vernacular Semitic languages and various creoles are written down and analyzed by foreigners who do not share the attitudes toward them of their own users. At this step one has elementary or anthropological philology (which can be roughly defined as the philology of peoples without indigenous philology of their own). At a later step an interplay between indigenous and exogenous traditions, concerned with the indigenous subject-matter, may arise. Noteworthy in this connection are Whitney's arguments as to the autonomy, equality, and in some respects superiority of Western studies of Indic philology, as against those conducted within the Indian setting (1872). Of course, those who work in the name of general linguistics may confuse themselves with the office, and ignore or distort indigenous testimony that is correct.[2]

General Linguistics

We think of the history of linguistics principally in terms of the third of the three stages, that of *general linguistics*. Particular philologies and lines of work are considered of interest insofar as they contribute to the development of this stage. Yet it is difficult to say when and where this stage begins. Generalizations about the nature of language and of grammar were made in ancient India and in classical Mediterranean antiquity. Given the continuity in the history of ideas in both Indian and European civilization, a general linguistics broad enough to include aspects of language beyond technical grammar can easily be traced, then, for some 2500 years.

A generation ago it would have been common sense to say that a general linguistics grounded in knowledge of but one or a few languages could not be truly 'general' in a scientific sense. The history of linguistics proper would have been felt to begin with the development of a methodology giving a new depth of insight into particular languages by means of comparison of many. In particular the kind of depth and of comparison associated with the separating out of language study as a discipline with academic chairs, the comparative-historical approach of the early nineteenth century, would have been seen as the start of linguistics proper. As will be seen with regard to section III of this book, that starting point seems now more an institutional than an intellectual 'breakthrough'.

We are familiar with the increase in interest in the history of linguistic ideas stimulated by Chomsky's notion of 'Cartesian linguistics' (Chomsky 1966). Chomsky brackets the hitherto celebrated history of true linguistics in the nineteenth and twentieth centuries, to find predecessors among grammarians and philosophers of the seventeenth and eighteenth centuries. Yet there is an element of contradiction in appeal for a starting point to the period of Descartes. To be sure, it fits well with the general history of the rise of natural and social science, which must be located in the period. That has long been recognized by historians of natural science, and is becoming widely recognized among students of the history of the social sciences. The nineteenth century is the century of the separating out of special disciplines, of great advances in institutionalization and in empirical scope and precision of method, but the seventeenth and eighteenth centuries saw the development of comprehensive frames of reference, initial institutionalization, and accomplishments of still some validity. But the appeal to 'Cartesian' precedent is strange in a science. Perhaps some physicists appeal to seventeenth century precedent as warrant and legitimation for their work, or out of a sense of honor to neglected merit, but one is inclined to doubt it. We have then the somewhat contradictory spectacle of an approach hailed and felt as a triumphant new 'paradigm' (cf. Koerner 1972), an approach which eclipses its immediate predecessor, as a paradigm should, but which is so far from having a sense of building upon cumulative efforts, as to seem to want to regret a century and a half, because of what is regarded as philosophical misdirection.

It is clear from Chomsky's own account, and even more so from the accounts of his critics, that the original 'Cartesian' linguistics does not represent a successful scientific paradigm; it represents rather a tradition of inquiry, a set of questions and problems, which were addressed for a time, and which are now addressed again. In effect, the clearest case we have of a linguistic 'paradigm' in the United States declares the history of general linguistics to be a history, not of paradigms and continuity, but of traditions and discontinuity.

I think that this view of the history of general linguistics is correct, and not only for the past, but also for the history that is accomplished in the present and the foreseeable future. Let me try to show some of the reasons why.

On Paradigms and Cynosures

It may appear anachronistic to assess a notion about the history of a science in terms of the recent and contemporary scene, especially when space cannot be taken to develop and support statements that are not neutral to current controversies. I can refer to other places where some basis for the view taken here is given (Hymes and Fought 1974; see also the historical treatments in Hymes 1970a, 1970b, 1971a, 1971b, 1972, 1973a). And I believe it is necessary to discuss the notion of 'paradigm' in this way, because its interest for linguists is partly a function of their sense of the contemporary scene, and because the notion has indeed entered into the contemporary scene as a factor in its development. Kuhn may have intended the notion of 'paradigm' to illuminate the past of science, but of course the notion also involves a conception of the nature of science, specifically, of the nature of scientific progress. This aspect of the notion has been taken up as something of a scenario of what future progress will be like. A good deal of controversial literature takes the form, not just of the adequacy or inadequacy of this or that finding or idea, but of contention for being the next stage in a process conceived as unilinear. All this has roots in the experience of linguistics itself, of course; the notion of 'paradigm' may be as much a convenient label as anything else. In any case, the joint result is unhealthy, I think, for genuine progress in linguistics, and I am sure that it is disastrous for progress with the history of linguistics. The lessons drawn from recent experience, and the interpretation given to the notion of 'paradigm' are both, I think, incomplete. To assess the two together may contribute something to current linguistics; it is indispensable, I think, for development of the history of linguistics.

The term 'paradigm' is deceptive. It answers to something real in the recent history of linguistics, but not to enough of reality. Many linguists have rightly sensed in the success of the Chomskyan approach something corresponding to Kuhn's concept of a paradigm, as a revolutionary, eclipsing, general view (cf. Thorne 1965, Grace 1969, Wells 1963, Voegelin and Voegelin 1963, and Lounsbury 1961). One can also see the dominance of a 'neo-Bloomfieldian' approach from late in the Second World War until the emergence of Chomsky's approach (as in important part a thoroughgoing reaction against it) as constituting a preceding 'paradigm' in the United States. One cannot readily identify a central 'paradigm' before then (and it is one of the grave defects of the discipline's current account of its own history that the 'neo-Bloomfieldian' approach is left to stand for all of American structuralism preceding Chomsky (on the fallacies involved in this, see Hymes and Fought 1974; on the Sapir tradition in this period, see Hymes 1971a).

These temporal facts indicate what is missing. The notion of 'paradigm' has been taken to refer to philosophies of science, to psychological assumptions, to analytic practices, but not to social realities. Yet it is no mere coincidence that the dominance of the 'neo-Bloomfieldian' approach came with the emergence of linguistics as a distinct academic profession, separate from philology, language departments, and anthropology departments, in the United States. The approach provided the ideology for a separatist movement. Numbers grew, departments and programs grew, focussed around the new concepts of structural units and relationships, and concomitant methodology; and the views that were furthest from those of the preceding period (and other contemporary disciplines) had the most appeal. The phenomenon is frequent enough in political life for us to recognize it in our own profession. The Chomskyan approach seized hold of linguistics coincident with a second surge in the profession. The preceding group had sought independence. The Chomskyan group inherited independence, and attracted numbers of new students, who entered linguistics as if it had begun with Chomsky, having in turn a novel conception of structural units and relationships, and methodology.

In their political aspect each approach in turn has dominated journals, professional meetings, textbooks, and the like. But neither has been exclusive holder of the stage. Each has had the center, but not the whole. Perhaps the same sort of thing is found in the history of the natural sciences—one cannot tell from Kuhn's account, which is largely silent on the articulation of paradigms to each other, within disciplines, and between disciplines. In the case of linguistics, at least, other approaches than the dominant ones continued, and indeed sometimes emerged, contemporaneously. One can say that each dominant approach was successively the *cynosure* of its discipline. One can say that its participants, and others around them, had a *consciousness* of a revolutionary change, and that there was indeed a *paradigmatic community*. The paradigmatic community, however, has never come to be equivalent to the whole of the discipline. Nor has this been due to holdovers from the past alone. Each new 'paradigm' simply has not succeeded in establishing complete authority. For example, the authority of the 'neo-Bloomfieldian' approach was never accepted by such major figures as Swadesh (cf. his 'mentalistic' critique of it [1948]) and Pike (1954 is a major source for his views). In important part they considered themselves to be continuing the valid structuralist tradition of Sapir; in part, their influence was limited because of political and religious commitments, respectively. In the time-honored manner of economically and politically successful approaches, members of the inner paradigmatic community could afford to mock them, rather than have to take them seriously. Similar conduct of course has been familiar within the succeeding Chomskyan approach, in regard, say, to the work on universals of Greenberg. But the lines of work represented by these and many others have not simply lingered on to die. They have had varying fortunes, but many have thrived or been revitalized. How can this be so, if paradigmatic succession is unilinear, in the image of an Einstein succeeding a Newton as law-giver?

Part of the answer is that each approach has not been a matter of scientific methods and findings alone, but also a complex of attitudes and outlooks. The congeries of attitudes and interests of each has been roughly in keeping with ingredients of the outlook of the youngest generation in the period in which each came to the fore. On this more specific scale, as on the broader scale of international changes over many generations, *climates of opinion* play a part. (Malkiel and Langdon 1969 discuss, for instance, the role of reaction against German culture in the acceptance of the Swiss-French linguist, de Saussure, after the First World War, as well as in the local popularity, for a time within Germany, of Vossler's idealism. Bloomfield's 'mechanism' and its appeal to young American linguists can hardly be understood apart from the skeptical climate between world wars). Particular *social origins* are a factor as well, although seldom considered by linguists engaged in their own history. It seems significant that the leaders of the 'neo-Bloomfieldian' approach after the Second World War had mainly entered the new profession of linguistics from backgrounds in European languages and literatures, and work in American dialectology, as against the anthropological and field work backgrounds of a number of established figures who did not accept their hegemony. There is in fact an irony here, in that the militant behaviorism of the 'neo-Bloomfieldians', along with their concentration on phonology, is often explained in terms of anthropological field work. The truth of course is that structuralists everywhere concentrated on phonology at the time—that is where the structural breakthrough had been dramatically accomplished, the new territory that traditional grammar had not conquered, and that leading fieldworkers such as Morris Swadesh and Kenneth Pike, men most notably concerned with practical field procedures, were vigorous opponents of behaviorism and algorithms.

In short, membership in the self-conscious paradigmatic community has entailed allegiance to a variety of ideas, only some of which have been essential to new insights and genuine problems. (In this volume, Kiparsky provides a fine example of this phenomenon with regard to the generation of the Junggrammatiker in the seventies of the nineteenth century.) One could rightly understand one's work as contributing to the advance of the subject without sharing the conscious ideology of, and membership in, the group commanding the center of the discipline. In this respect, linguistics in the United States clearly has not corresponded to the picture of a paradigm initially provided by Kuhn.

The complexity of the relationship between the community holding the center of the stage, and the discipline as a whole, goes further. Just in terms of scientific content, each has comprised a bundle of features, understood from the beginning by some to be not necessarily interdependent (cf. Wells 1963), of equal merit, or of equal relevance. In some cases, indeed, relevance could not readily be found. To illustrate: Chomsky has maintained that linguistics should be considered a branch of cognitive psychology. This view is accepted by many linguists. But how is, say, Romance Philology, to be understood as a branch of cognitive psychology? The world of the serious study of languages is in fact composed in large part of persons trained in, and responsive to, the traditions of work of particular languages and language families. To this extent work in linguistics inevitably reflects some of the diversity of national and cultural contexts, attitudes and interests, associated with the cultivation of these diverse subjects. A student of the Romance languages, a student of American Indian languages, a student of West African languages (in Francophone or Anglophone territory), a student of the creolization of languages, has each to come to terms with different contexts. Not least in these contexts may be the interests and aspirations of the speakers of the languages, which may place cognitive psychology, in the sense of generalizations about the human mind, below literature, say, or national development.

Such illustrations bring us to the nub of the matter. One response to such cases would be to say that they are external to linguistics; Romance philology, perhaps, is not part of linguistics at all. On this answer, the nature and history of linguistics clearly is not continuous and cumulative. (Hence, so we have noted, Chomsky's rediscovery of pre-nineteenth century philosophers and grammarians.) Might one conclude that linguistics has only properly existed in such times and places as current definition of its nature has flourished? That might suit a self-image of having appeared essentially *de novo*, and avoid questions of indebtedness to immediate predecessors and contemporaries outside one's paradigmatic pantheon. Some people indeed write histories, or paragraphs on history, that come to little more than hailing moments of 'true' linguistics, and speculating as to causes of the mysterious prevalence of 'false' linguistics at other times. One would think, however, that Kuhn's monograph would have warned adherents of the notion of 'paradigm' against such travesty. Carried out in a thoroughgoing way, indeed, it would lead to the necessity of devising a different name for the study of language in excluded times and places (a hand stamp, to imprint 'Not Linguistics' on offending materials, might be useful). One would have to pose as perhaps the crucial question of the history of the subject, why did (true) linguistics *disappear* during, say, the nineteenth century? Was the Humboldtian tradition from Wilhelm himself, through Boas, Sapir and Bloomfield (cf. Bloomfield 1914, ch. 10) responsible? How was it possible to reinvent linguistics so quickly in the 1950's, when it had not existed for so long?

More seriously, there is an obvious generalization, when the human sciences are considered as a whole, namely, that the intellectual periods we loosely designate as the 'Eighteenth', 'Nineteenth', and 'Twentieth' centuries have had characteristically different dominant orientations, and that these have been shared by linguistics among other disciplines. The generalization only states an obvious fact, it does not explain it. The generalization does avoid an absurdity, and narrow our choices essentially to two. The first is to think of different interests and orientations as competing to be 'linguistics', with one succeeding in displacing another at intervals. Such a choice is implicit in most histories of linguistics, which, like most histories of other disciplines, adopt a quasi-Hegelian perspective, telling a chronological story that moves from place to place, with the 'Spirit' of progress. (Such a choice may also agree with the outlook of those who reserve phrases such as 'linguistic theory' for their own work.) The result, however, is to make of the history of linguistics something very much like a game of 'King of the Mountain'. And, like the absurdity suggested above, it leaves much out of account, and much unintelligible; continuities and causes are hard to come by, and most of the development of linguistics is in shadow or off-stage most of the time.

The second choice is to think of different interests and orientations, different lines of work, as all part of linguistics, although competing for attention and such limelight as is available. From the standpoint of past history and present humility, this is the better conception. It makes possible a general study of the history of the study of language.

Our subject, then, is a general *field* of the study of language, of *field of linguistics* (cf. Hymes 1968). The very importance of language to human life, which linguists often note, implicates language in facets of human life that engage the attention of many disciplines and perspectives. At a given time, in a given place, the range of interests in language is variously institutionalized, variously distributed among disciplines, and flourishes differentially. Within the general field, the cynosure, or paradigmatic community, at any one time is just one of the communities and kinds of interest in language that serious scholars pursue. (For an instructive case study, see Malkiel 1964, and cf.

Malkiel and Langdon 1969; cf. also Hymes 1963 and 1970a for another case.) Many, but not all, of these interests are pursued within the professional, academic discipline. Their diversity has not yielded to any synoptic perspective, and, short of a millenium for the human sciences as a whole, is not likely to.

All this is not to dismiss or ignore the relevance of the notion of 'paradigm', as sketched by Kuhn. Despite the controversy over the notion, it is clear that it has caught essential features of the history of scientific and scholarly disciplines. Yet with linguistics, there is this irony. Kuhn intended his notion to counteract the bias of practicing scientists, in favor of a picture of their discipline's history as one of continuous, cumulative progress; the bias failed to capture the genuine discontinuities of meaning and purpose, by assuming that earlier work was to be assessed as answers to one's own questions (one's own questions being taken to be the only and permanent questions—cf. Collingwood 1939). The success of Kuhn's notion among a younger generation has encouraged a bias of practicing linguists toward their own history of a complementary kind, in favor of a picture of their discipline's history as one of great gaps and discontinuities, and, so far as the history informs the present and future, toward an image of 'permanent revolution'. But whereas Kuhn would have thought that recognition of discontinuity would carry with it recognition of the need to interpret other periods of linguistics in their own terms, the assumption has persisted that earlier work is to be judged in terms of one's own questions; periods perceived as discontinuous and different from one's own are ignored or left to the mercy of stereotypes. Instead of the whole of the history of the discipline seen as a progress toward the present (the so-called 'Whig' interpretation of history), we have selected moments of the history of the discipline, seen as types of a scholarly Old Testament anticipating the salvation in the New. This gives us the same kind of bias, and less history.

There is a great virtue in Chomsky's appeal to 'Cartesian' linguistics; it shows that the understanding of past efforts, not at first thought pertinent, can have interest for our own work. If this promise of a dual benefit, to both history and present science, is to be realized, however, what has been made of the notion of 'paradigm' must be analyzed critically. The conception of a field of linguistics, advanced above, suggests two themes of special importance. One has to do with recognition of the continuities that occur across changes of paradigm and paradigmatic community, and that need to occur; the other has to do with sources of change in paradigm that come from outside linguistics itself, stemming from its social contexts. In both respects we must criticize ways in which the notion of 'paradigm', as an implicit theory of the nature of science and scientific progress, may be used as a scenario.

'Paradigm' as Scenario

Certainly there is something to a conception of the history of linguistics as exhibiting a succession of paradigmatic triumphs. Since the academic institutionalization of linguistic study early in the nineteenth century in Prussia, successive groups of scholars have been able, with some justice, to identify advance in the field as a whole with their own activity. To a fair extent, there has been consistency across countries and periods. The comparative linguistics that first took root, as a cumulative discipline, in Germany, became the standard-bearer for study of all the world's languages in whatever country during the course of the nineteenth century. The structuralism that took root in Europe outside Germany, after the First World War, became the standard bearer for our own century.

The difference from a view of paradigms as successively replacing each other lies in this: comparative linguistics has continued to develop. If the qualitative study of grammatical structures should be succeeded as cynosure by a quantitative paradigm, concerned with variation and use, still structural linguistics will continue to develop. What changes from one to the other is not so much explanation of the same phenomena, but the phenomena one wants most to explain. One does not supersede the other, but shunts it from the center of the stage.

It is true that comparative-historical linguistics has benefitted from developments in structural linguistics, and has changed in consequence, since the early integration of the two in the work of Bloomfield in the United States, and Jakobson and Trubetzkoy in Europe. Yet the benefits and integration are not the whole story, and the influence is neither in only one direction or unequivocal. The autonomy of comparative-historical linguistics is in fact essential as a check against rash and unfounded claims, inspired by a new paradigmatic community (cf. Maher 1973); and if approaches in terms of variability and 'dynamic synchrony' (Jakobson's term) come to the fore, comparative-historical linguistics will have more than a dependent relation to synchronic interpretation of dialects, creoles, and languages generally.

The same sort of thing holds true with regard to the successive foci of structural linguistics itself. The early structuralist approach in the United States tended to focus on phonology as an autonomous subject, neglecting non-phonemic phonetic phenomena on one side, and grammar on the other, in its enthusiasm for the discovery of the phonological sphere itself. In the first flush of enthusiasm for syntax as a deep and central sphere, the initial Chomskyan paradigm denied the relative autonomy of phonological study, on the one side, and of semantic study, on the other. Now the second generation generative approach, 'generative semantics', has denied the relative autonomy of syntactic studies, on the one side, while seeking to preserve intuition and logic as sufficient bases for dealing with social context, on the other. The enthusiasms have been right in affirming a new sphere of relationships and (in some respects) its autonomy from others, or the dependence of others on it. The enthusiasms have been wrong in dissolving or denying the integrity of the other levels. A variety of structural, historical, and social factors combine to require recognition of the relative autonomy of each, and consequently, the possibility of some continuing independent study of each. (There is evidence of the truth of this analysis in the way in which previous approaches, and lines of inquiry within phonology, morphology, lexicography, and the uses of language, are coming to be reconsidered and revalued by some participants in the Chomskyan paradigm.)

Kuhn takes for granted that a new paradigm, a new outlook, is not just different from a preceding one, but successful because superior; in particular, the new paradigm explains new things that the old could not, but it continues to be able to explain what the old one could as well. Within linguistics, the successive 'paradigms', or cynosures, have not fully had both properties, which account, of course, for much of their failure to command complete authority within the field.[3] This gap between true 'paradigmatic' status and the lesser authority of a 'cynosure' may, indeed, help explain the polemical overkill that has characterized a new group's treatment of the predecessors and competitors. (The neo-Bloomfieldian reaction to traditional grammar, and the Chomskyan reaction to preceding structuralism, are cases in point.) It may be that, one's scientific base not being sufficient for complete hegemony, rhetoric and ideology have had to be called upon to fill the gap.

In any case, both on the broad scale of the 'neo-Bloomfieldian' and 'Chomskyan' approaches, and the scale of successive foci within the analysis of language, from phonology to conversation, we seem to be dealing with something more complex than scientific advance. The tendency for each successive focus of interest to present itself as a fundamental change, eclipsing and antiquating others, suggests that Kuhn's notion of paradigm, when diffused into linguistics, has suffered the fate of many an idea that crosses boundaries. It has lent itself to reinterpretation in terms of the successive, scientific-*cum*-ideological successes of the 'neo-Bloomfieldian' and Chomskyan groups, and, more recently, to individual role-modelling in terms of the image provided by the dramatic conjuncture of Noam Chomsky's brilliance, personality, training, and (later) moral-political stature; the arrival of structural linguistics in the United States at the frontier of formal models of syntax that would go beyond descriptive classification; and the influx of a new generation into a disciplinary scene, temporarily dominated by established scholars of middle years. The attractiveness of Kuhn's notion undoubtedly is due to the fact, as noted, that it summarizes, and dignifies, a genuine sense of the recent past. The difficulty is that it seems to come to summarize and dignify also an aspiration, that of a scientific triumph that will constitute the new 'paradigm', with oneself perhaps as Chomsky II (or III or IV). And where Kuhn intends his notion to designate unequivocal scientific revolution, there is reason to think that in linguistics now 'revolution' becomes confused with another phenomenon, that of being 'center of attention' (what is here dubbed cynosure).

The implicit scenario for succeeding as cynosure seems often enough to consist as much of discrediting, and forgetting or ignoring, other work, as of making new discoveries and of integrating what has already been discovered on a new foundation. The temptation to join, or create, a contender for 'King of the Mountain' and disciplinary cynosure seems almost irresistible, once the possibility of success in this regard is scented. In both the clear-cut cases, the only cases experienced by most linguists, the neo-Bloomfieldian and the Chomskyan, there has been a heady atmosphere at the center of building everything new. Linguistics in the United States, in short, seems to have developed its own 'tradition of the new', and to have taken on, perhaps not surprisingly, cultural characteristics shared with urban developers and the Army Corps of Engineers, (contrast the last sentence of Sapir 1924 [in Mandelbaum 1949: 159]).

There is satisfaction and, indeed, gaiety, in this. As Yeats put it, "All things fall and are built again/And those that build them again are gay" (in his poem, 'Lapis Lazuli'). The trouble is that not all things had in fact fallen, requiring to be rebuilt. One needs to bear in mind a point that Kuhn himself has now accepted, namely, that the phenomena of paradigms and paradigmatic succession can be found outside the sciences. We tend to think of paradigms in terms of intellectual innovation winning its way by merit, but what is fundamental to the whole thing, I think, is the existence of the paradigmatic community. Kuhn himself has nothing to say about the criteria by which the scientific status of the successive paradigmatic innovations is guaranteed. It would seem entirely sufficient, to produce the phenomena he describes, to have a community, guided in problem-solving by a dominant model, and sharing over any particular period of time some common commitment to the purposes of both. Given these ingredients, one might find an unending series of successive 'paradigms', as one takes up the anomalies of another, without any continuity of progress to be observed across the whole. To a skeptic or atheist, the history of theology may appear to be of this sort; to many a natural scientist, the humanistic disciplines may seem to afford many examples. I am afraid that current linguistics will provide a few, although I think that there is the possibility of cumulative advance in the fields indicated, and am far from denying the genuine advances in parts of current linguistics.

The problem is this: some of the sense of advance in current linguistics is due to true discovery. Some is due to rediscovery. The sense of progress and building anew is made possible partly by the opening up of new perspectives, but also partly by ignorance and incomplete training, on the one hand, and by the pursuit of artifactual phenomena, *ignes fatui*, on the other. It has become possible for a leading scholar, fully sympathetic to the mode of formal linguistics now dominant, to distinguish between work which contributes to knowledge of a particular model, and work which contributes to knowledge of language. (He finds relatively little of the latter.) Such a situation is due in part to the diffusion of the culture of mathematics and logic, in which precociousness with abstract relationships is naturally highly valued, as well as to the fact that Chomsky's personal goals for the use of linguistic findings place a premium upon pin-pointing universal underlying formal properties. There is a permanent role for formal ability of this kind in linguistics, a role established by the work of Harris, Greenberg, Hockett, Hiz, Chomsky and others, but a limited one. Many of the problems of linguistics do not yield to such an attack, and cannot wait upon or much use the results of such an approach. (See Hymes 1973c for fuller discussion.) Fortunately or unfortunately, depending on one's view, the problems of linguistics require a diversity of kinds of talent, and many of them always will require skill in the acquisition and interpretation of elementary data, on the one hand, and upon cumulative knowledge and experience, on the other. In this respect, much of linguistics is inescapably akin to the humanities, in which major work often must come later, rather than earlier, in a career. More generally, much of the difficulty is due to a tendency of longer standing, which may be called 'simpling'. Like sampling, 'simpling' is a technique for reducing the complexity of reality to manageable size. Unlike sampling, 'simpling' does not keep in view the relation between its own scope and the scope of the reality with which it deals, but denies the difference (as 'not linguistics', perhaps). It then secures a sense of progress by progressively readmitting what it has first denied. 'Simpling' is as much a professional fact as a scientific one, and is unfortunately easily confused with genuine simplification by valid generalization.

The prestige of the notion of 'paradigm', then, may well have a disabling effect on the discipline. We would do well to ponder instead the 'darker' side of the notion. For Kuhn (1962) can be read as describing scientists as sacrificed victims. For the sake of the ultimate progress of science, they commit themselves to a kind of 'tunnel vision'. The implications of a certain paradigm can thus be worked out completely, to the inevitable point at which it breaks down, and a more adequate one is propounded successfully, usually by someone outside their own group.

Possibly the authoritarian, even totalitarian, character of the notion of paradigm, as presented by Kuhn, is a good description of what the progress of particular lines of science has been like. If so, it remains unclear as to how the notion relates to the mutual articulation of the various branches of any science as a whole. At what level is a drastic change a paradigmatic change? And may it not be possible that the kind of rigid control described by Kuhn reflects a particular phase of the history of science, and is not inevitable? To be sure, any closely knit community is likely to develop its own view of itself and its relation to the rest of the world; it is likely to have its own internal discipline and values. But the rigid control described by Kuhn for science suggests something of the characteristics of the upwardly mobile, especially the petit bourgeois, in many societies. One's claim to respectable status being suspect, or not universally granted, one's insistence on rectitude is all the more intense. Such motives have had much to do with the doctrines of correctness in language over the generations. Perhaps they have had something to do with the self-consciousness of scientists. Perhaps, then, Kuhn's account of 'paradigm' can lead us, not to emulate it as a badge of status, but to transcend it. Perhaps it can lead us to recognize the ingredients of paradigm in any cohering community of scholars, and also to recognize the multiplicity of such communities within our discipline, conceived as the field of linguistics as a whole. We could then accept that different of these communities answer to the interests and needs of different extra-disciplinary communities, different aspects of the role of language in human life. In our media-mediated world it would no doubt be impossible to escape entirely the pressure to have some one community touted as 'the' community. Linguistics no doubt will continue to appear in the pages of *Time* Magazine and the *New York Times*. But we can lend ourselves to the need of the media for stereotyped struggles and victors as little as possible. In sum, critical reflection on the concept of 'paradigm' may lead us to transcend the 'paradigmatic' phase, and enter into a phase that is pluralistic in ideal and in practice—even, to borrow an analogy from Chomsky's political interests, anarchistic.

Such a perspective is at least clearly required for the understanding of the past development of linguistics. It is to repeat, not adequately understood as a succession of *paradigms*. Rather, it has had a history of the rise, and variegated development, of a plurality of *traditions*. These traditions of inquiry, sets of problems, have each their own record of continuity in and of themselves. In relation to the center of the intellectual or disciplinary stage, to the succession of cynosures, as it were, the record is one of discontinuity. So much, as we have seen, is implicit in Chomsky's recourse to 'Cartesian' linguistics. And so much is evident in the differential sense of relevance of different current vantage points. The twentieth century development of glottochronology, for example, motivates analysis of hitherto neglected nineteenth century developments (Hymes 1974). A particular professional affiliation and subject matter created a particular vantage point on the history of the study of language as a whole (cf. Hymes 1963 for one such; part of this introduction draws on that essay). New linguistic interest in discourse, rhetoric, and poetics may bring their past histories within the felt scope of the relevant past.

All this leads to the conclusion that the self-consciousness of the members of a paradigmatic community—the aspect of historical change to which Kuhn's notion essentially appeals—is a treacherous guide. It is an element, but only one element, in a situation. Its sources may not be solely scientific, intra-disciplinary, but may be extra-disciplinary as well (a prospective instance is noted below), and its understanding of what it is doing, and why, may be very partial, even quite msitaken (cf. Hoenigswald in this volume). The actual history of advance, and more generally, of change, in linguistics in the present period, as in past periods, appears a far more tangled matter than can be sorted out at first glance.

Cynosures and Contexts

To delimit the subjective element is not to eliminate it. For one thing, it is an essential part of the history itself, and, for another, an essential part of motivation to write the history. The effective scope, and the internal organization, of what is taken to be the history of linguistics, will change, as contemporary interests and cynosures change. One can simply accept the rewriting of history with each change in cynosure, since it no doubt will always occur. More responsibly, one could insist that histories, although inescapably subjective in part, be also consistent with the data and each other. In this, at least, lies the irreducible difference between the art of the novelist and the scholarship of the historian. The former is free to express insight through imagining the detail, motive, or relationship that should have been true, and to accept different logics of situation in different books. In histories of linguistics it should be possible to recognize a common subject matter by more than the recurrence of certain key characters. It would be rash to say that this is possible today.

The two requirements would seem to be, first, cultivation of basic scholarship, so that eliminable conjectures and misrepresentations are indeed eliminated; and second, a comprehensive conception of the scope of what is to be written about. Research such as that represented in this book, the first of its kind, so far as I know, is prerequisite, as is the development of basic sources of information (such as the *Biographical Dictionary of Linguists*, now under way under the general editorship of T. A. Sebeok and others), stock-takings of current knowledge (as in the volume on the history of linguistics, vol. 13, of *Current Trends in Linguistics*), and the provision of forums for sustained discussion of research (such as the new journal,

Historiographia Linguistica, being launched under the editorship of E. F. K. Koerner). The second requirement would seem to be to find vantage points for the conception, and writing, of history that are more adequate than the Hegelian highlighting of disconnected great books and moments that the usual history resolves itself into, and that the 'paradigm' notion has been made to lend itself to. The history of linguistics in relation to any one *continuing* community of scholars, or social community, such as a nation or region, clearly would not show an unrelieved chain of successes and advances. By comprising ups and downs, and shifts within a sociologically continuous group, such a history would make possible an actual account of causes of change. In short, to use current terms, a 'sociolinguistic' approach to the history of linguistics is necessary, if it is to approach 'explanatory adequacy'. Such an approach might be dubbed the study of 'cynosures and contexts', insofar as it takes its starting point from the former.

In the writing of such history one would seek to discover the range of interests in language of a given place and time; to place both central and peripheral traditions, or competing central traditions, in relation to each other; and to interpret the pattern, or organization, of diversity thus found. Clearly merit alone will not explain the centrality of a tradition, and concentration of personal merit in the tradition may be a response to its centrality as much as a cause of it. In treating a cynosure, or central 'paradigm', over time, one will attend not only to the fascination of its introduction and the salient facts of its development, but also to the recognition and embracing of it by one or more groups, which see in its application an opportunity for the protection or advancement of its own interests. One will see not only the benefits, but also the costs, of the innovation, and attend to the specific problems which exploitation of the development of the paradigm may create, together with the responses thereto. And one will attend to the justifications which participants in the paradigmatic community offer for their roles, and which others offer for their relationships to the paradigm; what, from another or later point of view, may appear as rationalizations. In sum, one will deal with the occurrence of a paradigm, or cynosure, as more than an intellectual accomplishment; one will deal with it as a process of sociocultural change.[4]

Attention to community contexts is likely to be necessary if one is to understand the factors shaping the present and future history of linguistics. Within linguistics in the United States, the almost exclusive study of their own language, English, by so large a proportion of the world's linguists, has seemed to the participants a source of deepened insight into the underlying structure of all languages. Leaving aside the methodological difficulties that have become increasingly apparent, we must consider that to many other communities, including those of American Indians, such a concentration may seem an expression of ethnocentrism at best, a hostile turning of the back at worst. Proclamation of universals without need to engage the languages of the peoples of the world may strike some as reactionary. In any case, many participants in formal linguistics are liberal or radical in social views, and yet their methodological commitments prevent them from dealing with the verbal part of the problems of the communities of concern to them. This extra-disciplinary source of tension is increasingly felt in linguistics (cf. Hymes 1973b). If it has significant effect, the resultant changes will not be due to appearance of a more successful explanation of anomalies within the currently dominant approach. The changes will be due to changes in self-consciousness and motivation, having to do with reconciliation of scholarly and personal concerns. One will have seen the working of a factor that has played a part in past periods of the history of linguistics as well; I have cited this current instance to highlight its perennial presence.

Within the study of cynosures in contexts, as part of a recognizable common subject matter, the subjective element will remain. The issue will not be between what was said and thought, and what was done and accomplished; or between different definitions of perimeter; but between different weightings given to phenomena recognized by all. This kind of difference is inescapable, since history obviously does not come in 'natural', 'objectively given' periods and patterns. There are many lines of work and interest connecting generations, and mixtures of novelty and continuity in each. Depending on differences in experience and empathy, capable scholars may differ in the weightings of importance, of continuities and innovations, to which they come. And often they will find themselves in competition for the use of standard terms, whose general acceptance makes them assets, and hence counters. (This phenomenon has been nicely analyzed by Levich 1962, with regard to controversy over the definition of the notion of 'Renaissance'.) With the advent of transformational generative grammar, 'structural' linguistics came to signify an eclipsed predecessor for many younger linguists. Commonly it was characterized in terms of the 'neo-Bloomfieldian' outlook, or, more adequately, in terms of an approach limited to 'taxonomy' and 'surface structure'. There was of course already a complication in defining as 'structural' an approach considered not to deal with the most important part of structure, and denying the term to the approach which did. Recently the rise of challenges to Chomsky's conception of structure has led some to give greater weight to his continuities with preceding 'structuralists', and less to his differences from them. Viewed from the standpoint of work which gives up the notion of a general system to a language, or which regards variation, time, and diversity of function as the bases for an account of the linguistic means of a community, Chomsky may appear as the great defender of twentieth century structuralist principle (see further discussion in Hymes and Fought 1974).

Such issues repeatedly arise, notably recently in discussion of Chomsky's attempt to characterize a 'Cartesian' type of linguistic thought. One man's relevant resemblances will be trivial to another, and the second's crucial difference trivial to the first. (Cf. discussion as to whether or not Du Marsais was a 'Cartesian'.) For Chomsky the important thing about William von Humboldt is the respect in which he fits with the 'Cartesian' developments of the Enlightenment. For myself, the important thing about him is the respect in which he leads on to the general linguistics of the nineteenth century, and the tradition of Boas and Sapir. The latter view seems to me to have the better historical foundation, since it encompasses all of von Humboldt's importance, not just a part; but if that argument is in itself an historian's criterion, it is advanced partly in a polemical spirit.

There can be as many histories of linguistics, then, as reasons for interest in the history, and should be. Still, chaos is not the inevitable outcome, and history is not illimitably plastic. We may delight at the discovery of forgotten merit, and relish fresh vantage points on erstwhile familiar ground, but major patterns of cynosure and context, and major traditions will remain fairly fixed points of reference. The fundamental difficulty is that what we can today take to be fixed, common knolwedge is so vulnerable. For there has been very little in the way of adequate historical research. Most of what we understand as the fixed reference points of the history of linguistics is a palimpsest of past selective vantage points (cf. again Hoenigswald in this volume, and Romeo and Tiberio 1971). The primary task of research is to overcome this limitation. We may wish to choose our own histories, but there is a great difference between choice made in a clear light and groping amidst chiaroscuro.

The papers in section II of this volume represent important contributions in this regard. Each has to do with major traditions of the relevant past which our extended horizon now encompasses.

Traditions: The Nature of Language and of Grammar

The general grammar and philosophical grammar of the early modern period cannot be adequately understood as direct reflections of their own period alone. On the one hand, they show little impact of the accumulating knowledge of the world's languages beyond Europe until well into the eighteenth century. On the other hand, they show much of a tradition of grammatical study continuing from the Middle Ages. The medieval sources of much grammatical theory, indeed, have been emphasized by Roman Jakobson (cf. Salmon 1969: 169-176; Uitti 1969: 81-2). BURSILL-HALL, a leading scholar in the investigation of the primary data for knowledge of medieval linguistics, calls attention to how much must be done, before a full, continuous history of linguistics in the period can be written. Grammar enjoyed a privileged position throughout the Middle Ages, and its status in the curriculum is well known, but not the facts as to the nature and development of theory. Most general historians of linguistics, indeed, have been unsympathetic to the period, dismissing it, (with R. H. Robins and F. J. Dineen as notable exceptions). Bursill-Hall provides us with an account of our present state of knowledge, and of work underway to enlarge it. Implicit in his paper is a general point needing to be taken to heart by linguists. The materials of our history do not remain, waiting to be taken up when one gets around to it; continuing activity is necessary, to preserve them. (Nor is this a problem for remoter periods alone; the records of quite recent developments may be lost, through carelessness or disposal, if no interest is taken in their historical significance.)

AARSLEFF here presents in full, almost monographic scope an analysis of part of the 'Cartesian' period that has become already of more than historical concern, and a factor in controversy over current directions of linguistics (cf. Aarsleff 1970, 1971; and Bracken 1972). Controversy aside (I shall return to it below), Aarsleff makes a major contribution to the substance of the history of linguistics. Bursill-Hall deals with a tradition which has been known but neglected; Aarsleff brings into focus a tradition which has been effectively forgotten. Condillac's role has been sometimes noted (significantly by Uitti 1969) but has hardly entered at all into general historical treatment. The essays on the origin of language by Herder and Rousseau are celebrated, but their intellectual background, in debate in the Berlin Academy, and ultimately in the Abbé Condillac's *Essai sur l'origine des connaissances humaines,*—the fact of an extended tradition—has been missed. Aarsleff restores to us a knowledge of this major tradition, set in the problem of the origin of language, as a problem of the nature of language; in his own words, this tradition is "the linguistic theory that underlies and finds expression in efforts to deal with the question of the origin of language".

A consequence of recognition of this tradition is revaluation of Rousseau and Herder in this regard. A further consequence is to unravel the necessary connections that one is often led to assume between views. Those of us old enough to remember, know that structuralism in the hands of most linguists of the period before Chomsky was compatible with, indeed interwoven with, a mentalistic view (cf. Swadesh 1948, for one 'taxonomic linguist's' attack on mechanism), and directed toward the discovery of semantics and language universal. Aarsleff's scholarship enables us to 'remember' that a view of language as the distinguishing feature of man, and as a subject whose study gave insight into mind and nature of man, was part of the origin of language tradition as much as of the tradition of universal grammar. Both saw language as striking proof of man's creativity, and a condition for further creativity; both had rationalist qualities.

The two traditions became interwoven, and Aarsleff suggests that the interest in universal grammar in the later eighteenth century, and the insistence of the Romantics, chiefly in Germany, on the creative aspect of language and speech, both derive from the influence of Condillac.

Aarsleff's work has become part of controversy over the political consequences of ideas, associated with various theoretical dichotomies, and symbolized by the figures of Descartes and Locke. As for the political consequences of ideas, one can only observe that some critics employ an amazing double standard. Aspects of Locke unsavory today are singled out, while his anti-royalism and forced exile and his stimulus to the American and French revolutions are ignored, as is the fact that in his own day and long after he was attacked as subversive of religion and authority. Nothing of the political position or implications of Descartes are noticed (Bracken 1972). No matter, Locke, liberalism, and empiricism are attacked as 'counter-revolutionary' (Bracken 1972). But the association between theoretical views and political implications is seldom so tidy. The meaning of views is interdependent with context. One would indeed have thought it a common-place that the revolutionary method or concept of one period may become the conservative force of another, and conversely. (Presumably it is the present, not eighteenth century context that motivates attack on Locke as counter-revolutionary.) Despite the attempt, in Marxism or Christianity, to unite ontology, epistemology, social position, and convictions into a single package, both experience and analysis have shown such 'packaging' to be a matter of empirical concatenation, not logical necessity. Attempts to enforce such packaging are totalitarian in scholars as in governments. One might indeed play this particular game by treating 'Cartesian' linguistics as an ideology of elitist intellectuals, who wish to claim credit for views of the greatest radical consequence, while keeping professional hands utterly clean from the actual problems of language in society today (cf. Hymes 1973b). If 'Lockean empiricism' = liberalism = counter-revolutionary subordination of scholarship (Bracken 1972), then perhaps 'Cartesian rationalism' = 'radical chic'. (I say all this as a member of the editorial board of a Marxist historical journal.)

But let us return from polemic to history. The fundamental point is that the package of ideas presented as Cartesian linguistics does fall apart under historical scrutiny, through positive analysis of a major and distinct tradition of the period following upon Descartes and the work of Port-Royal.

For the period preceding Descartes and the Port-Royal work, Vivian Salmon (1969), cited as 'an exemplary model of the kind of good scholarship Chomsky's work has provoked' (Bracken 1972: 15), politely but utterly demolishes the putative link between Cartesian philosophy and grammatical analysis, together with the claim to originality of the latter. She concludes an extended analysis (1969: 185):

> The major 'distortion' (here picking up a word from Chomsky 1966: 73) . . . is the attribution of the form taken by the Port-Royal grammar to Cartesian inspiration with little or no attempt to take into account the total intellectual context in which it appeared. No one would deny the general debt of Port-Royal to Descartes, in whose philosophy they were interested because they saw it as 'a revival of Augustinian thought and therefore an ally of their own kind of theology' (Kneale, 1962: 316). But when we examine the actual details of the grammar we find that they were mainly a reworking of certain features of (then) current grammar, logic and rhetoric which was already characteristic of the grammars of Campanella and Lobkowitz . . . (who) were consciously reverting to the Middle Ages . . . .

Much more remains to be learned of the concrete character and development of linguistics in early modern times. Editions of essential texts are much needed (cf. again Uitti 1969: 80-81). When we attempt to interpret the connections and contexts of the work of the period, to provide history (rather than projection), the short history of 'Cartesian' linguistics, and the kind of scholarship manifested in the work of Aarsleff and Salmon, will be essential. Actual connections and underlying causes will have to be sought. We cannot settle for apparent surfaces.

Like the origin of language, and universal grammar, the question of the ranking of the parts of speech was given new direction and impetus with the eighteenth century. In the study by STANKIEWICZ we have a bringing to recognition of a topic lost sight of with the rise of structural linguistics in the United States. Stankiewicz shows how one of the oldest topics known to the history of linguistics took on a different character in a different climate of opinion, being formulated as a genetic, rather than a logical, problem. In this respect his study is a substantial documentation of Aarsleff's point as to the invigoration of general grammar within the tradition of the origin of language, and the linking of the two. Stankiewicz shows how assignment of priority to one principal part of speech, the noun, came to be replaced by assignment of priority to the verb. He regards the problem-tradition as one which, unlike that of general grammar and the origin of language, has a chronological end with recognition of the mutual necessity of both noun and verb in the twentieth century. Still, echoes of this problem have continued into recent years with discussions of the priority of one or the other part of speech in the reconstruction of a language or language family, and with discussions of the starting point within a formal grammar for the assignment and mapping of features of selection between parts of sentences. Mutual interdependence does not preclude differential weighting. The long history of this controversy (extending also into the early history of Indian linguistics, e.g., the *Nirukta*) may seem to us to demonstrate mainly the projection onto linguistic structure of cultural attitudes and values (with consequences for classification of language, analysis of Indo-European, and syntactic analysis); but it may be that such attitudes and values have indeed differentially weighted the form classes of individual languages, and that a revival of the interest of Boas and Sapir in grammatical categories as evidence of cognitive styles (cf. Hymes 1961) may further extend the history of this question.

The recurrence of problems, and their transformation in new contexts, is the general theme of the essay by VERBURG. He draws on a major work (Verburg 1952), unfortunately still untranslated from the Dutch (but cf. the account by Faithfull 1955). The dependence of the scope of history on current interest is especially well displayed here. A few years ago many linguists might have said that one of the two recurrent orientations traced by Verburg is central to the history of linguistics—the orientation toward the analysis of internal structure—and that the other is philosophy or something else. The growth of interest in sociolinguistics, as analysis of language functions, and the growth of interest among linguists in practical problems, wherein functional questions loom large, makes this pioneering, unique study freshly relevant. Most of all, the study indicates that the question of the nature of language is not exhausted by the question of the nature of grammar.

To sum up the significance of this section: recent years have made linguists aware that their relevant history begins before the institutionalization in the nineteenth century of their profession, but adequate knowledge of that greater history is hardly available. A combination of linguistic knowledge and scholarly competence, rarely to be found, is required. The studies presented here represent substantial additions, and in some respects changes, to what the history has been taken to be.

First Paradigm (?): Comparison and Explanation of Change

Although our retrospective horizons have been enlarged, standard accounts of the history of linguistics have not been wrong to locate a crucial, qualitative change somewhere within the last part of the eighteenth century and the first part of the nineteenth century. The papers in section III, "First

Paradigm (?): Comparison and Explanation of Change," give reason to think that the nature of the change has not been well understood or explained. Addressing as they do the long-standing conventional origin myth of 'scientific linguistics', indeed, these papers constitute the centerpiece of the book.

METCALF, GULYA, and DIDERICHSEN show from complementary vantage points that the novelty of a purely conceptual or methodological breakthrough cannot be an adequate explanation. Metcalf, the principal scholar in his subject, demonstrates that the Indo-European hypothesis, far from being new or sensational, was derivative and even typical of at least one important strand of linguistic tradition in Northern Europe. Religious tradition itself, in the Biblical myth of the Tower of Babel, may be thought to have facilitated the linguistic interest. Metcalf does find a methodological break between the centuries he treats and the later, nineteenth century profession. Addressing the etymological tradition from before modern times, and within the eighteenth century, Diderichsen finds the essentials of the nineteenth century method, however, to develop within the eighteenth century. He can see no sharp break at the time of supposed paradigmatic breakthrough. Gulya casts profound light on the problem from the vantage point of an adjacent language family, the Finno-Ugrian, where the question to be asked is why the paradigmatic breakthrough did NOT take place, given the presence of necessary concepts and methods. Both Metcalf and Gulya discuss the general character of the work they treat, and place it with regard to the notion of paradigm, Metcalf finding a good fit in the sixteenth and seventeenth centuries for Kuhn's depiction of a pre-paradigmatic state, while Gulya adds dimensions to the conception of paradigmatic formation, stressing among other things the need for continuity of accumulation of relevant materials. Diderichsen treats the paradigm usually thought first, that of historical-comparative linguistics of the nineteenth century, as at best second. One original paradigmatic approach in the study of language, he argues, was that of traditional grammar, connected with the establishing of a standard literary language and the teaching of its most important rules. A second such approach, deserving the name of tradition of inquiry and explanation certainly, and perhaps that of paradigm, was the etymological. Not the least interesting aspect of his paper is the informative account given of the roles of Turgot, de Brosses, and Adam Smith, men not usually placed in any paradigmatic relation to linguistics in conventional accounts.

Just as Diderichsen shows us the central relevance of men not usually considered, so PERCIVAL shows us that the merits of men usually praised may be misconceived. It takes nothing away from Rask's great achievements to recognize that he was not a literal founder of the tradition of work that followed him, but that principles in his work which seem such foundations to us were, for him, parts of a quite different general conception, one which was not to be taken up. And just as Diderichsen shows us the continuity in what was later to be perceived as revolution, for all linguistics, so MALKIEL shows us the same in a particular branch of linguistics. His essay.is not less, but more significant for its particularity. The great fallacy and disservice of cursory accounts (to which the notion of 'paradigm' too easily lends itself), is that only the 'great' changes are noticed. The greater part of the actual history of linguistics is lost from view and from accounting. But, as has been argued above, it is inherent in the nature of the subject that it is a congeries of histories, a collection of the traditions of lines of work on particular languages, language families, and language areas. The general changes are partly influenced by their location in their data and traditions of some one or a few such lines of work. Their successes, through diffusion, and the character they come to have in their many particular instaurations, depend in important part on continuities independent of them. The interaction of these two forces, a novel method and genre, on the one hand, and long cultivated sources of data on the other, is nicely brought out here. We need many more studies of this kind. Notice that Malkiel finds Diez' truly original contribution, the first union of several ingredients, to be something unadmitted and inexplicit at the time.

The problem of appearance and reality, with regard to continuity, is given a new twist by KIPARSKY. Whereas Diderichsen demonstrates continuities across the onset of the conventionally recognized 'paradigm', Kiparsky discovers a hidden discontinuity within it. More precisely, he shows that the discontinuity has been mistakenly located. It does not lie in the formulation of the famous thesis of the exceptionless nature of sound laws, associated with the *Junggrammatiker*, which has often been taken to have defined a paradigmatic 'breakthrough'. Kiparsky points out that men on both sides of that issue contributed to a new kind of historical linguistics. This development, not articulated at the time, was a drastic change in the nature and direction of the explanations sought.

The essay by HOENIGSWALD sums up the section, with reflections on the earlier standard views of the subject—the most cultivated area of the history of linguistics perhaps—and with cautions born of experience. Hoenigswald stresses particularly the recurrence of discrepancy between the conscious controversies of a period, and the changes taking place that prove truly significant. Scholars like Schleicher, for example, he finds, make crucial contributions, yet receive a bad scholarly press for what they said and thought they were doing. Before him, Sir William Jones cannot, in Hoenigswald's view, be credited with having meant the splendid things his famous statement (often quoted as the founding charter of linguistics) seems to say to us. Hoenigswald indeed comes down on the opposite side of the fence from Diderichsen. Whereas Diderichsen locates the crucial change earlier than is commonly thought to be the case, Hoenigswald locates it later (in Schleicher). This difference of judgment may be taken to demonstrate three vital points: the continuity of the whole development was indeed far greater than textbooks suppose; the placing of formation of a paradigm in time is inescapably a matter of weighing of criteria: and the perspective of time changes the weighting one gives. One has to choose which new things are most important, as against the background of the many things to continue. It is fair to suggest that the twenty-first century is unlikely to agree in locating the major points of change in the twentieth century where we do today.

The whole section points to one great limitation of what we can do today in the history of linguistics. The subject is studied mostly by linguists, and we are equipped to recognize and trace ideas perhaps, but not usually equipped to probe social contexts and institutions. Yet, as Paul Thieme pointed out in discussions of Hoenigswald's paper at Burg Wartenstein, the indispensable foundation of what took place in the German area in the early nineteenth century was institutional. It had to do with the short tenure of an important ministry in the Prussian government by Wilhelm von Humboldt, famous to linguists for his ideas, but not his administration. By establishing chairs in Sanskrit and general linguistics in universities, a model emulated outside Prussia, von Humboldt may be said to have created the first successful paradigmatic *community* in linguistics; and he ought to be celebrated for this as much as for his ideas as to the nature of language and languages.

The Slow Growth of Grammatical Adequacy

Next to institutional perspective, the greatest lack at present in the history of linguistics probably is knowledge of the growth of the methods and practices on which linguistic work, and theory, have depended. Throughout its history, success of linguistics has come down to its ability to say accurate and worthwhile things about languages. Counted by centuries, far the greater part of this history has been concerned only with one or a few great languages of literature, religion, and cultural hegemony. It is with the modern period that we begin to get the 'democratization' of linguistics, as it were, in which gradually each and all of the languages of the peoples of the world come to have the right to contribute to knowledge of language. This principle reached something of a peak in the structuralism of American anthropologically oriented linguistics in the second quarter of this century, and in the interests of Trubetzkoy and Jakobson in Europe in typology and universals. Despite some apparent backsliding in recent years, it appears to be a permanently won gain; but it has been slowly and painfully won. We are far from being able to give an adequate account of the subject, but the papers in this section demonstrate that what may now be taken for granted was only recently achieved at all.

ROWE provides a fundamental step in assessing the development of grammar in the early modern period. We need to know not only what was variously said about grammar, but also what kinds of grammars were written. Rowe comments on the implications of his findings, as to the slow and in part accidental way in which opportunities for broadening and deepening knowledge of language were taken up and publicly realized. Much depended in practice on what may have been the first institutionalized body of fieldworkers in ethnography and linguistics, the missionaries; but the public availability of their work had as much to do with expulsion of the Jesuits from the New World, Rowe suggests, as with anything else. The missionary grammatical work of the period is a fascinating scene of the interaction between received genre and novel information. Rowe's study of the publicly available, printed grammars is complemented nicely by Hanzeli's monograph (1969) on unprinted grammars of northeastern America; Hanzeli's discussion of the relation between concepts of 'grammar' and of 'economy' (the character of the language actually being described) is especially noteworthy.

In his second contribution to the volume PERCIVAL brings out yet another side of Wilhelm von Humboldt. In addition to the theoretician and the administrator, there was also the describer of languages, and Percival analyzes Humboldt's treatment of a problem in the language to which his most famous theoretical work (1836) was an introduction. One of our most widely experienced fieldworkers, HAMP, provides evidence bearing on the recurrent problem of preconception vs. data, here with regard to phonology. He finds that an amateur, Prince Bonaparte, in some respects was more successful than professional linguists of his day, whose work conditioned their expectations of what they would find.

Alongside the development of the comparative-historical approach, the development of the structural approach is the problem of greatest general relevance to modern linguistics, and the structural approach began, effectively, with the development of phonology. Just as the comparative-historical approach has its mythical founder in Sir William Jones, so the structural approach has had its mythical founder in Ferdinand de Saussure. The great respect one must have for both men does not bar inquiry into the actual part they played; in both cases, it was, most dramatically, in the symbolic use made posthumously of each. The explanation of the symbolic significance of each is not fully available, but institutional and social factors clearly are important. And if with comparative-historical linguistics the causes had something to do with the institutional and cultural aspects of German scholarship, so with structuralism they seem to have had something to do with a reaction against things German, after the First World War (Malkiel and Langdon 1969). And if the institutional success of both developments came after the symbolic intellectual breakthrough, so the true intellectual origins appear in both cases to precede it. The European ground has already been investigated with valuable results by Jakobson, Stankiewicz, Coseriu, Koerner and others. Here we are able to contribute two studies of the much more neglected development in the United States. The neglect perhaps is due to the tendency to retrospectively assign origination of all things structural to de Saussure. Whatever the case, it is clear that synchronic, penetrating accounts of novel languages were being written by Boas and Sapir well before de Saussure's lectures were given, let alone published. WELLS treats the development of the recognition of structure in phonology, culminating, so far as he carries the story, in the work of Boas. Wells finds Boas' own insight into the principle of phonology incomplete, though path-breaking for its time. In retrospect we can see the step taken by Boas not only as a matter of structural insight, but also as the equally crucial matter of the *universalization* of the principle of structure. Well into the twentieth century, *a priori*, ethnocentric notions of the inadequacies of languages other than the relatively familiar and well-studied Indo-European languages were current. Well into the twentieth century, and in some respects still today, the equality of all varieties of language in terms of structure, has had to be argued. It was through their study of the individual characters of lowly-regarded languages that Boas, Sapir and others were able to demonstrate, as against received general linguistic notions, the truth of this principle. It is a kind of linguistic relativity, a reciprocal relativity of perception, that informs the remarkable article by Boas with whose discussion Wells ends, and in a sense, STOCKING begins. For Stocking finds in embryo in the article the principles that were to inform the long remainder of Boas' career as a shaper of the study of languages in American linguistics and anthropology. His study has the great merit of being based on research into unpublished materials, including correspondence—a hallmark of the maturity of a historical discipline, which the history of linguistics has only partially approached. And it has the great interest of dealing with a problem of authorship— collective or individual, and so of reminding us that even the seemingly most obvious facts are not to be taken at face value. In the course of his study Stocking sheds light on the institutional bases of descriptive linguistic work in the United States, reminding us not to take this for granted either.

All together, the individual studies in this volume are valuable contributions to the growth of the history of linguistics; and at the same time, they point up how far we have yet to go. There is a seeming paradox in what they collectively show. It is our own activity and period that we likely least adequately understand. This, of course, is the point of Hegel's remark that it is at dusk that the owl of Minerva takes her flight, that it is when a period draws to a close (or is over) that it can be wisely understood. The paradox, of course, is only seeming, because the reasons that scholars cannot both pursue original research and stand back from it are obvious enough. The maxim of the history of linguistics, then, might be an adaptation of Marx' last thesis on Feuerbach. Linguists undoubtedly will continue to change the world (of linguistics); the problem is to understand it. And for understanding, history of linguistics is indispensable, even perhaps the main means.

Complementary Perspectives

It seems likely that we shall see a continuing growth in studies of the history of ideas in linguistics, especially of the major ideas, that have been central to whole periods. It is worthwhile, then, to urge studies of three complementary kinds: of the institutional bases of linguistics; of the diverse lines of work and traditions of work that enter into the field of linguistics at any time; and of the available means, methods, and in general, the practice, of a line of work, a scholar or a time. Focus on general ideas alone will never suffice to explain why and when events occur, and is likely to mislead us badly. It is by situating scholars and ideas that we can come to assess them adequately and to hope to give valid accounts of what has happened to create the history that linguistics has had. The three papers of the last section of the volume are contributions in this regard. The eminent historian of science, JOHN GREENE, draws on his experience to suggest ways in which the history of linguistics can benefit from longer established areas of the general field to which it belongs. As a sociologist of knowledge, KURT WOLFF, and his associate, BARRIE THORNE, suggest some of the considerations that that discipline provides for gaining insight and explanation. Finally, STOCKING responds to editorial request by discussing his own experience and views as trained historian, approaching a discipline as a novel subject matter. The history of linguistics always will depend on the contributions of linguists, for the assessment of technical matters and the recognition of significance in many ways, but the subject is unlikely to prosper without the complementary contributions of other standpoints. We may even hope that the day is not too far distant when the study of the history of linguistics, having become already more than an avocation, will be recognized as of interest to more than linguists, and as a vital part of the general field of the history and sociology of the human sciences.

NOTES

1. I want to thank Al Romano for help in preparing the manuscript of this introduction, and John Fought for discussions of the history of linguistics during the writing of it.

2. There is a story that can serve as a parable. A learned French Catholic is supposed to have said of the claims of Protestantism to be valid, because based on the original gospels, 'Do you expect me to take the word of four ignorant fishermen against all the glories and traditions of the Church?'

3. Not only is there persistence of work which the new 'paradigm' does not adequately incorporate, but there is also what has been called in the study of culture change, the 'loss of useful arts'. Where the study of structure has shaped linguistic training, and particularly since the new 'paradigm' of formal grammar; and where anthropologists have not maintained interest in practical linguistics and ethnography; the phonetic training once considered mandatory for both linguists and ethnographers has largely lapsed. Relatively few linguists, relatively few anthropologists, could today record oral data. Yet within linguistics new interest in rhetoric, poetics, and conversation call attention to oral aspects of speech that are not available in ordinary writing; and there are of course many languages not yet adequately described, for whose study transcription is necessary.

4. In doing so, one will find the elaboration of Kuhn's notion by Wallace, on which I have drawn in the preceding paragraph, to be a cogent, penetrating guide (see Wallace 1972). A longer and more general treatment of sociocultural order and change, but also cogent, is that by Cohen (1968). The major assumptions as to social groups that a historian of linguistics is likely to use find a place there. On assumptions and inferences generally, see Fischer (1970).

REFERENCES

Aarsleff, Hans. 1970. The history of linguistics and Professor Chomsky. Language 46: 570-85.

_____. Locke's reputation in 19th-century England. The Monist 55: 392-422.

_____. 'Cartesian Linguistics' History or fantasy? Language Sciences 17: 1-12.

Austerlitz, Robert. 1972. Review of Sebeok (1966). International Journal of American Linguistics 38: 212-7.

Bloomfield, L. 1914. An introduction to the study of language. New York: Holt.

_____. 1927. Literate and illiterate speech. American Speech 2: 432-9. (Reprinted in Hymes 1964: 391-6).

Borst, Arno. 1957-1963. Der Turmbau von Babel. Stuttgart.

Bracken, Harry M. 1972. Chomsky's Cartesianism. Language Sciences 22: ll-6.

Chomsky, Noam. 1966. Cartesian Linguistics. New York: Harper and Row.

Cohen, Percy S. 1968. Modern social theory. London: Heinemann.

Collingwood, R. C. 1939. An autobiography. Oxford: At the Clarendon Press.

Coseriu, Eugenio. 1970. Semantik, innere Sprachform und Tiefenstruktur. Folia Linguistica 4(1/2): 53-63.

Donzé, Roland. 1967. La Grammaire générale et raisonnée de Port-Royal. Contribution à l'histoire des idées grammaticales en France. Berne: Francke. (Reviewed by Uitti 1969).

Elmendorff, W. W. and Suttles, Wayne. 1960. Pattern and change in Halkomelem Salish dialects. Anthropological Linguistics 2(7): 1-32.

Faithfull, R. G. 1955. Review of Verburg (1952). Archivum Linguisticum 7: 144-50.

Ferguson, C. A. 1971. Absence of copula and the notion of simplicity: a study of normal speech, baby talk, foreigner talk, and pidgins. In Hymes 1971b: 141-50.

Fischer, David H. 1970. Historians' fallacies. New York: Harper Torchbooks, TB 1545.

Frachtenberg, L. J. 1917. Abnormal types of speech in Quileute. International Journal of American Linguistics 1: 295-9.

Gipper, Helmut. 1971. Gibt es ein sprachliche relativitätsprinzip? Untersuchungen zur Sapir-Whorf hypothesis. Frankfurt am Main: S. Fischer.

Gossen, Gary. 1972. Chamula genres of verbal behavior. Journal of American Folklore 84: 145-67.

_____. 1974. To speak with a heated heart: Chamula canons of style and good performance. In Sherzer and Bauman (1974).

Grace, George W. 1969. Notes on the philosophical background of current linguistic controversy. Working papers in linguistics 1 (January), 1-41. (University of Hawaii, Dept. of Linguistics). Honolulu.

Gudschinsky, Sarah C. 1959. Toneme representation in Mazatec orthography. Word 15: 446-52.

Hale, Kenneth. 1973. Some questions about anthropological linguistics: The role of native knowledge. In Hymes 1973a: 382-97.

Hallowell, A. I. 1960. The beginnings of anthropology in America. In F. de Laguna (ed.), Selected papers from the American Anthropologist, 1888-1920, 1-90. Evanston: Row, Peterson.

Hanzeli, V. 1969. Missionary linguistics in New France. A study of seventeenth- and eighteenth-century descriptions of American Indian languages. The Hague: Mouton.

Hoenigswald, H. M. 1966. A proposal for the study of folk-linguistics. In W. Bright (ed.), Sociolinguistics, 16-26. The Hague: Mouton.

Hymes, D. 1961. On typology of cognitive styles in language (with examples from Chinookan). Anthropological Linguistics 3(1): 22-54.

_____. 1962. Review of R. H. Lowie, Crow texts. American Anthropologist 64: 900-2.

_____. 1963. Notes toward a history of linguistic anthropology. Anthropological Linguistics 5(1): 59-103.

_____ (ed.). 1964. Language in culture and society. New York: Harper and Row.

_____. 1968. Linguistics — the field. International Encyclopedia of the Social Sciences 9: 351-71. New York: Macmillan.

_____. 1970a. Linguistic method in ethnography. In P. L. Garvin (ed.), Method and theory in linguistics, 249-311. The Hague: Mouton.

_____. 1970b. Linguistic theory and the functions of speech. International Days of Sociolinguistics, 111-44. Rome: Istituto Luigi Sturzo.

_____. 1971a. Morris Swadesh: From the first 'Yale School' to world prehistory. In M. Swadesh, The origin and diversification of language, 228-70. (ed. by J. F. Sherzer). Chicago: Aldine.

_____. (ed). 1971b. Pidginization and creolization of languages. Cambridge: At the University Press.

_____. 1972. Review of J. Lyons, Noam Chomsky. Language 48: 416-27.

_____. (ed.). 1973a. Reinventing anthropology. New York: Pantheon.

_____. 1973b. Speech and language: On the origins and foundations of inequality in speaking. Daedalus (Summer).

_____. 1973c. Toward linguistic competence. Working papers in sociolinguistics, (University of Texas, Department of Anthropology). Austin.

_____. 1974. Lexicostatistics and glottochronology in Paris (1834, 1862). In I. Dyen (ed.), Lexicostatistics in genetic linguistics. The Hague: Mouton.

Hymes, D. and Fought, J. 1974. American structuralism. In T. A. Sebeok (ed.), Historiography of linguistics. (Current Trends in Linguistics, vol. 13). The Hague: Mouton.

Koerner, E. F. K. 1972. Towards a historiography of linguistics. 19th and 20th century paradigms. Anthropological Linguistics 14(7): 255-80.

Kroeber, A. L. 1940. Stimulus diffusion. American Anthropologist 42: 1-20.

_____. 1944. Philology. Configurations of culture growth, ch. 4, 215-38. Berkeley and Los Angeles: University of California Press.

Kuhn, T. S. 1962. The structure of scientific revolutions. Chicago: University of Chicago Press. (2nd ed., 1970).

Lakatos, I. and Musgrave, A. (eds.). 1970. Criticism and the growth of knowledge. Cambridge: Cambridge University Press. [A discussion of Kuhn's thesis, with response by Kuhn].

Levich, Martin. 1962. Disagreement and controversy in history. History and theory 2(1): 41-51. Reprinted in Nadel, G. H. (ed.), Studies in the philosophy of history, 35-45. New York: Harper Torchbooks, TB 1208.

Lounsbury, F. G. 1962. Linguistics. In B. Siegel (ed.), Biennial review of anthropology 1961, 279-322. Stanford: Stanford University Press.

Lowie, R. H. 1935. The Crow Indians. New York: Rinehart.

Maher, J. Peter. 1973. Review of Stockwell and Macaulay, Linguistic change and generative theory. Language Sciences (April), 47-52.

Malkiel, Y. 1964. Distinctive traits of Romance linguistics. In Hymes (1964), 671-88.

Malkiel, Y. and Langdon, M. 1969. History and histories of linguistics. Romance Philology 22(4): 530-73.

Pike, K. L. 1954. Language in relation to a unified theory of the structure of human behavior, 1. Santa Ana: Summer Institute of Linguistics. (Rev. ed., The Hague: Mouton, 1967).

Rollins, P. C. 1971. Benjamin Lee Whorf: transcendental linguist. Unpublished Ph. D. thesis. Cambridge, Mass.: Harvard University.

Romeo, Luigi and Tiberio, Gaio E. 1971. Historiography of linguistics and Rome's scholarship. Language Sciences 17: 23-44.

Salmon, V. G. 1969. Review of Chomsky 1966. Journal of Linguistics 5: 165-87.

Sandys, Sir John Edwyn. 1921. A history of classical scholarship. Cambridge: At the University Press. (3rd, revised ed.). 3 vols.

Sapir, E. 1915. Abnormal types of speech in Nootka. (Canada, Department of Mines, Geological Survey, Memoir 62; Anthropological Papers, no. 5). Ottawa: Government Printing Bureau. In D. G. Mandelbaum (ed.), Selected writings of Edward Sapir (Berkeley and Los Angeles: University of California Press, 1949), 179-96.

_____. 1924. The grammarian and his language. American Mercury 1: 149-55. (In Mandelbaum 1949: 150-55).

Sapir, J. D. 1973. Big and thin; Two Diola metalinguistic terms. Paper presented at annual meetings, American Anthropological Association, New Orleans.

Sebeok, T. A. (ed.). 1966. Portraits of linguists. A biographical sourcebook for the history of Western linguistics, 1746-1963. Bloomington: Indiana University Press. 2 vols.

Sherzer, J. and Bauman, R. (eds.). 1974. Explorations in the ethnography of speaking. New York: Cambridge University Press.

Steinthal, H. 1863. Geschichte der Sprachwissenschaft bei den Griechen und Römern mit Besonderer Rücksicht auf die Logik. Berlin: Dümmlers Verlagsbuchhandlung. (2nd rev. ed., 1890; reissued, 1961).

Stross, B. 1974. Speaking of speaking: Tenajapa Tzeltal metalinguistics. In Sherzer and Bauman 1974.

Swadesh, Morris. 1948. On linguistic mechanism. Science and Society 12: 254-9.

Thorne, J. P. 1965. Review of P. Postal, Constituent structure. Journal of Linguistics 1(1): 73-6.

Uitti, K. D. 1969. Review of Chomsky 1966, and of Donzé 1967. Romance Philology 22: 75-85.

Verburg, P. A. 1952. Taal en functionaliteit. Wageningen: Veenman and Sons.

Voegelin, C. F. and Voegelin, F. M. 1963. On the history of structuralizing in 20th century America. Anthropological Linguistics 3(1): 12-37.

Von Humboldt, W. 1836. Über die Verschiedenheit des menschlichen Sprachbaues und ihren Einfluss auf die geistige Entwickelung des Menschengeschlects. Berlin.

Wallace, A. F. C. W. 1972. Paradigmatic processes in culture change. AA 74: 467-78.

Wells, R. S. 1963. Some neglected opportunities in descriptive linguistics. Anthropological Linguistics 3(1): 38-49.

White, A. D. 1896. A history of the warfare of science with theology in Christendom. New York. (Reprinted, New York: Dover, 1960).

Whitney, W. D. 1867. Indo-European philology and ethnology. North American Review 105: 521-54. (Reprinted in his Oriental and Linguistic Essays, First Series, 198-238 [1872]).

Williams, R. 1965. The long revolution. London: Pelican Books.
Zimmer, K. E. 1968. Review of Chomsky 1966. International Journal of American Linguistics 34(4): 290-303.

I : CONTRASTIVE BEGINNINGS

1. Very Ancient Texts: Babylonian Grammatical Texts

Thorkild Jacobsen

Linguistics as a study of the structure of language would seem to have come into being independently at various times and places in the course of human history. There is the well-known beginning of such studies in the West, where Krates of Mallos and Dionysios Thrax wrote the first grammars of Greek around the middle of the second century B.C., and there is the far more impressive earlier beginning in India, which culminated in Pāṇini's remarkable grammar of Sanskrit composed some time around the beginning of the third century B.C. Lastly there are Ancient Mesopotamian attempts at grammatical analysis of Sumerian, attempts which are far less well known and to which we would like to draw the attention of linguists.[1]

These Ancient Mesopotamian attempts are preserved in grammatical texts which date from Old-Babylonian times, around 1600 B.C., and which are thus earlier by more than a thousand years than any other known attempt at structural analysis of language. They were studied and developed in the succeeding periods and their ultimate versions are attested in later manuscripts dating from the Neo-Babylonian Period or roughly to the sixth and fifth centuries B.C.

The circumstances that gave rise to grammatical study in Mesopotamia seem to have been fairly similar to those that surrounded the rise of such studies in later times in India and in the Classical World: serious concern with the preservation of a classical literature written in a language that was becoming obsolete at the time. In the Old-Babylonian Period the Sumerian language, in which a major part of Ancient Mesopotamian literature was written, was rapidly dying out as a living language and was being replaced by Akkadian. It was still spoken and taught in the schools but that was all.

We are inclined to consider this general similarity of cultural situation significant. As motto for his book *The Philosophy of Grammar* (1924) Otto Jespersen aptly chose a passage from Rousseau: "Il faut beaucoup du philosophie pour savoir observer une fois ce qu'on voit tous les jours", for true as this is generally it is particularly true of language. Language is so much a part of us that we are rarely aware of it for itself, only for what we are trying to convey with it; it has become second nature to us. To properly observe it, to become aware of it for itself and as a system a special situation is necessary, a situation inviting comparison, a situation such as the one in which the beginnings of grammars are found to appear, where there is choice of statement in the classical rather than in the colloquial form of the language, or even in an entirely different language.

Such a situation of choice, it may be added, already had come into being with the introduction of writing, for the existence of writing offered a choice between statement in language, as a system of symbolic sounds, and statement in writing, as a system of visual symbols, thus offering all the analytic incentive inherent in a choice between closely related systems. Historically the resultant analysis stayed with analysis of the expression side of the language (phonology), setting up – on a purely practical basis–such fundamental analytical concepts as vowels and consonants where the writing was alphabetical, words and syllables where, as in Mesopotamia, it did not progress beyond the syllabic stage.

I. The Old-Babylonian Paradigm Analyses

The analytical method which characterizes the Old-Babylonian grammatical efforts is the well-known device of the "grammatical paradigm," a listing in which the various forms of a word are given in order according to the grammatical categories represented in them. As a homely and familiar example of such an approach, we may use the paradigm of nouns of the First Declension found in the school grammar of Latin:

	Sing.	*Plur.*
Nom.	īnsula	īnsulae
Acc.	īnsulam	īnsulās
Gen.	īnsulae	īnsulārum
Dat.	īnsulae	īnsulīs
Abl.	īnsulā	īnsulīs

Here the forms are so ordered that lateral movement, position in the left-hand or right-hand column, is governed by the category of Number: whether the form is in the Singular or in the Plural; whereas vertical movement, position on the first, second, third, fourth, or fifth line, is governed by the category of Case: whether the form is Nominative, Accusative, Genitive, Dative, or Ablative.

In the example here given the two categories according to which the forms are analyzed are represented each by a different dimension, horizontal or vertical. It is also possible, however, to use only one dimension so that, for example, the first five lines are allotted to cases in the Singular, the following five to cases in the Plural as follows:

Sing.	Nom.	īnsula
	Acc.	īnsulam
	Gen.	īnsulae
	Dat.	īnsulae
	Abl.	īnsulā
Plur.	Nom.	īnsulae
	Acc.	īnsulās
	Gen.	īnsulārum
	Dat.	īnsulīs
	Abl.	īnsulīs

In this one-column arrangement the primary category of ordering is that of Number, the secondary that of Case. It would also be possible, of course, to choose the category of Case as the primary one, that of Number as the secondary one and list the forms as:

Nom.	Sg.	īnsula
	Pl.	īnsulae
Acc.	Sg.	īnsulam
	Pl.	īnsulās
Gen.	Sg.	īnsulae
	Pl.	īnsulārum
Dat.	Sg.	īnsulae
	Pl.	īnsulīs
Abl.	Sg.	īnsulā
	Pl.	īnsulīs

In the Old-Babylonian grammatical texts — although two-dimensional arrangement with descriptive headings was beginning to find favor in certain account-texts at this time[2] — only one-dimensional arrangement without headings is used, perhaps because of conservative adherence to a traditional form. In the ordering of the categories controlling the arrangement, furthermore, the texts show a fair degree of freedom so that for practical reasons one section of a larger list may well choose to reverse the order followed by the other sections and make primary the category they have as secondary, and secondary the one they have as primary in their arrangement. For the interpretation this means that very little external help is offered. In each text, and each section of text, only the ordering of the forms itself serves as clue to the analysis underlying it and to the categories with which that analysis operates.

As may be seen by a perusal of the nineteen or so texts and fragments that have come down to us, the Old-Babylonian grammatical materials are of rather varied character and range from almost entirely lexical lists such as OBGT XV, which shows occasional grammatical "paradigms" of two or three variant forms only, to a text such as OBGT VI, which lists 227 carefully ordered variant forms of one and the same verb, ğar "to place". Furthermore, comparison between relatively substantial verbal paradigms such as OBGT VI, VII, VIII, IX, and X shows that no single pattern-arrangement existed, but that each verb, apparently, was independently arranged. Attempting, therefore, no generalization we may look briefly at some of the more systematically ordered texts seeking to ascertain some, at least, of the grammatical categories underlying the analysis they present and, since our intention is merely to call attention to these materials, attempting no exhaustive treatment of them.

Since the claim to attention of these texts as early evidence of linguistics — that is to say: of systematic inquiry into the structure of language — must rest essentially on the depth of analysis and degree of systematic classification and ordering of complex linguistic data to which they bear witness, it is obvious that the tracing and demonstration of such order must be a main concern of our presentation. This raises, however, some practical difficulties. The original texts cannot very well be reprinted here, and yet they are crucial for following our argument and judging of its merits. We must therefore hope that the interested reader will have MSL IV to hand as he reads. Even so the dry and technical nature of the data with which we must deal may disconcert him; and for the reader who seeks only a general impression of the nature of the materials we would recommend reading of the sections presenting sample passages only. These are (1) Sample passage from OBGT I on p. 47 for the treatment of the pronouns; (2) the passage on the verb taken from OBGT VII on pp. 53-54 for the verb, and (3) the sample passage from NBGT I on pp. 58-59 for the treatment offered in the later grammatical texts.

PRONOUN AND ADVERB

The text OBGT I comes from the upper right-hand portion of a large sixteen-column tablet which, when complete, contained some 1200 lines of text dealing with pronouns, adverbs, and pronominal and adverbial expressions, analyzing them, among others, according to the categories of Person, Number, and Case. The arrangement of its materials seems to have been as follows:

(Aa) Personal Pronoun Sg.

The first three columns, now lost, can be assumed to have treated the personal pronoun first, second, and third person singular in much the same manner in which the corresponding plural forms are dealt with in cols. vi, vii, and viii, listing first (1) the independent nominative forms ğae : *anāku* "I", zae : *attā* "thou", ene : *šū* "he", and various other nominative forms, then (2) comitative/ablative forms formed with the case-element -da in Sumerian and translated by accusative or various prepositions in Akkadian, and lastly (3) dative/directive forms formed with the case elements -a (illative), -ra/-r (dative), or -šè (directive) in Sumerian and translated by dative and by prepositional constructions with *ana* "to", "for" and composites of it in Akkadian.

(Ab) Demonstrative Pronoun

Following the section dealing with the singular forms of the personal pronoun is not, as one might have expected, the corresponding plural forms, but rather an intermediate section dealing with the demonstrative pronouns -e, pl. -e-meš, and -ne, pl. -ne-meš. Both of these pronouns are listed in their dependent form in attribution to the substantive lú "man" even though ne and -ne-meš can also be used independently, and both are translated by *annū*, pl. *annūtum*, in Akkadian. The first part of this section, (1), which presumably occupied col. iv and dealt with various nominative forms, is lost except for a few uninformative traces at the end of the Akkadian side of the column. When the text is fully preserved at the beginning of col. v it lists (2) comitative/ablative forms marked by -da "with" and -ta "from" in Sumerian and by the prepositions *qādum* "inclusive of", and *itti* "with", "from" in Akkadian (301-316). These forms are followed (317-345) by (3) dative/ directive forms marked by -a (illative), and -ra/-r (personal dative) or -šè (directive) in Sumerian, by accusative and the prepositions *ana* "to", "for", *eli* "above", "against", and *ana ṣēr* "toward" in Akkadian.

(Ac) Personal Pronoun Plural

With column vi — or rather, it would seem, already with the lost last three lines of col. v — the text returns to the personal pronoun proper to deal with its plural forms. It lists first

(1) nominative forms beginning (373-384) with (α) the simple forms, first person **mende, menden, mededen** : *nīnu* "we", second person **menzen, zae-menzen** : *attunu* "you", and third person **enene, enenene** : *šunu* "they", to which it adds the demonstratives **lú-ù-ne, lú-bi-ne, ur₅-meš** and **ur₅-bi** : *šunu* "those". The simple forms are followed (385-418) by (β) various constructions — mostly, it would seem, adverbial in nature — in which the pronoun or the related pronominal subject-element of the verb occurs as subject or predicate nominative of the verb **me** "to be". They are all translated into Akkadian by the nominative form of the pronoun followed by the particle *-ma* "only", "also". Other nominatives listed are (γ) negated forms (419-426) with **-nu** "is not" and **-in-nu** "if not" both translated *ul* "not", and — after a lacuna (437-450) — deprecative (454-456. Suffix **-nam-mu** : *mīnu* "what matter . . ."), direct quote (457-459. Suffix **-e-še** : *-mi* "as they say . . ."), irrealis (460-462. Suffix **-g̃iš-en** : *-man* "were it . . ."), and constructions with the conjunction **ù** (463-469). The nominative forms are followed by

(2) comitative forms with **-da** "with" (470-497) and continuing into the lacuna covering 498-535. Some difficulties are caused here by lines 488-496 which do not construe with **-da** and which perhaps represent a later insertion. When the text resumes after a lacuna it lists

(3) forms in **-ra/-r** (personal dative), in **-a** (illative) and **-še** (directive) which continue (536-560) to the next lacuna.

(B) In col. ix, where the text resumes with line 635, it deals with the prepositional relations of "before" **igi-** . . . . **-ta** (635-637) and "after" **bar-** . . . **-ta** : *ištu warki-* (638-640) as applied to first person singular, second person singular, and third neuter singular pronominal suffix (possessive). Then follow four seemingly unrelated entries (641-646) until in 647 it begins treatment of

(Ba) Adverb of Place

The adverb of place **me** : *ali, aii-* etc. "where?" It deals first (1) with forms in **-a** (illative) (647-669), then, after a lacuna (670-709), with forms in **-da** (comitative) and in **-še** (directional) (710-720). The adverb of place is followed by

(Bb) Adverb of Time

The adverb of time **me-da** : *mati* "when?" (721-727), **me-na** : *mati* "when?" (728-735) **en-na-me-še** : *adi mati* "until when?" (736-737), and **en-** : *mati* "when?" (738-739). After a lacuna follows then in column xi

(784-825) all kinds of adverbial expressions for points of time: "tomorrow", "yesterday", "daily", etc., etc.

(Bc) Adverb of manner

With col. xii, lastly, the text treats after a lacuna adverbs of manner (853 onwards) such as **ne-nam, tukun-tukun,** and forms with **ur₅** all translated as forms of, or constructions with, Akkadian *kīam* "thus".

With line 900 the text is interrupted by a new, final, lacuna and the last three columns, from *ca.* 901 to 1200 are lost.

A few examples from various sections of the text may serve to illustrate in somewhat more detail its treatment of the materials.

Sample Passage from OBGT I

Lines 317-330 of the section dealing with the demonstratives in OBGT I read:

317 (Sg.)	lú-ne-	ra	*a-na an-ni-i-im*	"to this one"
318	lú-ne-	er	*a-na an-ni-i-im*	"to this one"
319	lú-ne-	a	*a-na an-ni-i-im*	"to this one"
320	lú-ne-	šè	*a-na an-ni-i-im*	"to this one"
321 (Pl.)	lú-ne-meš-	rà	*a-na an-nu-ú-tim*	"to these ones"
322 (Sg.)	lú-ne-	šè-àm	*a-na an-ni-i-im-ma*	"to this one only"
323 (Pl.)	lú-ne-meš-	šè-àm	*a-na an-nu-ú-tim-ma*	"to these ones only"
324 (Sg.)	lú-ne-	a	*an-ni-a-am*	"(to) this one"
325	lú-ne-	er	*an-ni-a-am*	"(to) this one"
326	lú-e-	ra	*an-ni-a-am*	"(to) this one"
327 (Pl.)	lú-e-meš-	a	*an-nu-ú-tim*	"(to) these ones"
328	lú-ne-meš-	ra	*an-nu-ú-tim*	"(to) these ones"
329 (Sg.)	lú-ne-	er	ì-me-a *an-ni-a-am-ma*	"(to) this one only"
330 (Pl.)	lú-e-meš-	ra	ì-me-a *an-nu-ú-tim-ma*	"(to) these ones only"

The pronoun dealt with is **ne** "this" except in lines 326, 327, and 330, where **e** "this" has been substituted for it. There is no obvious reason for this substitution and it would seem that the scribe considered **ne** and **e** equivalent interchangeable variants. Both are given in their dependent form in attribution to the substantive **lú** "man" and the combination is translated in Akkadian by the demonstrative pronoun *annūm* "this", "this one".

Governing for the section from line 317 to line 330 and onwards is the marking of the forms by one of the Sumerian case-endings **-ra/-r** "personal dative", **-a** "illative" or **-šè** "directive" in contrast to the immediately preceding section in which the forms were marked by **-da** "comitative" or **-ta** "ablative". The case marks **-ra/-r, -a, -šè,** are apparently considered more or less equivalent and interchangeable alternants by the scribe. He varies their order freely (**-ra, -r, -a,** in 317-319; **-a, -r, -ra** in 324-326) and he chooses now one, now another to serve as case-representative with plural or delimiting forms (-ra in 321 and 328, -a in 327, -šè for both sg. and pl. delimiting in 322-323; -r(a) in 329-330). They are also all translated alike in Akkadian, either by the preposition *ana* "for", "to", or by accusative.

As for the form of these case-elements it may be noted that the personal dative mark is -r after vowels, -ra after consonants, as may be seen in forms such as lú-ne-meš-ra (321,328) and lú-e-meš-ra (330) as against lú-ne-er (318,325,329). In lines 317 and 326 the writings lú-ne-ra and lú-e-ra indicate forms with a genitive element -ak before the dative element: lunêkra < lu.ne.ak.ra and luêkra <lu.e.ak.ra both denoting "for the . . . ('son', 'wife', or other word for a person) of this one". The a of the genitive element is regularly assimilated to and contracted with the e of the demonstratives, the k is never indicated in writing when final in a syllable. In the Akkadian column *a-na an-ni-i-im* in line 317 may be considered short for *a-na ⟨mār⟩ an-ni-i-im* "for ⟨the son or similar⟩ of this one" while *an-ni-a-am* of line 326 is probably a dittography of *an-ni-a-am* in the line above, the line should read *an-ni-i-im*.

Section 317-323 differs from section 324-330 primarily in the Akkadian column where the translation changes from a construction with the preposition *ana* to a simple accusative. This difference presumably reflects the fact that Sumerian and Akkadian verbs of the same or similar meaning often construe their object differently. Thus Sumerian **sum** "to give" takes the word for the recipient in the dative if the recipient is a person, e.g., lú-ne-er mu-na-an-sum "he gave to this one", whereas Akkadian, which possesses a dative only in the pronouns, will construe its verb for "to give", *nadānum* with the preposition *ana : ana annîm iddin* "he gave to this one", so that in these instances Sumerian lú-ne-er will correspond to Akkadian *a-na an-ni-i-im* as stated in line 318. The Sumerian verb-phrase for "to love" ki . . . ača, on the other hand, construes the word for the person loved in the dative: lú-ne-er ki mu-na-an-ača "he loved this one", while the Akkadian verb for "to love" *râmum* construes the word for the person loved in the accusative: *annîam irâm* "he loved this one", so that in these instances Sumerian lú-ne-er will correspond to *an-ni-a-am* as stated in line 325. In similar manner there are cases where Sumerian -a or -šè will correspond to Akkadian constructions with *ana* and cases where they will correspond to constructions with Akkadian accusatives.

Sections 317-321 and 324-328 contrast with sections 322-323 and 329-330 in that the latter sections list forms marked by -àm and ì-me-a in the Sumerian column, forms with the particle -*ma* in the Akkadian column. The Sumerian -àm "(that) he/she/it is", "who/which is" and ì-me-a "that it/he/she is", "who/which is" are forms of the verb me "to be" which can be used to form adverbial clauses with delimiting force: "only". This same delimiting force pertains in Akkadian to the particle -*ma*. As an example of -àm in this usage may serve *Inventaire de Tablettes de Telloh III* 5279.11 é kug-šu-na-ta-àm in-sa$_{10}$ -a "that she bought the house only (-àm) with (-ta) silver of her hand". The statement records an oath by a widow that she had bought a certain house with her own personal means and had not used property of her late husband to pay for it. A similar use of i-me-a is perhaps *Tablettes Cunéiforme de Louvre V* 6169.7-9 áb Ša-bar-tur mu-bi i-me-a Lugal-ba-ta-è máš-šè-àm-da i-⟨na⟩-an-gub-a "that Lugalbatae had pledged with him the cow named Shabartur for the interest only".

Sections 317-320, 322, 324-326, and 329, finally, contrast as singular forms with respectively 321, 323, 327-328, and 330, which list the corresponding plural forms marked by -meš.

VERB

The most remarkable of the Old Babylonian grammatical texts that we possess are unquestionably the five large and detailed verbal paradigms OBGT VI, VII, VIII, IX, and X. They show remarkable analytic penetration and skill in organizing and presenting the results.

The paradigms do not, as we have mentioned, follow a single set pattern of arrangement but differ considerably from one another in this respect. Nevertheless there are a number of grammatical categories that are common to all, or almost all, of them.

Of such common categories may be mentioned those of person – in the indicative verbal paradigm always in the order 3p. 1p. 2p. – and of tense or – more precisely – of aspect: permansive (stative) present/future (fientic durative) and preterit (punctive). Of special interest are the moods which include a category common to all the verbal paradigms which might be named volitive. It embraces what we should call Sumerian imperative, cohortative, optative; Akkadian imperative, optative, in such a manner that 2d person sg. volitive is represented by imperative of Sumerian and Akkadian, 1st person by cohortative in Sumerian and optative 1st person in Akkadian, and 3rd person volitive by optative 3rd person of Sumerian and Akkadian both.

Other categories generally attested are those of ventive,[3] represented in Sumerian by forms with prefix containing an m, in Akkadian by the well-known ventive-suffixes; and non-ventive. To this comes causative, expressed in Akkadian by the Š-stem and in Sumerian by a variety of prefixes and infixes, dative and directive, expressed in Sumerian by dative and directive infixes, in Akkadian by dative forms of suffixes; and finally comitative expressed in Sumerian by the comitative infix and rendered in Akkadian by means of the accusative of the relevant suffix.

As an example of the overall organization of one of these paradigms we may select that of the verb ğen : *alākum* "to go" OBGT VII. The paradigm is organized through the successive application of a series of categories as follows:

I. Number (Sg:Pl.) of Goal

The paradigm divides into two main parts according to whether the dimensional goal of the verb is singular (including cases where no goal is specified): lines 1-190, or plural, lines 191-318.

II. Participation (1 and 2p.:3p.) of Goal

A further subdivision according to whether the indicated goal includes a speech situation-participant (1 or 2p.) — lines 191-246 — or not (3p.) — lines 247-318 — is made in the plural sections mentioned above but not in the section.

III. Number (Sg.:Pl.) of Subject

Each of the three major parts resulting from the divisions mentioned above: 1-190, 191-246, and 247-318, are in turn divided into two according to whether the subject of the verb is singular or plural as follows: sg. goal, sg. subject 1-95, pl. subject 96-190; pl. goal, 1 and 2 p. sg. subject 191-222, pl. subject 223-246; pl. goal, 3p. subject sg. 247-282, pl. subject 283-318.

IV. Modes (Vol.:Indic.)

Each of the singular and plural sections listed is further divided according to whether the forms listed are in the volitive or in the indicative mood.

V. Aspect (Pres:Pret)

A further subdivision is made in the indicative section according to whether the forms are in the fientic durative (Pres.) or the punctive (Pret.) aspect; in the volitive section no such subdivision is made, so that application of the categories of modes and aspect result in a triple subdivision of each of the six sections so far mentioned as follows:

Sg. goal, sg. subj. vol. 1-30; indic. pres. 31-67; indic. pret. 68-95: pl. subj. vol. 96-125, indic. pres. 126-162; indic. pret. 163-190 — *pl. 1 and 2p. goal*, sg. subj. vol. 191-198, indic. pres. 199-210, indic. pret. 211-222; pl. subj. vol. 223-230, indic. pres. 231-238, indic. pret. 239-246 — *Pl. 3p. goal*, sg. subj. vol. 247-258, indic. pres. 259-270, indic. pret. 271-282: pl. subj. vol. 283-294, indic. pres. 295-307, indic. pret. 308-318.

VI and VII. Ventive and separative

The various volitive sections are divided and subdivided according to whether the forms are in the ventive or not in the ventive, and then as to whether the ventive forms are in ventive separative or not, and as to whether the non-ventive forms are in separative or not. Thus, e.g., the volitive section 1-30 divides into VENTIVE non-separative [1-9]; separative [10]-18 : NON-VENTIVE, non-separative 19-24, separative 25-30.

In the indicative sections, both present and preterit, the same categories are applied but curiously enough in reverse order, first that of separative: non-separative then, as subdivision, that of ventive: non-ventive. As example may serve the indicative present section 31-67, which shows the ordering NON-SEPARATIVE non-ventive 32-45, ventive 46-51: SEPARATIVE ventive 52-59 . . . non-ventive 62-67.

As a whole the application of the categories VI-VII result in divisions as follows:

(1a) Sg. goal, sg. subject

Volitive

Ventive non-separative 1-9,	ventive-separative 10-18,
non-ventive non-separative 19-24,	non-ventive separative 25-30

Indic. Pres.

Non-separative non-ventive 32-45,	non-separative ventive 46-51,
separative ventive 52-59. . . .	separative non-ventive 62-67.

Indic. Pret.

Non-separative non-ventive 68-73,	non-separative ventive 74-79,
separative ventive 80-87. . . .	separative non-ventive 90-95.

(1b) Sg. goal, pl. subject

Volitive

Ventive non-separative 96-104,	ventive separative 105-113,
non-ventive non-separative 114-119,	non-ventive separative 120-125

Indic. Pres.

Non-separative non-ventive 126-140,	non-separative ventive 141-146,
separative ventive 147-154. . . .	separative non-ventive 157-162.

Indic. Pret.

Non-separative non-ventive 163-168,	non-separative ventive 169-174,
separative ventive 175-182. . . .	separative non-ventive 185-190.

(2a) Pl. goal, 1 and 2 p.; sg. subject

In this section, where the goal point is 1 and 2p. sg., the scribe lists only ventive forms. We have thought it convenient to indicate in angle brackets also the corresponding non-ventives for comparison with other parts of the paradigms but have no opinion as to whether such ventives could actually be formed. In lines 207-210 and 219-222 the scribe lists ablative 1 and 2p. pl. forms he/you go/went away from us: and he/I go/went away from you (pl.)"

which fall outside the framework of the paradigm for the paradigm deals with goal points, not also starting points of the action. We have therefore indicated these lines as intrusive by enclosing them in double angle brackets.[4]

Volitive

Ventive non-separative 191-194,	ventive separative 195-198
⟨non-ventive non-separative⟩	⟨non-ventive separative⟩

Indic. Pres.

⟨Non-separative non-ventive⟩	non-separative ventive 194-202
separative ventive 203-206	⟨⟨separative non-ventive 207-210⟩⟩

Indic. Pret.

⟨Non-separative non-ventive⟩	non-separative ventive 211-214
separative ventive 215-218	⟨⟨separative non-ventive 219-222⟩⟩

(2b) Pl. goal 1 and 2p.; pl. subject.

Volitive

Ventive non-separative 223-226,	ventive separative 227-230
⟨non-ventive non-separative⟩	⟨non-ventive separative⟩

Indic. Pres.

⟨Non-separative non-ventive,⟩	non-separative ventive 231-234
separative ventive 235-238,	⟨separative non-ventive⟩

Indic. Pret.

⟨Non-separative non-ventive,⟩	non-separative ventive 239-242
separative ventive 243-246,	⟨separative non-ventive⟩

(3a) Pl. goal 3p.; sg. subject

Volitive

Ventive non-separative 247-249,	ventive separative 250-252
non-ventive non-separative 253-255,	non-ventive separative 256-258

Indic. Pres.

Non-separative non-ventive 259-261,	non-separative ventive 262-264
separative ventive 265-267,	separative non-ventive 268-270

Indic. Pret.

Non-separative non-ventive 271-273,	non-separative ventive 274-276
separative ventive 277-279,	separative non-ventive 280-282

(3b) Pl. goal 3p.; pl. subject

Volitive

Ventive non-separative 283-285,	ventive separative 286-288
Non-ventive non-separative 289-291,	non-ventive separative 292-294

Indic Pres.

Non-separative non-ventive 295-297,	non-separative ventive 298-300
separative ventive 301-303,	separative non-ventive 304-306

Indic. Pret.

Non-separative non-ventive 307-309,	non-separative ventive 310-312
separative ventive 313-315,	separative non-ventive 316-318

VIII. Person (#p.:3p.:1p.:2p.) of goal

The category would seem originally – or ideally – to have consisted of two separate categories, namely #p. (i.e., no personal goal):3p. and 1p.:2p. These original categories appear to underlie the arrangement of the plural goal sections, where 1p.:2p. appears in the first plural goal section, #p.:3p. in the second plural goal section. However, since #p. is neither sg. nor pl. or – if one wishes – is the same in both sg. and pl., the scribe had already listed its forms under sg. goal and did not repeat them.

In the singular goal part the two categories #p.:3p. and 1p.:2p. have been treated as one. The full number of contrasts of this joint category is dealt with, however, only in the volitive sections 1-28 and 96-123; in the indicative present (31-65 and 126-160) and indicative preterit (68-93 and 163-188) sections, only #p.:3p.:2p. are dealt with, 1p. is disregarded.

Since movement toward 1p. or 2p. normally presupposes ventive the paradigm lists no forms with 1p. or 2p. goals except ventive ones, and for reasons which may be connected with a desire to keep forms with prefix **mu** together on the Sumerian side, the paradigm chooses in its indicative sections to list 2p. goal non-separative ventive forms after the 2p. goal separative ventive forms (58-59, 86-87, 153-154, 181-182) instead of after the 3p. non-separative ventive forms (49-51, 77-79, 144-146, 172-174), where one would have expected them in indicative present and preterit.

IX. Person (3p.:1p.:2p.) of subject

Each of the sections formed by division according to category VIII is further, and finally, subdivided according to person of the subject. The order is in the volitive sections 2p.:1p.:3p., in the indicative sections 3p.:1p.:2p. In cases where the form has 1p. goal only 2p. and 3p. subject forms are listed while similarly, where the form has 2p. goal only 1p. and 3p. subject forms are listed.

We dispense with the very long list necessary to show the divisions resulting from the application of categories VIII and IX and content ourselves instead with giving as an example of the details of the list the passage lines 62-79. The headings in parentheses and the translations have been supplied by us and are not in the text:

(Singular goal, singular subject)
(Indicative, Present)
(Separative (I_2) non-ventive)
(#p. goal)

62 3p. [ba]-du	*it-tál-lak*	"he goes away"
63 1p. [ba-d]u-un	*at-tál-lak*	"I go away"
64 2p. [ba-d]u-un	*ta-at-tál-lak*	"you (sg.) go away"

(3p. sg. goal)

65	3p. [ba-š]i-du	*it-tál-lak-šum*	"he goes away to him"
66	1p. [ba-ši]-du-un	*at-tál-lak-šum*	"I go away to him"
67	2p. [ba-ši]-du-un	*ta-at-tál-lak-šum*	"you (sg.) go away to him"

(Indicative Preterit)
Non-separative non-ventive)
(#p. goal)

68	3p. [i]n-g̃en	*il-lik*	"he went"
69	1p. ⌈in-g̃en⌉-en	*al-lik*	"I went"
70	2p. ⌈in-g̃en⌉-en	*tál-lik*	"you (sg.) went to him"

(3p. sg. goal)

71	3p. ⌈in-ši⌉-g̃en	*il-lik-šum*	"he went to him"
72	1p. ⌈in⌉-ši-g̃en-en	*al-lik-šum*	"I went to him"
73	2p. ⌈in-ši-g̃en⌉-en	*tál-lik-šum*	"you (sg.) went to him"

(Non-separative ventive)
(#p. goal)

74	3p. [i-i]m-g̃en	*il-li-kam*	"he came"
75	1p. [i-i]m-g̃en-en	*al-li-kam*	"I came"
76	2p. ⌈i-im-g̃en-en⌉	*tál-li-kam*	"you (sg.) came"

(3p. sg. goal)

77	3p. [i-] ⌈im-ši⌉-g̃en	⌈il-li-kaš-šum⌉	"he came to him"
78	1p. [i-] im-ši-g̃en-en	⌈al-li-kaš-šum⌉	"I came to him"
79	2p. [i-i] m-ši-g̃en-⌈en⌉	*tál-li-kaš-šum*	"you (sg.) came to him"

II. The Neo-Babylonian Element Analysis

The device dominating the preserved Old-Babylonian grammatical texts, the paradigm, is capable of ordering and analyzing all the varied forms in which a word may occur while leaving these forms intact. For analysis to break through the form as given by the language, to take it apart in elements which have no independent existence, and to consider and order these elements in isolation, is a bold and radical step indeed. Yet it seems to have been taken in Ancient Mesopotamia already in the Old-Babylonian period, for in lexical lists of that period one occasionally meets up with grammatical elements, bound forms, which can only derive from such analyses. Examples are MSL II p. 126 5-6 where the bound element (postposition) -a is listed with meanings *ina* "in" and *ana* "to", p. 129 18 where the bound pronominal subject-element 1p. pl. of the preterit active, -me- is listed with translation *ni-i-nu* "we", p. 132 32 -ba translated *ša-a-ti* "him", 43 -zu translated -[*ka*]-*a* "thy", p. 139 ii 3 -da translated *i-ti* "with", p. 145 26 -ta translated *a-na* "to", 35 -ra translated *e-li* "over", "beyond" etc.

For evidence of full utilization of element analysis, isolation of grammatical elements and their systematic ordering in a grammatical table, we must turn to texts which have come down to us in copies — and probably also in "editions" — of much later time.

To these late texts we must go also for evidence of the development of a grammatical terminology even though internal indications suggest origin of the terms in the Old-Babylonian period already. Such terms are AN-TA MÚRU-TA KI-TA "prefix", "infix", "suffix", *ša išten* "singular" lit. "of one", and *ma'dūtu* "plural", *hamṭu* "preterit", "punctive", lit. "fast" and *marū* "present", "durative", lit. "slow", *riātum* "ventive" lit. perhaps "closeness", *gamartum* "finished", "off", "away" "separative", and *šushurtum* a term of unclear meaning.

As an example of a grammatical table listing isolated grammatical elements may serve NBGT I, the first tablet of a series called ù : *anāku* which presumably dealt with grammar throughout, a tablet known to us in a copy from the time of Darius.

In trying to recover the underlying principles of ordering one must, we believe, pay special attention to the economy with which the text uses translation into Akkadian; only key entries are translated, so that the translations take on in many respects the character of headings indicating basic structuring points in the ordering. Such points are particularly helpful for finding the way back to the basic underlying scheme which would seem to have been somewhat blurred — perhaps already by the author — through addition after such key terms not only of grammatical elements belonging there properly, but sometimes also of elements that merely had, or could have, the same Akkadian translation as the key term.

And as if this were not enough to urge caution, there is no guarantee that the text as we have it is correct — in fact, in various places it seems clearly to have suffered corruption at the hands of incompetent copyists in the course of its transmission.

Attempting an outline of the arrangement of NBGT I we would suggest, then, following the lead of the translated key terms, that the core of the ordering is a treatment of the Sumerian personal pronoun and pronominal elements represented by lines 1-201 and 267-307 of the present text. Lines 202-257, which deal with the conjunction and subjunction ù, with genitive and illative cases and with ventive and separative prefixes unrelated to the personal pronoun, and lines 258-266, which deal with the possessive pronoun, would seem to be additions — possibly original ones made by the author of the listing, possibly later ones made by a copyist or editor.

As such additions we would consider also lines 308-402, which list cases in which Sumerian directives (-šè), ablatives (-ta), and comitatives (-da) cannot be translated as *ana* or *ina* in Akkadian as stated in the core section.

Lastly the section 403-462, which lists verbal elements of various kinds, modal elements, negations, etc. unrelated to the personal pronouns may be considered a unit of its own, whether original or addition.

THE CORE SECTION

The core section lists forms of the Sumerian personal pronoun and pronominal verbal element ordering them according to the categories of (I) Number (sg. and pl.), (II) Marked and unmarked case, (III) Free or bound form, (IV) Verbal aspect of simple form, šushurtu, or riātum (ventive), (V) Orthographical differentiation of plene or vide (VI) Aspect (punctive : durative), (VII) Person (1p.:2p.:3p.), (VIII) Case (# of nom., # of acc., illative, dative, directive, comitative, ablative).

Of these categories IV, V, and VI are applied only to sg. zero-case pronominal element in the verb (lines 1-101). Of the more generally applied categories I, II, III, VII, and VIII, category I, number, is curiously treated. Instead of two successive sections, one of singular forms and one of plurals, the plural section (lines 125-201) has been oddly inserted in the singular section between the unmarked (lines 1-124) and the marked (lines 267-307) case forms. The order in which the categories are applied varies from section to section. With the singular unmarked forms that constitute the section from line 1 to line 124 the order is I(number), II(unmarked:marked case), III(bound:free form) . . . VII(person), VIII(case). In the corresponding sections of singular marked forms of lines 267-307 the categories III and VII have changed place so that the order of application is I(number), II(unmarked:marked case), VII(person), III(bound:free form), VIII(case). In the inserted plural section of lines 125-201, finally, category II (unmarked: marked) is not applied, so that unmarked case form becomes just one more instance, zero-case, under category VIII. In this section, furthermore, the order of categories III and VIII are reversed so that the order of application is I (number), VII (person), VIII (case), III (bound:free form).

Applications of these categories in the order indicated results in a set of divisions as shown in the foldout chart that follows.

COMPLEMENTARY ADDITIONS

We have mentioned that certain sections seem to represent additions to the basic scheme of arrangement.[5] Such supposed additions are lines 202-266 and 308-402. They show a characteristic pattern of their own with focus on a case as such rather than on case as implied in the declension of the pronoun. This pattern is (1) Case-marks listed alone or as applied to non-pronominal stems (2) Case-marks applied to pronoun or pronominal infix 1, 2, or 3d p. sg.

In section 202-266, added before lines that treat of the dimensional cases of the pronoun (lines 267-307), the additions provide a section on the possessive pronoun (258-266), viewed, apparently, as a kind of genitive of the personal pronoun. It then prefaces this with two non-pronominal sections of case-marks listed alone, one (lines 202-222) to head the new possessive section and one, (lines 223-257), to head the existing section on dimensional cases.

In the heading for the possessive section the additions seem to operate with an extension of the genitive to a general "junctive" relation, for the heading starts out with the conjunction ù (202) translated as *ù* "and also" in Akkadian, then follow other conjunctive elements such as Sumerian -bi and -bi-da "and" (203-204) and the conjunctive verbal prefix -n--ga- "and", "also" (205-208). Next comes the subjunctive ù- of previousness, "when ... then", translated *lu*, and its allomorphs (209-212); the prefix ša-, "it on its side" translated *ša* (213) níg "that (of)" translated *ša* (214) and a series of combinations of the genitive mark -(a)k with following allative -e, illative -a and the enclitic emphatic element -àm (214-217). Last is listed a number of syllables which presumably are meant to represent cases of vowel followed by the genitive element -ak in which the a of -ak is assimilated and the k left unexpressed in the writing: da, u, a, i, e (218-222).

The heading for the dimensional cases is introduced by ka representing a combination of the genitive element (a)k with a following illative -a and is translated *ina ana* "in(to)", "to" (223). There follows a great many case-marks of various kinds and various combinations, all capable — in one context or another — of being translated into Akkadian by either *ina* or *ana*. Here belongs also the series of ventive prefixes with m beginning in line 241: um: [*a-na i*]*a-a-⟨ši⟩* "toward me" and continuing to line 256, and the ba of line 257, literally "in its" which is used after clauses and denotes "when such and such had taken place". It is explained as *ga*(!?)-*mar*(!?)-tum KI-TA "finished, "suffix".

The later supposed additions, lines 308-402 deal with cases in which the Sumerian case-marks -šè, -ta, and -da, are not to be translated simply as *ana* or *ina* in Akkadian but as *aššum* "because of", (308-313) or *ištu bīt* "since . . .", (314) or *innani* "from now on" (315), etc. Particularly regularly constructed are the sections from line 322 and onward, they show preposition, preposition with 1p. sg., with 2p. sg., and with 3p. sg. pronoun in that order in Akkadian. The constructions treated are *e-li* "against (322-325), *eli-ia* "against me" (326-331), *eli-ka* "against you" (322-336), *eli-šu* "against him" (337-352), *qá-du* "inclusive of" (353-356) *qá-du-ú-a* "inclusive of me" (357-360) *qá-du-uk-ku* "inclusive of you" (361-363), *qá-du-uš-šu* "inclusive of him" (364-377), *it-tum* "with" (379-382), *it-ti-ia* "with me" (383-385), *it-ti-ka* "with you" (386-389), *it-ti-šu* AN-TA! "with him", "infix", *ap-pu-na* "also" (395-398), and the potentialis forms *le-e-ú* "to be able to" (399), *e-li-i* "I can" (400), *te-li-i* "you can" (401), and *i-li-i* "he can" (402). The case-mark corresponding to all of these Akkadian prepositions etc., is in the Sumerian of the translated lines always the comitative **da**, but in the lines following it there is considerable variation. The translation will, however, apply throughout.

FINAL SECTION

The final section of NBGT I, from line 403 to 462, is made up of various verbal elements unconnected with pronouns or pronominal elements. They seem to comprise nominalizing – in Akkadian participial – elements 403-404, various modal elements 405-410, prefixes of previousness 411-414, negative elements expressive of negation, of "not yet", of deprecatory attitude, and of deprivation and exception 415-435. Then follow elements translated by the Akkadian particle *-ma* in various of its meanings 439-459, the irrealis particle -ǧiš-en : *-ma-an*, and the particle of direct quotation -e-še : *-mi-i*. As the last is listed the indefinite pronoun **na-me** : *man-ma* "any (one)" 462.

SAMPLE PASSAGE FROM NBGT I

As an example of the kind of analysis offered in NBGT I and in other texts of similar nature we may quote the section from column i line 47 to line 84. It reads:

47 un *a-na-ku ma-lu-ú* AN-TA MÚRU-TA ⟨KI-TA⟩ "I (nom.), plene, prefix,
   an   infix, and suffix"
   in
50 en
   ab
   mu
   u₈
54 un *ia-a-ti* AN-TA KI-TA MÚRU-TA "Me (acc.), prefix, suffix, and infix"
   an
   in
   en
   mu
59 un *at-ta ma-lu-ú* ⟨MÚRU-TA⟩ KI-TA "you (nom.), plene, infix, suffix
   an
   in
   en
   ab
   u₈

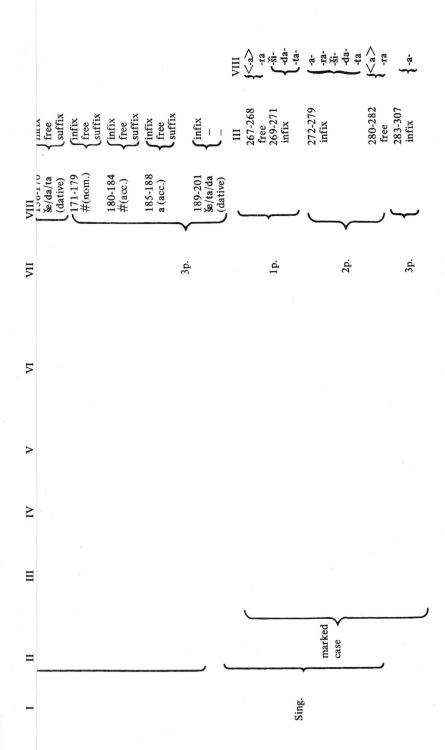

65 un *ka-a-ta* MÚRU-TA KI-TA "you (acc.) infix (or) suffix"
   an
   in
   en
   ab
   u$_8$
71 un [*šu*]-*ú* ʿ*ma-lu*ʾ-*ú* AN-TA MÚRU-TA "he/she/it (nom.) plene, prefix
   an   (or) infix"
   in
   en
   ub
   ab
   u$_8$
78 un *šu-a-ti ma-lu-ú* AN-TA MÚRU-TA "him/her/it (acc.), plene, prefix
   an   (or) infix"
   in
   en
   ub
   ab
84 íb

The following comments on details may be attempted:

1) The section appears to deal with elements marking subject, direct object, and various indirect objects in the preterit singular of the intransitive or passive and the transitive active conjugation. The corresponding present/ future forms seem to have been dealt with in lines 35-46. The section limits itself to forms written "plene" (*malū*), i.e., with the final consonant specifically indicated by the writing. The corresponding "vide" (*rīqu*) writings are listed in lines 1-34.

2) The subject elements recognized by present day Sumerologists are as follows:

	Preterit Singular	
	Intransitive and Passive	*Transitive Active*
1p.	$-\sqrt{}-$ **en**	$-\#-\sqrt{}$
2p.	$-\sqrt{}-$ **en**	$-$ **e** $-\sqrt{}$
3p.	$-\sqrt{}-\#$	$-$ **n** $-\sqrt{}$
3n.	$-\sqrt{}-\#$	$-$ **b** $-\sqrt{}$

The 1p. and 2p. elements **-en** of intransitive and passive serve as direct object elements 1p. and 2p. if suffixed to a transitive active form.

It may be noted that the text NBGT I deals only with explicit marks and that accordingly forms in zero such as intr. and pass. 3p. sg. and 3n. sg., and trans. act. 1p. sg. are not treated. Furthermore, trans. act. 2p. -e- √ is treated as if it were -#- √ in conformity with most of our Old Babylonian verbal paradigms and with the majority of writings of the form in Sumerian texts generally.

3) The suffix -en of 1p. and 2p. intr. and pass. is regularly assimilated to any immediately preceding vowel; after stems ending in -u, -a, -i, it will therefore appear as -un, -an, and -in. With these allomorphs the subject element -en of 1p. is listed in lines 47-50 under the heading *anāku* "I", and the subject element -en of 2p. sg. is listed in lines 59-62 under the heading *attā* "you" with the same series of allomorphs.

As direct object elements these elements -en appear in lines 54-57 under the heading *iāti* "me" and in lines 65-68 under the heading *kāta* "you".

The rank of these elements as suffixes is duly indicated by the term KI-TA "suffix" in lines 54, 59, and 65. The same term must be restored in line 47 where it seems to have been lost in the course of the tradition of the text.

4) The infixes -n- and -b-, which mark the subject 3p. sg. and 3n. sg. in the preterit transitive active cannot be rendered in isolation by the cuneiform writing, which is syllabic, not alphabetic, in character. The best the scribe can do, therefore, is to list these elements as they occur in writing combined with a preceding vowel: **un, an, in, en** and **ub, ab,** and thus they occur under the heading *šū* "he/it" in lines 71-76. The other possible syllabic combinations: **nu, na, ni, ne** and **bu, ba, bi, be,** were not, apparently, considered worth listing since the elements -n- and -b- never, of course, form a syllable with the initial consonant of a following verbal root, and very rarely form a syllable with one beginning with a vowel. The combinations of -n- and -b- with a preceding vowel, **un, an, in,** etc. could — since Sumerian has verbal prefixes of the form **u-, a-,** and **i-** — stand for combinations of prefix (**u-, a-, i-**) and infix (**-n-, -b-**) and the notation on rank given in line 71 reads accordingly AN-TA MÚRU-TA "prefix (or/and) infix".

5) In lines 78-84 the forms **un, an, in, en, ub, ab,** and **íb** are given under the heading *šuāti* "him/it" and with AN-TA MÚRU-TA "prefix (and/or) infix" notation about rank. The use of the infixed elements 3p. and 3n. sg. thus indicated is generally recognized. Poebel, GSG 523 assumed that thus used they mark factitive, originally 3p. or 3n. object, Falkenstein GSGGL 64 assumes that they are object elements 3p. We ourselves AS XVI p. 95 note 17 recognize them as indirect object elements with zero mark of collative case.

6) There remains a number of entries less easily identified. To these may be counted **ab** listed as 1p. sg. subject (51) and 2p. sg. subj. (63) and

object (69). Presumably reference is to an infix, but more than that is difficult to say. A further group of elements are **mu** and **u₈** listed as 1p. subj. elements in lines 52 and 53. Of these **mu-** is clearest. It reoccurs as 1p. object element in line 58, but is not listed as either 2p. or 3p. element. It seems clear that we are here dealing with the prefix **mu-**, which indicates spatial and emotional closeness to speaker and which can be used to focus attention on the speaker i.e. on 1p. subject, as shown by us in AS XVI p. 82, note, second column. For its use with 1p. indirect object, but not with 2d. and 3rd person such object cf. e.g. **e-da-g̃ál** : *na-ši-a-ta* "is with you": "you carry", **mu-da-g̃ál** : *na-ši-a-ku* "is with me": "I carry", **an-da-g̃ál** : *na-ši* "is with him" : "he carries" in MSL IV page 70 lines 59-61. As will be seen the Sumerian indirect (comitative) object corresponds here to the Akkadian subject. Other examples are listed in AS XVI page 81 note, second column (1). Cases of similar uuse of **mu-** with indirect object (allative) are e.g. **mu-un-ti-ti** : *ú-re-še-an-ni* "he teased me" but **an-ni-ib-ti-ti** : *ú-re-ši-* [*šu*] "I teased him" MSL IV page 74 lines 232-235. Further examples may be found in AS XVI page 81-82 in the note.

The element **u₈** listed as subject element 1p. in line 53, as subject element 2p. in line 64, as object element 2p. in line 70, and as subject element 3p. in line 77 admits of too many and too partial identifications to repay comment here.

NOTES

*The ms. of this chapter was completed in June of 1968. It has been left unchanged.

1. A convenient, recent edition of the grammatical texts is Landsberger et al. 1956: 45-202, with addenda in Landsberger et al. 1957: 196-199 (abbreviated as MSL 4 and MSL 5, respectively). The texts are divided by Landsberger into OBGT, i.e., Old-Babylonian Grammatical Texts, and NBGT, i.e., Neo-Babylonian Grammatical Texts. We use his abbreviations here. Of treatments see especially Poebel 1914: 29ff. for OBGT I; Jacobsen 1956 and 1965: 71-102 for OBGT VI, VII, VIII, and IX; and Thureau-Dangin 1935 for NBGT I. [See now also the important article by A. Shaffer, "TA *ša kīma A ītenerrubu,"Orientalia,* 38 (1969), pp. 433-446. – author]

2. Cf. – to mention just one example of a great many – Jean 1926, no. 236.

3. The term was coined by Benno Landsberger. It denotes a form indicating movement toward the speaker or – we tend to assume – to a point directly opposite the speaker. See our discussion Jacobsen 1960: 105-106, 107-109, and literature there quoted.

4. For a more detailed treatment of the problems raised by these entries, see Jacobsen 1960, von Soden 1961, and Jacobsen 1963.

5. More likely, perhaps, survivals of an earlier less, or differently, systematized form. It is our impression that ultimately NBGT I belongs in a tradition harking back to texts of the type of OBGT I.

REFERENCES

Jacobsen, Thorkild. 1956. Introduction. Materialien zum Sumerischen Lexikon 4, edited by Benno Landsberger et al., 1*-50*. Rome: Pontificium Institutum Biblicum.

———. 1960. *ittalak niāti*. Journal of Near Eastern Studies 19. 101-116.

———. 1963. The Akkadian ablative accusative. Journal of Near Eastern Studies 21: 18-29.

———. 1965. About the Sumerian verb. Studies in honor of Benno Landsberger . . ., The Oriental Institute of the University of Chicago. (Assyriological Studies, 16). Chicago: University of Chicago Press.

Jean, Charles-François. 1926. Contrats de Larsa. (Musée du Louvre, Département des antiquités orientales, Tablettes cunéiforme de Louvre, 11). Paris: Paul Geuthner.

Jespersen, Otto. 1924. The Philosophy of Grammar. London: Allen and Unwin.

Landsberger, Benno et al. 1956. Materialien zum Sumerischen Lexikon 4. Rome Pontificium Institutum Biblicum.

———. 1957. Materialien zum Sumerischen Lexikon 5. Rome: Pontificium Institutum Biblicum.

Poebel, A. 1914. Grammatical texts. (University Museum, Publications of the Babylonian section 6 [1]). Philadelphia: University of Pennsylvania.

Soden, W. von. 1961. Zum Akkusativ der Beziehung. Orientalia 30: 156-162.

Thureau-Dangin, F. 1935. Formes grammaticales Sumeriennes. Revue d'Assyriologie 32: 89-114.

2. The Origin and Development of Linguistics in India

J. F. Staal

Generalizations about linguistics and its history from the Western tradition alone go often astray, as evidence from the Indian tradition – and specifically from the "Sanskrit grammarians" – is neglected. The following notes provide some data which may help to pave the way for a more unified outline of linguistics in India and for more adequate statements about the history of linguistics in general.

I

   The earliest evidence of intensive and extensive linguistic activity in India is the constitution of a *padapāṭha* or "word for word recitation" corresponding to the *saṃhitāpāṭha* or "continuous recitation" of the Veda. This may have taken place in the period between the tenth and the seventh centuries B.C. Its primary aim was to preserve the Vedic heritage, which in turn was required for recitations at the ritual. In the *padapāṭha*, the words of the *saṃhitāpāṭha* were separated, forms considered compounds were analyzed, and the end of utterances was marked. The following is an example from the Ṛgveda (10.127.2):

SAṂHITĀPĀṬHA: *órv aprá ámartyā niváto devȳ̀ udvátaḥ//*
PADAPĀṬHA: */ā́/urú/aprāḥ/ámartyā/ni-vátaḥ/devī́/ut-vátaḥ//*
  "the immortal goddess has pervaded the wide space, the depths and the heighths"

   The Prātiśākhya literature aimed at a complete description of the derivation of the *saṃhitāpāṭha* from the *padapāṭha*. This implies that its extent was circumscribed by Vedic texts handed down in this double form, and that its attention was confined to fixed corpora of utterances, each analyzed with respect to a definite underlying structure. This led to the study of few, well-defined grammatical topics, such as external sandhi and accentuation. Thus concentrating on the given finite corpus transmitted within a Vedic school (*śākhā*), the authors of the Prātiśākhyas paid no attention to the infinite character of language; they studied utterances (*uccāraṇa*) rather than sentences (*vākya*); they were concerned with enumeration (*saṃkhyā*) rather than with the formulation of general rules (*sāmānyasūtra*).

This is not to say that rules were not formulated. But such rules as were formulated account for specific relationships between the *padapāṭha* (e.g. /*tava* / *ayam* /) and the *saṃhitā* (i.e., *tavāyam*). Such rules happen to coincide with general rules of external sandhi and Western linguists and philologists tend to interpret them as such — except, e.g., Whitney commenting on the chapter of the Taittirīyaprātiśākhya which describes the conversion from dental *n* to retroflex *ṇ*: "I have not discovered in the Sanhitā any case of a lingual nasal arising in the conversion of pada text into saṃhitā which is not duly provided for in this chapter". That Whitney, to whom such views were congenial, was right and that the "general" interpretation is inadequate may be shown by the fact, among others, that between such apparently general rules numerous ad hoc rules are interspersed to account for specific and irregular relationships between the *padapāṭha* and the *saṃhitāpāṭha* without corresponding to general rules of the Vedic language.

In connection with the formulation of such rules certain technical methods of description developed. Some rules were given a specific form, e.g., when a sound A was conceived of as having changed into B, A was sometimes referred to with the help of the Nominative and B with the help of the Accusative. In other words, certain case-endings were used meta-linguistically. In the following fragments of rules the passage from the dental *s* in the *padapāṭha* to the retroflex *ṣ* in the *saṃhitāpāṭha* is described:

> *sakāraḥ ṣakāram*: Ṛkprātiśākhya 5.1
> *saḥ ṣam*: Vājasaneyiprātiśākhya 3.55.

Sometimes the order of application of rules had to be specified, e.g., when the *padapāṭha* has:

> *bhakṣa* / *ā* / *ihi* // Taittirīyapadapāṭha 3.2.5.1
> "food come hither"

and the corresponding *saṃhitāpāṭha*:

> *bhakṣehi* /

but not:

> **bhakṣaihi* /

This led to the formulation of certain meta-rules, e.g.:

> *tatra pūrvaṃ pūrvaṃ prathamam*: Taittirīyaprātiśākhya 5.3
> "here what comes first should be taken first".

There is at least one case where not merely the order of application of rules, but the order of rules itself is specified; this occurs in Vājasaneyiprātiśākhya 3.3 and may well be due to Pāṇini's influence (cf. the famous sūtra 8.2.1: *pūrvatrāsiddham*). The rule states:

na parakālaḥ pūrvakāle punaḥ
"(what was applied) at a former time is not again (applied) at a later time".

An example is provided by Vājasaneyiprātiśākhya 4.124 which converts *mahāy indraḥ* into *mahā indraḥ*. If 4.51 were to apply to this result, *mahā indraḥ* would be converted into **mahendraḥ*. But this incorrect conversion does not take place since 4.51 precedes 4.124.

There are two features of the Prātiśākhya literature which continue to characterize the Indian tradition of linguistics: (1) the emphasis on synchronic relationships to the exclusion of a diachronic point of view; (2) the desire for explicit rules and for formal modes of expression. The first feature is related, e.g., to the circumstance that the *padapāṭha*, though recognized as artificial and man-made (*laukika*), is taken as the source from which the *saṃhitā* (which is of divine origin: *apauruṣeya*) is derived. This is undoubtedly due to the fact that such a derivation is unambiguous, because the Pada-Saṃhitā relationship is a many-one relationship. It also explains the metaphysical speculations (e.g., in the Brāhmaṇa and Araṇyaka literature) on the importance of *sandhi* ("union"), which leads from the human level of the *padapāṭha* to the divine level of the *saṃhitāpāṭha*. There is at the same time an important difference between the interpretation of sandhi rules by the authors of the Prātiśākhya and the later grammarians. The former held that such rules involved *pariṇāma* "change, transformation" (in a synchronic sense); the latter argued that they could only involve *ādeśa* "substitution", for words are eternal and hence cannot change.

The second feature of the Prātiśākhya literature, i.e., its devotion to rules and formalization, originated in the ritual sūtras. Here minute descriptions of the deviant, artificial, ritual language had already played an important role. It is here, too, that "rules" were introduced for the first time in order to provide a well-defined domain with precise and fully explicit descriptions.

II

Apart from phonology and the analysis of nominal compounds, phonetic descriptions were given. The earliest may have occurred in the ritual texts, for the ritual required extraordinary pronunciations. Āsvalāyana-śrautasūtra 7.2 describes the *nyūṅkha*, which is substituted for the second syllable of certain half-verses, as follows:

ó3oooooó3oooooó3ooo.

In this domain the origin must be sought for the investigations into place (*sthāna*) and "effort" (*prayatna*) of articulation.

Morphological relationships were discovered even earlier. The Śatapatha-brāhmaṇa (13.4.1.13) refers to a Vedic verse as *sadvatī* "(the verse) containing (the verbal root) *sat*". But the verse itself (Vājasaneyisaṃhitā 13.15) contains the word *bhuvas* "be thou". This shows (as Weber noted in 1855) that the relationship between the roots *bhū* and *as* was known during the period of the Brāhmaṇa literature.

It seems certain that linguistics originated in India because of the requirements of the ritual. As far as language is concerned, these requirements were twofold: first of all the textual material needed for the ritual had to be transmitted; secondly rules had to be given which enabled the priests to convert this material into ritually more effective forms. Such rules were artificial by definition. It seems likely that they preceded by centuries the discovery of rules which account in a similar fashion for the workings of natural language.

Since the requirements of the ritual were most stringent in connection with the Sāmaveda, it is probable that the study of language developed first in the Sāmavedic milieu. This is in accordance with the fact that the oldest *padapāṭha* appears to be that of the Sāmaveda.

III

Some of the forms of expression and technical devices of the Prātiśākhya literature were influenced by the Sanskrit grammarians. For, although the Prātiśākhyas contain very old material, their present form was largely determined in the period 500-150 B.C., i.e., after the oldest extant grammar of Sanskrit, i.e., that of Pāṇini, was composed. Pāṇini's grammar, on the other hand, does not merely refer to predecessors, but also contains rules put forward by them. The accompanying lists of words (*gaṇapāṭha*), of verbal roots (*dhātupāṭha*) and of certain affixes (*uṇādisūtra*) may also be largely pre-Pāṇinian. It is moreover highly probable that complete grammars of Sanskrit were composed (e.g., by Āpiśali) before Pāṇini.

Despite these historical relationships, about which little is known with absolute certainty, the grammatical tradition as we know it from Pāṇini's grammar (fifth century B.C.?), Kātyāyana's rules of interpretation (*ca.* 300 B.C.?) and Patañjali's commentary (second century B.C.), presents numerous characteristics which distinguish it from the Prātiśākhya tradition. First of all the interest had shifted from the fixed corpus of Vedic utterances (called *chandas*) to a type of language that was much closer to the spoken language (*bhāṣā*). It was realized that the forms of language are infinite and cannot be described by enumerations, but only with the help of "rules and exceptions" (*sāmānyaviśeṣaval lakṣaṇam*). Moreover, whereas there are specific

Prātiśākhyas concerned with specific portions of the Vedic corpus, Pāṇini's grammar was general and universal, also with respect to the Vedic language (*sarvavedapāriṣadam hīdaṃ śāstram*). At the same time the analysis was no longer confined to a "word-for-word" underlying structure: the words themselves were analysed (*śabdānuśasana*) and attention was paid to the grammatical relations between them (*kāraka*). It was discovered that grammatical relations may be syntactically expressed by a variety of surface forms, themselves either paraphrases of each other, or closely related in semantic terms.

Adopting a modern terminology, it could be said that phonology was supplemented with morphology, syntax, and semantics. However, Pāṇini's linguistic method was to a large extent unified. This is mainly due to its highly technical character: rules (*sūtra*) were formalized; numerous meta-linguistic elements (e.g., *it*), destined to be removed from the finally derived forms, were introduced; meta-rules (*paribhāṣā*), which describe how the rules must be manipulated and applied, became explicit. Clear distinctions were moreover made between use and mention (*svaṃ rūpam*) and between object-language and meta-language (*upadeśa*).

IV

A somewhat simplified example from Pāṇini's grammar may illustrate some of these devices. Consider the following three rules:

(1) *ato dīrgho yañi*: 7.3.101

(2) *supi ca:* 7.3.102

(3) *bahuvacane jhaly et*: 7.3.103.

(1) In the first rule *ato* is *at*, followed by the Genitive ending, which is used meta-linguistically to denote the substituendum; *at* itself denotes short *a;* *dīrgho* is a term for lengthening followed by the Nominative ending, which is used meta-linguistically to denote the substitute; *yañi* is *yañ* followed by the Locative ending, which is used meta-linguistically to denote a limiting context which follows; *yañ* itself denotes any of the following sounds (in accordance with principles of abbreviation laid down at the beginning of the grammar): *y v r l ñ m ṅ ṇ n jh bh*. The rule itself occurs in a section which deals with the modifications of verbal stems.

The first rule therefore expresses that final short *a* of a verbal stem is lengthened whenever any of the sounds *y v r l ñ m ṅ ṇ n jh bh* follows. This accounts for *pacāmi* "I cook" instead of **pacami*, *pacāmaḥ* "we cook" instead of **pacamaḥ*, etc.

(2) In the second rule *ca* means "and" and *supi* is *sup* followed by the Locative ending; *sup* itself denotes any case ending, in accordance with a

principle of abbreviation laid down elsewhere in the grammar. Since in this rule no Nominative or Genitive occurs, and the rule is ordered immediately after the previous one, the substitute, the substituendum and the limiting context from the previous rule carry over (in accordance with a meta-rule which was formulated only later). But since the second rule speaks of case endings, it can no longer apply to verbal stems.

The second rule therefore expresses that final short *a* of a nominal stem is lengthened whenever a case ending beginning with any of the sounds *y v r l ñ m ṅ ṇ n jh bh* follows. This accounts for *vṛkṣāya* "to the tree" instead of **vṛkṣaya, vṛkṣābhyām* "to the two trees" instead of **vṛkṣabhyām*, etc.

(3) In the third rule *bahuvacane* means "in the Plural", *jhali* (which becomes *jhaly* because of the following vowel: the meta-language is itself subjected to the rules of the language) is the Locative of *jhal* and *jhal* itself denotes any of a long list of sounds, including *bh* and *s*.

The third rule therefore expresses that the final short *a* of a nominal stem is replaced by *e* in the Plural when a case ending beginning with *bh* or *s* follows. This accounts for *vṛkṣebhyaḥ* "from the trees" instead of **vṛkṣabhyaḥ, vṛkṣeṣu* (from *vṛkṣesu*) "on the trees" instead of **vṛkṣasu*, etc.

The formation of *vṛkṣebhyaḥ*, however, raises a problem. The second rule also mentions *bh*, and its application to *vṛkṣabhyaḥ* would yield *vṛkṣābhyaḥ*. Now even if the rules were to apply in the given order, the third rule could not apply to this result since it only applies to a short *a*. There is a contradiction, then, between the second and the third rules, for different forms are derived from them.

We know – and the Sanskrit grammarians knew – that *vṛkṣebhyaḥ* is the correct form, not *vṛkṣābhyaḥ*. A basic principle of the Sanskrit grammarians is that the rules should be formulated in such a way, that the correct forms automatically result. Grammar is descriptive, not prescriptive. Its definitions or rules (*lakṣaṇa*) are constructed so as to conform to what is defined (*lakṣya*), i.e., common usage (*loka*). However this does not afford any help, for if we were to argue that the correct form shows which rule has to be applied, we ought to be consistent and abolish grammar altogether. Grammar requires an explicit principle which leads to the correct decision.

Fortunately Pāṇini's grammar is indeed constructed in such a way, that a meta-rule helps out, viz.:

vipratiṣedhe paraṃ kāryam: 1.4.2

"in the case of contradiction (between two rules) the later (rule) is to be applied".

Hence the third rule prevails over the second and the correct form *vṛkṣebhyaḥ* is correctly derived.

V

The Pāṇinian tradition has always remained the central tradition of Indian linguistics. Following Patañjali, a long (though not uninterrupted) sequence of grammarians on the one hand refined, and on the other simplified Pāṇini's grammar. This tradition reached another peak with Nāgojī (or Nāgeśa) Bhaṭṭa in the 18th century; it continues to the present day.

Throughout the centuries non-Pāṇinian schools of grammar have also flourished. Hindus, Buddhists, and Jains contributed. The Sanskrit grammarians moreover inspired grammatical work in, and with respect to, other languages, not excluding Dravidian (e.g., Tamil) or, e.g., Tibetan. At the same time fruitful exchanges developed between the grammatical tradition on the one hand and ritual studies, philosophy, logic, poetics, and numerous other disciplines on the other. Semantics flourished especially in the age-long discussions between grammarians, logicians, philosophers, and poeticians. Grammar was considered the most scientific among the sciences in India. The other traditional sciences aspired to the ideal of linguistics as embodied in Pāṇini's grammar in a manner similar to that in which the Western sciences aspired to the ideal of mathematics as embodied in Euclid's Elements.

A comparison with mathematics may be relevant in connection with the historical problem of the origin of zero. The discovery of the mathematical zero in India came many centuries after the discovery of the linguistic zero (probably by Pāṇini, who introduced several kinds of *lopa*; but the verbal form *lupya(n)te* "disappear(s)" occurred already in similar contexts in the ritual sūtras). It is not improbable that the linguistic discovery led to the mathematical discovery, though historical evidence in this respect is totally lacking.

About historical relationships with the non-Indian world relatively little is known. Indian astronomy and mathematics were influenced by the Greek, from Alexander onwards. It is extremely unlikely that the study of grammar, which was exclusively concerned with Vedic and Sanskrit, underwent any influence from outside the Indian tradition. The same may be said with regard to Indian logic, which was also closely related to Sanskrit studies, despite the fact that there are striking similarities between the systems of categories in Aristotle and in the Nyāya school of logic. (These are in fact due to a common linguistic background.)

The relationship between logic and linguistics is especially interesting. It is certain that linguistics came earlier (as perhaps in the West, where linguistics however developed much more slowly, while logic developed rapidly: cf. Aristotle's De Interpretatione and Categoriae). The grammarian

Patañjali was a much better logician than the early adherents of the Nyāya school. Among topics that were discussed repeatedly by logicians and linguists, mention may be made of the controversy about whether sentences in the final analysis are verbal or nominal. The later grammarians adopted the former point of view; the later Hindu logicians the latter (they wrote themselves a style which was nominalized to a semi-artificial degree). The discussion was not merely speculative: illustrative sentences were analyzed in terms of either theory. The discussion can be traced back to much earlier times. Pāṇini himself did not adopt an extreme view in this respect; that might have been incompatible with his careful work in linguistics. However he could not but treat as a noun, and hence decline, whatever he had occasion to quote. This explains the use of such surprising forms as *asteḥ* "(in the place) of *asti*", the Genitive Singular of the Third Person Singular Present Indicative of the verb "to be". Such forms could have been avoided only by circumlocution (e.g. *astīti padasya (sthāne)* "(in the place) of the word *asti*"). Expressions such as *asteḥ* clearly belong to the meta-language of grammatical instruction (*upadeśa*), unlike an object-language form discussed by the grammarians, viz., *apacati* "he is a bad cook", in which the nominal negative particle *a-* is prefixed to the verbal form *pacati* "he cooks".

The topic of nominalization, itself so characteristic a feature of later Sanskrit, is also related to the controversies between the Hindu realists and the Buddhist nominalists. In later Sanskrit, *ghaṭasya nīlatvam* is on a par with *ghaṭo nīlaḥ* "the pot is blue". The Hindus, in particular the Hindu logicians, accepted *nīlatvam* ("blueness") as a universal; the Buddhists, who did not accept any form of permanence, endeavored to refute the Hindu position with the help of a host of arguments, often reminiscent of those that were employed in the corresponding Western controversy. The grammarians occupied in this respect an intermediary position. However they agreed on the whole with the Hindu philosophers that language, viz., Sanskrit, is eternal and could not have been other than what it is (*svābhāvika*). For the Hindus, the Veda remained unique and its *mantras* untranslateable. They embodied not only mundane meaning, but ritual and sometimes magical force as well. The Buddhists, on the other hand, held the view that language is based upon convention (*saṃketa*). While Buddhist views in general tend to be empiricist and positivistic, the theory about the conventionality of language is not surprising in view of the fact that the Buddhists had never confined themselves to Sanskrit. The Buddha himself had addressed members of all castes and had (like Dante) made use of the vernacular. His authoritative words were handed down in a Prakrit dialect and were subsequently translated into numerous languages.

At the peak of the grammatical tradition, in the period marked by Pāṇini and Patañjali, words of foreign origin were recognized along with dialectical variations. As for the latter, Patañjali reports, for example, that Southerners have a predilection for *taddhita* suffixes (*priyataddhitā dākṣiṇātyāḥ*): they say *laukikavaidikeṣu* "in matters pertaining to ordinary speech and to Vedic" rather than *loke vede ca* "in ordinary speech and in the Veda".

Linguistics developed in India in the course of almost 3000 years. At their worst, linguists in India were given to classifications and to dogmatic adherence to what earlier authorities had laid down. But at their best the Indian linguists studied Sanskrit in width as well as depth and in terms of a general scientific methodology which was remarkably consistent, explicit, and hence fruitful. Linguistics in the West, despite its early beginnings in classical antiquity, presents the image of a young science, until recently concerned with its own autonomy and eager to reach the level of the physical or the mathematical sciences. Linguistics in India has from the beginning occupied the center of the scientific tradition.

SELECT BIBLIOGRAPHY

Texts and Translations (in customary order of letter of Sanskrit alphabet).
Atharva-prātiśākhya = Cāturādhyāyikā. Edited and translated by W. D. Whitney. Journal of the American Oriental Society 7 (1869).
Aṣṭādhyāyī of Pāṇini. Edited and translated by O. Boehtlingk. Leipzig, 1887 (Reprint, Hildesheim, 1964).
_____. Translated by L. Renou, I - III. Paris, 1948-1954.
Ṛk-prātiśākhya. Edited and translated by M. D. Shastri. Allahabad, 1931; Lahore, 1937.
Kāśikāvṛtti of Jayāditya. Edited by Śobhita Miśra. Banaras, 1952.
_____. Translated (I) by Y. Ojihara and L. Renou, I-III, Paris 1960-1967.
Taittirīya-prātiśākhya with Tribhāṣyaratna, Edited and translated by W. D. Whitney. Journal of the American Oriental Society 9 (1871).
Durghaṭavṛtti of Śaraṇadeva. Edited and translated by L. Renou, I-III, Paris, 1940-1956.
Paribhāṣenduśekhara by Nāgojībhaṭṭa. Edited and translated by F. Kielhorn. Re-edited by K. V. Abhyankar, I-II. Poona, 1960-1962.
Mahābhāṣya of Patañjali. Edited by F. Kielhorn, I-III. Bombay, 1880-1885. (Reprint, Poona, 1966).
Vājasaneyi-prātiśākhya. Edited and translated by A. Weber. Indische Studien 4:65-171, 177-331 (1858).
Siddhāntakaumudī of Bhaṭṭoji Dīkṣita. Edited and translated by S. C. Vasu. (Reprint, Delhi-Varanasi-Patna, 1962).

Other Works

Abhyankar, K. V. 1961. A dictionary of Sanskrit Grammar. Baroda.
Allen, W. S. 1953. Phonetics in Ancient India. London-New York-Toronto.

_____. 1955. Zero and Pāṇini. Indian Linguistics 16: 106-113.

Birwé, R. 1961. Der Gaṇapāṭha zu den Adhyāyas IV und V der Grammatik Pāṇinis: Versuch einer Rekonstruktion. Wiesbaden.

_____. 1965. Fragments from three lost kośas I: Vācaspati's Śabdārṇava. Journal of the American Oriental Society 85: 524-543.

_____. 1966. Studien zu Adhyāya III der Aṣṭādhyāyī Pāṇinis. Wiesbaden.

_____. 1967. Fragments from three lost kośas II: Vyādi's Utpalinī II. Journal of the American Oriental Society 87: 39-52.

Brough, J. 1951. Theories of general linguistics in the Sanskrit grammarians. Transactions of the Philological Society (London) 27-46.

_____. 1952. Audumbarāyaṇa's theory of language. Bulletin of the School of Oriental and African Studies 14: 73-77.

_____. 1953. Some Indian theories of meaning. Transactions of the Philological Society (London) 161-176.

Buiskool, H. E. 1939. The Tripādī. Leiden.

Cardona, G. 1965a. On Pāṇini's morphophonemic principles. Language 41: 225-238.

_____. 1965b. On translating and formalizing Pāṇinean rules. Journal of the Oriental Institute (Baroda) 14: 306-314.

_____. 1967. Negations in Pāṇinian rules. Language 43: 34-56.

_____. 1969. Studies in Indian grammarians I: The method of description reflected in the Śivasūtras. Philadelphia, American Philosophical Society.

Devasthali, G. V. 1967. Anubandhas of Pāṇini. Poona.

Emeneau, M. B. 1955. India and linguistics. Journal of the American Oriental Society 75: 145-153.

Faddegon, B. 1936. Studies on Pāṇini's Grammar. Amsterdam.

Fowler, M. 1965. How ordered are Pāṇini's rules. Journal of the American Oriental Society 85: 44-47.

Frauwallner, E. 1960. Sprachtheorie und Philosophie im Mahābhāṣyam des Patañjali. Wiener Zeitschrift für die Kunde Süd-, und Ostasiens und Archiv für indische Philosophie 4: 92-118.

Al-George, S. 1967. The semiosis of zero according to Pāṇini. East and West 17: 115-124.

_____. 1968. The extra-linguistic origin of Pāṇini's syntactic categories and their linguistic accuracy. Journal of the Oriental Institute 18: 1-7.

_____. 1969. Sign (Lakṣaṇa) and propositional logic in Pāṇini. East and West 19: 176-193.

Katre, S. M. 1968-69. Dictionary of Pāṇini, I-III. Poona, Deccan College.

Kielhorn, F. 1876. Kātyāyana and Patañjali. Osnabrück. (Reprint, 1965).

Kiparsky, P., and J. F. Staal. 1969. Syntactic and semantic relations in Pāṇini. Foundations of Language 5: 83-117.

Kunjunni Raja, K. 1957. Diachronistic linguistics in ancient India. The Madras University Journal, Centenary Number, 127-130.

_____. 1963. Indian theories of meaning. Madras.

Matilal, B. K. 1960-61. The Doctrine of Kāraṇa in grammar and logic. Journal of the Gananatha Jha Institute 17: 63-69.

——. 1966. Indian theories on the nature of the sentence (vākya). Foundations of Language 2: 377-393.

Misra, V. N. 1966. The descriptive technique of Pāṇini. The Hague-Paris.

Paranjpe, V. G. 1922. Le Vārtika de Kātyāyana. Paris.

Pawate, I. S. 1935? The structure of the Ashtadhyayi. Hubli (?).

Renou, L. 1940. La Durghaṭavṛtti de Śaraṇadeva. Traité grammatical en sanskrit du XIIe siècle. I,1: Introduction. Paris.

——. 1941-1942. Les connexions entre le rituel et la grammaire en sanskrit. Journal Asiatique 233: 105-165.

——. 1955. Les nipātana-sūtra de Pāṇini et questions diverses. Etudes Védiques et Paṇinéennes I: 103-130. Paris.

——. 1956. L'arrangement des paribhāṣā chez Nāgojībhaṭṭa. Etudes Védiques et Paṇinéennes II: 137-149. Paris.

——. 1957a. Terminologie grammaticale du sanskrit. Paris.

——. 1957b. Grammaire et Vedānta. Journal Asiatique 245: 121-133.

——. 1960a. La forme et l'arrangement interne des prātiśākhya. Journal Asiatique 248: 1-40.

——. 1960b. La théorie des temps du verbe d'après les grammairiens sanskrits. Journal Asiatique 248: 305-337.

——. 1961. Grammaire et poétique en sanskrit. Etudes Védiques et Paṇinéennes VIII: 105-131. Paris.

——. 1963. Sur le genre du sūtra dans la littérature sanskrite. Journal Asiatique 251: 165-216.

——. 1969. Pāṇini. Current Trends in Linguistics 5: South Asia, ed. by T. A. Sebeok, et al. The Hague-Paris.

Rocher, L., and R. Debels. 1960. La valeur des termes et formules techniques dans la grammaire indienne, d'après Nāgeśabhaṭṭa. Annali, Instituto Orientale di Napoli 15: 129-151.

Rocher, R. 1964a. 'Agent' et 'Object' chez Pāṇini. Journal of the American Oriental Society 84: 44-45.

——. 1964b. The technical term 'hetu' in Pāṇini's Aṣṭādhyāyī. Vishveshvaranand Indological Journal 2: 31-40.

——. 1965. La formation du futur periphrastique sanskrit selon Pāṇini: un exemple de description linguistique. Annali, Instituto Orientale di Napoli 6: 15-22.

——. 1968. La théorie des voix du verbe dans l'école paṇinéenne (le 14e āhnika). (Travaux de la Faculté de Philosophie et Lettres, 35). Bruxelles, Presses Universitaires de Bruxelles.

Ruegg, D. S. 1959. Contributions à l'histoire de la philosophie linguistique indienne. Paris. (Reviewed in Philosophy East and West 10: 53-57).

Scharfe, H. 1961. Die Logik im Mahābhāṣya. Berlin. (Reviewed in Journal of the American Oriental Society 83: 252-256).

Shefts, B. 1961. Grammatical method in Pāṇini: his treatment of Sanskrit present stems. New Haven. (Reviewed in Language 39: 483-488).

Sreekrishna Sarma. 1957. The words ākṛti and jāti in the Mahābhāṣya. Adyar Library Bulletin 21.

_____. 1959. Syntactical meaning – two theories. Adyar Library Bulletin 23: 41-62.

Staal, J. F. 1962. A method of linguistic description: the order of consonants according to Pāṇini. Language 38: 1-10.

_____. 1965a. Context-sensitive rules in Pāṇini. Foundations of Language 1: 63-72.

_____. 1965b. Euclid and Pāṇini. Philosophy East and West 15: 99-116.

_____. 1966a. Room at the top in Sanskrit: ancient and modern descriptions of nominal composition. Indo-Iranian Journal 9: 165-198.

_____. 1966b. Pāṇini tested by Fowler's automaton. Journal of the American Oriental Society 86: 206-209.

_____. 1967. Word order in Sanskrit and universal grammar. Dordrecht.

_____. 1969. Sanskrit philosophy of language. Current Trends in Linguistics 5: South Asia, edited by T. A. Sebeok et al. The Hague-Paris.

_____. 1970. Review of Cardona (1969). Language 46: 502-507.

_____. 1972. A reader on the Sanskrit grammarians. Cambridge, Mass., M.I.T. Press.

Subrahmanya Sastri, P. S. 1960-1962. Lectures on Patañjali's Mahābhāṣya, I-VI. Thiruvaiyaru.

Thieme, P. 1931. Grammatik und Sprache, ein Problem der altindischen Sprachwissenschaft. Zeitschrift für Indologie und Iranistik 8: 23-32.

_____. 1935a. Pāṇini and the Veda. Allahabad.

_____. 1935b. Bhāṣya zu vārttika 5 zu Pāṇini 1.1.9 und seine einheimischen Erklärer. Ein Beitrag zur Geschichte und Würdigung der indischen grammatischen Scholastik. Nachrichten von der Gesellschaft der Wissenschaften zu Göttingen 171-216. Berlin.

_____. 1956. Pāṇini and the Pāṇinīyas. Journal of the American Oriental Society 76: 1-23.

Van Nooten, B. A. 1969. Pāṇini's theory of verbal meaning. Foundations of Language 5: 242-255.

_____. 1970. The vocalic declensions in Pāṇini's grammar. Language 46: 13-32.

Varma, S. 1929. Critical studies in the phonetic observations of Indian grammarians. London.

Wackernagel, J. – Renou, L. 1957. Altindische Grammatik: Introduction générale 34-42, 112-125.

II : TRADITIONS: THE NATURE OF LANGUAGE AND OF GRAMMAR

3. Toward a History of Linguistics in the Middle Ages, 1100-1450

G. L. Bursill-Hall

I. Introduction

The purpose of this paper is to make a factual account of the present state of knowledge, as I see it, of the grammatical theories of the Middle Ages. It is, therefore, a problem-oriented account, i.e., data-oriented rather than theory-oriented. Throughout the Middle Ages grammar enjoyed a privileged position, but we are not yet in a position to write the full, continuous history of linguistics of that period; this will remain so until many more annalistic facts are at our disposal. I have tried, therefore, to state some of the major problems which have to be resolved before we can attempt a systematic account of the theoretical work of the high Middle Ages.

The status of grammar in the curriculum of the mediaeval university is well known to the historians of the period and to students of the manuscript tradition. We cannot say the same about our knowledge of the nature and development of grammatical theory in that period. Scholars such as Thurot (1869), Grabmann (1926, 1943), Lehmann (1944), Hunt (1941-43, 1950a, 1950b), Paetow (1909, 1914), Roos (1952), and Pinborg (1967)[1] have provided us with accounts of the development of grammar during the later part of the Middle Ages but these are for the most part non-linguistic accounts and rarely attempt a description, let alone discussion, of vital theoretical developments. They have also done much to preserve an awareness of the wealth of manuscripts which still await the scholar's scrutiny; but how much of this is known to the modern linguist? The answer is: very little indeed, and it is not difficult to enumerate those linguists of today who are aware of the sophistication of mediaeval grammatical writing. Since 1962, at least seven books have appeared purporting to be histories of linguistics. Of these, only two (Robins 1967; Dinneen 1967) have given a sympathetic and understanding account of mediaeval linguistic theory; to these must be added Robins' (1951) earlier study. The others have been content to repeat older accounts which always dismissed mediaeval grammarians as of no interest to modern linguistic scholarship.

The study of grammar in the Middle Ages can be divided into two periods, the second of which, coinciding as it did with the revival of dialectic, the rediscovery of Aristotle, and the tremendous revival of learning from the twelfth century onwards is much more interesting to the historian of linguistics. Of the period prior to 1100 it would appear that grammatical work consisted very largely of a faithful adherence to the fourth-century Ars minor of the Roman grammarian Aelius Donatus and the sixth century "Institutiones Grammaticae" of the Latin grammarian Priscian. That there was the odd exception to this has been shown by R. H. Robins (1967, ch. 4) and Haugen (1950), but Thurot's description (1869: 60), though a trifle harsh perhaps, seems to be the case, and I have not encountered Latin manuscripts of the period which suggest that the position was any different. It is only fair to add that other disciplines were no better off, and philosophy, which in the golden age of mediaeval scholasticism came to be the big sister of grammar, fared little better in this earlier period. It would, moreover, be unfair to dismiss the role that grammar played in the intellectual life of the earlier Middle Ages, even though no original grammatical work was produced. The Quadrivium was eclipsed as an educational activity and of the Trivium only grammar and rhetoric survived to become the key to the preservation of classical learning. The literary background of the poets and humanists of the eleventh and twelfth centuries came from a fully developed grammar and rhetoric. The grammar was, as stated above, based on Priscian and Donatus who had themselves built on the theoretical basis created by Aristotle, Plato, and the Stoic philosophers on the one hand and Dionysius Thrax and Apollonius Dyscolus on the other. The earlier mediaeval grammarians preserved the tradition of classical grammatical work, as a result of which grammarians throughout the period of creative linguistic scholarship, that is, the twelfth, thirteenth, and fourteenth centuries, possessed a successful model; and it must be remembered that the grammars of this later period were written in the first place as commentaries on Priscian.

Thurot (1869: 59) has stated that the history of grammar in the Middle Ages is divided by the period of Abelard. In other words, we can say that the revival of dialectic in the eleventh century was probably the first of the factors which were to alter the course of grammatical thinking up to the fifteenth century. This should not be taken to imply that literary grammar died, but after the twelfth century there arose a tremendous enthusiasm for grammar which coincided with the revival of interest in dialectic. Grammar (or, as many scholars have called it, *Sprachlogik*) in this period became much more theory oriented than data oriented, and it can be said that it was the influence of dialectic and the concomitant intimacy with logic and philosophy along with the general intellectual ferment which caused this change in direction.[2]

In this brief preamble much has obviously been omitted but it can safely be left unsaid since it has been well recorded elsewhere.

II. Schemes for understanding

The development of grammar in the second part of the Middle Ages has been variously described. Wallerand (1913: 34) stated that four important facts summarize the history of grammar of the period as follows:

(1) Preponderance of the Latin grammarians, Priscian and Donatus

(2) Influence of Peter Helias

(3) Appearance of new grammarians

(4) Establishment of speculative grammar.

This is quite clearly an inadequate framework on which to build a history of the period.

The scheme can be stated in a slightly different and more explicit manner, viz.:

(1) The discovery of Aristotle and the concomitant introduction of logic into grammar

(2) The influence of Peter Helias

(3) The triumph of the grammarians over the humanistic schools of the "authors"

(4) The constitution of speculative grammar embodying the new knowledge which followed upon the rediscovery of Aristotle's philosophical works and which culminated in the treatises on the modes of signifying (*Summa Modorum significandi*).

This version is really no better although it does suggest an explanation for the apparent "inactivity" immediately following the period that Peter Helias was teaching in Paris.

Pinborg (1967: 55-56) has described the development differently and in more technical detail, i.e.:

(1) Retention of the old definitions

(2) Fusion of grammatical and logical termini

(3) Grammar established as autonomous, though logical terms preserved and incorporated into grammatical metalanguage

(4) Introduction of idea of universal grammar

(5) Refinement of universalist concept and extension of the modus significandi which served to refine the description of word-classes

(6) The synthesis of the Modistae, producing a unified grammatical theory.

Into this scheme we can begin to weave the names of scholars who made significant contributions to the development of grammar in this period, i.e.:

(1) Priscian and Donatus

(2) Abelard, Anselm, William of Conches, Gilbert de Poitiers, Hugo de St. Victor, and perhaps Berengar of Tours

(3) Peter Helias and his followers — but who were they?

(4) Jordan of Saxony

(5) Nicholas of Paris, Lambert of Auxerre, Robert Kilwardby

(6) Martin of Dacia, Boethius of Dacia, Michel de Marbais, Siger de Courtrai, and Thomas of Erfurt.

There are a number of gaps in such a presentation of the development of grammatical theory in the later Middle Ages. Although it is the single most satisfactory account as yet, it is not sufficient to allow a complete picture of the period to be constructed on its framework. One might say that it is not sufficiently linguistic. I wish therefore to suggest certain areas which have to be carefully researched as necessary prerequisites to any projected history of linguistics in the Middle Ages.

In the twentieth century, linguistics has achieved a remarkable degree of autonomy and it is possible (although not necessarily desirable) to write an account of linguistics today with little or no reference to its epistemological basis or its intellectual background. Any account of the development in grammatical theory in the Middle Ages must consider the philosophical bed in which it was engendered; this is particularly true when one examines the changes in theory between dialectical grammar and Peter Helias's commentary on Priscian and the Nominalist grammars of the fourteenth century. Similarly, it is impossible to appreciate the work of the Modistae who, beyond question, represent the highest achievements of mediaeval grammatical theory, without a detailed examination of their metaphysics. It should indeed be remembered that none of the grammarians of the Middle Ages were "pure" grammarians in the sense that they were concerned only with the formulation of a theory of language; they were also logicians and in some cases primarily so.

The little that we know of Peter Helias is that he taught in Paris about 1150. He was not the first, however, to incorporate logic into grammar; his achievement would seem to be rather that he integrated and systematized the work of his predecessors. He was frequently referred to by later grammarians as the authority and yet the historian is handicapped in his assessment of Peter's contribution by the lack of an available edition of his grammar and a critical commentary by a modern linguist. It will not, moreover, be possible to assess Peter's contribution until the work of William of Conches has been thoroughly incorporated into our knowledge of grammatical work of the twelfth century. He was Peter's teacher, a grammarian of the first importance, and his influence was profound (cf. Hunt 1941-43; de Rijk 1967, ch. 2; Robins 1967:76). However, Peter does stand as a manifestation among grammarians of the new spirit in the schools of Northern Europe which gave the impetus to philosophy and logic and led to the temporary relegation of literary studies. The "new" Aristotle was systematically incorporated into grammatical theory; grammar now became a speculative philosophical discipline and it was not until the fourteenth century that teaching or literary grammars began to compete with Priscian and the commentaries on Priscian of scholars such as Peter Helias and Robert Kilwardby.[3]

Between Peter Helias and the next name quoted by Pinborg, that is, Jordan of Saxony (1220), there is a gap of some 70 years. This was presumably a period of consolidation during which logical grammar came to supersede literary grammar; we appear to know little if anything about theoretical developments during that period though there are a number of manuscripts extant and it is, moreover, a period which includes scholars such as Robert Grosseteste,[4] Ralph of Beauvais, Hugutio of Pisa, Bonus de Lucca, all of whom wrote grammatical treatises. As in all periods of the Middle Ages, we are hindered in our examination of grammatical theory by the total absence of editions of these works.

There seems to be little doubt that Robert Kilwardby (Harrison Thomson 1938) was a grammarian of the first order as well as a considerable logician. He wrote numerous commentaries on Aristotle as well as an extensive commentary on the Priscian Minor and the Priscian Major and grammatical (as well as logical) Sophismata. He was often referred to by later grammarians as an authority but again we are hampered in our appreciation of his contribution to the development of grammatical theory in the thirteenth century by the total absence of any modern edition of his work.[4a] It was probably Kilwardby who first *insisted* on the universal nature of grammar, that is, of deep structure as opposed to the relative unimportance of the surface differences between languages, which alone justified considering grammar a science. This was more fully developed by Roger Bacon who was unquestionably influenced by Kilwardby; the status of Bacon as a grammarian of the mid-thirteenth century also is one which requires careful definition. Grabmann (1926:118) refers to him as the first of the speculative grammarians, but this is an opinion which tells us nothing about his contribution to grammatical theory. The question arises as to his position in the development of pre-Modistic theory. There is no doubt of his dependence on Kilwardby;[5] however, the earlier Modistae, for example Martin of Dacia and Boethius of Dacia, refer to him, somewhat disparagingly, as one of their predecessors (Pinborg 1967:57). His exact position will clearly not be established until his grammatical theories have been more extensively examined, particularly in terms of the work of Kilwardby and other pre-Modistic grammarians of the thirteenth century as well as in terms of Modistic grammatical theory.

The remaining gap[6] in Pinborg's schematic representation would be filled by the post-Modistic grammarians. This gap in our knowledge of the grammatical theories of the Middle Ages, especially the later Middle Ages, concerns developments during the second half of the fourteenth and throughout the fifteenth centuries. In particular, the nominalist grammarians have been overlooked and yet, as in other spheres of intellectual activity in the Middle Ages, they are of the greatest importance. In this instance, it is not only because of the opposition they provided to the Modistae and other realist grammarians but also because it may well be that they provided a link with the grammarians of the Renaissance and perhaps more so with the universalist grammarians of the seventeenth and eighteenth centuries. Nominalism of the fourteenth century represented a new departure in the philosophy of the later Middle Ages, and so too did the grammatical theory of the period; the nominalist grammarians constituted the most effective opposition to the Modistae, and the fourteenth century seems to have been the scene of unyielding controversy between the Nominalists and Modistae, not so much about the facts of grammar as their epistemology. "In this area of fourteenth century scholasticism (i.e., meaning and grammar) almost everything remains to be investigated and understood" (Moody 1964: 74). (This is also true, let it be said en passant, of the thirteenth century). The controversy broke the back of Modistic grammar, largely because the "modus significandi" was no longer of interest to the philosopher of language; it became instead a facile target for the barbs and arrows of the Humanists. The controversy, however, was not the only reason for the disappearance of Modistic grammar. Apart from the disadvantages of a grammatical theory that relied entirely on meaning, the rigor of their method left them open to attack. On the other hand, the work of the Modistae did leave positive results (cf. Dinneen 1967: 146-147).

III. A Program of Study

The question arises whether the linguist is yet in a position to write a fuller history of his science in the Middle Ages and the answer is clearly that he is not. It is however possible to suggest a program or paradigm of investigation and to draw attention to the many problems that have to resolved and the many lacunae in our knowledge to be filled before it will be possible to write the history of grammatical theory in the later Middle Ages. It should be noted that I am writing in terms of grammatical theory stated in terms of Latin and that it is no part of the project to include grammatical descriptions of the vernacular languages.

It is clear that certain priorities can be stated:

(1) The greatest impediment to a complete understanding of theoretical developments in the period 1100 to 1450 is the dearth of accessible versions of these grammatical treatises. There is one notable exception to this unfortunate state of affairs; I refer of course to the work of Danish scholars, for example, Fathers Roos (1962) and Otto (1955, 1963) and Dr. Pinborg. So far, in the course of my compilation of manuscripts, I have noted some 2400 manuscripts of a grammatical nature and I expect this figure to increase to 3500 by the time that I have completed my visits to all the major libraries of Europe. It is a motley collection and includes elementary grammatical texts, commentaries, as well as versions of the works of grammarians of substance so that I fully expect this corpus to be reduced to some 1000 manuscripts when a more careful examination can be made of them. The gross figure includes multiple copies of various treatises and others to be discarded because they have been or are in the process of being published, for example, Roos refers to some 54 manuscripts of Martin of Dacia and his commentators. An examination of the manuscript holdings in European libraries reveals an extensive literature on the subject of grammatical theory; this is testimony enough to the importance that the mediaeval schoolmen attached to the study of grammar, and to the necessary connections between grammar, logic, and philosophy so as to produce a theory of grammar harmoniously set in its contemporary intellectual frame. These manuscripts represent an immense fund of important matter not yet in print; many years of solid work will be required before they become available. In addition to the works of Peter Helias, Robert Kilwardby, Michel de Marbais, all of whom were grammarians of substance but whose works remain unedited, there are a number of minor grammarians whose work cannot even be assessed until it is made more readily accessible; in addition, I can point to several treatises on syntax, grammatical treatises, commentaries on Priscian, *Questiones* and *Summa Modorum Significandi*, all of which are recorded as anonymous.

(2) The next stage would appear to be the production of annotated editions and commentaries on these individual grammarians. Critical editions of John of Dacia (Otto 1955), Martin of Dacia, (Roos 1962), Simon of Dacia (Otto 1963), and Boethius of Dacia (Pinborg and Roos 1969) are available, a commented edition of Thomas of Erfurt (Bursill-Hall 1972),[7] an uncommented edition of Roger Bacon's *Summa Grammaticalis* (Steele 1940) also exists. Pinborg's (1967) important study contains a number of short treatises including Johannes Aurifaber's *Determinatio de Modi Significandi*, and an edition of Petrus de Alliaco's *Destructiones modorum significandi* is projected.[8] An edition of Siger de Courtrai's *Summa Modorum Significandi*

(Wallerand 1913) is available but dates from 1913; in this version his treatise is incomplete, though it is possible to complete his theory of the word-classes by reference to his *Sophismata* which are included in this edition. He himself referred to a section on syntax which would complete his treatise and it may well be found among the anonymous treatises on syntax or modi significandi. In any case a commented version is clearly desirable in view of the important position that he assumes among the Modistae.

The historian of linguistics in the Middle Ages really could not do better than to emulate the mediaeval schoolmen, that is, by producing commentaries on their grammars as they themselves produced commentaries on Priscian and Donatus. Indeed, I am projecting a series of monographs which purport to be commentaries on the grammars of scholars such as Peter Helias, Robert Kilwardby, Roger Bacon, so that it can be established what exactly was the nature of their grammatical theory. Similarly, a more detailed examination of the Modistae is required.[9] They numbered at least ten[10] and span a period of some 60 to 80 years; whether they represent a school in the modern sense of the term remains to be seen but it is important that the historian take proper notice of their differences of presentation although they appear to share the same theoretical point of view and conception of grammar. All these critical commentaries must perforce take into account philosophical problems, for example, the nature of universals and problems of intellectual interrelationships, that is, the mutual cross-fertilization of logic and grammar, since learning and knowledge in the Middle Ages was not as readily compartmentalized as it is today. An additional useful source of information may well be the numerous pedagogical grammars, including commentaries on the *Doctrinale*, since they do appear to reveal, as R. W. Hunt (1964) has shown, the impact of contemporary theoretical work on language teaching problems.

(3) Once these major texts have been established, problems of a much more historical nature can be tackled. There is, to my mind, no question about the importance of Peter Helias as a grammarian; for long, he was considered the initiator of the new grammar, but Hunt (1941—43: 1950a) would rather have it that he was not so much a pioneer as the first to bring order out of chaos. His real worth can only be seen when he can be compared to his immediate predecessors, those whom I would call the dialectical grammarians and in particular his own teacher William of Conches, and to the grammatical writings of the period immediately following his own, that is, late twelfth and early thirteenth centuries. Similarly, the status of Robert Kilwardby and Roger Bacon must be clearly established, since the nature of the developments in grammatical theory after Peter Helias but prior to the Modistae is relatively unknown; it is clearly of real importance for an appreciation of the achievements of the Modistae.

(4) No account of linguistics in the Middle Ages can hope to be complete unless it takes into account (a) mediaeval theories of meaning, (b) mediaeval technical terminology, and (c) mediaeval theories of syntax.

(a) It would be quite easy and equally wrong to dismiss mediaeval grammatical theories as mentalistic. The mediaeval schoolmen were linguistically sophisticated and their grammarians were conscious of and exercised by questions such as universals, adequacy, deep and surface structure; but meaning was all pervasive in their work and linguistic descriptions were to them, as to, for example, the late J. R. Firth, in the final analysis statements of meaning. Just as their descriptive processes were shot through with concepts borrowed from contemporary metaphysics, for example, the dichotomies of matter and form, act and potentiality were frequently used as descriptive devices, so too meaning (which in their context should not be taken as notional or translational) rather than formal analysis enabled the mediaeval grammarian to seek for the oneness of human language, the universal validity of the rules of grammar. As a result of the intimacy between the reality of things and their conceptualization by the mind, grammar became, particularly for the Modistae, the study of the formulation of these concepts. The descriptive procedure for such a grammar can be called semantic but it was a semantics in keeping with the philosophical spirit of the thirteenth century. Mediaeval scholars, as Robins (1967: 88) points out, consciously sought a system of knowledge constructed on the same philosophical and religious principles.

(b) By virtue of this necessary association with other disciplines, the technical language of mediaeval grammar was subtle and often obscure (Bursill-Hall 1966a); this was to some degree inevitable when one considers the subtlety of the contemporary dialectics, but its unraveling is rewarding in the picture it gives of the interpenetration of logic, metaphysics, epistemology, and language.

(c) Mediaeval linguistic theory was grammar oriented; one looks in vain for studies of a phonological nature, and the Modistae were emphatic on their rigorous exclusion of sound matter as being outside the province of the grammarian.[11] Thurot refers to the importance attached by the mediaeval grammarian to the analysis of the *constructio* and it is clear that the description of the word-classes of Latin was subordinate to the study of syntax. The manuscript tradition may appear to belie this and Thurot (1869: 237) states, "Il est singulier qu'aucun grammairien du moyen âge ne paraisse avoir cherché à établir systématiquement et a priori une division de la syntaxe, comme on aimait à le faire à cette époque".[12] I am not in a position yet to comment on the completeness of the treatises on syntax that I have noted in manuscript form, but a number of the Modistae have sections on syntax in their treatises which they obviously regarded as complete (Bursill-Hall 1966b; Robins 1967: 81-84). That their treatment of syntax was much more brief than would be the case of a modern linguist, for instance, can be attributed to the intellectual framework within which they worked and to the avowed object of their syntactic theory. It remains to be seen to what extent the earlier mediaeval grammarian was data oriented but the later grammarians, especially the Modistae were, as Robins (1967: 89) has pointed out, intentionally theory oriented. It was not their purpose to state the rules of Latin syntax but simply to state the requirements of a *sermo congruus et perfectus*. Syntactic theory represents a major development on the part of speculative grammarians and any history of the linguistics of the period would not only be incomplete without a consideration of syntactic theory but would be tantamount to a denial of their most significant achievement. Again, the full story cannot be told until the wealth of the manuscript tradition is more readily available. Here, too, the pedagogical grammars may provide important clues to developments in syntactic theory.

Such would appear to be the state of the knowledge for a history of linguistics in the Middle Ages; certain areas are fairly well known, others not at all, and our knowledge of the intellectual background far exceeds our knowledge of developments in the grammatical theory.

Conclusion

We can summarize briefly certain scholarly necessities and other prerequisite areas of research. I do not wish to imply that these must necessarily follow in the order in which I shall offer them nor that I have stated them exhaustively, but it will be obvious that the first two items must take priority.

(1) Publication of texts: the work of some seven grammarians can be found in some modern edition, but in addition to those already named there remains the work of at least another ten grammarians known by name, for whom no edition exists (Gosvin de Marbais, Hugo de Abbatisvilla, Jean Josse de Marvilla, Johannes de Rus, Ionnes de Soncino, Magister Hoygensis, Matheus de Bononia, Nicholas of Bohemia, Radulphus Brito, Vincentius Heremita). This is in a sense, of course, pre-linguistic, but the historian of mediaeval linguists may well have to be his own paleographer.

(2) Commentaries on the works of key figures among the grammarians of the period.

(3) The placing of these scholars in the chronological progression of theoretical developments.

(4) Study of developments in grammatical theory between Peter Helias and the Modistae.

(5) Detailed comparison of Modistae in order to establish changes in presentation.

(6) Study of Realist and Nominalist grammatical theories.

(7) Study of interpenetration of grammar and the general intellectual and philosophical atmosphere of the Middle Ages. It is not sufficient to restrict the study of the relationship of grammar to contemporary logical and philosophical theories and much can be learned from the history of science in the Middle Ages. It is significant, for example, that both Robert Grosseteste and Roger Bacon were also scientists of originality; moreover, the Modistae, especially Thomas of Erfurt, developed a syntactic theory based on a hierarchy of a binary nature and one might well ask whether this was a concept that they took from the contemporary mathematician. The examination of mediaeval grammatical theory must be fitted into a framework which embraces all intellectual activity, since the mediaeval schoolmen themselves sought for a unified system of knowledge.

(8) There are a number of concepts and topics that require study:

    (a) syntactic theory

    (b) adequacy and deep structure

    (c) meaning

    (d) the concept of "pars orationis"

    (e) the meaning and use of the term "modus significandi"

    (f) termini technici

    (g) a detailed account is needed of Priscian's grammar

    (h) pedagogical grammars, e.g., Alexander de Villa-Dei's *Doctrinale,* John of Garland's *Compendium Grammaticae,* and John of Genoa's *Catholicon.* It is true that the Modistae were teachers but they were teachers of grammar *not* of Latin. What I am suggesting is that teaching grammars of Latin and elementary grammatical treatises may well reveal current changes in theory.

(9) There are a number of other relationships that require study:

    (a) interpenetration of mediaeval grammatical theory and philosophy of language

    (b) the role of Byzantine grammarians—there is no evidence that a group of western grammarians such as the Modistae were influenced by, or for that matter knew of, the Byzantine grammarians, but no history of linguistics in the Middle Ages could hope to be complete without a detailed examination of their work. Professor Jakobson has spoken of the sophistication of their theoretical work (cf. also Hjelmslev 1935-37), but these are, so far as I know, the only modern scholars to have expressed an awareness of this. There is here an extensive and original field of research, since it would be quite wrong to imagine that Greek grammatical work ceased with the Alexandrian school; it would be especially interesting to know more about the mutual impact of Priscian (who taught in Constantinople in the fifth century) and these later Greek grammarians.

(c) the influence of Boethius on mediaeval grammatical theory; according to Thurot (1869: 150), he created the term "modus significandi."

(d) comparison of grammatical work in Northern and Southern Europe. I have in mind work at the end of the Middle Ages, particularly in the second half of the fifteenth century; this should help to bridge the gap between the philosophical grammarians and the humanist grammarians, (cf. C. Thurot, 1869, Troisième partie). There is another aspect of linguist activity which is relevant here, that is, the writing of grammars of vernacular languages. In Spain, for instance, there is no evidence of any solid interest in theoretical work as such, but in Spanish libraries there are unpublished grammars of Spanish and other languages which may well have been written in a mediaeval idiom. It would be interesting to speculate on the extent of the influence of mediaeval theory in terms of the model it provided for these grammars. The grammarians of Italy may well prove to be of particular interest to the historian in the Middle Ages. It is true that they do not figure prominently among the Modistae, but at the same time it would be quite wrong to ignore the pioneer work of men such Hugutio de Pisa and Bonus de Lucca; in addition, Gentilis de Cingulo was an important commentator on the Modistae, especially of Martin of Dacia. The Italian grammarians tended always to have a more practical aim in view (Hunt 1950b); if the manuscript tradition is to be believed, many grammars were produced in Italy in the fifteenth century including many glosses and commentaries on the *Doctrinale* of Alexander de Villa-Dei. Until more actual knowledge of Italian grammatical work becomes more readily available, the significance of the Italian grammarians would seem to have been their incorporation of "northern" terminology and doctrine into teaching grammars; nor should it be forgotten, and this is obviously something that the historian cannot afford to overlook, that Italian theoretical work was always closely associated with the study of stylistics.

Finally, I would propose a commission with a twofold task: (a) to ensure that microfilms are obtained of all grammatical manuscripts dating from 1100 to 1500, and (b) the publication of all major texts not yet available in modern edition. There is considerable urgency to the former in view of the parlous state of some of the manuscript collections of European libraries and we should all take serious note of Kristeller's (1965: XVIII) warning; the second is similarly urgent, because until this is done, the history of linguistics in the Middle Ages can be little more than a secondhand chronicle.

The study of linguistic theory in the Middle Ages is quite fascinating for its own sake, but for the linguist of the twentieth century, it affords him the opportunity of seeing a fully developed theory worked out against a very different intellectual and academic background (Bursill-Hall 1963). To ignore one's past is an act of arrogance and we must respect our predecessors and their contributions to linguistic science; we may discard their theories, but an examination of their theories against their intellectual background should enable us to refine the criteria with which we should view our own.

NOTES

The research for this paper was carried out during my tenure of a Canada Council Senior Fellowship; this and other support received from the Canada Council is hereby gratefully acknowledged.

1. Pinborg's book contains an extensive bibliography including the works of those scholars mentioned here.

2. It must be pointed out that this is true really of the schools of Northern Europe; in Italy, though the new terminology was known, the teaching of grammar remained essentially practical. The manuscript tradition in Spain and Southern France certainly suggests that their schools did not experience such a drastic change in direction.

3. The *Doctrinale* of Alexander de Villa-Dei and the *Graecismus* of Evard de Bethune, although written at the end of the twelfth century, did not *supersede* Priscian in the schools until the middle of the fourteenth century; they were of course used as teaching grammars throughout the period.

4. Harrison Thomson (1940) queries the attribution to Grosseteste of the *De Lingua*; he mentions, however, a *Summa Grammaticalis* and lists some seven manuscripts. Grosseteste was a very able linguist, logician, and scientist, and it will be interesting to know more of his views on language.

4a. I am preparing an edition of Robert Kilwardby's Priscian commentaries to appear in the *Classics in Linguistics* series.

5. R. W. Hunt has insisted on this in course of private conversations with me; few scholars, if any, are better able to make such an assertion.

6. It is not intended as any animadversion of Pinborg's work to refer to "gaps"; his is a major contribution to the history of the linguistics of the period, but it aims primarily at an account of the development of Modistic grammar. It must also be said that, even if he does exclude the Nominalist grammarians from his schematization, he includes a more detailed account of them in the body of his book.

7. I have completed (Bursill-Hall 1972) an edition of Thomas of Erfurt, *Grammatica Speculativa* for the series *Classics in Linguistics* published by Longmans Ltd. There is also a version available under the authorship to which it was so long ascribed, J. Duns Scotus (Garcia 1902).

8. J. P. Thorne of Edinburgh University has undertaken to do this for the Longmans series, *Classics in Linguistics*.

9. I have completed (Bursill-Hall 1971) a detailed examination of the word-class theory of Siger de Courtrai and Thomas of Erfurt; it does contain

references to Martin of Dacia, but it cannot be considered a comparative study of the Modistae.

10. Grabmann (1943: 95) lists thirteen grammarians by name as well as anonymous treatises but he included in his list grammarians who were in fact Nominalist grammarians, e.g., Johannes Aurifaber.

11. Although the Modistae are not explicit on the function of *vox*, they did see it as performing a function which would today be regarded as phonological. Professor Jakobson, as ever full of fruitful ideas, has suggested that we may well be able to derive more information about mediaeval phonological theory from the work of the philosophers of language, especially Thomas Aquinas who does discuss the function of *vox*; Jakobson also has suggested that some of the mediaeval commentaries on Priscian may well contain comments of phonological import. It is perhaps worthy of mention that Grosseteste's *Summa Grammaticalis* has the intriguing subtitle: "De Generatione Sonorum".

12. Thurot seems to be somewhat inconsistent (contrast Thurot 1869: 213 and 237); it would seem that Thurot did not appreciate the aim of the Modistae in writing their sections on syntax.

REFERENCES

Bursill-Hall, G. L. 1963. Mediaeval grammatical theories. Canadian Journal of Linguistics 9:39-54.

_____. 1966a. Notes on the semantics of linguistic description. In Memory of J. R. Firth. Edited by C. E. Bazell, J. C. Catford, M. A. K. Halliday, and R. H. Robins, 40-51. London, Longmans.

_____. 1966b. Aspects of modistic grammar. Report of the Seventeenth Round Table Meeting on Linguistics and Language Teaching (Monograph series in languages and linguistics 19), 133-148. Washington, D.C., Georgetown University Press.

_____. 1971. Speculative Grammars of the Middle Ages. Approaches to Semiotics 11. The Hague, Mouton.

_____. 1972. Grammatica Speculativa of Thomas of Erfurt. The Classics of Linguistics. London, Longmans.

Dinneen, F. P., S. J. 1967. An introduction to general linguistics. New York, Holt.

Garcia, M. F. (ed.). 1902. J. Duns Scotus, Grammatica speculativa. Quaracchi.

Grabmann, M. 1926. Mittelalterliches Geistesleben. München.

_____. 1943. Thomas von Erfurt und die Sprachlogik des mittelalterlichen Aristotelismus. Sitzungsbericht der bayerischen Akademie der Wissenschaften, Heft 2. München.

Haugen, E. (ed.). 1950. First grammatical treatise. Language 26 (1950), Supplement.

Hjelmslev, L. 1935-37. La catégorie des cas. Etude de grammaire générale. Aarhus.

Hunt, R. W. 1941-43, 1950a. Studies on Priscian in the Twelfth Century. Mediaeval and Renaissance Studies 1:194-231; 11:1-55.

Hunt, R. W. 1950b. Hugutio and Petrus Helias. Mediaeval and Renaissance Studies 11:174-178.

———. 1964. Oxford grammar masters in the Middle Ages. Oxford Studies Presented to Daniel Callus. Oxford, Oxford Historical Society, New Series 16.

Kristeller, P. O. 1965. Latin manuscript books before 1600. New York, Fordham University Press.

Lehmann, P. 1944. Mitteilungen aus Handschriften VIII. Sitzungsberichte der bayerischen Akademie der Wissenschaften, Phil-Hist. Abteilungen, Heft 2. München.

Moody, E. A. 1964. A quodlibetal question of Robert Holkot, O. P. on the problem of the objects of knowledge and of belief. Speculum 39:53-74.

Otto, A. (ed.). 1955. Johannes Dacus, Opera. Corpus philosophorum danicorum medii aevi I. Copenhagen.

———. (ed.) 1963. Simon Dacus, Opera. Corpus philosophorum danicorum medii aevi III. Copenhagen.

Paetow, L. J. 1909. The arts course at mediaeval universities with special reference to grammar and rhetoric (The University of Illinois Studies, vol. 3, no. 7). Urbana.

———. 1914. The battle of the seven arts (Memoirs of the University of California, vol. 4, no. 1). Berkeley.

Pinborg, J. 1957. Die Entwicklung der Sprachtheorie im Mittelalter. (Beiträge zur Geschichte der Philosophie und Theologie des Mittelalters, 42). Munster–Copenhagen.

Pinborg, J. and Roos, H. (eds.) 1969. Boethius de Dacia, Modi Significandi. (Corpus philosophorum danicorum medii aevi, IV). Copenhagen.

Rijk, L. M. de. 1967. Logica Modernorum. A Contribution to the history of early terminist logic. Vol. II. Assen, Van Goncum and Co.

Robins, R. H. 1951. Ancient and Mediaeval Grammatical Theory in Europe. London, Bell.

———. 1967. A short history of linguistics. London, Longmans.

Roos, H. 1952. Die Modi Significandi des Martinus de Dacia. (Beiträge zur Geschichte der Philosophie und Theologie des Mittelalters, 37). Munster–Copenhagen.

———. (ed.) 1962. Martinus de Dacia, Opera. (Corpus philosophorum danicorum medii aevi, II). Copenhagen.

Steele, R. (ed.) 1940. Roger Bacon, Summa grammaticae. Opera hactenus inedita Rogeri Baconis XV. Oxford.

Thomson, S. Harrison. 1938. Robert Kilwardby's commentaries, In Priscianum and In Barbarismum Donati. New Scholasticism 12:52-65.

———. 1940. The writings of Robert Grosseteste, Bishop of Lincoln, 1235-1253. Cambridge, University Press.

Thurot, C. 1869. Extraits de divers manuscrits latins pour servir à l'histoire des doctrines grammaticales au moyen âge. Paris. (Reprinted Frankfurt am Main, 1964).

Verburg, P. A. Hobbes' Calculus of Words. I.T.L.5 (Review of the Institute of Applied Linguistics, Louvain): 62-69. (Previously read at the Third International Conference on Computational Linguistics, Sanga Säby, September 1969).

———. 1971. De Mens in taalkunde (Man in Linguistics). Truth and Reality, Philosophical perspectives on Reality, dedicated to Professor Dr. H. G. Stoker, Braamfontein, de Jong.

Wallerand, G. (ed.) 1934. Les oeuvres de Siger de Courtrai. (Les philosophes belges, VIII). Louvain.

4. The Tradition of Condillac: The Problem of the Origin of Language in the Eighteenth Century and the Debate in the Berlin Academy before Herder

Hans Aarsleff

Passion, interest, inadvertency, mistake of his meaning, and a thousand odd reasons or capriccios men's minds are acted by (impossible to be discovered) may make one man quote another man's words or meaning wrong. He that has but ever so little examined the citations of writers cannot doubt how little credit the quotations deserve where the originals are wanting, and consequently how much less quotations can be relied on. This is certain, that what in one age was affirmed upon slight grounds can never after come to be more valid in future ages by being often repeated.

Locke, *Essay* IV, xvi, 11.

The ordinary words of language and our common use of them would have given us light into the nature of our *ideas*, if they had been but considered with attention.

Locke, *Essay* III, viii, 1.

Introduction

It is the primary aim of this essay to identify and examine the intellectual background of one of the best-known and most influential works in the history of the study of language, Herder's *Über den Ursprung der Sprache*.* It was written in response to a prize-essay topic set in 1769 by the Berlin Academy, which at the time had debated the problem of the origin of language for some twenty years. In Berlin as well as in Paris, London, and Edinburgh, the characteristic eighteenth-century formulation of this problem had been introduced by a single immensely influential work, Condillac's *Essai sur l'origine des connoissances humaines* (1746). This work has largely been forgotten; the Berlin Academy debate it caused has been ignored; and Herder's *Ursprung* has been read with very slight knowledge—or none at all—of its historical context. It has been almost universally misinterpreted both in regard to its doctrines and its originality. My essay consists of two parts of roughly equal length. Part I deals, first, with Condillac's *Essai* in history, that is, with the reasons for its being so widely neglected or misunderstood; and, second, in order to remedy the effect of

93

these misconceptions, with three basic features of linguistic theory in the mid-eighteenth century. Space does not permit detailed and systematic exposition of the argument of the *Essai*, which I hope the reader will find encouragement to read on his own, in its entirety. Part II deals with the first and most striking effect of the *Essai*, the debate on the origin of language in the Berlin Academy. Beginning in the years round 1750, this debate continues unbroken until the spring of 1771 when Herder's *Ursprung* was awarded the essay prize. I shall close my essay with some preliminary observations on the position of Herder's essay within the context I have attempted to identify and explain. A full discussion of the *Ursprung* must be reserved for another essay.

It will be useful to make a brief remark about the term "origin of language." It is cumbersome always to say "the linguistic theory that underlies and finds expression in efforts to deal with the question of the origin of language," but the term must be so understood. Unfortunately we lack such neat terms as "universal grammar" and "universal grammarian," which are readily understood to involve linguistic theory. In order to remedy the absence of a much-needed term that is formally parallel to "universal grammar," it may be suggested that the term "origin of language" be used without the definite article. It is characteristic that the late eighteenth century and the early nineteenth understood the terms "universal grammar" and "grammaire générale" to include the problem of origin of language in its Condillacian formulation. The historical legitimacy of this usage will become clear in the course of my analysis.

I. Origin of Language in the Mid-Eighteenth Century

It is common knowledge that the eighteenth century was vitally interested in the origin of language. It is safe to say that no other century has debated that question with greater zeal, frequency, consistency, and depth of insight. The truly creative period was intense and brief. It began in 1746 with the publication of Condillac's *Essai*, and it ended twenty-five years later in the final month of 1770 when Herder, during his sojourn in Strasbourg, hurriedly wrote his prize-essay, which appeared in print in January of 1772. With a singleness of origin that is rare in the history of ideas, the fountainhead of this debate was the *Essai*,[1] which in turn drew its inspiration from Locke's *Essay*. This indebtedness is not my present subject, but it may be briefly indicated by citing the subtitle to the *Essai* in the first edition: "Ouvrage où l'on réduit à un seul principe tout ce qui concerne l'entendement." Similarly, the subtitle of Thomas Nugent's English translation (1756) correctly made the same point in slightly different words: " A supplement to

Mr. Locke's Essay on the Human Understanding." Within this philosopical context in Locke, Condillac was heavily indebted to one other English work, William Warburton's *Divine Legation of Moses* (1737-1741), where Condillac had found the doctrine of the language of action or gestures which occupies a crucial position in his argument.[2] In a general way, like most of his French contemporaries, Condillac was also under the influence of the current conception of Newtonian philosophy as known chiefly through Voltaire's *Eléments de la philosophie de Newton* (1738).

In France the debate was taken up by Diderot, Rousseau, Turgot, de Brosses, by Condillac himself in subsequent works, by a large number of articles in the *Encyclopédie*, as well as in a variety of pieces by other figures. In Berlin the problem was introduced in 1748 by the expatriate Frenchman Maupertuis in his *Réflexions philosophiques sur l'origine des langues et la signification des mots*. Cross influences soon passed between Berlin and Paris, and the debate also reached Scotland as seen in two distinguished works, which fall outside my present plan. The first was Adam Smith's "Considerations concerning the first Formation of Languages," first published as an appendix to the third edition of the *Theory of Moral Sentiments* in 1767.[3] The second was the first volume of Lord Monboddo's brilliant *Of the Origin and Progress of Language* (1773).[4] To these two, a third, less substantial work may be added, Joseph Priestley's *Course of Lectures on the Theory of Language, and Universal Grammar* (1762). But apart from the decisive roles of Locke and Warburton, other English writers also exercised a continuing influence both on general and on particular aspects of the debate, whether in the original or in French and German translations. A few names and titles will immediately call this strain to mind: Shaftesbury, Berkeley, Francis Hutcheson's *Inquiry into our Ideas of Beauty and Virtue* (1725 and often reissued, French translation 1749, into German 1762), Thomas Blackwell's *Inquiry into the Life and Writings of Homer* (1735), James Harris's *Three Treatises* (1744), Robert Lowth's *De sacra poesi Hebraeorum Praelectiones academicae* (1753, reissued in Germany with notes by J. D. Michaëlis 1758-1761), and John Brown's *Dissertation on the Rise, Union, and Power, the Progressions, Separations, of Poetry and Music* (1763).

Condillac's Essai *in History*

THE *ESSAI* NEGLECTED AND MISUNDERSTOOD

The chief piece in the puzzle is Condillac's *Essai*. With that piece lost, forgotten or ignored there is no hope of gaining a clear and coherent understanding of the debate, of its basic issues, and of the historical sequence of events that tie it together. Secondary, tertiary, or irrelevant pieces have been introduced to fill the empty space in an attempt to achieve some semblance of order—Rousseau, Hobbes, and even Plato and Aristotle. Benfey's *Geschichte der Sprachwissenschaft* uses all four, but makes no mention of Condillac.[5] Before coming to Herder, Heymann Steinthal's *Ursprung der Sprache* makes brief mention of Plato and of Dietrich Tiedemann's *Versuch einer Erklärung des Ursprunges der Sprache* (Riga, 1772), which, judged on Steinthal's account, is wholly secondary and which in any event had no influence.[6] Cassirer's chapter on "The Problem of Language in the History of Philosophy" in the first volume of *The Philosophy of Symbolic Forms* has been widely regarded as a history of the debate that is our present concern. It should not be considered in that light. Herder again emerges in a manner that is contrary to the facts, but in a footnote to the opening of this chapter Cassirer rightly observes that "a comprehensive work on the history of the philosophy of language is still a desideratum."[7] P. A. Verburg in *Taal en Functionaliteit* (1952) deals with Condillac in scattered fashion, quite failing to grasp the nature of his thought and especially of the *Essai*. Verburg explores the relationships with Hobbes and Leibniz, who have no historical relevance to the *Essai*, but ignores the impact of Locke.[8]

Hans Arens' *Sprachwissenschaft* (1955) sees Condillac as a typical representative of the French "rationalistisch-psychologische Betrachtung," which, we are told, is characterized by "einer Ungeduld und Unduldsamkeit des Geistes gegenüber dem Leben, das man mathematisch nur bewältigen kann, wenn man es als einen reinen Mechanismus auffasst." For the study of language, we are told, the result is that "die Sprache wird also überhaupt nicht als Lebensform und -ausdruck gesehen, sondern immer noch und nur als ein—an sich logisches—System von Zeichen für Vorstellungen und zum Ausdruck von Urteilen."[9] Against this travesty of Condillac, indeed of the dominant strain of mid-eighteenth century French thought, there is no remedy except the obvious one: a reading of the *Essai*. Arens' judgment denies Condillac the very qualities that were central to his conception of the nature of man and of his progress and achievements in all modes of expression from poetry and art to philosophy and mathematics. It totally misconceives the nature of Condillac's doctrine that, "le bon sens, l'esprit, la raison et leurs contraires naissent également d'un même principe, qui est la liaison des idées les unes avec les autres; que, remontant encore plus haut, on voit que cette liaison est produite par l'usage des signes; et que, par conséquent, les progrès de l'esprit humain dépendent entièrement de l'adresse avec laquelle nous nous servons du langage. Ce principe est simple, et répand un grand jour sur cette matière: personne, que je sache, ne l'a connu avant moi."[10] One consequence of such neglect of Condillac is that prominent aspects of Herder's *Ursprung* will appear more original and new than they in fact were. Herder was not the first to stress the primacy and legitimacy of poetic expression in comparison with philosophical discourse. Arens illustrates the nature of Condillac's thought by citing one passage from the posthumously published *Langue des calculs* (1798) and another from the *Essai*, both of which quite fail to indicate the nature of Condillac's argument. These citations are so bizarre as to preclude any suspicion of influence in the very quarters where that influence was most powerful.[11]

Of course, it may be argued that some of these works were not really setting out to explore historical relationships, and it is true that some of them are not very clear about their methods and intentions. There can be no doubt, however, that these works have indeed been read as if they were giving quite adequate and reliable historical coverage. They have been considered authoritative, and they are typical of a large number of other works that present either the same story or the same kind of story. All of them appear to be the victims of quite obvious misconceptions about the eighteenth century that were first confidently asserted as truth during the nineteenth century. In the second chapter of his *De l'origine du langage*, Ernest Renan deals briefly with the French philosophes, then dismisses their work as irrelevant: "Ils s'attaquèrent aux questions théoriques avant de s'être livrés à l'étude patiente des détails positifs. . . . La philosophie du XVIIIe siècle avait une tendance marquée vers les explications artificielles, en tout ce qui tient aux origines de l'esprit humain," words that contrast strangely with the mystical rhapsodies which Renan substitutes for clear statement whenever he approaches the need for explanation or for some sort of conclusion, as for instance in the final pages of *De l'origine*.[12] His manner is characteristic of the nineteenth-century belief that the eighteenth century was trying to "explain" the origin of language when in fact it was trying to explore and perhaps explain the nature of mind and man.

It is reasonable to ask why Condillac's *Essai* has been ignored. In general, I think that the strong international position of historical and comparative philology in German scholarship of the last century and the reflection of this prominence in the historiography of the subject have tended to favor earlier German work pertaining to the study of language. But more specifically I think there are two reasons: The overwhelming attention paid to Herder as the single focus of all attempts to deal with the history of the problem; and, second, the seemingly trivial fact that the title of the *Essai* gives no indication that a theory of language and its origin is the center of the entire argument of the *Essai*. I shall deal with each in turn.

(a) *Herder as focus.* The longest, most detailed attempt to come to grips with the refractory philosophy of Herder's *Ursprung* is a typical example of this failure to see the relevance of Condillac. Hansjörg A. Salmony has devoted nearly the first half of his book on *Die Philosophie des jungen*

Herder (1949) to a discussion of the *Ursprung* and its argument, making a determined effort to resolve its seeming—or perhaps real—contradictions and ambiguities in order to explain what Herder really meant. In the process Salmony produces an explication of Herder which in fact closely resembles Condillac's argument. This turn is so extraordinary that it would not seem possible were it not for the fact that Salmony clearly reveals his total ignorance of the *Essai*. He simply has not read it, though he has a great deal to say about what he takes to be its doctrine, depending largely on his faith in the reliability of Herder's own statements concerning it—thus following the curious procedure of taking a primary text, *in casu* the *Ursprung*, to be also a trustworthy secondary text on a work which for the prupose of the examination at hand should itself have been considered a primary text. Salmony regularly makes reference to well-established scholarly works that support his analysis, a fact which clearly shows how widely and authoritatively Condillac has been ignored.

A few typical instances will reveal the absurdities that result. It is the thesis of the *Essai*, we are told, that "Die Sprache ist nichts als Entwicklung des 'Schreies der Empfindung,' sie ist ihrer Entstehung nach nicht übermenschlich, nicht göttlich, sondern untermenschlich, tierisch." Both the *Essai* and Condillac's other works reject this view. This common error is in part made possible by ignoring Condillac's basic distinction between natural gestures and "les cris naturels" on the one hand and on the other the artificial and, in this sense arbitrary, vocal signs of the language and speech that is uniquely human. In the same context, again revealing ignorance of what the *Essai* says, Salmony tells us that, "in der *Langue des calculs*. . .wird gezeigt, wie aus einer ursprünglicher Gebärdensprache (langue d'action) allmählich die artikulierte Sprache hervorgeht, die ausdrücklich keineswegs allein der Mitteilung und äusseren Verständigung, sondern vor allem dem Verstehen dient. . . .Vom tierischen Ursprung der Sprache, von den 'Schällen' und 'Schreien der Empfindung' ist hier nicht mehr die Rede."[13] In his own book, Salmony says, "ist immer nur von der Sprachursprungs-Theorie im *Essai* und. . .nie von der weitaus bedeutsameren in der *Langue des calculs* die Rede."[14] It is a good guess that the *Langue des calculs* has attracted attention by virtue of its title, though that work in fact only briefly mentions the principle that was explained and argued at length in the *Essai*. Salmony seems aware that if the argument he recognized in the *Langue des calculs* had been presented in the *Essai* in 1746, as in fact it was at great length, then this fact would have had very considerable consequences for the possibility of a link between Condillac and Herder. But Salmony's ignorance of the *Essai* and hence of the true chronological relationship protected him against that painful possibility. (The *Langue* was written in the last years before Condillac's death in 1780 and first published in the *Oeuvres* of 1798.)

Naturally, any evidence that Herder during the 1760's was acquainted with Condillac's *Essai* would be of the utmost importance to Salmony, but here again he shares the universal silence of scholars, though the evidence has been in print for nearly one hundred years. In a note to *Fragmente III* (1767), Herder observed: "Ich bin durch die D[eutsche]Bibliothek auf ein Buch aufmerksam gemacht, das ich jetzt mit Vergnügen durchblättere. Der zweite Theil von dem *Essai sur l'origine des connoissances humaines* enthält Betrachtungen, die mein Fragment 'von den Lebensaltern der Sprache' sehr ins Licht setzen."[15] This acquaintance with Condillac would seem to go back to the years 1763-1764, when Herder wrote a brief piece called "Allgemeine Betrachtung über die Sprachen," which consists of excerpts from the *Essai*.[16] In his perplexity, Salmony uses the common expedient of paying more attention to Rousseau than a strict examination of the historical context will justify. Salmony's one hundred pages on Herder's philosophy of language is not only long and detailed and pursued with great determination in regard to historical correctness; his treatment also offers a compendium of common errors, thus raising neglect of Condillac to the level of confident doctrine.

(b) *The Title.* The second reason for neglect of Condillac is perhaps more obvious than the first and also rather distressing: the title of the *Essai* says nothing about language. It does not reveal that more than a third of it bears the title "De l'origine et des progrès du langage,"[17] nor of course that the origin of language is pivotal in the entire argument concerning "l'origine des connoissances humaines." This lesson could, however, have been learned from Condillac's contemporaries, who were not mistaken. Rousseau's *Discours sur l'origine et les fondemens de l'inégalité parmi les hommes* (1755) has been the most common substitute to fill the gap left open by ignorance of the *Essai.* The most famous and often cited passage has this rarely cited beginning: "Qu'il me soit permis de considerer un instant les embarras de l'origine des langues. Je pourrois me contenter de citer ou de répéter ici les recherches que Mr. l'Abbé de Condillac a faites sur cette matière, qui toutes confirment pleinement mon sentiment, et qui, peut-être, m'en ont donné la première idée."[18] Similarly, Diderot in the opening paragraph of his *Lettre sur les sourds et muets* (1751) observes, "J'aurais pu m'adresser à M. l'abbé de Condillac, ou à M. du Marsais, car ils ont aussi traité la matière des inversions."[19]

Other obvious references can easily be cited; but they are hardly needed since all major and minor items in the debate clearly reveal their debt to the *Essai*, to its problems and its issues, including significant passages in Condillac's own *Traité des sensations* (1754), *Traité des animaux* (1755), and his *Cours d'études* (1775). The argument of the *Traité des sensations* has perhaps offered the chief cause for misunderstanding. In the *Lettre sur les aveugles* (1749),[20] Diderot had pointed out that the *Essai* came very near to saying the same thing as Berkeley in the *Three Dialogues between Hylas and Philonous*, though ostensibly Condillac would be opposed to Berkeley's idealism, a point well taken and its occasion already obvious in the opening sentence of the *Essai*: "Nous ne sortons point de nous-mêmes; et ce n'est jamais que notre propre pensée que nous apercevons." In the *Sensations* Condillac had gradually endowed a statue with the senses of smell, taste, hearing, and vision, none of which alone or together give any assurance of the existence of anything outside ourselves. But adding finally touch and motion, it gains—in the words of Georges le Roy—"de façon irrésistible le sentiment de l'extériorité." Thus Condillac passes from "l'idéalisme au réalisme," paradoxically borrowing suggestions from Berkeley's *New Theory of Vision*. Still, as le Roy rightly observes, "la psychologie de Condillac n'est pas un matérialisme, comme d'aucuns avaient pu le penser en la rapprochant des vues d'un Diderot; elle implique un spiritualisme très net."[21]

The statue demands a moment's attention. The *Traité des sensations* is generally reputed to contain the fullest and most characteristic version of Condillac's conception of man. This conception, it is believed, offers a purely mechanistic and materialist account of the nature of man and his knowledge, as if Condillac in that work had offered "enough to account for the richest intellectual and emotional experiences man knows," to use the words of a recent publication on Condillac.[22] In other words, the *Sensations* has been read as if it were a "traité des connaissances humaines," when it is in fact precisely what its title says and no more. It is not, as has been believed, about the whole subject of man and the understanding. The statue is a structural device designed to show that the sensations suffice to produce a habitual and instinctive assurance of the existence of the outside world, which was all Condillac set out to do in order to meet Diderot's charge of Berkelianism. Existing not in society but in total isolation and lacking all but the most rudimentary form of reflection as well as the use of signs and language, the statue is forever debarred from attaining the nature of man. It is quite literally and in a profound sense speechless.

This conception of the statue was already clear in the first, 1754 edition of the *Sensations*, as le Roy clearly demonstrated in 1937 in his book on *La psychologie de Condillac*: "En fait, le *Traité des sensations* n'a pas le caractère exclusif qu'on lui prête quelquefois. Il ne nie pas le rôle du langage dans le développement des facultés mentales, et par conséquent, il n'apporte pas une réfutation de l'*Essai sur l'origine des connoissances humaines*. Il envisage seulement les opérations de l'esprit qui précèdent l'acquisition des langues, et il se borne à les analyser."[23] In this book, however, le Roy did not consider some very significant additions on this very point to the final version of the *Sensations* which Condillac prepared during the last years of his life. These additions very strongly underscore the meaning of the statue's lack of language, as if Condillac was eager to make this point especially clear, thus further reducing any possibility of conflict with the *Essai*. In one of these revisions, the marginal summary reading "conclusion de ce chapitre" has been replaced by these words: "Ses connoissances ne sont que pratiques; et la lumière qui la conduit n'est qu'un instinct." A new paragraph has then been added, containing these passages: "Elle [la statue] analyse naturelle-ment, mais elle n'a aucun langage. Or, un analyse, qui se fait sans signes, ne peut donner que des connoissances bien bornées. . . .Lors donc que je traite des idées qu'acquiert la statue, je ne pretends pas qu'elle ait des connoissances dont elle puisse se rendre un compte exact: elle n'a que des connoissances pratiques. Toute sa lumière est proprement un instinct, c'est-à-dire, une habitude de se conduire d'après des idées dont elle ne sait pas se rendre compte. . . .Pour acquérir des connoissances de théorie, il faut nécessairement avoir un langage: car il faut classer et déterminer les idées, ce qui suppose des signes employés avec méthode."[24] In fact, late in life Condillac appears to have been eager to insist on his continuing commitment to the argument of the *Essai*. In his final revisions in *De l'art de penser* he added a note to a chapter entitled "De la nécessité des signes." The note said: "Depuis l'impression de mon *Essai sur l'origine des connoissances humaines*, d'où la plus grande partie de cet ouvrage est tirée, j'ai achevé de démontrer la nécessité des signes, dans ma *Grammaire* et dans ma *Logique*."[25]

In fact, the statue hardly differs from the animals in the *Traité des animaux* (1755), as a few passages from that work will show: "Il y a en quelque sorte deux mois dans chaque homme: le moi d'habitude et le moi de réflexion," and "le moi d'habitude suffit donc aux besoins qui sont absolument nécessaires à la conservation de l'animal. Or l'instinct n'est que cette habitude privée de réflexion." This is precisely what was also true of the statue. But "la mesure de réflexion que nous avons au-de-là de nos habitudes est ce qui constitue notre raison." Like the statue, the animals have only "des connoissances pratiques," but not of theory, "car la théorie suppose une méthode, c'est-à-dire, des signes commodes pour déterminer les idées, pour les disposer avec ordre et pour en recueillir les résultats." Thus "notre âme n'est donc pas de la même nature que celle des bêtes," and it is no wonder that man, "qui est aussi supérieur par l'organisation que par la nature de l'esprit qui l'anime, ait seul le don de la parole."[26]

Thus the decisive difference between man and beast lies between the statue and man, not between the statue and the beast. The *Essai* had already been perfectly clear on this point: "De toutes les opérations que nous avons décrites, il en résulte une qui, pour ainsi dire, couronne l'entendement: c'est la raison. . . .elle n'est autre chose que la connoissance de la manière dont nous devons régler les opérations de notre âme," and "on est capable de plus de réflexion à proportion qu'on a plus de raison. Cette dernière faculté produit donc la réflexion."[27] The unique instrument of this reflection is "la liaison des idées," which ensures control over the memory by means of those signs which men in society by mutual aid have instituted for that purpose. And "le langage est l'exemple le plus sensible des liaisons que nous formons volontairement," unlike the mere association of ideas which, not being voluntary, also is not subject to our control, a distinction Condillac makes frequently and clearly. This "liaison" itself is, like reason behind it, natural and innate; it is "uniquement dans la nature de l'âme et du corps. C'est pourquoi je regarde cette liaison comme une première expérience qui qui doit suffire pour expliquer toutes les autres."[28] Thus in Condillac as in Locke, reflection is a powerful, active, creative, innate faculty, Professor Chomsky *non obstante*; and it is precisely for this reason that Condillac, building on Locke, could present a theory of the creation of human language.

ROUSSEAU

If the full title of Condillac's *Essai* made it possible to overlook the relevance of that work in the history of linguistic philosophy, one may ask why the same fate did not befall Rousseau's *Discours sur l'origine et les fondemens de l'inégalité parmi les hommes*. It has not been ignored, no doubt because Rousseau has continued to maintain his place in literature. The *Inégalité* was published in German in 1756, while the *Essai* appeared in German only in 1780. Rousseau and his contemporaries took Condillac for granted, while later generations have tended to remember only Rousseau. The fact that some passages on language in *Inégalité* have been used to fill the gap left open by neglect of Condillac has caused perhaps the most widely held misconception of the question concerning the origin of language. On the basis of Rousseau, it has been believed that the entire question had only received shallow treatment, as if all previous accounts had assumed that primitive man must have been a full-fledged philosopher—in the manner of contemporary man—in order to create the first language. Rousseau put the dilemma succinctly: "Si les Hommes ont eu besoin de la parole pour apprendre à penser, ils ont eu bien plus besoin encore de savoir penser pour trouver l'art de la parole."[29] This dilemma in turn resolves itself into the question whether language or society came first. Rousseau gives up: "Je laisse à qui voudra l'entreprendre, la discussion de ce difficile problème, lequel a été le plus nécessaire, de la société déjà liée, à l'institution des langues, ou des langues déjà inventées, à l'établissement de la société."[30] The dilemma is obvious enough, but it has been forgotten that Rousseau is, at this point, making the prior assumption that the primitive man he is here considering leads an absolutely solitary life, that men, "n'ayant ni domicile fixe, ni aucun besoin l'un de l'autre, se rencontreroient, peut-être à peine deux fois en leur vie, sans se connoître, et sans se parler."[31] It is only after he has made this basic assumption that Rousseau lapses into his first and best-known digression on the origin of language.

At the beginning of Part Two of the *Inégalité*, however, Rousseau returns to the question of the origin of language, and this time he can give an account that closely follows that of Condillac since he is now making a different assumption about the stage of development man has achieved: man already has the rudiments of social organization. Need has given him "quelque idée grossière des engagements mutuels." He has also, still independently of language and speech, developed "quelque sorte de réflexion, ou plutôt une prudence machinale qui lui indiquoit les précautions les plus nécessaires à sa sûreté."[32] Now the origin of language creates no difficulty: "Des cris inarticulés, beaucoup de gestes, et quelque bruits imitatifs, durent composer pendant longtems la Langue universelle, à quoi joignant dans chaque Contrée quelques sons articulés, et conventionnels dont, comme je l'ai déjà dit, il n'est pas trop facile d'expliquer l'institution, on eut des langues particulières, mais grossières, imparfaites, et telles à peu près qu'en ont aujourd'hui diverses Nations Sauvages."[33] This agrees well with Condillac, and it is this second conception that is taken up in Rousseau's posthumous *Essai sur l'origine des langues* (1781).[34]

It is obvious that Rousseau's two passages on the origin of language are not contradictory, since they rest on very different assumptions. The former is not a valid critique of Condillac, and the second closely follows him, but it is only the former that has been remembered and cited as if it touched Condillac's argument. It is easy to see the fatal consequences of that error. Condillac later gave a good answer to Rousseau's first passage.[35]

LINEARITY OF SPEECH

Now, if Condillac is misunderstood and ignored, there is a good possibility that Rousseau will also be misunderstood. This has in fact occurred, even where it was perhaps least to be expected. Citing an observation of Rousseau's on what is usually called the linearity of speech, Jean Starobinski has remarked: "Il reconnaît parfaitement la différence spécifique, d'ordre temporel, qui caractérise la parole. En quoi il anticipe les remarques de Ferdinand de Saussure."[36] If the implication is that this idea is original with Rousseau, then the statement is not correct. Rousseau had himself been anticipated by several others. Condillac's *Essai* had already shown how the inescapable linearity of speech had forced man to decompose the initial unitary signs of the language of action into discrete, arbitrary signs of human language, thus making analysis and ordered reflection possible.[37] Later he gave this idea prominence in his theory of language: "Si toutes les idées, qui composent une pensée, sont simultanées, dans l'esprit, elles sont successives dans le discours: ce sont donc les langues qui nous fournissent les moyens d'analyser nos pensées."[38] An entire thought is instantaneous, like a painting; it has no succession in time. This idea had also been forcefully stated by Maupertuis in his *Réflexions*, as we shall soon see. And in the *Lettre sur les sourds et muets*, Diderot had observed that "notre âme est un tableau mouvant, d'après lequel nous peignons sans cesse. . .l'esprit ne va pas à pas comptés comme l'expression. Le pinceau n'exécute qu'à le longue ce que l'oeil du peintre embrasse tout d'un coup. La formation des langues exigéait la décomposition."[39] Thus the linearity of speech was, also before Rousseau, a central doctrine in the philosophy of language which found expression in conjectures on the origin of language. This doctrine held a place of equal importance in universal grammar. We shall later see that this common agreement was one of the reasons why origin of language and universal grammar were completely fused soon after the publication of the *Essai* in 1746, a fusion that would seem highly unlikely, indeed impossible, if certain current dogmas about the history of linguistics, about the so-called "Cartesian" linguistics and Lockian thought, had any validity.

I have tried to correct some basic misconceptions which for the most part have their origin in purely factual errors and inadequate knowledge about the heroic age—a name it deserves—of linguistic theory in the eighteenth century. I shall now take up three misconceptions of a more general nature. They concern: the true import of analysis and understanding in terms of origins; the meaning, more specifically, of asking questions about the origin of language; and, thirdly, the reputed conflict between universal grammar and Lockian philosophy.

Three Basic Features of Linguistic Theory in the Eighteenth Century

ORIGINS

The eighteenth century explored the origins of all aspects of man's institutions and works: Society and the state with their laws and rules of obligation, the arts (whether poetry, music, painting, sculpture, or architecture), the crafts, the mind, thought, and language. It was the best mode of explanation and analysis they knew, just as understanding in terms of structure is perhaps the dominant and most natural mode in our time. This approach in terms of origins was man-centered, and its chief object was to get down to principles, to what was basic and natural or innate in man's being as he came from the Creator's hand, as distinct from what man had created by means of his "active faculties" as Locke called them, from what in the terminology of the eighteenth century was called artificial. What man had by nature, in addition to his body, was the light of nature, which to Locke, Du Marsais, and Condillac meant the two innate, active, creative powers of reason and sense experience.[40] "Principe," said Condillac, "est synonyme de *commencement*, et c'est dans cette signification qu'on l'a d'abord employé."[41] A large number of specific statements to this effect can be found, but we may take one from an early piece by Herder, his "Versuch einer Geschichte der lyrischen Dichtkunst," which he wrote in 1764 at a time when he had been reading Condillac's *Essai*. This passage will also show how the metaphor of organic growth is used to enforce this conception: "Nicht aber allein ergötzend, sondern auch nothwendig ist's, dem Ursprunge der Gegenstände nachzuspüren, die man etwas vollständig verstehen will. Mit ihm entgeht uns offenbar ein Theil von der Geschichte, und wie sehr dienet die Geschichte zur Erklärung des Ganzen? Und dazu der wichtigste Theil der Geschichte, aus welchem sich nachher Alles herleitet; denn so wie der Baum aus der Wurzel, so muss der Fortgang und die Blüthe einer Kunst aus ihrem Ursprunge sich herleiten lassen. Er enthält in sich das ganze Wesen seines Produktes, so wie in dem Samenkorn die ganze Pflanze mit allen ihren Theilen eingehüllet liegt; und ich werde unmöglich aus dem *spätern* Zustande den Grad von Erläuterung nehmen können, der meine Erklärung *genetisch* macht."[42] During the years he spent in Königsberg, 1762-1764, Herder took notes from Kant's lectures, including a passage that clearly shows how the question of origin was designed to separate the natural from the artificial. In a section on "Quellen der Sittlichkeit," at this point in relation to Hutcheson's *Inquiry*, Herder took this note: "Um das Künstliche von Natur zu unterscheiden, muss man so auf den Ursprung dringen, wie [man] die Vorurteile (Sprüchwörter) von Gewissheit zu unterscheiden [pflegt]. Man müsste das Gefühl des Natur Menschen Untersuchen, und dies ist besser als unser gekünsteltes. Rousseau hat es aufgesucht."[43]

The search for origins is thus an attempt to get down to basic principles, to what is by nature as opposed to what is by art. But this method would make no sense without the unquestioning acceptance of a particular doctrine that is one of the great commonplaces of the eighteenth century: the doctrine of the uniformity of human nature in all ages and climes. Again, there is hardly a major figure of that century who has not given it direct statement, for instance David Hume in his familiar statement that "mankind is so much the same, in all times and places, that history informs us of nothing new and particular." Similarly Du Marsais observed: "Les différens tours que les peuples différens ont pris pour s'exprimer sont soumis à ces deux règles souveraines d'uniformité et de variété; il y a uniformité dans l'essentiel de la pensée, et variété dans le tour et dans l'expression."[44] In Locke's words, "Men, I think, have been much the same for natural endowments, in all times."[45] This doctrine of uniformity had an important consequence, again shared by all the men we are concerned with. Referring to his *Essay*, Locke wrote: "All therefore that I can say of my book is, that it is a copy of my own mind, in its several ways of operation. And all that I can say for the publishing of it, is that I think the intellectual faculties are made, and operate alike in most men."[46]

The doctrine of uniformity and its corollary in the universal relevance of self-examination are equally fundamental in Descartes and Locke, but the use of the genetic method in philosophical inquiry was an example set by Locke and eagerly pursued in the eighteenth century with the full weight of his authority. This procedure was applied in the philosophy of mind and the understanding as well as in paedagogy and political philosophy. It should be recalled that knowledge of Locke had a much wider base in the eighteenth century than it has had since. In fact, today the most that can generally be assumed is a skimpy acquaintance with the *Essay*, even for people who pretend to know what it says. Many are still the victims of nineteenth-century conservative thought, to which denigration of Locke was a matter of doctrine. Many still use A. C. Fraser's edition of the *Essay*, now over seventy years old. Toward that edition there can only be one intelligent attitude: to consider it a curious piece of late Victoriana. Both the text and the information about it are very unreliable, and the notes are outright laughable.[47] Being spared that monster, readers in the eighteenth century were much better off than many readers and scholars are today, whether they read the *Essay* in the original or in translation. But the eighteenth century also read the *Thoughts concerning Education* (12 printings in French and at least one German by 1747), which as we shall see had a significant influence on Du Marsais; and the *Two Treatises of Government* (five printings in French by 1755, one German in 1718). Locke was much more than the *Essay*, and something quite different from the sort of empiricist he has later—much later—been made out to have been. In our terms Locke was, like Descartes, a rationalist, a matter to which I shall return.

It is too obvious to require demonstration that the *Essay* exhibited the genetic approach and that Locke is chiefly responsible for its popularity during the eighteenth century. There is so to speak, in Locke's own words, "a progress of the mind" both in the individual and in mankind at large. This progress is suggested in a variety of ways, but especially by the consideration of children and languages. In Book II of the *Essay*, for instance, we find a number of suggestive observations. Locke says he "is apt to think [words] may very much" direct "our thoughts towards the originals of men's *ideas*," while in another passage he remarks, "that mankind have fitted their notions and words to the use of common life and not to the truth and extent of things. . . .This, by the way, may give us some light into the different state and growth of languages."[48]

But Locke himself had not pursued the origin of language. In the *Second Treatise of Government*, however, he had used the postulate of a hypothetical or conjectural state of nature for the purpose of identifying the basic rules of moral and political obligation. This procedure aimed at reaching back beyond the artificial accretions—the customs, laws and rules of government—of particular societies as they had been known in history. The conception of this conjectural state was of course supported by much relevant knowledge, drawn from all periods and places in history, but especially from travel accounts of distant and presumably more primitive and certainly different societies. This sort of information corresponded, so to speak, to the experimental knowledge which the scientists could produce in the laboratory, where nature could easily be separated from art to reveal its uniform natural laws.[49] Similarly, the philosophical question of the origin of language as first formulated by Condillac sought to establish man's linguistic state of nature in order to gain insight into the nature of man, indeed into the unique nature of man. Consequently, in addition to the method, the political philosophy of Locke and Condillac's origin of language have much in common, most strikingly perhaps a common interest in what has rightly been called comparative anthropology, nourished by travel literature. Owing to this similarity between the uses of the state of nature in political and in linguistic philosophy, they have also frequently been misunderstood in similar ways.

The state of nature itself was hypothetical construct, a model it might perhaps be called today, and the charge often brought later that Locke fooled himself about history is entirely beside the point. Neither Locke nor the eighteenth century made any such mistake. In *Inégalité*, for instance, speaking of the state of nature, Rousseau said: "Il ne faut pas prendre les recherches, dans lesquelles on peut entrer sur ce sujet, pour des verités historiques, mais seulement pour des raisonnemens hypothétiques et conditionnels; plus propres à éclaircir la Nature des choses qu'à montrer la véritable origine, et semblables à ceux que font tous les jours nos physiciens sur la formation du monde." He wanted to be sure this point was not misunderstood. A few pages earlier, in the Preface, he had observed: "J'ai hazardé quelques conjectures, moins dans l'espoir de resoudre la question que dans l'intention de l'éclaircir et de la réduire à son véritable état. . . .Car ce n'est pas une légère entreprise de démêler ce qu'il y a d'originaire et d'artificiel dans la Nature actuelle de l'homme, et de bien connoître un état qui n'existe plus, qui n'a peut-être point existé, qui probablement n'existera jamais, et dont il est pourtant nécessaire d'avoir des notions justes pour bien juger de notre état présent."[50] This is the capital point: the search for origins concerned the present state of man, not the establishment of some "historical" fact or "explanation" of how things actually were at some point in the past. The nineteenth century was so saturated with a factual historical view that it could not see the attempt to deal with origins in any other light, thus failing utterly to comprehend what the previous century had been up to. Renan's critique is typical, clearly demonstrating this failure of understanding. Referring to Condillac, Maupertuis, and Rousseau on the origin of language, Renan observed: "On prenait l'homme avec le mécanisme actuel de ses facultés, et on transportait indiscrètement ce mécanisme dans le passé, sans songer aux différences profondes qui durent exister entre les premiers âges de l'humanité et l'état présent de la conscience."[51] It was in fact precisely this difference between early man and modern man that the eighteenth-century philosophers were interested in, and they took it to be the result of a process of development or progress that had occured owing to man's artificial accomplishments, which in turn had their source in man's nature, in his innate mental make-up. By rejecting the uniformity of human nature, Renan lost the distinction between natural and artificial man; consequently the eighteenth century could no longer be understood. More than that, it became, in so far as this view was involved, an object of contempt.

Locke's political philosophy and Condillac's origin of language share another significant agreement. In both cases the method rules out that divine origin can be admitted, even though one may on other grounds accept it. In the *First Treatise of Government* Locke had rejected the argument that the grounds of political authority could be derived from the lordship of Adam and his descendants; he had also strongly insisted on Adam's ordinary humanity, as it has been called. Condillac, at the very beginning of his section on the origin and progress of language in the *Essai*, had rejected the relevance of the story of Adam and Eve, for when they came from the hand of God, they were, "par un secours extraordinaire, en état de réfléchir et de se communiquer leurs pensées." It was not, he said, sufficient for "un philosophe de dire qu'une chose a été faite par des voies extraordinaires." It was his duty to explain "comment elle auroit pu se faire par des moyens naturels."[52] Similarly, Rousseau observes with regard to his hypothetical state of nature that religion tells another story, but religion "ne nous défend de former des conjectures tirées de la seule nature de l'homme et des Êtres qui l'environnent, sur ce qu'auroit pu devenir le Genre-humain, s'il fût resté abandonné à lui-même."[53] Herder was of the same opinion. In the early "Versuch einer Geschichte der lyrischen Dichtkunst" already cited, he devoted several pages to the task of showing the uselessness of referring to divine origin, for it fails to explain anything: "Und wozu nützt diese Hypothese: die Poesie hat einen göttlichen Ursprung; sie erklärt nichts: sie fodert selbst noch Erklärung. Sie erklärt nichts, denn sie sagt eigentlich blos: ich sehe Wirkungen, die ich nicht aus natürlichen Ursachen herleiten kann: folglich kommen sie von Gott: ein Schluss der Barmherzigkeit, der alle weitere Untersuchung aufhebt. . . . Unwissenheit, Furcht und Aberglauben, drei Schwestern, die so viel Zeiten und Völker beherrscht, haben ja für viele Dinge in der Natur vormals eine Wolke vorgezogen gehabt, deren Ursachen wir jetzt ohne Wunder und Zaubereien erklären können. Ein Philosoph muss so ungeduldig hiebei werden, als Shandy gegen seinen Bruder Tobias, wenn jener untersuchen wollte, und dieser ihm mit aufgehabnen Händen und entzückten Augen entgegen seufzte: Bruder! das kommt von Gott!—Bruder Tobias! rief er, das heisst den Knoten unphilosophisch abhauen."[54] The method is conjectural, the postulate of divine origin can have no relevance. Its acceptance would of course also have meant than man's career would not be a record of progress, but a sorry story of decay and corruption, a doctrine which early in the next century was in fact advocated by the two conservative and anti-Lockian writers Joseph de Maistre and Louis de Bonald, who both had a considerable influence on anti-Lockian English thought in the nineteenth century.[55]

ORIGIN OF LANGUAGE

With these considerations in mind, it will, I hope, be obvious that the question of the origin of language did not aim at historical and factual explanation of states of language in the past. It was as hypothetical as the state of nature in political philosophy, and like the latter, its aim was to understand man in the present. But among all the accomplishments of man that might be inquired into, language was the most important because it was admitted that man could have achieved very little without signs and language. In Condillac's words: "Les progrès de l'esprit humain dépendant entièrement de l'adresse avec laquelle nous nous servons du language."[56] To inquire into the origin of language is therefore the same as inquiring into man's understanding and knowledge. It may be a bit crude, but still have truth and brevity, to say that Condillac transformed Locke's theory of knowledge, his inquiry into "the original, certainty, and extent of human knowledge" as Locke called it at the beginning of Book I of the *Essay*, into a theory of the origin of language just as Locke had turned political philosophy into a question about the state of nature. Condillac's gestures and "les cris naturels" form the only "language" that is natural to man; it is the immediate expression of the passions. It is not, therefore, the specifically human language and speech that form the aim of Condillac's inquiry, but thanks to man's unique possession of reason this gestural language suggests the utility of signs and the possibility of developing artificial, voluntary signs. Of these natural signs, Condillac said: "L'usage de ces signes étendit peu à peu l'exercice des opérations de l'âme, et, à leur tour, celles-ci ayant plus d'exercice, perfectionnèrent les signes et en rendirent l'usage plus familier. Notre expérience prouve que ces deux choses s'aident mutuellement."[57] This passage indicates why the origin of language has a crucial function in Condillac's account of the origins of the human understanding. Without language and signs, man's innate capacity for reflection, his reason, could not have shown itself and developed. The connection between the first part of the *Essai* ("Des matériaux de nos connoissances et particulièrement des opérations de l'âme") and the second ("Du language et de la méthode") is indicated by this sentence: "Il semble qu'on ne sauroit se servir des signes d'institution, si l'on n'étoit pas déjà capable d'assez de réflexion pour les choisir et pour y attacher des idées: comment donc, m'objectera-t-on peut-être, l'exercise de la réflexion ne s'acquérroit-il que par l'usage de signes? Je réponds que je satisferai à cette difficulté lorsque je donnerai l'histoire du langage."[58]

Thus the question of the origin of language is a question about the nature of language and the nature of thought, a means therefore of gaining knowledge of the progress of mind and the history of thought. Without the linearity of speech, no progress could have occurred. In Condillac's words: "Si une pensée est sans succession dans l'esprit, elle a une succession dans le discours, où elle se décompose en autant de parties qu'elle renferme d'idées. Alors nous pouvons observer ce que nous faisons en pensant, nous pouvons nous en rendre compte; nous pouvons par conséquent, apprendre à conduire notre réflexion. Penser devient donc un art, et cet art est l'art de parler," a view in which Condillac entirely agrees with the Port-Royal Grammar, whose subtitle was "l'art de parler," just as its companion piece, the Port-Royal Logic, had the subtitle "l'art de penser."[59] All participants in the debate accepted the principles expressed in Monboddo's two statements that "it appears, that, from the study of language, if it be properly conducted, the history of the human mind is best learned," and that he "could not give the philosophical account I proposed, of the origin of language, without inquiring into the origin of ideas."[60] The origin of language and universal grammar agreed that language cannot be seriously studied without reference to mind.

The function of Condillac's treatment of the origin of language in his argument about the human understanding clearly shows that the question of the origin of language had serious epistemological implications. Maupertuis' *Réflexions* opened with this statement: "Les signes par lesquels les hommes ont désigné leurs premières idées ont tant d'influence sur toutes nos connoissances, que je crois que des recherches sur l'origine des langues, et sur la manière dont elles se sont formées, méritent autant d'attention, et peuvent être aussi utiles dans l'étude de la philosophie que d'autres méthodes qui bâtissent souvent des systèmes sur des mots dont on n'a jamais approfondi le sens."[6] [1] When pressed by a critic that he had in fact not said much about the origin of language, Maupertuis answered: "La composition et décomposition des signes de nos perceptions, et leur rapport aux perceptions mêmes, forment presque toutes nos connoissances, et les font tourner à leur gré. C'est pour apprécier la valeur de ces connoissances que je me suis étendu sur cette méchanique et nullement, comme le pense M. Boindin, pour expliquer la méchanique des langues mêmes."[6] [2] Another good example of this epistemological concern is Diderot's *Lettre sur les sourds et muets*, which takes up the origin of language in connection with the problem of inversion. Franco Venturi has rightly stressed this aspect of the origin of language. The subject of that *Lettre* is, in Venturi's words, "des problèmes plus particulièrement esthétiques et gnoséologiques."[6] [3]

UNIVERSAL GRAMMAR AND ORIGIN OF LANGUAGE

Though historically related to different philosophical doctrines—one Lockian and the other now popularly supposed to be Cartesian—both the origin of language and universal grammar saw language as the distinguishing feature that set man apart from the animals and both assumed that the study of language could give insight into mind and the nature of man. Both saw language as the most striking proof of man's creativity; the use of language was itself creative and in turn the condition for all further creativity. Accepting the axiom of the uniformity of human nature, both aimed first at understanding the universal properties of language. They were, as Maupertuis warned his readers, not interested in knowing why Londoners said "bread" but Parisians "pain."[6] [4] Today no one will deny that these are prominent qualities of universal grammar. We are all indebted to Chomsky for restoring universal grammar to its rightful place of importance in linguistic theory and history, for dismissing the ignorant, hostile, uncomprehending, and incompetent accounts which were the run of the mill not so long ago. Partisan history is no history.

But I am not so sure that these rationalist qualities will also be granted to the mid-eighteenth century concern with the origin and progress of language. Yet, there cannot be any doubt that this concern exhibits those qualities as clearly as does universal grammar. Both modes in the study of language were directed to the same subject matter and aim; only their methods of approach were different. When Condillac during the 1760's prepared a grammar for the young Prince of Parma, he began with two chapters on the origin of language; necessarily so, he said, "car, avant que d'entreprendre de décomposer une langue, il faut avoir quelques connoissances de la manière dont elle s'est formée."[6] [5] Why so? Because "l'histoire de l'esprit humain me montroit. . .l'ordre que je devois suivre moi-même dans l'instruction du Prince," and because "l'art de parler n'est donc que l'art de penser et l'art de raisonner, qui se développe à mesure que les langues se perfectionnent."⁶⁶ These passages, incidentally, remind us of the very important—and I take it obvious—fact that both universal grammar and the origin of language are closely allied to the theory of learning and the problem of the acquisition of language. Universal grammar and the origin of language became fused. What one did atemporally in terms of structure alone, the other did on the scale of time. It is no accident that the first great collected editions of Du Marsais and of Condillac appeared within one year of each other—in 1797 and 1798—during the Directory, and it was natural that Destutt de Tracy should remark a few years later on the greatness of the Port-Royal Grammar, but regret, "que dans leur grammaire non plus que dans leur logique ils ne soient pas entrés dans plus de détails sur la formation de nos idées."⁶⁷

This view of the basic utility of forming conjectures on the origin and progress of language is already evident in Condillac's *Essai*, though he was later to become more explicit in this regard. It comes out in such statements as, "les mots ne doivent-ils pas être aux idées de toutes les sciences ce que sont les chiffres aux idées de l'arithmétique?"⁶⁸ and "comment les arithméticiens ont-ils des idées si exactes? C'est que, connoissant de quelle manière elles s'engendrent, ils sont toujours en état de les composer ou de les décomposer pour les comparer selon tous leur rapports."⁶⁹ This conception did not mean that Condillac took the first speaking men to have been full-blown philosophers, for the first language was still intermixed with gestures and owed its origin to the passions: "C'est aux poëtes que nous avons les premières et peut-être aussi les plus grandes obligations,"⁷⁰ a view that has often been denied to Condillac in favor of Herder.

One of the central concerns of universal grammar was the problem of inversion, which in current terms involves the matter of deep and surface structure, like the problem of ellipsis. This problem was equally important in the origin of language. In the *Lettre sur les sourds et muets*, Diderot dealt with that question by considering it in the light of gestures. To discuss the matter of inversion, he said, "je crois qu'il est à propos d'examiner comment les langues se sont formées."⁷¹ Similarly, the Port-Royal Grammar had assumed that some word classes—such as those of the noun and the verb—were primary in relation to other classes, which were only abbreviations or convenient substitutes for the former, as most of the pronouns were for nouns. These latter classes had therefore been "invented" to fulfill those functions. The origin of language converted this problem into the problem of which came first and how the others were formed and introduced. This intimate and happy alliance of universal grammar and the origin of language is clearly stated in Turgot's article "Étymologie," first published in volume six of the *Encyclopédie* in 1756. Referring to the origin of language, he wrote:

"On sent aisément combien ces préliminaires sont indispensables pour saisir en grand, et sous son vrai point de vue, la théorie générale de la parole et de la marche de l'esprit humain dans la formation et les progrès du langage. . . .Cette théorie est la source d'où découlent les règles de cette grammaire générale qui gouverne tous les langues, à laquelle toutes les nations s'assujettissent en croyant ne suivre que les caprices de l'usage."[72]

In this fusion of universal grammar and the origin of language, Du Marsais is a special and very instructive case. As a universal grammarian he has no rival except Claude Lancelot and Antoine Arnauld, and Chomsky leaves no doubt about his importance. But Du Marsais gained recognition only late in life when he was engaged to write articles on language and related philosophical subjects for the *Encyclopédie*. At the time of his death at eighty in 1756, he had completed a large number of articles—both short and long—covering the beginning of the alphabet through the entry "Grammairien." As early as 1749, Condillac praised his *Des Tropes* (1730), regretting that Du Marsais had not yet given the public a complete grammar.[73] Diderot also often referred to Du Marsais in terms of great respect.[74] But until the concluding years of his life, Du Marsais' work on universal grammar was ignored, and he himself lived in poverty, moving from one insignificant post to another. His short "Exposition d'une méthode raisonnée pour apprendre la langue latine," appeared in 1722; a brief Preface to a larger work on "Les véritables principes de la grammaire, ou nouvelle grammaire raisonnée pour apprendre la langue latine" was published in 1729, but of the great work he had in mind only *Des Tropes* appeared during his lifetime—and on that work he was complimented by a well-wisher who thought it was a history of the tropical regions.[75] The *Logique*, the essay on "Inversion," and the "Fragment sur les causes de la parole" were not published until 1769, and still other writings only in the *Oeuvres* of 1797.

In philosophy Du Marsais was strongly anti-Cartesian—he maintained, for instance, that animals are not automatons.[76] His work on universal grammar was closely tied to the practical job of teaching Latin by which he tried to make a living for the better part of his life. His method was this: He arranged the Latin phrases according to the "ordre naturel" and placed the corresponding French words underneath in interlinear translation. This method obviously involves the related problems of inversion and construction or syntax, two subjects on which Du Marsais gave special proof of his brilliance as a universal grammarian. On his authority for this method, he said: "Je pourrois ajouter bien des autorités, et entre autres celle de M. Locke dans son Traité de l'Éducation des enfans, pour justifier ce que je dis ici, que la routine doit précéder les règles; mais dans une affaire qui est du ressort du bon sens, et qu'on peut justifier par des expériences, les autorités sont inutiles."[77] It is true that Locke had not advocated changing the Latin word

order to make it more nearly follow the "ordre naturel," but he had implied
the same principle by suggesting that the child should begin with "some easy
and pleasant book" and that the English interlinear translation should be
"made as literal as it can be." Instruction in formal grammar should be kept
to a minimum until the pupil could, as Locke said, "read himself 'Sanctii
Minerva,' with Scioppius and Perizonius's notes."[78] By using this method, Du
Marsais similarly argued that the child would first gain a sufficient command
of the new language by "routine"; only after instruction and learning by
routine should the pupil turn to grammar. His mode of teaching was attacked
by the Jesuit *Journal de Trévoux* in May of 1723 in a review of Du Marsais'
"Exposition." The following year Du Marsais published an answer, defending
his method and citing Locke at greater length. This defense included a list of
"un grand nombre de savans du premier ordre," who had advocated the same
method: "Scaliger, Sanctius, Vossius, Scioppius, M. le Fèvre de Saumur, le P.
Lamy, Locke, M. l'abbé de Dangeau, et un grand nombre d'autres."[79] Du
Marsais enrolled Locke among the universal grammarians.

    This is not the place to demonstrate in detail that Du Marsais followed
Locke not only on this particular point, but in philosophy in general. But a
few quotations will show that Du Marsais held basic views of mind, thought,
and the understanding that are entirely incompatible with the version of
innateness which Professor Chomsky takes to be essential to the fundamental
principles of universal grammar. In 1743 Du Marsais published a short piece
on the chief virtues of the good philosopher. In this piece, "Le philosophe,"
he said among other things: "Le philosophe est une machine comme un autre
homme; mais c'est une machine qui, par sa constitution méchanique, réfléchit
sur ses mouvement." In the same piece he had this to say about the nature of
thought: "La pensée est en l'homme un sens comme la vue et l'ouie,
dépendant également d'une constitution organique."[80] In another short
piece, "De la raison," first published in 1770, he said: "Les seuls moyens que
nous avons de nous instruire sont, ou notre propre expérience ou l'autorité.
L'expérience. . .est ou extérieure, c'est-à-dire, nous fournit les idées des objets
sensibles; ou intérieure, c'est-à-dire, nous fournit des idées des opérations de
notre entendement; voilà la source commune de toute connoissance; il nous
est impossible d'acquérir des idées d'aucune autre façon."[81] No Cartesian, in
Chomsky's sense, could hold those views. In sum, Du Marsais was heavily
indebted both to the Port-Royal Grammar and to Locke, and he was
decidedly anti-Cartesian in philosophy on the very points that have in recent
years been held most essential to the strength of universal grammar as a
linguistic theory.

    Far from being averse to each other, universal grammar and origin
of language interpenetrated each other. This union apparently did not spoil
universal grammar, for we are told by Chomsky that "the tradition of

philosophical grammar. . .flourished from the seventeenth century through romanticism."[82] There is in fact strong evidence in favor of the argument that universal grammar as a philosophical and theoretical discipline, on the level of a Du Marsais, had fallen into desuetude during the first half of the eighteenth century, *gaining fresh importance only after the origin of language, thanks to Condillac, had created renewed interest in linguistic theory*. After its initial publication in 1660, the Port-Royal Grammar was published again in 1664, 1676, 1679, and 1709, but then not again till 1754 with the notes of Duclos. At that time the publishers said that it had long been unobtainable, which is what they always say when an old text has recently come into demand. In England, the Port-Royal Grammar did not appear in English until 1753, though there had been translations of Lamy's *Art of Speaking* in 1676, 1696, and 1708. Universal grammar was revived only after Condillac's *Essai*, and the debate it caused had again raised significant problems in linguistic theory.

Of course, Du Marsais' own lack of success is the best demonstration that universal grammar had declined into merely practical and specific applications. It might perhaps be argued that the revival of universal grammar in 1754 was designed to counter the origin of language as a linguistic theory, but the historical facts do not offer the slightest foundation for such an interpretation. Equally groundless would be the argument that what remained of value was exclusively the contribution of universal grammar. Chomsky rightly admires Herder, F. Schlegel, A. W. Schlegel, Coleridge, and Wilhelm von Humboldt as exponents of certain doctrines and views which Chomsky derives from "Cartesian" linguistics, but which in fact derive from the tradition of linguistic theory that took shape around the origin of language problem. Indeed the references to Herder and to both the Schlegels occur in works that deal specifically with the origin of language, in one case even with "etymology in general." Both of these are subjects which nowhere appear in "Cartesian" linguistics or universal grammar, which would in fact seem immune to time perspective.

LOCKE, CONDILLAC, AND PROFESSOR CHOMSKY

There is especially one basic confusion which has followed in the wake of Chomsky's pronouncements on the history of linguistics. It has come to be believed that it is a uniquely "Cartesian" doctrine that human language consists of arbitrary, voluntary signs and not of vocal gestures that are the mere expression of the passions. This doctrine is not only much older than Descartes, but fundamental in Locke and Condillac. Locke insists over and over again that the "signification of sounds is not natural, but only imposed and arbitrary," brought about by "a voluntary imposition whereby such a word is made arbitrarily the mark of such an idea."[83] In Condillac, the voluntary and arbitrary nature of the vocal sign in human language is even more prominent than in Locke, who had not systematically discussed the origin of language. In the *Essai*, Condillac says that there are three kinds of signs, accidental, natural, and "les signes d'institution." Neither of the first two is "species-specific" to man since he shares them with the animals. Thus instituted signs alone effect the uniqueness of human language and speech. "Mais aussitôt qu'un homme commence à attacher des idées à des signes qu'il a lui-même choisis, on voit se former en lui la mémoire. . . .Voilà où l'on commence à percevoir la supériorité de notre âme sur celle des bêtes; car, d'un coté, il est constant qu'il ne dépend point d'elles d'attacher leurs idées à des signes arbitraires; et de l'autre, il paroît certain que cette impuissance ne vient pas uniquement de l'organisation. Leur corps n'est-il pas aussi propre au langage d'action que le notre? "[84] Thus in Locke as well as in Condillac, "the force that generates language is indistinguishable from that which generates thought," to use Chomsky's own words, though he would presumably deny this view to Locke and does not find it in Condillac for the painful reason that Condillac is not once mentioned in any piece of writing by Chomsky that I have ever seen. The insistence on the creative aspect of language and speech among the Romantics—chiefly of course in Germany—derives from Condillac's *Essai* and is transmitted by Herder. Recalling Condillac's discussion of artistic creativity in the long section on the origin and progress of language, one wonders how it has been possible to miss this point—except of course owing to what in fact happened, both in the past and today: neglect of Condillac's *Essai*.[85]

As an expression of his own interpretation, Chomsky cites a passage from d'Alembert's "Éloge de Du Marsais," to the effect that his object of study was "la marche de l'esprit humain dans la génération de ses idées."[86] In the literature of the time, this phrase is used over and over again to refer to the origin of language, but never to universal grammar alone. In *Language and Mind*, Chomsky says that he has "been describing the problem of the acquisition of knowledge of language in terms that are more familiar in an epistemological than a psychological context, but I think that this is quite appropriate."[87] This statement also perfectly describes the enterprise of Condillac and his followers in their concern with the origin of language.

It is true that Chomsky in *Cartesian Linguistics*[88] states that his chief concern is with the content and present-day significance of Cartesian doctrines, not with their transmission and the historical situation. But unfortunately, if one sets out to do part of the history, one does not escape the consequences of making a selection that ignores other contemporary work. These consequences mean not only historical distortion and error—which might be considered by some an academic matter of little relevance—but also the loss and neglect of other work which would seem to be relevant and deserve attention by the same criteria that are applied to universal grammar. Condillac and others are ignored, while features of later linguistic theory are assigned exclusively to the "Cartesian" tradition, when in fact, as we have seen, they have a very different source.

I think it will be granted that all the writers in question—including the ones who figure in Chomsky's work—were neither unintelligent nor befuddled. Consequently we have no reason to assume that they carelessly or stupidly overlooked the sort of incompatibility between "Cartesian" and Lockian linguistics which Chomsky's argument certainly entails. I therefore see only one possibility, that there is something seriously wrong with Chomsky's facts and argument. We have before us a private myth which is already well on its way to becoming a public one. This debilitating distortion of the history of the study of language need not surprise us. That "history" has always, with very few exceptions, been a succession of partisan stances, as in the standard nineteenth-century works on the subject as well as in the later denigration of universal grammar that was fashionable until recently. By Chomsky's own frequent admission, this situation is unfortunate, for he often deplores the virtual absence of reliable, precise, in-depth work on the history of the study of language. In these misunderstandings, the crucial figure is Locke, who receives very strange treatment from Chomsky, so strange in fact that it is very hard to see what the point about him is, except that he is assigned the role of villain, or at best is made out to have been a fool or nincompoop in matters of linguistic theory. This matter deserves closer attention.

Both *Cartesian Linguistics* and *Language and Mind* make a number of statements about Locke's conception of innateness, but the reader will look in vain for as much as a single precise reference to Locke's text, or even for a correct report of what he says. *Language and Mind*, however, makes a reference to two notes by Fraser in his edition of the *Essay*, the edition I have mentioned above. In the text to which Chomsky appends this note, he says: "Locke's critique had little relevance to any familiar doctrine of the seventeenth century. The arguments that Locke gave were considered and dealt with in quite a satisfactory way in the earliest seventeenth-century discussions of innate ideas, for example those of Lord Herbert and Descartes, both of whom took for granted that the system of innate ideas and principles would not function unless appropriate stimulation took place. For this reason, Locke's arguments, none of which took cognizance of this condition, are without force [note 14]; for some reason, he avoided the issues that had been discussed in the preceding half-century."[89] In note 14, Chomsky says that "this observation is commonplace," and then proceeds to cite two notes in the Fraser edition as authority.[90] The observation may be commonplace with some because Fraser's edition, with its silly notes, has been so widely used. But this observation will not be found in informed works—including eighteenth-century works—that deal seriously with Locke and with what he said and meant. The remark that Locke on this point took no account of what had been said during the rest of the seventeenth century is astounding, so astounding that one must wonder how—and whether—it can be made by anyone who has read the *Essay* (even in Fraser's edition), and who has made an effort to acquaint himself with the best secondary literature, which though not necessary could have offered welcome aid.

A reading of the *Essay* itself is enough to show that Locke was not the sort of empiricist we have generally been told that he is, for instance in the "commonplace" observations of Fraser's notes. If there is a typical empiricist version of the philosophy of mind, it is surely that of Hume, who took the mind to be nothing but a train of ideas held together by association. This is a view that is totally foreign to Locke, and the very position of the association of ideas in the *Essay* is the best reminder of it. To Locke the association of ideas is a disturbing, non-constructive, uncontrollable feature of thought precisely because such association interferes with the normal exercise of reason, even to the point where it may subvert reason. Locke calls it a "madness": "I shall be pardoned for calling it by so harsh a name as *madness*, when it is considered that opposition to reason deserves that name and is really madness."[91] If by rationalism is meant the doctrine that reason is the principal source of certain knowledge as well as of all ordered knowledge even when not certain in that sense, then Locke was surely nothing but a rationalist, in spite of all that we have been told to the contrary—though chiefly by Victorian conservatives.

It might have seemed more germane to the entire question to have talked about rationalism but Chomsky for some reason generally prefers to talk instead about innateness, even about the "Cartesian postulation of a substance whose essence was thought."[92] On the matter of innateness the confusion is complete and so basic that it may not be worth further consideration until Chomsky abandons dependence on Fraser's notes as authority for what are commonplace views of Locke's philosophy. The confusion is complete because the doctrines of innateness which Chomsky attributes to both Descartes and to Locke are doctrines which neither of them held. *Cartesian Linguistics* quotes a long passage from Descartes' "Notes directed against a certain Programme" in support of the interpretation of Descartes' conception of innateness which that book presents. But Chomsky does not cite the passage which immediately precedes it. This is a long passage, but it will be necessary to quote it in its entirety: "*In article twelve* he [Regius who had criticized Descartes on innateness] appears to dissent from me only in words, for when he says that *the mind has no need of innate ideas, or notions, or axioms,* and at the same time allows it the faculty of thinking (to be considered natural or innate), he makes an affirmation in effect identical with mine, but denies it in words. For I never wrote nor concluded that the mind required innate ideas which were in some sort different from its faculty of thinking; but when I observed the existence in me of certain thoughts which proceeded, not from extraneous objects nor from the determination of my will, but solely from the faculty of thinking which is within me, then, that I might distinguish the ideas or notions (which are the forms of these thoughts) from other thoughts *adventitious* or *factitious,* I termed the former '*innate.*' In the same sense we say that in some families generosity is innate, in others certain diseases like gout or gravel, not that on this account the babes of these families suffer from these diseases in their mother's womb, but because they are born with a certain disposition or propensity for contracting them."[93] In other words, what is produced by the "faculty of thinking" (*facultas cogitandi*) is what Descartes calls innate. This agrees precisely with Locke, who uses the terms reason, reflection, that powerful faculty, and similar terms, and who derives all knowledge from the light of nature, from the "faculties [man] is endowed with by nature." To Locke these innate faculties were reason and the capacity for sense experience—sensation or sense-perception to Locke being much more than a picture in the back of the eye or something automatic for which a passive mind would suffice.[94]

Locke's agreement with Descartes on this point will be clear to anyone who has read the *Essay*, but it also emerges from certain notes, which Locke wrote in response to a critique of his conception of innateness: "Of those who say there are innate laws or rules of right and wrong, 'tis reasonable to demand a list of them, & he that cannot produce what he soe tells of 'tis plain folly." And: "If moral Ideas or moral rules (which are the moral principles I deny to be innate) are innate, I say children must know them as well as men. If by moral principles you mean a faculty to finde out in time the moral difference of actions. . .this is an improper way of speaking to cal a power principles; I never deny'd a power to be innate, but that which I deny'd was that any Ideas or connection of Ideas was innate."[95] It is surprising that it could have been missed that Locke and Descartes do not use the term innate in the same manner, and that owing to this difference, it is possible for them to have the same conception of what is in fact natural and innate to the mind. Locke will not allow the term to be used of any idea or notion or principle unless it is already full-blown, actual, and known to the child from the mother's womb. In the long passage I have cited, Descartes made the same point, though having stated that qualification, he did allow himself the use of the term innate.

Writing to Locke in 1704, his intelligent friend Anthony Collins observed: "There can be nothing advanced contradictory to the design of the

Essay of Human Und. but on the Principle of Innate Ideas, in that sense they are refuted by the Author in the 1st book."[96] In the *Essay* Locke took up Lord Herbert of Cherbury's *De Veritate* on innateness. Lord Herbert had listed five innate principles "imprinted on the minds of men by the hand of God." Locke lists them and then observes: "Though I allow these to be clear truths and such as if rightly explained, a rational creature can hardly avoid giving his assent to, yet I think he is far from proving them innate impressions *in foro interiori descriptae*."[97] To Locke self-evident propositions, for instance, are innate in Descartes' sense. To Locke all men are by nature rational and God "commands what reason does." When the *Essay* first came out, some quite intelligent men took it to be a metaphysical treatise in the Cartesian manner. It may also, owing to many misrepresentations on this point, be recalled that Leibniz did not say that the *Essay* offered the philosophy expressed in the familiar words "nihil est in intellectu quod non fuerit in sensu." Leibniz cited the whole statement, concluding "excipe: nisi ipse intellectus." This, Leibniz said, "s'accorde assez avec vostre Auteur de l'*Essay*, qui cherche la source d'une bonne partie des idees dans la reflexion de l'esprit sur sa propre nature."[98] It may also be recalled that Locke had great sympathy for the Jansenists and their philosophy, which of course is the philosophy characteristic of the Port-Royal and preeminently of Antoine Arnauld. During his years in France, Locke translated some of the essays in Pierre Nicole's *Essais de morale*, which would appear to have had a decisive influence on his political philosophy. Nicole was, except for the last years, a close associate of Arnauld, with whom he collaborated on the *Logique ou l'art de penser*.

If Locke had a single passionate thought that informed his entire life and work, it was toleration and the belief that men could live in peace. Innateness as commonly used was inimical to this belief, and Locke's philosophy was immediately in conservative, orthodox, and bigoted circles taken to be dangerous heresy. If the inhabitants of South America, for instance, did not share the moral rules and religious beliefs which their Spanish conquerors took to be a necessary and innate part of the make-up of decent men, then they were treated accordingly, as animals rather than as men. In the eighteenth century Professor Chomsky's innateness did not have a single philosophically respectable defender. To Locke it was in the interest of toleration and peace to postulate that all men could learn or come to assent to what had been revealed by the light of nature. But it was intolerable and had violent and inhuman consequences to claim that there are certain rules they must know. At the end of Book I, "Of Innate Notions," Locke said: "Nor is it a small power it gives one man over another to have the authority to be the dictator of principles and teacher of unquestionable truths, and to make a man swallow that for an innate principle which may serve to his purpose who teacheth them." These principles or "universal truths" were "discovered by the application of those faculties that were fitted by nature to recieve and judge them, when duly employed about them."[99] Claims to truth must be argued on public, not on private and esoteric, grounds.

Chomsky's version of Locke's philosophy—in so far as it is possible (and fair) to judge on the slender evidence we are offered—is plainly false. The consequence of that error is historical chaos.[100]

II. The Debate in the Berlin Academy

Arens has observed that universal grammar was the dominant French concern in the mid-eighteenth century, while origin of language received only slight attention. But in Germany, he says, the emphasis lay on the origin of language since universal grammar made a late appearance in Germany. We are further told that German work on the study of language in this period was, by contrast to French work, informed by a strong anthropological view.[101] I hope I have shown that the historical facts do not offer the slightest support to Arens' thesis; it is a conventional myth. The problem of the origin of language is brought to Germany from France only a few years after the publication of Condillac's *Essai* in 1746, by the president of the newly reconstituted Berlin Academy, Pierre-Louis Moreau de Maupertuis (1698-1759).

On his arrival in Berlin, Maupertuis had found German metaphysics "une étrange science," which he took to be the fault of the Germans rather than of metaphysics. With a true sense of the moment, he introduced his new audience to the question of the origin of language and its attendant philosophical problems. Outside the Academy the climate was very favorable indeed. Within it, Maupertuis raised a debate that was to lead directly to the prize topic which Herder answered in his *Ursprung*.

The Debaters and Their Writings

I shall now, in chronological order, take up the communications on the philosophy, nature, and origin of language which belong to the Academy debate before Herder. For each item, I shall provide an exposition of its main argument and a brief discussion, but space does not permit detailed observations. On the whole, I shall assume that the reader will draw his own conclusions on the basis of the material I have presented in the first part of this paper.

MAUPERTUIS AND THE REVIVAL OF THE ACADEMY

When Frederick the Great became King of Prussia in 1740, he soon made plans to put new life into the Berlin Academy. Though founded by Leibniz in 1700 with great expectations and ambitious plans, it had declined into narrow provincialism, and it had quite failed to gain any stature among the learned societies of Europe. The King reorganized the Academy, himself wrote its new statutes, and invited Maupertuis—then a French scientist of acknowledged international standing and a member of both the Académie des Sciences in Paris and the Royal Society in London—to become its first president. Maupertuis assumed the presidency in May of 1746, and he officially remained in that post until his death in the house of Johann Bernoulli at Basel on 27 July 1759. During most of his years in Berlin, he was plagued by the disease from which he died, consumption, as well as by the unpleasant and bitter controversy with Voltaire, who by his greater prestige and by merely being read, has put Maupertuis' reputation under a cloud ever since. Still, in terms of work and influence, these were fruitful years for Maupertuis and for the Academy, which prospered under his guidance and under the benevolent patronage of the King.

The statutes of the Académie Royale des Sciences et Belles-Lettres, to use its official name, were unique in one respect; they made provision for all branches of knowledge, for the sciences as well as for the humanities. In addition to the two classes of natural science and mathematics (which in London and Paris were the subjects of the Royal Society and of the Académie des Sciences), the Berlin Academy had a third class for "philosophie spéculative" and a fourth for "belles-lettres." It was expressly stated that the new society should include the subjects which in London and Paris were covered by the scientific societies as well as the subjects which in Paris were the province of the Académie des Inscriptions et Belles-Lettres. This organization did not come about without controversy and discussion, but the solution brought the Academy into line with Leibniz' organization of the first Berlin Academy. It was determined that the third class, "la classe de philosophie spéculative s'appliquera à la logique, à la métaphysique et à la morale," while the fourth class, "la classe de belles-lettres comprendra les antiquités, l'histoire et les langues."[102] It is significant that both prize-topics and all the communications on language dealt with here, except two, belong to the third class, that is, to philosophy rather than to what we would call literature and philology. It was further stipulated that any member could make communications outside his own class and that the weekly Thursday-night meetings should be plenary sessions, that is, not be divided according to class, and that each should in turn be devoted to one of the four subject classes. The importance and uniqueness of this arrangement are obvious.

Without it Maupertuis, for instance, would have had no opportunity to speak to his fellow members on the philosophy of language. Writing late in 1747, Maupertuis expressed reservations about the inclusion of metaphysics, but at the same time affirmed his determination to make the best of it, "peut-être que si j'avois créé la forme de l'Académie, je n'aurois pas eu le courage d'y introduire une telle classe; mais puisque je l'y ay trouvée, je suis bien aise qu'elle y soit; et je voudrois seulement qu'elle jouât dans le monde un bon personnage." The remaining years of his life were chiefly devoted to "philosophie spéculative," which he wished to raise to a higher and international level, above the German provincialism he had found on his arrival.[103]

For obvious reasons, the official language was French, but papers in German and Latin were permitted, and regular provision was made for their translation into French. It should be emphasized that Maupertuis' contemporaries in Berlin considered him to have a deeply religious and spiritual outlook. "M. de Maupertuis," said Formey, "a eu de grands sentimens de religion." Formey also believed that Maupertuis' two papers on the origin of language were not only the best of their kind but also the best of all his writings.[104] Maupertuis was inordinately fond of animals (birds, dogs, deer, and monkeys), kept a whole menagerie around him in his living quarters, and made great efforts to interbreed them in the most unlikely combinations. Maupertuis made extended visits to France and Paris during the summer of 1746, and from the spring of 1753 until the summer of 1754. He again left for France in June of 1756 and never returned to Berlin. It is significant information that Maupertuis, during his second visit to Paris, took "grand plaisir à la conversation de Condillac et s'interessa fort à l'entreprise de l'Encyclopédie, dont les premiers volumes étaient parus depuis peu."[105]

MAUPERTUIS, *RÉFLEXIONS* (1748)

In the late 1740's Maupertuis wrote his *Réflexions sur l'origine des langues et la signification des mots*,[106] which was first published at Paris in 1748 in a dozen copies in order to see what reception it would get. Since the problems it takes up are so clearly linked to those of Condillac's *Essai* of 1746, there would seem to be little doubt that the *Réflexions* was suggested by the *Essai*. In fact, they offer a critique and conclusions very similar to the Berkeleian consequences which Diderot had also found in the *Essai*. Maupertuis had been in Paris during the summer of 1746, and we are told that he meditated on the interrelations of material existence and thought during the winter of 1746-1747.[107]

Maupertuis' essay strikingly illustrates how conjectures on the origin of language are put in the service of epistemology. His problem is this:

Accepting the uniformity of human nature and the identical workings in all of perception and reason, that is the light of nature, all men will also have the same experience of nature (vii); their perceptions will be the same and thus also their knowledge of the structure of reality. But men's knowledge is in fact not based directly on these common perceptions; men have of necessity become creatures of language, and their knowledge is about signs which owe their origin "à des hommes simples et grossiers, qui ne formèrent d'abord que le peu de signes dont ils avoient besoin pour exprimer leurs premières idées" (iv). Men have fixed their attention on and given signs to widely differing parts of the original perceptions. Hence translation among distant languages is virtually impossible, and signs have no strict philosophical validity in regard to reality—an idea also found in Bacon, Robert Boyle, and very clearly in Locke. We are barely born before we hear an infinity of words which express rather the prejudices of our speech community than the first ideas of our minds: "Nous retenons ces mots, nous leur attachons des idées confuses; et voilà bientôt notre provision faite pour le reste de notre vie, sans que le plus souvent nous nous soyons avisés d'approfondir la vraie valeur de ces mots, ni la sûreté des connoissances qu'ils peuvent nous procurer, ou nous faire croire que nous possédons" (iii). These considerations underlie the opening statement of the *Réflexions*: "Les signes par lesquels les hommes ont désigné leurs premières idées ont tant d'influence sur toutes nos connoissances, que je crois que des recherches sur l'origine des Langues, et sur la manière dont elles se sont formées, méritent autant d'attention, et peuvent être aussi utiles dans l'étude de la Philosophie que d'autres méthodes qui bâtissent souvent des systèmes sur des mots dont on n'a jamais approfondi le sens." We may therefore expect to learn a great deal from the comparison of distant languages, "parce qu'on peut retrouver dans la construction des Langues des vestiges des premiers pas qu'a fait l'esprit humain." Comparison of contiguous and related languages—such as English and French—will not offer insight, for "les expressions des idées y sont coupées de la même manière, et dès-lors la comparaison de ces Langues entre elles ne peut rien nous apprendre" (ii). Consequently, speakers of such languages "ont fait assez le même chemin, et les sciences ont pris à peu près le même tour" (v). In these observations Maupertuis reveals the characteristic eighteenth-century interest in comparative anthropology and in the relativity of men's achievements, a theme also prominent in Locke. Maupertuis' concern was not entirely theoretical, however, for during his scientific expedition to Lapland in 1736 to measure the flatness of the earth toward the pole, which had been predicted by Newton, he had not failed to pay attention to the Lapp language.

But in his approach to the problem, Maupertuis actually takes another course, for two reasons. No language is really primitive enough to give us the information we need, and, second, the only substitute Maupertuis can think of also has nothing to offer. He admits that he has no memory whatsoever of his own first ideas, of what happened when he first opened his eyes and formed his first conclusions "dans cet âge, où mon âme plus vide d'idées m'auroit été plus facile à connoître qu'elle ne l'est aujourd'hui, parce qu'elle étoit, pour ainsi dire, plus *elle-même*" (vi). He finds only one remedy, to imagine that, having totally lost all memory of all his previous perceptions and of all the judgments of reason he has made, he suddenly again confronts the world with the light of nature alone at his disposal. He will then, as also postulated by Condillac, have the sort of single, unanalyzed, simultaneous perception or thought which we can only express by a collection of words such as "je vois un arbre" (vii). He would have other perceptions and ideas, for instance "je vois un cheval." These would all have single expressions—A, B, etc.—so long as they had the form "je vois" plus object. But the large number of single perceptions and their signs would soon become unmanageable, forcing man to have recourse "à un autre Langage" (viii). The two examples above would become CD and CE, and similarly "je vois deux lions" and "je vois trois corbeaux" would become decomposed into CGH and CIK. Again, H for "lions" and K for "corbeaux" will no longer do if we want to describe those animals, "car si je veux analyser ces parties de perceptions, il faudra encore subdiviser les signes" (x). Further, new signs will be needed for the use of other senses, as in "j'entends des sons, je sens des fleurs." Thus our knowledge soon ceases to be about our immediate perceptions. Language and words take over, and hence also the possibility of error. The very nature of our knowledge becomes determined by language, which it alone makes possible. What we call our sciences depend so intimately on the manner in which we have designated our perceptions, "qu'il me semble que les questions et les propositions seroient toutes différentes si l'on avoit établi d'autres expressions des premières perceptions" (xii).

Man has now, for better or worse, become a creature of language, and he finds himself in a dilemma. If human memory had been sufficient to the task of remembering all its single perceptions, we would never have fallen into the perplexities which are caused by language. As a remedy for our shortness of memory, we achieve economy by means of decomposition. The consequences have been momentous, "il me semble qu'aucune des questions qui nous embarrassent tant aujourd'hui ne se seroit jamais même entrée dans notre esprit" (xiii). As soon as we began to analyze and give signs to different parts of our perceptions, "nous avons méconnu notre ouvrage: nous avons pris chacune des parties des expressions pour des choses; nous avons combiné les choses entre elles, pour y découvrir des rapports de convenance ou d'opposition, et delà est né ce que nous appellons *nos sciences*" (xiii). Thus the result: "On peut dire que la mémoire est opposée au jugement," or as he expressed it more carefully in the answer to Boindin, "Cette construction des

Langues est la cause de nos erreurs, et l'origine de tant de difficultés que nous trouvons insolubles . . . . Ce qu'on a fait pour soulager la mémoire a jeté le jugement en erreur."[108] It would appear that the alternative to error is piecemeal, scattered, unmanageable knowledge and the impossiblity of science. The danger becomes evident when we consider the traditional concepts of substance and mode.

The substance of a tree is said to inhere in its extension, not in its greenness, but "cela vient de ce que dans le langage établi on est convenu d'appeller *arbre* ce qui a une certaine figure indépendamment de sa verdeur" (xvi). It is not obvious that we—or the first speaker—might not have fixed on the greenness and made it as inseparable from the concept of tree as we now consider its extension to be. If men of the same country who have long reasoned together have difficulty agreeing on their ideas, what can we imagine if we gained contact with a distant and to us entirely unfamiliar nation whose first ancestors had built their language on different principles? We could not possibly understand each other. The different quality of their philosophy and knowledge would not, however, derive from a difference in their first perceptions, "mais je crois qu'elle viendroit du Langage accoutumé de chaque nation, de cette destination des signes aux différentes parties des perceptions: destination dans laquelle il entre beaucoup d'arbitraire, et que les premiers hommes ont pu faire de plusieurs manières différentes; mais qui une fois faite de telle ou telle manière, jette dans telle ou telle proposition, et a des influences continuelles sur toutes nos connoissances" (xix).

So far, it is clear that Maupertuis has offered a critique of the argument of Condillac's *Essai*, which had not explored the errors that are consequent upon words. We have seen that Diderot's remark on the Berkeleian consequences of the *Essai* had made Condillac somewhat advance the fund of knowledge which man could gain in his pre-linguistic state. This revision occurred in the *Traité des sensations* with the device of the statue; but it is tempting to assume that Maupertuis' observations may have given additional force to Diderot's remarks.[109]

In the concluding pages of the *Réflexions*, Maupertuis explores the problem in a somewhat different manner which very clearly shows the influence of Berkeley. A man may not only have the perception that is expressed in the words "je vois un arbre," but also "je pense à un arbre," "j'ai revé d'un arbre," which together strengthen the conviction of the reality of the tree's independent existence, thus producing the perception "j'ai vu un arbre" joined with circumstances of place, having seen the same tree before, having returned and seen it again, etc. He will arrive at "il y a un arbre," in other words he will gain conviction that the tree does in fact have existence apart from perception, or as Maupertuis says: "Cette dernière perception transporte pour ainsi dire sa réalité sur son objet, et forme une proposition sur l'existence de l'arbre comme indépendante de moi" (xxi-xxv). But we may also say "il y a des sons," though we know very well that what is 'out there' are only vibrations not at all like what we hear and call sounds. Our tree may be in the same situation, "ni cette image, ni l'arbre, ne ressemblent à ma perception" (xxvi), and even the sense of touch will not convince him otherwise. He concludes with the admission, "qu'il y a une cause d'où dépendent toutes nos perceptions, *parce que rien n'est comme il est sans raison. Mais quelle est-elle cette cause? Je ne pui la pénétrer, puisque rien de ce que j'ai ne lui ressemble. Renfermons-nous sur cela dans les bornes qui sont préscrites à notre intelligence" (xxviii).[110]

The *Réflexions* was not published for a wider public until 1752, when it was included in the first volume of Maupertuis' *Oeuvres*, published at Dresden. In the meantime it had been seen by the Parisian man of letters Nicolas Boindin, who wrote some brief critical remarks on it, suggesting that its entire thesis might have dangerous consequences to religious belief. The final words of his critique were: "Ainsi, quoiqu'au premier coup d'oeil cet ouvrage ne paroisse point donner de prise à la critique, il est néanmoins certain qu'on pourroit tirer des inductions très-scabreuses." These remarks were first published in Boindin's *Oeuvres* in 1753, two years after his death, and Maupertuis found them so important that he in turn wrote an answer, first printed in 1756.[111] Boindin was the most notorious and unregenerate atheist of his day, and the only member of the Académie des Inscriptions et Belles-Lettres never to have been the subject of an official eulogy, facts which suggest that Boindin's real intent was to embarrass Maupertuis—or whomever he took to be the anonymous writer—in order to promote his own atheism.[112] In any event, in his answer Maupertuis reiterated his position that his analysis of the origin of language not only explained "ce que c'est que l'existence des corps, mais qu'elle anéantit toute distinction qu'on voudroit faire de deux manières d'exister, l'une dans l'esprit, l'autre au dehors." Maupertuis compared himself to Berkeley, who had attacked the system of our errors only by toppling its pinnacles, while Maupertuis, as he says of himself, "nous le sappons par les fondements: édifice bien différent de cette tour fameuse que la confusion des Langues empêcha d'élever dans les plaines de Sennaar, celui-ci n'est élevé que par l'abus ou l'oubli de la signification des mots."[113]

The *Réflexions* was not read in the Academy, but it could have been known there after the Dresden edition of 1752. In addition, his interest in language also found expression in other ways. In a very well-attended public assembly on 18 June 1750, he spoke on "Les Devoirs de l'académicien," concluding with remarks on the desirability of exploring the possibility of framing a universal language of learning, "une langue plus régulière que toutes nos langues, qui ne se sont formées que peu à peu; plus facile, et qui put être entendue de tous," a subject which had occupied Leibniz and which, as we shall see, continued to occupy the Berlin Academy, in fact as late as the first decades of the nineteenth century.[114] A few years later, in the *Lettre sur le progrès des sciences* (1752), he reported that travelers to the Pacific Islands had there seen "des hommes sauvages, des hommes velus, portant des queus; une espèce mitoyenne entre les singes et nous. J'aimerois mieux une heure de conversation avec eux qu'avec le plus bel esprit de l'Europe."[115] He also observed that the Patagonians ought to be better known, not so much for their large stature but rather because "leurs idées, leurs connoissances, leurs histoires, seroient bien encore d'une autre curiosité."[116] In the same work, in a section entitled "Expériences métaphysiques," Maupertuis remarked on language and the original knowledge of men and on their interdependence. He then suggests that one could raise several groups of children in isolation to find out whether, for instance, the differences among languages that are now so obvious, were introduced by the fathers of separate families on a common original language, or whether the different modes of expression were different from the very beginning. "Cette expérience ne se borneroit pas nous instruire sur l'origine des Langues; elle pourroit nous apprendre bien d'autres choses sur l'origine des idées mêmes, et sur les notions fondamentales de l'esprit humain." The philosophers have talked long enough on this subject without giving an answer; perhaps the natural philosophers will provide the answer, "ils nous donneroient du moins leurs connoissances sans les avoir sophistiquées."[117] This sort of experiment was again, as we shall see, to be mentioned in the Berlin Academy.

BEAUSOBRE (1755)

On 18 September 1755, Louis Isaac de Beausobre read a paper called "Réflexions sur les changemens des langues vivantes par rapport à l'orthographie et à la prononciation," a subject he pursued in three additional papers delivered over the next three years.[118] This is a rather conventional and unexciting piece. The most perfect language can be found only among the dead languages, and Beausobre prefers Latin. We should aim to prevent those changes which it is within our power to control and find suitable restraining remedies for the rest. Orthography is obviously a great stabilizer, and we ought rather to let pronunciation follow spelling than change spelling to conform to our speech, as had been advocated by Duclos in the notes to his edition of the Port-Royal Grammar (1754). Our alphabet does not in any event have enough letters to record the number of distinct spoken sounds—a point Herder was later, in the *Ursprung*, to bring against Süssmilch. Etymology is a great aid to memory and should not lightly be allowed to disappear from view—"c'est un flambeau qui nous éclaire dans un chemin obscur, et qui nous épargne ainsi la peine d'en retenir les tours et les détours," an old argument about the mnemonic utility of etymology. It also has another familiar importance: "Tout ce qui peut nous servir à connoître les progrès de l'esprit humain, est précieux."

Beausobre's essay contains no interesting philosophical observations, no profound critical insights, but it compares well with many other similar pieces written during these years, whether in Germany, in France, or in England. It also offered a certain amount of information that could be useful and suggestive to others. This essay would appear to be indebted to Diderot's famous article "Encyclopédie," which had appeared in volume five (1755) of the *Encyclopédie*. Oddly, it also shows some affinity with Turgot's article on "Etymologie," which was published in volume six the following year. As a remedy against the changes that occur in living languages, Diderot had advocated referring the roots of a modern changing language to those of a dead one—either Latin or Greek—which is fixed and does not change. He also was much concerned about the growing difference between spelling and pronunciation, advocating the creation of a phonetic alphabet, "un alphabet raisonné, où un même signe ne représente point des sons différentes, ne des signes différents." Diderot considered it essential to transmit our present pronunciation to posterity. It was his concern to ensure that the *Encyclopédie* would not be rendered obsolete by becoming linguistically inaccessible to later generations.[119]

MAUPERTUIS, "DISSERTATION" (1756)

On 13 May 1756, Maupertuis read a paper with the title, "Dissertation sur les différents moyens dont les hommes se sont servis pour exprimer leurs idées."[120] This piece lacks the philosophical depth of the earlier *Réflexions*. It is rather a collection of very astute observations on several subjects. Its opening is reminiscent of Condillac, which is perhaps no accident when we recall that Maupertuis a few years earlier had met Condillac in Paris. We can, Maupertuis says, imagine a variety of means of communication—"des cris naturels," gestures, musical notation, etc.—but no such language has been known both to arise and to be maintained naturally. The choice has for a number of reasons fallen on speech. The number of words in a given language is proportioned to the number of ideas, hence among "les peuples les plus spirituels," we find more words and finer distinctions than among "les plus grossiers," who would have only just enough to get along, and in some cases perhaps not even that. In the course of time it was observed that a large number of ideas referred to objects that could be conceived independently of others, and for these were formed the words we call substantives. Adjectives were originally modifications of these words. Verbs were formed separately to refer to actions, and so forth, but Maupertuis does not intend to go into detail about the parts of speech, which differ from language to language. They are the grammarian's business. Maupertuis will rather deal with the general principles which have guided all peoples in the formation of languages.

He then briefly reverts to the argument of the *Réflexions*. Actually men did not at first make all these distinctions, but expressed everything in a single "word," for example "j'ai tué un gros ours" would not have been divided up into so many words but would have been a single expression (xiii). Soon shortness of memory caused decomposition, just as the reverse may occur in a language that is already well developed. "C'est ainsi que dans les Langues les plus parfaites on introduit les mots techniques, et tant d'expressions abrégés qui contiennent des phrases entières."

After a digression on systems of writing (xiv-xxix), Maupertuis raises the difficult question of the causes of the diversity of languages if we are to assume that all mankind has its ultimate origin in a single family. Even if a million changes should have occurred, would we not expect to find a large number of words that are still the same? Of course we would, but we find that it is in fact not so. A certain number of "auteurs plus savans que philosophes" (xxxi) have claimed to find words in modern languages that have the same signification as in the languages that are said to be old and original. But this, says Maupertuis, proves nothing; it is purely a matter of statistical chance among such a vast number of words, so that all these etymologists prove is that they themselves know a very large number of words in many different languages. To understand the diversity of languages, we must then either believe in the miracle that is told of the Tower of Babel, or we must assume that when the dispersal took place men had not yet begun to speak. Though he does not say so outright, he clearly believes that the latter is the case. The independent origin of many languages is an unstated assumption of the earlier *Réflexions*, whose problem would disappear if they could all be known to have had a single origin. Maupertuis concludes that each language has had its beginning in the family: "Chaque famille séparée devenant un peuple, ses besoins, ses idées se multipliant, elle se forme une langue et une écriture, de la manière que nous l'avons expliqué; et aujourd'hui il n'y a si petite nation qui n'ait la sienne" (xxxiii).

This diversity is obviously very inconvenient, and learned men have tried to find a remedy. Maupertuis will not imitate them, but merely make some general observations. To hope that one could ever gain adoption of a spoken universal language is utterly foolish. It is, however, possible to consider a written one, though it would have to be more than a mere device for easy translation. If the nature of ideas could be fixed and ordered according to their priority, their generality, etc., it would be possible to create a corresponding set of characters. But how is it possible to hope that men could ever come to agree on the same ideas, when they cannot even agree on such ideas as space and the vacuum, which some say are the first and most fundamental of ideas, while others maintain that they do not even exist. If Descartes and Malebranche had made a written philosophical language, Locke and Newton would never have understood it (x1). This sort of thing is possible only where a few, very simple ideas are involved, as in arithmetic, algebra, and music. Maupertuis is convinced that each nation will keep the language it has, though many of the factors that cause difficulty are not essential to languages and could perhaps be removed or simplified—inflections and conjugations, for instance, could be made uniformly similar and regular. Here the essay ends, seemingly unfinished. It became the immediate occasion for the next event in the debate.

SÜSSMILCH (1756)

In the autumn of the same year, on 7 and 14 October 1756, Johann Peter Süssmilch—best known for his highly original demographic studies—read two papers on the divine origin of language. These papers were not published until 1766, with the title *Versuch eines Beweises, dass die erste Sprache ihren Ursprung nicht vom Menschen, sondern allein vom Schöpfer erhalten habe*. In the Preface, signed 13 May 1766, Süssmilch explained that the first draft went back some ten years when his interest in the subject had first been roused by a paper read by Maupertuis—it later becomes clear that Süssmilch is referring to the "Dissertation." Desiring to re-examine his own argument, Süssmilch had held up publication, but a stroke three years ago had now made him decide to publish his papers without further revision. The mere act of publication as well as the dedication of the essay to the members of the Academy would seem to suggest that Süssmilch was eager to reintroduce his argument into the debate at this time. He was right that publication was timely, for both Herder's prize-topic and the answer are closely related to the *Versuch*, which is an excellent piece—cogently argued, lucid, and tightly organized.[121] Its author died less than a year after publication in March of 1767.

Süssmilch's thesis is simple: "Die Sprache ist das Mittel zum Gebrauch der Vernunft zu gelangen, oder, ohne Sprache kann der Gebrauch der Vernunft nicht statt haben, man kann ohne selbige nicht zu abgesonderten und allgemeinen Begriffen und zu deren fertigen Gebrauch gelangen, man kann folglich auch nicht Schlüsse in Verbindung setzen und ratiociniren, also auch nicht andere Dinge verrichten, die schlechterdings von dem Gebrauch der Vernunft abhängen."[122] Briefly, the argument takes this form. Language is either divine or human. If human it must be either natural or artificial. But since we say that the sounds made by animals are natural and also observe that they are the same for the same species all over the world, human language cannot be natural in that sense. Only arbitrary audible forms will do. Language must then be artificial, and if so it must have come about either by complete accident or by design, that is by free choice and the exercise of reason. Accident can be ruled out since it would entail complete disorder and irregularity, which apart from the uselessness of such a language is disproved by our observation that all languages, also primitive ones, have "Regeln der Vollkommenheit und Ordnung," that is design. Consequently any human language must be the work of reason and wise choice. But the prerequisite for such design is the perfect use of reason, which involves abstraction, reflection, and ratiocination. These, however, cannot occur without the prior possession of the use of signs. Thus man cannot have invented language, either instantly or gradually. Its origin must then lie outside man in a higher and more intelligent being. God was the creator and first teacher of language, which by a miracle was communicated to man in the beginning.[123] How this may have happened Süssmilch does not propose to examine since his proof is entirely philosophical, though he hopes it will offer a convincing refutation of all enemies of revelation.

A few points in this cogent argument deserve attention. Condillac had argued that an adequate capacity for silent reflection precedes the first invention of arbitrary vocal signs, which in turn is followed by a steady extension of the effect of reflection. The process is gradual and has its origin in a latent capacity for the use of reason. Süssmilch will allow nothing of the sort. His argument rejects that possibility; the conclusion of his argument is in accord with Revelation—but not derived from it. The *Versuch* presents a philosophical argument, not a string of scriptural citations.[124] To Süssmilch, language as a human accomplishment has nothing in common with the arts, which indeed do seem to have had simple beginnings and to have undergone gradual growth toward greater perfection.[125] Second, the very uniformity of grammar—i.e., universal grammar—and the arbitrariness of the signs become sources of proof: "Ja diese Übereinstimmung der Form zwinget uns, auf den einigen Lehrmeister und Urheber der Sprache zurück zu gehen. Die freye Willkühr in der Wahl der Zeichen und deren Zufälligkeit benimmt alle Ausflüchte. Die Form der Sprache ist nicht wie die Form eines Vogelnestes oder Bienenbaues, die vermöge angebohrner Triebe, jederzeit auf einerley Art gebildet werden müssen."[126]

An Appendix citing *Inégalité* has Condillac's name to which Süssmilch notes that he has not seen the work in question, the *Essai*; it might have been useful, he admits, but has decided to make do with Rousseau. Having been the occasion for the *Versuch* in the first place, Maupertuis' analysis is rejected, while the dilemma of the first passage on language in Rousseau's *Inégalité* is accepted, though Süssmilch ignores the pre-social state of man in that passage as well as the Condillacian argument offered later in the passage on post-social man. The *Inégalité* had come to Süssmilch's attention—in Moses Mendelsohn's German translation of 1756—only after he had finished the first complete draft. He had then decided not to take account of it in his *Versuch*, except to mention in an appendix at the end that he found himself in basic agreement with it. For the first time since Condillac's *Essai*, genuinely new views had been introduced into the debate by Süssmilch's brilliant *Versuch*. The power and influence of his argument are clearly revealed also before their publication in 1766.

MICHAËLIS' PRIZE-TOPIC (1757-1759)

In the public assembly of 9 June 1757, a significant event occurred: the Academy announced its first prize-topic on language. The problem was set for "la classe de philosophie spéculative" and had the following form: "Quelle est l'influence réciproque des opinions du peuple sur le langage et du langage sur les opinions? " It was further specified that the answer should first, by means of suitable examples, show "combien il y a dans les Langues de tours et d'expressions bizarres, nées manifestement de telles ou telles opinions reçues chez les peuples où ces Langues se sont formées." This, it was felt, would be the easier part and merely preliminary to the more essential task "de montrer dans certains tours de phrase propres à chaque Langue, dans certaines expressions, et jusques dans les racines de certains mots, les germes de telles ou telles erreurs, ou les obstacles à recevoir telles vérités." Finally, these two parts would, it was hoped, lead to "des réflexions fort importantes. Après avoir rendu sensible, comment un tour d'esprit produit une Langue, laquelle Langue donne ensuite à l'esprit un tour plus ou moins favorable aux idées vraies, on pourroit rechercher les moyens les plus pratiquables de remédier aux inconvéniens des Langues."[127]

It will hardly require demonstration for the reader to see that both the topic and the directions have their source in issues raised by Maupertuis—in fact the opening sentence of the *Réflexions* had formulated the problem. But we have even more precise evidence. In his *Cours d'études pour l'instruction du Prince de Parme*, Condillac devoted the last chapter of Book III of the *Cours d'histoire* to "L'influence des langues sur les opinions et des opinions sur les langues." It opens with this statement: "C'est M. de Maupertuis qui a proposé, au nom de l'académie de Berlin, la question que je vais traiter." Considering the meetings of Condillac and Maupertuis during the 1750's, there would seem to be no room for doubt that these words refer to our present concern, the prize-topic for 1759.[128]

In the public assembly of 31 May 1759, the secretary, Samuel Formey, announced that the prize had been awarded to an essay submitted by the distinguished Göttingen professor of Semitic languages, Johann David Michaëlis.[129] On the same day a rather fantastic and otherwise unimportant member of the Academy, André-Pierre le Guay de Prémontval, wrote his congratulations to Michaëlis: "Je me félicite, d'y avoir doublement concouru, et comme Auteur de la question proposée, et comme un de ceux, qui Vous ont donné leur suffrage."[130] Given Prémontval's understandable eagerness to attract what little importance he could to himself, I see no reason to accept this claim, which in any event would not change the fact that the problem had been introduced by Maupertuis. A footnote to the English translation of Michaëlis' essay, taken over from the French translation by J. B. Merian (1762),[131] explains that the problem had arisen in connection with a point in the philosophy of Wolf, on which Prémontval had read two very confused papers on 16 May 1754, one on the principle of sufficient reason and the other on the law of continuity.[132] This note also gives an interesting insight into partisanship in the Academy and shows how observations on language were expected to provide solutions to philosophical problems: "It is proper even to take notice that M. de Prémontval having shewn that the falsity of the demonstration becomes manifest, on thinking, or on translating into French, whereas in the Latin and German expression, it remains strangely enveloped and intricate; and this it was which gave rise to the important question, on the influence of language on opinions, and of opinions on language. Never had the bulk of the German nation been misled by the Wolffian philosophy, had not the two languages, which are most familiar to them, the German and Latin, been more accommodated than the French, to the sophism, on which the whole is founded. This, perhaps, is one of the most remarkable passages in the history of the human mind."

Michaëlis' answer was greatly admired and was soon published in German (1760), in French (1762), in English (1769 and 1771), and in Dutch (1771). The French translation, from which the English was made, contained some important supplements, of which the chief dealt with the possibility of framing a successful universal language of learning—the answer is no, and Michaëlis' discussion still stands as one of the best on that subject.[133]

Michaëlis' answer is spirited, well informed on the general nature of the debate, and clearly reveals the hand of an accomplished philologist. It has been almost wholly forgotten, and even in contexts, such as Herder, where it is highly relevant, it figures not at all, wrongly, or only briefly—often with misinformation. Space does not permit analysis and discussion here. One point, however, demands attention. Michaëlis had not dealt with the origin of language, but near the end of his essay he had emphasized the close connection between that problem and his own. He suggested that the

Academy might some day direct its attention to this topic: "Wie eine Sprache zuerst unter Menschen, die vornhin keine Sprache gehabt haben, entstehen, und nach und nach zu der jetzigen Vollkommenheit und Ausarbeitung gelangen würde?"[134] It is obvious that this question is an invitation to reconsider the entire problem of the origin of language since Condillac's *Essai*. It is also obvious that the formulation of the question makes an assumption which had been rejected by Süssmilch's *Versuch*. The Academy took the suggestion, and some readers may already have recognized the topic for which Herder's *Ursprung* gained the prize in 1771. The next item in the debate repeated Michaëlis' question and again invited the Academy to make it the topic of a prize-essay.

FORMEY (1762)

On 15 July 1762, the Academy's perpetual secretary, Samuel Formey, read a very lively paper which presented a summary of the present state of the question accompanied by an outline of a practical experiment designed to give a factual and irrefutable answer. The title of Formey's paper is: "Réunion des principaux moyens employés pour découvrir l'origine du langage, des idées et des connoissances des hommes."[135] Its aim was to offer proof of the Süssmilch thesis, and its occasion was a passage Formey had found in Michaëlis' supplement on the universal language, added to the French translation. "Le penchant à associer les idées aux sons est naturel à l'homme," Michaëlis had said, "et si en naissant nous n'avions pas trouvé une langue toute préparée, nous n'eussions pas tardé à en inventer une." Having confidently offered this assertion as if it were incapable of contradiction, Michaëlis had proceeded to suggest the essay topic which has been cited above. "Je nie également le principe et la conséquence," Formey commented. If men had been abandoned on the surface of the earth without language, without a certain fund of knowledge, and without reason to handle that knowledge in order to satisfy their most basic needs, they would have remained the most imperfect of animals, indeed they would rather have failed to survive beyond the first generation. To Formey the state of nature is a phantasm, it has no explanatory value since it will always begin with conjectures that man started out with something, with certain abilities. Consequently Formey concludes, "qu'il n'y a d'autre langue primitive que celle que le premier homme a parlée parce que Dieu la lui avoit apprise." Plain reasoning has brought Formey to this conclusion, but for the sake of gaining more universal grounds of conviction he would rather have facts. He would therefore suggest an experiment which, though Formey does not mention it, by a clever argumentative turn harks back to a proposal already made by Maupertuis in 1752 under the title "Expériences métaphysiques."

The experiment must last at least two generations, says Formey. Take a dozen children of the same age, bring them up with everything they need—food, clothing, and every other care—but do not ever allow anyone to say a word in their presence, and when they grow up, do not show them any product of art and science; do not even allow them to see how their food is prepared. What will happen when they reach adolescence and youth? They will no doubt follow the only passion we can attribute to them, and soon they will have children—if we can imagine that they will know how to go about satisfying their desires. But how will the mother know how to take care of the child, never having had occasion to learn it by observation? How will the child find the mother's milk when even the mother probably will not know enough to give it to the child? And if the natural families cannot find subsistence, do we need to ask questions about the invention of language and the satisfaction of man's most basic needs? Add further that in actuality the first generation of men, unlike the one in the experiment, would not have enjoyed the benefit of having been taken care of in infancy and childhood. If at any point the merest vestige of language should occur, Formey would willingly admit defeat. As for himself, "plus j'y pense donc, plus je crois l'état de pure nature, une vraye chimère, une grossière absurdité, une contradiction manifest; plus je m'affermis dans l'idée que l'Être suprême, Auteur de notre existence, l'est aussi de nos premières idées, et même du pouvoir habituel que nous avons de les exprimer." He is also convinced that he has found the answer to Rousseau's remarks on the state of nature in the Preface to *Inégalité*, especially to Rousseau's question: "Quelles expériences seroient nécessaires pour parvenir à connoître l'homme naturel? Et quels sont les moyens de faire ces expériences au sein de la Société? "[136] Formey's essay and Süssmilch's *Versuch* supported the same thesis, and they were published in the same year. The debate was rapidly reaching the impasse which found its issue in Herder's *Ursprung*.

TOUSSAINT (1765)

On 13 June 1765, François-Vincent Toussaint read a paper called, "Des inductions qu'cn peut tirer du langage d'une nation par rapport à sa culture et à ses moeurs."[137] In spite of the promising title, this essay is a very conventional performance, almost as if Toussaint—who had recently become a member—knew that papers on language were popular, but did not quite know how the problems were discussed. We are told, for instance, that German is the most methodical of all languages, the least mixed in with exotic terms, the best preserved, and that it has undergone the fewest changes: "Elle annonce des hommes solides et sensés, sur qui les inconstances des modes, et l'influence du commerce avec l'étranger n'ont point eu de prise." These are familiar themes, but they appear out of place in the debate on the nature of language.

SULZER (1767)

The last paper to concern us was read in 1767 or possibly in 1768, by Johann Georg Sulzer, "Observations sur l'influence réciproque de la raison sur le langage et du langage sur la raison."[138] The title is enough to show that Sulzer opposed Süssmilch and Formey, but beyond that his argument is not very clear. On the whole Sulzer presents a weak version of Condillac, seeming rather to follow some of the more doctrinaire articles in the *Encyclopédie*. The origin of language is a difficult problem, Sulzer observes, for without reason how could language develop and how reason without language? Finding themselves in this dilemma, even great philosophers have found no other explanation than miraculous origin, but Sulzer believes that supernatural causes cannot be admitted till natural causes have been proved to fail. The purpose of his essay, however, is not to examine the entire question, but merely to make some thoughtful observations on the interdependence of language and reason. Sulzer seems not entirely aware how many problems he is raising, but a cry of despair in the middle of the essay shows that he did feel the consequences: "Il est infiniment plus facile de sentir comment les choses se sont passées que décrire clairement la marche de l'esprit dans ses opérations."

His problem is this: "Qu'elle peut avoir été la marche de l'esprit pour que l'homme s'avisat de chercher des signes propres à représenter des idées, et par quels moyens a-t-il trouvé ces signes? " He finds the method rather easy. We cannot follow history back to the twilight of reason, but fortunately we have another source of information. What instructed man does today can tell us what "l'homme brute" did before he had language. Experience must begin by analysis of perception before words can be made. This is the first step toward language, and the next is equally simple. To find words for objects, all he needed to do was to imitate "les mêmes sons par lesquels ces objets s'annoncent." It is no surprise to the reader that Sulzer believes the first invention of language was not at all difficult and did not surpass the capacities of "un homme brute." His assurance is, of course, incompatible with the arguments of Condillac, Maupertuis, Süssmilch, and Formey; one wonders how it was possible to ignore them in a paper on this subject at that time unless even a poor argument against Süssmilch's thesis was considered better than none at all.

How then, asks Sulzer, did man first find words for things which are not associated with sound in any way? Quite easily, we are told. He changed an "old" word a bit and gave it a new meaning, or he used metaphor, the association of ideas being common to all men: "Ce talent est inné dans l'homme, les peuples les plus grossiers et les plus proches de l'état brute, les hommes même qui sont nés sourds et muets, le possèdent. Une attention un peu réfléchie suffit pour le mettre en usage. Il étoit donc aussi l'appanage de l'homme avant que son langage fut formé." If we could recover these first radical words, Sulzer believes it would be possible to "faire voir exactement la marche que l'esprit a suivie pour arriver jusq'aux significations les plus éloignées du premier sens." Etymology then receives its conventional tribute: "Remarquons ici que l'histoire étymologique des langues seroit sans contredit la meilleure historie des progrès de l'esprit humain." It is especially by virtue of this optimism, this characteristic rhetoric about "la marche de l'esprit humain"—a phrase we have met before—that Sulzer has much in common with contemporary French discussions and very little with the Berlin debate which had preceded his own contribution.

So far Sulzer has shown how man could find or make the elements of language. He will now consider their role in man's progress toward cultivated reason. The question of the relationship between language or words and reason is quite lost sight of, in any serious sense. Words are an aid to memory, abridge the operations of the mind, and promote invention and discovery, as exemplified in the work of Linnaeus. These points are all very conventional. Though Sulzer does not himself say so, the words he has so far considered are all nouns; he has followed the simplest form of the argument that finds the origin of language in invention with reference to first sensations of objects. Verbs, he says, are formed by modification of already existing forms; exactly how we are not told, though Sulzer believes that these modifications are for the most part the result of chance. He concludes that the grammatical perfection of a language is the outcome of reason and genius. Language and reason interact to improve each other. The degree of sophistication of a language is measured by its capacity for compact expression. Hence to learn such a language is to learn to think and improve one's taste. The perfection of language and eloquence is as important as the discovery of new truths. The progress of reason depends both on the scientists and on "les beaux-esprits." Sulzer's paper quite lacks the force of argument that would be required to decide the issue in favor of the human invention of language, against Süssmilch and Formey. The question remained open. One or two years later, in the late spring of 1769, the Academy set the topic for 1771, Herder's topic. With this topic the debate also closed, and the Academy never again returned to the problem it had given so much prominence over the past twenty years. Condillac's *Essai*, the fountainhead of the debate, was now nearly twenty-five years old.

HERDER (1769-1771)

Following Michaëlis' suggestion, the topic for 1771 was given this form: "En supposant les hommes abandonnés à leurs facultés naturelles, sont-ils en état d'inventer le langage? Et par quels moyens parviendront-ils d'eux-mêmes à cette invention? " It was further specified that "on demande une hypothèse qui explique la chose clairement et qui satisfasse à toutes les difficultés."[139] Corresponding to these two divisions, Herder divided his answer in two parts with these superscriptions: "Haben die Menschen, ihren Naturfähigkeiten überlassen, sich selbst Sprache erfinden können? " and "Auf welchem Wege der Mensch sich am füglichsten hat Sprache erfinden können und müssen." The answer to the first question is yes, as summarized in these assertions: "Der Mensch, in den Zustand von Besonnenheit gesetzt, der ihm eigen ist, und diese Besonnenheit (Reflexion) zum erstenmal frei würkend, hat Sprache erfunden. Diese Besonnenheit ist ihm charakteristisch eigen und seiner Gattung wesentlich: so auch Sprache und eigne Erfindung der Sprache. Erfindung der Sprache ist ihm also so natürlich, als er ein Mensch ist!"[140] At least since the nineteenth century it has become an unquestioned dogma that this doctrine is Herder's entirely new and original contribution to the problem of the origin of language, indeed that "mit der Preisschrift Herders beginnt die Epoche der Sprachphilosophie."[141] Belief in this dogma has been coupled with the equally unfounded dogma that all previous natural (as distinct from divine) explanations had given language a purely animalistic origin, most often with specific reference to the example of Condillac. It will now, I hope, be clear to my readers that all participants in the debate (perhaps with the exception of Sulzer) had emphatically asserted that man's possession of reason and reflection is the foundation of human language and that animals, not having reason and reflection, also are without such a language. Herder had arrived at a doctrine which had been fully argued in Condillac's *Essai* in so far as it involves reflection and language.

It would be easy to draw up a catalog of close similarities between Herder and Condillac, in spite of the fact that the existence of such similarities has been ignored or denied, though always (as in the case of Salmony) with little or no knowledge of the *Essai*. The doctrine of the intimate connection between "Volksgeist" and language has generally been held one of Herder's most important contributions to the thought of his age. But the second part of the *Essai*, the part Herder had read by the middle 1760's, contains such statements as these: "Tout confirme donc que chaque langue exprime le caractère du peuple qui la parle." "De tous les écrivains, c'est chez les poëtes que le génie des langues s'exprime le plus vivement." And "Les langues, pour quelqu'un qui les connoîtroit bien, seroient une peinture du caractère et du génie de chaque peuple. Il y verroit comment l'imagination a combiné les idées d'après les préjugés et les passions."[142] It is true that at the time these ideas were, so to speak, in the air, but Condillac was the first to give them a firm place in the theory of language and its origin.

There is, however, one very significant difference between the Condillacian argument and the argument Herder presents in the first part of the *Ursprung*. Though this difference has very considerable consequences, it has not to my knowledge been noted in the secondary literature. To Condillac and his followers language meant language *and* speech. Without including articulated, arbitrary, vocal signs language could have meant nothing in their argument. But in the first part of the *Ursprung*, the part that has generally been considered a deliberate and successful refutation of Condillac's doctrine, Herder deals exclusively with "die innere Entstehung der Sprache."[143] Only in the second part does "Sprache" also mean speech, though Herder throughout the *Ursprung* uses the term "Sprache" without remarking on the distinction, except when he later adds "äussere" and "innere." The reader is alerted to this use of "Sprache" in such passages as these: "Die erste Merkmal der Besinnung war Wort der Seele! Mit ihm ist die menschliche Sprache erfunden!" "Der Wilde, der Einsame im Walde hätte Sprache für sich selbst erfinden müssen, hätte er sie auch nie geredet. . . .[Es ist] mir unbegreiflich, wie eine menschliche Seele, was sie ist, sein konnte, ohne eben dadurch, schon ohne Mund und Gesellschaft, sich Sprache erfinden müssen." And "In mehr als einer Sprache hat also auch 'Wort' und 'Vernunft,' 'Begriff' und 'Wort,' 'Sprache' und 'Ursache' einen Namen, und diese Synonomie enthält ihren ganzen genetischen Ursprung."[144] This "innere Sprache" is in other words a complete language of concepts, a doctrine that is entirely foreign to the argument of Condillac's *Essai*, which therefore is not touched by Herder's assertions. Herder's doctrine would also seem to conflict with his own argument about the creation of speech in the second part of the *Ursprung*, for here Herder holds a doctrine of the mutual development or progress of reason and speech. It would further seem to conflict with Herder's belief that language in the beginning has no grammar, that is, language considered as speech.[145] It is this sort of disagreement and inconsistency between the parts of the *Ursprung*—and it has long been admitted (though almost as if it were a special virtue) that the essay contains many such inconsistencies—that has necessitated a number of not very successful attempts at interpretation which fill up the literature. Curiously, more than one interpreter has, like Salmony, unknowingly offered a reading that comes close to presenting Condillac's argument.

The Academy's official report on the *Ursprung* reveals the distance that separates well-informed, contemporary judgment from later opinion. According to this report, Herder had argued that the origin of language was not divine, but "purement animale, c'est à dire qu'elle procède de la combinaison de la structure organique de l'homme avec les facultés de l'âme domiciliée dans un corps ainsi organisé, et des circonstances où l'animal qui possède cette organisation et ces facultés, se trouve placé." Herder's name deserved to be mentioned with those of Diderot, Rousseau, and Condillac, "tant par la force de raisonnement avec laquelle il sonde comme eux les profondeurs de la Métaphysique, que par les égards qu'il leur témoigne en s'écartant plus ou moins de leurs opinions."[146] A dozen years after the award of the prize, the Academy published the report, which Johann Bernhard Merian had read on the day of the award, 6 June 1771. What Merian saw in the Ursprung were, for instance, such Condillacian principles as these: "Le langage humain dépend si immédiatement de la réflexion, qu'il ne nous reste qu'un pas à faire pour conduire l'homme à cette important découverte," and that man has "une nature essentiellement différente de la nature animale. Et ce n'est que le pouvoir de réfléchir, d'enrégistrer les pensées, et de les lier par le moyen du langage, qui produit cette différence."[147] I find Merian's report correct and neutral, but modern readers conditioned by the conventional views would hardly recognize it as an analysis of the *Ursprung*, let alone as an exposition of Herder's linguistic philosophy.

A detailed examination of Herder's essay falls outside the limits of this paper. Such an examination will demand consideration of his reading, of his writings both before and after 1770, of his position vis-à-vis Kant, Hamann, Mendelsohn, Abbt, and others. Thanks to the important work of Professor Irmscher we may hope to see the publication of much relevant, hitherto unpublished material. But in the present context it will seem reasonable to try to give a few preliminary answers to the problems we are facing: Why has the *Ursprung* received such curious and on the whole (it must be said) ignorant treatment? And why did Herder give very inadequate, indeed on significant points, false accounts of contemporary work on the origin of language? These two questions are interrelated, but I shall begin with the second.

There are first of all the known facts about the conditions under which Herder wrote the essay, hastily in Strasbourg during the last months or even weeks of 1770. Many of the texts he did not have at hand, and physically he was troubled by a recent eye operation; and there may have been other personal factors. Condillac is the test. We have seen that Herder some five years earlier had come upon the *Essai*, been excited by it, and taken notes from it. But in all the references he makes to the *Essai*—whether earlier or in the *Ursprung*—he talks only of volume two, that is the volume of the original edition which contained the second part of the *Essai*, the part with the long section on the origin and progress of language. If it can be assumed that Herder had never read the first part, he would have had no way of understanding the important role of reflection in Condillac's argument. Herder would also have been ignorant that the origin of language in the *Essai* merely forms part of a larger argument about the origin of human knowledge and understanding. Further, the later writings on the origin of language, including those I have dealt with in this paper, had addressed themselves directly to the problem of the origin of language without systematically placing it in Condillac's full context. Thus, if Herder had not read Part One of the *Essai*, it becomes understandable that he could criticize the adequacy of the argument he found in Part Two at the very same time as he unwittingly reconstructed the missing part in Condillac's manner. Herder's surprising misrepresentation of the argument of the *Essai* could in fact have come about without his knowledge. It might be argued that even Part Two would have given Herder a better understanding of Condillac than he shows. This objection carries little weight, however, for in the *Ursprung* Herder is never very precise even about the arguments of texts he did have at hand. We know, for instance, that he did have a copy of Süssmilch's *Versuch*, though he still misrepresents its argument.[148] My suggestion that Herder had not read the first part of Condillac's *Essai* will solve the most perplexing problem about the *Ursprung*.

But why has the context of the prize-essay been studied so carelessly, if at all? First of all, I think, because the *Ursprung* by its very style carries the reader along; it is forceful, direct, irreverent, and clever. More important, no doubt, is its central position in the national tradition of German literature. After the *Ursprung*, Herder's reputation steadily increased until he became the authority, the seeming originator of the ideas he had laid down in his youthful essay. Herder was believed, even on Condillac. But this neglect of the context could hardly have persisted right down to the present day if the nineteenth century had not corrupted our understanding of the eighteenth. For complex reasons I shall not go into, post-romantic scholarship has lent its enormous prestige to the truly silly belief that Condillac, among many others, was a mechanistic, materialist philosopher. Herder became one of the intellectual heroes of romanticism because it was believed that he had rescued the origin of language from, "der aufgeklärten Auffassung der Sprache als eines besondern, dem fertigen Menschen gleichsam noch-zu-addierten Vermögens," from "einer Ungeduld und Unduldsamkeit des Geistes gegenüber dem Leben, das man mathematisch nur bewältigen kann, wenn man es als einen reinen Mechanismus auffasset," statements that speak plain nonsense about the material we have examined though they purport to say something true about that very material.

One thinks with gratitude of Franco Venturi's brilliant insight concerning the significance of studying the discussions of the origin of language among the *philosophes*: "Suivre de près cette discussion doit être un des meilleurs moyens pour pénétrer l'époque des lumières, découvrir la force et la vigueur intellectuelle qui font, encore aujourd'hui, sa grandeur; et je crois qu'on pourrait arriver ainsi à saisir le moment extrêmement complexe, mais fort intéressant, où les revendications faites au sujet de la force créatrice de l'esprit humain coïncident avec les premières découvertes esthétiques qui ouvrent la voie aux théories romantiques et modernes."[149]

Thus I end where I began, with Condillac. His influence is decisive, the issues he raised in the *Essai* first created the problem of the origin of language in its most powerful and philosophical form. Rarely in intellectual history has a single work raised a European-wide debate so quickly yet continued to dominate the debate for so long, whether in Germany, France, or England. And that debate has much greater unity and quite a different meaning and wider implications and greater relevance than has generally been admitted and understood.

NOTES AND REFERENCES

*This paper was first prepared for the Newberry Library Conference (February 1968) under the title "The debate on the nature of language in the Berlin Academy during the 1750's and 1760's." Most of the text of that paper appears in Part II of the present essay. For this final version, the additional reading, research, and writing were done October 1968—January 1969, with some additional revision in January—February 1970 and some minor additions in January of 1971. I am grateful to the editor, Professor Dell Hymes, and to the Indiana University Press for permitting me to use the style of references and notes which I consider best suited to the sort of historical investigation in which I am engaged. Unfortunately, a great deal of time has elapsed since I wrote the first version of this essay five years ago, and since its completion in its present form four years ago, except for the revisions made in 1970 and 1971. In the meantime, several aspects of the subject matter have attracted the interest they deserve, and a fair number of items on similar and related subjects have already appeared in print. It is a good sign of the growing interest that these subjects now enjoy that the eighteenth-century texts, which a few years ago were only accessible in the original editions or in expensive reprints, are now available in handy editions and anthologies at reasonable cost. For an up-to-date bibliography, I can refer to my contribution, "The Eighteenth Century, including Leibniz," to *Current Trends in Linguistics*, volume 13, *The Historiography of Linguistics*, ed. Thomas A. Sebeok and others (The Hague: Mouton), which will appear at approximately the same time as this volume. See also " 'Cartesian Linguistics': History or Fantasy" in *Language Sciences*, No. 17 (October 1971), 1-12; and "Post-scriptum, April 1973" in H. Parret, ed., *History of Linguistic Thought and Contemporary Linguistics* (The Hague: Mouton, 1974).

1. The best edition of Condillac is *Oeuvres philosophiques de Condillac*, ed. Georges le Roy, 3 vols. (Paris: Presses Universitaires de France,

1947–1951). Hereafter referred to as Condillac, followed by volume and page number (with a and b for each column); to facilitate cross reference to other editions of Condillac, I shall also give the section, chapter, and paragraph numbers necessary for identification. Of the relevant secondary literature, the following may be mentioned: Georges le Roy's *La Psychologie de Condillac* (Paris, 1937) and his Introduction to the *Oeuvres* I, vii-xxxv. Franco Venturi's excellent chapter entitled "La lettre sur les sourds et les muets" in his *Jeunesse de Diderot (1713–1753)*, tr. Juliette Bertrand (Paris, 1939), pp.237-282; this chapter, which also deals with Condillac and Rousseau, offers one of the best discussions of the problem of language and its origin in the mid-eighteenth century. Ulrich Ricken, "Condillac's *liaison des idées* und die *clarté* des Französischen" in *Die Neueren Sprachen 1964*, pp.552-567. Hans Aarsleff, *The Study of Language in England 1780-1860* (Princeton, 1967), pp.18-34; on p.18 I say that Condillac wished to reduce reflection to sensation, but now consider that false. The single principle by which he wished to explain the mind was "la liaison des idées," a principle that was designed to imitate the power of the concept of gravity in Newtonian philosophy. Condillac makes it very clear that "la liaison des idées" is not the same as association of ideas.

2. On Warburton, see Aarsleff, pp.21-22.

3. This essay was based on lectures Adam Smith had delivered in 1762 and was suggested by a reading of the early volumes of the *Encyclopédie* for a review for the early, short-lived *Edinburgh Review*. Adam Smith, *Lectures on Rhetoric and Belles Lettres*, ed. John M. Lothian (Edinburgh, 1963). Cf. Aarsleff, pp.103-104.

4. This work was suggested by Monboddo's reading of a review of Nugent's English translation. See Aarsleff, pp. 36-42.

5. (München, 1869), pp.283 ff.

6. 2nd ed. (Berlin, 1858), pp.1-10.

7. Ernst Cassirer, *The Philosophy of Symbolic Forms*, tr. Ralph Manheim, vol. I *Language* (New Haven, 1953), 117-176. First German edition 1923.

8. (Wageningen, 1952), pp. 357-367. Verburg deals with Condillac after Monboddo.

9. (Freiburg/München, 1955), p.89. Arens' section on the "Französische Richtung: rationalistisch-psychologische Betrachtung," including the selections from Condillac, is repeated unchanged in the second "durchgesehene und stark erweiterte Auflage" (Freiburg/München, 1969), pp.106-119, (1st ed., pp.88-102).

10. Condillac I, 36b (*Essai* I, ii, § 107).

11. See also Guy Harnois, *Les théories du langage en France de 1660 à 1821* (Paris, 1928), pp.43-50. Harnois admits the importance of the *Essai* in a few sentences, but then goes on to the *Grammaire*, first published in 1775.

12. Renan, *De l'origine du langage* in *Oeuvres complètes*, ed. Henriette Psichari, vol. VIII (Paris, 1958), 9-123; the quoted matter is on pp.41-42. This is the expanded version of 1858 (first version 1848).

13. Salmony, *Die Philosophie des jungen Herder* (Zürich, 1949), p.42.
14. *Ibid.*, p.67. This is one of the many passages that show Salmony's ignorance of the *Essai*.
15. *Herders Sämmtliche Werke*, ed. B. Suphan, vol. I (Berlin, 1877), 529. The part to which Herder refers is Condillac's long section on the origin of language. This edition will hereafter be referred to as Suphan.
16. Suphan II (Berlin, 1877), 370. Cf. A. Warda, "Ein Aufsatz J. G. Herders aus dem Jahre 1764," in *Euphorion*, Ergänzungsheft No.8 (1909), pp.75-82, where Condillac's *Essai* is also mentioned.
17. Condillac I, 60-104. The entire *Essai* covers pp.3-118.
18. *Inégalité*, ed. Jean Starobinski in Rousseau, *Oeuvres complètes*, vol. III (Paris: Pléiade, 1964), 146; *Inégalité* covers pp.109-223, hereafter referred to as *Inégalité*. It should be recalled that Rousseau spent a year as tutor to Condillac's nephews, made his acquaintance, and later met him again in Paris: "Je suis le premier, peut-être, qui ait vu sa portée et qui l'ait estimé ce qu'il valait. . . .Il travaillait alors à l'*Essai sur l'origine des connoissances humaines*, qui est son premier ouvrage." Condillac had difficulty finding a publisher, but Rousseau put him in touch with Diderot, who then arranged for publication. At the time the three philosophers met regularly for a weekly dinner and conversation. See *Confessions*, end of Book VII.
19. Denis Diderot, *Oeuvres complètes*, vol. I (Paris, 1875), ed. J. Assézat, p.349. This edition will hereafter be referred to as AT.
20. AT I, 275-342, see esp. 304-305. On 21 August 1749, Condillac wrote to Gabriel Cramer: "Avés vous connoissance d'un ouvrage de Diderot intitulé *Lettre sur les aveugles à l'usage de ceux qui voyent*? Je ne vous en dirai rien car j'y suis trop loué." See Condillac, *Lettres inédites à Gabriel Cramer*, ed. Georges le Roy (Paris, 1953), p.54.
21. Le Roy, "Introduction" in Condillac I, xix-xx and xxiii. For the interesting relationship between the *Essai* and *Sensations*, see *ibid.*, pp.xvii-xxi. On the non-materialist and religiously devout tendency of Condillac's teaching, see also Henri Bédarida, *Parme et la France de 1748 à 1789* (Paris, 1928), pp.412-416.
22. Isabel F. Knight, *The Geometric Spirit, the Abbé de Condillac and the French Enlightenment* (New Haven, 1968), p.106. This work can only tend to perpetuate conventional errors about Condillac. The title is curious; in the *Essai* II,ii, § 52, Condillac says: "Nous avons quatre métaphysiciens célèbres, Descartes, Mallebranche, Leibnitz et Locke. Le dernier est le seul qui ne fut pas géomètre, et de combien n'est-il pas supérieur aux trois autres! " Condillac I, 117b.
23. p.175. See pp.166-176, with citations given p.166, to which other citations could be added.
24. Condillac I, 267b-268a (*Sensations* II,viii, § 35). The other additions reinforce this point: an entirely new introduction to Part IV on p. 298, and a new paragraph on p. 307a in IV,v, § 4. In this second version of the *Sensations*, Condillac made even more extensive revisions and additions on the matter of touch and motion; these are duly noted in le Roy's book

from 1937. I have not had access to the 1754 edition of the *Sensations*, but am following the indications given in le Roy's own excellent edition of the *Oeuvres philosophiques*. It is hard to understand why le Roy himself both in the Introduction to the *Oeuvres* as well as in some footnotes to Condillac's text should have forgotten the good insight of 1937. It would seem to be mere inadvertence since he offers no argument one way or the other. Also, though le Roy has noted the additions I have just listed, he does not take account of them though they greatly strengthen his argument of 1937. I therefore find his note in Condillac II, 536 inexplicable.

25. Condillac I, 731, in note to *L'Art de penser* I, vi.

26. The first three passages are in Condillac I, 363-364 (in *Animaux* II, v); the last two on p.371b (end of II vii) and p. 361b (II, iv).

27. Condillac I, 33a and 36b (in *Essai* I, ii, § 92 and § 107).

28. Condillac I, 29a and 14a-b (in *Essai* I,ii, § 77 and § 15). On Condillac's distinction between the voluntary and the involuntary connection of ideas, of which only the latter corresponds to Locke's "association of ideas," see also Condillac I, 29-30 (*Essai* I, ii, §§ 79-84); I, 400 (in "Discours préliminaire" to *Cours d'études*); I, 727-729 (*L'Art de penser* I, v); and II, 221 (in *Histoire moderne* XX, beg. of ch. x).

29. *Inégalité*, p.147.

30. *Ibid.*, p.151.

31. *Ibid.*, p.146.

32. *Ibid.*, pp.165-166.

33. *Ibid.*, p.167. The different layers, so to speak, of natural man in Rousseau have been pointed out by A. O. Lovejoy in "The supposed Primitivism of Rousseau's *Discourse of Inequality*," in *Essays in the History of Ideas* (New York: Capricorn Books, 1960), pp.14-37. It would have illuminated Lovejoy's argument if he had considered the place of language in this context.

34. *Oeuvres complètes* (Paris: Hachette, 1905), I, 370-408. The parts of this essay that concern language were almost certainly written in 1754 to form one of the long notes to *Inégalité*. See P. M. Masson, "Questions de chronologie rousseauiste" in *Annales de la Société Jean-Jacques Rousseau* IX (1913), 45-49.

35. Condillac I, 433a-b (in *Grammaire* I, ii). Jean Morel in "Recherches sur les sources du Discours de l'inégalité," in *Annales de la Société Jean-Jacques Rousseau* V (1909), 119-198, deals with both passages in the section "Condillac et Rousseau," but does not discriminate between them (pp.143-160).

36. "Rousseau et l'origine des langues" in *Europäische Aufklärung. Herbert Dieckmann zum 60. Geburtstag*, eds. Hugo Friedrich and Fritz Schalk (München -Allach, 1967), p.294.

37. See Venturi, pp.247-249, and Ricken, pp.559-561.

38. Condillac I, 436b (*Grammaire* I, iii). See also I, 430a (*Grammaire* I, i). This idea is also fully developed in *Logique* (1780) I, chs. ii-iii in Condillac II, 374-378, and earlier in a somewhat different manner in the original ch.xvii "De l'usage des systêmes dans les arts," in *Traité des systêmes* (1749) in Condillac I, 212-214.

39. AT I, 369. A few years later, Diderot stated the same principle in much greater detail in the article "Encyclopédie" in the *Encyclopédie* vol. V (1755); see AT XIV (Paris, 1876), 433-435. With a somewhat different conception, the idea is first developed in Bernard Lamy, *L'Art de parler* (Paris, 1676) pp.4-9. It is also in Du Marsais, *Oeuvres* (Paris, 1797), III, 381, 385 (in "Fragment sur les causes de la parole"). Further references in Aarsleff, p.15n.

40. Cf. Du Marsais: "Quand on dit *la lumière de l'esprit*, ce mot de lumière est pris métaphoriquement; car comme la lumière, dans le sens propre, nous fait voir les objets corporels, de même la faculté de connoître et d'apercevoir éclaire l'esprit, et le met en état de porter des jugemens sains." *Oeuvres* II, 120, in *Des Tropes* (1730).

41. Condillac II, 403b (*Logique* II, vi).

42. Suphan XXXII (Berlin, 1899), 86-87; "Versuch" covers pp.85-140.

43. Hans Dietrich Irmscher, ed., *Immanuel Kant. Aus den Vorlesungen der Jahre 1762 bis 1764. Auf Grund der Nachschriften Johann Gottfried Herders* (Köln, 1964), p.92 (= *Kantstudien. Ergänzungsheft* No.88).

44. *Oeuvres* I, 23, in "Exposition d'une méthode raisonnée pour apprendre la langue latine" (1722), which covers pp.1-41.

45. *Works* (London, 1794) II, 361, in *Conduct of the Understanding*, written 1697, first published 1706, in French 1710, 1732; in German 1755.

46. *Works* II, 139, in "Mr. Locke's Reply to the Bishop of Worcester's Answer to his Letter" (1697). The qualifications "much the same" and "most men" are designed to take account of men whose minds are for some reason or other deficient. Locke took for granted that man is wholly different from the animals in his capacities.

47. The best edition of Locke's *Essay* is the 5th (1706), the last to receive Locke's own revisions. Fortunately, this text is now again available in John Locke, *An Essay concerning human Understanding*, 2 vols., ed. John W. Yolton (London & New York: Everyman's Library Nos. 332 & 984, 1961). The claim made by Fraser for his edition and prominently repeated on the cover of the Dover reprint, no doubt in good faith, that it is "collated" is simply not true in any meaningful sense of that word. In French the *Essay* was read in Pierre Coste's translation of 1700, which had Locke's approval and which included a number of revisions which were first published in English in the 5th edition. German translation 1755 and 1757; Latin at London 1701, Leipzig 1709 and 1731, Amsterdam 1729. There were ten printings in French by 1787, all but two before 1759.

48. *Essay* II, xv, 4, and II, xxviii, 2. The key passage is III, i, 5, which is perhaps the most frequently quoted passage of the *Essay*. It is cited in Condillac I, 87a (*Essai* II, i, § 103). Of course, these passages became suggestive only because they were imbedded in a work which invested them with profound meaning and rich implications.

49. It is well known that books on voyages and travels constituted a very large part of Locke's own library and that he took special care to acquire everything of this sort that was published. See John Harrison and Peter Laslett, *The Library of John Locke* (Oxford, 1965), pp.18, 27-29 (= *Oxford*

Bibliographical Society Publications, New Series, XIII). Richard Ashcraft, "John Locke's Library: Portrait of an Intellectual," *Transactions of the Cambridge Bibliographical Society* V (1969), 47-60.

50. *Inégalité*, pp.133 and 123.

51. Renan, *De l'origine*, p. 42 (ch. ii).

52. Condillac I, 60a (*Essai* II, i, § 0). It is worth noting that Locke in the *Essay* III, vi, 44-51, argues strongly for Adam's ordinary humanity also in regard to language, concluding: "The same liberty also that Adam had of affixing any new name to any ideas, the same has anyone still especially the beginners of languages, if we can imagine any such."

53. *Inégalité*, p. 133.

54. Suphan XXXII, 99, but see the entire passage pp.92-101. It should be noted that this was written before the publication of Süssmilch's *Versuch* in 1766. Cf. *Über den Ursprung der Sprache* in Suphan V (Berlin, 1891), 52: "Der Göttliche Ursprung erklärt nichts und lässt nichts aus sich erklären". The anecdote of Shandy and Tobias would seem to come from Kant; see Herder's letter to Hamann (17 April 1768), which deals with the subject of divine origin, in Johan Georg Hamann, *Briefwechsel*, eds. Walther Ziesemer and Arthur Henkel, II (Wiesbaden, 1956), 408-409. In a lecture on the origin of language, Joseph Priestley observed: "Notwithstanding the powers of speech might have been communicated, in a considerable degree, to the first parents of the human race; yet, since it is natural to suppose it would be only sufficient for the purpose of their own condition, we may perhaps conceive more justly of the manner in which language was improved from so small a beginning as is represented in the lecture." *A Course of Lectures on the Theory of Language, and Universal Grammar* (Warrington, 1762), pp.237-238.

55. On de Maistre's and Bonald's influence in England, see Aarsleff, pp.227-229.

56. Condillac I, 36b (*Essai*, I, ii, § 107).

57. *Ibid.*, I, 61b (*Essai* II, i, § 4).

58. *Ibid.*, I, 22b (*Essai* I, ii § 49).

59. *Ibid.*, I, 403b ("Discours préliminaire").

60. See Aarsleff, p.38n. On the principle that language cannot be studied without reference to mind, see a firm statement in Du Marsais, *Oeuvres* V, 95-96 (at the end of his article on "Construction" (1754)). It may be useful to recall Du Marsais' definition of "Esprit": "Par ce mot, *esprit*, on entend ici la faculté que nous avons de *concevoir* et d'*imaginer*. On l'appelle aussi *entendement*." *Oeuvres* V, 316.

61. *Oeuvres de Mr de Maupertuis* I (Lyon, 1756), 259-260.

62. *Ibid.*, p.294.

63. Venturi, p.238.

64. *Oeuvres de Mr de Maupertuis* I (Lyon, 1756), 260.

65. Condillac I, 435a (*Grammaire* I, ii). The *Grammaire* as well as the *Art d'écrire*, l'*Art de raisonner*, l'*Art de penser*, and the *Histoire ancienne* and the *Histoire moderne* all formed part of the *Cours d'études pour l'instruction*

du Prince de Parme. The *Cours* was written between 1758 and the end of 1766, but not published until 1775. *L'Art de penser* is largely made up of passages from the *Essai*.

66. Condillac I, 403a ("Disc. prélim.")

67. Harnois, p.33.

68. Condillac I, 42a (*Essai* I, iv, § 5).

69. *Ibid.*, p.105b (*Essai* II, ii, § 9).

70. *Ibid.*, p.101b (*Essai* II, i, § 153).

71. AT I, 349.

72. *Oeuvres de Turgot*, ed. Gustave Schelle, 5 vols. (Paris, 1913-1923), I, 505. ("Étymologie" covers pp. 473-516.) Of all the work on language produced in France in the eighteenth century, Turgot's "Étymologie" proved most congenial to the nineteenth-century philologists; to Renan, "Turgot seul doit faire exception; il semble avoir eu sur le langage les vues les plus avancées." *De l'origine*, p.42. I agree with Venturi, p.394, that Turgot is not typical; he made no original contribution to the origin of language, and even his article on etymology was based on work by de Brosses. See Aarsleff, p.36n.

73. Condillac I, 214 (in a note to the original ch.xvii of the *Traité des systêmes*). Condillac and Du Marsais knew each other personally; see Condillac I, 735b (in note to the end of *l'Art de penser* I, vi, a note that is interesting also for other reasons).

74. AT I, 349, 414 and XIV, 429.

75. The "Exposition" is in Du Marsais' *Oeuvres* I, 1-41; the "Véritables principes" *ibid*. I, 265-279.

76. d'Alembert, "Éloge de du Marsais" in Du Marsais, *Oeuvres* I, lxvii.

77. *Oeuvres* I, 27.

78. *Works* (1794), VIII, 152-164, in §§ 163-169 of *Thoughts concerning Education*. This edition of Sanctii *Minerva* is from 1687 and was in Locke's library; he also had another edition from 1664 before Perizonii notes were added. He owned Lancelot's grammars of Italian and Spanish, Lamy's *l'Art de parler*, and Cordemoy's *Discours physique de la parole*. See Harrison and Laslett, *Library of John Locke*, Nos.845b, 1114, 1307, 2202, 2543, 2544, 2987.

79. *Oeuvres* I, 145; cf. pp.102-104. Du Marsais' "Remarques sur les articles LII et LIII des Mémoires de Trévoux du mois de May 1723" are in that volume pp.83-146. M. le Fèvre de Saumur presumably refers to Tannegui le Fèvre, *Méthode courte et facile pour apprendre les humanités grecques et latines* (Saumur, 1672), published in English in 1721, 1723, and 1750. It was in Locke's library, No 1114.

80. *Oeuvres* VI, 25 and 28. There has been some doubt whether Du Marsais wrote "Le philosophe"; see Herbert Dieckmann, ed., *Le Philosophe*, Texts and Interpretation (St. Louis, 1948) and Werner Krauss, "L'énigme de Du Marsais" in *Revue d'histoire littéraire de la France* LXII (1962), 514-522. There is no doubt whatever about his Lockianism and his strong anti-

Cartesianism; see for example these articles written for the *Encyclopédie*: "Abstraction" and "Adjectif" in *Oeuvres* IV, 29-41 and 85-110; and "Éducation" and "Fini" in *Oeuvres* V, 183-212 and 291-294. Very outspoken is a section "Remarques sur l'idée" (in V, 319-322), which occurs in the *Logique*, a work from which Professor Chomsky often cites other passages at length.

    81. *Oeuvres* VI, 9; cf. also pp.16-21 on reason and faith, closely following Locke. Cf. Ricken, p.554: "Es erscheint auf den ersten Blick paradox, ist aber eine Tatsache, dass Du Marsais sich bei der Begründung seiner rationalistischen Wortstellungstheorie auf Locke stützte." See also quotation from Degérando in Krauss, p.519. Our knowledge of the intellectual milieu in which Du Marsais moved just prior to his first publication in 1722, also indicates closeness to Lockian thought; see Ira O. Wade, *The Clandestine Organization and Diffusion of philosophic Ideas in France from 1700 to 1750* (Princeton, 1938), pp.98-101.

    82. *Language and Mind* (New York, 1968), p.19.

    83. *Essay* III, iv, 11 and ii, 1.

    84. Condillac I, 21b (*Essai* I, ii, § 46). In the correspondence with Gabriel Cramer, having been asked to explain the prerogative of arbitrary signs over natural ones, Condillac observes that this problem is the key to his insistence on "la nécessité absolue des signes" (by which he means arbitrary signs). So long as man has only natural cries, he is bound to nature and thus not free; the arbitrary signs over which he has control and which alone constitute human language, free him from that dependence, but in turn make him culture bound; granted that man has reason and reflection, language and knowledge are products of man's social being and of social intercourse. See Condillac, *Lettres*, pp.83-86 (in letter written between September 1750 and January 1752) and again pp.101-105 (which was also written during those years).

    85. *Cartesian Linguistics* (New York, 1966), pp.13 ff.

    86. *Ibid.*, pp.53-54.

    87. *Language and Mind*, p.77.

    88. *Cartesian Linguistics*, pp.1-2, 75-76.

    89. *Language and Mind*, p.70.

    90. *Ibid.*, p.86.

    91. *Essay* II, xxxiii, 4. It must be recalled that Condillac's "liaison des idées" is not the same as Locke's association of ideas. In the standard French translation of the *Essay* Locke's term was rendered "association des idées." See also note 28 above.

    92. *Language and Mind*, p.6. Professor Chomsky sometimes says "innate" and "innateness," and "innate ideas," at other times "rationalist" and "rationalism," though in all cases he seems to intend his words to carry the same meaning. That usage is curious, and it disregards necessary and time-honored distinctions. There would in fact seem to lie some deeper and more serious confusion behind this terminological mistiness.

93. *The Philosophical Works of Descartes*, trs. Elizabeth S. Haldane and G. R. T. Ross, 2 vols. (Cambridge, 1967), I, 442. Since I cited the long passage from "Notes directed against a certain Programme" in January of 1969 in order to show that this text cannot be used to set Descartes and Locke apart on this important matter, it has come to my attention that the very same passage has been cited at least twice for the same purpose. It was used in 1801 by Coleridge to show that Locke's "Innate Ideas were Men of Straw," because Locke and Descartes "held precisely the same opinions concerning the original Sources of our Ideas." See Earl Leslie Griggs, ed., *Collected Letters of Samuel Taylor Coleridge*, vol. II (1801–1806) (Oxford, 1956), pp.681-686 (in letters to Josiah Wedgwood of 18 and 24 February 1801). The same passage was cited again in 1821 by Sir James Mackintosh, who found that "it may well be doubted, whether [Locke's ideas of reflection] much differed from the innate ideas of Descartes." See *Edinburgh Review* XXXVI (October 1821), 235-236. Dugald Stewart also believed that Locke had been misrepresented on innate ideas and that he was essentially a rationalist. See Stewart's *Dissertation*, Part II (1821) in *Collected Works*, ed. Sir William Hamilton, 11 vols. (Edinburgh, 1854-1860), I, 206-251 and 553-556, esp. pp.223 ff. Mackintosh's discussion occurs in a review of the *Dissertation*, Part II. See my paper "John Locke's Reputation in Nineteenth-Century England," in *The Monist* LV (Summer 1971), 392-422. It is evident that present-day assumptions—or more often dogmas—about the opposition between rationalism and empiricism form a characteristic late-Victorian heritage of largely conservative inspiration.

94. In this respect Locke agreed with, for instance, Antoine Arnauld. See Arnauld's argument against Malebranche in *Des vraies et des fausses idées*, especially ch. v in Arnauld, *Oeuvres* XXXVIII (Paris, 1780), 198.

95. John W. Yolton, *John Locke and the Way of Ideas* (Oxford, 1956), p.56.

96. *Ibid.*, p.57.

97. *Essay* I, iii, 15. In this chapter, sections 15-20, Locke cites and discusses Lord Herbert on innateness, using the very chapter and passages in Herbert which Professor Chomsky cites with approval in *Cartesian Linguistics*, pp.60-62. Thus Professor Chomsky takes Herbert to be relevant and familiar, yet says that "Locke's critique [of innate ideas] had little relevance to any familiar doctrine in the seventeenth century" (*Language and Mind*, p.70). Since the *Essay* also discusses Herbert on innateness in I, iv, 8-18, these sections offer by far the most extensive discussion of any named philosopher anywhere in the *Essay*. Of course, even if the *Essay* had not said a word about Lord Herbert, it is a matter of plain knowledge that its discussion of innateness was indeed relevant to doctrines held in the seventeenth century.

98. *Nouveaux essais* II, i, 2 (in the Akademie Ausgabe of Leibniz, series 6, vol. VI (1962), 111; cf. also *ibid.*, p.55). In 1821 Stewart cited the entire "nihil est. . .nisi ipse intellectus" passage from a Leibniz letter of 1710, observing that Leibniz' words "only convey in a more precise and epigrammatic form, the substance of Locke's doctrine" (*Dissertation*, Part II,

pp.233-236). In his review of the *Dissertation*, Mackintosh for the first time in England cited the similar passages from the *Nouveaux essais* to the same effect (*Edinburgh Review* XXXVI, 247-248). Again in 1854, Henry Rogers made the same point with similar citations (*Edinburgh Review* XCIX (April 1854), 421-422). In 1819, Coleridge had drawn the opposite lesson; see *The Philosophical Lectures of Samuel Taylor Coleridge*, ed. Kathleen Coburn (London, 1949), p.383. Coleridge several times repeated that interpretation elsewhere.

99. *Essay* I, iv, 25; cf. I, iii, 20.

100. For matter relevant to the argument I have presented here, see my essay "The State of Nature and the Nature of Man in Locke" in John W. Yolton, ed., *John Locke: Problems and Perspectives* (Cambridge, 1969), pp.99-136. In my essay "Leibniz on Locke on Language" in the *American Philosophical Quarterly* I (1964), 180-182, I have tried to identify the specific doctrine of innateness—a linguistic one—against which Locke was arguing; I am still convinced that my suggestion is correct. See now also my article, "The history of linguistics and Professor Chomsky," *Language* 46 (1970), 570-585, esp. p.575 on this last point; pp.571-572 on criteria for historical research; and pp.583-584 on the retrograde consequences of Chomsky's version of the history of linguistics.

101. *Sprachwissenschaft*, pp.102-103. So also in the 2nd ed. (1969), pp.119-120.

102. Adolf Harnack, *Geschichte der Königlich Preussischen Akademie der Wissenschaften zu Berlin*, 3 vols. (Berlin, 1900), I, 300.

103. Harcourt Brown, "Maupertuis *philosophe*: Enlightenment and the Berlin Academy," in *Studies on Voltaire and the Eighteenth Century* XXIV (1963), 258-259. The history of the Berlin Academy is set forth in Harnack's magnificent *Geschichte*, which is of the first importance for all studies in the thought of the eighteenth century; for the present subject see especially I, 247-394, where the statutes will be found pp.299-302. Convenient biographies of most of the members mentioned below will be found in Christian Bartholmèss, *Histoire de l'Académie Prusse depuis Leibniz jusqu'à Schelling, particulièrement sous Frédéric-le-Grand*, 2 vols. (Paris, 1850-1851). See also Samuel Formey, "Éloge de Monsieur de Maupertuis" in *Historie de l'Académie Royale des Sciences et Belles-Lettres* 1759 (imprint 1766), pp.464-512. I have given the official title of the Academy's proceedings normally referred to as the *Mémoires*, hereafter abbreviated *Mém.*, followed by year and in parenthesis the year of publication. Emil du Bois-Reymond gives a good biography of Maupertuis in *Sitzungsberichte der Königlich Preussischen Akademie der Wissenschaften zu Berlin 1892* (Januar bis Mai), pp.393-442. This item is also in *Reden von Emil du Bois-Reymond*, 2 vols. (Leipzig, 1912), II, 426-491. An indispensable guide and source of information concerning the early years is Eduard Winter, *Die Registres der Berliner Akademie der Wissenschaften 1746-1766* (Berlin: Akademie-Verlag, 1957). For each of the 855 meetings (until 17 July 1766), it gives a list of the

members present and the business of the meeting. I shall refer to it as Winter, followed by number and date. It should be remembered that somewhat less than half of the communications read in the weekly sessions were actually printed in the *Mém.*, though some papers were later published separately.

104. Formey, "Éloge," pp.505 and 495-496.

105. Pierre Brunet, *Maupertuis*, 2 vols. (Paris, 1929), I, 161. Condillac was unanimously elected member on 4 December 1749 (Winter No. 153). During the time when he had sought refuge in Berlin, de la Mettrie was proposed for membership on 27 June 1748 and elected regular member on 4 July 1748 (Winter, Nos. 92 and 94).

106. The relevant items are in vol. I of *Oeuvres de Mr de Maupertuis*, nouv. éd. corrigée et augmentée (Lyon, 1756). This volume contains: "Avertissement" by Maupertuis, with some useful information, pp.255-257; *Réflexions*, pp.259-285; Boindin's "Remarques," pp.287-291; Maupertuis' "Réponse," pp.293-309. Both the *Réflexions* and the later "Dissertation" are divided in short paragraphs, to which I shall make reference in the text with the appropriate Roman numeral.

107. M. L. Dufrenoy, "Maupertuis et le progrès scientifique," in *Studies on Voltaire and the Eighteenth Century* XXV (1963), 572.

108. *Oeuvres* (Lyon, 1756) I, 299-300.

109. See letter of Condillac to Maupertuis (à Segrez 12 August 1750) in which he thanks him for the gift of "l'Origine des Langues," which he knew by reputation but had not yet seen, copies being scarce. Condillac adds that he is now himself working on "la génération du sentiment"(Condillac II, 535). Owing to his poor eyesight, Condillac does not write a long answer until 25 June 1752 (*ibid.*, 535-538). He finds the *Réflexions* very philosophical, precise and fruitful, but regrets that Maupertuis has not dealt with the question, "comment les progrès de l'esprit dépendent du langage. Je l'ai tenté dans mon *Essai*. . .mais je me suis trompé et j'ai trop donné aux signes." We have already seen that Condillac later in life was eager to reassert the doctrine of the *Essai*.

110. The words underlined by Maupertuis remind us of his well-known familiarity with Leibniz. The concluding four paragraphs of the *Réflexions* deal with the problem of duration and have been seen to relate to Kant.

111. In the *Oeuvres* (Lyon, 1756) in vol. I, as Maupertuis explains in the "Avertissement."

112. L. Gossman, "Berkeley, Hume and Maupertuis," in *French Studies* XIV (1960), 322, suggests that Boindin's remarks were actually written by Turgot, but the only reason given is reference to Turgot's "Remarques critiques sur les Réflexions philosophiques de Maupertuis" (1750). I see no force in that suggestion. Boindin's "Remarques" were published in his *Oeuvres*, and Maupertuis in his answer clearly assumes that the writer was the famous atheist. Turgot's critique was not published until du Pont de Nemours' edition of the *Oeuvres* (Paris, 1807-1811). Turgot's critique offers a strange instance of utter incomprehension or perhaps of

stubborn unwillingness to argue on Maupertuis' grounds. According to Turgot, words are tied directly to things, things are directly experienced as they are; since all men have the same sense experience, their ideas are correspondingly identical.

113. *Oeuvres* (Lyon, 1756), I, 298-299. For a typical nineteenth-century opinion of eighteenth-century discussions of language, see Benfey's remarks on the *Réflexions* in his *Geschichte der Sprachwissenschaft*, pp.283-285. The quality of his remarks is suggested by this passage: "Wüsste man nicht, dass der Menschen Weisheit und Thorheit stets Hand in Hand gehen, so würde man nicht begreifen können, wie ein so ausserordentlich intelligenter Mann zu solchen wahrhaft unüberlegten Thorheiten gelangen konnte."

114. Winter No.176. Printed *Mém.* 1753 (1755), pp.511-521; also in Maupertuis, *Oeuvres* (Lyon, 1768. Olms Reprint, 1965) III, 283-302 (this matter p.297).

115. *Oeuvres* (Lyon, 1768) II, 383.

116. *Ibid.*, II, 388.

117. *Ibid.* II, 429-430.

118. Winter No. 399. Printed *Mém.* 1755 (1757), pp.514-529. The other three papers were not printed in the *Mém.* See Winter Nos. 424 (25 March 1756), 476 (7 July 1757), and 501 (16 February 1758).

119. AT XIV, 435-441.

120. Winter No.430; printed in *Mém.* 1754 (1756), pp.349-364. It is worth noting that, though given in 1756, this essay was printed in the volume for 1754, which was published in 1756. It is also in *Oeuvres* (Lyon, 1768) III, 435-468.

121. Winter Nos.444 and 445: "Mr. Süssmilch a lu en Allemand un Mémoire ou l'on prouve, que les Langues ne sçauroient avoir une origine humaine mais qu'elles viennent immédiatement de Dieu." In 1745, Süssmilch had read a paper (published in *Mém.* for that year, pp.188-203) under the title, "Réflexions sur la convenance de la Langue Celtique, et en particulier de la Teutonique avec celles de l'Orient, par lesquelles on démontre que la langue Teutonique est matériellement contenue dans les Langues Orientales, et qu'elle en descend" (Harnack, *Geschichte* III, 554). Between 1746 and his death, Süssmilch read no less than 32 papers, most of them on demography, but seven of them on linguistic matters. These were not printed in the *Mém.* In addition to Nos.444 and 445, see Winter Nos.143, 255, 469, 696, and 709.

122. *Versuch*, pp.33-34.

123. *Ibid.*, pp.14-17.

124. Thus in the study of language Süssmilch's *Versuch* would seem to be the first work to show the conflict between faith and natural explanation, between the divine act and gradual development. This conflict has since taken many forms, but when, during the 1830's and 1840's in England, it involved the opposition of Genesis and geology, language was invoked on the side of Genesis. See Aarsleff, pp.207-209, 223-225. See also C. C. Gillispie's excellent *Genesis and Geology* (Cambridge, Mass., 1951).

125. *Versuch*, p.54.

126. *Ibid.*, p.83. The excellence of Süssmilch's argument needs to be stressed; one fears that scholars who make disparaging remarks about him are ignorant of his outstanding contributions to demography and have not read the *Versuch*. His work on demography easily makes him the most important and creative member of the Academy during the years we are here concerned with, possibly with the exception of Euler. Robert T. Clark, Jr., in his *Herder, his Life and Thought* (Berkeley, 1955), p.131, observes: "...Süssmilch, a member of the Academy, although one wonders how he got in." Clark has the *Versuch* in mind! More recently, it has been remarked: "...diejenige, die den Ursprung der Sprache—letztlich aus Ratlosigkeit und Bequemlichkeit des Denkens—in Gott verlegte (Süssmilch)." One must sincerely hope that people who associate the *Versuch* with "Ratlosigkeit und Bequemlichkeit" have not read it. See Manfred Krüger, "Der menschlich-göttliche Ursprung der Sprache, Bemerkungen zu Herders Sprachtheorie," in *Wirkendes Wort* XVII (1967), 8.

127. Winter No.472. The formulation of the question and the directions will be found in the first part of *Mém*.1770 (1772), "Histoire de l'Académie," with separate pagination, p.25. Also briefly in Harnack, *Geschichte*, II, 306.

128. Condillac II, 90-94. In a footnote the editor refers to Maupertuis' two papers. These are of course highly relevant, but Condillac's words—"a proposé"—are so specific that they can well bear my reading.

129. Winter No.554.

130. J. G. Buhle, ed., *Literarischer Briefwechsel von Johann David Michaëlis* I (Leipzig, 1794), 152.

131. (London, 1769), p.46.

132. Winter No.344. Printed *Mém*. 1754 (1756), pp.418-442. In his "Éloge de M. de Prémontval" (*Mém*. 1765 (1767), pp.526-540), Formey concluded with the somewhat unkind remark that it was "la société délicieuse d'une Epouse, qu'on peut incontestablement appeller son plus bel ouvrage."

133. It was read to the Academy on 13 March 1760 and was, like the original essay, in German. Winter No. 587.

134. *Beantwortung der Frage von dem Einfluss der Meinungen in die Sprache und der Sprache in die Meinungen* (Berlin, 1760), p.78. It may be recalled that Johann Georg Hamann in *Kreuzzüge des Philologen* (Riga, 1762), included an unfavorable discussion of Michaëlis' essay under the title "Versuch über eine akademische Frage." See Hamann, *Sämtliche Werke*, ed. Josef Nadler, II (Wien, 1950), 119-126. For a brief account of Michaëlis' essay, see Aarsleff, pp.143-147.

135. Winter No.682. Printed in *Mém*. 1759 (1766), pp.367-377. Since this and the remaining pieces are brief, I shall not give further page references. In 1757, Formey had brought out an edition of Du Marsais' *Des Tropes*; he had been shocked by French indifference to it and found it difficult to obtain a copy (see "Avis des éditeurs" in Du Marsais, *Oeuvres* I, xiii). Formey had some correspondence with Condillac; see the interesting letter from Condillac to Formey (Paris, 25 February 1756) in Condillac II, 538-541.

136. *Inégalité*, pp.123-124. See also the informative notes on pp.1295-1296.

137. Winter No.808. Printed in *Mém.* 1765 (1767), pp.495-505. This paper and Beausobre's were printed in the "Classe de Belles-Lettres." All the other papers as well as the two prize topics, Michaëlis' and Herder's, belonged to the "Classe de Philosophie Spéculative."

138. *Mém.* 1767 (1769), pp.413-438. Winter's *Registres* end with 18 July 1766.

139. *Mém.* 1770 (1772), "Histoire" p.28. It is striking proof of the popularity of the question that the Academy recieved no less than thirty-one answers.

140. *Ursprung* in Suphan, V, 34.

141. Bruno Liebrucks, *Sprache und Bewusstsein*, vol. I *Einleitung. Spannweite des Problems* (Frankfurt am Main, 1964), p. 48.

142. Condillac I, 98b, 103b (*Essai* II, i, §§ 143, 161, 162).

143. Suphan V, 64, 194.

144. *Ibid.*, V, 35, 38, 47.

145. *Ibid.*, V, 82-83: "Da jede Grammatik nur eine Philosophie über die Sprache und eine Methode ihres Gebrauch ist, so muss je ursprunglicher die Sprache, desto weniger Grammatik in ihr sein," a view which I should think will rule out that Herder can be cited as an example of "Cartesian" linguistics. Cf. Condillac I, 442-443 (*Grammaire* I, vi) : "La lenteur des progrès ne prouve donc pas qu'elles [les langues] se sont formées sans méthode; elle prouve seulement que la méthode c'est perfectionné lentement," and "Il faut que le système des langues soit, pour le fond, également le même par tout; par conséquent, toutes les langues ont des régles communes" (in Condillac I, 435a; *Grammaire* I, ii). Though not published until 1775, the *Grammaire* was finished no later than 1766.

146. *Mém.* 1771 (1773), pp.17-20, in "Histoire."

147. *Mém.* 1781 (1783), pp.388 and 404 in "Analyse de la Dissertation sur l'Origine du Language, qui a remporté le prix en 1771."

148. Suphan V, 20-21, 40-41.

149. Venturi, pp.238-240. Among the Herder interpretations I have seen, I know only one exception to the conventional view; it is Hans Dietrich Irmscher writing in the "Nachwort" to his recent edition of the *Ursprung* (Stuttgart: Reclam, 1966), p.140: "Condillac...behauptet...in seinem *Essai*...den *tierischen* Ursprung der Sprache. Was wir als ein höchst differenziertes Mittel der Verständigung benutzen, sei nichts anderes als eine kontinuerliche Entwicklung dessen, was der Mensch neben anderem auch mit dem Tier gemeinsam hat. Herder hat sich diese These ganz zu eigen gemacht." Though I cannot agree with this interpretation of Condillac, the second statement is correct, and to my knowledge unique. Irmscher's text in the Reclam edition follows that of the Suphan edition.

5. The Dithyramb to the Verb in the Eighteenth and Nineteenth Century Linguistics

Edward Stankiewicz

I. Introduction

The analysis of the parts of speech is one of the oldest and most controversial topics in the history of Western linguistics. The choice of logical or semantic criteria in classifying the parts of speech, their relation to the mind or to reality, and their universality or particularity have made this topic a battleground of linguistic and philosophical theories, leading eventually, as in our times, to a scientific agnosticism and even to its dismissal as a scientific problem. The question of the ranking of the parts of speech, which had been introduced by the Greek and Roman grammarians, was given a new direction and impetus in eighteenth- and nineteenth-century Europe when the relation of the principal parts of speech, the noun and the verb, was explicitly formulated as a genetic, rather than a logical, problem, with the priority being assigned at first to the noun. But the most interesting chapter in the history of our problem opened up at the end of the eighteenth century, when the genetic and functional priority was decided in favor of the verb. The primary factor responsible for this change of attitude was obviously the philosophical swing from realism to idealism, which reached its apogee in German Romanticism. The interpretation of the noun and the verb and of their origin and development as manifestations of the creative mind or national mentality (*Volksgeist*) subsequently became one of the focal points of the evolutionary approach to language, leading to far-reaching conclusions of a historical and anthropological nature. But it also exerted a strong influence on the treatment of such concrete linguistic problems as the classification of languages, the analysis of the Indo-European stem, and the structure of the sentence. All discussion of the parts of speech is thus throughout the nineteenth century informed by the two leading ideas of that epoch: philosophical idealism and an all-embracing historicism. Salutary as these ideas might have been in other areas of linguistic inquiry and within the framework of their time, they were the fountainhead of a linguistic metaphysics, which was from the beginning wrong-headed, and which absorbed the energies of the best linguistic minds of the nineteenth and part of the twentieth centuries. What is of particular interest to the modern linguist in the history of this topic is the role of philosophical commitments or, more broadly, of scientific "paradigms" in the formulation of linguistic questions and the solutions given to them, which solutions are, in turn, intended to strengthen the validity of the "paradigms" by which they are engendered.

In what follows I shall discuss primarily the theories of and debate around the principal parts of speech as they developed from the middle of the eighteenth century until the end of the nineteenth century. The treatment accorded the parts of speech before that period will be presented only as background material to indicate the profundity of the break with the traditional approach that took place in the second half of the eighteenth century. In the twentieth century our problem loses its grip on the mind of linguists as a result of the decline of glottogonic interests and of the general re-orientation of linguistics toward questions of synchrony. The fading echoes of the old controversy will be dealt with briefly, to round out our story.

Another topic closely connected with the interpretation of the relative importance of the verb and the noun, namely the problem of the word-order of the noun and verb (or subject, object and predicate) will be taken up in a future study.

II.   From Antiquity to the Middle of the Eighteenth Century

Classical grammar elaborated a theory of hierarchy between the various parts of speech. The subordinate position assigned to some parts of speech with respect to the principal ones, the noun and the verb, is indicated by the grammatical terms (such as pronoun, adverb, and participle) which were coined by the classical grammarians. The noun and the verb were, according to Apollonius Dyskolos, in a state of "natural harmony", but the other parts of speech were the "links" of a sentence. The noun and the verb, he argued, were like the head and the heart of a man, without which he could not exist, whereas the other parts of speech were like the limbs—important, but not vital (Egger 1854: 68; [Apollonius Dyskolos] 1878: 31ff.). Destutt de Tracy (1825: 355), centuries later, gave expression to the same idea by saying that the "accessory" parts of speech were "utiles, mais non nécessaires".

In classical grammar, the hierarchical relationship of the parts of speech was interpreted statically, like the "Ladder of Nature" established by Aristotle for all beings. Aristotle himself, the true founder of the theory of the parts of speech, had dealt with them from various points of view in his

Logic ("De interpretatione"), *Rhetoric*, and *Poetics*. In his *Logic* he admitted, however, only two parts of speech, the *ónoma* and the *rhēma*, and the interpretation he gave to them had a decisive influence on the Western conception of the parts of speech until the end of the eighteenth century (Pagliaro 1959/60: 93 ff.). The main semantic property which Aristotle singled out in the *ónoma* and *rhēma* was their reference to time. Thus he defined the noun negatively, as "a voice significant without time" (*semantikòn áneu chrónou*), and the verb as "a voice connoting time" (*prossēmaínon chrónon*) and as "a sign of things asserted about others" (Heidegger 1959: 57ff.; Pagliaro 1959/60: 105 ff.). The *rhēma* was thus first of all the predicate of the sentence, expressing attributes which were, to begin with, inherent in the subject. The position of the attributes could be filled not only by a finite verb, but also by an adjective or noun accompanied by the finite form of the verb "to be". The logical next step was, of course, to reduce also the finite verb to a nominal form (i.e., participle) plus copula. And in effect, Aristotle interprets a sentence such as *ánthrōpos badízei* as *ánthrōpos badízōn estí*.

Since any attribute, including the attribute of existence, was, as we said, imputed to the subject as its intrinsic property, the verb was consequently denuded of all semantic properties; the "copula" itself was merely an element of relation or the logical expression of assertion. This is, at least, the way the "copula" is interpreted by Aristotle's commentators (e.g., Quintilian) throughout the Middle Ages (when the term itself was coined by P. Abelard) and in modern times (e.g., the definition given by J. Harris in "Hermes" [1751; 1756: 90]). The grammatical treatment of the verb as a purely formal element of the sentence is echoed and endorsed by the grammar of Port Royal which follows the tradition by "rewriting" *Pierre vit* as *Pierre est vivant* : "J'ai dit que le *principal* usage du verbe étoit de signifier l'affirmation ... au lieu que, si on s'étoit contenté de donner au verbe la signification générale de l'affirmation, sans y joindre aucun attribut particulier, on n'auroit eu besoin, dans chaque langue, que d'un seul verbe, qui est celui qu'on appelle substantif" (Arnault and Lancelot 1810: 327).[1]

The reductionist treatment of the verb initiated by Aristotle was at the same time concomitant with a realistic interpretation of all the nominal parts of speech, including the adjective. It has been argued that Aristotle himself was the first to view any attribute (such as "white") as an ontological entity, as a "thing" ("whiteness") which was inherent in, and which operated through, the subject (Jeruzalem 1895: 142; Jodłowski 1960: 55 ff; Geiger 1869: 261; Ong 1958: 68). The semantic definitions that were afterward given to the noun were consistently those of *sōma ē pragma* (Dionysius Thrax), *corpus vel res* (Donatus), or simply, of substance. It became, henceforth, customary for linguists to treat the nominal parts of speech as the principal constituents of the sentence, and to analyze them in terms of their syntactic functions as subjects or as attributes.[2]

Priscianus was probably the first to suggest some kind of genetic relationship between the noun and the verb. Having selected, after the Stoics, the "quality of action" (i.e., voice), instead of tense, as the principal property of the verb, he views this property as being implicit in, or emanating from the noun, the proper agent or patient of the action: "agere vel pati substantiae est proprium, in qua est positio nominum, ex quibus proprietas verbi, id est actio vel passio, nascitur" ([Priscianus] 1857-80: 116) [to act or to suffer is the property of any substance that resides in the noun which brings forth the property of the verb, i.e., action or passion]. Whether the *nascitur* did indeed carry any genetic connotation is hard to tell, for it might simply have implied a relationship of logical dependence upon properties implicit in the primary, nominal part of speech. Explicit reference to a temporal order between the parts of speech must await the eighteenth century and the father of historicism, Giambattista Vico.

The supremacy of the noun over the verb hardened into a theoretical dogma (Ong 1958: 67 ff.). Leibniz, who foreshadowed the comparative method and cultivated an interest in the most diverse languages of the world, gives us a clear insight into what had become the standard interpretation of the noun-verb relationship. His program for the construction of a rational grammar, or *Characteristica Universalis*, reads almost like a summary of the traditional statements on the parts of speech. Following are some of Leibniz's proposals concerning the description of a "simplified Latin" which he treated as an intermediary between a universal rational grammar and the actual languages of the world (Coutourat 1901: 66 ff.).

> Verba possunt resolvi in nomina. *Petrus scribit*, id est *est scribens*. Unde omnia verba reducentur ad solum verbum substantivum. [Verbs can be resolved into nouns. *Peter writes* equals *he is writing*. Hence all verbs can be reduced to a single substantive verb.]
>
> In cogitando reducuntur omnia ad *qualitates* sensibiles, tum internas (*ut calor. . .*), tum externas (ut *essentia, unitas, nihil*). [In the thought processes everything can be reduced to properties of the senses, which are either internal (such as *heat*) or external (such as *essence, unity, nothing*).]
>
> Verbum nota rei sub tempore. . . .Verbum est quod involvit affirmationem aut negationem. [The verbs are notes (signs) of things from the viewpoint of time. The verb is something that implies affirmation or negation.]
>
> Omnia in oratione resolvi possunt in nomen substantivum *ens* seu *res*, copulam seu verbum substantivum *est*, nomina adjectiva, et particulas formales. [All parts of speech can be resolved into substantive names designating *beings* or *things*, the copula or substantival

verb *to be*, into adjectives and formal particles.] (Coutourat 1903: 281, 282.)

Leibniz goes even further, denying the verb most of its grammatical properties. Thus, he would like to see it stripped of gender, which he considers an "incongruity" of the Semitic languages; of number: "numerus inutilis in verbo, satis enim intellegetur a nomine adjecto" [number is unnecessary in the verb, for it is sufficiently understood from the adjacent noun], and of person: "personae verborum possunt esse invariabiles, sufficit variari *ego, tu, ille*, etc." [the persons of the verb need not vary; it is sufficient to vary the pronouns: *ego, tu, ille*, etc.] (Coutourat 1903: 289). Even tense, the last foothold of the verb (which marks even the copula) is not an indispensable verbal category and could be transferred to the noun:

> tempus et locus possunt ingredi non tantum verba, sed et nomina. Ut in participiis videmus, quae nihil aliud quam nomina sunt. . . . [Time and place can adhere not only to verbs, but also to nouns, as we see in participles, which are nothing else but nouns. . . .]

The hypothetical forms of the Latin conjugated noun would then be as follows:

> ut enim dicitur: *amatio*. . . ita esset *amavitio* vel *amaturitio* eius qui *amavit*, vel *amaturus est.* [so that as there is: *amatio*. . . there could also be *amavitio* or *amaturitio* of him who *amavit* (has loved) or *amaturus est* (will be loving)].

Referring, finally, to the Hebrew root, considered to be verbal, Leibniz states that he would prefer it to be nominal: "Radix Hebraeis est verbum, sed malim eam esse nomen, ut *vita*" [The Hebrew root is a verb, but I would prefer it to be a noun, such as *vita*]. Leibniz's program seems, then, to draw the logical conclusions of the traditional approach, which he would extend to a non-European language.[3]

A literary echo of the ill repute into which the verb had fallen among European grammarians is found in Jonathan Swift's *Gulliver's Travels*: "The first Project was to shorten Discourse by cutting polysyllables into one, and leaving out Verbs and Participles, because in Reality all things imaginable are but Nouns" (1961[1726]: 158).

Within the European tradition before the eighteenth century we find only one work which challenged the generally accepted view on the supremacy of the noun over the verb: *Grammaticale Bellum nominis et verbi regum: de principalite orationis inter se contendunt [The Grammatical War between the Kings, the Noun and the Verb, contesting for the Primacy of Speech]* written by Andrea Guarna of Cremona in 1512. This work went through a number of editions in the sixteenth, seventeenth, and eighteenth centuries, attesting to its great popularity. In 1841 it was put into verse by Andrea M. Ricci (Trabalza 1908: 246). The fact that it was not a serious theoretical tract, but a parody, does not diminish its significance. It was a typical product of Humanism, which marks a crisis in the European grammatical tradition. It is at this time that descriptions of national languages become more important than works of general theory and that universal rules of grammar give way to notions of "good usage" and of elegance. Reverence for antiquity and the study of original texts undermine the prestige of scholasticism and of its rational schemes. According to Swintheim, it is unimportant to know why a particular verb governs a certain case, so long as this usage was agreed to among the grammarians of antiquity (Sayce 1890: 25ff.; Trabalza 1908: 252 ff.). In this spirit it is easy to understand Guarna's disrespect for established tradition and his arguments in favor of the supremacy of the verb:

> Proferam autem ipsum veteris scripturae caput, ubi dicitur: in principio erat verbum et verbum erat apud Deum. Et Deus erat verbum. Arrige aures, cur faciem caperas. Deus inquit: erat verbum . . . et sine ipso factum est nihil. Non igitur nomen fecit omnia, sed verbum. Deus autem erat verbum, non nomen. Sed et verbo Domini coela firmata sunt, et omnia virtus eorum. [A part of this passage is quoted by Trabalza 1908: 6.] [However, I will quote the very beginning of the ancient Scripture, where it is said: in the beginning was the verb (i.e., word) and the verb was with God. And God was the verb. Hark, that you may understand. God says: there was the verb and without it nothing is created. Thus it was not the noun that created everything but the verb. God was the verb, not noun. And so the heavens and all their splendor were made by the verb of the Lord.]

The above words are obviously not intended as an exposition of the philosophy of the Logos, but as a critique of a dominant grammatical viewpoint. Guarna's appeal to the Bible (John 1:1) is purely facetious; he himself was, no doubt, well aware of another Biblical passage which seems to indicate the priority of the noun (Gen. 2:19-20):

> ... and [God] brought them unto Adam to see what he would call them; and whatsoever Adam called every living creature, that was the name thereof. And Adam gave names to all cattle, and to the fowl of the air, and to every beast of the field.

The "substantive-preferring principle" was repeated and advocated by philosophers of language after Leibniz, especially J. Bentham (1748–1832): "The import of the verb is in such sort covered, disguised and dunned that no separate view nor continued view can be taken of it. Where, on the other hand, a substantive is employed the idea is stationed as it were upon a rock" (Ogden 1959: CVII ff.).[4]

The middle of the eighteenth century could be viewed as a turning point, however, both in the history of European science and in respect to conceptions of the relative primacy of noun and verb. Newton himself, with his "hypotheses non fingo", anticipates the new era of empiricism and the crisis of the mathematical and physical models of nature established by Galileo and Descartes. "The certainty of physics is not based any more on purely logical premises, but on premises of biology and sociology..." (Cassirer 1932a: 61). Rationalist and universal principles are abandoned in favor of a naturalistic pluralism and of a dynamic vision of nature and man. The study of human society, in which we are immersed, is capable, according to Vico, of providing greater certainty than the "outside" knowledge provided by mathematics.

Dynamic laws governing society were formulated for the first time by Vico, who however came too early in then-provincial Italy to exert a serious influence on contemporary European thought. Vico's view on the relation of the principal parts of speech was traditional, but he was the first to interpret this relation diachronically and to try to support his claims with empirical observations, especially of children's speech and the speech of asphasics. (A genetic approach to the parts of speech, incidentally, was foreshadowed in the works of Vico's sixteenth-century predecessor and countryman, Castelvetro.) Since language was, according to Vico, of natural origin, the first parts of speech which emerged after the stage of communication by means of gestures and of physical objects, were onomatopoeia and interjections. After that came the pronouns (obviously deictic) "concerning things which we cannot name or whose names another may not understand" (Vico 1961: 109):

> Gradually nouns were formed. . . .And that nouns sprang up before verbs is proved by this eternal property: that there is no statement that does not begin with a noun, expressed or understood, which governs it.
>
> Last of all, the authors of the languages formed the verbs, as we observe children expressing nouns and particles but leaving verbs to be understood. For nouns awaken ideas which leave firm traces; but verbs signify notions which involve past and future, which are measured from the indivisible present, which even philosophers find very hard to understand. Our assertion may be supported by a medical observation (*osservazione fisica*). There is a good man living among us who, after a severe apoplectic stroke, utters nouns but has completely forgotten verbs. Even the verbs which are genera of all the others, as *sum* is of being, to which are

reduced all essences. . . .The verbs must have begun as impera-
tives. . . which are all monosyllables.

The proposed reconstruction of the origin of the parts of speech
departs clearly from the rationalist approach, which had sought to discover
universal and immutable properties of thought and language. The development of the human mind, according to Vico, is from "sensory topics" to
"genera" (495), and not the other way around. The founders of rationalism,
Aristotle and Zeno, who deduced "particulars from universals", were in error;
"neither yielded anything notable to the advantage of the human race"; the
advance of "experimental philosophy" lies in the application of the inductive
method, which has been elaborated by the "great philosopher and states-
man", Bacon, and followed with so much profit by the English (Vico 1961:
125). Thus we see that Vico's historical conception rests on the same
philosophical premises which are developed by the English Empiricists and
inherited by the French Sensualists. But while the latter emphasized
psychological and individual aspects in the formation of general ideas and of
language, Vico places their development in a sociological and historical
setting. Vico's empiricism is far from being purely observational or
descriptive. Theory and explanation are for him as important as they are for
his Rationalist predecessors: only the order is reversed (Vico 1961: 110):

> this [theory of the] genesis of language is in conformity with the
> principles of universal nature by which the elements of all things,
> out of which they are composed and into which they are bound
> to be resolved, are indivisible; and also with the principles of
> human nature in particular, according to the axiom that
> "children. . . begin with monosyllables". . .[Our theory] gives us,
> moreover, the order in which the parts of speech arose, and
> consequently the natural causes of syntax.

With the Sensualists, as with the Rationalists, language is not an
autonomous subject of study, but an instrument for understanding the nature
of our ideas, or of "reason". But as the latter is for the Sensualists nothing
but "transformed sensation", language is merely the instrument for
transforming sense-impressions into general ideas, the "méthode analytique
qui nous conduit d'idée en idée". As the world of objects constitutes, however,
the source of all knowledge, words are to be viewed as "images" and
reproductions of external reality. According to de Brosses, the "imposition
des noms aux choses" is determined, on the one hand, by the properties of
the vocal organs, and on the other hand by the nature of "choses réelles
qu'on veut nommer" (quoted after Harnois 1929: 54). The formation of our
ideas being rooted in the world of concrete objects and of their properties,
can thus best be traced through an analysis of the parts of speech, through

their genetic development. The temporal priority of the noun with respect to the verb was in this extreme empiricist position a foregone conclusion.

Condillac gives the clearest outline of this development:

> Je vais actuellement rechercher par quels progres le langage des sons articulés a pu se perfectionner et devenir enfin le plus commode de tous. . . .
>
> 82. La langue fut longtemps sans avoir d'autres mots que *les noms* qu'on avoit donnés aux objets sensibles. . . . Les notions complexes des substances étant connues les premières, puisqu'elles viennent immédiatement des sens. . . . On distingua ensuite, mais peu-à-peu, les differentes qualités sensibles des objets; on remarqua les circonstances où ils pouvoient se trouver, et l'on fit des mots pour exprimer toutes ces choses: ce furent *les adjectifs* et *les adverbes*; mais on trouva de grandes difficultés à donner des noms aux operations de l'âme, parce qu'on est naturellement peu propre a réfléchir sur soi-même. On fut donc longtemps à n'avoir d'autre moyen pour rendre ces idées, *je vois, j'entends, je veux, j'aime,* et autres semblables, que de prononcer le nom des choses d'un ton particulier, et de marquer à-peu-prés par quelque action la situation où l'on se trouvoit. C'est ainsi que les enfans qui n'apprennent ces mots que quand ils savent déjà nommer les objets qui ont le plus de rapport à eux, font connoitre ce qui se passe dans leur âme.
>
> 83. En se faisant une habitude de se communiquer ces sortes d'idées par des actions, les hommes s'accoutumèrent à les déterminer, et dès-lors ils commencèrent à trouver plus de facilité à les attacher à d'autres signes. Les noms qu'ils choisirent pour cet effet, sont ceux qu'on appela *verbes*. Ainsi les premiers verbes n'ont été imaginés que pour exprimer l'état de l'âme quant elle agit ou pâtit. Sur ce modèle on en fit ensuite pour exprimer celui de chaque chose.
>
> 85. Les verbes, dans leur origine, n'exprimoient l'état des choses que d'une manière indéterminée. Tels sont les infinitifs *aller, agir*. L'action dont on les accompagnoit suppleoit au reste, c'est-à-dire, aux temps, aux modes, aux nombres et aux personnes.

The pronouns were according to him, the last part of speech to develop, since it is difficult for man to apply the idea of a given name or even an entire sentence to something else (Condillac 1798: 362 ff.).

If we compare the reconstruction of the parts of speech given by Condillac with that proposed by Vico, we find interesting differences in detail but not in principle: the development of the parts of speech is for both a gradual and ascending progression from the concrete to the abstract, from sensible objects to general ideas. Inasmuch as the verb involves reference to action and not to concrete objects (Condillac), or to the self which must contemplate itself in time (Vico), it is the last, or almost last part of speech to be formed. The primitive form of the verb is for Vico the imperative, for it is both monosyllabic and situation-bound, whereas for Condillac it is the infinitive, which is the "indeterminate" or nominal form of the verb.

The theory on the origin of the parts of speech developed at the end of the century by the *idéologue* Destutt de Tracy, deserves mention here, for it occupies an intermediate position between the theories of Vico and of Condillac. Destutt de Tracy rejects the notion that the first words were designations of objects. He assumes instead, with Vico, that interjections were the first verbal expressions of man and that they served to designate not only objects but their attributes also. "Ensuite, quand dans un jugement nous séparons le sujet de l'attribut, et que nous le nommons, l'interjection par cela même n'exprime plus que l'attribut. Elle devient le verbe. . . .Les noms et le verbe, voilà les deux seuls élémens nécessaires de la proposition. L'un exprime l'idée existante dans l'esprit; l'autre, l'idée existante dans celle-là" (Destutt de Tracy 1825: 354, 355). The other parts of speech, according to him, followed the formation of the verb.

III. The Genetic Priority of the Verb in Linguistics of the Later Eighteenth and the Nineteenth Centuries

The belief in the priority of the noun over the verb is shaken in the second half of the eighteenth century; that is, around the same time that empiricism reaches its fullest and extreme expression in the works of the French *philosophes*. The new interpretation of the noun-verb relationship emerges almost simultaneously in three different centers: in England, in the Netherlands, and in Germany. Although these centers were in close intellectual contact, the final elaboration of the theory in the first part of the nineteenth century was left almost exclusively to the Germans.

Among the philosophical grammars of the eighteenth century, none achieved such distinction as Harris's *Hermes* (1751). Although this work was free of genetic speculations, it advanced views which were diametrically opposed to those of the Sensualists and which struck at the very heart of their conceptual framework. The linguistic (and philosophical) activity of Harris derives its inspiration from Cambridge Platonism, which rejected the analytical and pragmatist orientation of the English empiricists. In place of the passive senses of the Empiricists, the Cambridge Platonists asserted the priority of the active mind; in place of analysis, they posited synthesis, and in place of imitation, the creative powers of man. The head of the school, and Harris's uncle, Shaftesbury, became the founder of a new idealistic esthetics, which came to glorify the poet and the creative genius in place of the "morbus mathematicus" of the Cartesian era. Cudworth saw the source of all knowledge not in the perception of external objects, but in the judgment of the knowing mind; knowledge, he claimed, was "actio", not "reactio", and any attainment of truth (or, as Kant would say, of "synthetic judgments") concerning the sensual, particular "subject" was possible only through the use of a conceptual, general "predicate" (Cassirer 1932b: 40). These philosophical premises of the English Platonists permeate the entire work of Harris and are explicitly stated in Book III of Hermes (Harris 1765: 314 ff.):

> All language is founded in compact, and not in nature... there never [was] a language, nor indeed can one possibly be framed to express the properties and real essences of things, as a mirror exhibits their figures and their colors. . . .
>
> If words are not the symbols of external particulars, it follows of course they must be the symbols of our ideas: for this is evident, if they are not symbols of things *without*, they can only be symbols of something *within*. . .[i.e.,] of general ideas.
>
> The connective act of the soul by which it views *one in many* is perhaps one of the principal acts of its most excellent part. . . . Were it not for this, even the sensible world would appear as unconnected as the words of an index. . . .
>
> The axiom "Nil est in intellectu, quod non prius fuit in sensu" [is] so far all allowable, as it respects the Ideas of a mere contemplator. . . . 'Twill be proper that we invert the axiom. We must now say—"Nil est in sensu, quod non prius fuit in intellectu". . . unless we give precedence to atoms and lifeless ·bodies, making mind to be struck out by a lucky concourse.

In the light of the above statements, one can understand Harris's special interest in the verb, as that part of speech "which claims precedence over all attributes, for things must first of all exist". Among the "accidents" of the verb, time (i.e., tense) occupies a central position, for it is that category of the mind which transcends the limits of sense impressions, pointing to its own autonomy. Harris writes (1765: 107 ff.):

> Senses may grasp only the present and instantaneous, but they fail us in grasping the past and future. . . .To memory, to the imagination, and above all to the intellect, the several nows and instants are not lost. There is nothing appears so clearly an object of the mind or intellect only, as the future does, since we can find no place for its existence anywhere else. And thus it is the mind which acquires the idea of time.

The significance of Harris's position can well be measured by the critical remarks of his French translator, commentator, and otherwise great admirer, Fr. Thurot. As a good "grammairien-philosophe", he naturally rejects the philosophical speculations of Harris as so much metaphysical ballast, which in these modern times (of the French Revolution) "on ne sauroit lire sans le plus grand étonnement". But Harris's lengthy discussion of the categories of tense draws his special barb: "Harris se trompe ici très-evidemment avec Aristote: il est bien vrai que la sensation actuelle ne nous donne pas l'idée du passé; mais d'où nous viendroit cette idée, si ce n'est des sensations passées? " (Harris 1795: 100).

Some twenty years after the appearance of *Hermes*, Harris's follower, Lord Monboddo (James Burnet), published his *Origin and Progress of Language*, which, as many other works of the epoch, attempts to give an account of the origin of language including the parts of speech. The neo-Platonic position which characterizes the book is stated at the very beginning: "The greatest work of art . . . is man himself . . . and the mind furnishes the ideas which make the form of language (1809: 2,3). The author then proceeds to present what he claims to be a new approach to language (1809: 221):

> I have endeavoured to deduce the principles of grammar from the principles of philosophy, upon which all the sciences ought to be founded, otherwise they can never be perfectly understood, nor truly deserve the name of science. In this view I have divided and explained the parts of speech, in a manner a good deal different from the common.

In what consists Monboddo's novelty? First, he assumes that the verb expresses the "energies of the mind of the speaker", which necessarily bears a reference to action, or at least to the idea of existence (as is the case of the copula which he calls the "metaphysical verb"). Second, he maintains that the verb is that part of speech from which all other meaningful (i.e., auto-semantic) parts of speech are historically derived (1809: 188 ff.):

> This so copious derivation from the verb [in Greek] naturally leads one to suspect that it is the parent word of the whole language. . . . And not only does the fact appear to be so, but there is good reason why it should be so; for unless we believe that names were imposed upon things arbitrarily and capriciously, we must suppose that they were framed with some view to the nature of the things. Now how do we know the nature of any thing, but from what it acts or what it suffers. . . . [Thus] the names of the elements are derived from verbs that denote their

operations, and the effects they produce. . . the first words that men used, when they began to speak, were certainly words denoting actions and feeling.

The interjection which has been claimed to be the primordial expression of man is, according to Monboddo, likewise a verb, for "it expresses one of the two things essential to the verb, namely, the energy or affection of the mind of him who uses it, but it differs from the affection expressed by the verb in this, that it expresses only passion." Consequently interjections are "the remnants of the most ancient language among men, that by which they expressed their feelings, not their ideas. They are therefore the *verba* that Horace speaks of, as used by the first men who spoke. . ." (1809: 181,182). Monboddo goes even further: he thinks that the adjective and participle are "improperly ranged under the noun, and ought to be ascribed to the verb". Thus he uses a reductionist procedure as much as his predecessors, except that he applies it to the noun and not to the verb. Monboddo finds a striking confirmation of his thesis of the priority of the verb in the structure of Greek, the ideal language of mankind. He confesses to being unable to conceive of an *a priori* model of a perfect language and sees in Greek the closest equivalent. The modern languages of Europe are defective in etymology, but Greek is complete in itself, with its "wonderful generation of words"—from the verb. But the ultimate confirmation of his thesis comes from universal grammar and from Hebrew. "For it now seems to be a point agreed among all the learned in the Hebrew, that the roots of it are verbs; and if it is true that there is such a connection, as I suppose, betwixt the Hebrew and the Greek, it is natural to believe that the systems of the two languages should agree in this fundamental point." That is not all: there is also "a resemblance in this respect between the Bramin and Greek languages, which I think the more likely that I am persuaded both Indians and Greeks got their language, and all their other arts from the same parent-country, viz. Egypt" The comparison of Sanskrit and Greek might seem to suggest that Monboddo had hit (about a decade before Jones!) upon the comparative method. But this was not the case. He himself considered the comparison "a remote analogy", with Hebrew being, after all, another link and prototype. Monboddo's intention was rather to provide an analysis by which all words could be deduced from a minimal number of ultimate units (which he called dyads). His method of analysis was misguided, but his quest for simplicity was remarkable. What is, however, of special historical interest is that Monboddo's "discoveries" were not new but had been advanced before him by the Dutch Graecists and put forth around the same time with as much vigor by Herder. The cross-fertilization and convergence of ideas (extending to the very phrasing of their arguments) of the Dutch, English, and Germans in the second half of the eighteenth century should, indeed, make an exciting subject for study.[5]

The Dutch Graecists, who received such short shrift from Benfey for their arbitrary etymologizing and arcane teachings (Benfey 1869: 255ff.), had probably more in common with German linguistic philosophy, and with Benfey himself, than is generally recognized. Bopp, at least, was fully aware of and willing to acknowledge his indebtedness to the Dutch (citing Scheidius). By drawing a consistent distinction between primitive and derived terms, the Dutch were the first in modern times to resume an analysis of the word into its component parts, an analysis which also became the mainstay of the comparative method. They, furthermore, held to the conviction that all elements of language were interconnected thanks to the principle of "analogy". Greek and Hebrew were, according to the founder of the school, Hemsterhuis, related not genetically, but "universae analogia constitutione". As has been pointed out by Gerretzen (1940: 117, 131, 180, and esp. 287), "analogy" referred to the "innate, creative ability of the human spirit" to see and to establish a relationship between simple and complex structures, both on the level of words and on the level of syntax. Interest in the origin of language was for the Dutch (as for their contemporaries) not a naive curiosity about the unknown, but an attempt to treat language (and with it, society) as a dynamic and internally motivated process. Thus they interpreted the history of Greek as an evolution from the "smallest germ" into a powerful and versatile language. And, in contrast to the Rationalists, they did not treat the sounds of language as an external cloak appended to its internal form but sought instead to discover the relationship between form and function. All these tenets of the Hemsterhuis school played a decisive role in the development of nineteenth-century linguistics, which had an advantage over the Dutch in that it dealt from the beginning with a comparison of morphological forms and not, like the Dutch, with that of isolated lexical items. Another conviction held by the Dutch school was that the verb historically preceded the noun, that

> Nomina a verbis, non verba a nominibus esse formata; non nisi verba, eaque simplicissima, pro stirpibus haberi posse. . . .Reliqua omnia vocabula sunt derivata aut composita; sive nomina sint, sive aliae partes orationis . . . .Nomina, a verbis orta, horum significationem sequuntur. . . . Quae, praeter verba et nomina, numerantur partes orationis, ea vel ad verba, vel ad nomina, proprie referenda sunt; nisi sint quaedam interjectiones (Verburg 1949/50: 459; Lennep 1808: 4 ff.). [Nouns are formed from verbs, and not verbs from nouns. Roots can be nothing else but simple verbs. All other words of the language are derivatives or compounds and are either nouns or other parts of speech. . . .

Nouns, being derived from verbs, inherit their meaning. All other parts of speech aside from verbs or nouns bear a reference to verbs or nouns, the only possible exception being the interjections.]

We are told by Scheidius that the theory of the priority of the verbal root was adopted by Hemsterhuis from the Hebraist Albert Schultens ("Hemsterhusii civis, aequalis, condiscipulus, collega, amicus, unicus litterarum") (Lennep 1808: Preface, p.14). The belief in the antiquity and perfection of Hebrew was, indeed, sufficient reason to seize upon it as a model of linguistic structure and to follow the analysis applied to it by Hebrew scholars. The principle of "analogy" must have served, in turn, to corroborate this belief in the priority of the verb as reflecting the organizing capacity of the human mind.

This belief is expressed with greater force and a flamboyant style in the prize-winning essay of Herder (1772). The capacity of the mind is for Herder an unanalyzable and strictly human quality called "Besonnenheit". This quality (and here Herder shows himself as still a man of the Enlightenment) enabled primitive man to single out and to fix the attributes of the surrounding environment. Man is best attuned to sound impressions and singles out primarily attributes of sounding actions ("tönende Handlungen"), inasmuch as "the objects of hearing are connected with motion". By way of example, Herder projects primitive man's encounter with a sheep. Man comes to recognize the sheep as nothing but a bleating creature ("ein blöckendes Geschöpf"), and when he imitates its bleating, "language is born, as naturally and necessarily, as man is man." In the same manner "the child names the sheep, not as sheep, but as a bleating animal, and thus turns the interjection into a verb". Interjections are thus for Herder as they are for Monboddo, the source of verbs, while verbs generate, in turn, the other parts of speech (Herder 1891: 82).

> Aus den verbis wurden also Nomina [says Herder with the Dutch linguists] und nicht Verba aus den Nominibus. . . .Nicht abgezogene, allgemeine Begriffe sind ja auch der älteste Bestandteil der Sprache, wie der Verfechter des göttlichen Ursprungs annehmen musste [i.e., Süssmilch], sondern die Verben als Bezeichnungen mit Geräusch ins Ohr fallender Handlungen; dann erst haben sich als deren Träger aus verbalen Wurzeln die Nomina gebildet.

Not through the higher logic of modern man, but by tracing the gradual development of man's perceptions ("Sinnlichkeit") can we grasp the progress of mankind. "All old and primitive languages show the verbal origin of nouns, and a philosophically arranged dictionary of the Oriental languages that would properly assign each stem ("Stammwort") to its word-family would be a chart of the human spirit, a history of its development and the most excellent proof of the c r e a t i v e p o w e r o f t h e h u m a n s o u l". "Had we but such a history! ", exclaims Herder, "it would be, with all its advances and abberations ("Abweichungen"), a chart of the humanity of mankind" (Herder 1891: 82). The primitive form of the verbal root was, according to Herder, the past tense, for this is the form which pertains to actions, and which provides an outlet for the narrative, poetic impulse of man. The present is situation-bound, is pointed at ("zeigt man"), but the past is "context-free", is narrated. That is why all old and primitive languages have a number of past tenses, but only one or no present tense. The modern, philosophical languages have evolved in the direction of "cold observation of what there is" and have consequently restricted the use of verbs and increased the number of nouns. To the question of how one can imagine a language to consist only of verbs without nouns, Herder responds that primitive, creative, man ("Erfunder") was not given to analysis, but to synthesis. In the primitive sentence "everything merged" ("alles floss zusammen") and carried "all at once" a plurality of meanings. The formation of different meanings was afterwards achieved through spontaneous phonetic change, as proved by Hebrew and other Oriental languages, where the least nuance of sound, accent and aspiration brings about a change of meaning. Sound and meaning are thus intimately connected. Herder's emphasis on the symbolic function of sound recalls the arguments of Monboddo and of the Dutch grammarians and leads directly to the "organic" theories of Indo-European flection advanced by Schlegel and the Bonn school. Only now it was Sanskrit, and not Hebrew, that was to provide the proof and exemplification of linguistic theory, and which led only secondarily, and almost incidentally, to the discovery of the comparative method.

The primacy and genetic priority of the verb is a theme that recurs in many of Herder's writings on poetry and on language, the two strands of his thought that become twisted into a single cord. The praise of the verb reaches a high pitch in his *Vom Geist der Ebräischen Poesie* (of 1787). For the Hebrew, says Herder, almost everything is a verb. Their language is like "an abyss of verbs", an ocean of waves swelling with action.

> Ein Nomen stellt immer nur die Sache todt dar: das Verbum setzt sie in Handlung, diese erregt Empfindung, denn sie ist selbst gleichsam mit Geist beseelet (Herder [1879]:227).

The further elaboration of the "verb-first" hypothesis takes us to the greatest general linguists of the first half of the nineteenth century, Wilhelm von Humboldt and Heymann Steinthal. They were the last linguists to deal with the problem in philosophical terms, before the development of comparative grammar and of Indo-European linguistics limited its scope, making it a part of the inquiry into the origin of the Indo-European inflection.

For Humboldt the priority of the verb was no longer acceptable in Herder's genetic and naturalistic terms. Herder himself had, in his later years, come to abandon the last vestiges of his imitation theory, and to agree with Hamann that thought does not precede, but resides in language.[6] Speech was, therefore, a primitive faculty of man, and language was given all at once *in toto*. This was also the view of Humboldt (1843: 62):

> Die Sprache ist, wie es aus ihrer Natur selbst hervorgeht der Seele in ihrer Totalität gegenwärtig, d.h. jedes Einzelne in ihr verhält sich so, dass es Anderem, noch nicht deutlich gewordenem und einem durch die Summe der Erscheinungen und die Gesetze des Geistes gegebenen...Ganzen entspricht.

To derive language from impressions of external objects affecting our senses is, according to Humboldt, an unexplainable and chimeric enterprise. The only possible definition of language is, however, genetic, but its dynamism expresses itself in the unceasing labor of the Spirit, or of the "inner form", to find external realization, which, in turn, stimulates the development of the "inner form". Linguistic evolution is thus to be measured not only by the intensity of the "inner form" (which varies according to the national Spirit), but also by the synthesis achieved between the "idea" and its exteriorization (Humboldt 1843: 95):

> Die Verbindung der Lautform mit den inneren Sprach-gesetzen bildet die Vollendung der Sprachen und der höchste Punkt dieser ihrer Vollendung beruht darauf, dass diese Verbin-dung, immer in gleichzeitigen Akten des spracherzeugenden Geistes vor sich gehend, zu wahren und reinen Durchdringung werde.

The uninterrupted tension between sound and meaning, Spirit and matter, is thus the essence of linguistic evolution; the flexional languages, with their "symbolic" utilization of phonetic matter, achieve this fusion to the highest degree and represent the most complete form of language. The dialectical conflict of opposites, which are synthetically reconciled and surpassed, informs Humboldt's entire philosophical outlook: idea and matter, means and ends, universal and particular, individual and nation, "ergon" and "energeia"—these are the basic concepts which he elaborates and shares with the Romantic age.

The synthetic act of the Spirit reveals itself in each utterance, and the ability to form sentences is its foremost expression. This act is accomplished through the "energetic" predicate, which involves the use of the personal pronoun and the finite form of the verb. The verb is the most vital and dynamic part of speech, "the nerve of the entire language", for it guarantees the act of "self-generating" ("selbsttätige") synthesis (Humboldt 1843: 214):

> Es liegt daher zwischen ihm [dem Verbum] und den übrigen Wörtern des einfachen Satzes ein Unterschied, der diese mit ihm zur gleichen Gattung zu zählen verbietet. Alle übrige Wörter des Satzes sind gleichsam todt daliegender, zu verbindender Stoff, das Verbum allein ist der Leben enthaltende und Leben verbreitende Mittelpunkt. . . . Der Gedanke, wenn man sich so sinnlich ausdrücken könnte, verlässt durch das Verbum seine innere Wohnstätte und tritt in die Wirklichkeit über.

The verb, which bears reference to action, is itself the most energetic part of speech. Its internal unity is, however, assured through its form, for the verb more than any other part of speech, shows the fusion of root and affixes, and the ability to express various grammatical meanings through symbolic variation (i.e., apophony) in the root, as is the case in the inflected languages (especially in Sanskrit). The verb exerts, finally an energizing and seminal effect on the other parts of speech, for if the verb is "correctly constructed", the other parts of speech necessarily follow suit.

The languages of the world can, in Humboldt's view, be classified according to a number of criteria. But the advance of the human Spirit can best be measured by the type and degree of integration of "form" and "matter" (i.e., of the grammatical affixes and the root) and by the autonomy of the verbal expression. "It is on this point," he writes, "on whether these [nominal and verbal] ideas are confused and obscure, or whether they are definite and clear, that the grammatical perfection of a language depends" (Brinton 1885: 48). The typologically diverse languages do not in Humboldt's conception present genetically related links of a progressive chain; the expression of action, nevertheless, genetically preceded in all of them the expression of being, and the Sanskrit grammarians were right, he thought, in treating the root as verbal.[7]

Steinthal returns in many respects to the naturalistic interpretation of language abandoned by Humboldt. As he was prone to insist, Humboldt himself "had destroyed the foundation on which he stood", inasmuch as his universal "inner form" could not be dealt with outside its concrete realizations in the languages of the world (Steinthal 1850: 56 ff.). The "Sprachidee" could therefore be objectivized only through the empirical study of the grammatical (strictly speaking, morphological) systems of the various languages of the world, which would provide an insight into the mentality of the nations that use them. As a basic criterion for the classification of languages Steinthal chooses (with Humboldt) the distinction of nominal and verbal parts of speech, since the development of verbal forms provides the surest clue to the capacity of the human spirit (in Steinthal's terms, of the "Volksgeist") for synthetic "apperception". This capacity enables man to project the Self ("das Ich") into reality as the first firm point in the world of fleeting objects which are in this synthetic act established as predicates. "Predicates were thus the first words of the language." The first sounds or "word-sentences" produced by man were onomatopoeia imitating action, as is confirmed by the language of children. Through the act of synthesis these are then naturally associated with the predicates. "That's why substantives contain less onomatopoeia than verbs, which were more, original." Being of a spontaneous and imitative origin, the "verb goes through less apperceptions" than the noun, by which Steinthal means to say that since the noun was later in coming, it was also more complex.[8] He might have drawn from this. the conclusion (arrived at in the second half of the nineteenth century) that the more complex represents also a more advanced stage of development. But this he did not do, his interest being directed toward the origin of thought and language. Like other linguists of his time, he was primarily "a prophet of the past". The languages of the world are evaluated by Steinthal in terms of the formal means used to express predication (that "wahrhafte Angelpunkt der Sprachen"). Languages lacking a finite verb are "niggardly", even if they abound in many other forms, whereas the Sanskrit and Semitic languages ("die Rosen der Sprachen") have turned their full attention to the development of verbal expression even at the expense of developing the noun (Steinthal 1850: 80 ff.). With all his erudition, coupled with an obscure and involuted style of exposition, Steinthal contributed no new arguments to the prevalent belief in the priority of the verb. But his empirical and psychological approach to the problem exerted a strong influence and was resumed in the second half of the nineteenth century by Wundt. It is also worth mentioning that Steinthal owed some of his philosophical views to his teacher, Heyse, according to whom "man can only act freely, when he had developed the linguistic expression for the activity of the subject, i.e., for the verb" (Heyse 1856: 155).

IV. The Priority of the Verb in Comparative Indo-European Grammar

The discovery of Sanskrit and of "comparative grammar" caught the imagination of nineteenth-century Germany not only because it lent proof to the genetic theory of the Indo-European languages (a theory which had long been anticipated), but also because it agreed with and strengthened the then prevailing explanatory hypothesis of science, especially its historicism and the organic conception of the world. Just as Goethe could speak of the "Urpflanze" and "Urtier", it was now possible to speak of the "Urformen" and "Ursprache", whereas the structure of the Indo-European word, with its root and internal flection, suggested analogies to a "living germ" and to an "organic force" emanating from it. Bopp's avowed purpose was not merely to compare related Indo-European forms, but to give an explanation of their origin (Delbrück 1889: 62 ff.; Hirt 1939: 54).

The mechanical vs. organic origin of the Indo-European inflection, the ideal vs. real character of the root, were major theoretical issues surrounded by controversy and dissent. Another such issue was the origin of the Indo-European parts of speech and in particular of the Indo-European root. The first European Sanskritists (including Colebrooke) had no doubt that "all, or almost all words came from verbal roots".[9] In this they followed the tradition of Sanskrit grammarians, especially the Nairuktas, who derived all words from verbal roots. It is interesting that the philosophical arguments of the Indians in favor of the primordial verb embodying action (*kriyā*) bore some striking similarities to those advanced in the eighteenth and nineteenth centuries.[10] It is, furthermore, possible that the Indian grammarians had also influenced the Hebrew lexicographers who arranged their dictionaries according to verbal roots and their derivatives (Geiger 1869: 21).

Bopp was among those who expressed caution: primitive Indo-European (of the so-called "Wurzel-Periode") had, according to him, two classes of roots, verbal and pronominal. The former, however, he called verbal "for the sake of distinction and according to established custom", for the nouns and the verbs were only in "brüderlichem, nicht in einem Abstammungs-verhältnisse" (Quoted after Delbrück 1889: 77). This moderate position regarding the nature of the Indo-European root did not prevent him from accepting the more fundamental view that "die wichtigste Wortklasse der indogermanischen und überhaupt fast aller Sprachen ist das Verbum" (Quoted after Benfey 1869: 494).

The primacy of the verb having been accepted as an axiom of Indo-European linguistics, the glottogonic discussion has now shifted to the question of the priority of the verbal root vs. actual verbal forms. While Bopp had assumed (like his Dutch predecessors) the historical reality of verbal roots, for Pott (1861: 194) they were merely scientific conventions, "ideale, dem Grammatiker nöthige Abstraktionen". The two positions were most clearly counterposed in the controversy which erupted in the sixties of the last century between Th. Benfey and George Curtius. Benfey himself (1860: 81-132) has put the contended question in the subtitle of an essay which was meant to form a part of a comparative Indo-European grammar: "Sind die

Wurzeln oder die Verba die Grundlage der Indogermanischen Sprachen? "
Believing the latter to be the case, Benfey (1860: 125) claimed that "the
entire stock of Indo-European words with the exception of the interjections
and of their derivatives originated from verbs". He granted the existence of
primitive roots only in the function of expressive elements; from these
amorphous and polysemantic roots ("vieldeutige und unbestimmte Wurzeln")
there might, in turn, have sprung the secondary function-words
(Formwörter"). Curtius (1867) on the other hand, assumed the existence of
an initial verbal root period ("Wurzelperiode") which was followed by four
consecutive stages; the third stage produced simple or primary verbs, whereas
only the fifth or last stage produced the nominal forms. Whatever the
difference in their respective positions, neither author expressed the slightest
doubt about the originality of the verb.

The exploration of the beginnings of Indo-Eurpoean flection, which was
inspired as much by linguistic as by epistemological concerns, continues
unabated throughout the nineteenth and well into the twentieth century,
when Indo-European linguistics as a whole, with its increased interest in
sound-change and phonetic laws, becomes more and more empirically
minded. The works on Indo-European morphology continue at the same time
to be eminently philosophical and speculative.

A typical work of this kind is Westphal's book (1873) on the origin of
the Indo-European verb, which, in addition to rejecting Bopp's agglutinative
theory, attempts to reconstruct the Indo-European flection with the help of
concepts borrowed from Fichte's and Hegel's metaphysics. In the oldest stage
of Indo-European there were, according to Westphal, only monosyllabic roots
which carried the expression of "being in itself" (*Sein für sich*). Inasmuch as
being is, however, inconceivable without motion, the meaning of the roots
was verbal. The interference of the active, self-aware subject introduced, in
turn, the opposition between the third and the first person. In this way the
meaning of motion, which was at first abstract and non-specified, became
concrete and rooted in specific situations. "Being in itself" was thereby
converted into "being for me" (*Sein für mich*). In the third stage of
development there arose the possibility of expressing "being for others" (*Sein
für anderes*). This last stage coincides with the formation of nominal forms.

Another treatise remarkable for its assertion of the priority of the verb,
as well as for its philosophical abstruseness, was that of W. Scherer (1868).
The gist of Scherer's arguments amounts to this: the Indo-European
proto-language contained at first only predicative roots. Inflected forms arose
thanks to the acquisition of temporal and localistic notions, such as "here"
and "there", "I" and "you" which were the basis for a developed system of
conjugation which was, in turn, followed by the formation of cases. Another
factor accounting for the growth of flection was the principle of least effort,

which reduced the unwieldy number of primitive roots to a finite stock of inflected and compounded words.[11]

The genetic priority of the verb is also asserted by the American W. D. Whitney: "Roots, directly significant of quality or action were there [in the seventh lecture] shown to be the starting-points, the germs, of our whole vast system of nomenclature, for qualities, beings, and relations" (Whitney 1891: 423).[12] Any human attempt at conveying a conception of some sensible thing, "today as in the first making of language", is taken as beginning with the selection of some one of the specific qualities of the thing. Whitney polemicizes with those realistically-minded thinkers who "are unwilling to believe that language can have begun with the expression of anything so abstract as a quality [and] feel as if the first words must have been designations for concrete things." But being himself of a more pragmatic disposition than his German colleagues, Whitney proposes an ingenious, though obviously uneasy, compromise in the age-old debate. The things first "cognized", apprehended by the mind are concrete things, the "prima cognita"; but the process of cognition must not be confounded with the linguistic process of naming, with the "prima denominata" which designate qualities or actions. "No etymologist feels that he has traced out the history of any concrete appelation till he has carried it back to a word expressive of quality" (Whitney 1891: 424).

New elements in the discussion on the genetic priority of the verb are introduced by the French comparativist, Michel Bréal. Though in his *Essai de Sémantique* Bréal voiced some reservations with respect to glottogonic speculations, he posits the primitive origin of the personal pronoun (on the grounds that one cannot imagine how "the word for "I" could have been missing in any language" [1897: 207]), and of intransitive ("neutral") verbs. Desinences and a well-formed syntax would have emerged, he argues, only after the neutral verbs had acquired transitive force. The desirability of glottogonic hypotheses is asserted with far more vigor in Bréal's subsequent essay dealing with the formation of verbal categories (1900). Bréal is critical of a positivistically minded generation of linguists that has grown "prudent" and "discouraged" and weary of the eternally challenging question of the origin of grammar, at least in the Indo-European languages. Bréal rejects the viewpoint held by such Romantics as Schlegel that language was born instantaneously and in one piece (we may recall the concise formulation of Humboldt: "die Sprache wurde mit einem Schlage fertig"). According to Bréal, who invokes an older tradition (he quotes Lucretius approvingly), need was the mother of linguistic invention, and the progressive diversification of language reflects the development of man in society. Consequently, it is not biology or sociology that should serve as models for the linguist, but rather the history of social institutions (284).

Bréal, like his predecessors, sees the beginning of language in onomatopoeia and in vague, non-differentiated signs. Progress in language consists of
the progressive formation of grammatical categories of the verb. The first to
emerge were the imperative and the indicative, the twin categories that were
indispensable for social interaction. In the next phase of its development
language acquired a number of modal categories that were used to express
mental dispositions ("les categories de l'âme"). The tenses and persons were
the last to come, since the former are of an abstract, intellectual character
and the latter can be dispensed with in a system that contains pronouns.
Bréal's reconstruction of the formation of the verb exerted a certain influence
on a younger generation of linguists, especially Meillet (1920: 175-198); what
they found of interest in his scheme were not so much its philosophical
preconceptions as the attempt to discover the hierarchy of verbal categories,
its sociological orientation, and a lessened concern with the merits of the verb
versus the noun.

V. The Supremacy of the Verb in Works of the Late Nineteenth and the Twentieth Centuries

Toward the end of the nineteenth century, the debate over the relative
chronology of the nominal and verbal parts of speech is given a new slant and
impetus when the genetic priority is again assigned to the noun. Even in the
middle of the nineteenth century some voices had challenged reigning
opinion, but they were isolated and not taken seriously.[13] But by the end of
the century the long-forgotten viewpoint was readily absorbed into the
mainstream of linguistic thought. The change did not, however, signify a
return to old positions. On the contrary, it was meant to give a new lease on
life to the theory of the primacy of the verb.

The end of the nineteenth century marks a crisis in the "Ursprache"-
oriented and reconstructive science of Indo-European linguistics. The sense of
crisis is vividly reflected in the second edition (1879) of Sayce's *Introduction
to the Science of Language*. The preface to the second edition, according to
the author (1890: xvi) was written in order to correct the theoretical
shortcomings of the first edition which represented "the last page of the
history that has been played out." The traditional approach to Indo-
European, its emphasis on word-etymology and the dissection of stems, is
now considered to have been a sterile and wasted endeavor.

The reconstructed formulas of Indo-European forms constituted in the
opinion of Fick (1881) (who had himself composed a comparative Indo-
European dictionary), the "empty clatter of roots and suffixes." The
sentence, and not the individual words, became recognized as the basic unit

of primitive speech. The etymological and genetic approach thereby automatically lost ground, while much interest developed in the typological study of genetically unrelated languages. Anthropologists (such as Brinton) and psychologists (such as Wundt) moved into the field to offer a broader view of language and to substitute empirical material for the genetic speculations of linguists. "It is in modern savages and in young children that we have to look for the best representatives of primeval man... and as long as we remember that they are but imperfect representatives we shall not go wrong in our scientific inferences" (Fick 1884: xxciii). The development of mankind and of the human mind is a constant progression from observable, concrete facts to abstract thought. The primitive sentence (or, rather, word-sentence) could not have had a verbal character, since the verb represents the highest form of linguistic abstraction of which there is no correlate in external reality. There are many primitive languages which "have not yet attained the conception of the verb." What Sayce wrote in the first edition of his book (Vol. II, p.151) about the Aryan verb was in need of total revision, for it represented "the theory of the last half-century and must now make way for one in accordance with the actual [!] facts." "In short, the Aryan verb was originally a noun, just as it is still in many languages of the world, and how long it was in becoming a separate part of speech may be seen from the widespread influence of analogy or assimilation upon the verbal conjugation" (Fick 1881: xviii ff., 122, 151).

The above statements by Fick provide a good insight into what was happening in European linguistics of the fin-de-siècle, though Fick fails to mention the main idea that was responsible for the reversal of the chronology of the parts of speech. This was, no doubt, the idea of Progress, which captured the imagination of his contemporaries, or, as Bury (1928) put it, which "in the seventies and eighties of the last century was becoming a general article of faith." If the backward-looking linguists of the Romantic era could glorify the verb by placing it in the "golden age" of the just discovered proto-language, the forward-looking linguists of the Positivist era could claim its superiority by viewing it as the end result of a ceaseless and progressive development.

At the beginning of the twentieth century, J. van Ginneken (1907) attempted to bolster the theory of the primacy of the verb with notions drawn from experimental psychology. In effect, he restated the older metaphysical arguments in new psychological terms. Van Ginneken distinguishes two types of perception: "adhésion absolu" and "adhésion relative". The first type concerns the psychologically simpler perception of facts (i.e., of events), whereas the second (which is the equivalent of Steinthal's "apperception") represents the more complex faculty of perceiving things. Sentence-formation presupposes only the first type of adhesion, whereas the second type accounts for the introduction of nominal forms. The lack of the noun/verb opposition which is found in many (non-Indo-European) languages proves that only the category of predication is fundamental and that it can be expressed by any word. Substantives and adjectives have separated from originally predicative forms. This fact is further confirmed by certain kinds of aphasia (specifically by "aphasie croissante ou guerissante") in which the ability to use nouns, which requires greater mental energy, disappears earlier and returns later than the ability to use verbs (Van Ginneken 1907: 74 ff.; 53 ff.; 123).

R. de la Grasserie (1914) was truly fascinated with the force and uniqueness of the verb as the "generator of all other parts of speech" and the bridge "from the phenomenon to the noumenon."[14] Despite his avowed empiricism ("içi toute théorie a priori serait inutile"), de la Grasserie remains immersed in the idealistic tradition of the nineteenth century. His arguments in favor of the primordial character of the verb rest, in fact, on two a priori assumptions: 1) that the concept of motion is prior to the concept of substance and 2) that perception of properties or of "phenomena" precedes the perception of being or of the "noumenon" which is essentially inaccessible to the human spirit. From these premises flow the consequences that all words of the language are derived from verbs and that substantives bearing a reference to the substance (or to the noumenon) are late creations, presupposing the existence or parts of speech which bear a reference to properties, i.e., to the verb and the adjective (cf. especially the introduction and chapters I-IV). The bulk of the book is a kind of etymological dictionary of Indo-European verbal roots, together with their verbal and non-verbal derivatives. The etymologies are often strained, since de la Grasserie is bent on the proposition that all nominal forms are based on verbs.

The last outstanding proponent of the hypothesis of the priority of the verb was Hugo Schuchardt (the quotations are from [Schuchardt] 1922, ch. VI, "Sprachursprung", 200-246). With the appearance of the work of Wundt (cf. below), the discussion around the origin of the parts of speech had essentially been transferred from the domain of word-etymology to that of syntax. Like Wundt, Schuchardt subscribed to the theory that the primitive utterance was a one-unit (predicate), rather than a two-unit (subject plus predicate), sentence. But, unlike Wundt, he was convinced that the original word-sentence consisted only of a predicate. Schuchardt, too, adduces the oft-repeated epistemological argument (for which he credits Trendelenburg) that "action can be perceived by itself, as shown by the existence of impersonal sentences, but a thing can be perceived only through action" ([Schuchardt] 1922: 230n.). The immediacy of perception is always, at first, rendered by means of motion- and sound-imitating words (onomatopoeia) which lie at the basis of most lexical items of the language. Schuchardt's exposition also resounds with echoes from Herder: "Nicht in einer starren und stummen Welt, nur in einer schwingenden und klingenden, war die Entstehung der Sprache möglich, sie begann mit der Bezeichnung von Vorgängen, die sich an den Dingen vollzogen, nicht von Dingen, an denen etwas vorging" ([Schuchardt] 1922: 229). Nominal forms might have arisen through the use of deictic gestures (such as "here", "there") and through the introduction of personal pronouns.

An outstanding champion of the new position was W. Wundt, a psychologist and philosopher rather than an Indo-European linguist. His arguments (Wundt 1900) in favor of the superiority of the verb have, nevertheless, an all too familiar ring, except for the re-ordering of the priorities. The formation of thought, according to Wundt, is a gradual advance from the concrete *Gegenstandsbegriff* ("object-concept") to the abstract *Zustandbegriffe* ("situation-concepts"). The latter include the concepts of time and of the agent, which are embodied into the linguistic categories of tense and person. The original word-sentence was the expression of immediate thought, of "gegenständliches Denken", which bears a direct relation to the external world. Only in the course of time did man lift himself to the level of "zuständliches Denken" which produced the various categories of the verb. This course can be divided into four stages. The oldest form of the verb (the "Urform") is the past tense which has the closest relation to a concrete context ("der Gegenstand im gegebenen Augenblick"), while its most recent form is the auxiliary verb, which corresponds to the "philosophical stage of abstract concept-formation." The parts of speech did not emerge from some indeterminate noun-verb stem, but from a noun to which a verb was subsequently added, or from which it branched out.[15]

In his controversy with Delbrück, Wundt asserts the priority of the nominal word-sentence, rejects the notion of ellipsis, and accuses the traditional linguists of a lack of interest in the growth and progress of language. The Indo-Europeanists, he says, believe in a kind of "paradiesischer Urzustand" in which all the concepts of language appeared ready-made ("direct von Himmel gefallen") (Wundt 1901). It should be apparent that this critique was not quite justified, although the Neogrammarians (like the contemporary French Linguistic Society) had, indeed, suspended all discussion regarding glottogonic and epistemological questions of language. But even among the Neogrammarians there were some outstanding linguists for whom the origin of the parts of speech, and with it the history of the human mind, remained a live and overriding concern. One of them was, for example, H. Hirt, who attempted to show that the verbal categories of Indo-European have evolved from original nominal forms and that the modern European languages have advanced over the classical languages in their development of finite verbal forms as opposed to the older languages which abounded in the infinite (or nominal) forms of the verb.[16]

The latter thesis was most strongly advanced and elaborated in the works of the great Russian linguist, A. A. Potebnja, whose theory of *oglagolenie* ("verbalization") or *rost glagol'nosti* ("growth of verbality") was to affect a generation of Russian scholars. History, says Potebnja, is not a meaningless tautology, but the progressive evolution of life and civilization. "Just as in the realm of organic life differentiation of the organs produces greater complexity and an increase of perfection, so also here [in language] we observe an increase of differentiation and the growth of perfection." The analogy from biology is adduced to substantiate the contention that the development of language consists of an ever sharper differentiation of the noun and the verb and of the gradual emancipation of the verb as the principal part of speech and the center of the sentence. This is, according to Potebnja, accomplished through the transformation of nominal forms (such as the Old Russian past active participle and adjective) into purely verbal forms or into forms which modify the verb (such as the modern Russian past tense and the adverb), as well as through the emergence of impersonal constructions and the replacement of syntactic agreement (with the subject) by grammatical government with the verb as its moving force. The existence of nominal one-member sentences in the modern languages should not mislead one to assume that they are identical with such sentences in the old stage of the language, for as a result of a long historical process, these sentences have acquired a purely predicative and verbal function (Potebnja, 1888; esp. pp. 33 ff., 82 ff., 516 ff.).

The theses of Potebnja were taken up and popularized by his disciple, A. M. Peškovskij who, as a syntactician, emphasized in particular the growing importance of the impersonal construction (of the type *ego ubilo*) in the history of Russian (Peškovskij, 1956, esp. 344 ff.). The proliferation of nominal derivatives and compounds which, after the Revolution, affected the style of newspapers and literature, was for Peškovskij a sign of a regrettable "marginal counter-tendency", and he exhorted his contemporaries to keep in line with progress by a "return [*sic!*] to the verb" (*nazad k glagolu*) (Peškovskij 1959: 101 ff.). Peškovskij's call seems also to have been the last outcry, the swan song of a linguistic controversy that has exhausted itself.

With this the dispute around the primacy of the principal parts of speech was not, however, quite over. Having left the quarters of linguists, it lingered in the domain of literature and poetics. Early twentieth-century poetic tracts of Expressionists, Futurists, Imagists (such as F. Werfel, E. Fenollosa, Gertrude Stein) reverberate with echoes of the old arguments that give the edge to the verb (Nilsson, 1970: 74 ff.) and which tend generally to accept Humpty Dumpty's verdict (in *Through the Looking-Glass* by L. Carroll), "They've a temper, some of them [words] — particularly verbs, they're the proudest — adjectives you can do anything with, but not verbs...."

Linguists, on the other hand, have come more and more to realize that language is a system of implicational terms, and that the noun and verb presuppose each other as opposite members of a higher functional unity. It was Meillet who, though not averse to emphasizing the pivotal role of the verb as a part of speech ("la categorie du verbe comme essentielle dans le langage"), set the tone for a more sober evaluation of the relationship between the noun and verb: "La phrase nominale et la phrase verbale différent de nature, et il est aussi vain de vouloir ramener l'une à l'autre, qu'il le serait de vouloir ramener le nom au verbe, et inversement" (Meillet [1920], 1948: 180). Sapir put it even more cogently: "It is well to remember that speech consists of... propositions. There must be something to talk about and something must be said about the subject of discourse once it is selected.... No language wholly fails to distinguish noun and verb, though in particular cases the nature of the distinction may be an elusive one. It is different with other parts of speech. Not one of them is imperatively required for the life of the language" (1921: 126).

NOTES

1. This, as one may say, emasculation of the verb as a part of speech was one of the points which in the nineteenth century provoked the strongest objections to traditional grammar. Thus the Italian historian and man of letters Francesco de Sanctis wrote, "Such decomposition of *amo* into *sono amante* for me turns the word into a corpse, takes from it all which comes from the will in action" (Trabalza 1908: 6). To this critique was often added the historical argument that various forms of the copula, such as Greek *phúo* or German *(ge)wesen*, were originally verbs with a concrete lexical meaning (Delbrück 1889: 29). But even earlier Thurot, the French translator of Hermes, could defend the traditional decomposition of the verb only by arguing that the copula *être* was but a scientific construct, an "element fictif de verbes" (in Harris 1795: 296).

2. See, for example, Harris's distinction of the parts of speech into substantives and attributives, pp.31 ff. In the suppositional logic of Peter of Spain and his followers there is "the tendency not only to 'treat terms as substances' in the way Mullally notes, but also to keep at the center of the discussion terms for substances such as man or donkey, readily evocative of images of concrete, individual existents. Such a tendency ... is connected with the interest in predication which lingers in suppositional logic" (Ong 1958: 68).

3. It is interesting to notice that this approach was not unknown to the Hebrew grammarians and lexicographers, for whom the verbal root was the primitive element of the language. Thus we find the eleventh-century author of the "Book of Roots of the Hebrew Language", Abulvalid, expressing the view that substantives denoting concrete objects were the primary parts of speech and that the infinitive or nominal form of the verb was its oldest form. As Geiger (1869: 212, n.9) observes, this theory had no impact whatsoever upon his successors.

4. [On J. Horne Tooke (1736–1812), whose *Diversions of Purley* (1786, 1805) reflects much of English thinking in this regard, see Aarsleff 1967, ch. 2, esp. pp.46-8, 65-8.–DH]

5. The resemblance of style and formulation is apparent in a number of details. Thus, both the Dutch linguists and Herder state in a negative, "polemic" form the possibility of deriving verbs from nouns ("nomina a verbis, non verba a nominibus" and "aus den Verbis wurden also Nomina, und nicht Verba aus den Nominibus"), while Herder's quotation from Horace (on p.58) figures also as the motto of Monboddo's book: "Donec verba, quibus voces sensuque notarent, nominaque invenere". Herder became familiar with Monboddo's work thanks to Hamann, who had pointed out to him the importance and congeniality of Monboddo's views on several occasions (cf. Hamann 1778–82: 209, 287, 318). In 1784 Herder wrote the introduction to the German translation of Monboddo. Monboddo's work attracted the attention not only of Hamann and Herder, but also of Bernhardi (1850) and Benfey (1869).

6. According to Hamann, "Sprache ist zeitlich, ursächlich und dem Range nach gegenüber der Vernunft das Frühere und Erste. Sprache macht Vernunft, nicht umgekehrt" (quoted from Hilpert 1933: 72, 74).

7. [Cf., however, his treatment of the Javanese verb as nominal in origin, see Percival, this volume.–DH]

8. [In his own espousal of the priority of the verb, the American anthropologist Brinton takes Steinthal to have considered the noun primary in his treatise of 1855. Brinton writes: "So far as I have been able to analyze these primitive sentence-words, they always express *being in relation*; and hence they partake of the nature of verbs rather than nouns. In this conclusion I am obliged to differ with the eminent linguist Professor Steinthal, who, in his profound exposition of the relations of psychology to grammar, maintains that while the primitive sentence was a single word, that word was a noun, a name" (Brinton 1888, cited from 1891: 403-4, and referring to Steinthal 1855: 325).–DH]

9. "The roots of the Sanskrit language, wrote H. T. Colebrooke, are crude verbs and perhaps particles. All nouns without exception, say some grammarians, or with few exceptions according to others may be deduced by rules of etymology from the crude verb. The *dhátus* or crude verbs, are contained in a catalogue, at the head of which is placed *to be*. Those, and their derivations (or any significant sound however derived) being inflected

with the signs of persons and cases, are denominated words" (1805: 11); cf. also Delbrück (1880). It should be emphasized that even before the discovery of Sanskrit some forerunners of the comparative method, such as the Dutchman Lambert ten Kate (1674-1731), believed that the verbs represented the "veritable primitive roots" of the Germanic languages; cf. Raumer (1870: 144).

10. Cf. Müller, pp.78 ff.; Chakravarti 1930: 179, 213; Heimann 1964: 41: "The verbal root (*kriyā* 'activity') is the basic root of all forms of grammatical morphology. The verbal adjective and the noun are, it is true, derivations in which dynamics are less felt than in the verb itself, but their verbal origin is still traceable, and as such the noun can be revitalized by tracing it back to its verbal root. The verbal root can be compared with the pulsating which expands its life-force to the extremities, the limbs, the prefixes, and suffixes. All of them fulfill their own individual functions, but corroborate or modify each other in cooperation."

11. An analysis of Scherer's views and stature is given by Basch (1889).

12. In the seventh lecture Whitney had recognized two classes of original roots, one demonstrative or pronominal (ultimately indicative of position merely [deictic], as well as a class significant of action or being (p.258), the latter being, however, very much more numerous (p.259). The discussion being quoted here stresses qualities and does not mention parts of speech, but in the seventh lecture Whitney states that the predominant original class, "significant of action or quality", are styled predicative or verbal roots (258).

13. Such a dissenting voice was that of G. I. Ascoli, who wrote: "Noi dunque stimeremmo che il nome preesistesse in favella ariana al verbo. Per noi, il verbo ariano ricerverebbe un vasto e continuo sistema di formazioni nominali, di appelativi dell'agente; tutte le quali forme, da quella che appena può dirsi un'espansione del monosillabo primordiale, in sino alle ampie trisillabe, si ripeterebbero da elementi derivati che durano ancora con uguali funzioni in etá relativamente moderne" (1865: 33). The position of Ascoli is mentioned only in a footnote by Curtius (1867: 202-3).

14. Grasserie devoted a large part of his prolific literary output to the study of the verb and verbal categories in Indo-European and American Indian languages.

15. Pp.131, 134, 161, 270 ff. The notion that mental and linguistic development proceeds from the concrete to the abstract became a commonplace at the time of Wundt, as evidenced also by the later pronouncements of A. Meillet with regard to the development of verbal categories: "Le progrès de la civilisation met en évidence le temps; il tend à eliminer les catégories à valeur concrète ou expressive, et à donner aux catégories abstraites une importance du plus en plus grande" (1948: 176).

16. The full passage on the verb reads as follows: "Das Verbum ist also, wie ich darzulegen versucht habe, aus dem Nomen entstanden. Wir sind nun in der glücklichen Lage, solche Sprachen ohne Verba vor unseren Augen zu

haben. Im Griechischen und Lateinischen ist der Nominativ oder Akkusativ mit dem Infinitiv weit verbreitet, und er zeigt uns eine eigentümliche Ausdrucksweise. . .Gegeniiber dem. . .Griechischen und Lateinischen verwenden die modernen Sprachen vielmehr das Verbum finitum. Infinitive und Partizipien spielen heute eine viel geringere Rolle als im Altertum" (Hirt 1939: 110-11).

REFERENCES

Aarsleff, Hans. 1967. The study of language in England, 1780-1860. Princeton.

[Appollonius Dyscolus]. 1878. Appollonii Dyscoli quae supersunt. . . scripta minora. Grammatici Graeci, 1. (ed. Richard Schneider). Leipzig.

Arnauld, Antoine and Claude Lancelot. 1810. Grammaire générale et raisonée de Port Royal. 6th ed. Paris.

Ascoli, G. I. 1867. Studii ario-semitici. Classe di lettere del Reale Instituto Lonrbardo. 10. Milano.

Basch, Victor. 1889. Wilhelm Scherer et la philologie allemande. Paris—Nancy.

Benfey, Theodor. 1860. Ein Abschnitt aus meiner Vorlesung über vergleichende Grammatik der indogermanischen Sprachen, Zeitschrift für vergleichende Sprachforschung. 9: 81-132.

———. 1869. Geschichte der Sprachwissenschaft. München.

Bernhardi, A. F. 1805. Anfangsgründe der Sprachwissenschaft. Berlin.

Bréal, Michel. 1897. Essai de sémantique. Paris.

———. 1900. Les commencements du verbe. Mémoires de la Société de Linguistique de Paris. 11: 268-284.

Brinton, D. G. 1885. The philosophical grammar of American languages, as set forth by Wilhelm von Humboldt. Philadelphia.

———. 1888. The language of paleolithic man. Proceedings of the American Philosophical Society 25: 212-224. Reprinted as "The earliest form of human speech, as revealed by American tongues", in Brinton, Essays of an Americanist (Philadelphia, 1891), 390-409.

Bury, J. B. 1928. The idea of progress. An inquiry into its origin and growth. London.

Cassirer, Ernst. 1932a. Die Philosophie der Aufklärung. Tübingen.

———. 1932b. Die platonische Renaissance in England und die Schule von Cambridge. Leipzig—Berlin.

Chakravarti, P. Ch. 1930. The philosophy of Sanskrit grammar. Calcutta.

Colebrooke, H. T. 1805. A grammar of the Sanskrit language. 1. Calcutta.

Condillac, Étienne B. de. 1798. 2nd ed. Essai sur l'origine des connaissances humaines. Oeuvres. Paris.

Couturat, L. 1901. La logique de Leibniz d'après des documents inédits. Paris.

———. 1903. Opuscules et fragments inédits de Leibniz. Paris.

Curtius, Georg. 1867. Zur Chronologie der indogermanischen Sprachforschung. Leipzig.

Delbrück, Berthold. 1880. 1893. (3rd. ed.). Einleitung in das Sprachstudium; ein Beitrag zur Geschichte und Methodik der vergleichenden Sprachforschung. Leipzig.

Destutt de Tracy, Comte. 1825. Éléments d'idéologie. Paris.

Egger, E. 1854. Apollonius Dyscole: essai sur l'histoire des théories grammaticales dans l'antiquité. Paris.

Fick, August. 1881. (November 9). Gelehrte Anzeigen. München.

Geiger, Lazarus. 1869. Der Ursprung der Sprache. Stuttgart.

Gerretzen, J. G. 1940. Schola hemsterhusiana. Utrecht.

Ginneken, Jac. Van. 1907. Principes de linguistique psychologique. Paris–Leipzig–Amsterdam.

Grasserie, Raoul de la. 1914. Du verbe comme générateur des autres parties du discours (du phénomène au noumène). Paris.

Hamann, Johann Georg. 1778-82. Briefwechsel, 4 (ed. A. Henkel). Wiesbaden. 1959.

Harnois, Guy. 1929 (?). Les théories du langage en France de 1660 à 1821. Paris.

Harris, James. 1751. 1765 (2nd ed.). (All quotations from 2nd ed.) Hermes, or a philosophical inquiry concerning languages and universal grammar. London.

⸺. An IV (1795). Hermès, ou recherches philosophiques sur la grammaire universelle. Ouvrage traduit de l'anglois, avec des remarques et des additions par François Thurot. Paris.

Heidegger, Martin. 1959. Introduction to metaphysics. (trans. R. Manheim). Princeton.

Heimann, Betty. 1964. Facets of Indian thought. London.

Herder, Johann Gottfried. 1879. [1782, 1783]. Vom Geist der Ebräischen Poesie. In Sämmtliche Werke, ed. B. Suphan, 11: 213-475, 12: 1-309. Berlin.

⸺. 1878. [1772]. Abhandlung über den Ursprung der Sprache. In Sämmtliche Werke, ed. B. Suphan, 5: 1-147. Berlin.

⸺. See Monboddo 1774.

Heyse, Karl W. L. 1856. System der Sprachwissenschaft. Berlin.

Hilpert, Walter. 1933. Johann Georg Hamann als Kritiker der deutschen Literatur. Königsberg.

Hirt, Herman. 1939. Die Hauptprobleme der indogermanischen Sprachwissenschaft. (ed. H. Arntz). Halle-Saale.

Humboldt, Wilhelm von. 1843. Über die Verschiedenheit des menschlichen Sprachbaues und ihren Einfluss auf die geistige Entwicklung des Menschengeschlechts. Gesammelte Werke 4. Berlin.

Jeruzalem, W. 1895. Urteilsfunktion. Wien.

Jodłowski, Stanisław. 1960. Kryteria klasyfikacji wyrazów na części mowy. Biuletyn polskiego towarzystwa językoznawczego 19: 51-980.

Lennep, Daniel Jo. 1808. Etymologicum linguae graecae, sive observationes ad singulas verborum nominumque stirpes. Leiden.

Meillet, A. 1948. [1920]. Sur les caractères du verbe. In: Linguistique historique et linguistique générale [I]. (Collection linguistique, La Société de Linguistique de Paris, 8). Paris.

Monboddo, James B. 1774. (2nd ed., 1809). Of the origin and progress of language. Edinburgh. (German trans., 1784, with introduction by Johann Gottfried Herder).

Mullally, Joseph P. 1945. The Summulae Logicales of Peter of Spain. Notre Dame.

Muller, Max F. 1912. (2nd ed.). A history of ancient Sanskrit literature. Allahabad.

Nilsson, N. Å. 1970. The Russian Imaginists. Stockholm.

Ogden, C. K. 1959. Bentham's theory of fictions. New Jersey.

Ong, Walter J. 1958. Ramus' method and the decay of dialogue. Cambridge, Mass.

Pagliaro, Antonino. 1959-60. Teoria della lingua e grammatica. Corso di glottologia. Rome.

Peškovskij, A. M. 1956. Russkij sintaksis v naučnom osveščenii. Moscow.

――――. 1959. Glagol'nost' kak vyrazitel'noe sredstvo, Izbrannye trudy. Moscow.

Potebnja, A. A. 1888. (2nd ed.). Iz zapisok po russkoj grammatike 1-2. Moscow.

Pott, August F. 1833-36. Etymologische Forschungen auf dem Gebiete der indo-germanischen Sprachen. . . .

[Priscianus]. 1857-80. Prisciani grammatici Caesariensis Institutionum grammaticarum libri XIII–XVIII ex recensione Martini Herzii. Grammatici latini III. (ed. Heinrich Keil). Leipzig.

Raumer, R. von. 1870. Geschichte der germanischen Philologie, vorzugsweise in Deutschland. München.

Sapir, Edward. 1921. Language. New York.

Sayce, A. H. 1879. Introduction to the science of language. London.

Scherer, Wilhelm. 1890. Zur Geschichte der deutschen Sprache. Wien.

Schuchardt, Hugo. 1922. (ed. L. Spitzer). Hugo Schuchardt-Brevier, Ein Vademecum der allgemeinen Sprachwissenschaft. Halle–Saale. (chapter vi, Sprachursprung).

Steinthal, M. 1850. Die Classifikation der Sprachen dargestellt als die Entwicklung der Sprachidee. Berlin.

――――. 1855. Grammatik, Logik, und Psychologie, ihre Principien und ihr Verhältnis zu einander. Berlin.

――――. 1860. Charakteristik der hauptsächlichen Typen des Sprachbaus. Berlin.

Swift, Jonathan. 1961. [1726]. Gulliver's travels. (ed. R. A. Greenberg). New York.

Thurot, François. See James Harris, An IV.

Trabalza, Ciro. 1908. Storia della grammatica italiana. Milano.

Verburg, Pa. A. 1949-50. The background of the linguistic conceptions of Bopp. Lingua II(4).

Vico, Giambattista. 1961. (trans. T. G. Bergin and N. H. Fisch). The new science. New York.

Westphal, Rudolf. 1873. Das indogermanische Verbum. Jena–Oxford–Paris.

Whitney, William Dwight. 1891. Language and the study of language. New York. [First published, 1867].

Wundt, W. 1900. Völkerpsychologie. Die Sprache.

_____. 1901. Sprachgeschichte und Sprachpsychologie, mit Rücksicht auf B. Delbrück's *Grundfragen der Sprachforschung*. Leipzig.

6. Vicissitudes of Paradigms

Pieter A. Verburg

> To my surprise that exposure to out-of-date scientific theory and practice radically undermined some of my basic conceptions about the nature of science.
>
> Kuhn (1962:vii)

Introduction

Kuhn's story of the radical change in his outlook reminded me of my own experience: I have only to substitute "language" for "science" to make the description fit my own case. Moreover I found that at the time Kuhn, like myself, was very much impressed by the writings of Emile Meyerson (1859–1933), the French scholar who, on the threshold of this century, together with Emile Boutroux (1845–1921), Henri Poincaré (1854–1912), and Pierre Duhem (1861–1916), critically undermined the prevailing positivistic dogma.

Since in almost any description or discussion of philosophy or knowledge in general after World War II the theory of language plays a key role, and since the reason for the study of history lies in the acquisition of a deeper insight into the present, the theme of "Revolution versus continuity in the study of language" appears to be topical and important. In this contribution to that theme we will trace, very briefly, the ups and downs of the theories of language—hence the title, "Vicissitudes of paradigms"—first, as they occurred in Western thought from Antiquity until the birth of the specific discipline of language, i.e., linguistics, at the beginning of the last century, and secondly, from then until the present day. In the second period, because many disciplines either continue or start to occupy themselves with language problems, the "paradigms" become very numerous and difficult to survey, let alone to arrange critically. For the pre-linguistic period, from Antiquity to around 1830, the author was able to rely on his book *Taal en functionaliteit. Een historisch-critische Studie orer de opvattingen aangaande de Functies der Taal* (1952; English translation forthcoming). There the texts are analyzed and references are given which could not be included within the restricted scope of this paper.

SOME PRELIMINARY REMARKS ON THE GENERAL THEME

In the history of the vicissitudes of thought we come across trends that are *continuations* of ideas of many centuries standing on the one hand, and with new *revolutionary* ideas that seem to break radically with the past on the other hand. We believe, however, that continuity and revolution are not, strictly speaking, direct opposites. More complex "vicissitudinal" conceptions are needed. These we can show in terms of the different values of two binary oppositions, one of "enchrony", one of "modality."

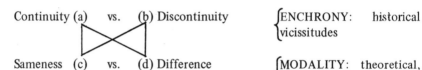

Continuity (a)   vs.   (b) Discontinuity $\begin{cases} \text{ENCHRONY:} \quad \text{historical} \\ \text{vicissitudes} \end{cases}$

Sameness   (c)   vs.   (d) Difference $\begin{cases} \text{MODALITY:} \quad \text{theoretical,} \\ \text{paradigmatic content} \end{cases}$

By definition, of course, (a) and (b) are mutually exclusive, so also are (c) and (d). The possible combinations give us four kinds of situations:

a c = Continuity + Sammeness $\begin{cases} \text{Persistence:conservation, lasting} \\ \text{immutability; "aere perennius".} \end{cases}$

b c = Discontinuity + Sameness $\begin{cases} \text{Reoccurrence: intermittent iden-} \\ \text{tity; "l'histoire se répète".} \end{cases}$

a d = Continuity + Difference $\begin{cases} \text{Evolution: continuous change,} \\ \text{imperceptible transition; "panta} \\ \text{rei".} \end{cases}$

b d = Discontinuity + Difference $\begin{cases} \text{Revolution: sudden change, a-} \\ \text{brupt alteration; "uniqueness",} \\ \text{"Einmaligkeit".} \end{cases}$

We can find instances of all these relationships of processes in history in general. The history of Western thought about language is no exception.

THE STUDY OF LANGUAGE AND THE PARADIGMS

In the beginning of Western culture the study of language was the task of philosophers and philologists, and more especially of the former, since philology was largely a school subject within the framework of the *artes liberales*, at least through the Middle Ages. The different themes and their continuities, revolutions, etc., that we want to describe must therefore be traced mainly in the works of philosophers until linguistics proper develops at the beginning of the nineteenth century.

Doctrinal theories of language resulted in *two* main trends, stretching back to the old philosophic opposition between Heraclitus (c.540–c.480 B.C.) and the Eleatic school (Parmenides, c.504 B.C.). The controversy may be called *genetic dynamism* or *functionalism* on the one hand versus a *static elementarism* or *"entitarism"* on the other hand. These two views are encoded in common language today, for example, the universe is *Wirklichkeit* (i.e., "what works") in German and reality (i.e., "things") in English. (We can see a kind of scientific reconciliation in the complementarity thesis of present day micro-physics.) The dilemma seems to occur pretty well everywhere and appears to be founded in some ontic and existential duality; thus it is no surprise to find it in the historical paradigms—or "models"—of the study of language.

After the Renaissance new disciplines appeared so that when linguistics proper emerged there were many other sciences around. Sometimes one of them would paradigmatically influence or even dominate language study. Examples are physics, biology, psychology. The impact of these diciplines results in a different sort of paradigm from the kinds that are a consequence of philosophical doctrines. We must keep this in mind when considering the theories of language in the nineteenth and twentieth centuries. As a rule the impact is gradually neutralized and incorporated into a specific sub-discipline within authentic linguistics. In this way sub-disciplines such as physical and organic phonetics as well as phonemics—counterparts of physics, biology, and psychology respectively—were integrated in linguistics.

Antiquity

PLATO (427–347 B.C.)

In the oldest Western monograph about the study of language, Plato's *Kratylos*, which deals with the *orthotès* (rightness) or *alètheia* (truth) of words, we come across the continuation of the controversy between Heraclitus and the Eleatics. Plato, more or less along the lines of Heraclitus, regards language as *legein* (speaking) that confronts the things meant as *diakrinein* (discerning) and human beings as *didaskein* (teaching).

Reality (Things) ← diakrinein : *legein* : didaskein → Other people
(cognitive)   (communicative)

Although Plato concentrates mainly on the discerning character of language, we have to give him credit for having also observed, in the didactic function, the socio-communicative character of language.

In the stream of *diacritical* legein the *onomata* (words) materialize as *organa* (tools). Tools are judged for appropriateness by checking whether they fit a task. Plato tries to elaborate his tool theory by setting up comparisons with other tools, but he does not feel happy about it. In our opinion this is because he fails to see that organizing, instrumental, operational faculty and function, as embedded in our locution—in legein—maintains its functional character, though in a bound and underlying way.

In his etymologies Plato starts by considering words to have been in an earlier stage *rhèmata*, i.e., phrases, that have been "thingified" in one-word-units. Dissection of the restored rhèmata yields unanalyzable elements, *onomata prota* (first, original words), which are only subject to reduction along the lines of Plato's well-known *mimetic* (imitating) and portraying sound-symbolism. So Plato's search for the orthotès or truth of words ends in the blind alley of a pictorial *adaequatio* (equation) of sounds and things meant.

Plato's theories and methods keep wavering between Heraclitan functionalism and Eleatic entitarism. Especially by focusing on *diakrinein* as an aspect of *legein* Plato turns away from the former toward the latter; all the same he did not quite forget the more anthropological aspect of *didaskein*: the teaching of others. He also draws attention to the role of the speaker—though perfunctorily.

In *Kratylos* 422 E Plato remarks that if we were deaf and dumb, but wanted (*eboulometha*) to clarify (*dèloun*) affairs (*ta pragmata*) we would contrive to signify (*sèmainein*, verb derived from *sèma*) by means of our heads, hands, feet, etc. There is a subsumption here, though implicitly, of natural speech—and gestures—under the normative notion of *dèlosis*, i.e., clarification. The actualization of *dèlosis* depends on man's will (*boulesthai*). Regrettably Plato did not elaborate this finalist view; he kept to cognitive rightness or truth. However, in his later dialogues Plato gave up his efforts to find orthotès or alètheia (truth) in words. Only the sentence, or rather, the proposition could be true or false. And so he almost reached the point from which his disciple Aristotle started.

ARISTOTLE (384–322 B.C.)

In Aristotle's theory a statement consists of a subject – (copula) – predicate. His categorizing principle (*kategoreuma* = *praedicatum*) holds for his logic as well as for his view on language, even for his ontology; in the latter it was parallel to substance and its properties. In this theory the Eleatic tradition plays an important part. Reality, thought, and lingual description are looked upon as congruent to such a degree that they seem to be telescoped into one. Also there is little room for the actuality of thinking and speaking. The thought process by means of which a conclusion is reached was not adequately pictured in the structure of syllogism.

It has been said that language was to Aristotle what mathematics was to Plato. In any case it was an Aristotelian logic that, so to speak, scientifically legitimized (especially by means of the form-matter scheme) the old pre-scientific and undifferentiated logos-notion which covered both thought and language. To Aristotle every man experiences the same world of things; every man thinks things with the same thoughts; only the sound of the words that represent the thoughts is different in different languages.

Plato's ideas on language remained a brilliant endeavor, not a completed theory, though certain features were sometimes remembered centuries after. Aristotle's writings about logic provided doctrinal theorems arranged systematically with great didactic talent. They dominated the Middle Ages, and have continued to play a part until the present day. One might even regard the history of the study of language as a struggle for liberation from Aristotelian dogmas. We will not dwell upon these matters here; in the section devoted to the Middle Ages we shall return to the Aristotelian tradition.

RHETORIC

Rhetoric never developed a philosophical theory of language; nevertheless it established a strong and persistent, though rather fluctuating, tradition. It originated from the teaching practices of the sophists; and it is as old as Socrates (*c*.470–*c*.399 B.C.) himself. Plato had contemplated the *onomata* as *organa*; the sophists and their successors, the rhetores, experienced and taught speech as an instrumental use of language, as a human ability, not only for the transfer of cognitive information but also for practical persuasion, to influence their hearers' decisions and actions.

Thus, while Plato and Aristotle searched for truth in language, the rhetores were interested in the practical effects of speech: *ton hèttō logon kreittō poiein* (to turn the weak argument into a strong one). Rhetoric is not so much concerned with knowledge like the doctrines of the Academy or the Lyceum; it is more of a skill, more human, more practical. Plato hated rhetoric; Aristotle incorporated it in his philosophy, "kicking it upstairs".

STOICS AND EPICUREANS

Since both schools were at least initially interested in Roman conduct rather than in abstract theories, they are classified as ethical schools.

There is an old division, probably of Stoic origin, passed on through the Middle Ages by way of the encyclopaedias, springing up again later in, for example, Locke (1632–1704) and Leibniz (1646–1716), and forming the background of Kant's (1724–1804) "Kritiken", namely,

Practica sive ethica / Logica / Physica.

To the *Stoa* the universe is full of *dynameis,* which work in a determinist way. Language, in spite of its more dynamic character compared with thinking proper, seems to be dealt with under logic, although Stoic logic, apparently as a consequence of the dynamic principle, deals with simple propositions and hypothetical reasonings rather than subject–predicate statements and syllogisms. This same principle also made the Stoics defend the allegorical use of language. Furthermore they thought that language had to proclaim truth, and in so doing they kept close to speech—and rhetoric. Their *etymon* is not identical with Plato's *onoma prōton* and there is much reason to attribute *anomaly* to the Stoic view, *analogy* to the Aristotelian.

The Epicurean theory is not dynamistic, but atomistic, and instead of the Stoic determinism Epicureans cherish a similarly dogmatic *tychism* (the doctrine of contingency). To them language is only of cognitive value insofar as it contains sensorily acquired and, in this sense, verifiable knowledge.

FATE OF SOME OF THESE DOCTRINES

What about the continuity or the disappearances and reappearances of these linguistic doctrines? As for Plato, one may ask whether he had a definite linguistic doctrine at all. The ironical style of his etymologies puzzled many people; nevertheless this kind of etymology continued to the end of the last century in spite of many Bopps and Potts and root- and stem-theories. To Plato, his "etymologies"–-better termed "rhèmatic analyses"—were merely an intermediate stage between the ordinary words and the *onomata prōta.* In the third stage of his analysis, sound-symbolism, he must have been serious since he started in search of the truth in words, and thought he could apply his theory of *mimesis* to the *onomata prōta.* Sound-symbolism reappeared now and then, as we will see, and will always find consideration among psychologists. The tool theory vanished for a considerable time and so did the concept of *dèlosis* (clarity).

PHILOLOGY

Aristotle's taxonomy of disciplines likely fostered the philology of Alexandria. The first grammatical *technai* ("arts") which distinguished and elaborated word classes (Dionysios Thrax, first century B.C.) and initiated the study of syntax (Apollonios Dyscolos, second century A.D.) originated there. But Alexandria became isolated from philosophy and logic and started its own tradition: philology and grammar. Grammar became one of the *artes sermocinales* ("linguistic" abilities) of the Trivium, especially during the Roman Empire. It continued as such in the Middle Ages and kept its position in the schools and in education through the ages; in a way philology and grammar were precursors of linguistics.

Few places are so conservative as schools. So for renewals in the study of language we had better consider again the impact of philosophy and logic, at least before the genesis of linguistics proper. Aristotle had distinguished two genuine parts of speech: nomen (noun, onoma) and verbum (verb, rhèma), being praedicabilia, that is, they could serve as elements in an S-P proposition. Propositions of this kind he "computed" into syllogisms. It may be correct that the truth of the conclusion is dependent on the truth of the premises, but matter-of-fact speculation about concrete sublunar things and their properties ran only a small risk of error. Aristotle, in contrast to Plato, took little interest in nebulous *transcendentalia*. For that reason the medieval Church could easily accommodate Aristotle *in naturalibus* because he generally left the supernatural alone.

CHURCH FATHERS

Clement (*c*.150 A.D.) and especially Origen (185/186–254/255 A.D.) developed theories of allegorical interpretation based on Philo Judaeus (*c*.25 B.C.–*c*.40 A.D.) who, in his turn, was influenced by Stoic paradigms.

Augustine (354–430 A.D.) borrowed more from Platonism, actually from neo-Platonism. With him we find a new sign concept: a creature is *signum Dei* and symbolizes supernatural reality. But God is beyond any categorizing, and human logic has to give in to revealed paradox.

The Middle Ages, 500–1500 (1400)

After the fall of the Roman Empire and in the centuries of cultural disorder that followed, the study of languages was abandoned until the twelfth century. The Church had to teach culture to barbarians as well as to preach faith to unbelievers: Scholasticism. Latin was the language, and it derived its authority and credibility from divine language, the Holy Writ, the Truth. In the first half of the Middle Ages *sermo, verbum,* or *locutio* is defined as *intellectus, mens,* or *cogitatio exterior*; and, conversely, *intellectus,* etc., as *sermo,* etc., *interior.*

About 1100 there was a revival of "belles lettres" in Chartres and Orléans, and some Platonic influence appeared. This revival anticipated the Humanist movement some centuries later.

The first century of the Crusades resulted in a widening of the cultural horizon and a renewed interest in knowledge. In the thirteenth and fourteenth centuries the *universalia* controversy drew attention once more to language and grammar, both from the realist and the nominalist standpoint.

REALISM

The *Grammatica Speculativa* is in the main realistic, and its writers are known as *Modistae*. The term Grammatica Speculativa, though of a later date, is correct, if one bears in mind that "speculari" is the term for the "mirroring" experience of concrete physical things. Thus Grammatica Speculativa means a grammar which is as reliable as a record of factual things and real facts.

The well-known three *modi*, which gave the speculative grammarians their name—*modus essendi, modus intelligendi,* and modus significandi— justify the following basic paradigm:

Reality/Things → Intellect/Thoughts → Language/Signs
(spoken language → written words)

Although there is some room left for an active modus intelligendi, the basic concept is the *tabula rasa* theory: the modus intelligendi passively receives impressions from the modus essendi, and passes them on to the modus significandi; thus language is an expression of thought; the intellect is a transitional phase. There is a radical congruence between the modi: *materialiter et realiter congruent.* Consequently the basic attitude toward language is fiducial. Language is regarded as words, intellect as thoughts, and reality as things; a concrete thing is thought of in a subsistent image which results in a substantive noun.

Basically this is a justification of the traditional classification of words with the help of Aristotle's *categories*. Our main objection is , that the human agent is not taken into account. We find a static, non-dynamic theory, coming from a crypto-hearer's standpoint. The three modi are equated to such a degree that language, at least categorically, appears as a static reflection of an ontology which in its turn is a rigid, immutable concept of the world.

NOMINALISM

Whereas the realistic grammar just described is a logical grammar, its counterpart, the nominalistic language theory, is a grammatical logic; its attitude toward common language is not fiducial but critical; it is less static and more dynamic, less entitary and more functional, less Aristotelian and more Stoic. The nominalist model is twofold:

I Reality/Things ←———————————— Intellect/Thinking
II Reality/Things ← Language/"nomina" ← Intellect/Thinking

(I) illustrates the thesis that the intellect can know reality in a direct authentic way; this enabled the nominalist to posit his axiom as to the individual constituents of reality. (II) analysis of reality is also possible by means of naming-items ("nomina") as lingual labels for things, on the understanding, however, that nothing real corresponds to a general or universal nomen like "homo".

Although nominalism is critical of language, realists and nominalists agree (cf. the realist model) that language is expression of thoughts. The difference is, that in realist theory the intellect expresses language under the impression of reality, whereas in nominalist theory the intellect is spontaneously initiating and freely deciding whether to express its thoughts lingually or not. Thus, nominalism takes up the speaker's position, although the human factor as such is not represented in the theory. Anthropologically, the nominalist theory is therefore as unsatisfactory as the realist theory. Both theories neglect the human factor. In the nominalist case, even an active intellect is not identical with the human self. Both theories regard the world as a set of entities, and only disagree on the reality of universals.

William of Occam (c. 1300–c.1350), for example, rejected the reproach of heresy and of modernism and claimed to be a faithful and even better interpreter of Aristotle than his adversaries. However, he did not accept the Aristotelian congruence theory and he did not telescope language, thought, and reality into one. Prantl (*Geschichte der Logik im Abendlande*, Leipzig 1855–70) believed that the so-called "logica modernorum" was influenced by Byzantine rhetoric. We now know that this logic is essentially of Stoic origin and thus a reappearance of old ideas rather than a revolution.

Humanism and Renaissance, 1400–1600

HUMANISM

Humanism originated mainly from a revival of rhetoric which formed part of the Trivium, which in its turn was a part of the cyclical curriculum of the schools. During the Middle Ages on the whole the two other components of the Trivium, dialectics and grammar, were considered more important. Rhetoric was only emphasized in passing during the literary movement of Chartres and Orléans (see above). Since Quintilian (*c*.35–*c*.100 A.D.) rhetoric had been the guardian angel of belles lettres, and as Humanism mainly harked back to Quintilian, the rise of Humanism resulted in friction with the medieval Scholastics, who neither spoke nor wrote a very elegant Latin.

Valla (1407–1457) was a professor of rhetoric; he had to educate his pupils to eloquence, that is, literally: well-speaking. Speech was considered an ability for a task which involved the pursuit of an optimum; all this resulted in a functionalistic and normative view of language. It was natural for Valla, faced with ugly medieval Latin, to set the ideal of an elegant, select, regenerated classical Latin: an esthetical finalism of *pulchre loqui*. This indeed was a revival of the Quintilian paradigm.

Erasmus (1466–1536) developed a more profound view. He had grown up in the atmosphere of the ethical revival of the Devotio Moderna in the Low Countries. An essay of his, *De Linguae Usu et Abusu*, moralizes that we should not lie, slander, etc., but it does not say what the authentic optimum of language is or should be. Many Humanists have left us manuals on the art of writing letters, packed with precepts and advice. These were intended for the lettered and the unlettered, for the diplomat as well as the kitchenmaid. Erasmus too wrote such a manual, *De Conscribendis Epistulis*, a work which has so far remained pretty well unnoticed, as indeed has Erasmus the linguist. In this manual he does state what the normative optimum is. Three cardinal virtues are concerned: *Perspicuitas* (!), *Compositio, Elegantia*.

Vives (1492–1540) opened the door for the vernaculars. Valerius van Oudewater (1512–1578) and Pierre de la Ramée (1515–1572) wrote Humanistic encyclopaedias for teaching purposes. However, Humanism was never a general philosophical trend. Any logical claim to an adequate intellectual and dialectical reflection or analysis of things disappeared; thinking neither enhances nor overgrows language any more. Instead, clarifying and/or artistic speaking and/or writing avails itself of and molds thought for its own aims. Humanism started as a revival of speech as a human function, and as such was something of a revolution, for that matter a palace revolution within the Trivium, that is, within teaching. As an educational movement it gave cultural self-confidence to the third estate. But it eventually sterilized itself by concentrating on the philology of the classical languages. Nevertheless the issues of the Humanistic interest in teaching temporarily re-humanized society's attitude toward language.

The genuine novelty of Humanism is that it sees language, whether spoken or written, as a normative or teleotic function. This is accompanied by the characterization of the human being as animal *loquens*—especially by

Erasmus—in the ethical sense of a person who assumes responsibility for his lingual acts. The Humanist language model takes this shape:

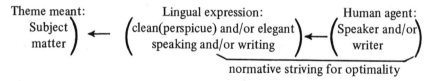

Moreover, we have here what is initially a pronounced speaker's standpoint, which, alas, was being undermined even in Erasmus' time by the literary imitators of classical Latin, the *simiae Ciceronis*.

During a period of three to four centuries, the Humanistic language revival became bogged down in the highly respected Classical Philology conducted on Latin and Greek texts, and the Humanistic view of language gradually changed from dynamic to static. Free functional normativity in active speech deteriorates into a pseudo-normativity of prescriptive grammatical rules, derived from classical texts by docile readers who want to write impeccable Latin. In Classical Philology language turned from an *ars* (ability) into a *scientia* (knowledge), and the speaker's standpoint shifted to the hearer's, or rather the reader's.

Humanism shares with Nominalism emphasis on spontaneous human mental activity; it shares with Realism the fiducial attitude toward language; its own contribution is a dynamic, normative view of language as an elucidative revelation of what a person means to say.

RENAISSANCE

Although in cultural history the ideologies of Humanism and the Renaissance were first intermingled and hardly kept apart, one gradually became compelled to distinguish them because of the fundamentally different principles. But it was only about a hundred years ago that Michelet, Voigt, and Burckhardt began to differentiate between the two.

The Renaissance ranges roughly from Leonardo da Vinci (1452–1519) to Francis Bacon (1561–1626) and has a scientific and political aspect. Whereas Humanism is, as we have seen, a functional revival, a lingual movement, the Renaissance is a revolutionary and existential attitude and outlook on life and the world, a genuine rebirth of Man. Like Humanism, the Renaissance finally lost the impetuousness and rashness of its earlier years; this meant that the ideal of man as a heroic and dynamic personality, independent and free from the restraints of law or norm, was gradually replaced by the ideal of man as a free thinker, whose autonomous reason was the highest authority.

At the end of the period (1400—1600) a philosopher drew up a balance sheet and at the same time gave an estimate for the future. This threshold philosopher was Francis Bacon. It is not sufficiently known that in his *Novum Organon* and *Division Scientiarum* Francis Bacon, besides turning against Aristotelian Scholasticism, also turned against the rival encyclopaedias of Humanism. The most important Humanistic encyclopaedias were those of Valerius van Oudewater and Pierre de la Ramée, and in my opinion (cf. the author's article, 1961) Bacon's polemics are directed against these authors. According to the *Organon*, language is *"traditio cogitationum"*, a concept which real Humanists abhorred; to Bacon language once more became the *"ancilla logicae"*. As a result of this reversal to nominalism Bacon designed his theory of fallacies as a warning against the pitfalls in natural language that endanger accurate and adequate thinking (cf. our Nominalism diagram). Bacon's much praised empiricism in the knowledge of nature operates with hardly a modern idea of form, although it is linked with an elimination method which is modern indeed; it is, however, only a vague prophecy of the scientific analyses and experimental investigations of the seventeenth and eighteenth century. Nevertheless we may regard him as a forerunner of rationalism.

Francis Bacon's scheme runs as follows:

$$\text{Speaker/Writer} \rightarrow \frac{\text{Discourse as}}{\textit{vehicle} \text{ of } \textit{thoughts}} \rightarrow \text{Hearer/Reader}$$

Like Nominalism Bacon is critical of language and therefore recommends checking for contraband; the Humanist idea of the superiority of language over thought was dismissed, though a recognition of the interhuman communicative role of language was retained.

Rationalism

SCIENTIAL RATIONALISM

From the seventeenth century onwards rationalism (cf. the author's article, 1968) overran philosophy: a real revolution, as we shall see. This began with the research of Galileo (1564—1641) and other thinkers, especially in the field of macro-motion. Their impact is comparable to that of Einstein and his contemporaries at the beginning of this century. Galileo was the father of modern mechanics. Mathematics had survived the Middle Ages in the two quadrivial elementary school subjects of arithmetic and geometry. Despite the Pythagorean and Platonic traditions, philosophers were not interested and kept to the Aristotelian logico-verbal observations. As against them Galileo applied mathematics as a means of counting and measuring and of exactly describing and explaining his observations and experiments on motion. Galileo was fully aware that he broke the chains of the medieval "words, words". He repeatedly remarked that the book of Nature—an obvious reference to the "bookish" pseudo-knowledge of Scholasticism and Humanism—was written in numerals and figures, that is, in mathematical characters or symbols. And so physicists grew certain that they had found the key to the secrets of nature: applied mathematics.

Philosophy appropriated the new scientific discoveries, but went too far by trying to make the key of "la bonne science" (Descartes, 1596-1650) fit the universe at large, thus including the practica sive ethica sive moralia (see the above section on Stoics.). The most striking example of this universalized mathematical approach is Spinoza's (1632–1677) *Ethica*, in which he discusses even ethics *"more geometrico"*.

The development, since Nominalism, of the paradigmatic views of language in its diacritical and cognitive function (see the section on Plato) took the following shape:

1. Nominalism II : Reality ← (Natural Language / Signs (words)) ← Intellect

2. Galileo et al. : Physics ← (Mathematical (artificial) symbols) ← Intellect / Reason

3. Philosophers of : Reality   "Symbols" in
   sciential (i.e.,   (Physica ← general, incl.   ← Ratio
   mathematical)   and   natural signs
   Rationalism   Practica)

Not only physical phenomena but also "politica" and other "practica" now became calculable—and predictable! Did not Galileo regard the universe as an accurately working *horologium*? In theology the consequence was Deism. In natural philosophy determinism and predictability combined with atomism, another remarkable novelty of the seventeenth century's revolution.

Since Antiquity the combinations had been:

Epicureans : atomism + tychism (as a theory of contingency)
Stoics   : dynamism + determinism (including predictability)

But now Epicurean atomism, divorced from tychism, married Stoic determinism which in its turn had been divorced from dynamism. From now on the new complementarity became atomism + determinism (see section on Heraclitus vs. the Eleatics; cf. van Mater 1958).

HOBBES (1588–1679), DESCARTES (1596–1650)

The first philosopher to apply the new model to language was Hobbes (cf. the author's article, 1970). *Ratio* in the sense of a counting mind, operating as a mental calculus, became the keyword. Arithmetical and geometrical symbolism functioned as the noo-intellectual instrument par excellence, a means of *invention*[1] for reason in its approach to reality:

$$\text{REALITY} \longleftarrow \text{SYMBOLS} \longleftarrow \text{REASON}$$

The certainty in natural science was now based upon accurate calculation with mathematical symbols, characters, marks, "notae". This certainty, according to Hobbes, could also be attained with the help of natural words, provided they were used rationally (cf. the Platonic *diakrinein*). Was not Adam's "first use of speech" a correct diacritical use of "names" as marks or notes, of words as "counters"? To Hobbes words are essentially fit to perform (*praestant*) this counting function. *Ratiocinari* (reasoning) about reality is a calculus (i.e., adding and subtracting) with words. In this inventive way one acquires science. The varying and arbitrary shape of words in different languages presents no problem; it is the consistent calculus with words that counts. Of course, metaphors and "tropoi" should be avoided because of their inconstancy. Only fools value words by the authority of an Aristotle, a Cicero or a Thomas.

It is clear that Hobbes subsumed natural words belonging to a natural language under the concept of an artificial symbolism consisting of marks or notae like Galileo's mathematical numerals and figures. This subsumptional fallacy may be compared to a statement like "Look how this mother resembles her daughter! ", while only the inverse assimilation is correct. The creation of mathematical symbols, whether applied to physics or not, is feasible just because man possesses the natural faculty of language and lingual signification. Therefore only a subsumption of abstractive artificial symbolism under natural "symbolism", that is, lingual signification, seems correct.

Plato's functional distinction of *diakrinein* vs. *didaskein* returns in Hobbes' language model (see *Figure 1*). The common words function as notae (marks) in the rational calculus; this accurate and exact use is the privilege of philosophers: "words are wise men's counters" and therefore their specific means of invention. The same words are used as demonstrative "signs" toward other people in a loose and "foolish" way.

Figure 1

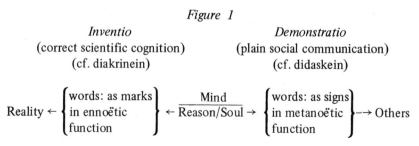

Inventio
(correct scientific cognition)
(cf. diakrinein)

Demonstratio
(plain social communication)
(cf. didaskein)

Descartes objected to Hobbes' inventional nota-theory and, as a better mathematician, for cognitive purposes, preferred genuine mathematical symbols. On the other hand Descartes opined that a reliable *demonstratio* might profit from an artificial language, though he was most skeptical about its realization because it had to wait until the development of the true philosophy was complete.

Indeed many artificial languages were drawn up in the seventeenth century. John Wilkins in his *An Essay towards a real charcter and a philosophical language* remarks that this real character and philosophical language "would prove the shortest and plainest way for the attainment of real knowledge! " Thus Wilkins, unlike Descartes, confidently assigns to his artificial language the task of invention.

LOCKE (1632–1704), LEIBNIZ (1646–1716)

Locke's attention was concentrated on *demonstratio*. He developed the principle of acquisition of knowledge by sensory perception into an empirical epistemology. From this viewpoint he investigated natural language words which did not lead him further than a registration of ideas analogous to the different sensory organs; nevertheless his ideal of knowledge remained the certainty of the mathematical sciences (cf. Gibson, *Locke's theory of knowledge and its historical relations*, Cambridge, 1917). Locke distinguished between a strict, that is, "philosophical" use of language and an inaccurate, that is, "civil" use. Both philosophical and civil use actually belong to the demonstrative application of natural language. Locke, like Bacon, resigned himself to the civil use of natural language, provided it is kept under rational philosophical control; consequently he points out—again like Bacon—certain fallacies. Descartes, however, had thought—though skeptically—that a correct artificial language for *demonstratio* might be practicable.

   The following is a diagrammatical presentation of the language problem
by sciential philosophy when Leibniz encountered it. Scholars' names have
been added to the subjects with which they were mainly concerned.

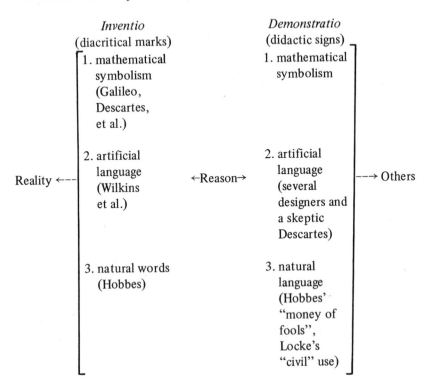

   A further attempt at gaining more rational insight into the essence of
language was made by the greatest genius of the seventeenth century, Leibniz,
a philosopher who was as competent a mathematician as he was a linguist.
Leibniz not only accepted Hobbes' inheritance but worked out the problems
which the latter had left unsolved. Therefore he tried to set up a real calculus
of ideas, a calculus ratiocinator, and to take stock of primary elementary
ideas, *"notiones primitivae,"* which are beyond analysis and definition, in
order to let them serve as elements in this calculus: these ideas would form an
alphabetum cognitationum (see Plato's onomata prōta). For this range of
ideas Leibniz seeks a universal, and consequently ideographic, representation:
a *characteristica universalis*. He experiments with notations of equally
unanalyzable prime numbers, which allow purely arithmetical dealings with
compound ideas. Whereas Hobbes had restricted his calculus to quasi-
syntactical adding and subtracting, Leibniz tried to let multiplication

correspond to combinatory lexical devices. His endeavors ran like the following example: let Change be 5, and Place 7, then Movement (as Change of Place) is 5 x 7 = 35. Let 2 be Entity, then a Moving Entity is 35 x 2 = 70. At another time we find Leibniz busy transposing notations into oral-aural code words. For example, he might substitute for 345: di-fe-ga. Here the third, fourth, and fifth consonants of the alphabet have been substituted for 3, 4, and 5, and added to these consonants are the vowels i, e, and a for the hundreds, tens, and units respectively. It is clear that five other sequences will also do, e.g., ga-fe-di, etc. By these games of transposition Leibniz ascertained that the six mark or sign systems (cf. the last diagram) were, in principle, interchangeable, especially as regards written and spoken signs or symbols. Consequently, Hobbes' fundamental opposition of cognitive-inventional use versus socio-communicative demonstration and his preference for the former were dismissed.

But Leibniz discovered that the creation and transposition of the notational marks and signs were easy compared with the difficulties that arose the moment he tried to operate with them syntactically; quite obviously the multiplication of prime numbers did not satisfy in this respect. In other words, he lacked an appropriate technique of combining, an operative syntax, an *"ars combinatoria"*. (For that reason he was very much interested in a predecessor in this "ars", Raymundus Lullus (1235–1315), a contemporary of Thomas Aquinas and an adherent of a realistic conception of language similar to that of the Grammatica Speculativa.)

Leibniz's search for a mathematically combinatorial technique resulted in postulating a universal omnipresent underlying grammatical system. He thought to have found it in a *"grammaire rationelle"*, which, in his opinion, underlay the seemingly defective and anomalous common languages as an original and universal basic order since the *lingua Adamica*. Leibniz saw this deep grammar as follows:

Materia: Elementa	*Forma: Relationes*
1. Nomina: Substantive	3. Particulae: Praepositiones
Pronomina	Coniunctiones
Adjectiva	Adverbia
	(local and temporal)
2. Verba: (void of Mode and Tense)	

The procedures he applied are often similar to the simplifications his contemporaries used in designing artificial languages; they often purified natural languages from all irregularities. Leibniz's aim was not to design an easily intelligible and simple grammar for demonstration and communication, but to detect the universal system in every language, which in his opinion, corresponded to both the ontic *ordo rerum* and the cognitive *ordo notionum*. This congruence of frameworks was Leibniz' *fundamentum veritatis*.

In this matter there are some similiarities and differences compared with the Grammatica Speculativa, which Leibniz knew and valued highly. Both grammars proclaimed congruence between the three "modi", but in the Grammatica Speculativa the congruence lay in the categoriality (in the Aristotelian sense) of elements (things / thoughts / words), while Leibniz was concerned with congruent relational frames or formal systems, which he saw as a mold of the constituent elements. Furthermore, there was the difference in the succession of the three orders:

Grammatica Speculativa : Things / → / Thoughts / → / Words
Leibniz :   Reality / ← / Symbolism or Language / ← / Reason

Gradually Leibniz' theory developed along the following lines:

a. The solely active and intentional intellect of Nominalism and its successor, namely, the likewise active and inventive reason put forward by Galileo and Hobbes, becomes in Leibniz' view also passive, impressionable, and receptive, just like the reflecting mirror-intellect of the realist Grammatica Speculativa. The former one-way relation between intellect / reason and reality becomes reciprocal (⇆).

b. Reason or reasoning and its symbolizing output, whether artificial or natural, are telescoped into one and reduced to one denominator: representation.

c. In a way anticipating the re-humanization of the language model by Rousseau and others, Leibniz introduces man as the most competent carrier of the representative power in terms of his monadology: the human monad (= unit). The outcome of this development may be summed up as follows:

Universe, incl. other monads) ⇆ Representation ⇆ Human Monad

In the three components of the final paradigm the underlying universal *ordo* remains an a priori guarantee of truth. With this, the application of the long-standing *verum-aut-falsum* criterion becomes pointless. Therefore Leibniz introduces a new criterion—which actually was not so new if we recall Plato's *dèloun* and Erasmus' *perspicuitas*. Leibniz had to account for the great variety among languages, natural or artificial, including symbolisms of any kind, regarding the degree to which their systems reveal the underlying universal *ordo*, and again for the differences, in the same respect, between individual and occasional locutional activities of one man compared with another's. Leibniz' criteriology describes quite elaborately the gradations between the two poles of *clarum* and *obscurum*, though the definitions of the gradations are kept in terms of rational cognition. Leibniz teaches that a fully clear monadic representation corresponds to an equally conscious "apperception" and a more obscure representation to a, less conscious, "perception". The existence of a representationally poor language he explains as a matter of "point de vue". When one sees a circle with some inscribed framework of figures from the side, the circle appears as an oval and the framework and its elements are presented in an obscuring optical distortion. Nevertheless the relations among its elements remain, in principle, proportionally adequate. Just so languages may be more or less clear in appearance, but their fundamental truth is unaffected.

Leibniz' theory was taught through the century of Enlightenment by his disciple Wolff (1679–1754). Although Wolff diluted much of Leibniz' thinking, he nevertheless had a widespread effect on his contemporaries, and not without reason he was called the second *praeceptor Germaniae* between Melanchthon (1497–1560) and Kant (1724–1804). Bopp (1791–1867), the founder of linguistics proper, acquired his doctrinal paradigms from Wolff.

PRACTICAL RATIONALISM

By the eighteenth century the practical disciplines, some just barely emerging, revolted against the preponderance of mathematics, e.g., ethics, law, aesthetics, economics, sociology, cultural studies; also pedagogics, medicine, architecture, and other "technologies". Their representatives regarded them not as static systems, but as domains of specific human faculties, energies, activities, dynameis, and the like. Empirical experience of enlightened common sense led to practical reliable knowledge, and for exact calculative investigations they had little use; one was content with the relative certainty of highest probability (vraisemblance) and did not need precise predictability. Even in the stronghold of natural science where Galileo (1564–1641) had scored his brilliant successes, the monopoly of mathematical mechanics was broken: for example, chemical experimenters proceeded by trial and error and drew their conclusions by arguments *per analogiam*. It was especially Dutch physicists like Chr. Huygens (1629–1695) Leeuwenhoek (1632–1723), Swammerdam (1637–1680), and Boerhaave (1668–1738), who advocated the new principles of analogy and probability, as P. Brunet very convincingly shows (1926).

As early as the end of the seventeenth century, the Port Royal scholars, anticipating this new spirit, considered grammar as "l'art de parler" and even logic as "l'art de penser"; that is, they introduced functional views. As regards language, dynamic *grammaire raisonnée* takes the place of the static *grammaire rationelle*.

It is with this principle of analogy that the grand old man of the eighteenth century's philosophical grammar, Condillac (1715–1780), operates. The application of this concept results in statements which form the practical counterpart of sciential theorems. For example, whereas Hobbes subsumed natural language under a mathematical symbolic system (language < mathematical symbolism), Condillac taught that mathematics, the pet of the scientialists, is a language: "le calcul, c'est une langue" (calcul < langue). No wonder that from Port Royal onwards and through the eighteenth century the dynamic rhetorical views of speech and the old Humanist traditions were revived.

The introduction to the *Hermes, or a philosophical inquiry concerning universal grammar* of Harris (*c.*1666–1719) is a very remarkable document of this revolution. He fights mathematics, and though he adheres to the idea of a universal grammar, there is little similarity to a concept like Wilkins'. Harris applies neo-Platonic theorems. He characterizes language as an *energeia*: "speech is the joint *Energy* of our best and noblest Faculties (that is to say, of our *Reason* and our *social Affection*)". In this twofold distinction something of the Platonic *diakrinein* vs. *didaskein* and mark / inventio vs. sign / demonstratio seems to survive.

Earlier than Harris, Shaftesbury (1671–1713) had drawn from the rhetorical humanist tradition: speech aspires to beauty (cf. Valla's and Erasmus' *elegantia*). Monboddo (1714–1799), whose impresario in Germany was Herder (1744–1803), regarded the systematic element in language, grammar, as an active form and a formative activity into which speech integrates. The higher the culture, the more thoroughly formed its language. But when Monboddo came across an exuberant, thoroughly formed language of primitive tribes (Guarani), he was at a loss. Herder translated Monboddo's idea of active formation as *"Vergewältigung der Welt"*. Monboddo's concept of a dynamic ordering as the most characteristic function of integrated speech is simply the dynamic, practicalist counterpart of the scientialist static order (ordo) or system of words and ideas of Leibniz and other seventeenth century philosophers.

From Doctrinal to Disciplinary Paradigms

SPIRITUALISTIC SENTIMENTALISM

Though Condillac already considered language as "une opération de l'âme", precision was still appreciated as the crowning glory of "la langue d'après la plus grande analogie", that is, algebra. Rousseau (1712–1778) rejects this view. In his *Essai sur l'Origine des Langues*, which was originally titled "Sur le principe de la mélodie", the first language was poetry, "une opération de l'esprit de l'homme en qualité d'agent libre". Corruption began when precision took the place of expression, "la clarté" (!) —this is the rationalized *claritas* of Descartes, Leibniz, Wolff, and others—instead of "la force et l'énergie", "convaincre au lieu d'émouvoir, représenter au lieu d'exciter". Language to Rousseau is again a living function, "une faculté", "une énergie". He reverts to Humanistic rhetoricism, when he observes its "effects", which in his view, however, result from its affective load, which is bound up with its musical intensity. Rousseau's language "effects" are not of a lingual nature, however, but really social. A language promotes or does not promote *la liberté, l'estime, la considération, la pitié, l'égalité,* etc. Rousseau considers the essential function of language to be "pour rendre—et pour exciter les *sentiments*".

At this point several observations about Rousseau's theory of language should be made:

1. The inventive diacritic approach has disappeared, demonstratio has remained.

2. a. Representative thought has made room for another, psychological characterization: "rendre des *sentiments*".

    b. This means that Rousseau was no longer a rationalist or even a practical rationalist, but rather a sentimentalist.

3. a. Rousseau introduced the human factor into his model, that is to say, he went further than his "enlightened" contemporaries who characterized speech as operation, activity, "action", but actually left the actor, the "agent", outside their concept.

    b. Rousseau did more. He introduced not only the speaker but also the hearer as the fellow-man upon whom the speaker operates. In this he goes back beyond Humanism to ancient rhetorical paradigms (émouvoir—exciter). Thus we have:

$$\left.\begin{array}{l}\text{Fellow-man,}\\ \text{Hearer}\end{array}\right\} \xleftarrow{\quad\text{Speech}\quad} \left\{\begin{array}{l}\text{Human agent,}\\ \text{Speaker}\end{array}\right.$$

Language is posited here, therefore, as inter-subjective communication.

4. a. For Rousseau the utterance fulfills different tasks at one and the same time. In addition to being able to delight aesthetically (speech was once poetry; here we are reminded of Humanist *elegantia*), language can, and should, respect and appreciate the other person. Interestingly, Rousseau thinks that the more musical a language, the more fit it is to function in this "social" manner, this reverential way, and carry social and moral virtues.

    b. This means that for Rousseau functions of a different nature are or can be combined in a speech-operation, although one function may be on a lower level, e.g., prosody, another on a higher level, e.g., the "dignative" attitude (with the term "dignative" we mean to denote phenomena such as reverence vs. contempt and the like). Furthermore, in the past speech was poetry and so it has an aesthetic aspect.

c. Rousseau either denounced or praised the functions of language. We have tried to list the different functions that Rousseau was especially concerned with, with the evaluations that Rousseau gave them.

Features	Good	Evil
aesthetic, artistic:	poetical, beautiful	prosaic, ugly
social, dignative:	reverential, appreciative, etc.	contemptuous, depreciative, etc.
intellectual, informative:		rational, exact, etc.
psychical, expressive:	feeling, emotional	
prosodic, musical:	intonationally rich	intonationally poor

It is clear that Rousseau's theory starts from the speaker's standpoint, that it is spiritual, and that it really leads to a philosophical anthropology which has to draw up a hierarchy of man's faculties.

Hamann (1730–1788), in his consideration of language, went much further than Rousseau in this spiritual direction. He saw the optimum function of language as a heralding of the Gospel, as a proclaiming of the Word of God.

We have already noted the revival of rhetorical humanist notions; through his emphasis on the freedom of the speaker as *"agent libre"* Rousseau followed in the footsteps of Humanism. His socialization of the speech-act meant that he saw this freedom especially as aiming at the social elevation of fellow-man. This was, in a double sense, revolutionary, even though such social elevation was caused by "émouvoir" and "excitation" of social and ethical sentiments. With this Rousseau posited more emphatically than Humanism had done a normative finalism. Rousseau's claim that we are concerned with a free acting human being in speech, meant a definite break with rationalistic determinism in general. One of Rousseau's contemporaries, Diderot (1713–1784), overemphasized this trend by teaching that optimum speech is the exclusive personal competence of a genius.

PHYSICS AND MECHANICS

There were contemporaries of Rousseau who did not regard man as a spiritual being with spiritual faculties, but as a machine or a plant. De Lametrie, once a medical student of Boerhaave in Holland, wrote two essays,

L'Homme plante and *L'Homme machine*. Surgeons and engineers had participated in the scholars' revolt against mathematical scientialism and the results of their works also had impact on the study of language. In 1765 de Brosses (1709–1777) wrote his *Traité de la formation mécanique des langues et des principes physiques de l'étymologie*. His materialism is the counterpart of Rousseau's and others' spiritualism. He is a forerunner of positivism in linguistics, of mechanical linguistics. To characterize his analysis we give a single example: negation is the use of the nasal cavity in the sound mechanism!

We have seen that during the eighteenth century more and more simultaneous functional features were noted in speech and language activity in general. This undeniably had to do with the rapid establishment of new disciplines or new specializations within established disciplines. The various inherent or adherent functions were then classed as lower or higher. This approach compels us to describe language functions by means of vertical, hierarchical diagrams.

PHILOLOGY AND ORIGIN

The study of language itself was also subject to this development and therefore gradually acquired a more definite and disciplinary form. For example, classical philology had already emerged from Humanism. This study was especially taken up in the young Dutch republic; in the seventeenth century Latin was the main concern, in the eighteenth century Greek. This Dutch philology was a forerunner of linguistics proper.

The eighteenth century is also the century of the problems of origin. Especially where language was concerned, the solutions were quite diverse, whether in philosophical anthropology or in philology proper. The anthropological considerations such as those of Rousseau, Herder, Süssmilch (1707–1767), and many others, no matter how speculative, led to reflections about the structure of man's faculties and the position of the lingual faculty among them. But we shall limit ourselves here to philology.

The Dutch students of Greek developed an etymological method restricted to Greek, which they considered to be older and somehow even the source of Latin. They searched for the oldest verb forms along the line of analogy (see above). Through the students who flocked to the Dutch universities from all over Europe, the method became very widespread. Rask (1787–1832), the great Danish linguist, also adhered to it. The original founders, Valckenaer (1715–1785) and Hemsterhuys (1722–1790), however, were reserved about it to the very end. Being a sort of reductive-historical extrapolation, the method yielded very simple one-vowel verbs; through *"componendi et glutinandi rationes"* (composing and gluing devices) one could arrive at the classical forms.

It was the Dutch etymological method that was the primary obstacle for Bopp (1791–1861) when he founded linguistic science proper. He polemicized only against these predecessors.

ESTABLISHMENT OF LINGUISTICS PROPER

Bopp's own method corresponded to Leibniz' *grammaire rationelle*, as interpreted by Wolff in the German schools, and consisted of a system of material elements and formal relations, parallel to the system of ideas. Bopp applied it to his comparative morphology (cf. the author's article, 1950). Through his extensive knowledge of Sanskrit and native Sanskrit grammar, Bopp was able to separate the stems and roots from the formal affixes; they corresponded to "Grundbegriffe" and "accessorische Begriffe" respectively. His method was an analysis of wholes into parts, elements, segments. Bopp practised this analysis on data which were documented in former stages of different Indo-European languages. Language was therefore, for Bopp, a static collection of written words. His segmentation principle failed with regard to what we now call morphophonemic phenomena.

Grimm (1785–1863), inspired by the Romanticism of Rousseau and Herder, shared the Romanticist's interest for genetic problems, for historical changes and transitions. He directed his attention to "Ablaut" phenomena and declared these to be intrinsically grammatical and formative. Bopp had thought that they could be explained by saying that a heavy "Grundform" is accompanied by a light ending, and vice versa, as in the case of a seesaw. Bopp called this a "Gesetz der Gravität", a mechanical law, though in his dispute with Grimm Bopp was careful not to exclude the possibility of a dynamic law. Grimm's influence gradually turned comparative morphology into a more historical lexicology (at least for Indo-European languages) which tried to understand the sound transitions and through this paid increasing attention to phonetics.

With the establishment of linguistics the study of language enters a phase that places particular demands on the description of the vicissitudes of the paradigms that had by then become influential. Now that linguistics had become a special discipline and had acquired an independent existence, it developed a more self-contained continuity, a tradition of its own and became less exposed to outside influences. Because of this it is very difficult to actually trace the penetration of outside philosophical-doctrinal or disciplinary trends or movements into linguistics. Sometimes a change was simply "due" or "in the air".

The indentification of paradigms is easy in the case of Bopp and Grimm; with Bopp we return to the static rationalism of the Wolff–Leibniz type, with Grimm to the dynamic romanticism, reminiscent of Herder and Rousseau. But for the second half of the nineteenth century and the first decades of the twentieth century a survey must suffice. About these periods the histories of linguistics give us little help, because they mostly deal with achievements and expansions instead of principles and methods.

IDEALISM

The autonomy of the young discipline of linguistics, resisting outside influences, is illustrated by several examples. Bopp wanted nothing to do with the various origin-speculations, anthropological or philological, which led to what Bopp called the twilight land of glottogony. Another, less well-known example, and incorrectly described (by Jespersen), is the influence of Bopp's lifelong friend and protector, Wilhelm von Humboldt (1767–1835). That influence was in fact nonexistent.

Humboldt was influenced by Kant (1724–1804), who strove for a compromise between seventeenth century mathematico-theoretical and eighteenth century moral-practical thought. Humboldt's philosophy of language represents, as it were, an unpaid bill of Kant's. Kant never discussed language in particular since he had assumed from Leibniz and Wolff the portmanteau concept of representation, that is, of language as a mere expression of thought. Scientialists like Leibniz as well as practicalists like the Port Royal grammarians, Harris, Condillac, and many others had, though in different ways, pointed to a universal grammar as an inner order, present in any language. This inner organizational form of language was studied by Bopp in his comparative morphology as a *static ergon*. Humboldt, however, taking over Rousseau's—and Herder's—dynamism, regarded language and its "innere Form" rather as a driving force, as a spiritual articulation, an "innerliche Gerstaltung", in a word as *energeia*. This forming force, with Humboldt, is not located in individual monads that automatically mirror the world-order, though with fluctuating clarity (Leibniz), nor in society as such, insofar as lingual intercourse persuades to higher or lower valued social feelings (Rousseau), rather it issues from a national community as characterized by its own language. Through its specifically patterned language such a community creates by necessity its own specific world-view (Weltbild) and here Kant with his Copernican revolution provides the paradigm. Humboldt's main theory can be represented as follows:

$$
\left. \begin{array}{l} \text{Reality} \\ \text{in ordered} \\ \text{perspective} \end{array} \right\} \longleftarrow \left\{ \begin{array}{l} \text{"Innere Form"} \\ \text{of national} \\ \text{language} \end{array} \right\} \longleftarrow \left\{ \begin{array}{l} \text{Representative} \\ \text{Mind of national} \\ \text{community (Volksgeist)} \end{array} \right.
$$

Steinthal (1823–1899) wanted to make the richness of Humboldt's ideas accessible to the professional linguist but he did not succeed. Some idealistic psychologists and philosophers at the turn of the century, for example, Wundt (1832–1920), Croce (1866–1952), and Cassirer (1874–1945), referred back to Humboldt as an important and vital source. Among linguists Sapir (1884–1939) is indirectly influenced via Croce, as was the anti-positivist Voszler (1872–1949). We find a remarkable reoccurrence of the Humboldtian theorem in the work of Sapir's student Whorf (1897–1941). Weisgerber (*b*.1899) started directly with the Humboldtian paradigm, as witness his ever-continued studies of the relations between "Muttersprache" and "Geistesbildung".

DEVELOPMENT OF LINGUISTICS: NINETEENTH CENTURY

The development within linguistics followed more and more the lines of Bopp rather than of Grimm. Important are three contemporaries: Schleicher (1821–1861), Max Müller (1823–1900), and Georg Curtius (1820–1880). They share an "es ist erreicht" attitude, the Indo-European languages were regarded as static sets of signs that could be placed into a family tree frame. Schleicher reconstructed with certainty Indo-European parent language forms; Max Müller introduced in the same spirit the comparative method in England: "anomalies are vanishing, there is nothing accidental, irregular. . . ."; and Curtius modernized classical philology.

In the seventies a rebellion set in which had some similarity to the opposition of eighteenth century practicalism and the Enlightenment to the preponderance of mathematics in the seventeenth century. Dynamic views returned, change and growth became the watchwords. Joh. Schmidt (1843–1901) launched his wave theory to correct and amend the rigid tree theory.

Hugo Schuchart (1842–1927) pointed out the extreme complexity of language phenomena and criticized dogmatic views of relationships. H. Steinthal introduced psychological theorems that influenced Paul (1846–1921), the philosopher of the neo-grammarians, and ended the one-sided interest in Indo-European languages. Whitney (1827–1894), who introduced linguistics to America, spoke with emphasis about the life and growth of languages and sharply opposed Max Müller, his British counterpart. Whitney also saw language again as a social phenomenon.

The linguistic discoveries of the revolutionary neo-grammarians had mainly to do with the laws of the sound-shifts, that is to say, with the natural conditions of speech; the positivistic conception remained, only changing the static substratum for the dynamic subsistence of sounds. The investigations remained comparative. Grimm's law of consonantal shift was reformulated by Verner (1846–1896); Sievers (1850–1932) observed the physiology of sounds; Brugmann (1849–1919) and Osthoff (1847–1909), the pioneers of the school, studied consonants; Thomsen and others worked out the law of palatals and a new theory that unraveled the Ablaut-problem. The accent, that is, stress and pitch phenomena, which Humboldt had unsuccessfully tried to interest Bopp in, received much attention in the following decades. The enthusiasm of the discoverers led to a belief in "Ausnahmslosigkeit"; "Ausnahmen" received a positive explanation in the theory of analogy: Osthoff imputed sound-changes to physiology, analogy to psychology. Morphology had not advanced much beyond Bopp's static elementarism and, in the seventies, even fell back a little. Brugmann brought the century's results together in his *Grundriss der vergleichenden Grammatik der indogermanischen Sprachen*. Delbruck (1842–1922) added a syntax, an almost forgotten aspect of language.

FURTHER DEVELOPMENTS OF LINGUISTICS: TWENTIETH CENTURY

In the first decades of the present century a kind of synthesis emerged: the French-Swiss Saussure (1857–1913), who had contributed to the movement of the neo-grammarians, developed a theory that broke through the diachronic-genetic one-sidedness and posited that a language, besides speech (*parole*), is also a system of signs (*langue*) that must be synchronically investigated; it is the systems that succeed each other. Consequently Saussure began his inquiry with signs, i.e., words: a word is a combination of sound (*son*) and concept (*idée*); the former is the "signifiant", the latter the "signifiée". Although Saussure regarded *parole* and *langue* as equally essential, the latter was his main concern.

Hjelmslev (1899–1965) elaborated Saussure's theory and further applied a mathematical analysis which was indeed in line with Saussure's own ideas. The similarity with Leibniz is striking, but there is also a definite difference. Here is no ontic parallelism. For Saussure and Hjelmslev language is a self-contained unity of two autonomous systems. In fact, part of Leibniz' ideas were reintroduced by Russell (1872–1970); Wittgenstein's (1889–1951) Tractatus showed the latter's influence in some respect; but here we enter the realm of philosophy.

Saussure considered language as belonging to both psychology and sociology. This as a remote after-effect of the opposition of diakrinein/inventio to didaskein/demonstratio. The emphasis on the social aspect has been a French tradition since Rousseau. Saussure's speech model is therefore intersubjective with alternating speaker's and hearer's roles.

Phonology—later, in the U.S.A., called Phonemics—originated in the Prague Linguistic Circle and made its debut in 1928; pioneers were Trubetzkoy (1890–1938) and Jakobson (b.1896). It represented an endeavor to conceive of the Saussurean hemisphere of sounds of a particular language in terms of a functional system. While in the sound unit of traditional phonetics articulatory, acoustic, and quantitative features mattered, the phoneme was defined by those features that functioned as semantic distinctives. Since obviously the inventories of functioning distinctives that appear in different positions in the word are not all the same, attention was focused sharply on the problem of distribution. Gestalt psychology contributed to the theoretical foundation of the new subdiscipline.

In 1933 Bloomfield's *Language* appeared. Saussure and Bloomfield (1887–1949) both studied in Leipzig under the neo-grammarians. Saussure returned a mentalist and rationalist, Bloomfield a mechanist and positivist. For Bloomfield lingual intersubjectivity is cooperation: notions like idea, concept, meaning (signification), etc., give way to stimulus, response, association, etc.

Observation of factual and observable behavior is a better lead than introspection. It is clear that Bloomfield opted for the dynamic side; language is a means of cooperation of two nervous systems. Operational acts, however, are only performed by man as *homo faber*. Bloomfield's dynamism lost ground again in Harris' distributional theory of successive segments. Pike, however, maintains a vivid dynamism in his rather esoteric technemic theory. Chomsky's (*b.*1928) point of departure lies in the highest-but-one level of language phenomena, that is, the sentences; this suggests in doctrinal respect a new idealistic approach, vide Humboldt.

Disciplinary Paradigmaticality, Correlations and Criteria

Since World War II the impact of disciplinary paradigms on linguistics has undergone an extremely rapid development and has acquired such magnitude that a satisfactory description in the limited scope of this paper is impossible. Therefore, from this point on we will follow another method. We will first list a number of autonomous disciplines outside linguistics. Some have an old, continuous, evolutionary tradition, some have been recently revolutionized. We shall subsequently consider their impacts on the study of language, both new as well as long-established ones, and also some perspectives. These disciplinary impacts become manifest in correlate subdisciplines within autonomous linguistics.

We first list the relevant disciplines in ascending order of complexity:

1. Arithmetic, the old discipline of counting and numbering based on the practical encounter with more-or-lessness, with "amount" or "numerality", which in reality appears as discrete quotity.

2. Geometry handles spatial quantitativity appearing as the volume of things, the expansion or range of events, being of a three-dimensional nature;

numerality (1) is presupposed here. These two disciplines are combined as Mathematics.

3. Physics, including mechanics, chemistry, electronics, etc., that is, all the disciplines concerned with inanimate nature, revolutionized at the beginning of the century. Micro-physics launched the complementarity principle of energy and element and consequently ontological doctrines had to be revised. "One is left with the feeling that the greatest enigma of physical matter is non-existence in any material sense" (Van Mater 1958). The phenomena concerned presuppose space (2) and numerality (1).

4. Biology, inclusive of physiology and other disciplines of living organsims and phenomena of life in general like growth, respiration, metabolism, propagation, etc. Physicality is the underlying layer (3).

5. Psychology's essential field is that of animal and human feeling, which is constituted by impressions, affects, emotions; here memory leads to associations, habits, learning. Psychology, through a rapid evolution, diverted into many branches and developed partially new notions, as for example the notion of Gestalt, for which the old idea of image could have perhaps sufficed. Psychical phenomena are clearly based on vital functions (4).

6. Noology is an old though not very widespread name for the discipline of thinking. Once there was even a normative denotation, namely alethiology, the discipline of truth. Furthermore one of the subjects of the Trivium was the teaching of thinking: dialectics. But logic is the broadest term, although it has covered an erroneous mixing of language and thought since Antiquity. Logic studies the ways, rules, and criteria of correct thought. Finally there is a philosophical theory of thought that mainly deals with the principles and the position of thinking; the latter approach is more doctrinal than disciplinary. But it is generally felt that the results of thinking ought to be correct and truthful. Feeling is considered as the next lower level (5).

7. Technology as the discipline of technique currently only covers engineering,[2] while it should label an all-inclusive understanding of man's organizing abilities, of his cultural creativity, of his existence as *homo faber*. This innate faculty appears in the most primitive stone axe as well as in the most subtly organized enterprises. Just as thinking seeks truth and correctness, in free organizing there is an aptitude and a striving for appropriateness, for fitting application and adjustment, for efficient order. Technical acts are based on intellectual knowledge (6).

These seven autonomous disciplines and their correlated fields seem to constitute a suppositionally ordered hierarchy: the first two (1 and 2) are concerned with zones of nondynamic phenomena, 3, 4, and 5 dynamic zones, though ateleotic, non-finalistic. Thinking (6), however, has an intrinsic end, aim, purpose, viz., truth, correctness, accuracy; human organizing and technique (7) likewise strive for appropriateness, and we can add that authentic language (8) aspires to clarity. Because oral language is the most integrated specimen of man's clarifying activity we specify linguistics as *glotto-delotics* (the latter term being derived from dèloun [cf. Plato] = clarifying).

Secondly we now draw up a list of the different authentic disciplines, with their corresponding inherent subdisciplines in linguistics:

	Dependent disciplines within linguistics:
Independent disciplines:	
8. Glotto-delotics	
7. Technology	: Grammar (Syntax)
6. Noology	: Semantics (Lexicology)
5. Psychology	: Phonemics
4. Biology	: Organic ⎫ Phonetics
3. Physics	: Acoustic ⎬
2. Geometry ⎫ Mathematics	: Quantitative Metrics
1. Arithmetic ⎭	: (Quotitative) Distribution

The interrelationship of these disciplines has had a varied and diverse history. On level 7 grammar was already called a technè in ancient Alexandria; on level 6 lingual words and noetic notions have been closely related since olden days (cf. Plato). On level 5 the psychical image character of the phoneme—and the syllable—has been to a large extent recognized. On levels 4 and 3 the impact of the natural sciences was notoriously strong. On level 2 the notion that the *mora* is a metric measure of spatial character and as such correlated to the field of geometry has remained and developed. The distributional (1) approach in linguistics has, from its recent beginnings, always had a full awareness of its close relationship with arithmetic.

RE: THE COMPLEMENTARITY PRINCIPLE OF MICRO-PHYSICS
(PARTICLE-WAVE THEORY)

Although it is a scientific paradigm, the complementarity principle has essentially solved the doctrinal controversy with which we began, namely, between a dynamic and a static conception of language (cf. Bridgman 1962). Without dynamic workings or processes there is no experience. But any process—in the case of language: speech—itemizes, once accomplished, into an entitarily complex (a whole) or simplex unit. This leads to some noteworthy conclusions. We take as a specimen the case of an imperative utterance (8) like "I! " (= go!) in ancient Latin. We find here a simultaneous performance of seven subroles on seven subfunctional levels, which we number from 7 to 1. This "I" may be said to be at one and the same time: (8) a clarifying utterance, (7) a structured sentence, (6) an identifying word or lexeme, (5) a monosyllabic phoneme, (4) an articulatory "phone", (3) a unit of vibrating air, (2) a measurable item, (1) a countable item, a "position".

From this we can infer:

a. that the simultaneous functional roles lend themselves after the event to complementary itemization;

b. that expressions like "a sentence consists of one or more words", contains a just as illegitimate reduction as "a hundredweight consists of so many quarters";

c. that dualisms like matter vs. form, substance vs. accidens, body vs. mind, "son" vs. "idée" (Saussure), are not satisfactory[3] because they do not account for the actual pluralism of functions and properties;

d. that a linguistic analysis should begin at the authentic level (8) of the utterances and proceed downwards.

And this brings us to a consideration of cybernetics.

RE: CYBERNETICS

A cybernetic circuit is especially obvious in the process by which a child learns a language. A child perceives a sound, imitates it at the same moment or repeats it later after it has been stored in his memory. When he speaks, in his nervous system a "command" goes from level 5 (phonemic imagery) to level 4 (organic articulation); a feedback control is involved since every articulatory (4) speaker is his own controlling hearer (5)! A similar to-and-back or rather down-and-up cybernetic relation seems to exist between every higher and every lower layer, beginning with the authentic glotto-delotic level (8). When one means to clarify a certain theme or subject matter, one formulates a sentence or sentences, applying the appropriate grammatical patterns (7). These grammatical schemes one fills with the proper sememes (6) and so on—or rather, further downwards; and in all these cases there is a conditioning feedback which, as it were, returns back—and upwards. One can, it is true, use older terms such as *causa formalis* (for a higher level) and *causa materialis* (for a lower level), but the application of the notions seems more appropriate.

While the language function and subfunctions emerge from human beings, we want to add some anthropological remarks.

RE: ANTHROPOLOGY

We refer here to the philosophical anthropology that, especially after World War II, has stressed human decision-making. Since then we can hardly speak any longer of the human factor in linguistics in terms of, for example, communicating nervous systems. The new concentration on man's free spontaneous initiative means for linguistics that theorems of the kind we found in Humanism and in the eighteenth century Enlightenment and Spiritualism might be revived. Phenomenology and existentialism have created a new atmosphere.

The basic model that offers a place to the human Person who, in principle, decides freely which subject matter he wants to clarify, is as follows:

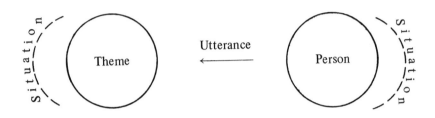

SOME POSTULATES

Three postulates take shape here:

The Person, the free initiating human agent, the speaker—or writer— who acts on his own authority, responsibility, and control. "Person" does not mean a solitary isolated individual, but a *solidary* social being, an a priori member of human society.

The Speech Act as a multi-featured functional deed, issuing from the speaking Person and directed at the Theme.

The Theme as the subject matter, projected on the screen of the Situation, and as the very purport of the Speech Act.

A fourth postulate is that the Person acting freely performs his Speech Act as a normative activity by which he strives for an optimum; for language use this optimum is clarity.

As a fifth postulate we could suggest the general enchronicity of events and things. But since this postulate would be valid for the totality of the universe, it lacks a specific linguistic aspect. However, we should remember that there is no escape from Time into some abstract static "synchronicity" of systems.

These postulates, derived from a careful digestion of both old and new paradigms of both doctrinal and disciplinary nature, offer, in our opinion, tenable principles for linguistic theory.

RE: SOCIOLOGY AND THE COMMUNICATION CONCEPT
(cf. the author's article, 1962)

There are communicative or cooperative models drawn up (Saussure, Bloomfield) that start with dialogue. So, the intersubjective communicative circuit (Saussure) shows speaker and hearer as alternating poles, as follows:

$$H \longleftarrow S$$
$$\downarrow \qquad \uparrow$$
$$S \longrightarrow H$$

In our opinion the hearer or reader is not a necessary postulate for a speech act. Many utterances in speech or writing lack an addressee. A hearer or reader may be present in the situation as a witness, but his presence is not a necessity. However, from the moment a witness is addressed, he enters ipso facto into the theme. The Person–Theme model can fully account for the ensuing dialogue: when such a witness joins in a conversation it is up to him whether he cooperates and sticks to the same theme, shifts the theme, or chooses another theme.

As for "communication" we wish to point out that this is an all-encompassing concept which contains little that is specific to language. Communication ranges from inter-molecular physical (e.g., electric) communication between things to inter-human ethical communication. For this reason subsumption like "language is communication" is rather pointless.

On the other hand, a real functional sociology that studies functional phenomena such as courteousness, disdain, pride, humility, status-seeking, familiarity, dignating reverence, honor, shame, impudence, etc. (cf. Rousseau), can contribute to an understanding of the adherent features of language that dominate some languages (e.g., Japanese) to such an extent that they determine their type considerably.

There is a communication theory, of mathematical origin, that we can better call Information Theory.

RE: INFORMATION THEORY

Telegraph engineers have measured the economic efficiency of certain code systems, and have discovered the concept of redundancy. Artificial languages especially lend themselves to an evaluation of the amount of intellectual information that they can transmit. As long as one realizes that artificial systems of signs or symbols can only occur as deliberately excogitated analogues of natural language, and that they are consequently of secondary nature, one can avoid the repetition of Hobbes' paradigm, namely, the subsumption of natural language under a system of artificial symbols. However, now that several linguists already discuss natural language use and interpretation as encoding and decoding respectively, the way has been opened for the reoccurrence of this paradigm.

Summary of the Main Paradigms

To conclude, we shall attempt to briefly trace the main paradigms we have encountered. To this end we will discuss:

I. The contrastive paradigm that concerns the controversy of dynamic-functional vs. static-entitative conceptions of language.

II. The coordinative paradigm of distinguishing along with teaching that we meet for the first time in Plato and that evolves through the ages from then on and which is mostly presented as a duality of aspects.

III. The paradigm that concerns the essential nature of language as orientation in the world or, in other words, the problem of meaning or of the *causa finalis* of language.

IV. The paradigm that concerns the human factor in language, the anthropological problem of the *causa efficiens* of language.

We realize that these four headings do not give a complete picture, that they partly overlap, but in our opinion they do represent the most important trends.

I. DYNAMIC VS. STATIC

Although Plato, like Heraclitus, considered *legein* as a progressing stream, the overall impression from the *Kratylos* is that the author could not choose between the two conceptions. For that matter, many notions that as major or minor paradigms have influenced Western study of language can be found in the *Kratylos*; but Plato left most of them unsolved. Aristotle preferred the static conception and elaborated it with the help of schemas like matter vs. form, substance vs. accidentia, etc. In his logic the subject-predicate proposition is his primary concern. As against this, Rhetoric was completely dynamic and saw language as speech function, as an ability which is directed toward influencing fellow-man. Ethical Stoicism, which regarded the universe as consisting of *dynameis*, stood close to Rhetoric. Epicureans considered language as a derivative of animal sounds.

When scientific and philosophical activity began to recover after the fall of the Roman Empire, in the second half of the Middle Ages, the contemplation of language came under the influence of that specimen of language that embraced all truthful and reliable thought: the Holy Scriptures.

The realistic Grammatica Speculativa supplied a static theory that was based upon formal congruence of things, thoughts, and words according to their category. As against that, the Nominalists in their logic posited an active and dynamic intellect that approaches reality, spontaneously and arbitrarily, with or without the help of language.

Humanism considered speech and writing rather than thinking the most typical human faculties. It freed language from the dominance of thinking, which meant a palace revolution within the Trivium. The Renaissance (Francis Bacon) put language back into its former prison: the active scientific mind. In accord with Nominalism, it considered language as a static vehicle for conveying thoughts.

Galileo saw the book of nature written in numbers and figures, that is to say, in mathematical symbols. He established mechanics as a science, namely, the science of physical motion, by applying mathematics to physical phenomena as an analytical and descriptive tool. Philosophers like Hobbes regarded words as counters and, in doing so, subsumed them under the static idea of a system of mathematical symbols. Leibniz took this over: he drew up a theory in which language is incorporated in reason, and whereby in any lingual or symbolic system the same static framework (ordo), consisting of elements and relations, which he thought formed the fundamental of the universe, was represented. The parallelism of frameworks is the *fundamentum veritatis*; the representational frameworks differ between them in degrees of clarity. In a language the inner framework appears in the *grammaire rationelle* which all languages have in common.

The eighteenth century Enlightenment was a rejection of the seventeenth century preoccupation with mathematics. The rationality of language was no longer seen as a rigid form, but rather as a rational capability. Language is speech, and as such an "art" and ability, capacity, energy. The Humanist tradition was picked up again in the spiritualism of Rousseau and even considerably extended, but this comes under other paradigms. Humboldt attempted a synthesis of the static and dynamic conceptions; language is energy indeed but has an "innere Form" which it imposes on reality.

Bopp, the founder of comparative linguistics, remained faithful to the static tradition of Leibniz–Wolff throughout his life. He was a morphologist who split up words as static data into elements operating with a schema of "Grundbegriffe" (in the stem) vs. "accessorische Begriffe" (in the affixes). Here he drew considerable support from similar elementary analyses of the Sanskrit grammarians.

Already in the seventeenth century, but especially in the eighteenth century, the originally doctrinal model became more and more involved with continually increasing impacts of disciplinary nature.

Another approach entered the picture when the transitional development of language data from older times until the present became subject to competent historical investigations: the notion of diachronic change in its application to language was new within the given paradigm (Grimm). Bopp did not go so far, he stuck to comparing static forms in static stages of development. But in the second half of the century a dynamic concept of diachronic and regular change in language was accepted, sometimes in biological terms of growth.

Partly like Humboldt, Saussure attempted a synthesis after the end of the nineteenth century. He contrasted a dynamic aspect "la parole" in historical diachrony with the static system of "la langue" which should be examined synchronically. The static synchronic system was Saussure's preference. A more dynamic viewpoint seems to cause linguists like Bloomfield to emphasize speech as a behavioral response to stimuli which brings about human cooperation.

In general, when one compares Plato's time with the present, it can be said that the dynamic-static controversy has itself undergone an evolution, a gradual metamorphosis, so that it can no longer be expressed in the old terms. This evolution comes clearly to the fore in the beginning of this century under the influence of the complementarity thesis of modern quantum-theory; it permits us to look at what is an energy a priori, as an entity a posteriori or conversely. We can even take both viewpoints simultaneously, without any temporal division into earlier and later, thus the contrast between dynamic vs. static is neutralized in complimentariness.

II. COGNITIVE DISTINGUISHING AND COMMUNICATIVE TEACHING

The second paradigm involves the two vital relations in which language stands, namely, the cognitive or representative relation of language to things and events meant or, in other words, the relation of its content to the world, to reality (IIa) and the relation of language to fellow-men in communication (IIb).

In the history of philosophy and study of language the two relations are often pictured as a coordinated pair. We will confine ourselves to four examples that have been discussed above, or at least touched upon:

	(a) cognition	(b) communication
Plato	: diakrinein	: didaskein
	(distinguishing)	(teaching)
Hobbes	: inventio (mark)	: demonstratio (sign)
Saussure	: psychological aspect	: sociological aspect
Bloomfield	: $S \longrightarrow r \longrightarrow s \longrightarrow R$[4]	

It is certainly not necessary that (a) cognition and (b) communication form one paradigm; in the course of history the relation to reality (a) and to one's fellow-men (b) have often been handled independently of each other. Logic, for example, inclined to (a), Rhetoric to (b). The reason for their combination in a single paradigm lies in the fact that language is practically always seen as communication (b) of thoughts (a). Relation IIa can, as we have shown, be of different kinds; language can mirror the categoricality (Grammatica Speculativa) or the system or structure (Leibniz) of things. Language can also be an instrument by which the active mind deals with things (Nominalism, Hobbes). In the opinion of others again language is a response to stimuli from reality (Bloomfield) or, inversely, a materialization in sound of thoughts about reality (Saussure). IIb is for the greater part informational in behalf of fellow-men. But Rousseau, for example, even thinks of an ethical impact on fellow-men. Bloomfield stressed the cooperational effect of language without a special appeal to meaning. For critical observations of this concept we refer to earlier sections.

III. THE PROBLEM OF MEANING

The third paradigm may be called the paradigm of essential characterization: it focuses on the problem of meaning and as such is an offspring of IIa. Here we also find the alternative characterization of what language either is or does (cf. I). The vicissitudes of this clearly philosophical paradigm stand out against all the disciplinary characterizations of language that history offers. Western thought begins by subsuming language to a *logos*-notion in which language and thought unite as exterior form and interior contents. This *logica*, according to an ancient philosophical theorem, forms a middle zone between higher *ethica, practica* or *moralia* and lower *physica*.

Until Humanism there were two alternatives: language is either intellectual whether of a passive mind (e.g., Grammatica Speculativa) or of an active mind (Nominalism); or thinking itself is of a lingual nature (Humanism). Rhetoric taught a sort of instrumentalism: language is a means, a tool, to be used and tested for its appropriateness in influencing others. Intellectualization reoccurred though in the new shape of rationalization in Hobbes' and Leibniz' subsumption under mathematical artificial symbolism. In the eighteenth century all kinds of equations emerged as disciplinary derivations: we recall de Brosses' physical mechanics; Romanticism fostered a psycho-sentimentalism which was succeeded in the nineteenth century by equally psychological associationism, while the twentieth century yields a psychological stimulus-response behaviorism.

From the criteria that one applies to lingual utterances it can be concluded what one judges the nature of language to be. Mathematicians and logicians demand exactitude and correctness from the speech act; Rousseau required that language evince respect and reverence for fellow-men; ancient Rhetoric asked for efficiency and appropriateness; artists of all time required beauty and aesthetic satisfaction. What does the man in the street in everyday life intuitively demand of his own and others' use of language? He simply demands and expects: *clarity*; therefore, it seems that the authentic nature of language can only and should be described as *clarification*.

The reason that so many erroneous definitions and paradigms could occur is that speech is respiration and therefore a biological function; speech is movement of matter and therefore a physical event; speech is habituation, remembered perception, etc., and therefore of psychical nature; speech is intelligence, cognition, etc.; speech is an orderly means toward a goal and therefore qualifiable as a technico-formative tool. Speech is all this quite properly and it functions in all these roles simultaneously; for this reason we drew up a scale of properties as a stratificational theory which accounts for the successful impacts of so many disciplinary paradigms. But the authentic ipso-function of language remains clarification.

IV. THE HUMAN FACTOR

The last paradigm we want to discuss is perhaps the one with the weakest tradition, one that has not been so manifest throughout the ages. We mean the one that includes the human factor as the nuclear motor without which language would not have appeared at all. The free agent and initiator of speech acts, who as such takes responsibility for his utterances, is the primary competent generator of language. We designed above a model that stood for the Person as the primary postulate of a functional and finalist conception of language.

In the history of paradigms the human factor as a free agent emerged during Humanism, but more definitely and overtly with Rousseau. Ever since it has disappeared and reoccurred a number of times; in the present the conviction that language is thoroughly human gains ground again.

Conclusion

There is growing consensus in linguistics as to the importance and value of the study of historical ideas, images, trends, paradigms, models, or whatever these often unnoticed but always active doctrinal or disciplinary preconceptions may be called. As variables or invariables they march through time, continuously or intermittently (cf. Chomsky 1966). They function as landmarks when one traces the historical routes of some branch of knowledge, and give a clearer insight into the present and may even allow a prediction of future developments. We have tried to focus on the anthropological implications of the study of language. To this end we have emphasized the occurrence of conceptions that recognize the human factor as the indispensable core of the language model. In the future we expect increasing emphasis on man and his free striving for the optimum of language: clarity.

NOTES

1. *Inventio* is orginally a rhetoric term, meaning the finding of the theme at the beginning of an address.

2. We can find a more general, philosophical, and doctrinal approach to the problem of the typical human technical faculty and ability in some pragmatist philosophers; cf. Thomas E. Hill, *Contemporary Theories of Knowledge* (New York: The Ronald Press Co., 1961), chap. 11, on instrumentalism (Dewey) and operationalism (Bridgman).

3. We mention here Professor Ryle's antagonism to philosophical dualism, as discussed, for example, in "Professor Ryle's Attack on Dualism," chap. 14, in *Clarity Is Not Enough*, ed. H. D. Lewis (London: George Allen and Unwin, Ltd., 1963).

4. S = stimulus, r = substitute response, s = substitute stimulus, R = reaction; cf. Bloomfield 1933, chap. 2. We assume that this schema is well known to the reader.

REFERENCES

Bloomfield, L. 1933. Language. New York, Henry Holt.
Bridgman, P. W. 1962. "The Way things are", chap. 5, in The Limits of language, ed. Walker Gordon. New York, Hill and Wang.
Brunet, P. 1926. Les physiciens hollandais et la methode experimentale en France au 18ième siècle. Paris.
Chomsky, N. 1966. Cartesian linguistics. New York, Harper & Row.
Faithfull, R. G. 1955. Review of Verburg 1952. Archivum Linguisticum 7: 144-150.
Gibson, J. 1917. Locke's theory of knowledge and its historical relations. Cambridge, Cambridge University Press.
Kuhn, Thomas S. 1962. The structure of scientific revolutions. Chicago, University of Chicago Press.
Van Mater, John P. 1958. What is matter? Sunrise (October 19).
Verburg, Pa. A. 1950. The background to the linguistic conceptions of Bopp. Lingua 2: 438-468. (Also in Sebeok 1966, I: 221-250.)
——. 1952. Taal en fuctionaliteit. Een historisch-critische Studie orer de opvattingen aangaande de Functies der Taal. [Language and Functionality. A historical-critical study of ideas regarding the functions of

language.] Wageningen, H. Veenman and Zonen. (English translation forthcoming; cf. review by Faithfull 1955.)

———. 1961. Bacon als vernieuwer van de encyclopedische idee [Bacon as renewer of the encyclopedical idea]. Algemeneen Nederlands Tijdschrift voor Wijsbegeerte en Psychologie (June): 169-180.

———. 1962. Some remarks on "communication" and "social" in language theory. Lingua 11: 453-468. (Festschrift de Groot).

———. 1965. Dèlosis and clarity. Philosophy and Christianity. Philosophical essays dedicated to Prof. Dr. Herman Dooyeweerd, 1-22. Kampen, Uitgeversmij J. H. Kok.

———. 1968. Ennoësis of language in 17th century philosophy. Lingua 21: 558-572.

———. 1970. Hobbes' calculus of words. I. T. L. 5 (Review of the Institute of Applied Linguistics, Louvain): 62-69. (Previously read at the Third International Conference on Computational Linguistics, Sanga Säby, September 1969.)

———. 1971. De Mens in de taalkunde [Man in Linguistics]. Truth and Reality, Philosophical perspectives on reality, dedicated to Prof. Dr. H. G. Stoker. Braamfontein, de Jong.

III : FIRST PARADIGM(?):
COMPARISON AND EXPLANATION OF CHANGE

7. The Indo-European Hypothesis in the Sixteenth and Seventeenth Centuries

George J. Metcalf

Introduction

A linguistic scholar today, coming across the following attempt to explain the interrelationship of certain languages, might object to minor details, but he would basically tend to support the proposition:

> An ancient language, once spoken in the distant past in the area of the Caucasus mountains and spreading by waves of migration throughout Europe and Asia, had itself ceased to be spoken and had left no linguistic monuments behind, but had as a "mother" generated a host of "daughter languages," many of which in turn had become "mothers" to further "daughters." (For a language tends to develop dialects, and these dialects in the course of time become independent, mutually unintelligible languages.) Descendants of the ancestral language include Persian, Greek, Italic (whence Latin and in time the modern Romance tongues), the Slavonic languages, Celtic, and finally Gothic and the other Germanic tongues.

The similarity with views held today concerning the Indo-European family is obvious despite certain quaintnesses: the pinpointing of the origin, for instance, and the obvious omission of the Indic family. Yet the views are the summary of a public lecture delivered in 1686 in Wittenberg, Germany (and published there that same year), by one Andreas Jäger. Far from being new or sensational, they are highly derivative and typical of at least one important strand of linguistic tradition in Northern Europe during the sixteenth and seventeenth centuries. It will be one aim of this chapter to show how much Jäger stands in this tradition and how unexceptional many of his views were. It will be an equally important aim to show the nature of the evidence presented to support such views and to persuade the public and other scholars of their rightness and validity. We shall note, particularly in the course of the seventeenth century, how certain basic modes of procedure, still recognized in comparative philology, came to be demanded as essential. But this concern with methods will also reveal the wide gaps that separate the earlier tradition from the present approach.

The "Scythian" Tradition

Andreas Jäger, not German but Swedish, was born in Stockholm and received his *Magister* in 1686 for the work paraphrased above. He did not personally receive much fame as a result of his lecture, and on his return to Sweden, Jäger's unsavory actions as a pastor brought him into disrepute, but he finally obtained his own parish in Uppsala *Stift*, where he died in 1730. (Cf. Hagström [1899, vol. 3: 139-140]; I am indebted for the information about Jäger to my colleague, Professor Gösta Franzén.)

The derivative nature of the lecture induced Arno Borst to relegate Jäger to a footnote in his *Turmbau von Babel* (1957–63: 1465, n. 119), the most extensive treatment of opinions on the interrelationship of languages. Yet the lecture possessed precisely the right combination of erudition and simplicity to seem pertinent for scholarly discussion for almost a hundred years following its first appearance. In 1742, for instance, two summarizing accounts appeared. One, with only few and very minor criticisms, appeared in the *Beyträge zur Kritischen Historie der Deutschen Sprache, Poesie und Beredsamkeit*, VIII (Leipzig), 76-94. The other, in the *Critische Versuche angefertiget durch Einige Mitglieder der Deutschen Gesellschaft in Griefswald*, I, 154-175, takes a somewhat more critical attitude:

> Man suchet auch bey einigen Sätzen die Gründe der Wahrschein-
> lichkeit nicht vergeblich. Bey andern aber sind sie sehr oft
> gezwungen, verwirret und unter einander geworfen (156).

Yet precisely what seems to us the most "modern" feature of Jäger's work is emphasized:

> Hätte dieses [the actions of the Hamites at Babel] seine
> Richtigkeit, so bliebe kein Zweifel übrig, dass Japhets Sprache
> unverändert bey den Scythen, als seinen Nachkommen geblieben
> sey, bis sie mit der Zeit in verschiedene Dialekte vertheilet
> worden, und die, nach dem Unterschied der von den scytischen
> [*sic!*] Völkern vorgenommenen Veränderungen, die in Europa
> üblich gewesene phrygische [from which Greek developed], alte
> italiänische, celtische, gothische, und slavonische Sprache her-
> vorgebracht hätten. Diese machen die Anzahl der in Europa

üblich gewesenen Sprachen aus, und die in einer jeden vorkommenden Wörter stimmen so mit einander überein, dass man nothwendig auf eine genaue Verwandschaft u. auf einen gleichen Ursprung derselben von einer Hauptsprache zu schlüssen, Recht hat (160).

Jäger's discussion of the relation of "language" and "dialect" also leads the reviewer to compare the relationship of Italian, Spanish, and French as "dialects" to "Latin"—"Alle diese Sprachen aber sind aus der lateinischen entstanden" (161)—with the relationship of the "dialects" "die unter dem Namen des phrygischen, celtischen, alten italiänischen, gothischen, slavonischen, und parthischen bekannt geworden sind" "zu der scythischen Sprache" (161).

Jäger's entire work was reprinted (without the slightest alteration so far as spot checks reveal) as late as 1774 in Oelrichs (2: 1-64). The comment (2: 341-355) is again concerned merely with minor details. (I have elsewhere treated the somewhat tangled bibliographical fate of Jäger's work; cf. Metcalf, 1966).

In presenting the initial brief summary of Jäger's views, I modernized, to be sure, by omitting a key element in his terminology. The indispensable term employed by Jäger himself (and most of his fellow scholars) for the ancient language was "Scythian," although this might be variously hyphenated, as Jäger's title reveals. But the hypenation (Lingua. . . Scytho-Celtica) also exposes an element of ambiguity. At times Celtic appears as a regular offspring of Scythian:

> *Japheti* lingua igitur in posteris duravit usque eo, dum in varias abiret alias: h.e. Lingua *Scythica* in *Phrygiam, Italicam* antiquam, *Celticam, Gothicam, Slavonicam*; tot cardinales etenim agnoscimus ac deprehendimus in media et extima *Europa* (16, similarly 17-18). [The language of *Japheth* persisted accordingly among his descendants until the time when it was transformed into various others: that is, the *Scythian* language into the *Phrygian* [i.e., Greek], ancient *Italic, Celtic, Gothic, Slavonic*; for we identify and apprehend just so many cardinal languages in central and outer Europe.] (All translations in this article are my own.)

At times Celtic seems to have a wider application and to stand as the older ancestor of all later European languages, especially Germanic (particularly 29 ff., where the attempt is made to show that both *Galli* and *Germani* were *Celtae*).

This very uncertainty is symptomatic. For despite a clearly developed sense of genetic relationships in languages, and a rich vocabulary of metaphors to reinforce this sense, scholars of the age by no means viewed linguistic history solely from the genetic perspective, and consequently did not feel the need to determine all details as precisely as was to be the case in the nineteenth century.

The genetic emphases and the genetic images that Jäger uses are nevertheless typical and impressive. He speaks of the "mater" with her "filiabus" (35) who are "sorores" (19). Even where the strictly "genetic" does not play a role, there is a one-directional, non-reversible imagery: the stream ["profluxerit"] (24); the family tree with its "radix" and its "rami" (dialects) (18). From Claudius Salmasius (cf. Borst, 1957–63: 1300-1301) Jäger takes the image of the woman who went through different stages of life while remaining the "same":

> Illa mater, quamvis primo infans fuerit, mox iuvencula, deinde floris vegeti mulier, postremo anus decrepita. Per tot mutationes eadem persona mansit, idem corpus circumtulit, idem nomen obtinuit (18). [That mother, although she had first been an infant, was soon a young maid, then a woman of vigorous prime, finally a decrepit crone. Through so many transformations she remained the same person, bore the same body, preserved the same name.]

Such an image, of course (despite its intent of emphasizing that which was permanent in language), permitted also the concept of the death of a language, a conclusion Jäger himself draws:

> Ex his iudicium formari queat de infantia, adolescentia, virilitate, flore ac devergio *interitu*que omnium Linguarum [my underlining] (18). [These considerations urge a judgment concerning the infancy, youth, manhood, flowering and divergence and *death* (my underlining) of all languages.]

The same image is employed by one of Jäger's chief sources, Georg Stiernhielm (1671):

> [Whoever has read extensively in ancient Latin documents] mecum fatebitur, Linguas senium pati, exolescere, et *emori* [my underlining] [ix]. Cum hominibus oriuntur, mutantur, differuntur, adolescunt, exolescunt, *occidunt* linguae [xvii]. (This preface, like several others to be cited in this discussion, is unpaginated; I have indicated the paging here and in other unpaginated prefaces by bracketed Roman numerals.) [. . .will grant me that languages suffer old age, grow out of use, and *die* (my underlining); just as with men languages are born, change, differ, mature, grow out of use, and *die* (my underlining).]

It is interesting to note here how the "organic" images are mixed with more neutral ones ("mutantur, differuntur")–once more a predominantly but by no means exclusively genetic perspective.[1]

Such a conception of language emphasizes its characteristic of constant change. The changeableness of language had been a consistent theme of Western tradition and was a commonplace of scholars in the sixteenth and seventeenth centuries, but one language or another had frequently been exempted from the general rule. Often it was Hebrew as the first and oldest (cf. Gesner [1555: 3v]: "From among the languages Hebrew, just as it is the first and most ancient of all, so it alone seems pure and unmixed [pura et syncera]"). In the implicit enthusiasm of a Johannes Goropius Becanus (1569), and the explicit statement of Abraham Mylius, it was even Dutch-Flemish. Mylius (1612: 146-147) confidently asserts that Brennus and Belgus, ancient "Belgian conquerors of Rome and Greece," could easily understand the "Belgian" (=Dutch-Flemish) speech of his own day. Indeed, the unchangeability of Belgian amid the general mutability of tongues approached the miraculous or Providential.

Jäger's particular model, Stiernhielm, was effective in ridiculing such claims, devoting nine pages of his "Praefatio" to evidence that Hebrew had changed and also pointing out the changes which had obviously occurred in the Germanic languages since the time of Charlemagne. Stiernhielm likewise mocked specifically the claims of Becanus and Mylius, and turned on Dutch-Flemish the epithet which usually had to be accepted by English: *spuma* ("scum") *nostrae Germanicae*, for Dutch-Flemish was noted for its large number of Romance loanwords (Stiernhielm is quoting [xxxv] Andreas Helvigius, whom Jäger [17] also quotes. Schottelius [1663] applied the term [*spuma linguarum*] to English, writing [141]: "Denn als in einem Topfe/ wie man sagt/ alle Sprachen gekocht worden/ were der Schaum davon die Englische Sprache geworden: weil dieselbe ein lauter Geflikk und Gemeng/ wiewol im Grunde Teutsch ist.")

At the same time Jäger and Stiernhielm tried to prevent this insistence on the mutability of *all* languages from thwarting the effort to establish their own vernacular as the "most ancient" and the "purest." Stiernhielm, for instance, claimed that "nostra Sueo-Gothica" is "ab externis pura & intaminata, nihilque, nisi aevo, a prima sua origine distans" [xxxiv] [pure and uncontaminated by foreign languages and different from its first origin in no respect except in age]. Jäger asks which of the Scythian languages can be considered the most ancient ("antiquissima"). His answer is at first theoretical: the one which deviates least from the mother ("quae a matre propius recedat"), which has been less corrupted by others, and among the "sisters" retains more vestiges of its original character ("sui generis"); such eminence, unsurprisingly, he would like to attribute to the "Lingua Celtica & Gothica" (19).

The "Scythian" tradition which Jäger represents was of course merely one way of viewing linguistic interrelationships in the sixteenth and seventeenth centuries; there could be other genetic filiations, or the genetic perspective could be largely lacking.

A special position was often accorded the "sacred three": Hebrew, Greek, and Latin, used for the inscription on the cross (Luke 23:38 and John 19:20). This special status was part of the whole Western tradition. For example, the Venerable Bede (d.735) remarks: "Tres sunt autem linguae sacrae: Hebraea, Graeca, Latina, quae toto orbe maxime excellunt. His enim tribus linguis super crucem Domini a Pilato fuit causa eius scripta" (1862, 1: 1179) [There are indeed three sacred languages: Hebrew, Greek, Latin, which greatly excel in the whole earth. For it was in these three languages that the cause of it was written above the cross of our Lord by Pilate]. (Borst, 1957–63: 1983-84, gives a detailed index to references to the special position occupied by the "sacred three.") This status was still vigorously championed, particularly in the sixteenth century. Thus Theodor Bibliander constantly stresses the unique position of the three, but this uniqueness is not based on a special genetic link. To be sure, Hebrew is the oldest and original language (1548: 37-38), and all others have developed from it: "reliquae ex ea [Ebraea] propagatae & genitae sunt" (142). But Greek and Latin, originating from descendants of Japheth (7), would be among those languages deviating most strongly from the original: "aliae [linguae] longius degenerarunt a principali sermone, ut dialecti filiorum Iapheth" (142). In the *Mithridates* of Konrad Gesner, Bibliander's fellow Züricher, the three sacred languages are again emphasized but there is likewise no reference to a possible genetic interconnection. Gesner points out rather the role of the three in spreading the gospel: Hebrew through the Old Testament, Greek through the New Testament, and Latin through its missionary tradition (1r-2v, 46v).

Another possible system (or rather lack of system) was the one suggested by the influential Joseph Justus Scaliger in his "Diatriba de Europaeorum Linguis" (1610), for he – confining himself to Europe – set up a pattern of four major and seven minor *Matrices*. ("We can call those languages *Matrices* from which many dialects like offshoots [propagines] have been developed" [119]). These were completely uninterrelated ("There is no relationship [cognatio] at all of the *Matrices* with one another, neither in the words [verbis] nor in the inflectional system [analogia]" [119]). It is, to be sure, not clear that Scaliger really believed in the total unrelatedness he here so stoutly maintains, for in another "Diatriba De Varia Literarum Aliquot Pronuntiatione" he remarks: "For what is o among the Greeks has been changed to (factum est) v among the Latins, as θεὸς, Deus" (131). This would imply that the Latins took over and changed such a fundamental word as that for God – precisely the word that Scaliger chose to identify the various "unrelated" *Matrices*. Even Scaliger may have been influenced here by the traditional belief that Latin developed from Greek. Scaliger found resonance particularly in England. Thus Stephan Skinner, in the "Praefatio ad Lectorem" of his *Etymologicon Linguae Anglicanae* (1671) lists the *matrices* of Europe [iii] following Scaliger (but with some omissions), and, a little later, ridicules precisely the Scythian hypothesis with which we are concerned [vii-viii].

But the impelling new direction of the sixteenth and seventeenth centuries was the trend toward giving greater prestige to the various vernaculars. In France, for instance, where the development of the common language from Latin was particularly well attested and recognized, a school arose which sought to prove that French had developed, not from Latin, but from the more prestigious Greek. (One of the outstanding advocates was the theologian Joachim Périon [1499-1559] in his *Dialogorum*. . . [1555]).

Even those in the Germanic countries who made no extravagant claims aided in this trend. Biblfander, although recognizing the priority of Hebrew, Greek, and Latin, at the same time stressed the importance of learning the vernacular and emphasized that it too could be encompassed by the *ratio* which applied not just to the "sacred three" but to all languages as well (i of his preface). Gesner, although he is concerned with all the languages of the world, still devotes a high proportion of his *Mithridates* to the Germanic languages (cf. Metcalf, 1963a, especially 149).

But it was Goropius Becanus in his *Origines Antwerpianae* (1569) who caused the greatest sensation with his claim that Dutch-Flemish had been the original language of Paradise, the language from which all others descended. Becanus received more than his share of ridicule for his seemingly tortured etymologies and his rambling account of the earliest Dutch origins. But in one sense he can be said to have supplied the basic germ for the later Indo-European theory. For it was he who emphasized the vague concept of Scythia as the real linguistic source of the later variety of languages. However much later writers differed on details, they came back again and again to the region which ancient authorities had reported as spreading out northward – both east and west – from Asia Minor. We shall return shortly to the more specific criticisms to which Becanus was subjected and to the more specific details of his methodology. But he had loosed an idea which might rouse opposition but was not allowed to die. In his own Dutch-Flemish area both Abraham Mylius in his *Lingua Belgica* and Adrianus Rodornius Scrieckius in his *Van t' beghin der eerster volcken van Europen, insonderheyt van den oorspronck ende saecken der Nederlandren, xxiii Boecken* (1614) were willing to grant ultimate priority to Hebrew but traced back their own tongue to the "Scythic-Celtic-Belgic" language of the age immediately after the Flood. Schottelius in his *Ausführliche Arbeit* (1663) chided Becanus, granted special status to Hebrew, but basically approved the Scythian doctrine. In Sweden Stiernhielm and Rudbeckius ridiculed Dutch-Flemish claims but still championed the Scythian theory. Andreas Jäger is firmly in this tradition.

That Jäger could be reprinted as late as 1774 (cf. above) is evidence of the persistence throughout the eighteenth century of this Scythian tradition, just as its influence on Leibniz' thinking is clear (cf. Waterman, 1963; cf. also Borst, 1957–63: 1475-78).

Etymological Methodology

As we mentioned at the beginning, our concern here is not merely with the Scythian tradition but with the whole complex of ideas which are bound up with that tradition. Thus the evidence adduced to support the one or the other view of linguistic history becomes significant. Our interest will be centered especially on the linguistic methodology itself, the type of etymologizing, the standards and rules, both explicit and implicit.

But we must constantly bear in mind that our scholars of the period were concerned not merely with this linguistic evidence but with the historical evidence as well: statements on language and the history of languages made by the infallible Bible and the more or less trustworthy ancient authors. But however infallible the Bible might be, the crux of any conclusion obtained from it was the proper interpretation, which could and did vary to the widest extent. The direct references to the relationship and development of languages in the Bible are relatively few; the most famous, of course, is the confusion of tongues at the time of the construction of the tower of Babel (Genesis 11:1-9), but the peoples named in the preceding tenth chapter and their spread over the earth were early associated with this confusion of tongues. (It is this particular tradition with which Borst [1957–63] is most immediately concerned.) Thus an initial linguistic unity followed by a later linguistic diversity was a basic presupposition of sacred scripture, and a historical framework for a genetic history of languages was thus provided. But the specific content of such a history could and did vary in extreme measure (as the numerous conflicting traditions testify), for the Biblical text as such is so little restrictive. The authors from classical antiquity were frequently contradictory in their linguistic judgments, and since their infallibility did not have to be assumed, they could be (and were) dealt with even more independently.

In the actual practice of their etymologizing and their setting up of linguistic interrelationships, the scholars of the period interwove their linguistic evidence and their historical evidence so neatly that the two strands cannot be unraveled with impunity. Although our concern in this paper will be the linguistic strand, we must expect to find the other strand constantly appearing as well.

BECANUS

Goropius Becanus himself, the real popularizer of the Scythian theory and the most controversial figure of the two centuries, is a useful starting point. He quickly became the butt of later commentators. Jäger offers a typical example of the ridicule he conjured up: Becanus proposes ridiculous jests ("nugas agit" [27]); Jäger warns his readers to hold their laughter at another Becanian etymology ("Tenete risum" [26]). Skinner, no admirer, hints nevertheless at the complexity of the man whom he terms uselessly subtle and laboriously inept ("inaniter subtilem & operose ineptum") [v]. Stiernhielm, admiring Becanus' unconventionality which reminds him some-what of his own, calls him "infelicem" [iii], although he later taunts both him and Mylius for their excessive claims to Dutch-Flemish purity and antiquity [xxxiv-xxxv]. Scrieckius, finally, devotes considerable space and effort to a just evaluation but summarizes initially: "Ioannes Goropius Becanus Magni vir ingenii origines conscripsit, conamine & labore incomparabili, sed successu nullo" [xiii] [Ioannes Goropius Becanus, a man of great talent, wrote of the origins with incomparable exertion and labor but with no success]. It was especially Becanus' lack of organization, his uncontrolled and too-imaginative erudition, to which Scrieckius objected. How difficult it was even for contemporaries to follow all the details of Becanus' argument is shown by the reproach which Scrieckius makes [xiv] because Becanus etymologizes *Cimbri/Cimmerii* as *Cum* plus *Ber* (can hardly be borne: "vix tolerari potest"), a name applied by their neighbors on account of their depredations. Actually Becanus weighs at some length this etymology proposed by others (368), only to reject it in favor of his own connection of the name with Gomer (as is discussed below).

It is true that Becanus' ideas are presented in what is almost a stream of associations, without a clear and orderly organization of material. It is also true that in his zeal he not infrequently proposes etymologies without attempting a detailed linguistic justification. Yet it is also true that his normal procedure is to present just such a detailed linguistic justification for many of his proposals.

Thus Becanus attempts to connect the *Cimbri* and *Cimmerii* (who in his view were the founders of Antwerp) with the family of Japheth and specifically with Gomer, Japheth's oldest son. But he is likewise concerned with the problem of linguistic "similarity" in all three items: *Cimbri, Cimmerii, Gomer*. The equating of the first two items is relatively simple: "E Cimmeriis igitur concisione vocis Cimri, & melioris soni gratia Cimbri sunt nominati" (367) [From *Cimmeriis* therefore *Cimri* developed by concision of the word, and then they were called, for the sake of a pleasanter sound, *Cimbri*]. But the equating of *Gomer* was complicated. There was, to be sure, little difficulty with the initial letter, once it was conceded that "gamma & cappa" were "cognatae litterae" (for the origin of the concept "cognatae litterae", see Diderichsen's chapter in this volume), and "ita minimo discrimine pro media littera eam positam esse, quae tenuis vocatur" (374-375) [thus that letter which we term "tenuis" has been substituted for the "media" with a minimal amount of variation]. (Becanus' starting point, of course, is the proper name *Gomer* and his task to see how it could appear as Greek-Latin *Cim*[*m*]*er-*). A further possibility might have been the attempt of foreigners to render the Hebrew "Gimel": "& fuit fortasse antiquissimis Hebraeorum ea Gimel pronunciatio, ut ab exteris per Cappa redderetur" (375) [and perchance there was a pronunciation of *Gimel* among the most ancient of the Hebrews that was imitated by foreigners by means of *Cappa*], yet this was not a necessary step: "cum frequentissimae fiant cognatarum litterarum permutationes" (375) [since permutations of cognate letters occur very frequently]. But Becanus also recognized that other sound interchanges were more difficult to account for: "Verum alterum non aeque facile, qua de causa o micron transiverit in Iota" (375) [but it is not equally easy to explain the other change as to why *omicron* shifted to *iota*]. Here the phonetic approach has to be given up: "Alia igitur ratio quaerenda" (375) [Another explanation must therefore be sought]. Now Becanus turns to his own interpretation from the Hebrew inflectional system:

> Quod enim Gomer in coniugatione Cal dicitur, id in coniugatione Piel Gimer erit: in Cal igitur Gomer nihil aliud est quam finitus, sive absolutus & perfectus est; in coniugatione vero Piel Gimer, idem est quod perfecit Latinis (375). [For what is called *Gomer* in the conjugation *Cal* will be *Gimer* in the conjugation *Piel*: in *Cal* therefore, *Gomer* is nothing other than "finished" or "absolute and complete"; but in the conjugation *Piel* it is *Gimer*, the same as "he has accomplished it" is for the Latins.]

Gomer, as the oldest son of Japheth, accomplished more than any other in spreading wide the name and fame and seed of Japheth: "Dicendus igitur potius Gimer, id est perfecit; quam Gomer, id est absolutus sive perfectus est" (375) [Therefore he is to be called *Gimer*, that is "he has accomplished it" rather than *Gomer*, that is "absolute" or "complete"].

We are here made aware of one of Becanus' implicit but basic assumptions. Like Plato's Cratylus and a long tradition, Becanus believes in a basic natural fit between form and meaning (at least in the original language).[2] Since the ultimate decision as to the "propriety" of a given fit must remain highly subjective as a reflection of one's own *Weltanschauung* —

Becanus' own deeply religious convictions are reflected repeatedly in his etymologies (cf. Borst, 1957–63: 1217) — this assumption is one of the basic factors in the later rejection of so many of Becanus' etymologies, even by those (like Scrieckius) who agree in theory but disagree as to the specific "propriety."

It may be useful at this point to consider another example of Becanus' etymologizing: his attempt to determine the "real meaning" of the classical proper name *Sacae* (equivalent — according to Becanus — to the *Saxones*). We will be forced to oversimplify (Becanus uses more than 70 folio pages, with many bypaths and digressions, to discuss this question). We must also note that Becanus in his etymologizing aimed to discover, not just the one "true" etymon, but as many "true" meanings as possible, for precisely the fusing or focusing of a large number of "pertinent" meanings was a mark of the original language to which he hoped to penetrate. It was of course his ultimate purpose to show that precisely Dutch-Flemish elements most clearly satisfied this demand and hence were in reality the elements of the original language.

Becanus starts out from the attempts of the ancients to connect the *Sacae* with the Latin *saga* (sooth-sayer). But Becanus rejects any attempt to explain the word in Latin terms, claiming rather that the whole complex of Latin *saga, sagio, praesagio*, and *sagax* was actually derived from the *Cimmerii* (585). *Saga* was in fact the original form ("priscum nomen" [573]) and in turn was derived from Dutch-Flemish *Segunen* (to bless [577]). The root of this form, moreover, was *Sagun* (*sagun* alternates with *segun* just as the *Angli & Zelandi* often pronounce *Sec* for *Sac* [581]). But by its very nature this must be a compound, for the original language contained only the shortest possible elements. *Sagun* therefore was composed of *Sac* and *Gun*. *Sac* had, to start with, a double meaning: with a short vowel it was "saccus" (sack), with a long vowel, "causa" (cause). The form and meaning with the short vowel were earlier ("quia breve tempus longo prius est natura & ortu" [577]), and this priority had its deeper meaning as well: "Qui nomen fabricavit, monuit illo quidem, nobis quaedam colligenda esse atque reponenda, sed pauca & exiguo tempore" (578) [Whoever constructed the word, assuredly admonished by means of it that we are to collect and put away certain things, but only few and for a short time]. But with the discovery of this meaning another secret becomes apparent: the *Sac* into which all things are drawn and put and which thus is "increased" is the phonetic reverse of *Cas* (which means to "diminish" [577]: I have not identified this Becanian form *Cas*). This is ordained by the "primae linguae proprietas. . .quae in conversione litterarum consistens, contrarium ei, quod priore ordine notabatur, significatum inducit" (577) (that is, it points to the "propriety" of the original language in expressing semantic opposites by phonetic reversals). But the development to the long vowel points to a further dimension: the "cause," that is the "prime cause," or God, who likewise draws all to himself and encompasses all. This double meaning of the first element of the word has its own entirely appropriate and symbolic phonetic form: "Prima littera sibilo suo motionem ad aliquid, media littera quadrato suo sono stationem & moram, ultima spiritus in se retractione suum cuique commodum ad se trahendum docet" (579) [The first letter with its sibilance indicates a motion toward something; the second with its square sound, halt and pause; and the final, by the retraction of the breath, teaches that that which is suitable to each one is to be drawn to one]. Becanus proceeds to decompose further: *Sac* itself is composed of *so hac*: "quo inclinatio ad aliquid & apprehensio eius notatur" (579), while *Hac* in turn is a contraction of *Ha ic* = "O si haberem!" (577) — all, of course, pertinent to the "true" meaning of the multi-compounded *Sac*. The second element is the verb *gun* ("faveo"), and the two elements together can have somewhat varying interpretations, depending on the way the linkage is interpreted: "I am well disposed toward the first cause" (faveo primam causam [580]) or "I grant the first cause to my favor" (favore meo primam causam do [580]); or, in the "preterite form," *Sagan*, the meaning would be: "God or the first cause favored" (Deus sive prima causa favit [584]). This "obviously" referred to the first column of the *Cimmerii*, sent out with the *blessing* of the father (Japheth) and grandfather (Noah) and called *Sagan* ("Deus favit"), a term then taken over by the Greeks who omitted the final *-n* (585). "Primi illi nostrorum magistri" therefore produced the term *sagun* most excellently (580).

Contorted as the mystically semantic interpretations seemed to his contemporaries and to later scholars, Becanus, as we have noted, was genuinely concerned with the *ratio* which might explain the actual phonetic similarities and dissimilarities. But he nowhere makes explicit his system of what is phonetically comparable; he does not give specific rules or formulas for the admissible and the inadmissible.

But it is precisely in this area that the seventeenth century appears to have taken more and more thought. There seems to be growing need for more explicit statements of the *rationes* which could be applied in phonetic correspondence, and also for rules to decide *what* could legitimately be compared. To be sure there is frequently a wide gap between the proclaimed rules and the actual practice of etymologizing. But the theoretical discussion, at least, becomes increasingly sophisticated.[3]

MYLIUS

Abraham Mylius in his *Lingua Belgica* (1612) attempted to set up appropriate rules for evidence, to prevent turning "derivanda" into "contorquenda" as Becanus had done (23). Thus he listed the possible causes for phonetic similarity between items in two different languages. Only a few such similarities were due to chance or to onomatopoeia, the fit of form and meaning (56, 66-67). Descent from an earlier common parent tongue, on the other hand, was a major factor,[4] while borrowing (as a result either of warlike conquest or peaceful trade) introduced by far the greatest number of similarities (68-69). It was with these latter two categories that the comparative scholar should concern himself.

But Mylius proposed certain phonetic limitations as well. Not only could phonetic variation be summarized under the terms traditional with grammarians—metathesis, metaplasm, aphaeresis, syncope, apocope (21), for example—but actual comparisons should be limited to those specific interchanges which had already been attested among dialects of the same language or in successive temporal stages of the same language. Thus the interchange of *r* and *s* was evidenced by Attic Greek *tharrein* in contrast to *tharsein* in other dialects, the interchange of *s* and *t* by High German *wasser* against Belgian *water*, the interchange of *h* and *f* by Spanish *hijo* and Latin *filius* (21-22). It is important to note that (in contrast to the modern concept of "sound laws") such interchangeability, once established, could be applied to any potential cognates in any languages in any age.

Liberal as these "rules" were, Mylius made little attempt, in his own etymologizing, to comply with them. He stretches "metathesis" in declaring Belgian *groen* (green) cognate with Hebrew *ragnan* [*ra^{<a}nân*, actually fresh, luxuriant] (207). His insistence that congruence had to extend to meaning as well as form (20) contrasts with his arguing, "per antiphrasin," that Belgian *hel* (bright) is connected with *hel* (hell) because hell showed so little light ("minime lucidum") (207), quite literally a *lucus a non lucendo*.

SCRIECKIUS

Rodornius Scrieckius, Mylius' immediate contemporary and linguistic compatriot, follows (in his xxiii *Boecken* of 1614) basically the same etymologizing procedure as Becanus: the breaking down of a given item into ever smaller "original" elements, and the justification of these latter in "Cratylan" semantic terms. But Scrieckius gives a detailed and specific list of what he considers these basic elements to be.[5]

These elements can be used to build up an item, as Scrieckius illustrates with the word for "earth." *A/Ae* is one of the basic Scythian elements, meaning "water"; with an added *r* this becomes somewhat "harder" ("duriuscula") and hence *ar* (a form I cannot further identify; glossed as "arena" [sand]), and with a *d* added to this, "harder" still: *ard/aerd* ("terra") [iii]. The Biblical CHANAAN illustrates a breakdown into the elements *Ga-na-an* ("Accessus-ad-propinque"), referring to Abraham's approach to the land of Canaan [v].

SCHOTTELIUS

The very nature of the task of etymologizing required some system of word analysis, either explicit (as with Scrieckius' elements) or merely implicit (with most writers), for some method was required to determine precisely which elements in a given form were to be identified and used as the basis for comparison. But a reasoned proposal, based on the careful analysis of one language, did not appear until the latter half of the seventeenth century: Schottelius' approach (in his *Ausführliche Arbeit* of 1663) to German (and Germanic). For this language (family) showed a typical structure of three elements: the *Stammwort* or *literae radicales*, the *Hauptendung* or *terminatio derivandi*, and *zufällige Endung* or *literae accidentales* (68-71). To be sure Schottelius, like Mylius, believed that the inflectional endings showed such infinite and irregular variation that they could be of little or no use in etymologizing (43); even the root and the derivational ending permitted phonetic variation to the point of complete disappearance (42-43). But at least the principle that root should be compared only with root gave a basic standard. For this reason Schottelius could reject the attempt to derive the German *Königen* in its dative plural form from the Greek infinitive *kunēgên* (to hunt), despite the close consonantal parallel, and similarly the proposal to derive the Latin *induciae* from *inde, uti, iam* could be rejected as violating the principles of Latin compounding (54).

DE LAET

Earlier in the century a challenging pragmatic voice had attempted to set up certain basic rules for comparing two languages to see if they were related. The challenger was Johannes de Laet (1582–1649). The opponent was the renowned Hugo Grotius and his theories on the settlement of the New World. Grotius assumed that the Indian languages of North America stemmed from the Norwegians, who had migrated by way of Iceland, "Frislandia," and Greenland. (For an account of Grotius' views as a whole, cf. Borst, 1957–63: 1298-1300; also Hodgen, 1964: 314-315 and Slotkin, 1965: 97-98. On the controversy, see also Huddleston 1967: 118-128 and Metcalf 1969).

De Laet's strength was his own personal experience in the New World and his reputation as a geographer (he had published numerous geographical works; cf. van der Aa, 1865: 26-28). His method was to take up and quote Grotius point by point, following the quotation by his own attempt at refutation, first in his *Notae. . .* (1643), and then, when Grotius had in turn replied to this, in his *Responsio. . .* (1644). (All citations, unless otherwise designated, are from the *Notae*). It will be worth our while to consider the particular statements which induced verbatim quotations, both by Georg

Horn (1620–1670), another opponent of Grotius' views (cf. Borst, 1957–63: 1305-1307), and by Andreas Jäger.

The immediate occasion was a small list of words which Grotius had adduced to show a Norwegian-Germanic connection with languages of the New World. De Laet not only takes up each item one by one and shows the unreliability of each (31-35), but also remarks:

> . . .non satis est, paucula vocabula . . . reperiri, sed oportet ipsum linguae aut dialecti genium, pronunciandi rationem, constructionis modum, & imprimis nomina earum rerum quae domesticae & maxime communes illi genti sunt, attendere: nam alias non difficile est in omnibus linguis reperire vocabula, convenientia aliquo modo cum aliis linguis . . . (30-31). [It is not sufficient that a few words. . .be found, but it is necessary that one observe the genius itself of the language or dialect, the system of pronunciation, the nature of the structure, and above all the names of those things which are domestic and most common to that nation: for otherwise it is not difficult to find words in all languages agreeing to some extent with other languages.]

Precisely Becanus and Scrieckius are then cited as examples of those who pursue etymologizing in complete disregard of such fundamental principles. After dealing with the individual items proposed by Grotius, De Laet continues:

> Si literas mutare, Syllabas transponere, addere, demere velis, nusquam non invenies quod ad hanc aut illam similitudinem cogas: sed hoc pro indicio originis gentium habere, id vero mihi non probatur" (35; similarly 24 and *Responsio*, 44-45, 49-50). [If you are willing to change letters, to transpose syllables, to add and substract, you will nowhere find something that cannot be forced into this or that similarity; but to consider this as evidence for the origin of peoples – this is truly not proved as far as I am concerned.]

Skinner likewise points out that the too "licentious indulgence" in the traditional categories of linguistic permutations could provide evidence to make any language agree with any other –even Icelandic (as a language of the Arctic Circle) with the language of the inhabitants of the Antarctic (if there was and were such) [x].

De Laet was not content with his more general statement as to the "ordinary" vocabulary to be compared: he specifies the parts of the body, the numerals, and the method of counting (54). He urges that these items be applied in testing both Grotius' theory of the Norwegian origin of the North American Indians and the legendary reports of the Welsh voyager Madoc. To facilitate such a test, he lists the parts of the body, the numerals from 1-10, close family relationships (father, etc.), and geographical terms (hill, etc.) in Norwegian and Icelandic, also in Welsh and Irish: these should be the basis for any pragmatic investigation into possible relationships with the languages of the New World (137-147). To show the difficulties, he also lists, item by item (e.g. caput), the appropriate forms from Welsh, Danish, and various North American Indian languages (147-151), illustrating vividly the lack of any obvious similarity. To show the discrepancies among the languages of North America themselves, he also lists the "basic vocabulary" terms in Huron and "Mexican" (172-186; cf. the more recent history of basic vocacabulary lists as sketched in Hymes, 1960a, b). De Laet illustrates how easily chance can play a role by comparing certain German and Ethiopian items and "deducing" that the Ethiopians had descended from the Germans, a *reductio ad absurdum* (*Responsio*, 44-45).

De Laet was also concerned with the relative rate of change. He pointed out the many obvious similarities that English showed to German even though it differs in dialect ("licet dialecto differat": *Responsio*, 48); yet the Anglo-Saxons migrated to Britain many years, even centuries, before the Norwegians were presumed to have gone to the New World. It was unreasonable to assume that the Norwegian language could have changed so rapidly and completely in the relatively brief space of time that would have to be assumed by Grotius' hypothesis (48).

STIERNHIELM

Even more iconoclastic was Stiernhielm, who dared to assert, in the "Preface" to his edition of the Gothic Bible: "Duo praecipua sunt ingeniorum obstacula, quominus veritatem & solidam sapientiam assequi valeant: Praeconcepta opinio, & virorum magnorum authoritas" [ii] [The two chief obstacles to the achievement of truth and solid wisdom are preconceived opinion and the authority of great men].

Stiernhielm's greatest merit, in this preface, is the clarity with which he defines "language" and "dialect." All language is for him subject to change, even his own Swedish, even those languages like Swedish that remain uncontaminated by outside influences: "lingua aliqua simplex, & ab aliis illibata perennans, solo diuturni temporis, seu vitio, seu virtute, sua sibi manens, aliam atque aliam successive faciem induit" [viii] [Any language, even one unmixed and uncontaminated by others, by the sole vice or virtue of a long span of time, assumes successively – while still remaining itself – another and again another appearance]. This constant change permits languages to be compared figuratively with men, even to the metaphor of birth and death. Stiernhielm likewise stresses in terms of "language" and "dialect" what he feels is the basic rhythm of human speech: "Temporum & Locorum intervallis, Dialectos abire in Linguas. Conversio Haec est perpetua: unam linguam abire in diversas Dialectos. Et ultra; singulas Dialectos, diuturnitate temporis, convalescere in linguas [xxvii-xxviii] [Because of the intervals of time and space, dialects develop into languages. This conversion is perpetual: one language is transformed into diverse dialects. And further: individual dialects, by the long passage of time wax into languages].

At the same time, of course, these new languages continue to be cognate through their common ancestor. But the varieties of linguistic development are not limited, and the images can include rejuvenation: [Whoever has studied the evidence] "mecum fatebitur, Linguas senium pati, exolescere, & emori; iterumque renasci, adolescere, iuvenescere, & in vegetam virilitatem roborascere" [ix] [. . .will grant me that languages suffer old age, grow out of use, and die; and on the other hand are reborn, develop into youth and manhood and grow strong into vigorous maturity]. A special case of this emergence of a "new" (but related) language is cited to emphasize that various "dialects" are still part of one "language." Stiernhielm proposes that speakers of "Brabantian," of Swedish, and of "Mechlenburgian" be brought into one city. In the course of time they would have developed a new dialect in itself unified ("una"), but different from each of the three original dialects and yet still Germanic [xxxi-xxxii].[6] Stiernhielm even provides a diagram:

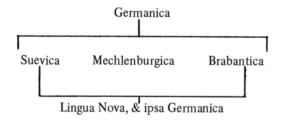

Germanica

Suevica   Mechlenburgica   Brabantica

Lingua Nova, & ipsa Germanica

Stiernhielm specifically excludes the languages of the New World from his considerations. It is not altogether clear whether he is moved pragmatically by lack of sufficient evidence, or by the frequent contemporary view that the "barbarian" languages really lacked a grammar, a *ratio*. But his own statement points to the latter consideration. He deals, he says, only with languages used in Asia, Africa, and Europe: "Quo Americanas, & in Indiis Insulanas, ut hodie sunt, omnino excludo: quippe in quibus nec rationis, nec cohaerentiae, aut cognationis ullum vestigium, deprehendo" [iv] [So I exclude altogether the American Languages and the Insular Languages of the Indies as they are today: for I detect in them not any trace of system or of coherence or of relatedness].

RUDBECKIUS

If Stiernhielm deserves credit for clarifying the concepts of language and dialect and of the historical rhythm of linguistic development, his countryman Olaf Rudbeckius deserves equal credit in his *Atlantica sive*

Manheim (1675) for making explicit many of the assumptions of the age concerning the principles of etymologizing. Like Mylius he was concerned with distinguishing borrowed items from inherited ones (21) and like De Laet he favored a concentration on words pertaining to ordinary needs ("ad designandas res in vita communi maxime necessarias & obvias" [21]) for establishing linguistic relationships. A foreign word ("peregrinum") could frequently be detected by the fact that it did not fit into a widespread pattern of derivation centering on a common root ("radix"), such as that provided by the Swedish *Byggia* ("aedificare"): *Bygningh, Bygd, By, Byaman,* etc. (27). In contrast to such patterns the proper name *Petrus* shows no derivatives and hence reveals itself as a foreign borrowing (27).

Rudbeckius is particularly clear and decisive in showing what may or may not be used in establishing phonetic parallels. For he is aware of the lengths to which the merely classificatory categories might lead and ridicules ("Nugae!") the attempt of Philipp Clüver to transform *Theut* into *Dan* and *Dan* into *Godh* and declared that such can lead only to "turpissimam . . . confusionem" (17). Using Clüver's procedure one could easily identify Swedish *Folk* with Latin *Gens* by merely mechanically changing F to G, O to E, L to N, and K to S (17). On the contrary, attention must be paid to the "ratio literarum." There are two possibilities. Some "literae" are apt to change "natura sua"; other changes we can discover "scriptorum fide ac testimoniis" (i.e., in the actual historical records of observed sound parallels [18]). The classes of consonants which "tend by nature to interchange" and can be termed "cognationes" are listed in detail and encompass groups which we recognize as of similar phonetic character: "(B P F W) (C K Q G) (I G) (D T) (L R) (M N) &c" (18). A full page lists specific instances of such correspondences. An inspection of the chart reveals quite clearly that we are dealing here (as we were with Mylius) simply with equations — not with historically conditioned parallels. For while the Swedish example regularly appears in the left column, items from any language or age may appear in the right. Thus Rudbeckius lists, along with other items:

T	ock	D
LåTa		LaDe (Danish)
FooT		FooD (Danish)
ÅTa		eDere [Latin]
F	ock	B
SkriFwa		ScriBere [Latin]
GaFFel		GaBlin (Danish)
LiuFlig		LiBlig (German)

Although the explicitness of procedure marks a distinct advance over Mylius, the basic *ratio* is the same: a parallel once established historically can be applied anywhere or any time in establishing a new etymology.

Conclusions

RELATION TO "COMPARATIVE METHOD"

We come at this point to a crucial distinction between the patterns of thought which dominated this early period and those which gradually crystalized in the nineteenth century as the "comparative method." There is much that prepared the way for nineteenth century developments: the concept of a no-longer-spoken parent language which in turn produced the major linguistic groups of Asia and Europe; a concept of the development of languages into dialects and of dialects into new independent languages that could help to explain the historical situation; certain minimum standards for determining what words are borrowed and what words are ancestral in a language; an insistence that not a few random items but a large number of words from the basic vocabulary should form the basis of comparisons.

But while the language as a whole was viewed genetically or at least historically, as moving in only one direction in the stream of time, the phonetic elements of the language were viewed a-historically, non-genetically, as interchangeable counters (subject, to be sure, to certain restrictions either by nature or by historical evidence); phonetic change was thus not viewed as limited to a specific direction in a specific dialect at a specific period of time. There is therefore no deeper parallel, but only a superficial resemblance to the later concept of the "sound laws."[7] As far as the sixteenth and seventeenth centuries were concerned, a language might show historical progression, but its parts changed at random.

Looking back on the record, we find it tempting to try to fix Jäger's position in the history of the Indo-European hypothesis and to consider the extent to which he anticipates not only the nineteenth century, but even Sir William Jones, whose famous statement (1786) is often taken as the start of the modern concept of the Indo-European family:

> The Sanscrit Language whatever may be its antiquity, is a wonderful structure, more perfect than the Greek, more copious than the Latin, and more exquisitely refined than either; yet bearing to both of them a stronger affinity, both in the roots of verbs and in the forms of grammar, than could have been produced by accident; so strong, that no philologer could examine all the three without believing them to have sprung from

some common source which, perhaps, no longer exists. There is a similar reason, though not quite so forcible, for supposing, that both the Gothic and Celtic, though blended with a different idiom, had the same origin with the Sanscrit. The old Persian may be added to the same family (quoted from Hoenigswald, 1963: 2).

But if we look at the proposal by Jäger, we can observe that precisely a century before Sir William Jones a theory is outlined which in some respects is even more "modern"; for the concept of an original parent language no longer spoken is an essential ingredient (in contrast to Sir William's uncertain phrase: "... some common source which, perhaps, no longer exists"). The whole rhythm of linguistic descent is likewise better defined than with Sir William. The review in the Greifswald *Critische Versuche* of 1742 (cited above regarding Jäger) emphasizes precisely these features (the lost parent, the development of "dialects" into "languages"). The fact that the original parent language has a name ("Scythian") makes it a more definite concept, even if it strikes modern ears as the most incongruous aspect of the theory.

But the one great flaw in Jäger's proposal is the ultimately decisive strength in Sir William Jones: Jäger is unfamiliar with the Indic branch of languages, and does not include it in his calculations. The overwhelming evidence of similarity between this branch and the more familiar branches in Europe was, however, the most convincing proof of relationship; and it was this evidence which Sir William and his successors opened up to European scholarship. Only gradually did the actual convincing method develop out of this new evidence, as Hoenigswald has shown. But since he lacked both decisive evidence and decisive method, Jäger was unable to effect a real "revolution," despite the repeated attention to his work in the century following its publication. It could impress but not entirely convince. To argue whether the credit for the discovery of the "Indo-European hypothesis" should go to Jäger or to Sir William is somewhat like arguing whether Leif Ericson or Columbus "discovered" America.

RELATION TO PARADIGMS

We turn finally to the pertinence for this study about Jäger and his contemporaries of the theses of Thomas S. Kuhn in his *The Structure of Scientific Revolutions* (1962).

I have found Kuhn's description of the "pre-scientific period" of a science interesting and relevant, as far as the "Study of Language" is concerned, to the era of the sixteenth and seventeenth centuries with which I have been dealing. I will return to this aspect shortly.

But the further question arises as to the applicability of Kuhn's proposals (whatever their ultimate validity) to the "Study of Language" as a whole.

In my opinion there has not yet emerged a "paradigm" (in the Kuhnian sense) all-embracing enough to encompass the whole field of the "Study of Language": in Kuhnian terms, therefore, the field as a whole has not yet emerged as a "science." At best and most hopefully we are merely on the threshold of such an emergence.

Nevertheless, there are parts of the field which have developed ascendant "paradigms" and which accordingly have emerged into the "scientific" age. It is my contention that comparative philology was the first to develop this "maturity," and that the practices of the comparative philologists during the nineteenth century established, even if much more slowly than usually assumed, the methods and the doctrines of this "science."[8] Later other aspects of the "Study of Language" developed dominant "paradigms": phonetics is an obvious and clear example.

But the overall pattern has still not appeared. There has not been a doctrine sufficiently embracing and sufficiently convincing to win general allegiance. In addition to the concentration on the sub-disciplines there has often been a wide geographical breach, as between Europe and America in a good part of the thirties, forties, and fifties of the current century.

Therefore, if Kuhn's doctrines are strictly applied to the history of the "Study of Language," it would not be correct to assert that a nineteenth-century "diachronic paradigm" has been "supplanted" by a twentieth-century "synchronic paradigm." There has not been a shift in "paradigm," since both diachronic and synchronic study are but aspects of the more general problems involved in the "Study of Language"; instead there has merely been a shift of major concern, with the "paradigm" of diachronic linguistics persisting and a "paradigm" of synchronic linguistics possibly emerging.

In returning to our original question: the pertinence of Kuhn to the study of the development of the Indo-European concept in the sixteenth and seventeenth centuries: we find ourselves in the "prehistory" of the "science" (Kuhn, 1962: 21) of comparative philology. The indices are all present: the early writers were not specialists writing for other specialists in learned professional journals, but rather men of broad learning, writing books for other men of broad learning (Kuhn, 1962: 20-21);[9] the authors felt the need for establishing their branch of study from its foundations and often derived their strength from theological or philosophical assumptions for which the often random linguistic data served as a convenient arsenal (Kuhn, 1962: 12-13). And although we have been concerned with a particular strand or tradition,[10] we were aware that this was merely one of a number of competing traditions. Even within the tradition itself, individual deviations were often marked and there frequently seemed to be more chaos than orderly progression.

Since the fundamental thesis of Kuhn requires that we take the prehistory of a discipline seriously in its own terms, we are encouraged to focus our attention on the details of method and rationale in the earlier period. Not surprisingly this provides us with a much better perspective in depth for contrasting the earlier and our later views.

In the field of comparative philology we noticed no fundamental change or shift in basic methodology during the two centuries we have been considering, but we did notice a growing sophistication in certain important if not crucial areas. At the same time a look at the *ratio* of the age prevented us from assuming "anticipation" of modern methods where the similarities are actually superficial. Thus, despite tables such as Rudbeckius drew up, there was really no parallel to the modern concept of "sound laws." While the scholars of the age could frequently view the larger structures (languages, dialects) from a genetic point of view, they consistently maintained a non-historical, non-genetic, two- (not one-) dimensional approach to the smaller phonetic ingredients. Since phonetic change was not treated with a sense of its historical pertinence, competing "schools" or traditions could not establish their etymologies so convincingly as to lead to a dominant paradigm.

But we have seen that their etymologies did have, in their own terms, a *ratio*, that they were not mere "nugae," however fantastic most of them seem to us today. For if we are willing to take seriously the prehistory of comparative philology, we can ourselves recover a lost dimension and gain a new perspective.

NOTES

1. Similar imagery employed by Stiernhielm is cited in the paper presented at the Burg Wartenstein conference by the late Paul Diderichsen (chapter 10, this volume). Diderichsen's account is particularly pertinent to the problems in the sixteenth and seventeenth centuries raised in my paper, and complements many of my observations. At the Newberry conference Roman Jakobson emphasized the great importance of the Swedish (Uppsala) school of linguistics in the sixteenth and seventeenth centuries, particularly for the later development of Slavic linguistics. Stiernhielm (as well as Rudbeckius mentioned later) was, of course, an important member of this school and his influence on Jäger is obvious and acknowledged.

2. Most commentators of the period deal explicitly with this question. Some, like Mylius, admit theoretically such a "fit" only in a rare number of cases. But Scrieckius confesses himself an adherent of "Plato's" theory that "the right principle of a name inheres by nature in individual things" ("Rebus singulis naturâ inesse rectam nominis rationem" [xii]), and hopes to prove that "omnia Scythica, Celtica et Belgica nomina" contain precisely the theoretically demanded "proprietates". Scrieckius recognizes in this respect his kinship with Becanus [xiv] and his opposition to Mylius [xv].

3. That this trend toward analyzing similarities was a characteristic feature of seventeenth-century thought is documented in considerable detail by Margaret T. Hodgen in the chapter "Similarities and Their Documentary Properties" of her recent book, *Early Anthropology in the Sixteenth and Seventeenth Centuries* (1964: 295-353). Particularly relevant to my own presentation are also the preceding chapters: "The Ark of Noah and the Problem of Cultural Diversity" (207-253) and "Diffusion, Degeneration, and Environmentalism" (254-294).

4. In accordance with his belief that Hebrew had been the original language and that the "confusion" at Babel had been a splitting into "dialects" rather than into completely new and unrelated languages (85-86), Mylius distinguished between words that had descended from this original Hebrew into every language (relatively few) and words that were characteristic of the many later language families or "matrices" such as the "Lingua Belgica."

5. They include all the forms, contracted and uncontracted, of the definite article (*I, Hy, Tie, Die*, etc., *D', T', -m, -n, -r, -s* [ii]). Like Becanus, Scrieckius was fond of assuming that a form in question had originated from the merging of the article with another element.

6. Skinner indulges in a similar fantasy: if three speakers of English, one cultivated speaker from London and two rustic speakers (one from Devonshire, one from York) were thrown together on an otherwise uninhabited island, they would at first have trouble understanding one another. But as time went on, either the two rustic speakers would adopt the urban speech or a new language would emerge: "una Lingua ex tribus mixtis & simul contemperatis conflata" [ii].

7. Many early grammarians have been erroneously credited with anticipating the formulation of certain "sound laws," thus Konrad Gesner by Jan Agrell. Cf. Metcalf, 1963b, n.30.

8. Henry Hoenigswald had emphasized at the Burg Wartenstein conference that the theory of comparative philology had developed during the nineteenth century in a much more complicated manner than is usually assumed. The unambiguous, "linear" development of the "science" of comparative philology was even more strongly challenged at the Newberry conference in papers by Paul Kiparsky, Keith Percival, Robert Austerlitz, and Hoenigswald himself. Many of the attitudes of the preceding centuries, it was demonstrated in the reports, persisted far into the century. Nevertheless, the

contrast with the sixteenth and seventeenth centuries is still strong enough to permit us, in Kuhn's terms, to speak of comparative philology as a "science."

9. Gesner, in addition to being a bibliographer, a biologist, and a professor of physics, was a physician, as were Becanus (personal physician to the sisters of Emperor Charles V), Skinner, and Rudbeckius (a famed botanist as well). Mylius was a theologian, De Laet a geographer, and Scrieckius and Schottelius learned jurists and high state officials. Bibliander was professor of Old Testament and Oriental Languages in Zürich and Stiernhielm, "S. R. *Maj.Consil. & Colleg.Antiquit.Praeses Holmiae*" (Jäger, 2).

10. The term "school" applied by Kuhn (pp.12 ff.) to these traditions is not, in my opinion, a happy choice, for it tends to connote a group of people rather than a complex of theory, practice, and procedure. Since I have no ideal term to propose, I have avoided "school" in this article but employed other terms used by Kuhn, especially "tradition" or "theory" (varying these occasionally with "strand").

REFERENCES

Becanus, Johannes Goropius. 1569. Origines Antwerpianae. Antwerp.

Bede, the Venerable. 1862. Opera Omnia 1. Edited by J. P. Migne. Paris.

Bibliander, Theodor. 1548. De ratione communi omnium linguarum et literarum commentarius. Zürich.

Borst, Arno. 1957–63. Der Turmbau von Babel. Geschichte der Meinungen über Ursprung und Vielfalt der Sprachen und Völker. 4 vols. in 6. Stuttgart: Hiersemann.

De Laet, Johannes. 1643. Notae ad Dissertationem Hugonis Grotii. Amsterdam.

_____. 1644. Responsio ad Dissertationem secundam H. Grotii. Amsterdam.

Diderichsen, Paul. 1964. The foundation of comparative linguistics: revolution or continuation? Paper prepared in advance for participants in Burg Wartenstein symposium no. 25. (See Diderichsen, this volume.)

Gesner, Konrad. 1555. Mithridates. Zürich.

Hagström, K. A. 1899. Strengnes Stifts Herdaminne 3. Strengnes.

Hodgen, Margaret T. 1964. Early anthropology in the sixteenth and seventeenth centuries. Philadelphia: University of Pennsylvania Press.

Hoenigswald, Henry M. 1963. On the history of the comparative method. Anthropological Linguistics 5(3): 1-11.

Huddleston, Lee Eldridge. 1967. Origins of the American Indians, European concepts, 1492–1729. Austin: University of Texas Press.

Hymes, Dell H. 1960a. Lexicostatistics so far. Current Anthropology 1: 3-44.

_____. 1960b. More on lexicostatistics. Current Anthropology 1: 338-345.

Jäger, Andreas. 1686. De Lingua Vetustissima Europae, Scytho-Celtica et Gothica. Wittenberg.

Kuhn, Thomas S. 1962. The structure of scientific revolutions. Chicago: University of Chicago Press.

Metcalf, George J. 1953a. Abraham Mylius on historical lingusitics. PMLA 68: 535-554.

———. 1953b. Schottel and historical linguistics. The Germanic Review (April), 113-125.

———. 1963a. Konrad Gesner's views on the Germanic languages. Monatshefte 55: 149-156.

———. 1963b. The views of Konrad Gesner on language. Studies in Germanic languages and literatures in memory of Fred O. Nolte. Ed. by Erich Hofacker. St. Louis: Washington University Press. Pp.15-26.

———. 1966. Andreas Jäger and his *De Lingua Vetustissima Europae* (1686). Modern Language Notes 81: 489-493.

———. 1969. A linguistic clash in the seventeenth century. German Life and Letters 23: 31-38.

Mylius, Abraham. 1612. Lingua Belgica. Leiden.

Oelrichs, Ioann. 1774. Germaniae litteratae opuscula historico-philologico-theologica emendatius et auctius recusa 2. Bremen.

Périon, Joachim. 1555. Dialogorum de linguae gallicae origine, eiusque cum Graeca cognatione, libri quatuor. Paris.

Rudbeckius, Olaf. 1675. Atlantica sive Manheim. Uppsala.

Scaliger, Joseph Justus. 1610. Diatriba de Europaeorum linguis. Pp.119-122. Diatriba de varia literarum aliquot pronuntiatione. Pp.127-132. In: Opuscula varia antehac non edita. Paris.

Schottelius, Justus Georgius. 1663. Ausführliche Arbeit von der Teutschen HaubtSprache. Braunschweig.

Scrieckius, Adrianus Rodornius. 1614. Van t' beghin der eerster volcken van Europen, insonderheyt van den oorspronck ende saecken der Nederlandren, xxiii Boecken. Ypres.

Skinner, Stephan. 1671. Etymologica Linguae Anglicanae. London.

Slotkin, J. S. 1965. Readings in early anthropology. Viking Fund publications in anthropology 40. New York: Wenner–Gren Foundation for Anthropological Research.

Stiernhielm, Georg. 1671. De linguarum origine Praefatio. In: D. N. Jesu Christi SS. Evangelia ab Ulfila Gothorum translata. Stockholm.

van der Aa, A. J. 1865. Biographisch Woordenboek der Nederlanden. Vol. 11. Pp.26-28. (The whole, 1852–77. 20 vols.)

Waterman, John T. 1963. The languages of the world: a classification by G. W. Leibniz. Studies in Germanic languages and literatures in memory of Fred O. Nolte. Ed. by Erich Hofacker. St. Louis: Washington University Press. Pp.27-34.

8. Some Eighteenth Century Antecedents of Nineteenth Century Linguistics: The Discovery of Finno-Ugrian

Janos Gulya

The especial trend of empirical linguistics in the eighteenth century was word-collecting and comparison of languages, as a means of historical research. On the basis of the history of Finno-Ugrian linguistics, I shall sketch the main lines of this trend, and then discuss its relation to the establishment of comparative linguistics in the early nineteenth century. In particular, I shall consider why the trend had revolutionary consequences in one family of languages and not in another.

Leibniz

The trend was inspired by the view of G. W. Leibniz, the eminent German philosopher of these times, on the investigation of the origin of peoples, according to which "nihil maiorem ad antiquas populorum origines indagandas lucem praebeat, quam collationem linguarum ..." [nothing provides a greater light for the inquiry into the ancient origins of peoples, than the comparison of languages ...] (Leibniz 1768: 228; cf. Pápay 1922: 6; Pedersen 1931: 9; Aarsleff 1969).

In order to obtain material for his researches in this field Leibniz issued an appeal insisting on the collecting of glossaries and translations of prayers, etc. for the purpose of comparison. The Appeal, which has become famous, gives a detailed program, too. In point 5 of the Appeal Leibniz asks for translations of the Lord's Prayer and "nonnulla vocabula rerum vulgarium ..." [some names of common things]. In point 15 he also enumerates the words the collecting of which, for the purpose of comparison, he considers most important. These are:

> Nomina numeralia, unum duo, 3, 4, 5, 6, 7, 8, 9, 10, 20, 30, 40, 50, 100, 1000. Propinquitates, aetates: Pater, mater, avus, filius, filia, frater, soror. ... Partes corporis: Corpus, caro, cutis, sanguis, ossa, caput. ... Necessitates: Cibus, potus, panis,

aqua. . . . Naturalia: Deus, homo, coelum, sol, luna, stella, aer, pluvis, tonitrus, fulgur, nubes, gelu, grando, nix, glacies, ignis . . . lapis, arena . . . canis, lupus, cervus, ursus, vulpes, avis, serpens, mus. Actiones: Edere, bibere, loqui, videre, esse, stare, ire, occidere, ridere, dormine, scire, velle c. [Numeral words, one, two, three, four, five, six, seven, eight, nine, ten, twenty, thirty, forty, fifty, one hundred, one thousand. Relationships, ages: Father, mother, uncle, son, daughter, brother, sister. . . . Parts of the body: Body, flesh, skin, blood, bone, head. . . . Needs: food, drink, bread, water. . . . Natural things: God, man, sky, sun, moon, star, air, rain, thunder, lightning, cloud, frost, hail, snow, ice, fire . . . stone, sand . . . dog, wolf, deer, bear, fox, bird, snake, mouse. Actions: to eat, drink, speak, see, be, stand, go, strike, laugh, sleep, know, pluck, etc.]

The researchers of the eighteenth century — and Leibniz among them — were especially attracted by the multinational and multilingual Russia, still having in store a great many unknown mysteries (see Guerrier 1873; Richter, passim; Aarsleff 1969: 186). So it is not due to mere chance that the word-collecting trend attained its height just in Russia and just among the foreign scholars who made visits there. The influence and hints of Leibniz were one factor, see, for example, the preface to Fischer 1770, where Schlözer says about Fischer: "viam . . . quam *Leibnitius* olim magno animo cepit, tu primus patefecisti. . . . [the way . . . which Leibniz with great spirit grasped long ago, you are the first to make truly accessible.] (Cf. Zsirai 1937: 489; Setälä 1921: 103, etc.). Another factor was the political and economic development of Russia in the seventeenth and eighteenth centuries. Owing to this development, at the beginning of the eighteenth century, it became more and more necessary to create a national independent economic life, one that would meet the requirements of the time and those of the State, growing ever stronger. The preliminary condition of the accomplishment of this task was the assessment of the natural resources of the country, her geography and population, industrial possibilities, and the like. Among other things it was this need which led Peter I to organize the Russian Academy of Sciences (1724—25) and to send out expeditions of research, frequently lasting for several years, to Siberia, and other places (cf. BSE² 32: 583, 1: 572; Ostrovityanov 1958: 20, 30; Vdovin 1954: 17, 18, 13, etc.). It was in the course of this "sizing up" initiated by Peter I, that, besides geographical, geological, astronomical, zoological, botanical and other records, handwritten glossaries of Russian languages in the eighteenth century were collected. (On the word-collecting activity of Leibniz, cf. among others, Setälä 1892, passim; Pápay 1922: 68; Bulič 1904: 190-191; Zsirai 1937: 481-482; Stehr 1957: 27-29; Richter passim.)

Word-collecting in the eighteenth century had two well-defined periods. The first period comprises the first half of the century, having in its center the activity of V. N. Tatiščev, G. F. Müller, and J. E. Fischer. The second period begins in the 1770's and its last phase extends into the nineteenth century. At the center of the latter period stands the best-known result of the word-collecting trend, the Comparative Dictionary of Pallas.

Word-collecting in the First Half of the Century

D. G. Messerschimdt, the first scientific explorer of Siberia in the eighteenth century, engaged in word-collecting. It was on behalf of Peter I that Messerschmidt stayed in Siberia from 1720 to 1727. During this time, among other things, it was his contractual obligation "to describe the peoples of Siberia and to study their languages philologically" (Lebedev 1950: 75-77).

Messerschmidt's collection, both in extent and in reliability, surpasses Strahlenberg's similar work (see immediately below). It is to be regretted that his valuable vocabulary acquired at the price of great efforts (cf. Hunfalvy 1864: 8 ff.) was not published until the next century and has been so little appreciated even after its publication.

Ph. G. Strahlenberg (his family name was Tabbert) was a Swedish prisoner of war taken to Siberia. During his stay there he took part as an assistant in Messerschmidt's expedition of 1721-22. It is likely that he was motivated by this expedition to undertake linguistic research.

Chronologically, Strahlenberg's activity belongs to the word-collection trend of the eighteenth century, but actually it was much more than that. Strahlenberg was the first man in the first half of the century to engage in language-comparison, and his work (cf. Strahlenberg 1730) was the first stage of Finno-Ugrian comparative linguistics, the stage of chance discoveries, of tracing of relationships of single languages, and of connecting them in a network of affinity (cf. Zsirai 1937: 488).

V. N. TATIŠČEV

Word-collecting proper, meeting the requirements of the times, began with the activities of the famous Second Expedition to Kamchatka (1733-43) and those of Tatiščev, one of the most eminent Russian scholars of the eighteenth century.

V. N. Tatiščev (1686-1750) was first of all a historian and as historian he studied ethnography, archaeology, and late in life "engaged in the study of the languages of the peoples inhabiting Russia", collecting their words

(Averjanova 1950: 45-46). In the Ural in 1720–22 and in 1734–37, as manager of the mines of the Treasury, Tatiščev became acquainted with the multinational population of the Ural district. The impressions he got there turned his attention to the study of the history and languages of these peoples. In his letter to Tredyakovsky from Jekaterinburg (today Sverdlovsk) on February 18, 1736, he writes: "I am busy here collecting the words of other (i.e., non-Russian) languages and what I have collected I shall send to the Academy without delay . . ." (Obn.-Bar.² 91).

He set about collecting with remarkable methodical circumspection and resolution, bringing a keen ethnographic and linguistic sense to bear on his work. Among other things he elaborated a questionnaire of 92 items and sent copies to every part of Siberia; one was received by the members of the Second Kamchatka expedition, too (Popov 1861: 665).

He even obtained approval of his plans by the Czarist Court (cf. Bulič 1904: 422). This is shown by the preface of a Vogul glossary dating from 1736, in which, along with the name of Tatiščev, reference is also made to a Czarist ukase (cf. Gulya 1958: 43).

This eminent organizer also saw to it that the fieldworker should record materials accurately. The 198th point of his questionnaire mentioned above also contains some hints for the "collectors". He informs them in a little more detailed way in the Preface to the project of his dictionary entitled "Lexicon" (published by Obn.-Bar.² 95). He considers it important that "we should not write for one letter another one as it often happens with us that one mistakes *a* for *o*, 6 for *n*, *e* for 3 . . ." Among other things he calls his collectors' attention to the importance of indicating length (!) and stress accurately, he warns them against using persons of defective speech as informants, he notices that in other languages sounds not existing in Russian are also used and vice versa, he calls his collectors' attention to the semantic range of some words, differing from Russian, and suggests that more than one informant should be questioned and several times (ibid: 95-96).

In a later work, Tatiščev informs us about the results of his collecting activity. Here he relates that he is in possession of several Finnish, Esthonian, Votyak, Chuwash, Cheremiss, Mordvinian, Vogul, Permian (Zyrian), Ostyak, Tatar, and other glossaries (cf. Tatiščev 1950: 71).

Up to the recent years Tatiščev's linguistic (word-collecting) activity has been neglected or underestimated (e.g., by Bulič). A truer picture has been drawn of him by the more recent researchers who perhaps sometimes exaggerate his achievement (among others, Averjanova, Vdovin). In any case, his linguistic activity has the incontestable merit that he was not only one of the most active propagators of word-collecting in the first half of the eighteenth century, but he also drew attention to the importance of the accuracy of linguistic recordings.

G. F. MÜLLER

The other famous investigator of the first half of the eighteenth century was G. F. Müller (1705—83). (See his autobiography in Müller 1937: 145-55.) As a member of the Second Kamchatka expedition, in charge of the historical and linguistic researches, during his stay in Siberia from August 8, 1733, to February 14, 1743 (Müller 1937: 149), Müller collected exceedingly rich Russian historical source material in the archives of Siberia (Putev 1946: 152).

From various sources we know something about the way this material, including the word-collections serving historiographic purposes, came into being. It is known that the Second Kamchatka expedition worked under central instructions, the fifth to seventh points of which gave detailed particulars concerning the collecting of linguistic data. Moreover Müller's legacy (preserved in the Moscow Central Archives) includes a questionnaire containing the list of the words to be collected. To give some idea of it the first twenty-one words of the questionnaire are: God, devil, idol, sky, hell, air, earth, water, fire, cloud, wind, storm, rain, snow, hail, ice, dew, hoar, frost, fog, thunder. All this shows clearly that the Second Kamchatka expedition had been carefully prepared for collecting language material even before it set out on its mission.

Apart from his published works (cf. 1732-64, 3[4]: 382-410; etc.) Müller wrote several works of a linguistic character preserved in manuscript in his legacy in the Moscow Central Archives. Thus, a glossary containing Hungarian words and what is more important, a hitherto unknown manuscript study of Hungarian—Vogul—Ostyak—Permian (Zyrian)-Mordvinian—Tatar—Samoyedic is also preserved. The equations of words given in this study can still pass muster in the light of our present-day knowledge. The author points out that the Hungarian words indicate closest affinity with the words belonging to the Chusovaya (properly speaking: Southern) Vogul dialect. The author of this study was in all probability Müller. At that time, so far as we know, only Fischer had made such comparative studies of words. These, however, contained another stock of words (e.g., Müller: Hungarian *mely* (*mell*)~Vogul *magl, mögil, mel*; Fischer Vogul *magla*, etc.). The manuscript works bear testimony to a greater linguistic interest and significance of Müller's legacy than has been hitherto realized (cf. Stehr 1957: 52).

J. E. FISCHER

The third and perhaps the most significant historic-linguistic researcher was Fischer (1697—1771). As far as we know, it was by means of the reports of the Second Kamchatka expedition sent to the Academy that Fischer learned about the famous word-collecting work of the century (cf. Stehr 1957: 53). Not much later, in 1740, when Müller became ill, Fischer himself joined the expedition and from this time till 1748 he took part in its linguistic researches. Fischer's results relating to Finno-Ugrian linguistics were made public in "De origine Ungrorum", finished as early as in 1756, but published only in Schlözer's edition of 1770 and in his own work (finished in 1752) entitled "Sibirische Geschichte" respectively. In both the works just cited Fischer made use of the material of his Siberian Dictionary.

The Siberian Dictionary ("Vocabularium Sibiricum") is at present in Göttingen (Niedersächsische Staats- und Universitätsbibliothek Göttingen. Handschrift Philol. 261). The glossary went to Göttingen in 1761, at Schlözer's request, as Fischer's gift (cf. Bulič 1904: 219). Another version, also by Fischer, is in Leningrad (Archiv Akademii Nauk SSSR, Leningrad, Razryad III, op. 1, no. 135).

As to its character, Fischer's Siberian Dictionary is an *Etymological Dictionary*, and in addition, the first *Finno-Ugrian Etymological Dictionary* of a scientific standard. With regard both to the number and to the correctness of its etymologies it surpassed all the dictionaries of the same kind, which had been compiled up to that time (cf. Farkas 1952: 1-22; Gulya 1968: 87-90). Fischer's Siberian Dictionary is the greatest achievement of the word-collecting trend of the eighteenth century. In Finno-Ugrian linguistics of the century it is surpassed only by the activity of Sajnovics and Gyarmathi, the latter of whom used Fischer's Dictionary as one of his most important sources.

The death of Tatiščev (1750) and the belated publication of Fischer's works marked the end of the most significant period from the point of view of the history of philology. Then came a silence for a quarter of a century, to be followed by the second period of this trend, richer in external events, but much poorer regarding its scientific value, closing with the publication of the Comparative Dictionary of Pallas.

Word-collecting in the Second Half of the Century

The second period of word-collecting began in 1773, when, after some attempts of lesser significance, G. L. C. Bacmeister, on the initiative of the Czarina of Russia, Catherine II, appealed to the scholars of the world for help in collecting language material. The Appeal ("Idea et desideria de colligendis linguarum speciminibus") contained a list of entry-words and 22 illustrative sentences and some hints for the collecting of language material.

The Appeal was also sent to the expedition led by Pallas who had been engaged in researches for some years. Pallas and the members of the expedition complied with the appeal, supported by the Czarina's request, and accordingly, with the co-operation of interpreters and officials of the chancellery, they compiled several glossaries. Then they sent these glossaries (and the collected illustrative sentences) to the Academy, to G. L. C. Bacmeister. At the same time Bacmeister received word-material from other parts of Russia, from Europe and Asia as well. Later on, this material became the main source of the Comparative Dictionary of Pallas (cf. Bulič 1904: 224).

In 1784 Bacmeister renewed his Appeal and asked for additional language material. In 1784 Catherine II herself took part in the work of the Dictionary. She made up a list of 286 entry-words which she intended to have translated into 200 languages. In the course of this work she copied with her own hand and collected in a group the equivalents of each entry-word in various languages. In nine months she grew weary of the work and in 1785 she handed over the whole material collected till that time, together with the collection of a Berlin scholar, P. Nikolai, to Pallas and commissioned him to complete the Dictionary (cf. Bulič 1904: 225).

Out of these materials Pallas published his well-known Vocabularia Comparativa, the first edition of which came out in two versions, one Russian and one Latin (1787-89). Similarly, at the request of Catharine II, in 1790-91 the second edition of the Dictionary was published under the editorship of F. Jankovics de Mirijevo who was born in Hungary. Already in the course of the eighteenth century both editions of the Comparative Dictionary gave rise to criticism. Nevertheless, the Dictionary is significant in that it contributed to the development of comparative linguistics. (For the literature of the Dictionary see Bulič 1904: 219 ff., 228 ff.)

It is interesting to note that Pallas did not make use of all the manuscripts that were presumably at his disposal. A few of these glossaries (e.g., a Vogul glossary coming from the Southern Sosva) were not yet compiled according to the instructions issued by Bacmeister. Their material was collected on the basis of the list of entry-words used by the Second Kamchatka expedition. From this the conclusion may be drawn that the expedition led by Pallas had done some collecting prior to Bacmeister's Appeal; in the course of this activity the collectors may have used the questionnaire belonging to the period of Tatiščev, Müller, and Fischer. Nor is it out of the question that these glossaries had been made at various Siberian chancelleries and, for some reason, it was only later that they came into the possession of Pallas or the Saint Petersburg Academy of Sciences.

In the second half of the century besides the "official" (Academic) efforts some glossaries were compiled by some private persons. Of this category is the glossary compiled in 1785 by S. Čerkalov, high priest (protoyerey) of Solikamsk. With the publication of the Comparative

Dictionary of Pallas, however, the word-collecting trend of the eighteenth century came practically to an end.

In the second half of the century in the "Demonstratio" of Sajnovics (1770) not only the correspondence of words but also those of grammar are investigated. A fresh chapter and a new stage begins in the history of the investigation of related languages. In this period in Russia Lomonosov, too, calls attention to the importance of the study of grammar. This new methodological demand was not met by scholars continuing the word-collecting traditions of the first half of the century. Thus, the second period of word-collecting falls short of scientific needs of the time, not only as regards the application of the new method of comparison, but also in its own sphere. There it represents a decline when compared with the achievements of Strahlenberg, Tatiščev, Müller, and Fischer (cf. Zsirai 1937: 489).

For instance, the famous Comparative Dictionary of Pallas (1786-89), produced by the dilettantism of a monarch, not only gives a wrong picture of the relationship between the individual Finno-Ugrian languages, but also affords numerous regrettable examples of linguistic incompetence, as when the dictionary gives in the same category the material of several, often very remote, dialects. The editors of the Dictionary did not know the languages on which the Dictionary was based; for instance, they did not know the Vogul language. This is proved by the fact that, owing to a slip in the Russian entry-words, the Finno-Ugric words sometimes appear under the wrong meaning. Similar mistakes are to be found in I. Chr. Adelung's *Mithridates* (1806, 1817; cf. Zsirai 1937: 489).

In spite of all this, it is a great merit of the second half of the century that it continued the material-collecting activity of the preceding half-century. This activity received a new impetus from the progress of the contemporary natural sciences, especially from the systematizing endeavors of C. Linné (1707-78). In the course of their activity the researchers of these times compiled numerous glossaries regarded today as literary monuments. Several of them are the only records of some dialect or language that has since become extinct, for example, a Vogul glossary from the district of Kungur.[1]

The activity of the century constitutes a stage of Finno-Ugrian comparative linguistic researches, beginning with Strahlenberg and lasting till the appearance of the work of Sajnovics (1770) and Gyarmathi (1799) and in the nineteenth century of M. A. Castrén (1813–52) and A. Reguly (1819–55) respectively. (On Reguly's relation to the work of Sajnovics and Gyármathi, see Pápay 1905: 272-73.) Its significance is threefold: (1) it bequeathed to posterity a rich, systematically collected body of scientific material; (2) on the basis of considerable material it attempted for the first time to reveal the affinity among the Finno-Ugrian (and other) languages; (3)

it aimed at achieving its end by applying a scientific method in the course of which a number of valuable methodological procedures were worked out for both linguistic collecting and language comparison.

It was this trend of the eighteenth century, hardly known today, that raised the problems which the great historical and comparative trend of the nineteenth century (and in our days glottochronology, language geography, etc.) was to solve. At the same time, the activity of the century collected language material needed for this purpose, laid a methodological basis for the solutions, and, last but not least, it created a scientific public opinion.

The Lesson of Principle to be Drawn From the History of Linguistic Science in the Eighteenth Century

When we survey the linguistic activity of the eighteenth century just described—a period very rich in activity, but little known to modern scholars—we can see that (a) questions could be raised in a scientific way (cf. Leibniz); (b) methodical work could be accomplished (cf. especially Fischer), and (c) a great amount of linguistic material was made available. Nevertheless, a revolution in this branch of learning was not effected. In our opinion, the reason for this is that a scientific revolution can only take place when methodical, concrete results are available in sufficient detail. Accordingly, the process of accumulation constitutes what may be called a period of continuity in science. After some time this is followed by a revolutionary upswing when, with the "explosion" of accumulated knowledge, the ground is broken for a fresh continuity, perhaps at a higher level than previously. We would say that the great linguistic revolution in the early nineteenth century can with good reason be seen as having been prepared by the linguistic activity of the eighteenth century. Indeed, in our opinion, one can hardly understand the history of modern linguistics without knowledge of the history of linguistics in the eighteenth century. A great deal more research, especially into manuscript materials, remains to be done on this subject.

Another question on which further research is desirable is why the nineteenth-century revolution was accomplished, or paradigm established, when and where it was. As is well known, comparative linguistics became established as a continuous, productive discipline in the second, third, and fourth decades of the nineteenth century, within the Indo-European family of languages, in large part through the work of German scholars. Rask (1787-1832), Bopp (1791-1867), and Grimm (1785-1863) are generally agreed to be the founders (Robins 1967: 171), although their relative importance is not agreed upon.[2]

Less well known is the fact that comparative method of the sort first applied to Indo-European by Bopp in 1816 had been applied to the Finno-Ugrian family, through the work of Hungarian scholars at the end of the eighteenth century. Building on the tradition of word-collection and comparison stimulated by Leibniz and encouraged by Schlözer,[3] Sajnovics (1770) showed the relationship between Hungarian and Lapp, employing a method of grammatical comparison that was to be applied by Gyarmathi to as much of Finno-Ugrian as a whole as data permitted (Zsirai 1951: 59, 66).[4] It is fairly often recognized both that Gyarmathi (1751-1830) made early use of such a method (Pedersen 1931: 240 treats it as the first use), and that he showed the relationship between Hungarian and Finnish (Thomsen 1927: 44; Pedersen 1931: 11, 105-6, 240-41; Mounin 1967: 146; Robins 1967: 170). Such recognition, however, reflects only the part of his achievement that is expressed in the title of his work (1799). What appears not to be noticed is that his work had three parts, treating, respectively, the relation between Hungarian and Lappish-Finnish (Gyarmathi classed the latter two languages together), the relation between Hungarian and Estonian, and the relation between Hungarian and other "Finnish" (i.e., Finno-Ugrian) languages. Only Pedersen notes that Gyarmathi subjoined lexical comparisons, and does so in a discussion of Finno-Ugrian (1931: 106) quite separate from his discussion of the general history of comparative method, where only the grammatical comparison is mentioned. In point of fact, in Gyarmathi's work "a substantial proportion of the accepted and up-to-date Finno-Ugrian etymologies was established for the first time" (Zsirai 1951: 67). His lexical comparisons contain errors, due mostly to failure to recognize regularity of phonetic correspondence, but this principle was established only much later, and inexactness in phonetic correspondence is a criticism that a later generation made of all the recognized founders of comparative linguistics, even of Grimm. Moreover, Gyarmathi, in an appendix, distinguished sharply between similarities due to affinity and similarities due to borrowing. He carefully examined Turkish structure and Turkish-Hungarian lexical resemblances and, against public opinion and other Hungarian scholars, declared that the Turkish element in Hungarian was not evidence of genetic relationship, but of borrowing.

Here would seem to be an accomplishment comparable to that of Bopp in scope and method. Indeed, Gyarmathi was read and highly valued by Rask (who also read Sajnovics) (Pedersen 1931: 106; Mounin 1967: 164; Diderichsen, this volume). Yet the full nature of Gyarmathi's accomplishment is not made clear in any modern treatment of the history of linguistics in English, French, or German.[5] That fact itself is evidence that Gyarmathi's work, despite its merit, was in practical effect a culmination of eighteenth-century linguistics, not a foundation of the nineteenth-century linguistics that came to be regarded as linguistics proper, or as modern linguistics.

For Pedersen (1931: 241), "it was impossible for linguistics to develop first in the Finno-Ugric field." As reasons, he gives that the Finno-Ugrian languages were too far beyond the horizon and interest of most European scholars, and that the problems to be solved were too difficult, because the languages are very distantly related, and mostly lack old documents. "Their problems were therefore not adapted to the feeble powers of the infant science" (241). In contrast:

> In the age of its languages, its wide dissemination and rich variation, and its profound but not unrecognizable divisions, the Indo-European family is unique. And the problems concerning it easily attracted general interest, since languages of that family were the mother tongues of the nations which have been and still are the leaders in the development of civilization and scholarship. In this field, then, comparative linguistics advanced rapidly and without interruption. (241-42).

This explanation seems to us to smack too much of reasoning after the event, insofar as the purely internal characteristics of language families are concerned. (Pedersen also argues that Semitic was not sufficiently challenging [241].) Nor does reference to the interest of scholars, or the general interest of a family of languages, seem precise enough, so far as external factors are concerned. Imagine if the Hungarian scholarly community and government of the time had greeted Gyarmathi's work with an eager desire to develop and complete it. Suppose funds and personnel had been made available, and arrangements facilitated, for fresh work with the imperfectly known members of the Finno-Ugrian family, and if academic positions had been established for specialists in the analysis of the material. Suppose a cooperative community of scholars involving also Finland (Gyarmathi hoped for help from his great Finnish contemporary, Porthan) had emerged. Might we not be asking why Sir William Jones' insight of 1786 had to wait thirty years to be taken up, letting Finno-Ugrian steal a march? Indeed, must we not ask why Indo-European comparative linguistics did not begin in England, under Jones' stimulation? (On an intellectual factor, cf. Aarsleff 1967: 73 ff.) Or in France, where Bopp, W. von Humboldt, and A. von Schlegel went in the early nineteenth century to study Sanskrit?

It is difficult to say precisely what intellectual and scientific factors must be taken into account, as necessary and sufficient for a revolution or the establishment of a paradigm, in a scientific field. Some five conditions might be distinguished:

(1) The putting of a problem (*Aufgabe*), a desire for knowledge that makes a new approach historically necessary;

(2) methods adequate to the problem (*Methode für gute Resultat*);

(3) sufficient new materials (*Materiale*);

(4) sufficient previous results (*Resultate*);

(5) an ingenious, clever researcher (*Forscher mit bestimmte möglichkeit*).

In terms of these five conditions, we might say that in the period of the Renaissance, the problem of language comparison and language history had been posed, but that the other conditions were lacking. In the eighteenth century all the conditions were present, except that of sufficient accumulation of results. In the late eighteenth and early nineteenth centuries, all these conditions are met in the study of what were to be known as the Indo-European languages, including new materials of a specially valuable kind, those of the ancient Indo-Aryan branch (Sanskrit).

One might question whether the new materials and previous results in Finno-Ugrian were sufficient, compared to those in Indo-European. What we mean does not have to do with Pedersen's notion that the Finno-Ugrian languages were too distant in relationship, or the fact that they mostly lacked old documents. Nor does the clarity of the ancient Indian analysis of Sanskrit, stressed by Pedersen (1931: 21-22) and Waterman (1963: 31), seem to us necessarily more than an accident peculiar to the particular history of Indo-European work. Sajnovics and Gyarmathi were able to develop comparison of inflectional systems without the aid of a grammatical tradition from the East. Much more important seems the sufficiency of the materials possessed by scholars, not only in documents, but also, so to speak, in their heads. An essential advantage for those engaged in comparative Indo-European would seem to be that most were not only native speakers of a language in one major branch of the family (Germanic), but through education well versed in what happened to be two other major branches (Greek, Latin). The addition of Sanskrit put them in personal command of four branches. In contrast, the researcher in Finno-Ugrian began with intimate knowledge of only one of the languages, that which he spoke. (Recall Gyarmathi's desire to obtain the collaboration of the Finnish scholar Porthan.) Word-collecting, and such grammatical description as had developed (cf. Zsirai 1951; Sebeok 1960) was absolute prerequisite for comparative work. A founder of comparative Indo-European such as Bopp could go (with W. von Humboldt and A. von Schlegel) to Paris to study Sanskrit, fully analyzed, and could not but have comparisons stimulated to languages he already knew well. A founder of Finno-Ugrian such as Gyarmathi had to rely on published information from the field work of others among scattered nonliterate groups, if he could not undertake an expedition himself (Zsirai 1966: 60, 68).

Even so, the sufficiency of materials seems in this case not an unchangeable given fact. As has been suggested, it is possible to imagine that in the decade after Gyarmathi's publication (1799) great changes might have been brought about in enrichment of the Finno-Ugrian materials, and in cooperative mastery of them. What seems the crucial factor is the creation of a community of scholars, within which the comparative work could develop. And the basis of such a community seems to depend, at least in this case, on social and cultural, rather than scientific, factors. We dare to suggest that the intellectual and scientific advances associated with Indo-European in the nineteenth century—the increased understanding of principles of change, the solution of increasingly complex problems—would have come about in the comparative study of any diverse language family, given a community of scholars. Our belief in the universality of the methods and principles of historical linguistics might be taken to imply as much.

The creation, or maintenance, of a community of scholars perhaps can be considered an aspect of the first condition listed above, the putting of a problem. That is, there is the putting of a problem within a line of research; and there is the putting of a problem from the standpoint of the interests and attitudes of society. Gyarmathi's problem, the affinity of Hungarian with other languages, and a method for determining it had interested Leibniz (cf. Arens 1965: 82) and exercised German historians at Göttingen (cf. Zsirai 1951: 62), but his results did not point in a direction in which the Hungarian officials, scholars, or public of the time wished to go. By contrast, when Indo-European comparison emerged early in the nineteenth century as a sustained field, it was not for the sake of linguistics alone. There was great excitement in the prospect of unravelling the earlier history, the earlier independent history perhaps, of a branch such as Germanic, and of gaining knowledge of the history and origins of the Indo-European (Indo-germanisch in German scholarship) peoples as a whole. It was thought that light would be shed on religious and intellectual origins and history. A connection with the ancient conquerors of India was acceptable and even indeed greeted with enthusiasm by many; some spoke of "wisdom from the East" and Oriental studies in Europe to a great extent have their institutionalization in this period.

Hungarian opinion also welcomed affinity with Oriental peoples. Unfortunately, the genetic affinities of Hungarian were with peoples to the north and northeast, many of them of little or no historical importance. The official position, and the position of many scholars, stressed ties especially with the Turks. Gyarmathi's conclusions were attacked. There was no desire whatever to be linked with "fish-eaters" such as the Lapps (Zsirai 1951:

59-60, 69; Pedersen 1931: 105). Indeed, on Schlözer's suggestion, Gyarmathi used "Finn" in the title of his work, because "Lapp" had been discredited to Hungarians since the work of Sajnovics. Gyarmathi did not himself develop his work further. Rask did interest himself in Finnish and Lappish with valuable results, and from a classificatory standpoint, on the one hand, showed Finno-Ugric to be separate from Indo-European, and on the other, grouped it typologically with a number of other groups as "Scythian". But a period of intensive, sustained research was not to come until more than four decades later, as part of the upsurge of comparative Finno-Ugrian ethnography and linguistics that began in the late 1830's, centered at first in Helsinki. In a "Berich an die ungarische Akademie" of May 2, 1842, the young Reguly expressed the impact upon him of reading Sajnovics and then Gyarmathi. (On Reguly's field work in the 1840's, something of that of Castrén, and the beginnings of publication of new comparative studies, see Pápay 1905.)

Elsewhere in Europe, on the other hand, a sometime student of Sanskrit, a theorist and practitioner of linguistics, became for a time Minister of Education in Prussia. He established a chair for Sanskrit and Comparative Philology in each university, a pattern imitated in other German states of the day, and to the chair in the University of Berlin himself called Franz Bopp (Paul Thieme, personal communication, August 19, 1964). This combination of personal interest and political power may explain why comparative Indo-European developed as a continuing paradigm of research in Germany, rather than in France or England. W. von Humboldt's personal interest, and the success of his policy as Minister, of course reflect also the great German interest in their national and "Indo-germanic" origins (Mounin 1967: 170-71).

It is the view of Mounin (1967: 159) that Bopp was the founder of comparative linguistics, not for discovery of Sanskrit or of grammatical comparison, both of which were already known, but for using them to pose and solve new problems concerning languages. Mounin does not precisely state what the new problems were. According to Meillet, Bopp has the merit of giving precise form to ideas that would otherwise have remained sterile; but also according to Meillet, "il a trouvé la grammaire comparée en cherchant à expliquer l'indo-européen, comme Christophe Colomb a découvert l'Amérique en cherchant la route des Indes", and his most hazardous speculations "ont plus fait sans doute au début pur le succès de la grammaire comparée, que la partie solide de son oeuvre" (quoted in Mounin 1967: 175, 174). It is difficult to avoid the conclusion that originality and scientific correctness, as judged by later scholars, had little to do with the establishment of the paradigm of comparative linguistics. That, indeed, the institutionalization of a community of scholars, and the work of those who gave the community a scholarly foundation (of Rask, as well as of Bopp—see Percival, this volume), grew out of conceptions and aspirations which the inheritors of the paradigm could not share, indeed would reject, but of which, willy-nilly, they were beneficiaries.

In sum, it appears that the general conditions for the establishment of a paradigm of comparative linguistic research were present widely in Europe in the late eighteenth century. Gyarmathi's comparative grammatical analysis of Finno-Ugrian indeed precedes the comparative grammatical analyses of Indo-European by Rask (1814, unpublished) and Bopp (1816) by fifteen and seventeen years, respectively. What made Bopp a founder of a paradigm, rather than an isolated precursor like Gyarmathi, was not what today is considered the scientific merit of his work, but the social and cultural interests which motivated and supported work of that kind at that time. The difference between Bopp's inclusion of Sanskrit, and Gyarmathi's inclusion of Cheremis—both the inclusion of another member of a Family—is not just the fuller and clearer state of the information about Sanskrit, but the difference between a desired and a rejected ancestry.

Much more research on the period in its intellectual and social context is desirable. Nevertheless, we hope to have shown that a true understanding of the history of linguistics requires comparison of traditions and paradigms, including comparison between successful paradigms and paradigmes manqués.

NOTES

* The concluding sections have been elaborated from discussion by and with Dr. Gulya at the Burg Wartenstein symposium. The editor has also supplied the comparisons of works on the history of linguistics (notes 1-4). The preliminary version of the paper prepared for the Burg Wartenstein symposium has been published (Gulya 1965; cf. Sebeok 1966: xiv).

1. For a discussion of the history of word-collecting from the standpoint of the Cheremis language, see Sebeok 1960. The poor execution of the Pallas publication, by the standards of its own time, is indicated (293-294), but the permanent value of the word lists is signalled also (294).

2. Thomsen (1927) and Pedersen (1931) subordinate Grimm to Rask and Bopp in similar words: "Neben Rask und Bopp müssen wir noch eines Drittes gedenken. . .(Thomsen 1927: 57); "Besides Rask and Bopp we must name also. . ." (Pedersen 1931: 258). Cf. also "The modern period of linguistics" begins "with the labors of Rask and Bopp" (Pedersen 1931: 241). Both scholars emphasize Rask's chronological precedence and Grimm's debt to Rask. The order and tenor of their discussion generally appears to place Rask and Bopp together, ahead of Grimm (Thomsen 1927: 62; cf. 44 ff., 53 ff., 57 ff.; Pedersen 1931: 241, 248). While Bloomfield (1933: 14-15) cites

Bopp, Rask, and Grimm in chronological order of publication (1816, 1818, 1819) of their first major works, his own subsequent comments highlight the scientific importance of Grimm. In this emphasis he is followed by Waterman (1963), for whom Grimm, although enormously indebted to Rask, is the father of the subject (19); Bopp is quite subordinate, both in length and manner of treatment (30-31). In contrast Leroy (1963: 18-19) centers discussion on Bopp with the heading "Bopp et les premiers comparatistes". Rask's merits are discussed in that context, and only then is Grimm introduced, the words echoing Pedersen: "un autre nom est à ajouter. . .". Even more in contrast is Arens (1965), who not only gives Bopp pride of place, but who also describes him as the foundation wall (*Grundmauer*), "as all the world agrees" (154). Rask and Grimm are treated both after Bopp, in that order, Rask briefly, Grimm at some length, with Rask's great influence on Grimm again being noted. Ivić (1965: 40-41) treats Bopp, Rask, and Grimm in that order as well. For Mounin (1967), Bopp is clearly the founder of scientific linguistics and of comparative grammar (159, 170); cf. his section heading "La linguistique après Franz Bopp" (176). Again, Rask and Grimm follow, in that order, Grimm's debt to Rask being noted (166). Finally, Robins (1967), after citing Rask, Grimm, Bopp, and W. von Humboldt as the best known scholars of the period, singles out Rask and Grimm (170). Remarking that it is often and justifiably said that Rask, Grimm, and Bopp are the founders of scientific historical linguistics, Robins discusses them in that order, i.e., Bopp last.

In sum, for the two Danish scholars Rask and Bopp take precedence, with Grimm subordinate; for the two Germanicists Grimm's merit is predominant; for Robins Rask and Grimm take precedence, with Bopp subordinate; a German, a Yugoslav, and two scholars writing in French give pride of place to Bopp.

3. As noted earlier, Schlözer wrote the preface to Fischer 1770. On the role of the great Göttingen historian, see Zsirai 1951: 59, 60, 62, 66, 68. Cf. Butterfield 1960: 50, 59, on Schlözer's concern for language relationships, and 6, 8, 36-37, 42-60, on his significance as a historian. The full story of the role of the Göttingen historians in the development of historical linguistics remains to be told; there is manuscript material in Göttingen which should be further studied.

4. A symposium on the history of linguistics and commemorative session dedicated to the memory of Janos Sajnovics, sponsored by the Sajnovics Memorial Committee of the Hungarian Academy of Sciences, was held May 12-14, 1970, in Szekesfehervar, Hungary.

5. The role of Leibniz in stimulating word-collection and interest in language relationships is noted by Thomsen (1927: 38-41), Pedersen (1931: 9-10), Arens (1965: 77-88, esp. 82), Mounin (1967: 143), and Robins (1967: 177-179, a quite useful discussion); but not by Bloomfield, Waterman, or Ivić. Sajnovics is not mentioned in any but the two most recent works (Mounin 1967: 146; Robins 1967:170). Gyarmathi is mentioned by all but the German, Germanicist, and Belgian scholars (Arens, Bloomfield,

Waterman, Leroy), but only Ivić seems even to suggest the true scope of his work: "the comparative study of the Finno-Ugric group of languages had already begun" (33). Pedersen writes "By an accident the new principle of comparison of inflexions was first applied in a practical way in the Finno-Ugric field by Gyarmathi in 1799 (see above, p.105)", but the cross-reference is to specific proof of relationship with Finnish, and "practical" also suggests a limited application.

REFERENCES

Aarsleff, Hans. 1967. The study of language in England, 1780-1860. Princeton.

———. 1969. The study and use of etymology in Leibniz. Akton den Internationalen Leibniz-kongresses, Hannover..., 1966, 3: 173-189. Wiesbaden.

Adelung, I. Chr. 1806–17. Mithridates. Berlin. [Last three volumes edited by J. S. Vater.]

Arens, Hans. 1955. Sprachwissenschaft. Der Gang ihrer Entwicklung von der Antike bis zur Gegenwart. Frieburg-Munich, Verlag Karl Alber.

Averjanova, A. P. 1950. V. N. Tatiščev kak filolog. (Vestnik Leningradskogo Universiteta 7). Leningrad.

Bloomfield, L. 1933. Language. New York.

BSE² = Bol'shaya Sovetskaya Entsiklopediya, 2nd ed. Moscva.

Bulič, S. K. 1904. Očerk istorii yazykoznaia v Rossii, vol. 1. St. Petersburg.

Butterfield, H. 1960. Man on his past. The study of the history of historical scholarship. Boston. [First published, 1955.]

Farkas, J. V. 1952. August Ludwig Schlözer und de finnisch-ugrische Geschichts-, Sprach-, und Volkskunde. Ural-Altaische Jahrbucher 24 (3-4): 1-22.

Fischer, J. E. 1770. De origine Ungrorum. (Quaestiones Petropolitanae, I). Göttingae.

Guerrier, Waldemar. 1873. Leibniz in seinem Beziehungen zu Russland und Peter dem Grossen. Eine geschichtliche Darstellung dieses Verhältnisses nebst den darauf bezüglichen Briefen und Denkschriften. St. Petersburg and Leipzig.

Gulya, J. 1958. Egy 1736-ból szarmazó manysi nyelremlék. Nyeltudományi Közlemenyek 60: 41-45.

———. 1965. Some 18th century antecedents of the 19th century linguistics. Acta Linguistica 5: 163-170.

———. 1967. A magyar nyelv elsö etimológiai szótara. Nyelvtudományi Értekezések 58: 87-90. Budapest.

Gyarmathi, S. 1799. Affinitas linguae Hungaricae cum linguis Fennicae originis grammatice demonstrata. Göttingen.

Hunfalvy, P. 1864. A vogul föld és nép. Pest.

Ivić, M. 1965. Trends in linguistics. Transl. by Muriel Heppell. The Hague.

Lebedev, D. N. 1950. Geografiya v Rosii Petrovskovo Vremeni. Moscow-Leningrad.

Leibniz, G. G. von. 1768. Collectanea etymologica. G. G. Leibnitii Opera omnia. Ed. by L. Dutens, Geneva. Vol. 6, Part 2.

Leroy, M. 1963. Les grands courants de la linguistique moderne. Bruxelles and Paris.

Mounin, G. 1967. Histoire de la linguistique des origines au xxe siècle. Paris, Presses Universitaires de France.

Müller, G. F. 1732-64. Sammlung russischer Geschichte, vols. 1-9. St. Petersburg.

_____. 1937. Istoria Sibiri, vol. 1. Moscow-Leningrad.

Neff, L. 1870–71. G. G. Leibniz als sprach forscher und etymologe. Heidelberg. 2 parts.

Obn. Bar.^{2} = Obnorskiĭ, C. P., and Barchugarov. 1948. Chrestomatiya po istorii russkogo yazyka. 2nd ed. Mosckva.

Ostrovityanov, K. V. 1958. Istoriya Akademii Nauk SSSR, vol. 1. Moscow.

Pallas, P. S. 1787–89. Sravnitel'nye slovari vsyex yazykov i maryečiy. 2 vols. St. Petersburg.

_____. 1787–89. Linguarum totius orbis vocabularia comparative. 2 vols. Petropoli.

Pápay, J. 1905. Anton Reguly's Gedächtnis. Sammlung Ostjakischer Volks dichtungen I-II. Budapest and Leipzig. [Cited from Sebeok 1966(1): 268-310.]

_____. 1922. A magyar nyelvhasonlítás története. Budapest.

Pedersen, Holger. 1931. Linguistic science in the nineteenth century. Transl. by J. W. Spargo. Cambridge, Mass. [Reprinted as The discovery of language, Bloomington, Indiana, 1962.]

[Putev.] Ms. [1946.] Tsentral niy Gosudarstvennyi arxiv dvernix adtov. Putevoditel 1-2. Moscow.

Richter L. 1946. Leibniz und sein Russlandbild. Berlin.

Robins, R. H. 1967. A short history of linguistics. Bloomington, Indiana.

Sajnovics, J. 1770. Demonstratio idioma Ungarorum et Lapponum idem esse. Copenhagen.

Sebeok, T. A. 1960. Eighteenth century Cheremis: the evidence from Pallas. Ural-Altaic Studies 1: 289-345.

_____. (ed.). 1966. Portraits of linguists. A biographical source book for the history of Western linguistics, 1746-1963. 2 vols. Bloomington, Indiana.

Setälä, E. N. 1892. Lisiä suomalais–ugrilaisen kielentutkimuksen historiaan. Suomi.

_____. 1921. Nyelvtudományi Közlémenyek 23.

Stehr, A. 1957. Die Anfänge der finnisch-ugrischen Sprachvergleichung. Göttingen, Georg August Universitat.

Strahlenberg, Ph. J. von. 1730. Das Nord und Östliche Theil von Europa und Asia.

Thomsen, V. 1927. Geschichte der Sprachwissenschaft bis zum Ausgang des 19. Jahrhunderts. Transl. by Hans Pollak. Halle (Saale).

Vdovin, I. S. 1954. Istoriya izunčeniya paleoaziatskix yazykov. Moscow— Leningrad.

Waterman, J. T. 1963. Perspectives in linguistics. An account of the background of modern linguistics. Chicago.

Zsirai, M. 1937. Finnugor rokonságunk. Budapest.

———. 1951. Samuel Gyarmathi, Hungarian pioneer of comparative linguistics. Acta Linguistica 1: 5-16. Budapest, Academiae Scientiarum Hungaricae. [Cited from Sebeok 1966(1): 58-70.]

9. The Foundation of Comparative Linguistics: Revolution or Continuation?

Paul Diderichsen

I. Introduction

It is a general assumption that linguistics was not constituted as a proper science until the works of Rask, Bopp, and Grimm (1814–22); see, for example, Pedersen (1931) and Waterman (1963). Thus it is a central question in this connection whether the views, the methods, and the results of these works are entitled to the name of a "scientific revolution".

In order to throw light on this problem, it is necessary to trace "the route of linguistics to normal science" (Kuhn 1962: 10 ff.), to outline the characteristic methods and patterns of thought in traditional grammar and etymology before the nineteenth century, and to find out if they were radically changed in the works mentioned above. I am not sure if we are quite justified in calling these patterns "paradigms" in Kuhn's special sense (1962: 10). For one thing, they do not "include law, theory and instrumentation together". But as they have "prepared the student for membership in the particular scientific community with which he will later practice" and have "seldom evoked overt disagreement over fundamentals", I think it will be justifiable to call them so, at least in quotation marks. We shall find that there is a point at which a "paradigm" permitting linguistics to progress as normal science may be said to arise; but it is not when the textbooks say it is.

II. The Original "Paradigms" of Linguistics

TRADITIONAL GRAMMAR[1]

The study of language, from antiquity to modern times, is characterized by the survival of ancient concepts and habits of analysis. It has often been demonstrated that its terms and concepts are unsatisfactorily defined, and

277

that its analysis is not based on consistent rules and principles, but nevertheless it has provided a terminology that has made it possible to deal with language, at least the languages taught in European schools, in a way that has proved to be adequate for traditional language teaching, and for comparative and historical linguistics as well. The core of this paradigm is traditional grammar with its main subdivisions: orthography, partes orationis, accidence (inflection and derivation), and syntax (particularly the rules of regimen and concord). The history of grammar shows us how this pattern of thought was molded by the Stoics for the description of their mother-tongue, how it was adapted, first to Latin and later to an increasing number of modern and ancient languages. Probably about 90 percent of all the thousands of grammars dealing with this immense variety of languages, have arranged their materials according to the inconsistent framework and terminology of Dionysios Thrax, Donatus, and Priscian.

Traditional grammar serves two practical purposes:

(1) to establish a standard literary language, telling us what is right and wrong, and giving reasons for the choice of forms and the formulation of rules;

(2) to teach foreign students the most important rules of spelling, accidence, and syntax. In certain periods small groups of scholars have shown a more theoretical interest in the principles of analysis and the relations between the categories of language and thought. The most important of these are the Stoics, the scholastic philosophers of the twelfth and thirteenth centuries, and the adherents of grammaire générale (seventeenth-eighteenth centuries).

From the point of view of traditional grammar, language is an invariable and unchangeable system of forms and combinations: only one form is correct; other forms have no proper existence. Rules and inflectional paradigms are based on an accepted literary usage, and the description is restricted to features which, sometimes rather arbitrarily, have been regarded as important for the practical purposes of grammar. Traditional grammar, therefore, has up to now disregarded the fact that language changes.

ETYMOLOGY

Nevertheless, people have always been aware that languages differ, and that the same language varies in different geographic and social environments, just as it changes from generation to generation. And these observations have given rise to various myths and speculations about the evolution and origin of language. In the classical tradition the concept of linguistic change is based on semantics; namely, the relations between word and thing meant, language and thought. But semantics, on the other hand, is viewed in the light of a general theory of culture and education (*paideia*).

The basic concepts of this theory were: nature, art, and usage. Through observation and imitation of nature — the external physical world as well as human nature — man learns how to cultivate the soil, breed cattle, cure illness, educate children, and so on. So far as such activities are based on rational understanding of the nature of things, they are called arts; if they are merely a sort of practice or habit, they are called usage (*consuetudo*). Usage may be good or bad, and it is, of course, highly important to imitate the usage of the wisest people, those who understand how to imitate nature.

These three elements, nature, usage, art, are all of them necessary for culture and education; usage must be directed by rational art, and art must be practised if it is to succeed in bringing nature to ever higher perfection. From wild nature to nature cultivated by art and usage, that is the way of all education and all culture.

As to language, the classical tradition knew two different concepts of its origin and change: (1) an idealist approach, founded by Plato and Aristotle and elaborated by the Stoics; (2) a materialist approach, best known from the writings of Epicurus and Lucretius. According to the idealistic view the first "namegivers" (*onomatopoietai*) invented words which were imitations of natural phenomena, thus expressing primitive concepts in which cognition was not separated from sense perception. These words were phonetically articulated, consisting of a fixed number of elements (*stoikheia*, letters or phonemes).

Later on these "primal words" were applied to more abstract concepts by means of metaphors and the like, and their external form was altered by addition, subtraction, or interchange of letters; special forms of these alterations are inflection, derivation, and word composition. As these changes in sound and meaning took place in usage, they were often irrational and thus corrupted the original accordance between words, concepts, and things. On the other hand, philosophers, grammarians, and rhetoricians have striven to improve language, and ever since antiquity the cultivation of oral and written discourse has had a central position in all forms of education.

The fundamental axiom of the Greek educational philosophy was the identity of thought and language (*logos*). All progress in education as well as in general culture or civilization was based on the development of *logos*; the language of a people, therefore, was a "mirror of its culture".[2]

In Epicurean philosophy the first words were inarticulate expressions of individual feelings (*idia pathe*), like the cries of animals and infants; later on cognitive values were given to articulate words in order to obtain intersubjective communication, and finally by pure convention a philosophical language was constructed and accepted.

These theories of the origin and development of language are the framework of *Etymology*, the discipline in which comparative linguistics has its origin.

According to the Stoic definition *etymologia* means "explication (*anaptyxis*) of words, by means of which the truth (*to etymon* or *to alethes*) of a word is made evident". As for the primal words, this truth consists in the agreement between *logos* (word/concept) and thing meant, the word being a pure imitation of a thing or a natural phenomenon. As for derived words, composite words and words corrupted through vulgar usage, etymology tries, by means of analysis or small hypothetical alterations of sound and meaning, to restore the original accordance, and so to find the "true" meaning and form of the word (Steinthal 1890, 1: 331).

Ancient etymology thus consists of three assumptions: (1) a semantic theory: words are "natural" signs for the things meant; (2) a general theory of linguistic change regarded as a cultural process in which language was corrupted by bad usage, and improved by speakers, authors, grammarians, and philosophers who were able to imitate nature by art; (3) a general theory of derivation: an immense number of words are derived from a restricted group of primal onomatopoietic sounds. Words which are derived from the same primal words have family resemblance; a simple logical calculus of possible alterations of sound and sense was elaborated within this general framework, etymologies of Greek and Latin words were established, and the origin of many Latin words was sought – and found – in Greek.

COGNATIO AND CUMMUTATIO LITTERARUM

A special feature of ancient etymology was the *cognatio* and *permutatio litterarum*. Words which were derived from the same "primal word" were called cognate (Varro, *Lingua Latina* VI, 1). Hence also letters which were substituted for each other (*commutatae*) in derivation or inflection were called cognate: *"ab docendo, docere, discere, disciplina*, litteris commutatis paucis". This type of letter alternation in derivation was regarded as being on a par with the correspondence of letters in Greek and Latin words with same or similar meaning, the Latin word being regarded as derived from Greek, and it was observed that the alternating letters often were produced by the same part or position of the speech organs. This appears from the following utterances of Latin grammarians:

x littera cognata est cum *c* et *g*, quod lingua sublata paulum hac dicuntur, ut ab eo quod est *lux* et *lex* dicimus *lucis* et *legis*. *b* cum *p* consentit, quoniam origo earum non sine labore coniuncto ore respondet. a quo quem Graeci *Pyrrian* nos *Byrrian*. [The letter *x* is akin to *c* and *g*, because they are pronounced with the tongue a little raised, (in such a way) then from what is *lux* and *lex* we say *lucis* and *legis*. *b* and *p* go together (or agree) because their origin comes from a closure of the mouth with a certain strength (non sine labore = not without some labor); hence our *Byrrian* where the Greek says *Pyrrian*.] Ter. Scaurus, *De Orthographia* (Keil, Grammatici Latini VII 14.1).

proprie sunt cognatae, quae simili figuratione oris dicuntur, ut est *b f (s) m p*, quibus Cicero adicit *v* ... quotiens igitur *con* prepositionem sequetur vox cuius prima syllaba incipit a supra dictis litteris, id est *b f m p v*, quae vox coniuncta prepositione significationem eius confundat, vos quoque praepositionis litteram mutate, ut est *combibit ... comferit ... comvalescit ... suffert*, non *subfert ... collatum ... corradit*. [the letters which are pronounced with a similar pattern of the mouth are said to be properly akin, as are *b, f, (s), m, p*, to which Cicero added *v* ... this is why when the preposition *con* is followed by an utterance whose first syllable begins with one of the above mentioned letters, i.e., *b f m p v*, this utterance conjoins its (signification) the joint preposition, and one must change the (last) letter of the preposition (lit.: you must change the last letter); as it is in *combinit ... comferit ... comvalescit ... suffert*, rather than *subfert ... collatum ... corradit*.] Marius Victorinus (Keil VI: 18).

In medieval grammar cognatio litterarum is treated by, for example, Dacus (1955: 146-49). The further development of this theory is treated in the next part of the next section.

DIALECTS

The Greek were aware that their classical literature was written in various "dialects", the most famous of which were Attic, Doric, Aeolic, and Ionic. These dialects were not regarded as provincial idioms in relation to a standard language, as such a thing did not exist in classical Greek, and as, in the Hellenistic age, a common Greek was created, this was called "the common dialect" (he koine dialektos). *Dialektos* originally means "discourse, conversation", then "articulate speech', 'way of speaking". (Mankind has only one *phone*, "voice", Aristotle says, but many *dialektoi*). This concept of "variants of the same language" was to play an important part in the foundation of comparative linguistics.

III. Extension of Knowledge and Integration of Paradigms

The progress of general and comparative linguistics during the seventeenth and eighteenth centuries is due to two main trends: first, the extension of the above-mentioned patterns to a wider range of languages (particularly Semitic, Germanic, and Finno-Ugrian), and second, the growing integration of the dominating trends in ancient grammar and etymology.

DIALECTS AND GENEALOGY OF LANGUAGE: IMPORTANCE OF
STRUCTURAL SIMILARITY

In the Middle Ages Latin was the only language taken into consideration by scholars. But as Vulgar Latin was split up in local idioms, these were regarded in analogy with the Greek dialects; namely, as variant ways of speaking the same language. The first to express the observation was Roger Bacon (circa 1250): "Die Mundart (idioma) ist eine von jeder andern unterschiedene Sonderart einer Sprache, wie das Pikardische, Französische und Provenzalische; denn die lateinische Sprache ist in allen ein und dieselbe der Substanz nach, aber je nach der Mundart variiert" (Arens 1955: 43, quoted from the introduction to Dante, *Über das Dichten in der Muttersprache* [*De vulgari eloquentia*] [1924: 7]). Later on the Semitic languages were regarded in the same way.

The genealogical view has its origin in the Bible: Hebrew was the language of Adam and of all men until God confounded the language of the people who built the Tower of Babel. (A comprehensive history of beliefs concerning the origin and diversity of languages is given by Borst, 1957-63, reviewed in Language 38: 400-404 [1962]; 39: 467 [1963].) This myth was turned into a sound linguistic model of language genealogy by the Semitic philology of the sixteenth century, the biblical view of genetic relationship being fused with the Greek conception of dialects:

> Ebraea est primigenia, reliquae ex ea propagatae et genitae sunt. Quarum aliae longius degenerarunt a principali sermone ut dialecti filiorum Japheth, quaedam arctius adhaeserunt linguae primae ut dialecti filiorum Sem. [Hebrew is the progenitor, from which the remainder were propagated and generated. Of these, some have degenerated rather far from the original speech, such as the dialects of the sons of Japheth; others have stuck rather close to the first language, such as the dialects of the sons of

Shem.] (Bibliander 1548: 152; see Benfey 1869: 227. The views of Bibliander are inspired by the philosophy of Vives [see Verburg 1952: 166 ff.].)

The "Hebrew hypothesis" raises the question of the causes of linguistic change, and Bibliander gives a survey of factors which later generations have not been able to extend substantially; namely, mixture of peoples and languages, political and social change, neglect and education (see Arens 1955: 56). The next step, taken by the younger Scaliger, was to abandon Hebrew as the mother of all languages. On a purely empirical basis Scaliger classifies the European languages as descendants of four major, and seven minor "matrices linguae", which are not mutually related, "neither as to single words nor as to analogy (i.e., flectional paradigms)". (Arens 1955: 56; cf. Metcalf's chapter this volume, on this and subsequent points in this section. Becamus' Scythian theory [1569] was an important step away from the Hebrew hypothesis.)

This view was an incentive to closer investigations of the similarities of "words and analogy" in languages which were regarded as genealogically related. The preponderance of grammatical unity was explicit stated by J. Ludolf in *Dissertatio de harmonia linguae aethiopicae cum ceteris orientalibus* (1702):

> Si linguam alteri dicere affinem velimus, necesse est, non tantum ut ea contineat nonnulla alterius cujusdam linguae vocabula, sed etiam ut Grammaticae ratio, maxima sui parte, eadem sit, qualis convenientia cernitur in Orientalibus, Ebraea, Syriaca, Arabica et Aethiopica. [In order to say that one language is related to another, it is necessary not only that it have some words in common with the other, but also that the grammatical structure for the greater part be the same, as one finds it in the Oriental languages, the Hebrew, Syrian, Arabic, and Ethiopian.]

The same outstanding orientalist seems to be one of the first who has urged that words common to two or more languages may only be used as proofs of original community of race, if they denote simple natural objects (parts of the body and the like) (Benfey 1869: 236). The importance of grammatical similarity and of the most necessary words was already stressed by de Laet (1643) and Rudbeck (1675) (cf. Metcalf, this volume).

The same view was transferred to the old Germanic languages by the Swedish polyhistor G. Stiernhielm, in his preface and glossary to the synoptic edition of the Gothic Bible with parallel texts in Swedish and Icelandic (1671). Stiernhielm starts with the assumption that the Semitic languages are dialects of one and the same language, and gives an acute discussion of the relations between dialects and related languages. He declares that in the course of time dialects may grow so different that speakers cannot understand each other, and that they must consequently be regarded as having become separate languages. On the other hand, a new language may be formed on the basis of dialects, when this is useful to the community (as has been the case with the Greek *koine* and High German literary language) (cf. Metcalf, this volume).

The genealogical view is combined with the idea that languages also have a definite life cycle: "Ex his capi potest judicium de naturali generatione, adolescentia, flore, devergio, et interitu omnium linguarum. Quod enim hominum, civitatum, imperiorum; hoc idem linguarum fatum est." [And from this can be formulated an assessment about the natural birth, adolescence, blossom, decay, and death of all the languages. As a matter of fact this is the fare of men, towns, and empires, as well as languages.] (A similar biological analogy had already been used by Claudius Salmasius; cf. Metcalf, this volume.)

In the glossary under the word *haban* Stiernhielm demonstrates the close formal similarity between the inflections of Gothic *haban* and Latin *habere*, adding the important remark:

> notatu digna est similitude flexionum verborum Gothicorum, et Latinorum, quae manifesto arguit linguam utramque, primis temporibus fuisse unam, quae postea in diversas abierit dialectos. Similitudo haec patet in sequentibus: [the resemblance between the declensions of the Gothic and Latin verbs is worth noting; and this resemblance obviously argues that both languages (lit.: have been one in former times) and later on evolved into two divergent dialects. This resemblance is obvious in the following:

Goth.	Haba,	-bais,	-baith,	-bam,	-baith,	-band,	-baida
Lat.	Habeo,	-bes,	-bet,	-bemus,	-betis,	-bent,	-buit
Goth.	-ban,	-bands,	-bandis,	-bandiu,	-bandan,	-bandana	
Lat.	-bere,	-bens,	-bentis,	-benti,	-bentem,	-bentes	

This discovery of Stiernhielm's was extended from the verbs to the substantives (first declension) by his countryman Johan Ihre in *Glossarium Sviogothicum* (1769: xxv) and the following year a thorough structural comparison of some Lappish dialects with Hungarian was carried out in Joh. Sajnovic's *Demonstratio idioma Ungarorum et Lapponum idem esse* (Copenhagen 1770; also in Danish translation).[3] Sajnovics, who wrote this book during a stay in Copenhagen, quotes the work of Ihre on several occasions and seems to have been influenced by the etymological method of the Swedish scholar. He is aware that orthography often veils the identity of words and forms (8) and therefore bases his comparisons on the pronunciation (13). He gives a list (from Leem's *Lapponic Grammar*) of 15 observations:

quarum ductu vox Dialecti Lapponum Montanorum, in vocem Dialecti Lapponum Maritimorum, mutati potest (31). . . . Ubi alii B enunciant, alii enunciant P . . . . [by following which, a word of the dialect of the Mountain Lapps can be changed into a word of the dialect of the Coastal Lapps. . . . Where the one group pronounce B, the others pronounce P . . . .]

He shows that the forms of the latter dialect are more or less identical with the forms of Hungarian. He explicitly excludes from the comparison all words which may be considered as loanwords (33). He warns against uncritical use of *litterarum permutationes* (33), and claims that the words which he identifies must have the same meaning. His comparison of the grammatical system (54-73) comprises all the parts of grammar: *partes orationis, suffixes,* prefixes, particles, and so forth.

His investigations were continued after the same principles in the famous work of Gyarmathi (see Gulya, this volume).

ETYMOLOGY AND WORD FORMATION

In Greco-Roman grammar no clear distinction was made between what was later called inflection and derivation, features of both being mentioned among the "accidences" of the single partes orationis. Nor had ancient etymology succeeded in giving a clear structural analysis of the inflected or derived word. The basic form from which the inflected or derived forms were derived (*thema, positio*) was not a root or stem, but a form which for semantic reasons was regarded as prior to other forms (the nominative singular masculine and the first person of the present tense in the indicative). The borderline between stem and "*terminatio*" was therefore not fixed by clear rules.

In this respect, too, the grammars of Semitic languages introduced new and useful methods. Instead of deriving the forms of a paradigm from an arbitrarily chosen *thema*, Semitic grammar took its starting point in the radix, that are common to all inflected and derived forms of the word (*litterae radicales*). This method was transferred to the analysis of German words, and hence to Latin, Greek, and other languages. It forced the grammarians to give a more precise delimitation of root, stem, and endings or prefixes. (See the instructive section, Theorie der Ableitung, in Jellinek [1914: 132 ff.].) When applied to etymology this analysis of words, practised with so much energy in the grammar schools, gave rise to a fatal simplification: the roots were regarded as genetically prior to the fuller or derived forms, the structurally simple (or inarticulate) as prior to the complex (or articulate). Consequently, the first language of mankind must have contained only roots of an extremely simple structure; first an inarticulated vowel (be it onomatopoeic or an expression of a feeling), later "articulated" by means of one or two consonants.

(I have not had time enough to trace the history of this theory and must confine myself to referring to the following works on the subject: Leibniz 1875, 5: 262 ff.; [see now Aarsleff 1969]; Adam Smith (1767); the articles "Etymologie" [see below] and "Langue" by Beauzée and others in Diderot's *Encyclopedie* [1756, 1965]; de Brosses, 2nd Paris [1765]; Beauzée [1767]; Monboddo [1773-92]. Extracts from most of these works are given in German translation by Arens.)

ETYMOLOGY AND ABSTRACTION

The semantic side of etymology was also molded into more elaborate forms on the basis of the new theories of cognition and language propounded by the great philosophers of the seventeenth century, particularly by John Locke in his *Essay Concerning Human Understanding* (1690). Just as the grammarians and etymologists considered the structurally simple or inarticulate word or syllable to be genetically prior to the articulate word or syllable, the philosophers of language reconstructed a genetic order of ideas or meanings which was based upon the assumption that simple ideas, provoked by sense impressions, were prior to complex ideas, and ideas of things prior to ideas of relations, and so forth. This theory is treated in connection with formal derivation in the works quoted in the preceding paragraph.

GRAMMAIRE GÉNÉRALE AND TYPOLOGY OF LANGUAGE

In medieval manuscripts and old grammars we find the inflectional paradigms of Latin explained by forms (inflected or paraphrastic) of the vernacular; and later on most grammars of modern languages have kept the fourth-century framework of Donatus, merely filling out the Latin word classes, flectional categories, and syntactic rules with material from other languages (cf. Bursill-Hall, this volume).

In the seventeenth century this schoolroom practice was combined with a revival of the scholastic logical grammar in the *Grammaire générale et raisonnée de Port Royal* (1660). C. Lancelot had invented a new method of language teaching, and had written a series of primers in Latin, Spanish, Italian, and other languages, all made exactly after the same pattern. He asked his colleague Arnauld, a famous disciple of Descartes, how this should be explained, and got the answer that language was the outer form of thought; and as, according to *Discours de la Méthode*, human understanding is always the same in all people, the fundamental categories and forms of thought must be the base of every grammar, the particular systems of existing languages being merely accidental approximations to the universal ideal, partly corrupted by neglective usage (see Harnois 1929).

Universal grammar consequently was a sort of comparative grammar, but as it principally was concerned with universal semantic concepts, it was not interested in the diverging forms of the particular languages, regarding these as pure variants of a general system, not as descendents of a common "Ursprache".

In the eighteenth century, philosophical interest concentrated on the origin of the differences of culture, language, and character. And the discussions on that subject led to the idea of a particular "genius" of every language,[4] and hence to the establishment of various "types" of language. The different characters and types might be viewed both from a systematic and from a genetic or historical point of view. In this way the general genetic theories of traditional etymology and language genealogy were merged with the systematic approach of school grammar and logical grammar.

The evolutionary theories outlined above led to the hypothesis that human language in general (and every language in particular) must have passed through three stages, corresponding to what nineteenth-century linguists called *isolating, agglutinating,* and *inflecting* languages. A further consequence was that existing languages were classified in types, according to the structure of words. These types of language, accordingly, were regarded as stages in a genetic series, but the typology was not necessarily combined with a genealogic tree.

Other, more empirical approaches to language typology were based on the comparison of ancient languages like Latin, Greek, and Gothic with their modern descendants. The point of departure was the old school practice of rearranging the "artificially inverted" words of a poem or a rhetoric period into "natural order". When translating a Latin author into modern French, it was quite obvious that the word order of the modern language was the more "natural" or "logical", and in continuation of medieval philosophy of language some French grammarians of the seventeenth and eighteenth centuries introduced the distinction between (1) an ancient type of language, with free word order and frequent inversions, and (2) a modern type in which the fixed arrangement of words gave a true picture of the natural sequence of thoughts or ideas (Le Laboureur 1669). This order was called "l'ordre analytique, parce qu'elle est tout à la fois le résultat de l'analyse de la pensée, et le fondement de l'analyse du discours, en quelque langue qu'il soit énoncé" (Beauzée, "Langue" [1756]). Girard (1747) called the first type *langues transpositives*, the latter *langues analogues ou analytiques*. He makes the observation that the fixed word order may have the same function as the case endings which have largely been lost in the *langues analogues*. The ideas of

Girard were adopted by Beauzée in his article in the *Encyclopédie* (1756) and in his *Grammaire générale* (1767). (A summary of the whole discussion is given by Jellinek 1913, 2: 425ff.)

The theory that fixed word order is caused by the reduction of the case system was combined with the old ideas of structural evolution by Adam Smith in his *Dissertation on the Origin of Languages*, and translated into French as a supplement to Beauzée's article "Langue" in the second edition of the great *Encyclopédie* (1784). Smith had already exposited his ideas in his lecture of 1761–62 (ed. 1963). Most of them were taken from the *Encyclopédie*. Adam Smith explains the reduction of inflectional systems by means of the old theory of language mixture: when adult people are forced to learn a foreign language with complex and irregular inflections, they fail to reproduce some of the forms.

> Their ignorance of the declensions they would naturally supply by the use of prepositions [*ad Roma* or *de Roma* instead of *Romae*. Similarly *Io sono amato* instead of *amor*]. And thus, upon the intermixture of different nations with one another, the conjugations, by means of auxiliary verbs, were made to approach towards the simplicity and uniformity of declensions.
>
> In general, it may be lain down for a maxim, that the more simple any language is in its composition the more complex it must be in its declensions and conjugations; and, on the contrary, the more simple it is in its declensions and conjugations, the more complex it must be in its composition.
>
> This simplification. . .restrains us from disposing such sounds as we have, in the manner that might be most agreeable. It ties down many words to a particular situation, though they might often be placed in another with much more beauty. . . . The place, therefore, of the three principal members of the phrase is in the English, and for the same reason in the French and Italian languages, almost always precisely determined.

A popular synthesis of all these ideas concerning the origin and development of language is to be found in Adelung (1782a, 1782b). It is probable that Adelung was the first and most important source for Rasmus Rask's general views of the evolution of language (see the next section).

IV. From Cognatio Litterarum to the Conception of Regular
Correspondence of Letters Between Two Languages

The theory of *cognatio* or *permutatio litterarum* was adopted by the grammarians of the sixteenth century and new material was gathered from

Semitic and Germanic languages. (For Becanus [1509], on *permutatio litterarum*, see Metcalf, this volume.) Eric Pontoppidan, in his *Grammatica Danica* (1663, partly written in the 1640's) ends the *Observationes Orthographicae* with a section he calls *Cognatio litterarum*:

> 1. Cognatae sunt literae inter se, ideoque aliae in alias mutantur. Nam, ut Critici ajunt, elementa homogenea et ejusdem organi inter se facile mutabilia sunt. [1. The letters are related to each other; this is why they derive from each other. As a matter of fact, as the Critics (?) said, the homogeneous elements, pertaining to the same organic body change easily among themselves.]
>
> 2. *A* et *aa* cognationem habent cum *ae, e* et *o* ut ex hisce vocibus collatis, conjugatis, derivatis et juxta Dialectos variantibus innotescit: *Lang* (longus) *laenger. . . mand, maend. . . Angelus, Engel. . . .* [2. *A* and *aa* are related to *ae, e,* and *o* as it appears from these words, (lit.) ordered, conjugated, derived and varying according to the different languages: *lang* (longus) *laenger. . . mand, maend. . . Angelus, Engel. . . .*]
>
> 13. *C* consonans lingvodentalis infera interior mutatur in *H* consonantem etiam lingvodentalem inferam interiorem. *Cornu*, quod ex Hebraeo . . . peperit, Germanis et Danis *Horn. Calamus, culmus* dedit Germanis et nobis halm. *Cutis. . . huud. . . caput. . . hovet.* [13. The interior, inferior, linguodental consonant *c* changes into *h* itself an interior, inferior, linguodental consonant. *Cornu*, which comes from Hebrew, became German and Danish *horn. Calamus*, gave the German *culmus* and our *halm. Cutus. . . huud; caput. . . hovet.*]

Wachter, in the prolegomena to his large *Glossarium Germanicum* (1737), Section III, has observed that not all permutations take place between physiologically cognate letters; namely, "literae . . . quae ab eodem instrumento, tamquam communi generis auctore figurantur" [letters . . . which are shaped by the same instrument, the same way as by an agent (author) of a common species (or kind)]. Besides this rational or "natural" type of permutation, etymology must recognize another type of mutation peculiar to each language however much done contrary to nature ("quamvis praeter naturam factis"). They must be explained by the particular "genius lingvae" (cf. Rudbeck [1675]: *ratio literarum sua*, Metcalf, this volume).

Wachter's analysis of the traditional view may be regarded as two steps toward a more just concept of phonetic change: (1) He urged that a mutation ought to be physiologically motivated; but the stage of development reached by phonetics at the period did not allow him to observe physiological affinities other than those of consonants produced by the same organ, and when comparing forms of distantly related words he lacked evidence for the intermediate stages. Consequently, he was not able to realize that mutations caused by the particular "genius of language" were also physiologically motivated. (2) He was aware that special rules applied to the permutations of every particular language; but he did not perceive that "natural permutations" between "cognate letters" were also restricted to a particular language (or dialect) at a particular stage of its history, let alone that such particular rules of permutations must be without exceptions.

Finally Wachter repeated the fault of his predecessors, mixing examples from inflection and derivation within the same language with permutations of the same letters in words from different languages. Wachter's theory, therefore, was not able to prevent arbitrary identifications in etymology; every permutation could be explained either as "natural" according to the physiological principle, or as due to an irrational *genius lingvae*.

TURGOT

On all these points the theory of eytmology was decisively improved by the article "Étymologie" in Diderot's great *Encyclopédie* (1756). The article was anonymous, but in the second edition it was attributed to the famous philosopher Turgot, and it was reprinted in *Oeuvres de Turgot* 1: 473-516 (1913), together with some other articles on linguistic matters and an interesting note on Turgot's relations with de Brosses.[5]

Turgot rejects the view that all "lettres des mêmes organes" may be arbitrarily exchanged (and that it is possible to give general physiological rules for permutations). Instead he argues in favor of the regularity and exclusiveness of sound change in each particular language (Section II, 17):

> ...On verra que chaque langue, et dans chaque langue chaque dialecte, chaque peuple, chaque siècle, changent constamment certaines lettres en d'autres lettres, et se refusent à d'autres changements aussi constamment usités chez leurs voisins. On conclura qu'il n'y a à cet égard aucune règle générale. Plusieurs savants, et ceux en particulier qui ont fait leur étude des langues orientales, ont, il est vrai, posé pour principe, que les lettres distinguées dans la grammaire hébraique et rangées par classes sous le titre de lettres des mêmes organes, se changent réciproquement entre elles, et peuvent se substituer indifféremment les unes aux autre dans la même classe. Ils ont affirmé la même chose des voyelles, et en sont disposé arbitrairement, sans doute, parce que le changement des voyelles est plus fréquent dans toutes les langues que celui des consonnes, mais peut-être aussi parce qu'en hébreu les voyelles ne sont point écrites. Toutes ces observations ne font qu'un système, une conclusion générale de quelques faits particuliers qui peut être démentie par d'autres faits en plus grand

nombre. Quelque variable que soit le son de voyelles, *leurs changements sont aussi constants, dans le même temps et dans le même lieu que ceux des consonnes*: le Grecs ont changé le son ancien de l'*éta* et de l'*upsilon* en *i*; les Anglais donnent, suivant des règles constantes, à notre *a* l'ancien son de l'*éta* des Grecs [e.g., *grace*]; les voyelles font, comme les consonnes, partie de la prononciation dans toutes les langues, et dans aucune langue la prononciation n'est arbitraire. . . . Les Italiens, sans égard aux divisions de l'alphabet hébreu, qui met l'*iod* au rang des lettres du palais, et l'*l* au rang des lettres de la langue, changent, l'*l* précédé d'une consonne en *i* *tréma* ou, mouillé faible, qui se prononce comme l'*iod* des Hébreux: *platea, piazza; blanc, bianco*. Les Portugais, dans les mêmes circonstances, changent constamment cet *l* en *r, branco*. . . . Ne cherchons donc point à ramener à une loi fixe des variations multipliées à l'infini, dont les causes nous échappent; étudions-en seulement la succession comme on étudie les faits historiques. Leur variété connue, *fixée à certaines langues, ramenée à certaines dates, suivant l'ordre des lieux et des temps*, deviendra une suite de pièges tendus à des suppositions trop vagues et fondées sur la simple possibilité d'une changement quelconque. . . .

La multitude des règles de critique qu'on peut former sur ce plan, et d'après les détails que fournira l'étude des grammaires, des dialectes et des révolutions de chaque langue, est le plus sûr moyen pour donner à l'art étymologique toute la solidité dont il est susceptible; parce qu'en général, la meilleure méthode pour assûrer les résultats de tout art conjectural, c'est d'éprouver toutes ses suppositions, en les rapprochant sans cesse d'un ordre certain de faits très-nombreux et très-variés.

OTHER ASPECTS OF EIGHTEENTH-CENTURY ETYMOLOGICAL THEORY

As Turgot's article in many respects gives the most exact and the most advanced exposition of philosophical etymology in the eighteenth century, it may be regarded as the best point of departure when we are to decide whether nineteenth-century comparative linguistics may in a sense be called a "scientific revolution." I have therefore extracted further passages from some of its most important theses, particularly such as seem to foreshadow the work of the following century.

I. Sources des conjectures étymologiques
(1) L'examen attentif du mot même dont on cherche l'étymologie. . .est. . .le premier pas à faire. . .il faut le ramener à sa racine, en le dépouillant de cet appareil de terminaisons et

d'inflexions grammaticales qui le déguisent. . ..: ainsi, la connaissance profonde de la langue dont on veut éclaircir les origines. . .
est le préliminaire le plus indispensable pour cette étude.

(2) Souvent le résultat de cette décomposition se termine à
des mots absolument hors d'usage. . . .[These may be found in
old manuscripts or dialects. . . .]

(5) Il n'y a aucune langue, dans l'état actuel des choses, qui
ne soit formée du mélange ou de l'altération de langues plus
anciennes, dans lesquelles on doit retrouver une grande partie des
racines de la langue nouvelle, quand on a poussé aussi loin qu'il
est possible, sans sortir de celle-ci, le décomposition et la filiation
des mots, c'est à ces langues étrangères qu'il faut recourir. . . .

(7) Lorsque, de cette langue primitive plusieurs se sont
formées à la fois dans différents pays. . ., la comparaison de la
manière différente dont elles ont altéré les mêmes inflexions, ou
les mêmes sons de la langue-mère, en se rendant propres; celle des
directions opposées. . .suivant lesquelles elles ont détourné le sens
des mêmes expressions; la suite de cette comparaison, dans toute
le cours de leur progrès, et dans leurs différentes époques,
serviront beaucoup à donner des vues pour les origines de chacune
d'entre elles. Ainsi, l'italien et le gascon. . .présentent souvent le
mot intermédiaire entre un mot français et un mot latin, dont le
passage eût paru trop brusque et trop peu vraisemblable. . . .

II. Principes de Critique pour apprécier
la certitude des étymologies

(1) . . .Si. . .on propose une *étymologie* dans laquelle le
primitif soit tellement éloigné du dérivé, soit pour le sens, soit
pour le son, qu'il faille supposer entre l'un et l'autre plusieurs
changements intermédiaires, la vérification la plus sûre qu'on en
puisse faire sera l'examen de chacun de ces changements. *L'étymologie* est bonne, si la chaîne des ces altérations est une suite de
faits connus directement, ou prouvés par des inductions vraisem-
blables; elle est mauvaise, si l'intervalle n'est rempli que par un
tissu de suppositions gratuites. . . .

(15) . . .[Le mot] s'use, pour ainsi dire, en passant dans un
plus grand nombre de bouches, surtout dans la bouche du peuple,
et la rapidité de cette circulation équivaut à une plus longue
durée;. . .les mots qui reviennent le plus souvent dans les langues,
tels que les verbes *être, faire, vouloir, aller,* et tous ceux qui
servent à lier les autres mots dans le discours, sont sujets à de plus
grandes altérations. . . .

(16) C'est principalement la pente générale que tous les
mots ont à s'àdoucir ou à s'abréger qui les altère; et la cause de
cette pente est la commodité de l'organe qui les prononce. Cette
cause agit sur tous les hommes; elle agit d'une manière insensible,

et d'autant plus que le mot est répété. Son action continue, et la marche des altérations qu'elle a produites a dû être et a été observée. . . ; les mots, adoucis ou abrégés par l'euphonie, ne retournent pas plus à leur première prononciation, que les eaux ne remontent vers leur source. Au lieu d'*obtinere*, l'euphonie a fait prononcer *optinere*; mais jamais à la prononciation du mot *optare*, on ne substituera celle d'*obtare*. . . .

(18) C'est. . .l'erreur de l'oreille qui domine et qui altère le plus la prononciation. Lorsqu'une nation adopte un mot qui lui est étranger, et lorsque deux peuples différents confondent leurs languages en se mêlant, celui qui, ayant entendu un mot étranger, le répète mal, ne trouve point dans ceux qui l'écoutent de contradicteur légitime, et il n'a aucune raison pour se corriger.

(19) Il résulte, de tout ce que nous avons dit dans le cours de cet article, qu'une *étymologie* est une supposition; qu'elle ne reçoit un caractère de vérité et de certitude que de la comparaison avec les faits connus, du nombre des circonstances de ces faits qu'elle explique, des probabilités qui en naissent, et que la critique apprécie. Toute circonstance expliquée, tout rapport entre le dérivé et le primitif supposé, produit une probabilité; aucun n'est exclus; la probabilité augmente avec le nombre des rapports, et parvient rapidement à la certitude. Le sens, le son, les consonnes, les voyelles, la quantité se prêtent une force récipro-que . . .il faut donc se faire une loi de ne s'en permettre qu'une à la fois, et par conséquent de ne remontrer de chaque mot qu'à son *étymologie* immédiate; ou bien il faut qu'une suite de faits incontestables remplisse l'intervalle entre l'un et l'autre, et dispense de toute supposition. . .On doit vérifier. . .les *étymologies* qu'on établit sur les mélanges des peuples et des langues; par des exemples connus, celles qu'on tire des changements du sens au moyen des métaphores; par la connaissance historique et grammaticale de la prononciation de chaque langue et de ses révolutions, celles qu'on fonde sur les altérations de la prononcia-tion: comparer toutes les *étymologies* supposées, soit avec la chose nommé, sa nature, ses rapport, et son analogie avec les différents êtres; soit avec la chronologie des altérations succes-sives, et l'ordre invariable des progrès de l'euphonie [i.e., the change of sounds] ; rejeter enfin toute *étymologie* contredite par un seul fait, et n'admettre comme certaines que celles qui seront appuyées sur un trèsgrand nombre de probabilités réunies.

L'application la plus immédiate de l'art étymologique, est la recherche des origines d'une langue en particulier. Le résultat de ce travail, poussé aussi loin qu'il peut l'être, sans tomber dans des conjectures trop arbitraires, est une partie essentielle de l'analyse d'une langue, c'est-à-dire, de la connaissance complète du système de cette langue, de ses éléments radicaux, de la combinaison dont

ils sont susceptibles, etc. Le fruit de cette analyse est la facilité de
comparer les langues entre elles sous toutes sortes de rapports,
grammatical, philosophique, historique, etc. On sent aisément
combien ces préliminaires sont indespensables pour saisir en
grand, et sous son vrai point de vûe la théorie générale de la
parole, et la marche de l'esprit humain dans la formation et les
progrès du language; théorie qui, comme toute autre, a besoin,
pour n'être pas un roman, d'être continuellement rapproachée des
faits. Cette théorie est la source d'ou découlent les règles de cette
grammaire générale qui gouverne toutes les langues, à laquelle
toutes les nations s'assujettissent en croyant ne suivre que les
caprices de l'usage.

V Rasmus Rask and the Foundation
of Comparative Linguistics

THE SCHOOLBOY'S WAY TO THE STUDY OF LANGUAGE

Rasmus Rask (1787–1832) was introduced to the etymological
grammar of the eighteenth century by S. Bloch, his teacher of Greek, whose
Greek school grammar (1803) was based on that of Trendelenburg (1732).
This in turn was a popular rendering of the Greek inflectional system in
accordance with the etymological theories of a Dutch school of classical
philology, founded by Hemsterhuis and Valckenaer, Lennep, and Scheid (see
Benfey 1869: 244; Rask, *Udvalgte Afhandlinger* 3: 135, *Samlede Afhandlinger*
2: 123 ff.; and Gerretzen). It was the basic idea of this system that the
irregularities of Greek conjugation were to be explained by suppletive
combination of several related paradigms, each of which originally belonged
to a particular dialect. Rask's manuscript of a Greek grammar (*Samlede
Afhandlinger* 2: 118 ff.) shows that he was inclined to accept this system
even as a mature scholar (parts of the ms. were written 1810–16 and 1819).

This theory fitted rather well into the general etymological theories of
the eighteenth century, which Rask got to know through Wachter's and Ihre's
etymological glossaries (quoted in notes from his schooldays, *c*.1806),
through the works of Adelung (an outline of whose theories was given in a
school program by Rask's teacher of Latin) and through the articles
"Étymologie," "Langue" in the *Encyclopédie* (2nd edition, 1784, to which is
added the translation of Adam Smith's dissertation, as noted above). Rask
explicitly quotes the *Encyclopédie* in the introduction to his comparative
grammar ([1814] see section VI, Conclusion), and details in the notes from
his schooldays seem to come from this source, directly or indirectly. Another
of his teachers (Degen) wrote a program on etymology which was based

mainly on the ideas of the *Encyclopédie*. In my book I have shown how Rask and his teachers were much preoccupied with all the main intellectual trends of the Age of Enlightenment.

Among Rask's papers two drafts from his last years at school (1806–7; printed in the appendix to my book on Rask) have been preserved. Here he gives his views on two main features of eighteenth-century etymology; namely (1) the evolutional theories of John Locke, Leibniz, and Adam Smith (as popularized in the works of Adelung, Meiner, and others), (2) the discussions on language genealogy (see above).

The incentive to write the first paper was Rask's knowledge of Creole (i.e., Dutch without inflections, spoken by the Negroes of the Danish West Indies) and the Eskimo language of the Greenlanders. Rask makes the acute remark that Creole, although it represents the final stage of a long evolution, "from Greek, through Gothic, Saxon, and Dutch" has the characteristics generally attributed to the most primitive stage of human language. Conversely, according to the structural theory of linguistic evolution, Eskimo with its highly complicated system of derivation and inflection (more complicated than those of Greek and Latin) must be said to represent a rather advanced type of language, in spite of the very primitive stage of the Eskimo culture. Rask draws the conclusion that evolution in language takes the shape of a spiral: "languages originally consist of single sounds (i.e., word expressions), then they are molded, extended, composed, and once more dissolved into single sounds, but not the same as the original ones"; in modern wording: primitive languages on the one hand and analytical languages on the other are "isolating" languages but on two different levels. Rask parallels this "spiral" evolution with the evolution of religion from primitive concepts to "artificial and unnatural" religions, and finally to the clear analytic ideas of free-thinking and finds the same spiral motion of nature in the evolution and dissolution of organic beings.

Rask's theory of evolution calls to mind a remark at the end of the dissertation of Adam Smith (cited above): "the same thing has happened in it (language) which commonly happens with regard to mechanical engines. All machines are generally, when first invented, extremely complex in their principles. . . . Succeeding improvers observe that one principle may be so applied as to produce several of those movements, and thus the machine becomes gradually more and more simple."

But, in contradistinction to Smith, Rask is of the opinion that language evolution is a natural process which cannot be checked, and as nature is always right Rask (like Adelung) views the tendency of modern languages in a positive light, pointing to English as a highly simplified but nevertheless extremely workable language.

The second paper is Rask's first attempt to find evidence for the genealogic relationship between Gothic (and the other Germanic languages) on the one hand and Latin on the other.

RASK'S INVENTION: AN ETYMOLOGICAL GRAMMAR

In a paper written in 1810, but not published until 1820 (*Udvalgte Afhandlinger* 2: 50 ff.) Rask declares:

> The present dissertation contains an attempt at a Danish grammatical etymology and etymological grammar, viz. an explanation of the origin of the endings and forms which are found in present-day Danish. This attempt is not only the first for our language, but as far as I know the first attempt of this kind for any language. . . . Up to now it has been regarded as sufficient to etymologize, treating only the words, but nobody has bothered to find out about the origin of their inflectional features.

The title of the paper is "The endings and forms of the Danish Grammar explained by derivation from the Icelandic language." And it contains a thorough comparison of the Danish inflectional paradigms with the corresponding Icelandic forms.

Rask was right that this was an unprecedented method in the study of languages. It is true that some scholars of the seventeenth and eighteenth centuries had compared the grammatical systems of languages in order to prove that they were related. And in Trendelenburg–Bloch's Greek grammar the classical forms were derived from constructed primitive forms (the existence of which was disputed by contemporary grammarians). But it was the first time the inflectional system of a modern language was systematically compared with its parent language ("Stammesproget") and a sister language, so that not only were single forms identified, but the causes and principles of change were expounded in detail. I think it would be difficult to find, in the whole body of linguistic literature, so many original and important observations on so few pages.

The basis of the comparison was Rask's Icelandic Grammar, printed in 1809, but drafted already when Rask as a schoolboy taught himself Icelandic (i.e., Old-Norse) solely by means of an edition of Snorri Sturlason's *History of the Norwegian Kings* with Latin and Danish translations, but without glossary or grammar.

Rask states that a comparison between two systems of grammar presupposes that both are described in exactly the same way. Consequently he discusses more seriously than any linguist before the twentieth century the principles of a structural description, for example, whether the three genders of the different endings should be the dominant principle in the establishment of the Icelandic declensions, or whether the particular forms within a paradigm could be derived (structurally and/or genetically) from each other.

He demonstrates that seemingly irregular and irrational forms and constructions find their "historical explanation" as survivals of an older system. And he sharply marks the borderline between an etymological grammar which only compares the parent language with its descendants ("the uttermost links of the chain"), and an exposition of "the transitions of the Danish grammar from the moment when it was separated from the Icelandic and until now". This part of the task was executed by Rask's school friend N. M. Petersen (1829), the first history of a language in the modern sense of the word. Both its method, its headlines, and its basic ideas were sketched by Rask.

FUNDAMENTAL UNITY OF THE INDO-EUROPEAN LANGUAGE

No doubt, at an early stage of his studies Rask was struck by the close accordance, first pointed out by Stiernhielm and Ihre, between some inflectional endings of Gothic and Latin; but during his work with Icelandic grammar (1805–9) he was aware that the congruity between the systems of Germanic, Greek, Latin, and Romance languages was almost perfect when the apparent differences were explained by the new methods of etymological grammar: the more languages and dialects you took into consideration, the more gaps you were able to fill out by intermediate forms. "I resolved to go through as many languages as possible, and make an abridgement of each recast according to my own principles. . . . That I discovered such a fundamental coherence (en sådan Grundsammenhaeng) between so distant languages (Greek, Latin, Gothic, Icelandic, German) led me to investigate so many European tongues as time would allow", he writes in a letter, probably from 1809 (*Samlede Afhandlinger* 1: 15 ff.).

The point of departure of this rearrangement of grammars was Rask's observation that the distinction between the 'strong' and the 'weak' conjugations (as Grimm called them) was common to Icelandic (and the younger Scandinavian languages), Gothic, German, English, Dutch; namely, all the Germanic languages.

The next step was to find out that also the Icelandic (and the other Germanic) declensions ought to be arranged in a bifurcate system of "strong" and "weak" inflections and that each of the main categories both of conjugation and of declension appeared on closer analysis to consist of one or two triads of subclasses. By highly acute reinterpretations of the structure of the inflectional forms of Latin and Greek he succeeded in demonstrating that the grammars of these languages also might be rearranged into exactly the same system of primary bipartitions and tripartite subclasses, and that the endings of the paradigms in question matched on all essential points, when the "permutations of letters" and some other rules of transition and simplification were taken into account.

In my book on Rask (chapter III) I have analyzed the stages of this attempt at reducing Germanic, Latin, and Greek grammar to symmetric variants of one fundamental system of dichotomies and triades. I have shown that his method was highly successful, but that on essential points Rask violated his own principles in order to fit the facts into his system.

The results of these comparative investigations were published in Rask's chief work, *Investigation on the Origin of the Old Norse or Icelandic Language* (1814) which (in the words of Holger Pedersen) "may well be called a comparative Indo-European grammar in embryo."

LEVELS OF CLASSIFICATION AND DEGREES OF RELATIONSHIP

We have seen Rask urging that the flectional systems should be arranged according to hierarchical principles, the different levels of "division" (*Inddeling*) being sharply distinguished and defined.

In just the same way he claimed that the structural classification of languages and the genealogical tree that could be constructed according to degrees of similarity, should be described in a fixed terminology, comprising six degrees. This number was not chosen arbitrarily; it had proved sufficient in empirical work, and as Linné's *Systema Naturae* also comprises six degrees, Rask thought that this must be a principle founded in the laws of Nature.

In a manuscript from 1815 (reprinted in Diderichsen 1960: 194 ff.) Rask proposed the following English terminology: (1) *race* (e.g., Indo-European), (2) *class* (Germanic), (3) *stock* (Scandinavian or Westgermanic), (4) *branch* (Southern or Northern Westgermanic), (5) *language* (Danish or Swedish; Dutch or Low German), (6) *dialect* (Jutlandic or the dialect of Bornholm).[6]

UNITY OF SOUND SYSTEM AND RULES OF LETTER-TRANSITION ("BOGSTAVOVERGANGE")

In Rask's treatment of grammatical similarity he fused the systematic view (the particular paradigms viewed as variants or "dialects" of one and the same fundamental system) with the historical hypothesis of genealogic relationship between "descendants" of a parent language.

The same fusion characterizes Rask's analysis of the sound systems of the languages he compared. By means of a few (more or less well founded) modifications and reconstructions he found almost the same sound system in modern Icelandic (which he identified with the original parent language of Scandinavian), Old Greek, and some dialects of the Danish Island Funen (Fyn), where he was born. In particular, the existence of exactly the same peculiar system of diphthongs in these languages could not, according to Rask, be due to accident; it must be proof that this system was an original common feature of Indo-European, lost in the other branches.

No doubt Rask set much more store on this discovery than on the existence of "letter-transitions" between Icelandic and Greek (*Udvalgte Afhandlinger* 1: 180). On the other hand, Rask's treatment of "letter-transitions" was the part of his work which had the most important influence on the further development of the comparative and historic method in linguistics. It is evident, however, that Rask had difficulties in realizing the full importance and true character of what was later (with a misleading term) called "phonetical laws".

In the introduction to his *Origin of Old Norse* ([1814]: 47) he states that "the variations and permutations of letters are so manifold that we should be in perfect confusion unless Nature, in this point as well as otherwise, complied with certain rules; these you must carefully search out and closely stick to". Rask, in other words, tries to find general, physiologically founded, laws for the permutations of letters, but remains with the vague principle of the old etymologists, that "letters which are pronounced with the same organ of speech or belong to the same class may be exchanged with each other! But," he cautiously adds, "there are many transitions and crossings of these classes."

In the following examples some few instances of grammatical alternation (e.g., *bresta, brast, brostinn*) are mixed with the main stock of correspondences between letters in words from different languages (e.g., Swedish *svafvel*, German *Schwefel*, Danish *Svovl*); and the examples are taken at random from a great variety of languages, the relationship of which is sometimes highly remote (e.g., Armenian and Icelandic, Greek and English, etc.). But in a parenthesis added at the end of the section, Rask hesitates as to the general validity of the rules of transition, admitting that other transitions take place in Slavonic or Oriental languages. Louis Hjelmslev is of the opinion that this section "represents a standpoint which Rask had already left during his work" (*Udvalgte Afhandlinger* 3: 76), referring to other utterances in which Rask more or less explicitly is aware of the importance of the particular letter-transitions between two languages. But in my opinion there is no evidence that Rask had given up the assumption taken over from Wachter and Ihre that the etymologist on the one hand must seek the general laws of letter-transitions, and on the other hand must state the special transitions between two languages under comparison, that are due to a special *genius lingvae* ("every people has something peculiar in its pronunciation and therefore changes the expressions borrowed from the neighbors in a particular way" *Udvalgte Afhandlinger* 3: 19).

But Rask, being aware that Wachter's "law" is too narrow, claims that new rules must be sought by extensive investigations of empirical materials. And, in contradistinction to his predecessors, he restricts himself during his comparative work to registering the transitions between the particular languages whose relationship he wants to prove.

It has often been pointed out that Rask did not apply the rules of permutation rigorously in all details; but in return he stressed an aspect of the matter which was of more central importance precisely for the task of stating linguistic relationship: "A language, however mixed it may be, belongs to the same class of language as another when it has the most essential, concrete, indispensable, and primitive words, the foundation of language, in common with it. . . . When agreement is found in such words in two languages, and *so frequently that rules may be drawn up for the transition of letters from one to the other*, then there is a fundamental relationship between the two languages; especially when similarities in the structure and inflectional system of the languages support the agreement of words (*Udvalgte Afhandlinger* 1: 50).

According to ancient etymology the number of "fundamental" words which could be identified both as to form and meaning, was the measure of probability (or degree) of relationship; but how decide which number was sufficient: 10? 100? 1000? According to Rask a small group of fundamental words with regular permutations of physiologically related sounds gives a much higher probability of relationship than a large number of words, the similarity of which is not based on regular correspondence of letters.

I think it should be difficult, also in our day, to express the structural definition of language relationship in a more succinct and at the same time more complete way.

VI. Conclusion

Space does not allow me to give a similar analysis of the ideas of Rask's successors, Bopp, Grimm, and Schleicher. I must restrict myself to referring to Pedersen's account (1931: 254 ff.) and my own comments (1960: 132 ff.).

It seems to me that none of these scholars has made contributions to the methodology and theory of comparative linguistics that go far beyond Rask. It may therefore be legitimate to discuss our problems on the basis of a comparison between Rask and his eighteenth-century predecessors. That is, if it is proper to speak of a "scientific revolution", the revolution is already present with Rask.

In the introduction to his chief work, Rask gives a survey of "the nature, division, and principal rules of Etymology" (*Udvalgte Afhandlinger* 1: 24). He mentions the article *Étymologie* in the *Encyclopédie*, and says that this article "is perhaps the best that had been written in modern times on this matter". But he objects that the article "says little or nothing about the immediate and proper purpose of etymology and its importance for a careful study of language" (25).

I think that my extracts from Turgot, given above, particularly the last part, have shown that this judgment is not just; and a thorough comparison of the two articles reveals that Rask is not able to add much of importance to the *theory* and *method* of etymology. In several points Turgot's account is more penetrating and comprehensive than that of Rask.

The main difference between the two articles is in *aim*. Turgot's etymology is mainly concerned with the origin and development of words, whereas Rask's object is the genealogical classification of languages. Rask therefore stresses the importance of comparing the grammatical structures of languages according to the methods of Sajnovics and Gyarmathi, whose works he mentions with admiration (*Udvalgte Afhandlinger* 1: 112). With these trends he combines the ideas of Adam Smith. In the course of his detailed comparative work Rask refined the methods and integrated them in a new way; but, above all, he demonstrated how they could lead to an irrefutable result of the greatest importance.

The chief merit of Rask is that he was the first who applied the theories and methods of eighteenth-century philosophical etymology and grammar to all the main languages of Europe, Indo-European as well as others. In many cases he gave a new analysis according to his own methods of the languages he dealt with. His intuition and his methods gave him unique capacity for grasping the principal structural features of a language and its relationship to other languages, merely through the analysis of a few pages.

Rask's works, with a few exceptions, were written in Danish, and they were consequently read by few linguists outside Scandinavia. But they have had a decisive influence on Jacob Grimm, and, through him, on Bopp and Pott. (See Raumer 1870: 508-520; Tonnelat 1912: 316-327, 383-387; Diderichsen 1960: 132 ff.; Pedersen 1931: 38, 254-264).

In sum, we may perhaps say that the philosophical grammar of the eighteenth century, by integration and extension of some ancient ideas, worked out a "paradigm" of research, in Kuhn's terms, such that continous scientific progress could be made by "problem-solving". Rask was the first to demonstrate how the methods were able to solve problems of a highly complex type. Bopp, Grimm, Pott, Schleicher with their collaborators and pupils formed the first community of fellow workers within this field.

The predominant motivation for the work of the first comparatists was the romantic interest in old poetic, historical, and religious texts, and the national movements in Germany and Scandinavia. The edition and investigation of Old Norse "edda" and "saga", Old German poetry, Sanskrit, and Avestan forced Rask, the Grimms, and the Schlegels to painstaking grammatical and etymological inquiries; and this combination of text-philology and comparative linguistics has continuously been an essential characteristic of the whole paradigm. The paradigm was slightly altered in the course of the nineteenth century, particularly by the Junggrammatiker, who tried to find more strictly causal explanations of linguistic change.[7] But their activity did not lead to anything that could be called a revolution.

NOTES

* Professor Diderichsen died suddenly in Copenhagen, shortly after his return from Burg Wartenstein. His paper was complete, except for minor changes, chiefly concerned with references and footnotes, in the light of other contributions to the symposium, particularly by Metcalf, and in the light of suggestions by Aarsleff. Permission was given for the paper to appear in a volume of Professor Diderichsen's work, honoring what would have been his sixtieth birthday (Diderichsen 1966). The paper was edited for that volume by Professor Eli Fischer–Jorgensen, incorporating minor stylistic improvements suggested by Professor Francis Whitfield and correcting the quotations from Turgot in accordance with the 1913 edition.

At the request of Professor Fischer–Jorgensen, the present editor has generally eschewed changes that he was going to propose, except as dictated by the format of the present volume. At the end of the Introduction a sentence and a preceding clause, and at the end of the second paragraph of the Conclusion, a sentence has been added in order to point up the general thesis. Translations into English have also been added for passages quoted in Latin. Other differences are very minor: the reference to Adam Smith is the 2nd ed. as on p. 350 of the previously published version, not 3rd as on p. 348. The reference to Rudbeck is placed three paragraphs earlier as apparently intended by Prof. Diderichsen (i.e., second paragraph from top, not bottom, on the original page). But the Danish editors are followed in retaining the original "relations", and not substituting "reflections", per the Addenda and Corrigenda in the next to last line of "Etymology and abstraction" (p. 348 of the Danish edition, p. 286 of this chapter). In the second paragraph of "levels of classification and degrees of relationship" in the discussion of Rask, the corrections of the Danish editors are adopted, but

Diderichsen's additional examples retained (see n.6). The heading "From cognatio litterarum. . ." has been raised to a heading of a major part, and it and the other major parts have been numbered (I, II, III, IV, V, VI). I am indebted to Professor Eli Fischer–Jorgensen and her collaborators for all their help.

1. For basic literature, see Steinthal 1890; Robins 1951; Pohlenz 1939; Dahlmann 1932.

2. I do not think that his expression is used by classical authors. Professor Hans Aarsleff quotes Leibniz: "les langues sont le meilleur miroir de l'esprit humain, et une analyse exacte de la signification des mots feroit mieux connoistre que toute autre chose les opérations de l'entendement" (Gerhardt edition, 5: 313).

3. Prior to Sajnovics another Jesuit missionary, Coerdaux, made a grammatical comparison of Latin and Sanskrit (1767). According to Verburg, ten Kate (1731) was the first "vergleichende Grammatiker". In 1787 William Jones and Chr. J. Kraus stressed the importance of comparative grammar.

4. This idea is already mentioned by de Laet (1643); see Metcalf, this volume.

5. There is another edition by Maurice Piron (with commentary). Turgot mentions Locke and Condillac (1746) as sources for some of his ideas. Other ideas are taken from Leibniz (1710), de Brosses (1751) and Diderot. [On Turgot and de Brosses, cf. now Aarsleff 1967: 33-36.]

6. Rask's text is in Danish. He himself gives the English terminology, "race, class" etc., but the names of the languages and language groups are his own Danish terms, i.e., "japetisk" (= Indo-European), "gotisk" (= Germanic), "germanisk" (= Westgermanic), "øvre" and "nedre germanisk" (= Southern, Northern Westgermanic), the latter including Dutch, Low German, and English. (Corrections in the contemporary English equivalents involving Westgermanic are adopted from the Danish edition, p.411, as is the preceding information about Rask's text).

7. The first who tried to give physiological explanations of sound change was Raumer (1837).

REFERENCES

Aarsleff, Hans. 1969. The study and use of etymology in Leibniz. Studia Leibnitiana Supplementa, 3: Erkenntnislehre, Logic, Sprachphilosophie, Editionsberichte. Wiesbaden, Franz Steiner Verlag. Circulated to participants in the Newberry Library Conference.

Adelung, Johann Christoph. 1782a. Beweis der fortschreitenden Cultur des menschlichen Geistes aus der Vergleichung der älteren Sprachen mit den neueren. Magasin für die deutsche Sprache 1.

———. 1782b. Einleitung. Umständliches Lehregebäude der Deutschen Sprache.

Arens, Hans. 1955. Sprachwissenschaft. Der Gang ihrer Entwicklung von der Antike bis zur Gegenwart. Freiburg-München, Verlag Karl Alber.

Arnauld, Antoine, and Claude Lancelot. 1660. Grammaire générale et raisonnée de Port Royal. Paris. (New edition, Paris, 1756, with annotations by Duclos and supplement by Abbé Fromant.)

Beauzée, Nicolas. 1767. Grammaire générale ou exposition raisonnée des éléments nécessaires du langage pour servir à l'étude de toutes les langues. 2 vols. Paris.

Becanus, Johannes Goropius. 1569. Origines Antwerpianae. Antwerp.

Benfey, Theodor. 1869. Geschichte der Sprachwissenschaft und Orientalischen Philologie in Deutschland seit dem Anfange des 19. Jahrhunderts mit einem Rückblick auf die früheren Zeiten. (Geschichte der Wissenschaften in Deutschland, no. 8). Munich, Cotta'schen Buchhandlung.

Bibliander, Theodor. 1548. De communi ratione omnium literarum et linguarum commentarius. Zurich.

Bloch, S. N. J. 1803. Det Graeske Sprogs Grammatik aldeles fra nv af bearbeidet. Odense.

Borst, Arno. 1957–1963. Der Turmbau von Babel. Geschichte der Meinungen über Ursprung und Vielfalt der Sprachen und Völker. 4 vols. in 6. Stuttgart, Hiersemann.

Dacus, Johannes. 1955. Corpus Philosophorum Danicorum Medii Aevi 1.

Dahlmann, H. 1932. Varro and die hellenistische Sprachtheorie. Problemata, no. 5. Berlin.

Dante, Alighieri. 1924. Über das Dichten in der Muttersprache (De vulgari eloquentia). Translated and annotated by F. Dornseiff and J. Balogh.

de Brosses, Charles 1765. Traité de la formation méchanique des langues et des principes physiques de l'étymologie. 2 vols. Paris.

de Laet, Johannes. 1643. Notae ad Dissertationem Hugonis Grotii. Amsterdam.

Diderichsen, Paul. 1960. Rasmus Rask og den grammatiske tradition. (Communication from the Royal Danish Academy of Sciences and Letters). Copenhagen. (Summary in German).

———. 1966. Helhed og sturktur. (Selected Linguistic Papers with detailed English summaries). Copenhagen, G. E. C. Gads Forlag.

Gerretzen, F. G. 1940. Schola Hemsterhusiana. De herlering der Grieksche studien aan de nederlandsche universiteiten in de 18. eeux. Nymegen, Dekker and Van de Vegt.

Girard, Abbe Gabriel. 1747. Vrais principes de la langue francoise, or La vraie parole reduite en methode conformement aux lois de l'usage.

Harnois, Guy. 1929. Les theories du langage en France de 1660 a 1821. Paris.

Hjelmslev, Louis (ed.). 1932–1937. Rasmus Rask's Udvalgte Afhandlinger = Ausgewahlte Abhandlingen. 3 vols. Copenhagen, Levin and Munksgoard.

Ihre, Johan. 1769. Glossarium Sviogothicum. Uppsala.

Jellinek, M. H. 1913. Geschichte der neuhochdeutschen Grammatik von den Anfangen bis auf Adelung. 2 vols. Heidelberg.

Keil, H. (ed.). 1855—1870. Grammatici Latini. Leipzig.

Kraus, Christian Jakob. 1787. Rezension des Allgemeinen vergleichenden Wörterbuches von Pallas. Allgemeine Literaturzeitung Nr. 235/7. [Reprinted in Arens 1955: 118-127.]

Kuhn, T. S. 1962. The structure of scientific revolutions. International encyclopedia of unified science. Vol. II, no. 2. Chicago.

Le Laboureur, Jean. 1669. Advantages de la langue Francoise sur la langue Latine.

Leibniz, G. W. 1875. Philosophische Schriften. Ed. by C. I. Gerhardt. Berlin, Weidmann.

Locke, John. 1690. Essay concerning human understanding.

Ludolf, J. 1702. Dissertatio de harmonia linguae aethiopicae cum osteris orientalibus.

Monboddo, Lord James Burnet. 1773—1792. Of the origin and progress of language.

Pedersen, Holger. 1931. The discovery of language, linguistic science in the nineteenth century. (trans. J. W. Spargo.) Bloomington, Indiana University Press.

Petersen, N. M. 1829. Det danske, norske og svenske Sprogs Historie under deres Udvilking af Stamsproget.

Pohlenz, Max. 1939. Die Begrundung der abendlandischen Sprachlehr durch die Stoa. (Nachrichten d. Gesellschaft der Wissenschaften zu Göttingen.)

Pontoppidian, Eric. 1663. Grammatica Danica. Hauniae, Typis C. Veringii.

Rask, H. K. (ed.). 1836. Samlede tildels forhen utrykte afhandlinger af R. K. Rask. Copenhagen, Trykt i det Poppske Bogtrykkeri.

Rask, Rasmus. 1814. Undersgelse om det gamle Nordiske eller Islandske Sprogs Oprindelse. Investigation of the origin of the Old Norse or Icelandic language. Copenhagen, 1918. Reprinted in Udvalgte Afhandlinger 1. Cited by Diderichsen as of the date of completion of the ms., which was written 1811—1814.

——. Samlede Afhandlinger. See Rask, H. K. (ed.), 1836.

——. Udvalgte Afhandlinger. See Hjelmslev, Louis (ed.), 1932—1937.

Raumer, Rudolf von. 1837. Uber die Aspiration und die Lautverschiebung. In: Geschichte der germanischen Philologie. (Geschichte der Wissenschaften in Deutschland; Neuere Zeit, 9). Munich.

Robins, R. H. 1951. Ancient and medieval grammatical theory in Europe. London, G. Bell and Sons.

Rudbeck, Olaf. 1675. Atlantica sive Manheim. Uppsala.

Sajnovics, Joh. 1770. Demonstratio idioma Ungarorum et Lapponum idem esse. Copenhagen.

Smith, Adam. 1767. Dissertation on the origin of languages. Supplement to The theory of moral sentiments, 2nd. ed.

Steinthal, Heymann. 1863. Geschichte der Sprachwissenschaft bei den Griechen und Romern mit Besonderer Rucksicht auf die Logik. Berlin, Dummlers Verlagsbuchhandlung. (2nd rev. ed., 1890; reissued 1961).

Stiernhielm, Georg. 1671. De linguarum origine Praefatio. In: D. N. Jesu Christi SS. Evangelia ab Ulfila Gothorum translata. Stockholm.

Tonnelat, E. 1912. Les freres Grimm; leur oeuvre de jeunesse. Paris, A. Colin.

Trendelenberg, J. G. 1782. Anfangsgrunde der griechischen Sprache. (4th ed., 1769).

[Turgot, Anne Robert Jacques.] 1913–1923. Oeuvres de Turgot. Ed. by Gustave Schelle. Paris.

[Varro, Marcus Terentius.] 1951. Varro on the Latin language. With an English translation by Roland G. Kent. Rev. ed. (Loeb Classical Library, 333). Cambridge, Mass., and London.

Verburg, P. A. 1952. Taal en Functionaliteit. Wageningen, Vieman and Sons.

Wachter, Johann Georg. 1737. Glossarium Germanicum. Leipzig.

Watermann, J. T. 1963. Perspectives in Linguistics. Chicago, University of Chicago Press.

10. Rask's View of Linguistic Development and Phonetic Correspondences

W. Keith Percival

Previous studies of Rask have been overly concerned with questions of priority. Both Jesperson and Pedersen, for example, inquired whether Rask was the equal of or superior to his contemporaries Jakob Grimm and Franz Bopp.[1] It has been customary for historians of linguistics, and particularly those of them who happen to be Danes, to point out that Rask should be credited with the discovery of Grimm's law. Thus, Pedersen (1932: LV) states:

> Die Erkenntnis der Lautverschiebung ist Rask's Ehre. Und es ist nicht eine Apfelsine, die zufällig in seinen Turban herabgefallen ist; er hat nicht wie eine blinde Henne ein Korn gefunden. [Rask must be credited with discovering the sound shift. Moreover, the discovery was not an apple which accidentally dropped into his lap. He did not come across it like a blind chicken finding a grain of wheat.]

Jespersen went further still and stated (1918: 72) that it would have been better if linguistics had received the stamp of Rask's spirit rather than that of his two famous contemporaries.[2]

In recent years discussion has shifted to another topic, namely the question as to which aspect of Rask's work should be given priority. Hjelmslev (1951) would have us believe that it was with some reluctance that Rask worked on historical problems, and that he would have preferred to be known for his efforts to develop a uniform method of grammatical description rather than as one of the founders of historical linguistics (see also Bjerrum 1959; Hjelmslev's ideas were prefigured by Pedersen (1932: XXXIV). Paul Diderichsen's excellent work in the late fifties (Diderichsen 1960) was undoubtedly an attempt to redress the balance, but was in addition the first successful attempt to place Rask in a wide historical context and submit his writings to a painstaking internal analysis.

What I should like to do here is to examine Rask's notions about language relationship. In particular I should like to establish what the hallmarks of relationship were according to him, and how he explained why these were the criteria and no other.

Basic to Rask's notions of relationship were his views concerning linguistic change. The problem was to reconcile the obvious fact of change with the equally obvious fact that languages, or at least standard languages, possess a rigidly systematic structure. Rather than assume a gradual transformation of structure, Rask posited that when a language changes, its grammatical structure is abandoned and then replaced by a different one. Between the time the new structure imposes itself, there is a more or less lengthy period of fermentation.

Lest I be accused of reading into Rask's writings ideas which were not really his, let me at this point quote a passage from his review of the second edition of Jakob Grimm's *Deutsche Grammatik* which appeared in English in the journal *Foreign Review* in March 1830 (H. K. Rask 1836: 2.448-450). Rask is discussing the Germanic, or as he prefers to call them, the Gothic languages, and he makes the following statement:

> In order to obtain a clear view of this matter, the reader must be aware, that in old times, till about the year 1100, the Gothic languages of both branches, the Teutonic as well as the Scandinavian, bore a very different aspect from that which they now present. Nay, they have not only changed in appearance; but the old ones have fallen into disuse, and several new ones have sprung up in their stead.

In other words the Germanic languages of today are no mere continuations of the same languages spoken a thousand years ago; they are in some sense *new* languages. Rask goes on to explain in what this novelty consists:

> All these ancient languages, like the Anglo-Saxon, had a complex structure and an ancient grammar, resembling that of the Greek and Latin. . . whereas the modern dialects have simplified that old structure immensely, and worn off, as it were, the ancient terminations for cases and persons, instead of which they have introduced prepositions and pronouns, nearly as our modern English.

As Rask sees it, the modern periods of the Germanic languages began with the Reformation, and up to that time there had been a long period of chaos and confusion:

> In this manner, about four hundred years, more or less, in the different states, have elapsed between the dissolution of the ancient languages and the organization of the modern ones. This

period may be styled in the middle age of the Gothic languages, all of them being at that time in a state of fermentation, or confusion, the old inflections being now observed and now neglected, and the expressions and phrases being, in some instances indigenous and proper, in others foreign and barbarous.

The new grammatical structure which arises after the dissolution of the old is therefore not an arbitrary new creation, but rather a less complicated version of the old one. Hence this new system can be said to be derived from the previous one and is explainable in terms of it. In this way it is inconceivable that two historically unconnected grammatical systems could change in such a way that it would be impossible to assign the descendent languages to their correct ancestors.

Thus, although Modern Danish and Modern English have extremely simple grammatical systems, it is still obvious that what structure Danish has is relatable to that of Old Norse, and that the structure of Modern English is derived from that of Anglo-Saxon. It is therefore possible to assign languages to families and sub-families by inspecting their grammatical structures. Two languages belong in the same group if their grammatical structures are derived from that of the same parent language.

Furthermore, the complexity of the descendant systems varies and makes it possible to arrange the languages in a definite ordered scale of relatedness to the parent language. Thus Swedish is closer to Old Norse than Danish is. It is also possible for the original grammatical system to remain intact somewhere. The Old Norse system was abandoned on the mainland of Europe but preserved unchanged on the island of Iceland. For Rask, therefore, Modern Icelandic and Old Norse are the same thing. Moreover, the complexity of a language is a rough indication of how old it is, or how near it is in time to its parent language. Thus Pāli is less complex than Sanskrit and must therefore have been spoken more recently than Sanskrit.[3]

The task of classifying languages in families is complicated by the fact that languages are subject to the influence of other languages. Linguistic change involves in addition to the processes just described the adoption of features from neighboring languages. While it is conceivable that a set of languages spoken in the same general area might influence one another to such an extent that it would be impossible to tell what their original affinities were, in fact this stage is never reached. This is because the influence exerted by one language on another falls within certain limits. Only certain parts of language are susceptible to outside influence.

Language in general, according to Rask, consists of three parts: pronunciation, grammar, and lexicon (Ausgewählte Abhandlungen 1: 48, 71). Pronunciation, the outer form of language, has to do with the particular set of sounds which each language uses. Lexicon, the raw material of language, is a set of words; and grammar, the inner form of language, is the way in which words change their shapes when appearing in sentences.

The influence of neighboring languages extends only to the raw material of language, i.e., the lexicon, leaving both the outer and inner form, i.e., pronunciation and grammar intact. Moreover, a certain portion of the lexicon is relatively impervious to outside influence also. This is the essential stock of indispensable words, including the names of meteorological and climatic phenomena, flora and fauna, kinship terms, pronouns and demonstratives.

Related languages, therefore, show widespread agreements not only in grammatical structure (the most permanent and stable aspect of language), but also in their basic lexical stock, and this is the case no matter what outside influences have affected the languages in question.

However, it is equally important to point out that related languages do differ from one another, or otherwise they would constitute one and the same language (Ausgewählte Abhandlungen 1: 59).[4] Each language possesses peculiarities of its own, some of which concern individual items and processes, others more widespread features. Thus individual words are liable to have slightly different meanings in related languages. But these differences, while classifiable, are of an individual kind, one word changing in one way, and another in another. Some differences between related languages are more systematic. Thus the exact appearance of items in the basic lexical stock varies in shape from language to language in a family, but in a highly characteristic fashion. For example, *faðir*, the word for "father" in Icelandic has an *f* where πατήρ, the Greek form has a *p*, and the same correspondence recurs in many other pairs of words in Greek and Icelandic (Ausgewählte Abhandlungen 1:188). For each pair of languages in a family, and indeed for any two stages of the same language, one can draw up rules of correspondence, that is, a list of all the sound correspondences, and this list will necessarily vary from pair to pair. Putative cognates can be checked against this list and spurious ones rejected if the sounds of the one word do not correspond to the sounds of the other in the manner prescribed by the particular rules of correspondence for those two languages.

The reason the list of correspondences varies with each pair of languages is that general habits of pronunciation in the nature of things are specific to particular communities. Rask, like many of his contemporaries, believed that this phenomenon was due to inherent differences in the anatomy of the speech organs from nation to nation (Ausgewählte Abhandlungen 1: 59; note Hjelmslev's comment, 3: 75), a supposition which turned out to be false. However, no matter what the ultimate causation of sound correspondences is, the linguist who ignores them is unable to identify genuine cognates. This is, however, crucial since whenever two words are assumed to be cognates, the languages they occur in are necessarily assumed to be related. It is not surprising then that the most egregious error which Rask accused his predecessors of committing was that of carrying on lexical etymologizing in a hasty and uncontrolled fashion, and hence frequently making wrong inferences about language relationship on the basis of such spurious lexical agreements. If such scholars had observed the rules of sound correspondence in each case and extended their attention to all aspects of the language in question, i.e., not just the lexical aspect, such mistakes would have been avoided.

Thus the apparent emphasis on sound correspondences in the prize essay should not delude the modern reader into imagining that Rask had anything like the late nineteenth-century notion of sound laws. It is not merely that he did not insist that correspondences be absolutely regular, nor is it relevant or even justifiable to claim that he simply did not believe languages changed at all. Rather the two crucial elements in Rask's system were his conception of pronunciation habits as fixed dispositions, and his conviction that linguistic change was not a gradual process but some kind of radical reshuffling of structure taking place over a certain restricted period of time.

Thus Rask's preoccupation with total linguistic systems, and with comparisons among these, and his lack of interest in minute descriptions of historical development of the kind being done at that time by Jakob Grimm are perfectly understandable. To phrase the matter differently, Rask was a historical linguist with a conception of history which was not shared by some of his contemporaries and which has not been shared by any generation of linguists since his time. Thus it is not the case that Rask preferred to work on descriptions rather than on history. The descriptive apparatus was a logical necessity for *the particular kind of historical linguistics which Rask created.*

Likewise the pairing of the criterion of grammatical agreement and that of phonetic correspondence is also no less logically consistent. For Rask it is natural that when languages undergo radical change they retain their grammatical cores intact, and at the same time it is natural that related linguistic communities differ in phonetic habits in a consistent fashion. Thus Rask did not believe that there could be pairs of related languages such that one member of a pair had the same underlying grammatical structure as the other, but the lexical items in the two languages showed no recurrent sound correspondences. When Rask saw no grammatical resemblance between two languages, as say between Icelandic and Welsh,[5] he assumed that what lexical resemblances there were must be the result of borrowing, and accordingly he would not even inspect the lexical items for possible sound correspondences. Thus he never worried about the possibility that relationship might prove

difficult to demonstrate in those instances in which the surviving indications
of it had all but disappeared from the languages in question, and that in such
cases the question of logical priority among the criteria of relationship might
constitute a genuine problem. (This possibility was seriously considered by
Humboldt; see Leitzmann 1908: 52.)

To sum up, I think it is unprofitable to assign priorities to the various
components of Rask's scholarly activity, and that it is equally unprofitable to
speculate as to which kind of criteria of relationship Rask can be said to have
preferred. To categorize Rask as a forerunner of the neo-grammarians is thus
just as untrue as to portray him as a structural linguist born before his time.
Rask's linguistic theory, such as it was, formed an organic whole, and the
enterprise of breaking it down into separate disconnected parts and
associating them with more recent theoretical developments obscures the
fundamental unity of Rask's work.

NOTES

*Enlarged and revised version of Percival 1970.

1. See Jespersen (1918), especially pp. 64 ff, and Pedersen (1932),
especially pp. XIV, XLVI ff., LV. Besides this discussion of the relative merits
of Rask and Grimm, see also Pedersen's earlier remarks (1916: 41, 43-44,
46-58, 1924: 228-234 =1931: 248-254). The volumes to which Pedersen
contributed the introduction are the standard edition of Rask's selected
treatises, and will be cited hereinafter as Ausgewählte Abhandlungen
(=Hjelmslev (ed.), 1932-37).

2. "Men det havde sikkert været bedre, om sprogforskningen på
avgørende punkter havde været mere præget av Rasks and end av hans to
samtidiges." [It would certainly have been better if linguistics had basically
borne the stamp of Rask's spirit rather than that of his two contemporaries.]

3. Rask discusses Pāli in a letter written in Colombo (see Hjelmslev
1941, 2: 56-57). Rask's reasons for believing that Pāli was spoken more
recently than Sanskrit were three: first, Pāli has fewer sounds than Sanskrit;
second, Pāli has distorted the pronunciation of many forms by assimilating
consonant clusters; and third, the language itself is simpler in structure and
has lost a great many of the Sanskrit inflectional forms.

4. See Ausgewählte Abhandlungen 1: 59. See also Rask's own marginal
note in the Prize Essay (Ausgewählte Abhandlungen 3: 21): "Ti man vil finde
at Overgangene imellem tvende givne Sprog ere ikke de samme som finde Sted
imellem tvende andre; da ethvert Folk gjerne har noget særeget i sin Udtale".
[For the correspondences obtaining within a given pair of languages will be

found to be different from the ones obtaining within another pair. This is because every community tends to have some peculiar cast to its pronunciation.]

5. Rask's failure to see the relationship between Celtic and Germanic has puzzled scholars. Given the information at Rask's disposal, together with his criteria of relationship, the outcome was, however, inevitable. In the same year that the Prize Essay was published (1818) Rask changed his mind and included Celtic in his list of subgroups of what we now call the Indo-European family (see Hjelmslev 1941, 1: 315, 385). Unfortunately, we do not know what made him change his mind. In any case, the Indo-European position of Celtic was not settled to general satisfaction until the work of Pictet (1837) and Bopp (1839). It should be noted that in his history of linguistics Holger Pedersen fails to mention Pictet's name in this connection and misquotes both the title and date of Bopp's publication (Pedersen: 1924: 53, 1931: 57).

REFERENCES

Bjerrum, Marie. 1959. Rasmus Rasks Afhandlinger om det danske sprog. Copenhagen: Dansk Videnskabs Forlag.

Bopp, Franz. 1839. Die celtischen Sprachen in ihrem Verhältnisse zum Sanskrit, Zend, Griechischen, Lateinischen, Germanischen, Litthauischen und Slavischen. Gelesen in der Akademie der Wissenschaften. Berlin.

Diderichsen, Paul. 1960. Rasmus Rask og den grammatiske tradition. Copenhagen: Munksgaard.

Hjelmslev, Louis, ed. 1932–37. Rasmus Rasks Ausgewählte Abhandlungen [= Udvalgte Afhandlinger]. 3 vols. Copenhagen: Levin and Munksgaard.

———, ed. 1941. Breve fra og til Rasmus Rask. 2 vols. Copenhagen: Munksgaard.

———. 1951. Commentaires sur la vie et l'oeuvre de Rasmus Rask. Conférences de l'Institut de Linguistique de l'Université de Paris 10: 143-157. [Republished in Portraits of Linguists, ed. by Thomas A. Sebeok, 1: 179-195. Bloomington: Indiana University Press, 1966.]

Jespersen, Otto. 1918. Rasmus Rask i hundredåret efter hans hovedværk. Copenhagen.

Leitzmann, A. 1908. Briefwechsel zwischen W. von Humboldt und A. W. Schlegel. Halle.

Pedersen, Holger. 1916. Et blik på sprogvidenskabens historie. (= Festskrift udgivet af Københavns Universitet i anledning af Universitets aarsfest, November, 1916.) Copenhagen: Universitets bogtrykkeriet.

———. 1924. Sprogvidenskaben i det nittende aarhundrede. Copenhagen: Gyldendalske Boghandel, Nordisk Forlag. [Published in English as Linguistic science in the nineteenth century, trans. from the Danish by

John Spargo. Cambridge, Mass.: Harvard University Press, 1931. Reissued as The discovery of language. Bloomington: Indiana University Press, 1962.]

————. 1932. Einleitung zu Rasmus Rasks Ausgewählte Abhandlungen, ed. by Louis Hjelmslev, vol. 1. Copenhagen: Levin and Munksgaard.

Percival, W. Keith. 1970. Rasmus Rask and the criteria of genetic relationship. Actes du Xe Congrès International des Linguistes (Bucarest, 1967), 2: 261-266. Bucarest.

Pictet, Adolphe. 1837. De l'affinité des langues celtiques avec le sanscrit: mémoire couronné par l'Institut. Académie royale des inscriptions et belles-lettres. Paris: B. Duprat.

Rask, H. K., ed. 1836. Samlede tildels forhen utrykte afhandlinger af R. K. Rask. Copenhagen: Trykt i det Poppske Bogtrykkeri.

Rask, Rasmus. Ausgewählte Abhandlungen. See Hjelmslev, Louis, ed., 1932-37.

————. Samlede afhandlinger. See Rask, H. K., ed., 1836.

11. Friedrich Diez's Debt to pre-1800 Linguistics

Yakov Malkiel

I

Among the verdicts and assessments of posterity apparently least subject to revision has been the long-established, unanimous opinion that the first major impetus given to comparative Romance linguistics was Friedrich Diez's *Grammatik der romanischen Sprachen* (1836-44). Diez's work eclipsed at once, and irrevocably, such earlier and far more modest ventures as Raynouard's (1821) and Diefenbach's (1831). Part of Diez's success was due to superb timing. The precocious Diefenbach's book—to be sure, not his first—appeared when its author was barely twenty-five; on the other hand, Raynouard, at the ripe age of sixty, was too old in 1821 for the very recent discoveries and techniques of Bopp, Rask, and Grimm to have percolated into the innermost chambers of his thinking. Diez, in 1836, however, was just the right age (forty-two) to exhibit flexibility and, at the same time, to command respect. At that juncture, he already had to his credit two major studies in medieval literature (1826, 1829), as well as shorter and more popular pieces, such as the translation of selected Old Spanish ballads (1818), and a controversial pamphlet on Provençal "courts of love" (1825).

The pioneering venture of the *Grammatik*, plus the somewhat later, likewise unprecedented *Etymologisches Wörterbuch der romanischen Sprachen* [EWRS] (1853), solidly established Diez's reputation over a span of no less than half a century.[1] Witnesses to this record of uninterrupted prestige are, toward the beginning of the given period, the eloquent praise bestowed on Diez by the precocious August Fuchs (1840: 10 f.), a tribute the more noteworthy as the author, by his own admission, was in general beholden to Bopp and Humboldt for guidance and to the former even for personal encouragement. (Significantly, Fuchs's posthumous synthesis [1849] is dedicated to Diez.)[2] Diez was one of the two teachers whom Schuchardt, in 1866, honored with a dedication of his *Der Vokalismus des Vulgärlateins*.

Toward the end of the period, there is the affectionate respect for the revered "Altmeister"—by that time a victim of frustration and exhaustion[3]—voiced by an equally young and ebullient Michaëlis (1876: vii). Ascoli's dedication to Diez of his masterpiece (1873) marks the peak of this cult.[4]

II

Did the *Grammatik*, for all the approval it earned, really constitute a sort of "creatio ex nihilo" or was it merely—as is sometimes cavalierly stated—a pale reflection of J. Grimm's earlier exploration of the paleo-Germanic *terra incognita*? To answer this question we must examine different kinds of evidence, external and internal, starting with the author's own disclosures.

In the opening volume of the original edition of his grammar Diez was less than explicit about his sources. The list of abbreviations, confined to two parallel columns of a single incomplete page (vi), identifies a few repositories of primary data but not a single representative of "Sekundärliteratur". The short and unassuming Preface (iii-v) delimits the scope of the undertaking and characterizes the project as a whole, barely hinting at some work done by Diez's predecessors among Germanists (Rask and Grimm?), then singling out for mention W. von Humboldt. Finally, the long Introduction — a full-blown language history in miniature ("Uber die Bestandteile der romanischen Sprachen")—cites, ahead of any other authority, B. G. Niebuhr (1775-1831), the then recently deceased expert in ancient, especially Roman, history.[5]

Internal analysis of Diez's comparative historical phonology (including the ninety pages of rather weighty forematter) at once dissipates any suspicion one may have harbored either of the author's use of a completely "clean slate" or of his slavish dependence on some early nineteenth-century model. What was truly original about Diez's major undertaking one hundred thirty years ago was the — unadmitted, inexplicit — formula he devised for a blend of several ingredients never before combined, though each element had long been widely known in isolation. The first and most striking component is, of course, the newly discovered comparative approach, involving neatly established sound correspondences and lexical equations made plausible through them; the modern reader's only surprise in this context is due to the prominence Diez accords, at the outset, to the Norwegian trailblazer Christian Lassen, now long-forgotten except among students of Indics, rather than to, say, the widely remembered Bopp or Pott.

Another category of sources on which Diez drew quite liberally was the corpus of Late Latin texts. In this domain of "Spätantike" the spadework of textual criticism had been done by humanistic classicists — so far as Central

Europe is concerned, chiefly throughout the sixteenth and the seventeenth centuries — and Diez had at his disposal such tools of traditional philological, that is, exegetic, scholarship as monographs, grammars, and analytic illustrative dictionaries, in addition to the priceless texts themselves. Along this particular line, the early nineteenth century, despite the advent of comparative grammar, assuredly marked no sharp break with the preceding era.

The third and perhaps most noteworthy reservoir of knowledge that Diez profitably tapped was the work of assiduous antiquarians so characteristic of eighteenth-century Europe (e.g., L. A. Muratori in Italy, T. A. Sánchez in Spain, Frei Joaquim de S. R. de Viterbo in Portugal). These scholars — and an occasional precursor such as Du Cange in France — were oriented toward the paleographic and archival approach and thus unearthed, inspected, inventoried, and described a wealth of medieval material, some of it of great esthetic appeal to moderns, the remainder of strictly historical, especially paleographic, significance. Of crucial importance is the fact that the material thus salvaged was heterogeneous, containing both motley shreds of medieval Latin (ecclesiastic, notarial, "barbaric" — a qualifier which often points to the agency of bilingualism) and slivers of nascent Romance vernaculars. For details see below; the one circumstance to remember at this juncture is that, again, the new style of linguistic analysis launched by Bopp, Rask, and Grimm in no way interfered with the continuity of a tradition dating back to 1700 if not to 1650.

The last element to be identified in the composite structure of the grammar (and the one that indisputably lent it a touch of freshness) was the evidence furnished by uninhibited living dialect speech. As is well known, scholarly curiosity about some regionally colored specimens of untutored speech predates 1800 in the citadels of Romance culture, but Romanticism unquestionably gave that interest a new incentive and a higher degree of intensity. To the dialects one may, stretching the facts a bit, add "Walachian", that is, Rumanian as it then emerged before the astonished eyes of Western and Central Europeans; the corpus of purposefully assembled Rumanian data represented the single most exotic tidbit in Diez's collection of morsels and — what with the Slavic, the Turkish, the neo-Hellenic overtones — was admirably suited to satisfy some of his reader's romantic propensities.

III

Once the four substances so deftly blended by Diez have been tidily isolated, it seems appropriate to examine at least the first three in somewhat more searching detail. To start with the historico-comparative edifice of the grammar, it is the comparative rather than the historical perspective that, in the 1830's, marked an innovation. (Comparativism in this context means neither the confrontation of two successive stages of the same language nor the contrasting of an ancestral with a single daughter language, but the systematic joint dissection of several "same-generation" languages performed without ever losing sight of the parent tongue as a background.) For this task Diez prepared himself very methodically. To his superb expertise in Old Provençal he added such philological accomplishments as the editing of a few archaic Old French texts, plus a concern with Old Spanish balladry and with Old Portuguese courtly poetry, quite aside from his lifelong concentration on Late Latin glosses.[6]

For the technique of the skillful, mutually corroborative interweaving of the various language threads, Diez could comfortably fall back on the examples set by Bopp, Grimm, and their peers. Such recourse was the easier for him because he, like everyone else in his country hit by the romantic wave, shared his Germanist colleagues' passionate concern with Old German culture.[7] This attitude in some respects immediately affected the structure and content of his grammar.[8]

Diez's heavy indebtedness to Grimm need not be labored. Neither, however, must it be exaggerated: A glance at Volume I of the *Deutsche Grammatik* (rev. ed., 1822) shows that under Phonology Grimm offered his readers a bulging portfolio of succinct autonomous sketches, as it were—parading, one by one, Gothic, Old High German, Old Saxon, Old English, Old Frisian, Old Norse, Middle High German, Middle Low German, Middle Dutch, Middle English, Modern High German, Modern Dutch, Modern English, Swedish, Danish, in this order. Diez, barely fourteen years later, was more comparativistic in his slant, actually intertwining the data culled from diverse Romance languages. In this art of mutual illumination Diez could have learned a good deal from Volume I of Bopp (1833), except that Bopp's architectural design offered no scope for a separate full-length treatment of phonology, on a par with inflection.

But while bold and large-scale comparativism was new, a narrower historical approach—including crudely manufactured historical phonologies of individual Romance languages viewed in their relation to Latin—had been continually practiced ever since the Renaissance and could not have eluded the attention of Diez. Allusions to sound correspondences abound in A. de Nebrixa's Castilian grammar of 1492; lists, if not tabulations, of sound changes—simplistically formulated—can be traced, for Spanish, to a treatise (*Del origen y principio...*) by the noted antiquarian B. Aldrete (1606), copies of whose second, posthumous edition (Madrid, 1674), practically without exception, were bound with the *Tesoro* by Covarrubias Horozco

(1673-74), a source book on etymology which Diez consulted and made a point of citing at every step; and the string of pre-1800 coarse-grained outlines of diachronic phonology continues to include Mayáns y Siscar's two omnibus volumes (1737).[9]

Diez's copious borrowings from the stock of classical philology drive home, more eloquently than any other debt he owed, how arbitrary it is to draw too sharply an early nineteenth-century line in the history of linguistics. At the outset of his experiment in historical grammar (I, 5) he listed the names of leading Roman writers who deviated from the classical canon and can thus shed light upon the sermo plebeius and upon related varieties of Latin; but his actual probings went much further. The first major word-list containing "vocabula rustica, vulgaria, sordida" (7-10) is replete with references to such writers – in part archaic, in part late – as Accius (apud Nonium), Adamantius Martyrius (apud Cassiodorum), Afranius (apud Nonium), Ammianus Marcellinus, Apicius, Apuleius, Arnobius, Augustine, Ausonius, etc.[10] It is doubtful that Diez, hard-pressed for time, actually excerpted their writings, page by page. He is more likely to have laboriously combed the Paduan E. Forcellini's remarkably comprehensive and then authoritative dictionary, published posthumously in 1771 three years after the aged compiler's death and prepared chiefly in the 1720's and '30's.[11]

This is not an isolated instance of Diez's dependence on research carried on by Latinists from 1500 to 1800. For epigraphic evidence, he used the *Inscriptiones antiquae totius orbis romani* (ca. 1602) of the celebrated anthologist J. Gruterius (1560-1627) in much the same way that late nineteenth-century Romanists drew on Mommsen's *Corpus Inscriptionum Latinarum*. He was able to supplement this information with material prepared (1785) by Abbot G. Marini (1742-1815), chief curator of the Vatican Library. Marini also furnished a motley collection (1805) providing grist for the early Romanist's mill. Opportunely, at the last moment, there also appeared Volume I of Orelli (1828-50). To all three authors Diez repeatedly acknowledges his indebtedness. On the side of grammar, rhetoric, poetics, etymology, and embryonic phonology ("De permutatione literarum") one of his principal guides, invoked again and again, was Gerardus Ioannes Vossius (1577-1649), whose *Etymologicon linguae latinae* was readily available in the edition (1664) prepared by Isaac Vossius (1618-89), who also had his share in the six-volume edition (Amsterdam, 1695-1701) of his namesake's and presumable relative's collected works. On the other hand, Diez obviously did not spurn publications by later generations of Latinists, some of them straddling the late eighteenth and the early nineteenth centuries.[12]

Several genres of seventeenth- and, especially, eighteenth-century antiquarian literature, so eminently characteristic of that period's European

"Gelehrsamkeit", guided Diez in his search for raw material; it is not always possible to draw a sharp line of demarcation between broadly defined antiquarianism, classical philology, and lexico-etymological research, which was directed toward all manner of curiosities and whose practitioners often lacked a truly critical attitude. One may class under this "grab-bag" heading − in addition to the aforementioned prime specimens, especially Muratori's collection − such bibliographic compilations as that by Fabricius (1668-1736); as the two *Thesauri* (1694-99, 1704-25) by the prestigious classicist J. G. Graevius independently noted as a textual critic (Cicero, Caesar, Catullus, etc.); and as the collections of charters and letters assembled by L. G. Brequigny (1714-94), who is today perhaps most vividly remembered as a pioneer Sinologist. (One "magnum opus" is most conveniently consulted in the edition of 1834-49). It is difficult to separate these vast collections of preëminently historical material, more or less sifted, from lexicographic compilation replete with anecdotal bric-à-brac and all sorts of guesses, conjectures, and hypotheses testifying to the authors' ingenuity and erudition. Of acknowledged usefulness to Diez in 1836 and, even more, in 1853 (on the occasion of his EWRS) were the glossaries for Low and medieval Latin by Du Cange (1610-88); early etymological compendia for the vernaculars, such as Ménage's for French and Covarrubias' for Spanish, as well as the Royal Spanish Academy's pronouncements (1726-39); an occasional bilingual dictionary rich in incidental explicative detail, such as M. de Larramendi's for Basque and Spanish (1745), for which W. von Humboldt's bold Euskaric spadework (1821) may have whetted his appetite. Here again, it is utterly impossible to draw any cogent line marking the years of upheaval in linguistics (1800-20). No unbridgeable gap separates Viterbo (1798), an annotated collection of obsolete Portuguese words extracted by an archivist, from the two major undertakings − to this day appreciated − of E. G. Graff (1780-1841), the one "etymologically and grammatically slanted", the other in large part newly edited from, or at least collated with, manuscripts (1826-29). By Diez's own account, every single source here individuated actually stood him in excellent stead, at the very least on the level of information and, particularly in his dictionary, also on the higher plane of interpretation.

IV

Our argument favoring an overlap, in Diez's writings, of the older and the newer approach to linguistics might be countered with the remark that the pioneer's debt to pre-1800 scholarship was confined to miscellaneous collections of raw material, while his analytical acumen betrays his exposure to the "revolution" sparked by Bopp and Grimm. But such an attempt to winnow out, with a few bold strokes, certain residual traits does not lead very far, because in reality the old and the new are still intimately, inextricably enmeshed. Take, for instance, the matter of borrowing (i.e., of diffusion). In the barely three and a half pages (I, 177-180) devoted to the Romance vicissitudes of Lat. *P* Diez operates freely — indeed, on a sweeping scale — with the concept of loans: He sets apart Spanish words absorbed from Italian, such as *capitán* and *caporal*; French Italianisms, for example, *capitaine* (which has dislodged older, indigenous *chevetaine*); and Italian words apparently channeled through Old French, an itinerary posited for *malato*, on the strength of simple *t* in lieu of expected *-tt-*.[14] In fact, Diez makes a serious effort to distinguish throughout between (unmarked) vernacular words, transmitted orally, and (marked) later intruders ("jüngere Wörter"), that is, Latinisms among secondary accretions; and he is sophisticated enough to class, again and again, such deliberate borrowings from Latin with other categories of loan-words. While this procedure is unimpeachable, it did not originate with mid-nineteenth-century scholarship. In his accompanying glossaries Sánchez operated quite liberally with the concept of lexical borrowing.[15]

Another example of retrograde attitude: While Diez astutely explains the aberrant voicing of *p-* in It. *Befan(f)a* "Epiphany, present(ation of gifts), funny old woman" (EPIPHANIA), *bottega* "small shop, village store, studio" (Gr.-Lat. APOTHĒCA), *brobb(r)io* "disgrace, infamy" (OPPROBRIUM), *vescovo* "bishop" (EPISCOPU) in terms of relative chronology, insisting that sonantization here preceded vowel apheresis, he lumps together Rum. *cap* "head" (CAPUT), *lup* "wolf" (LUPU), and *plop* "poplar" (PŌPULU), on the one hand, with, on the other, Prov. *cap* and *lop*, without suspecting that, in the latter cases, the process at issue, on circumstantial evidence, was not simple, uninterrupted preservation of the voiceless bilabial stop, but rather its initial voicing followed by secondary devoicing after the loss of the final vowel. Rum. *cap, lup* and Prov. *cap, lop* in their joint relation to Lat. CAPU, LUPU look to Diez very much alike, because, instead of heeding the consecutive swings of the pendulum, he still tends to resolve all processes of sound change into the very same kind of loosely coördinated "permutatio literarum" (with emphasis on final results alone) that haunted the thinking of Vossius, Aldrete, Mayáns y Siscar, and Cabrera. Even his style of suggesting reconstructed, putative bases, by prefixing the qualifier "gleichsam"[16] instead of the now so familiar asterisk, reminds one of the practice of a Ménage or a Covarrubias, who would use "quasi" to convey an identical message.[17] (The 2nd ed. of Diez's grammar, however, contains in its opening volume on phonology [1856] the "star" — presumably adopted in imitation of A. Schleicher's practice.)

V

Without denying or belittling the tremendous novelty of the "new linguistics" of 1820 and without disregarding the unique climate of opinion produced by these stirrings and fermentations, one can firmly contend that there failed to appear in Diez's *œuvre* any clear-cut break with the earlier tradition. In the light of the evidence produced, one is forced to make due allowance for a fairly long period of transition and adjustments. The heritage of pre-1800 scholarship weighing on an adolescent Romance linguistics was dual: It is visible, first and foremost, in the use the pioneers made of a vast store of slowly accumulated factual, philological knowledge, but traces of it can also be detected on the level of analysis and reconstruction. Above all, there is no evidence of any arrogance or hostility on the part of either Diez or his closest followers toward the spadework done by preceding generations: Master and disciples alike staked out their claims calmly and with engaging modesty.[18]

NOTES

1. Of the *Grammatik* there appeared before long a revised 2nd edition (1856-60), and finally an enlarged 3rd edition (1870-72), of which the posthumous 4th and 5th (1876-77, 1882) are mere reprints, except for an added index. There existed, we know, a plan for having the entire grammar revised, but the project fell through at its very inception. All that F. Apfelstedt and E. Seelmann, by way of compromise, could accomplish was, I repeat, to compile a set of indices; see my comment (1967-68a). On the publication history of the *EWRS*, see n.4.

2. On this unjustly forgotten pioneer (1818-47), who at a tender age made bold to review vol. 2 of Diez's *Grammatik* in the March 1839 issue of the *Berliner Jahrbuch für wissenschaftliche Kritik* (432 ff.), see my vignette (1967-68b).

3. Aside from revising some earlier works Diez failed to produce anything impressively original after the mid-Sixties. His concluding book-length contributions to genuine knowledge were in 1863 and 1865, the latter piece flanked by a French edition (tr. A. Bauer, Bibl. École des Hautes-Études, 1:5 [1870]) which added the Glosses of Vienna to those of Reichenau and Kassel. Quite anticlimactic—and tragically mistitled to boot— was the pamphlet (1875), described as a "Supplement" to, of all writings, the author's grammar but actually amounting to little more than a miniaturized and selective semantic vocabulary. It stands in pathetic contrast to a younger (but already experienced) Diez's vigorous "Streitschrift" (1859), a 36-page tract embodying a spirited "Auseinandersetzung" with his critics (one copy

of this bibliophile's item is owned by the New York Public Library, another by Harvard's Widener Library).

4. One can cite many other tokens of the esteem that Diez, as a historical linguist, enjoyed in his lifetime. The 3rd edition of his grammar was translated into French by an outstanding team of experts—all three fine researchers in their own right—A. Brachet, G. Paris, and A. Morel-Fatio (Paris, 1874-76), while the lengthy introductory section of the 2nd edition had been separately made available, as early as 1863, to French readers (tr. G. Paris) and to English readers (tr. C. B. Cayley) alike. An epitome of the Italian ingredients, with special reference to morphology, was excerpted by Fornaciari (1872), barely one year after the publication of a major essay—exceeding eighty pages in length—from the pen of U. A. Canello. Ten years before the publication of Diez's own dictionary, Hauschild (1843), as his title-page expressly announced, shrewdly put to use the etymological equations scattered over Diez's grammar. In England, Donkin (1864) was squarely based on Diez's model venture, of which the 2nd edition had become available by 1861. Honors continued to pour in posthumously, starting with E. Stengel's recollections (1883) to which specimens of Diez's letters to L. Diefenbach were appended and reaching their climax on the occasion of the pompous celebration of the centennial of the Founding Father's birth (1894), a year which saw a eulogy delivered at Bonn by Diez's successor W. Förster, other commemorative speeches pronounced by D. Behrens, H. Breymann, and E. Ritter, the joint publication of *Diez-Reliquien* (ed. Stengel), and of the slimmer sampler of *Freundesbriefe* (correspondence chiefly with Karl Ebenau, collected by Förster), both preceded by the distinctly more useful miscellany edited by Breymann (1883). We also owe to Breymann the most ambitious appreciation (1878). Symptomatic of the learned world's unflagging attention to Diez's writings—until the arrival on the scene of W. Meyer-Lübke, though after 1866 Schuchardt played first violin—was furthermore the appearance of two sharply focused elaborations on the senior comparatist's dictionary: Caix (1878) and Thurneysen (1894). So were the publisher's repeated attempts to update the 3rd definitive edition of the dictionary (1869-70) by inviting the Belgian Romanist A. Scheler (1819-90) to compile, on his own responsibility, a succinct Supplement attached to the 4th edition (1878) and, after proper revision, to the 5th (1887); also, the appearance of J. U. Jarník's complete index to that dictionary thus expanded and modernized (1878), an index newly revised at a later date (1889). All this activity does not include the philological and literary facets of Diez's *œuvre*, whose legacy after 1880 became mainly the concern of K. Bartsch.

There was one lame attempt, at the height of the last war, to commemorate the one-hundred-fiftieth anniversary (1944) of Diez's birth. The tasteful speech pronounced by E. R. Curtius on this occasion—rich in discreetly spiced anecdotal detail and in references to out-of-the-way bibliographic clues—has gained in importance through the incineration, presumably in the concluding year of the war, of much archival material tapped therein (Curtius 1960: 412-427). Ten years later E. Lommatzsch published samples of epistolary communications between Diez and the much younger A. Tobler (a Swiss stationed in Berlin). I cannot begin to do justice here to the indirect reverberations of Diez's linguistic spadework—as one senses them in the investigations of P. F. Monlau, F. A. Coelho, U. A. Canello, C. von Reinhardstoettner, G. Paris, A. Brachet, A. Darmesteter, and of numerous other members—not all necessarily lesser figures—of the "second generation" of Romance linguists. Warm appreciations by G. Bertoni and A. Vàrvaro testify to the affectionate esteem that Diez continues to enjoy in Italy − as in the days of Ascoli.

5. Niebuhr's voluminous writings, throughout the Twenties and Thirties, produced an impact—as far west as the Atlantic Coast of the still young United States—comparable to the influence exerted in our own century by the explosive *magna opera* of Spengler and Toynbee rather than, to name a topically closer counterpart, by M. Rostovtsev's masterly and monumental, but restrained, social and economic history of the Roman Empire. Niebuhr's influence on Diez is the likelier to have been tremendous as both scholars happened to teach at the same tone-setting university (Rheinische Friedrich-Wilhelms-Universität, Bonn) and as Niebuhr's lectures on ancient, specifically, Roman, history seem to have galvanized his audiences (also, conveniently enough, Niebuhr was Diez's senior by a margin of eighteen years). These lectures were not only collected and published after the historian's death, but were also translated, as was of course his *Römische Geschichte* (1828-32), which has remained a recognized classic of historiography. Niebuhr's powerful impact on German humanistic culture—then in its zenith—was, in part, due to his wide circle of influential friends and correspondents, perhaps also to his active involvement in politics; the fact that he died relatively young, shortly before the actual appearance of the concluding volume of his masterpiece, must have added to the poignancy of his loss, creating a demand for many posthumous publications. One measure of the repercussions of his work was the publication of an English epitome by T. Twiss (Oxford-London, 1845) of his *History of Rome*. What must have mattered most to a historical linguist of Diez's mettle was Niebuhr's masterly use of multitudinous collateral sources in mosaic-like reconstruction. It might be interesting to compare some day, point by point, Niebuhr's and the distinctly later T. Mommsen's separate influences on two generations of Romance linguists.

6. The translations from Old Spanish form part of Diez's *juvenilia*. His editions of archaic texts from France − reminiscent of J. and W. Grimm's pamphlet of 1812−fall between the first versions of the grammar and of the dictionary: those of 1846 encompass, apart from an appended metrical excursus, the "Strassburg Oaths", the "Cantilène de Sainte Eulalie", and the Old Provençal "Boethius", while the slenderer companion volume of 1852 offers "emended and annotated" (i.e., critical) editions of the "Passion" and of "Saint Léger" − two texts mediating between North and South. There is a certain piquancy in the fact that, at least on the monographic level, Diez

failed to busy himself directly with Old Italian, because the arrangement of his grammar and of his dictionary alike bespeaks the prime importance he invariably attached to the testimony of that language – not unlike the hegemony which pioneering Indo-Europeanists, in their overflowing enthusiasm, were prone to grant to newly discovered Sanskrit.

7. Witness his little-known, telltale pamphlet (1831) (which I have not seen). Curtius reports, from his inspection of university records, that Diez at times taught Germanics.

8. For an analysis of this structure, see Malkiel 1960: 321-416, esp. 351, 368 f., 373 f., included in minimally revised form, in Malkiel 1968: 71-164, esp. 100, 117 f., 121 f.

In the original edition of his grammar, Diez accepted the dichotomy – in retrospect, arbitrary – of Latin (pp.116-269) and German[ic] (pp. 270-332) "letters", i.e., sounds, followed by a meager Supplement on Arabic sounds in Spanish (pp.332-334). The definitive version of his grammar shows a complete reorganization: A newly built section, "The Sounds of the Source Languages", serves as the ground floor of the restructured edifice (pp. 120-270), inviting a pervasive contrasting of Latin and Germanic, while in the complementary section, an upper story devoted to the six languages chosen for separate survey, a unified treatment prevails. More rewarding than this strategy, at least from our own vantage point, was Diez's tactical skill in aligning Germanic borrowings from Latin with the Romance descendants of those same words, as when, in his grammar, he grouped MHG *boije* with OF *buie* (p.9), Dutch *krijten* with Fr. *crier*, Sp. *gritar*, It. *gridare* (p.15), G. *Planke* with Fr. *planche* and It. *palanca* (p.17), G. *Probe* with It. *pruova* (ibid.), or added MHG *sittech* (>*Sittich* "parrot")<Gr.-Lat. PSITTACU to the evidence for the Romance treatment of *ps-* and similarly pressed into service OHG *niumo* (Notker)<PNEUMA (p.179). If one agrees to make allowances for a trailblazer's unavoidable margin of error (medieval diffusion mistaken for common descent), one can legitimately see in this forceful approach an anticipation of J. Jud's brilliant breakthrough (1914-17).

9. Strictly speaking, the composition of the lengthy prospectus of Latin-Spanish sound changes prefixed to Cabrera (1837–posthumous) likewise preceded by a sizable margin the appearance of Vol. I of Diez's grammar. The author – a priest first elevated to the presidency of the Royal Spanish Academy, then living in enforced retirement as a disgraced *afrancesado*, in the end amnestied and reestablished as an academician – died as early as 1833.

10. The sources include a number of less well-remembered authors, e.g., the panegyrist Claudius Mamertinus, the language teacher Dositheus, the fourth-century historian Eutropius, the neo-Platonic astrologist J. Firmicus Maternus, the grammarian F. Caper, the Jurist Julius Paulus, also Laberius, Lampridius, Macer, Mattius apud Gellium, Nemesianus, Nigidius, Nonius Marcellinus, Paulinus Nolanus, Petrus Chrysologus (1449), Salvianus, Scribonius Largus, Spartianus, Theodorus Priscianus (a physician), Trebellius Pollio and Vopiscus (two minor historians who flourished under Constantine); the scholiast *ad Persium*; legal texts ranging from the *Codex*

Iustinianeus and the *Pandectae* to the "barbaric" *Lex Salica*; and, in anticipation of Loewe and Goetz (1888-1923), the *Glossarium Isidori* beside the *Glossarium Philoxeni*.

11. Forcellini (1688-1768) collaborated only nominally with his slightly older teacher J. Facciolati (1682-1769). The *Lexicon* appeared in Padua in 1771, was reprinted in 1805, then again, with G. Furlanetto's Addenda, in 1827-31. The later revisions and enlargements, by V. De-Vit (Prato, 1839-79) and F. Corradini and G. Perin (Padua, 1864-98), were not yet available at the critical juncture. One may liken Diez's reliance on Forcellini to his successor Meyer-Lübke's dependence on the masterly *Thesaurus Linguae Latinae* (on whose staff he acted as consultant). The lifespan of that dictionary was prolonged through G. H. Liinemann's and F. P. Leverett's adaptations, in Germany and England, respectively. Scheller may be characterized as a predecessor of Georges.

12. Diez's laconic, occasionally cryptic style of citing sources and adducing authorities (as a rule, by the surname alone, unaccompanied by the title of the book), not infrequently impedes his present-day reader. One can be reasonably sure that "Frisch" stands for the *Teutsch-lateinisches Wörterbuch* (1741) by J. L. Frisch (1666-1743), a man of learning whose interest oscillated between lexicography, entomology, and didactic play-writing and whose dictionary may have served Diez well as a companion piece to Forcellini's and Scheller's (see above). But though I know several older classical philologists named Schneider, I am uncertain as to which of them wrote the particular grammar to which Diez time and again refers.

13. For the original edition of his grammar Diez could readily use the Frankfurt 1710 or the Venice 1736-40 edition; for the revised editions and for all versions of his dictionary he had available the vastly improved and expanded edition launched by G. A. L. Henschel (7 vols.; Paris, 1840-50), which incorporated D. P. Charpentier's and J. C. Adelung's *addenda et corrigenda*. Decades later, Meyer-Lübke was fortunate in having at his disposal L. Faure's even more elaborate revision (10 vols.; Niort, 1883-87).

14. We are assessing here Diez's general ability to discriminate between varieties of change and of lexical layers, not the specific accuracy of every single equation he was led to posit. Thus, Fr. *capitaine*, traceable to the thirteenth century, is now linked to Med. Lat. *capitaneus* rather than to an Italian prototype, while It. *malato*, for which modern etymology favors a rapprochement with MALE HABITUS rather than with Diez's base MALE APTUS, may have here been attracted into the orbit of past participial *-ato*, an assumption which obviates any need to appeal to French mediation.

15. Sánchez wavered between merely pointing out cognates—in, say, French or Italian—of obsolete Spanish words and actually labeling certain lexical items as imitations of foreign (e.g., Provencal) usage. See Levy 1964-65: 403.

16. Examples include (177) It. *savio*<*SAPIU (a gratuitous recon-struction) and (179) Fr. *nièce*<*NEPTIA beside NEPTIS. In other instances the strictly inferential status of the base is contextually defined, as when Diez

contends: "Vielleicht bestand im Lateinischen neben *capo* die Form *cappo*" (178).

17. I cannot within the narrow frame of this paper categorize the errors that mar Diez's grammar. These range from serious strategic blunders, as when he confuses primary clusters, say, -PT- (as in CAPTĪVU>It. *cattivo*), with their secondary counterparts (in, say, CAPITOLIU>OPr. *capdolh*), to a host of minor inaccuracies and slips; witness, within the same chapters, such infelicities as alleged Sp. *lépido*, also Fr. *pseaume*, It. *recevere*, Sp. *receber*, Rum. *sëpon* (i.e., *psaume, ricevere, recibir, să-* or *së-pun*).

18. Stray addenda at proof: A forthcoming issue of the quarterly *Romance Philology* is to contain a two-page editorial comment, "Jakob Grimm and Friedrich Diez". – In the series "Romanistische Versuche und Vorarbeiten" there has just appeared, as No. 47 (1973), the Bonn dissertation by Wolfgang Sykorra, *Friedrich Diez' EWRS und seine Quellen*. – Finally, I discuss some facets of the early-nineteenth century period of Romance scholarship in a paper of very recent vintage, "Summits of Romance Linguistics", *The Canadian Journal of Romance Linguistics* 1.33-48 (1973).

REFERENCES

Aldrete, B. 1606. Del origen y principio de la lengua castellana o romance. . . . Roma. 2nd ed. (posthumous), Madrid, 1674.

Ascoli, G. I. 1873. Saggi ladini. Archivio glottologico italiano, 1.

Behrens, D. 1894. Friedrich Diez. Festrede zur Feier von Diez's 100. Geburtstage gehalten mit bisher nicht veröffentlichtem biographischem Material. Giessen.

B[ertoni], G. 1931. Friedrich Diez. Enciclopedia italiana di scienze, lettere ed arti 12.787b-788a [with valuable bibliographic clues].

Bopp, Franz. 1833. Vergleichende Grammatik des Sanskrit, Zend, Griechischen, Lateinischen, Litauischen, Gothischen und Deutschen. Berlin.

Bréquigny, L. G. [1714-94] 1843-49. Diplomata, chartae, epistolae, leges aliaqua instrumenta ad res Gallo-Francicas spectantia. Revised by J. M. Pardessus. 2 vols. Paris.

Breymann, H. 1878. (ed.) Kleinere Arbeiten und Rezensionen von Friedrich Diez. München.

――――. 1894. Friedrich Diez, sein Leben und Wirken. Festrede. . . [with a Supplement containing poems by Diez and N. Delius]. Leipzig.

Cabrera, R. 1837. Diccionario de etimologías de la lengua castellana. Ed. by J. P. Ayegui. 2 vols. Madrid.

Caix, N. 1878. Studi di etimologia italiana e romanza; osservazioni ed aggiunte al "Vocabolario etimologico delle lingue romanze" di F. Diez. Firenze.

Canello, U. A. 1871. Il prof. Federigo Diez e la filologia romanza nel nostro secolo. Firenze. [A reprint of the 85-page article, orig. published by the Rivista Europea, is available at Widener Library.]

Covarrubias Horozco, S. de. 1673-74. Tesoro de la lengua castellana. 2nd ed.
    Rev. by B. R. Noydens. (Madrid).
Curtius, E. R. 1960. Bonner Gedenkworte auf Friedrich Diez. In Gesammelte
    Aufsätze zur romanischen Philologie. Bern. (Orig. in Romanische
    Forschungen 60:389-410 [1947].)
Diefenbach, L. 1831. Über die jetzigen romanischen Schriftsprachen. Leipzig.
Diez, Friedrich. 1818. Altspanische Romanzen. Frankfurt a/M. Enlarged ed.,
    Berlin 1821.
_____. 1825. Über die Minnehöfe. Berlin. (=Beiträge..., 1).
_____. 1826. Die Poesie der Troubadours. Zwickau.
_____. 1829. Leben und Werke der Troubadours.
_____. 1831. Antiquissima germanicae poeseos vestigia: commentatio. Bonn.
_____. 1836-44. Grammatik der romanischen Sprachen. 3 vols. Bonn.
_____. 1846. Altromanische Sprachdenkmale berichtigt und erklärt....
    Bonn.
_____. 1852. Zwei altromanische Gedichte berichtigt und erklärt. Bonn.
    Reprinted, 1876.
_____. 1853. Etymologisches Wörterbuch der romanischen Sprachen. Bonn.
    [EWRS]
_____. 1856-60. Grammatik der romanischen Sprachen. Rev. ed. Bonn.
_____. 1859. Kritischer Anhang zum Etymologischen Wörterbuch der
    romanischen Sprachen. Bonn.
_____. 1863. Über die erste portugiesische Kunst- und Hofpoesie. Bonn.
_____. 1865. Altromanische Glossare, berichtigt und erklärt. Bonn.
_____. 1869-70. Etymologisches Wörterbuch der romanischen Sprachen. 3rd
    ed., 2 vols. Bonn.
_____. 1870-72. Grammatik der romanischen Sprachen. 3rd, enlarged ed.
    Bonn.
_____. 1875. Romanische Wortschöpfung. Bonn.
Donkin, T. C. 1864. An etymological dictionary of the Romance languages,
    chiefly from the German of Friedrich Diez. London and Edinburgh.
Du Cange, Charles du Fresne. 1678. Glossarium ad scriptores mediae et infimae
    latinitatis. Paris. Rev. ed., 3 vols., Frankfurt a/M, 1710; 6 vols., Venice,
    1736-40; rev. by G. A. L. Henschel, 7 vols., Paris, 1840-50 (with
    material supplied by P. Carpentier, J. C. Adelung, and L. Diefenbach);
    rev. by L. Favre, 10 vols., Niort, 1883-87.
Fabricius, J. A. 1754. Bibliotheca latina mediae et infimae aetatis. Padua.
Foerster, W. 1894. Friedrich Diez: Festrede zur Feier des hundertjährigen
    Geburtstages des Begründers der romanischen Philologie. Two folio
    pages included in the March 6 issue (No. 54) of the daily Neue Bonner
    Zeitung (copy owned by Widener Library); reprinted as a separate
    pamphlet. Bonn.
Forcellini, E. 1771. Totius Latinitatis lexicon. Padua.

Fornaciari, R. 1872. Grammatica storica. . .estratta e compendiata. Torino.

[Freundesbriefe]. 1894. Freundesbriefe von Fr. Diez. Bound with Foerster 1894.

Frisch, J. L. 1741. Teutsch-lateinisches Wörterbuch. Berlin.

Fuchs, August. 1840. Über die sogenannten unregelmässigen Zeitwörter in den romanischen Sprachen. Berlin.

———. 1849. Die romanischen Sprachen in ihrem Verhältnisse zum Lateinischen. Ed. L. G. Blanc. Halle.

Graevius, J. G. 1694-99. Thesaurus antiquitatum Romanarum. 12 vols. Traiectum ad Rhenum [Utrecht].

———. 1704-25. Thesaurus antiquitatum et historiarum Italiae. . . . 10 vols. Lugdunum Batavorum [Leiden].

Graff, E. G. 1826-29. Diutiska: Denkmäler deutscher Sprache und Literatur. 3 vols. Stuttgart.

———. 1834-43. Althochdeutscher Sprachschatz. 7 vols. Berlin.

Grimm, Jakob. 1822. Deutsche Grammatik. Vol. 1. Rev. ed. Göttingen. (Orig. ed.: 1819.)

Grimm, Jakob and Wilhelm. 1812. Die beiden ältesten deutschen Gedichte aus dem achten Jahrhundert. Kassel.

Gruterius, J. *ca.* 1602. Inscriptiones antiquae totius orbis romani.

Hauschild, E. I. 1834. Etymologisches Wörterbuch der französischen Sprache nach F. Diez. . . . Leipzig.

Humboldt, W. von. 1821. Prüfung der Untersuchung über die Urbewohner Hispaniens vermittelst der baskischen Sprache. Berlin.

Jarník, J. U. 1878. Neuer vollständiger Index zu Diez's Etymologischem Wörterbuch der romanischen Sprachen. Berlin. Pp. vi, 237. Rev. ed., . . . mit Berücksichtigung von Schelers Anhang zur 5. Ausgabe. Heilbronn, 1889. Pp. x, 378.

Jud, J. 1914-17. Probleme der altromanischen Sprachgeographie. Zeitschrift für Romanische Philologie 38: 1-75 (with 5 folding maps).

Larramendi, M. de. 1745. Diccionario trilingüe del castellano, bascuence y latín . . . San Sebastián.

Levy, A. K. 1964-65. Contrastive development in Hispano-Romance of borrowed Gallo-Romance suffixes (I). Romance Philology 18: 399-429.

Loewe, G., and G. Goetz. 1888-1923. (eds.) Corpus glossariorum Latinorum. 7 vols. Leipzig and Berlin.

Lommatzsch, E. 1954. Briefwechsel zwischen Adolf Tobler und Friedrich Diez. Kleinere Schriften zur romanischen Philologie. Berlin.

Malkiel, Yakov. 1960. A tentative typology of Romance historical grammars. Lingua 9: 321-416. (Included in Essays on linguistic themes.)

———. 1967-68a. Comment on D. Gazdaru, Controversias y documentos lingüísticos. Romance Philology 21: 361.

———. 1967-68b. August Fuchs. Romance Philology 21: 285.

_____. 1968. Essays on linguistic themes. Oxford.

Marini, Abbot G. 1785. Iscrizioni antiche delle ville e de' palazzi Albani. Roma.

_____. 1805. I papiri diplomatici, raccolti e illustrati. Roma.

Mayáns y Siscar, G. 1737. Orígenes de la lengua española. 2 vols. Madrid.

Michaëlis de Vasconcelos, C. 1876. Preface, Studien zur romanischen Wortschöpfung. Leipzig. [Actually an inquiry into Spanish allotypes.]

Niebuhr, B. G. 1811-32. Römische Geschichte. 3 vols. Berlin. (Vol. 1, 1811, 1827 [2nd ed.], 1828 [3rd ed.]; Vol. 2, 1812, 1830 [2nd ed.]; Vol. 3, 1832 [ed. Claasen]).

Orelli, J. K. 1828-50. Inscriptionum Latinarum selectarum amplissima collectio. Zürich.

Raynouard, F. 1821. Grammaire comparée des langues de l'Europe latine, dans leurs rapports avec la langue des troubadours. Paris.

Ritter, E. 1894. Le centenaire de Diez; discours prononcé à la séance annuelle de l'Institut genevois. Bulletin de l'Institut genevois, Vol. 33.

Sánchez, T. A. 1779-90. Colección de poesías castellanas anteriores al siglo XV. 4 vols. Madrid.

Scheler, A. 1878, 1887. [Supplement to 4th and 5th eds. of Diez 1869-70.]

Scheller, I. J. G. 1805. Ausführliches und möglichst vollständiges deutsch-lateinisches Lexikon. Rev. 3rd ed. 2vols. Leipzig.

Schuchardt, H. 1866-68. Der Vokalismus des Vulgärlateins. 3 vols. Leipzig.

Stengel, E. 1883. Erinnerungsworte an Friedrich Diez. Erweiterte Fassung der Rede, welche zu Giessen am 9. Juni 1883 gehalten wurde, nebst mehreren Anlagen und einem Anhang: Briefe von F. Diez an L. Diefenbach. . . Marburg.

_____. 1894. (ed.) Diez-Reliquien. Ausgaben und Abhandlungen aus dem Gebiete der romanischen Philologie, Vol. 91. Marburg.

Thurneysen, R. 1884. Keltoromanisches; die keltischen Etymologien im EWRS von F. Diez. Halle.

Vàrvaro, A. 1968. Storia, problemi e metodi della linguistica romanza. Napoli. (See esp. Part 2, pp.51-83.)

Viterbo, J. de S. R. de.1798-99. Elucidário das palavras, termos e frases. . . . 2 vols. Lisboa.

Vossius, G. I. 1664. Etymologicon linguae latinae. Ed. by Isaac Vossius. Lyon.

_____. 1695-1701. Opera. 6 vols. Amsterdam.

12. From Paleogrammarians to Neogrammarians

Paul Kiparsky

Early nineteenth-century comparative linguistics is in some ways a predecessor of twentieth-century theoretical linguistics. This is not because it held any of the same views as modern linguistics, but because many of its basic concerns were the same, and because the radical changes it underwent contributed directly to the development of modern linguistics. The theoretical disputes among the nineteenth-century comparativists were rarely about the modern comparativist's problem of establishing reliable methods of linguistic reconstruction. More often they centered on topics which today would be considered questions to be settled outside of comparative linguistics. These included such issues of current relevance as the relation of form and meaning in language, the psychological reality and abstract nature of underlying representations, and the status of explanatory theories in linguistics.

That the field bore this character is mainly attributable to the influence of Franz Bopp. Ostensibly aimed simply at reconstructing Indo-European, Bopp's works also implicitly presented a specific and original linguistic theory. While this linguistic theory did not survive past the 1860's, Bopp's influential idea that the study of language change was the most worthwhile kind of linguistics managed to hold the field for a full century. Between the publication of Bopp's *Conjugationssystem* in 1816 and the publication of Saussure's *Cours* in 1915, the main empirical basis of linguistic theory was in diachrony. The purpose of this essay is to explore some controversies that arose in connection with Bopp's approach to comparative linguistics, and to relate them to the development of modern linguistics.

Bopp's basic assumption is often said to have been that the Indo-European endings are derived from pronouns and forms of the copula attached to the verbal root (the "agglutination theory"). This is a true but incomplete statement, which glosses over the sharp differences between Bopp's views and those of later comparative grammar. It is merely the one aspect of Bopp's hypothesis about the structure of the Indo-European proto-language which later historians of linguistics, such as Delbrück, emphasized and partly accepted. Bopp actually seems to have held that in the proto-language the primitive semantic elements were by and large expressed by separate morphemes. The morphology of a Proto-Indo-European word, Bopp believed, was a representation of the elements of its meaning. Obscured as this state of affairs was in the daughter languages, because of phonetic decay, it was nevertheless reconstructible by the comparative method (cf. Verburg 1950).

Although Bopp in the *Conjugationssystem* was still strongly influenced by the very different ideas of Fr. Schlegel, the germ of his notion of the proto-language can already be found in this work. In a section on the formation of the voices in Sanskrit (1816: 36-37), Bopp gives an interesting semantic analysis of the active, middle, passive, and causative, by means of two binary features referring to the functional relation of the grammatical subject to the action denoted by the verb. In the active and the middle, but not in the passive or causative, the grammatical subject is the agent of the action, and in the middle and the passive, but not in the active or the causative, the subject is the direct or indirect goal of the action.

		Subject = Agent	Subject = Goal
Active	karoti "makes"	+	—
Middle	kurute "makes (for) himself"	+	+
Passive	kriyate "is made"	—	+
Causative	kárayati "causes to make"	—	—

He further notes that the middle and passive voices, and the passive and causative, each have some morphology in common. The middle and passive are characterized by a special set of endings (e.g., *-te* vs. *-ti* in the third person singular), and the passive and causative are characterized by similar suffixes *-ya* and *-aya*.

	-(a)ya	-te
Active	—	—
Middle	—	+
Passive	+	+
Causative	+	—

Bopp then takes the crucial step of linking the morphological and semantic analyses on the level of their primitive components. He associates with -(*a*)*ya* the meaning "subject ≠ agent" and with the mediopassive endings the meaning "subject = goal".[1] Commenting on this analysis, he remarks:

> Es kann hierdurch gesehen werden, wie im Sanskrit ähnliche Modifikationen der Bedeutung durch ähnliche Modifikationen der Form angezeigt werden, und wie in gewissem Betrachte der Sinn der organischen Flexionen eben so bestimmt und unverändert bleibt, als jener der bedeutenden Stammsylben selbst. [This shows how in Sanskrit similar modifications of meaning are expressed by similar modifications of form, and how in a sense the meaning of the organic inflections remains as fixed and constant as that of the significant stem syllables.]

This was an important remark. No one had ever tried to penetrate Indo-European morphology in this way before. It subsequently became one of the main goals of Bopp and his school to show that such a one-to-one correspondence between morphological and semantic elements could be established more widely in the Indo-European proto-language by comparative reconstruction.

What Bopp brought to linguistics was, then, a *paradigm* of historical explanation, in the sense in which Kuhn (1962) has introduced this term. A historical explanation of an inflectional form was to him a demonstration that the form was derived from a proto-form in which each of the primitive concepts into which its meaning was analyzable was expressed by a separate morpheme. This paradigm was based on the belief that the methods of comparative reconstruction, applied to what Bopp considered the greatly decayed and disorganized morphological debris of the attested Indo-European languages, would yield a proto-morphology which reflects logical relations. As Curtius (1871: 213) succinctly put it:

> Ein Haupbestreben dieser Wissenschaft läuft darauf hinaus, aus den in mannichfaltiger Weise entstellten und verstümmelten Formen, wie sie in den einzelnen Sprachen vorliegen, die vollen, reinen Formen einer grundlegenden Periode zu reconstruieren. [A principal goal of this science (comparative linguistics) is to reconstruct the full, pure forms of an original state from the variously disfigured and mutilated forms which are attested in the individual languages.]

Especially significant is the remark: "Erklärungen aber, welche die Hauptsache, nämlich die Bedeutung, dunkel lassen, sind nicht geeignet zu befriedigen" [But explanations which fail to elucidate what is of greatest importance, namely the meaning, cannot be satisfactory] (1871: 215).[2]

This paradigm of historical explanation can be represented by the following schema:

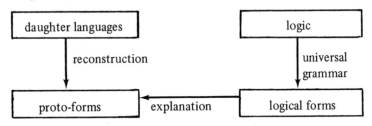

To say that Bopp and his followers operated according to this paradigm is not to say that such explanations were ever actually achieved. Needless to say, they were not. But linguists at the time thought that they had been achieved, and research in comparative grammar was for several decades oriented towards searching for them. It was the lack of any theory of reconstruction that made this whole schema of explanation quite empty in practice. Little thought was given to the rules whereby the actual forms of the daughter languages were derived from the reconstructed proto-forms, and hence these proto-forms could simply be set up ad hoc to fit the hypothesis that Proto-Indo-European had a morphology in which the salient elements of meaning corresponded to separate elements of form. A good illustration of this is the analysis of the personal endings of the verb which was developed by Bopp, Kuhn, and Schleicher, as summarized by Curtius, the last representative of this school of comparative linguistics (1877).

The basic assumption underlying this analysis was that the personal endings had originally been pronouns attached to the verb stem. This was at least given some phonological plausibility by an overall similarity between pronouns and the corresponding verb endings in the Indo-European languages. The first person singular was reconstructed as *-ma* and the second person singular as *-tva*. The derivation of the Greek second person singular endings from *-tva* was represented by Curtius (1877: 47) in the form of a tree as follows:

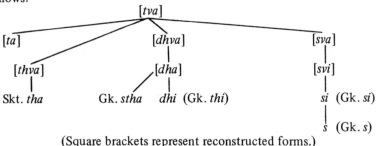

(Square brackets represent reconstructed forms.)

From here on the reconstruction proceeded on the basis of a purely semantic analysis. Plurals were analyzed as derived from conjunction, with 1.pl. *-ma-tva* and 2.pl. *-tva-tva*. The middle endings were also assumed to have had reduplicated pronouns, to reflect the double function of subject as actor and goal, e.g., sg.1.p. *-ma-ma* and 2.p. *-tva-tva*. But if the plural is formed by repeating singular endings, and the middle is formed by repeating the active endings, what of the plural middle endings? According to Curtius (who disarmingly remarks that this is one of the most difficult problems in IE morphology) they are to be reconstructed as 1.pl. *-ma-tva-tva* and 2.pl. *-tva-tva-tva*. Schleicher, more relentlessly logical, had set up *-ma-tva-ma-tva* and *-tva-tva-tva-tva*.

Characteristically, no one working in this framework of comparative grammar seems to have objected to all this on any phonological grounds. The argumentation was based on semantics (for example, an objection to 1.pl. *-ma-tva* was that this form should only have the meaning of an inclusive "we", which Schleicher and Curtius countered by postulating the existence of a lost exclusive "we" in the proto-language). No one was disturbed by the fact that the phonologically very different 2.p. active plural and middle singular endings were derived from exactly the same base form *-tva-tva*, or by the proposal that the 2.sg. present, past, perfect, and imperative endings all go back to *-tva*, as shown on the chart reproduced here from Curtius. Base forms as different as 2.sg. act. *-tva* and 2.pl.mid. *-tva-tva-tva* or *-tva-tva-tva-tva* were readily assumed to underlie forms as similar as Greek *-stha* and *-sthe*. Obviously it is not ignorance of phonetics but indifference to it that explains this. The actual shape of the forms in the daughter languages was not, in general, something that Bopp and his followers were interested in trying to explain. Attention was given to rules only insofar as they could serve to justify the choice of one base form over another. Otherwise they were satisfied with perfectly ad hoc statements. The idea did not occur to them that the anomalies of the daughter languages might have some interest in themselves.

What was the status of reconstructed forms thought to be? Usually, it seems to have been taken for granted that reconstruction results in the surface phonetic forms of the proto-language. But there was at least one important expression of dissent, which I should like to cite here to illustrate the fact that the same linguists who so neglected the formulation of sound changes were capable of highly sophisticated thinking on phonological theory. In a remarkable review of the first volume of Pott's *Etymologische Forschungen*,[3] Theodor Benfey in 1837 introduced the distinction between the phonetic value of a sound and its functional value, showing on the basis of a discussion of root and ablaut theory that they could differ greatly, and arguing that linguistic reconstruction yields functional as well as phonetic representations.

At the time, Indo-Europeanists accepted Pāṇinian root theory, in which roots are represented in the zero grade form in case they contain a sonant susceptible to vocalization (e.g., *kr̥*, *vid*), and in the full grade otherwise (e.g., *tap*). That is, base forms have the minimal vocalism, subject to the proviso that they must be pronounceable. This proviso was natural, indeed necessary, from the viewpoint of Indian linguistics, based as it was on an oral tradition.[4] Benfey pointed out that from a linguistic point of view it is indefensible, because it breaks the generality of the ablaut rules, and necessitates ad hoc statements like "*a* is its own guṇa". In considering more consistent alternatives to the Indian system, Benfey asks the fundamental question: "Denn wäre es nicht möglich, dass den unter sich zusammenhängenden *i*, *e*, *ya*, *ai*; *u*, *o*, *va*, *au*; *r*, *ar*, *ra*, *ar* etwas im Sprachgeiste zu Grunde liege, was von ihnen allen verschieden wäre? " [For is it not possible that the related series *i*, *e*, *ya*, *ai*, etc., might have an underlying representation in the mind that differs from them all?] (1837: 15). Benfey's question is whether base forms of morphemes can be different from any of the phonetic forms in which they actually appear. He bases his affirmative answer on the very good point that whatever ablaut grade is chosen as the basic one, it can happen that some roots for irrelevant morphological reasons happen not to occur phonetically in that grade:

> Wir haben bis jetzt Beispiele angeführt, wo sich neben den Formen mit *r* und anderm Vokal auch eine mit *r̥* wirklich zeigte. Es versteht isch aber von selbst, dass es leicht geschehen konnte, dass eine solche Form gar nicht hervortrat oder wieder verschwand. Wir sind also berechtigt, auch solche Formen unter eine Wurzel zu bringen, welche begrifflich verwandt nur in Beziehung auf den das *r* begleitenden Vokal wechseln, selbst wenn eine sie äusserlich zusammenhaltende Form mit *r̥* fehlt [Up to now we have cited examples where a form with *r̥* actually appears alongside those with *r*+vowel. But it is self-evident that such a form might fail to appear in the first place, or might disappear again. We are therefore justified in deriving from a single root semantically related forms with alternations in the vowel accompanying *r*, even where there is no actual form with *r̥* to superficially tie them together] (1837: 17).

Having thus justified abstract underlying representations, Benfey, after an analysis of the ablaut system, summarizes his conclusions as follows:

> Wir haben durch diese Untersuchung als Resultat erlangt, dass *r̥* im Sanskrit vom lautlichen Standpunkte aus ein wirklicher Vokal so gut wie *i*, *u* sei; dass alle drei functionell den Werth von

Consonanten in Wurzeln haben; dass alle Wurzeln im Sprachgeiste nur consonantisch liegen, und *a* wo es in Wurzeln erscheint, Guṇa ist [In this investigation we have reached the result that *r* in Sanskrit is phonetically a true vowel just like *i, u* are; that functionally all three have the value of consonants in roots; that all roots are purely consonantal in the underlying representation in the mind, and that *a,* wherever it appears in roots, represents full grade] (1837: 23).

Of especial interest is the following comment on the status of reconstructed forms:

Ubrigens fürchten wir nicht, dass man uns eine so barock materielle Ansicht unterschieben möchte, als ob wir glaubten, dass die consonantischen Wurzeln, welche wir annehmen, je nackend oder ihrer Stufenfolge gemäss aufgetreten wären. In dieser Abstraction ruhten sie nur im Geiste, in der Erscheinung traten sie sogleich, je nach den Gesetzen, welchen die zwischen Laut und Begriff zu erstrebende Harmonie sie unterwarf, nach ihren verschiedenen Phasen auf [Incidentally we do not fear that anyone will impute to us the grotesquely physicalistic view that the consonantal roots which we set up ever appeared unmodified or in the order of their ablaut grades (?). In this abstract form they were represented only in the mind, their successive phonetic forms were from the outset determined by the rules to which they were subjected, which established the required harmony between sound and meaning] (1837: 24).

In the 1860's the reaction against Bopp began. It was on the arbitrariness of the analysis of Indo-European verb morphology described above that the critics first seized. In 1860 and 1870, Fr. Müller published articles in which he argued for something that is today accepted by all Indo-Europeanists, but which at the time was a startling and paradoxical idea: that the secondary endings (*-m -s -t*) were more original than the primary endings (*-mi -si -ti*), and that the augment was not an original part of past tense inflection. The primary endings, Müller suggested arose only through the addition of a deictic, pronominal element to the end of the verb to denote the "here and now" of the present tense, just as the augment was added to the beginning as a sign of past tense. Müller criticized the baselessness of the standard derivation of verb endings and termed the basic assumptions of Boppian comparative linguistics "unsupported dogma" (1870: 194). A number of linguists, such as Scherer (1868) and Westphal (1869), agreed with Müller in this. In a reply, Curtius reiterated his fundamental position (1871: 213): "Dass das vollere das prius, das schwächere das posterius sei, das ist die gesammte vergleichende Grammatik umfassendeschwerlich anfechtbare Grundanschauung." [That the full forms are prior to the weaker forms is basic, hardly disputable assumption underlying all of comparative grammar.]

These critiques of Bopp reflect nothing less than a revolution, in the sense of Kuhn (1962), which was taking place in comparative linguistics in the 1860's. The Bopp paradigm of historical explanation, which had proved unproductive, was abandoned, and a new one was adopted in its place. The principal goal of comparative grammar now became the explanation of phonological or morphological features of the individual daughter languages on the basis of the reconstructed proto-language. The proto-language ceased to be of semantic interest, and its new importance was that it enabled the linguist to explain phenomena in the daughter languages which, viewed in isolation, had no explanation. All the sensational new sound laws discovered in the 1860's and 1870's were historical explanations within this new paradigm. Verner's Law was the explanation of certain anomalies in the Germanic consonantism on the basis of the Proto-Indo-European accent as reconstructed from Sanskrit and Greek. The "palatalgesetz" was the discovery that the Sanskrit palatals could be explained if the five-vowel system of the European languages was reconstructed for Proto-Indo-European. Grassmann's Law showed that some Sanskrit and Greek peculiarities could be explained on the basis of reconstructing the double-aspirate roots indicated by Germanic and Latin. The new paradigm illustrated by these discoveries, which might be called *formal explanation*, can be represented by the following schema:

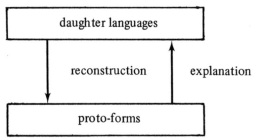

This new paradigm is so much a part of our thinking that it is hard to think of it as ever having been an innovation in method. Nevertheless, it was a very basic change. The results achieved in this new paradigm were partly incomprehensible and partly uninteresting to the comparativists operating in the older framework. Some of them even refused to accept Grassmann's Law. Bopp ignored it in the 1870 (posthumous) edition of his comparative grammar, and Pott attacked it in a long article, asking essentially: "how could monstrous roots like this have existed? " On the other hand, proponents of the new paradigm of formal explanation saw the new paradigm as a regeneration of the science of comparative linguistics. Writing in 1877, Ascoli criticized the older methods of reconstruction for their arbitrariness and contrasted with them the new explanatory paradigm as the properly scientific one, in a very modern-sounding passage:

> Ma chi vorrà per questo negare che la ricostruzione si debba dir solida, e nobilissimamente scientifica, quando ell'è, dall'un canto, la resultanza logicamente necessaria dei termini o de' fenomeni onde moviamo, e, dall'altro, riusce a rivelare, come per spontaneità sua propria, le ragioni istoriche d'altri termini o fenomeni, che non entravano nel calcolo pel quale siam riusciti a stabilirla? [But who would deny by this that the reconstruction must be termed solid, and eminently scientific, when it is, on the one hand, the logical consequence of the terms and phenomena on which it is based, and on the other hand, succeeds in revealing, spontaneously as it were, the historical reasons for other terms and phenomena, which did not enter into the calculations by which we succeeded in establishing this reconstruction?] (1877: 8).

The difference between the two paradigms can perhaps be clarified by an analogy from recent work in transformational grammar. The Bopp paradigm is roughly comparable to the line of investigation undertaken in Katz and Postal (1964). Bopp's program, ideally, was to show that reconstruction of Indo-European morphology, in principle a formal process, results in proto-forms with a one-to-one correspondence between morphemes and minimal semantic elements. Katz and Postal argue somewhat analogously that syntactic deep structures established on the basis of purely syntactic considerations will turn out to contain exactly the information needed for semantic interpretation. The difference is that Bopp's paradigm led to few results of any interest. The post-Boppian paradigm of formal explanation, on the other hand, is reminiscent of Chomsky's concept of explanatory adequacy as presented in *Current Issues in Linguistic Theory* (Chomsky 1964). As Ascoli put it very clearly, the application of the comparative method to a certain set of data enables the linguist, via the reconstructed proto-language, to explain other data found in these languages. Chomsky's point that a theory of phonology or syntax, applied to a set of data in a language, generalizes and makes predictions about data not in this initial set is formally comparable.

In linguistics textbooks the story of comparative linguistics usually gets told roughly as follows:

The early comparativists did badly because they knew no phonetics. ("One difficulty that limited Bopp, and especially Grimm, was an inferior understanding of articulatory phonetics" [Dinneen 1967: 182]). Increased attention to phonology, and a growing appreciation of articulatory phonetics, led gradually to greater rigor in the formulation of sound laws, and to a resulting refinement in the comparative method. ("From approximately 1820 through the 1870s scholars progressed from the notion of sound shifts between these language stages to sound laws that accounted for changes" [Dinneen 1967: 184]). This development culminated in the "breakthrough" (Hockett 1965) of the neogrammarian hypothesis that sound changes can have no exceptions.

I am inclined to question the alleged relevance of articulatory phonetics. I do not see that phonetics played much of a role in the sweeping revision of the comparative method between 1820 and the 1870's. There is nothing about the comparative method of Bopp or his followers which could be explained by their ignorance of some fact of phonetics. Arguments of many kinds were raised against Bopp by his critics in the 1860's, but no one at the time accused him of being a bad phonetician. As far as I know, *nothing* in the whole controversy about comparative linguistics ever turned either on any specific point of phonetics, or on any general considerations of phonetic theory. A much more plausible interpretation is that it was the new paradigm of historical explanation which made, for the first time, historical phonology a subject of interest. It was the realization that there were significant things to be said about the phonological detail of each language, and that explanation in this domain was possible, which caused comparative linguists to take an interest in articulatory phonetics.

Another facet of the story which needs rethinking is the role of the neogrammarians. Since so many important advances in comparative grammar were made by the neogrammarians, it is natural to think of them as the initiators of the revolution in the field. But the revolution was begun in the decade *before* the neogrammarians made their appearance. Furthermore, the new paradigm of historical explanation was in the 1870's accepted by linguists who stood on both sides of the controversy about the neo-grammarian theory of sound change. There exists a most regrettable myth that the belief in necessarily exceptionless sound change accounts for the discovery of the many new sound changes in the 1860's and 1870's. For example, Bloomfield (1933: 355) attributes Grassmann's discovery to this belief, and similarly Verner's discovery (1933: 359). But neither Grassmann nor Verner in fact believed that sound changes could not have exceptions. And why did linguists who specifically rejected the neogrammarian theory of sound change once it had been formulated in the 1870's, such as Collitz, Ascoli, J. Schmidt, discover sound laws which were just as significant as those discovered by neogrammarians, such as Brugmann, Osthoff, and Leskien? Neither side in the disagreement over the sound change issue seems to have had a bad effect on the linguists who embraced it. In fact, the two groups of linguists scarcely differed in the kind of actual historical linguistics they did. It is hard to see how a theory with so few actual consequences for comparative work should be considered a "breakthrough". A more important change in the field was surely the acceptance of the new paradigm of historical explanation. This far exceeds the sound change debate in productivity and concrete consequences, and is a far more likely historical source of the new discoveries in phonology. The disagreement between the neogrammarians and their contemporary opponents seems utterly insignificant compared to the rejection by both groups of the Bopp-Schleicher-Curtius paradigm.

The switch in outlook had further consequences. First, it opened the way to the theory of proportional analogy. The connection is obvious. Bopp's followers were being quite consistent in rejecting the concept of analogical change when it first began to be offered by the new comparativists. As long as the morphologies of the attested Indo-European languages were seen as nothing more than pitiful, jumbled remnants of an earlier stage, there was no way of supposing that these morphologies could undergo any sort of systematic modification. Analogy as a form of language change presupposes some synchronic regularity which is being generalized beyond its proper confines. But linguists of Bopp's school were not in principle prepared to admit the existence of the kind of synchronic regularities in the historical Indo-European languages which could form the basis for analogical generalization. Analogy only became a conceivable form of change when it was admitted that the morphology of the daughter languages could be described as a system in its own terms. It is no accident that the linguists who first began to use proportional analogy as a principle of explanation were Scherer, Whitney, and the other linguists who headed the rejection of the Bopp paradigm in the 1860's.

It can also be argued that the concept of a synchronic system is ultimately connected with these changes in the prevailing views about language. At the very beginning of the reaction against Bopp, the objection was already being raised that his theory, which saw all change as decay, could make no sense out of the fact that the daughter languages had system and structure too. In Westphal (1869), a historical grammar of German in the framework of a K. F. Becker-like system of universal grammar, this is the most serious charge against Bopp:

> Erst dadurch, dass die ursprünglichen Auslaute zerschlagen und zertrümmert worden sind und nicht einer einzigen Form ihr ursprünglicher Bestand gelassen ist, erst durch diese zufällige Vernichtung des ursprünglichen Zustandes soll jener in sich so ganz und gar consequente Organismus der Endungen t ta, ti tai, tu tau u.s.w. der doch sicherlich ein festes und vernünftiges

Princip zeigt, entstanden sien? Erst durch Depravation und Corruption soll es gekommen sein, dass die Endungen in ihrem Gegensatze zu einander als Träger logischer oder metaphysischer Kategorien dastahen und als solche mindestens dieselben Ansprüche auf Schönheit, ja auf unsere Bewunderung erheben, wie die bestimmten mathematischen Functionen folgenden Krystallformen der anorganischen Welt? [Is it only by the destruction and wreckage of the old terminations, which has not left a single form untouched, only by this random annihilation of the original state, that the internally quite coherent system of endings t ta, ti tai, tu tau etc., which surely shows a solid and rational principle, is supposed to have originated? Is it only by decay and corruption that the endings have come to stand in opposition to each other as carriers of logical or metaphysical categories, and as such deserve to be considered, indeed admired, as being beautiful, to at least the extent that inorganic crystals which follow certain mathematical functions deserve it?] (1869: 179).

Westphal seems to have had virtually no influence. But the paradoxical relationship between synchrony and diachrony which he was perhaps the first to point out continued to disturb linguists like Kruszewski (1881; cf. Jakobson 1965), and became the key problem of Saussure's *Cours*.

POSTCRIPT (1973)

The great handbooks of the neogrammarians form a kind of massive wall behind which the working Indo-Europeanist today rarely finds it necessary to go for either facts or theories. Consequently, our prevailing views of the earlier nineteenth-century Indo-Europeanists have been shaped mainly at second hand, through the historiography of men like Delbrück, Streitberg, and Pedersen, who take a very partisan view and understandably misrepresent the aims of their predecessors in terms of their own concerns. In discussing Bopp, for example, they play up issues which were of little concern to Bopp (such as the regularity of sound change, and what later came to be called the "comparative method"), and virtually ignore the issues that Bopp was mainly interested in (such as the relationship of form and meaning in language). The main purpose of my essay is to qualify their account of the nineteenth century (which may be caricatured as "Bopp + Ausnahmslosigkeit = Brugmann") and to emphasize the fact that the program that guided Bopp's work was very different from that which led to the *Grundriss*.

I think that my essay, which appears here substantially as written over five years ago, is right in its major points. However, I would now say that I depicted the contrast between the two approaches rather too luridly. Contrary to what I say in the essay, the development of a theory of phonetic features was rather important in the development of the new comparative grammar. A deeper analysis of the period would also have to take into account the long development of Bopp's own ideas, and (as Y. Malkiel rightly remarked during the conference) the role of men like Rask, Grimm, and Diez.

Perhaps the conflict between Bopp and the later Indo-Europeanists ultimately is a reflection of the two basic reasons why man has always found the study of language so fascinating: on the one hand the elusive relationship between form and meaning, and on the other hand the intricate but perhaps slightly less elusive intrinsic patterning of linguistic forms. Sometimes one must be bought at the price of the other, for reasons which we are still a long way from understanding. The nineteenth-century Indo-Europeanists were by no means the only linguists to feel this conflict. In the essay I compare the difference between Katz and Postal's and Chomsky's 1964 ideas of linguistic explanation. These have since been polarized into two major schools of generative grammar, which in practice at least have been distinguished by the fact that one has focused its search on the semantic basis of linguistic form, and the other on its intrinsic patterning. In a work now in preparation, S. D. Joshi and I hope to show that over two thousand years ago the same conflict arose in India, between Pāṇini and a school (probably antedating Pāṇini himself) represented by his greatest critic Kātyāyana. A major underlying theme of Kātyāyana's *vārttikās*, or critical remarks on Pāṇini's rules, is to tie syntax to semantics more closely, by attempting to show that *kārakas* (deep syntactic relations) are semantically based, and by arguing for highly "abstract" underlying representations quite similar to those which would be required by generative semantics today.

In the past, the study of intrinsic form came out with more lasting results than the search for semantic explanations: Pāṇini achieved more than Kātyāyana, and the neogrammarians achieved more than the Bopp school. The reason was the cavalier treatment of meaning which was possible and tempting in the absence of a well-motivated framework for representing meaning. That gap has still hardly begun to be filled. Semantics is as observable as phonetics, and yet we know much less about the nature of semantic representations than about phonetic representations. Quite possibly, the semantic representations appearing in present-day works on generative grammar will seem as amusing 100 years from now as Grimm's phonetic representation of German *Schrift* with the eight sounds [skhripht] seems to us today.

NOTES

*This work was supported in part by the National Institute of Mental Health (Grant No. MH13390-04). I would like to express my gratitude to Dell

Hymes for the great help he has given me in getting this essay into printable shape.

1. Bopp later proposed different solutions to these problems.

2. As Keith Percival has pointed out to me, Bopp did not require that base forms be uniquely interpretable. Ambiguities could be introduced, for example, by what today would be called the scope of negation. Bopp's (in fact erroneous) derivation of the tense-marking augment from the negative prefix had called forth a scathing attack by Lassen on the absurdity of assuming "I saw" to have been expressed as "I do not see". Today the issue would not even arise because of the phonological impossibility of the derivation. In Bopp's days, it provoked an interesting semantic discussion — probably one of the first treatments of scope phenomena in the Western linguistic tradition. In his comparative grammar (1870 edition. Vol. 2, pp.417-20) Bopp tried to defend his position by pointing out that one could view the present tense only, and not the verb, as negated, i.e., "I do not see *now* (but I saw earlier)". As a parallel he mentions that *not one* could mean either "no-one" (cf. English) or "several" (cf. Sanskrit *an-eka*). He then makes explicit that the ideal one-to-one correspondence between meaning and form is never reached. Reconstructions, he says, result not in full semantic representations, but only in representations of the most salient semantic properties: "Die Sprache drückt niemals etwas vollständig aus, sondern hebt überall nur das am meisten hervorstechende, oder ihr so erscheinende Merkmal hervor. Dieses Merkmal herauszufinden ist die Aufgabe der Etymologie. Ein Zahn-habender ist noch kein Elephant, ein Haar-habender noch kein Löwe, und dennoch nennt das Sanskrit den Elephanten *dantin*, den Lowen *keśin*. . . .somit dreht sich die Sprache in einem Kreise der Unvollständigkeiten herum, bezeichnet die Gegenstände unvollständig durch irgend eine Eigenschaft, die selber unvollständig angedeutet ist. Gewiss aber ist, dass die Nicht-Gegenwart die hervorstechendste Eigenschaft der Vergangenheit ist, und diese mit grösserem Rechte bezeichnet, als *Zahn-habender* den Elephanten." [Language never expresses anything completely, but everywhere brings out only the most salient feature, or what seems to her to be the most salient feature. It is the task of etymology to discover this feature. Just having teeth (tusks) doesn't make you an elephant, just having hair (a mane) doesn't make you a lion, and yet Sanskrit calls the elephant *dantin*, the lion *keśin*. . . .thus language turns in a circle of imperfections, denoting objects incompletely through some property which is itself incompletely expressed. But certainly non-presentness is the most conspicuous property of the past, and denotes it with greater justice than "tusk-carrier" denotes the elephant.] It is interesting to note that the Sanskrit animal names are also used by Humboldt in his discussion of sense and reference. The whole passage of Bopp is a nice illustration of the pitfalls of homemade semantics.

3. Benfey (1837), quoted from the reprint in Benfey (1890).

4. This restriction on pronounceable roots perhaps accounts for other peculiarities of Pāṇini's phonology, such as his relatively inelegant treatment of the Grassmann's Law phenomena.

REFERENCES

Ascoli, Graziadio Isaia. 1877. "Squarci d'une lettera concernente le ricostruzioni paleontologiche della parola". Studi Critici II, 1-29.

Benfey, Theodor. 1837. Review of Pott (1833). Ergänzungsblätter zur (Halleschen) allgemeinen Literatur-Zeitung, Dec. 1837, No. 114-7, Col. 905. Reprinted in Benfey (1890).

_____. 1890. Kleinere Schriften, ed. A. Bezzenberger. Berlin.

Bloomfield, Leonard. 1933. Language. New York, Holt.

Bopp, Franz. 1816. Über das Conjugationssytem der Sanskritsprache. Frankfurt am Main.

Chomsky, Noam. 1964. Current issues in linguistic theory. (Janua linguarum, 38). The Hague, Mouton.

Curtius, Georg. 1871. "Zur Erklärung der Personalendungen". Studien zur griechischen und lateinischen Grammatik 4.211-233.

_____. 1877. Das griechische Verbum. 2nd ed. Leipzig.

De Saussure, Ferdinand. 1915. Cours de linguistique générale. Paris.

Dinneen, Francis P. 1967. An introduction to general linguistics. New York.

Hockett, Charles F. 1965. "Sound change". Language 41:185-204.

Jakobson, Roman. 1965. L'importanza di Kruszewski per lo sviluppo della linguistica generale. Ricerche Slavistiche 13:3-23.

Katz, Jerrold, and Paul Postal. 1964. An integrated theory of linguistic description. Cambridge, Mass.

Kruszewski, Mikołaj. 1881. Über die Lautabwechslung. Kazan.

Kuhn, Thomas S. 1962. The structure of scientific revolutions. Chicago, University of Chicago Press.

Müller, Friedrich. 1860/70. "Zur Suffixlehre des indogermanischen Verbums". Sitzungsberichte der kaiserlichen Akademie der Wissenschaften, Philosophisch-historische Classe, 34.8-16 and 66.193-212.

Pott, August Friedrich. 1833. Etymologische Forschungen auf dem Gebiete der indo-germanischen Sprachen. Lemgo.

_____. 1870. "Die Umstellung des Hauches". KZ 19.16-41.

Scherer, Wilhelm. 1868. Zur Geschichte der deutschen Sprache. Berlin.

Verburg, Pieter A. 1950. The background to the linguistic conceptions of Franz Bopp. Lingua 2:438-468.

Westphal, Rudolf. 1869. Philosophisch-historische grammatik der deutschen Sprache. Jena.

13. Fallacies in the History of Linguistics: Notes on the Appraisal of the Nineteenth Century

Henry M. Hoenigswald

We may well agree that the nineteenth century is greatly overstressed. Yet for many reasons we cannot get away from it. Our extreme working dependence on nineteenth-century accomplishment is one of these reasons. There is another one, more germane to the present context: if it is true that the nineteenth century has become our central myth, what greater need for historiographers than to concentrate on its understanding. An obsession with one's past as one has come (or been told) to see it is not history; if linguistics is to rewrite its own history, it needs to master its obsessions; and the only way to do so is to face them, not to turn away from them.

For the moment, therefore, let us become historians once removed and examine the story of the great *fable convenue*. For one thing, it had not changed much for a long time. What our students learned—could learn—about their intellectual antecedents came, more often than not, from Pedersen's *Linguistic Science in the Nineteenth Century* (1931).[1] But Pedersen did not create our mythology; he elaborated and perpetuated it. His view is not fundamentally different from Thomsen's (1902), nor Thomsen's from Delbrück's (1880); and quite possibly we must go back to Benfey (1869) or beyond to find something significantly different. This may be disheartening, but it is also interesting; merely to put it down to laziness or to lack of historical sense would be to miss the point. We have here a true tradition, marked by the pathos which reflects a deeply exciting period (the early eighteen hundreds) as it was seen and relived not by historians but through the eyes and hearts of those close enough to feel that they had a part in it. One almost has to go to sectarian surroundings to appreciate the process; the "history" here is more *pro domo* than real history, though it is something for historians to know about and beware. We should not have too much difficulty empathizing. Those who spent their formative years under the influence of structuralism in Europe or America have on occasion gone through similar motions, with similar results. What we find in the connecting text of Joos' *Readings* (1957) or in the *Cahiers Ferdinand de*

Saussure, for instance, is surely not all historiography, although writers (experienced) and readers (often quite young) may be pardoned for taking it as such. Reminiscing, fighting old battles over again, recapturing the atmosphere in which one's earlier work was done (precisely in necessary ignorance of what it might one day mean in retrospect)—all these amount to something rather different. That it is not primary source material either is a point which eager interviewers making the rounds with their tape recorders should of course also bear in mind. It lies between the two, and it should be recognized as being essentially (though not always directly) autobiographical in nature. The genre is, of course, known to be delicate: aside from having incomparable informative value it is also suspect. And as for apostolic continuity within the nineteenth-century tradition let us only remember that Delbrück was a youth when Franz Bopp died in 1867, and that both were contemporaries of August Friedrich Pott.

·   The heroic age came to see itself as possessing two outstanding features in particular: its onset, it seemed, had been relatively sharp and its course relatively linear. Shortly after 1800 there supposedly occurred a break with the past and a great flowering of new activity, although there had been precursors. These were to be judged in the light of later events. Those later events, it was felt, consisted largely in the hammering out of established truth as it emerged at the end of the period. Such linearity, to be sure, is quite an oversimplification of the epigoni, as a direct study of the violent and programmatic polemicizing of the seventies shows more clearly. But, continuity is the keynote of the accepted retrospect. George Bolling, a man with a style and a fine sense of history, spoke of linguistics since Waterloo thereby drawing the obvious parallel with another accepted picture, namely that of general European history, and at the same time calling attention to certain specific factors in the background against which the first steps were taken: the function of the Napoleonic system in providing a center in Paris, where continental scholars learned oriental languages, the temporary decline of the English universities, the role of Wilhelm von Humboldt (both before but also after his official retirement in 1819) in the staffing of the Prussian universities. The main reason, however, why the start of the century will remain in the record as one of the great turning points in the study of language is that it was so regarded by the men who remembered it, directly or indirectly. Ever since its recognition in professional folk memory, the dividing line between mere Forerunners on the one hand and the Founding Fathers on the other has lain there.

Yet it is a fact that Forerunners are easy to find even if we limit ourselves to the specific interests most assiduously cultivated by the Founding Fathers. In the sixteenth century Sassetti knew Sanskrit and "compared" it with European languages.[2] A little later, the younger Scaliger set up his eleven matrices linguae for Europe, complete with descendants.[3] The following centuries abounded with activity directed toward the collection of information and its interpretation in terms of ancestry and descent. The eighteenth century, with increased wealth and a new conception of government, saw almost hectic action along those lines; it is sufficient to mention the Harmonies, Leibniz, the efforts made under the tsars which culminated in Pallas' Vocabularies, and the amazing Finno-Ugric work of Strahlenberg, Sajnovics, and Gyarmathi.

Hans Arens has put us in his debt by reprinting the review which C. J. Kraus, professor of history and political economy at Königsberg, devoted in 1787 to Pallas' collection (1955: 59-61). No better document can be imagined to illustrate what kind of notions prevailed at that time among scholars who were to some extent involved (it seems that Kraus had participated in what we would call field work), but who were by no means in the forefront. As we read his lucid essay, two matters strike us in particular. One is the strength of his anti-speculative feeling and his approval of the trend toward data and inductive study. When he insists in his artless style that "correctness is indispensable" because "no amount of reasoning will correct such error as has been allowed to intrude", it is not so much what he says as the urgency with which he says it and with which he pleads for more collective efforts on the imperial Russian model. It is this feeling which contributed to making the so-called reception of Sanskrit in continental Europe a reality. It was among scholars with Kraus' outlook (some, of course, much more expert than he) that the Halheds, Colebrookes, and Jones found the resonance which their English fellow countrymen did not at first provide.

The other interesting motif in Kraus is that of the "twofold purpose of language comparison". Comparison is in part philosophical and has, to put it anachronistically, both universalistic and Whorfian overtones; it teaches us both how man thinks and what different modes of thought there are. But comparison is also aimed at history. A classification of languages into groups (by "resemblance", it is implied) permits inferences with regard to ethnic origins, migrations, and prehistory in general. Not that these remarks are original; the very words with which Kraus puts them forward recall many earlier formulations, Leibniz' among them. But they make us realize how the relation between history and language was seen. Language classification (through something called comparison—one wishes for a thorough study of this notion in the history of science) is a key to the past, and suggestions are made or implied on how to achieve specific inferences. But nothing is said or implied concerning the ways in which time acts upon language, about the processes of change and replacement which in the later view create the conditions for "comparison" in the first place. Here we begin to touch an important aspect of the nineteenth century—an aspect under which it loses, not perhaps its essential unity, but certainly the sharpness of its onset.

If Kraus is mainly a bystander, Sir William Jones is of course seen as the Forerunner par excellence. His merits in Indian studies were so great as to command respect for his pronouncements on any subject. So it went with his famous paragraph of 1786 on the later so-called Indo-European languages. On an earlier occasion (1963) I have tried to call attention to its two aspects: one real and the other deceptive. It is the former that shows the latter for what it is. What came to be misunderstood were the expressions "a stronger affinity. . . than could have been produced by accident", and "some common source [i.e., source language] which perhaps no longer exists." By the end of the century these sounded like groping, intuitive anticipations of a procedure to which Greek, Latin, and Sanskrit may be subjected with the result that the reconstructed ancestor is found to be unlike each. This, to be sure, is the sense in which Antoine Meillet reconstructed, and in which we reconstruct. How far any of it was from Jones' mind can be seen from his own words: "The *Sanscrit* language. . . is of a wonderful structure; more perfect [read, naturally, 'even more perfect'] than the *Greek*, [even] more copious than the *Latin*." A hundred years earlier, Daniel Morhof had said: "It is most credible that the First Language was not one of the languages now known (which owe most to art), but rather some language other than they (Borst 19: 1465). George Metcalf has even now assembled other voices from the intervening years (see his chapter in this volume). And we also find Humboldt—not a Forerunner but a Founding Father—still writing in 1822: "Sanskrit is. . . among the oldest and first to possess a true edifice of grammatical forms, and that with such excellence and organic perfection that little has been added later on in this respect. . . . But it is Greek which has undoubtedly attained the highest perfection of structure."[4]

The tenor in all of this is too uniform for us to ignore its implication for Jones. Sanskrit, Greek, and Latin "owe most to art"; none of them can be a "First Language" (to use Morhof's words). Therefore (to switch to Jones) their "common source. . . perhaps no longer exists". There is no suggestion of a procedure for the recovery of that source, which is not to say that Jones did not have a picture of what kind of language it was. Still less would it be fair to think that his interest in the whole matter was perfunctory. Only a few pages earlier he expresses his belief that "Pythagoras and Plato derived their sublime theories from the same fountain with the sages of India", that is, as Edgerton understands it, that "Greek and Hindu philosophy, in part, were genetically related, not because either borrowed from the other, or both from any. . . third source, but by descent from a common source which he doubtless thought 'no longer exists' in records". Certainly Jones' thoughts

were "oriented in that direction" (Edgerton 1966 [1946] esp. 5-6). We might
even permit ourselves the fantasy that had he lived to see the day he would
have acclaimed the later uniformitarian, workaday "comparative" method of
reconstruction as some surprising fulfilment of promises made in a very
different vein. But surely a fresh glance at the "sages of India" and of Greece
would by then have shown how much the times had changed.

Along with many others before and after him Sir William may be said,
perhaps, to have divined some of the *results* of later comparative linguistics,
but he did not, and could not, differ from others (e.g., from Coeurdoux, as
has been said) by being the first to have divined its special mode of
reasoning (Edgerton 1966 [1946]: 16-18). To credit him with the "first of
the four really significant 'breakthroughs' in the modern development of
linguistics" is to do him an injustice, for his distinction lay in other fields and
in other kinds of discovery.[5] It also calls forth a caution against looking for
the 'real breakthroughs' in overt statement rather than in day-to-day work,
in preachment instead of practice. In any event it is worth noting that there
was no immediate, enthusiastic follow-up, as of something new and
revolutionary, despite the fact that Jones was widely known.

We have mentioned Humboldt's work of 1822. His treatise on the
Verschiedenheiten des menschlichen Sprachbaues of 1827-29 is more
discursive, and very explicit on matters of comparison and descent. The
author has at heart the investigation of the *Entstehungsgründe neuer
Sprachen in den Schicksalen der Völker* of which there are three: lapse of
time, migration, and mixture, to which a fourth (which does not occur alone)
must be added: the transformation of political and moral conditions such as
to alter national identity. The passages which follow are unusually interesting
because they are, for Humboldt, unusually factual. First Humboldt deals with
the interpretation of directly attested, observable changes; what he infers
from them are not pre-historic language phenomena (that is, more changes)
but the extra-linguistic causes, in terms of the types listed, behind the
changes. Order is created with the help of typological and universalistic
criteria (e.g., "A. W. Schlegel is right that languages... have a natural
propensity to become analytic. This, however, is nothing but the gradual
diminution of the form-preserving feeling in language") (Humboldt 1963:
3. 336-367, esp. 352). Then come, in bold relief, four generalizations on the
role of words, grammatical elements (like affixes), and grammatical type in
the recovery of the "different possibilities of historical connection among
languages". If there is a breakthrough, it is here, where Humboldt deals
elegantly and profoundly with the relationship between genealogical and
typological classification. Yet his specific preconceptions do not seem to be
radically different from those held by men like Kraus and, we repeat, Jones.

With Rasmus Rask we have been in a better position since the hold of official history was broken by Hjelmslev, Diderichsen, and lately by Percival who has shown, among other things, how much damage posterity's preoccupation with questions of priority can, and in Rask's case, did do.[6] The question is certainly not who was the first to formulate the Germanic consonant shift, when it is clear that Grimm and Rask held rather different views on what they were doing. If Percival is right in ascribing to Rask a "conviction that linguistic change was not a gradual process but some kind of radical reshuffling of structure taking place over a certain restricted period of time" (this volume, p. 311), this may indeed set his positive practice apart from that of Grimm—though not from Grimm's professed theory with its "Niedersetzungen" of the German language. In any event Rask is no closer than Jones was to the idea of an algorithm for reconstruction.

It is quite true that no such claim is generally made. On the whole the implication is that the idea of reconstruction by "comparison" in the later sense remained dormant until the neogrammarians took it up. The truth seems to be, however, that not only was there nothing *to* take up; the development of the comparative method as it became known later was itself a more tortuous affair than the protagonists knew. No doubt Pott plays a very important role in its early phases, although the relation among the various ideas that went into his Etymologies is surely one of the least well-known subjects in the history of linguistics. As a rough guide it is probably characteristic that Pott felt a special affinity with Humboldt and also with Grimm. He praises Grimm for his "historical exposition of the sound changes in the Germanic languages [which] has more value than many a philosophical grammar full of one-sided and futile abstractions" (Delbrück 1880: 77). Pott was 27 years old when Humboldt, in turn, wrote of Grimm as a "man who will always rest his assertions on a full and accurate knowledge of the historical" (Humboldt 1963: 3. 330). As so often, what is important are not the things which are said severally but the associations which they form and the emphasis which they receive. Pott credits Grimm with the restoration of "letters" to their rightful place, and he does so in a concrete, operational context. Thus he places himself along with Grimm in a somewhat special, anti-philosophical, a-posteriori tradition.

Until more is known we shall have to say that it is in the sixties, and with August Schleicher, that the great change occurred. I have attempted elsewhere to unravel some of the elements in this story (Hoenigswald 1963). There are several lessons to be learned from it. Most important, it is a prize example of the way in which reality and cant diverge. Schleicher thought much about the family tree as a concept with which to represent language relationship—a preoccupation which made his memory both famous and notorious. As a device to depict ancestry and descent among languages, the tree has itself the most distinguished ancestry imaginable. It is sufficient to recall the Tower of Babel and the theology of dispersal connected with it; and also the habit of Greek historians to use the similarity or intelligibility of speech to prove prehistoric migration and ethnic origins—a natural idea in a surrounding where colonial settlement had often and typically led to successive bifurcations of communities. The tree was a familiar notion to Jones and his contemporaries, who were, however, split on the question of uniqueness. Sir William's reference to the "stronger affinity [among the Indo-European languages] than could have been produced by accident" is to be taken as an option in favor of polygenesis as against one single lingua Adamica; it was most certainly not a premonition of an explicit discovery procedure that was not to be formulated until about eighty years later. When the time for this formulation came, the old metaphor served as a useful, perhaps even as a heuristically crucial vehicle. But when Schleicher thought that the new substance which he had provided for it was Darwinistic in nature, he was equally mistaken.[7] There was, perhaps, a better justification.

We must remember that Schleicher had two preoccupations among others, one with the tree and another with phonology, an area which had moved more and more to the foreground thanks to the exertions of Pott and others.[8] What these scholars had begun to see was a special property of certain kinds of sound change: unlike other alterations that can affect language, phonological mergers are ipso facto recognizable as innovations. This becomes clearest in matching two languages. If two contrasting stretches in one language are answered, in a related language, by two identical stretches the second language is seen to have innovated.[9] If, of two languages, one always innovates and the other never does, the first is the descendant of the second. This is the core of our present-day understanding of the "comparative" method. It also explains the obstinate (and frequently decried) predilection of comparative work for phonological data.

It is probable that Schleicher's early training conditioned him in the direction of seeing and cultivating the connection between sound change and the determination of descent. He was a classicist by training and had gone through the school of Friedrich Ritschl. This meant schooling in "the method"—the famous "via ac ratio" of textual criticism and archetype reconstruction governed by a set of formal rules. Principal among these is the doctrine of the shared error which serves as a criterion for the setting-up of subfamilies in a manuscript tradition. The subfamilies so recognized form a stemma, or tree. Its branches represent the origin, by copying, of manuscript from manuscript source (either extant or inferred, complete with all its readings, by the very act of reconstruction). In this way, they symbolize events in time.

So far as I know, Schleicher never acknowledged the analog. Probably he thought of his classicist past and later self-styled quasi-Darwinistic outlook as unconnected (and of the continuing personal ties to his former teacher as irrelevant). Whether he knew it or not, however, it seems certain that he acted on the logical parallel between a language and a text, between linguistic innovation and textual error.

We may assume that his personal history was not altogether untypical. Similar experiences may well have played a role in the research careers of others, no doubt with individual variations that would be worth going into. In no case may we expect them to lie very near the surface, for the real change in the concept of reconstruction had taken place some time before explicit theorizing caught up with it. The great neogrammarian debate, when it came, was only a somewhat turbid expression of the upheaval which had already occurred, and it is certainly not accurate to attribute the very real character of that upheaval to some kind of disciplined, deductive application of the new code embodying the exceptionlessness of sound laws and the alleged antagonism of sound law and "analogy" (let alone the further interpretation in terms of mechanistics vs. psychology to which this antagonism was subjected). Leonard Bloomfield was uniquely successful in reformulating the neogrammarian position and in rescuing it from its own misapprehensions, but it is difficult to see just what he meant with his insistence that A. Leskien's exceptionless nature of sound laws, not being a finding, is a postulate. Is it not rather a tautology with which to recognize the circumstance that some replacements from stage to stage ("changes") can be stated in terms of sound ("are regular") without reference to morph boundaries, and hence deserve a label of their own ("sound law")? That this raises a further question as to the typical settings in which such changes take place is another matter and belongs in a context which was not at the center of the discussion just then, although it proved difficult to kill in the long run. As is well known, some of the new discoveries were made by men who did not recognize Leskien's dogma but who nevertheless implicitly held the notion of reconstruction which was obliquely involved in that dogma. It is interesting to illustrate this with Verner's case. As he describes (in informal reminiscing, not in polished writing!) the experience of finding the famous principle which bears his name, he makes it beautifully clear that he was struck in an almost graphic way (on the printed pages of Bopp's Grammar, of all things) by the correlation between the Germanic "exception" and the Sanskrit accent. Very properly he checked whether Bopp's accents were right, and found that they were. Phonetic considerations seem to have had nothing to do with it, and even the examples of *grammatischer Wechsel* which quite rightly loom so large in the published article were secondary so far as the process of discovery was concerned. Yet as Jespersen ([1966]: 539, 543) reports this extraordinarily revealing bit of information—so neat a textbook case as to be almost unbelievable—he tells us, surely from good knowledge, that Verner "never accepted the [neogrammarian] doctrine in its most pointed form".

The operational, even procedural, meaning with which the ancient tree concept was now endowed carried certain corollaries. These were recognized in various, not always clearly correlated ways. Reconstruction had become uniformitarian in the sense that the ancestor was no longer expected to be typologically different just by virtue of being an ancestor; whether or not a reconstruction showed a given ancestor to differ in type from its descendants (insofar as it could show that, the phonemic structure of the vocabulary being the principal area accessible to the new reconstruction) had become a question of fact. This created a curious paradox: the starred forms had more historical reality of a positive and sometimes even verifiable kind (as when they turned up in newly discovered texts or in newly described dialects) but in one sense they made an unhistorical object out of human speech: the innovations that make up a family tree have a chronology, but they are only manifestations of the surface variability of language which is itself an unchanging characteristic.[10]

Another aspect of the new work was that subclassification and reconstruction had become one and the same problem—just as the establishment of "the text" (i.e., of the complete archetype) and the establishment of the stemma are ideally one and the same thing. Hence Schleicher's use of starred forms with the implicit requirement of total accountability; hence his much ridiculed attempt at setting down a complete proto-Indo-European fable which is in fact a most consistent effort to carry the principle to its conclusion.

The dependence of the new approach on the ability to distinguish innovations (of a sort) from retentions (of a sort) caused difficulties as it rose to the level of consciousness. Delbrück and Brugmann thought the matter important enough to state, mainly, one feels, because it appeared necessary to dispel the popular notion to the effect that closer relationship within a family is recognized by greater "similarity" in some presumably statistical sense.[11] Under the tree model, however, subclassification is a yes-or-no affair; if the model applies at all (if there is "clear-cut cleavage"), and if A and B share, in a non-accidental way, an innovation to the exclusion of C, B cannot share an innovation with C to the exclusion of A—subgroups cannot intersect. Thus "similarity", which is difficult to measure, does not need to be measured; besides, when similarity expresses a common retention it is of no importance under the procedure.

The kind of innovation meant here is not necessarily a "new" feature by the standards of common sense or by those of typology. In fact, uncompensated phonemic mergers (say, the loss of contrast between the two kinds of so-called voiced stops, plain and aspirated, in certain Indo-European descendants) spell reduction, not increase. A further source of confusion is the circumstance (already discussed) that, except in phonology, some outside knowledge, going beyond what "comparative" matching can by itself establish, is often required to discriminate between retention and replacement (see Hoenigswald 1966, esp. 9).

The lessons are many. "Talking about the talking about talking" (to elaborate on Goethe's rebuke) is a delicate business. Some of the pitfalls are terminological, but others are not so easily dismissed. The biblical notion of dispersal and the Greek notion of colonization as the source of language differences have this in common that they are both amenable to the model of the "rooted tree" which is, after all, only one possible metaphor among others if we remember that history has also been represented as springs and tributaries feeding a mighty river, as a kaleidoscopic dissociation and reassociation of particles, as a succession of cycles, and what not. But to say that the table of descent had firmly established itself in the western world as the concept to apply to language is not to attribute unchangeability to it. On the contrary: the content of the tree schema kept changing with the change of philosophies to an extent which is altogether obscured by the persistence of the label. For instance, Herder's eighteenth century thinking had altered matters profoundly by introducing the element of graduality and organic growth not originally present either in the Old Testament nor among the Greeks. And, as we have seen, as the much-attacked and much-defended technical concept of classical comparative linguistics, the family tree is another matter again.

A further subject on which there would be much to say is the function of biography and autobiography in the historiography of linguistics. It is clear that serious intellectual biography is far too little cultivated as a genre of research. Sebeok's *Portraits of Linguists* (1966), despite their inevitable special slant, have at least whetted our appetite. Self-description as a genre and as a source is still more challenging. That even great figures in scholarship can be sadly misleading about the nature of their own contribution is a commonplace. And yet, how fortunate would we call ourselves if we had at our disposal more precious flashes of recollection like Verner's, quoted earlier.

NOTES

1. In the paperback reprint of 1962. Meanwhile we also have Robins 1967, 1968, and Mounin 1967.

2. De Gubernatis 1867, referred to by Tagliavini 1963: 51.

3. See the passage translated from *Diatriba de Europaeorum linguis* in Arens 1955: 59-61.

4. Translated from the treatise "Über das Entstehen der grammatischen Formen", in Humboldt 1963, vol. 3, 63. —M. Beaulieu, in an unpublished study, calls attention to the fact that Alexander Hamilton (on whom now see Rocher 1968), in a context which is generally Jonesian, said that a "language so refined as the Sanskrit, must have undergone many changes in advancing from rudeness to a state of such metaphysical perfection" (*The Edinburgh Review* 13.378).

5. Robins, 1967, 1968: 134, where the reference is evidently to Hockett 1965: 185.

6. Hjelmslev 1950-51, cited from Sebeok 1966: 179-195; Diderichsen 1960; Percival, this volume.

7. Maher 1966 makes it abundantly clear that Schleicher, so far from being "influenced" by Darwin, only hailed him as a kindred spirit after he had discovered him and long after he had done his own work; see my remarks (1963: 6). Schleicher apparently knew a good deal about pre-Darwinian evolutionism, and Maher shows how it is this knowledge that is reflected in his theoretical pronouncements. The roots of his procedural approach to positive work are, however, more subtly hidden. [See now E.F.K. Koerner, in *Anthropological Linguistics* 1972: 255-280.]

8. The mutual animosity (Maher 1966, n.7) between Pott and Schleicher is in part a matter of age (Pott was 19 years older), in the relevant sense that Pott was already trained academically when the new textual criticism became the vogue.

9. E.g., Latin (*cr*)*ēd*(*it*) "he believes": Italian (*cr*)*ed*(*e*), and Latin (*v*)*id*(*et*) "he sees": Italian (*v*)*ed*(*e*).

10. Maher 1966: 5 explains how Schleicher dealt with this paradox by distinguishing between language *evolution* and language *history*.

11. Chrétien 1963 treats some of the history of this notion.

REFERENCES

Arens, Hans. 1955. Sprachwissenschaft. Der Gang ihrer Entwicklung von der Antike bis zur Gegenwart. Munich and Freiburg, Alber [2d ed., 1969].

Benfey, Theodor. 1869. Geschichte der Sprachwissenschaft und Orientalischen Philologie in Deutschland seit dem Anfange des 19. Jahrhunderts mit einem Rückblick auf die früheren Zeiten. (Geschichte der Wissenschaften in Deutschland, herausgegeben durch die Historische Commission bei der Königlichen Academie der Wissenschaften, no.8). Munich, Cotta'sche Buchhandlung.

Borst, Arno. 1957-63. Der Turmbau von Babel. Stuttgart, Hiersemann.

Chrétien, C. D. 1963. Shared innovation and subgrouping. International Journal of American Linguistics 29: 66-68.

De Gubernatis, A. 1867. Memorie intorno ai viaggiatori italiani nelle Indie Orientali. Florence.

Delbrück, B. 1880. Einleitung in das Studium der indogermanischen Sprachen. 1st ed. Leipzig.

Diderichsen, Paul. 1960. Rasmus Rask og den grammatiske tradition. (Hist. Filos. Medd. Dan. Vid. Selsk. 38, no.2). Copenhagen.

Edgerton, Franklin. 1946. Sir William Jones. Journal of the American Oriental Society 66: 230-239. Cited from Sebeok 1966, esp. p.506.

Hjelmslev, Louis. 1950-51. Commentaires sur la vie et l'oeuvre de Rasmus Rask. Conférences de l'Institut de Linguistique de l'Université de Paris 10: 143-157. Cited from Sebeok 1966: 179-195.

Hockett, C. F. 1965. Sound change. Language 41: 185-204.

Hoenigswald, Henry M. 1963. On the history of the comparative method. Anthropological Linguistics 5(1): 1-11.

_____. 1966. Criteria for the subgrouping of languages. Ancient Indo-European dialects, ed. by H. Birnbaum and J. Puhvel, 1-12. Berkeley and Los Angeles, University of California Press.

Humboldt, Wilhelm von. 1960, 1961, 1963, 1964. Werke in fünf Bänden. [Ed. by Andreas Flitner and Klaus Giel.] Darmstadt, Wissenschaftliche Buchgesellschaft.

Jespersen, Otto. n. d. Karl Verner. Selected writings, pp. 805-816. London, Allen and Unwin. Cited from Sebeok 1966: 539,543.

Joos, Martin (ed.). 1957. Readings in linguistics. Washington, D. C., American Council of Learned Societies.

Maher, T. P. 1966. More on the history of the comparative method. Anthropological Linguistics 8(3): 1-12.

Mounin, Georges. 1967. Histoire de la linguistique des origines au XXe siècle. Paris, Presses Universitaires de France.

Pedersen, Holger. 1931. Linguistic science in the nineteenth century. Translated from the Danish by J. Spargo. Cambridge, Harvard University Press. [Reprinted as The discovery of language. Bloomington, Indiana University Press, 1962.]

Robins, R. H. 1967, 1968. A short history of linguistics. London, Longmans; Bloomington, Indiana University Press.

Rocher, Rosane. 1968. Alexander Hamilton (1762-1824). New Haven, American Oriental Society.

Sebeok, Thomas A. (ed.). 1966. Portraits of linguists. Two volumes. Bloomington, Indiana University Press.

Tagliavini, Carlo. 1963. Panorama di storia della linguistica. Bologna.

Thomsen, Vilhelm L. P. 1902. Sprogvidenskabens historie. Copenhagen. [Translated as Geschichte der Sprachwissenschaft bis zum Ausgang des 19 Jahrhunderts; Kurzgefasste Darstellung der Hauptpunkte, Halle, Niemeyer, 1927; Historia de la lingüística, Barcelona, Madrid, Rio de Janeiro, Editorial Labor, 1945.]

IV : THE SLOW GROWTH OF GRAMMATICAL ADEQUACY

14. Sixteenth and Seventeenth Century Grammars

John Howland Rowe

The first printed grammar of a natural language other than Latin and ancient Greek was the Spanish one by Elio Antonio de Lebrija, published in 1492.[1] In the course of the sixteenth century grammars of 21 more languages were printed, and in the seventeenth century at least an additional 41. Thus, by 1700, grammars had been printed for not less than 63 languages. Yet each language was studied individually; there were no comparative studies of grammar involving more than two or three languages. Such comparative study as there was usually involved Latin and ancient Greek, or Latin and Hebrew. The earliest comparative study of a more general nature which has come to my attention is a work by Filippo Salvadore Gilii on the languages of America, published in 1782.[2] By this time grammars of at least 96 languages other than Latin and ancient Greek had been published, including grammars of 31 American languages. Gilii's treatment of American grammars is not based on this earlier literature, however, but partly on materials recorded by himself and partly on grammatical sketches furnished to him by other former missionaries.

There is obviously a historical problem here. How did it happen that so many languages were studied individually for so long, and so extensive a literature accumulated, without any comparative study of natural grammars being undertaken? The lack of comparative studies of grammar is the more remarkable, as there was some scholarly interest in linguistic diversity, reflected in the collections of texts and vocabularies published by Gesner and Megiser.[3] Brerewood made some shrewd observations on linguistic change, but again was primarily concerned with vocabulary.[4] The period under consideration was one of substantial activity in the collection and comparison of plants and animals and even some attempts to classify the varieties of human customs and institutions, the outstanding names in the last field being those of José de Acosta and Marc Lescarbot.[5]

To illustrate the dimensions of the problem, I have made a tabulation of the languages for which grammars were printed between 1492 and 1700.

The languages are listed in the order of their first printed grammars, and only the first printed grammar is listed for each language (see Appendix).

In deciding what constitutes a grammar, I have excluded works which deal with one aspect of grammar only, such as guides to pronunciation, and lesson books which do not give grammatical rules. The problem of determining which works are grammars in the sense intended is complicated by the fact that I have actually examined very few of the works listed. On the basis of some experience with old grammars, however, I have assumed that if one of the Latin words *ars, institutiones,* or *grammatica,* or an equivalent in another language, occurs in the title the work is a grammar. I have also been guided by statements about some of the works listed which appear in nineteenth and twentieth century works of scholarship.

A number of observations may be made on the tabulation:

(1) The first grammars of spoken American and Asiatic languages were not significantly later than the first grammars of spoken European languages. For example, grammars of four American languages were published before there were any printed grammars of Dutch or English.

(2) French grammar was first written by Englishmen, sixty years and more before anyone wrote an English grammar. The first French grammar by a Frenchman was a work in Latin by Jacques Dubois, published in 1531, which does not appear in the table because it was preceded by a grammar in English. A French grammar in French by Louis Meigret appeared in 1550.[6]

(3) The only languages in which the first grammar was written in the language being described were Spanish, Italian, Czech, Portuguese, Dutch, English, and Swedish — all European languages. A grammar of German in German was published by Johann Clay in 1578 and one of Danish in Danish by Peder Syv in 1685. With French, mentioned above, these items complete the list of langauges with monolingual grammars in the period under discussion.

(4) The languages most used for writing grammars of other languages were Latin (25), Spanish (21), and Portuguese (5). English was used in only two cases, and Dutch, Bielo-Russian, and French in one case each. Spanish was the language used to describe all American and Philippine languages, the only exceptions being two Brazilian languages described in Portuguese (Tupí and Carirí) and John Eliot's grammar of Massachusett in English (1666). Portuguese was used for languages in the areas where the Portuguese had colonies or commercial interests (Brazil, Angola, the Malabar coast of India, Japan); Latin was most commonly used for other European, Asiatic, and African languages.

(5) In terms of area, the spoken languages represented in the table group as follows: Europe 23, America 21, Asia 11, Africa 4. There are also 5 ancient languages represented. Only 2 of the American languages are from

North America north of Mexico (Timucua and Massachusett). It is curious that, in spite of the extensive missionary labors of the French Jesuits in Canada, no printed grammar resulting from this work appeared before 1700.[7]

The reader should bear in mind in using my table that it is probably neither complete nor accurate. I may have missed a number of languages that should have been included, and for some languages further research would probably turn up earlier grammars than the one I have listed as first. For example, there is an anonymous and undated grammar of Chibcha in the Bodleian Library which, on the basis of typographical evidence, may date to about 1603. The reliability of the entries naturally varies with the amount of research I have been able to devote to the language and the quality of the bibliographical tools available to me.

For many of the languages represented in the table there are other grammars besides the first one which were also published before 1700. For example, 8 grammars of Inca and 7 of Nahuatl were issued in the period under review. For English, French, German, and Italian the figures are undoubtedly higher. Some of the later grammars are, as might be expected, more complete and reflect the structure of the language better than the pioneer one; it would be interesting to follow the developments in some of these series of grammars, but such an endeavor falls outside the scope of the present paper. I have not even attempted a systematic listing of the later grammars.

Having examined the scope of the descriptive effort in sixteenth and seventeenth century grammatical work, we can turn now to consider the question posed at the beginning of this study. How did it happen that so many grammars were written for individual languages, but the gammars were not used for comparative study? There are several factors which influenced the situation.

In the first place, many of the early grammars were published in small editions and probably became unobtainable in a few years if they were not reprinted. Many of them are excessively rare today, in spite of the intensive book collecting of the last 150 years. For example, the first known grammar of English is the *Bref grammar for English* by William Bullokar, published in London in 1586. Only one copy of the original edition is known, and it is in the Bodleian Library. The British Museum does not have one. In a manuscript note in the author's hand which was added to the Bodleian copy, Bullokar explains that the *Bref grammar* is an abridgement of a more extensive work of his called *Grammar at large*, and the note clearly implies that the latter work had also been printed. No copy of the *Grammar at large* is known to exist (Plessow 1906: CXLVI-CXLVII; reproduction of the grammar, 331-385). The first Czech grammar went through five editions in 110 years; there is no copy of any of them in the British Museum, the

Bibliothèque Nationale in Paris, the Library of Congress, or the New York Public Library.[8] Many of the grammars of non-European languages are equally rare. Even today, with microfilming available, it would be a time consuming and costly task to assemble even a partial collection of early printed grammars for comparative purposes. It should also be remembered that libraries were uncatalogued in the sixteenth and seventeenth centuries, and there were few bibliographical guides. Probably no grammarian of the period before 1700 even knew of the existence of more than a few grammars of languages other than the language he worked on.

In the second place, the early grammars, with few exceptions, were written for pedagogical purposes rather than for scholarly use. The purpose of many of them was to teach one language to speakers of another, most commonly to teach missionaries the languages of the areas where they were assigned to work. In the case of European languages, a common motivation for grammar writing was to reform, purify, and standardize the literary dialect. In the sixteenth century in particular, many grammarians in England, France, and Italy had schemes for reforming the spelling of their languages and wrote grammars as part of their effort to win acceptance for their ideas on spelling reform. William Bullokar, the author of the first English grammar, was a dedicated spelling reformer.

In the third place, interest in comparison suffered from the fact that the methods of grammar writing then in effect obscured the structural diversity of the languages described. Non-European languages were studied primarily by missionaries whose aim was to "reduce" them, as the terminology of the time went, to the pattern of Latin grammar. Sometimes the procedure was made very explicit. For example, the author of the first Inca grammar, the Dominican Domingo de Santo Tomás, explained to his readers:

> Since this grammar is made for ecclesiastics who are familiar with the Latin language, it follows the grammar of Latin (Domingo de Santo Tomás 1560: [16]).

> This grammar is made and organized primarily for ecclesiastical persons who know Latin, so it is assumed that they know the definition and explanation of the eight parts of speech from the [Latin] grammar of Antonio de Nebrija [Lebrija] and the Latin language (Domingo de Santo Tomás 1560, f. 2v [p.20]).

This procedure was the more natural, as the only preparation most of the early grammar writers had for their work was the study of Latin, which, at the time, was the basis of education in both Protestant and Catholic countries.

The Latinizing tendency was very strong, but it should not be exaggerated. Lebrija, in his Spanish grammar of 1492, made an attempt to describe at least some features of the language in their own terms. Partial independence of the same sort is exhibited in the French grammars by Louis Meigret, published in 1550, and by Pierre de la Ramée (Ramus), published in 1562 (Kukenheim 1962: 22). John Wallis took a similarly independent approach to English grammar in 1653 (Lehnert 1936: 48; cf. Arens 1955: 68-70; Sugg 1964: 242-244). Domingo de Santo Tomás, in his deliberately Latinizing treatment of Inca, did not neglect to point out that there are certain peculiarities of the language which are not found in Latin or Spanish (1560, f. 36v [p. 87]). Ludovico Bertonio, the Italian Jesuit who wrote the first grammar of Aymará, claimed that he was following the Latin model in his treatment of morphology but departing from it in his handling of syntax (Bertonio 1879 (1603): 13).

In general, sixteenth and seventeenth century grammarians felt obliged to find correspondences to the parts of speech of Latin, the Latin declension of nouns, and the mood and tense system of traditional Latin grammar. A grammarian of the present day, trying to use the early works, generally finds that he can reinterpret the material presented in this Latin framework with some success, but he may be blocked by the very deficient treatment of phonology and by the fact that some forms and constructions alien to Latin are not given at all. For example, it is not possible to compile a complete table of the forms of Inca verbal nouns and adjectives from the information supplied by the sixteenth and seventeenth century grammarians, and this fact leaves open some questions regarding the rules governing the formation of these forms.

The factors we have been discussing certainly contributed to the lack of comparative grammar in the sixteenth and seventeenth centuries, but there was another one more important than any of them. The development of European thinking about grammar was in another direction. To understand what happened we need to review what may be considered the "main line" of European grammatical scholarship, the line of thought which prevailed in the schools.

Although modern scholarship has brought to light a few Medieval efforts in the description of spoken languages, grammar in the Middle Ages was almost exclusively Latin grammar (Robins 1951; Kukenheim 1962: 14-16; Bursill-Hall 1963). After about A.D. 1150 there developed a tradition of philosophical grammar, based on logic, which was particularly prominent at the University of Paris. Many contributors to this movement held that "there was *one* universal grammar dependent on the structure of reality and human reason" (Robins 1951: 77). The Renaissance, which was, as J. D.

Mackie says, "in essence a rebellion of the facts against the theories," broke with this scholastic tradition and in reaction encouraged the description of modern languages on the basis of usage (Mackie 1964: 118). The signs of independence of the Latin model which can be observed in some sixteenth and seventeenth century grammars reflect the Renaissance attitude toward language.

In the sixteenth century, however, a counter-Renaissance movement developed, represented in art by Mannerism and the Baroque style. In grammatical studies it is represented by a revival of the Medieval tradition of philosophical grammar, set off in 1540 by the publication of a Latin grammar, *De causis linguae latinae*, by the brilliant but contrary Italian-French scholar, Jules César de l'Escale (Scaliger). Scaliger accepted the Renaissance ideal of a pure Classical Latin but wedded it to the philosophical approach to grammar characteristic of the late Middle Ages; he wanted to make the structure of Latin conform to the principles of Aristotelian logic (García 1960: 23).

Scaliger's philosophical approach to Latin grammar was taken up in Spain by Francisco Sánchez de las Brozas (Sactius), whose *Minerva*, published in Latin in 1587, acknowledged its inspiration by using as a subtitle the title of Scaliger's earlier work. The *Minerva* had little influence in Spain, where a Latin grammar by Lebrija had been adopted as the only authorized text for use in the schools and held the field until the nineteenth century. In the rest of Europe, however, its influence was profound. This influence was reflected first of all in later works on Latin grammar; in Italy, for example, in the *Grammatica philosophica* of Gaspare Scioppio, published in 1628, and in France in the fifth edition of Charles Lancelot's *Nouvelle méthode pour apprendre facilement la langue latine*, 1654 (Trabalza 1963: 302; Lakoff 1966, 1969).

Since philosophical grammar was also supposed to be universal, it could be applied in theory to the study of other languages than Latin. The earliest example I have found of the application of philosophical grammar to a modern spoken language is an Italian one, the treatise *Della lingua toscana* by Benedetto Buonmattei, called "the prince of Italian grammarians," published in 1643. This work was directly inspired by the Latin grammars of Scaliger and Sánchez de las Brozas. More generally influential, because of the prestige of France in the age of Louis XIV, was the famous "Port Royal grammar" of French, the *Grammaire générale et raisonnée* by the grammarian Charles Lancelot and the philosopher Antoine Arnauld, published in 1660. Lakoff (1966, 1969) has properly criticized the supposition of Chomsky (1966) that the Port Royal grammar derived from Cartesian philosophy, emphasizing instead its dependence on Sánchez de las Brozas. There were subsequent editions of the Port Royal grammar in 1664, 1676, 1679, and in the eighteenth and early nineteenth centuries, a printing history which reflects the endurance of its influence.

A logical result of the preoccupation of European grammarians with philosophical and universal grammar was a neglect of the comparative study of natural languages in favor of a concern for the construction of artificial systems of communication. Natural languages were too diverse and contained too many irregularities to satisfy men who wanted to derive grammar from a single system of logic. R. H. Robins (1967: 113-116) has recently provided a summary of the seventeenth century efforts to construct artificial systems of communication, with special attention to John Wilkins' *Essay toward a real character and a philosophical language*, 1688.

The preoccupation of European grammarians with philosophical grammar remained dominant until late in the eighteenth century when Herder and others aroused a new interest in natural language which led to the development of a discipline of comparative linguistics. But that is another story.

NOTES

Acknowledgements and explanations. The topic of sixteenth and seventeenth century grammars was suggested by Dell H. Hymes, on the basis of my observation that the earliest grammars of non-European languages were not significantly later than the earliest ones of European languages. In my research on early grammars I have had the benefit of valuable suggestions and information from D. H. Hymes, Alan Dundes, George J. Metcalf, Edward H. Schafer, Dorothy Menzel, Luís Monguío, George Shkurkin, Eugene A. Hammel, H. Elizabeth Holtzman, André Simic, John J. Gumperz, and Patricia J. Lyon. The pressure of other obligations prevented me from consulting several other colleagues and friends regarding problems which arose in the research reported here.

A few works not specifically cited in the text or notes are added to the bibliography as sources of references to early grammars. I have not attempted to list all the books and articles on the history of grammar which have come to my attention.

Arens (1955: 48-49) gives a short list of sixteenth and seventeenth century grammars, citing them by language and year only, without names of authors and without bibliographical references. In this list he gives the date of the first Old Church Slavonic grammar as 1516 and says that a Basque grammar was published in 1587. I have been unable to locate references to works corresponding to either of these listings. Manuel de Larramendi, who published a Basque grammar in 1729, thought he was the first to solve what was considered an insoluble problem. Arens also lists a grammar of "Wallisisch" for 1567. Wallisisch should mean Valaisan, but it is possible that he means Welsh (properly Walisisch). I have not been able to find a grammar of either language for this date.

A preliminary version of this contribution was presented at the Newberry Library Conference on the History of Linguistics, Chicago, February 16-17, 1968. The present version was read at the Twelfth Annual Meeting of the Kroeber Anthropological Society, Berkeley, May 11, 1968.

1. On this work and its background, see Rowe 1965: 12-13 and references there cited. Further references are provided by García (1960: 25, note 19).

2. Gilii 1780-84, vol. III: 135-416. Nicolas Beauzée claimed to have consulted grammars of 17 languages, including 2 modern non-European ones (Chinese and Inca) for his *Grammaire générale* of 1767, but Arens (1955: 97, 99) says that Beauzée's analysis of grammar is actually based on French and Latin.

3. Gesner 1555; Megiser 1592, 1603. On Gesner, Sarton comments: "Gesner's activities were generally those of a naturalist dominated by humanistic traditions and habits. His *Mithridates* reveals a philologist inspired by the methods of natural history. Even as the naturalists were engaged in the enumeration, description, and differentiation of plants and animals, Gesner tried to enumerate and differentiate the languages used by men. He dealt with no less than 130 languages, quoting the *Pater noster* in twenty-two of them, anf provided a gypsy vocabulary. Gesner was interested not only in languages but also in dialects, and encouraged his friend Josua Mahler to investigate the German ones" (Sarton 1955: 111). Megiser appears in my table as the author of the first Turkish grammar.

4. Brerewood 1614. Brerewood's treatise is not as inclusive as the title suggests. Outside of Europe, he is mainly interested in the distribution of religions, and he makes no attempt to differentiate among "pagans." He does, however, use historical documentation to demonstrate linguistic change in a number of European languages.

5. On Acosta, see Rowe 1964: 8-9, 16-19. Lescarbot had travelled to Nova Scotia and neighboring areas and, inspired by Acosta, compared the native customs of the people he knew to those of other parts of the New World, particularly Florida and Brazil (Lescarbot 1609). For sixteenth and seventeenth work in natural history, a convenient reference is Sarton 1955: 52-132.

6. Kukenheim 1962: 21-22; cf. p.19: "C'est par conséquent en Angleterre, où le besoin s'en faisait sentir au moment du déclin de l'anglo-normand, qu'est née la grammaire française." There is a description and extract of Barclay's grammar, with emphasis on his treatment of pronunciation, in Ellis 1871: 804-814.

7. Cf. now Hanzeli (1969: 63) on the "surprising scarcity" of published materials, the little that was published being "too fragmentary to stimulate anyone. . .to use these materials for comparative or general linguistic studies." There were, however, "elaborate manuscript works. . .few of which ever got into print and even then not before the second half of the

nineteenth century." Indeed, "the bulk of the linguistic works of the French missionaries in New France is still awaiting publication" (102). An explanation is implied in the contrast drawn by Hanzeli between "writings destined for contemporaneous publication (mainly their *Relations*), and. . .grammars, lexicons, and various other linguistic manuscripts which they used in their mission houses for the recording, learning and teaching of these languages" (55). In general, Hanzeli's study of Algonquian and Iroquoian work confirms the conclusions reached in the present study, as to preparation in the study of Latin that obscured structural diversity (Ch. III, esp. p.43); the pedagogical purpose of the work (Ch. IV and p.101); the very strong but not wholly overriding influence of the Latinizing tendency (pp.65-66 on tension between "la Grammaire" and "l'Oeconomie", and pp.99, 101); and the role of philosophical, or general, grammar (p.101). [Note added by the editor at the author's request.]

8. Blahoslav 1857: XIII, note. The work in question, by Beneš Optat and others, was first published in 1533, with later editions in 1543 (2), 1588, and 1643.

BIBLIOGRAPHY

Arens, Hans
1955 Sprachwissenschaft; der Gang ihrer Entwicklung von der Antike bis zur Gegenwart. Orbis Academicus, Band I/6. Verlag Karl Alber, Freiburg/München.

Beauzée, Nicolas
1767 Grammaire générale; ou, exposition raisonnée des éléments nécessaires du langage pour servir de fondement à l'étude de toutes les langues. Paris. 2 vols.

Bertonio, Ludovico
1879 Arte de la lengua aymará. . . publicada de nuevo por Julio Platzmann. Edición facsimilaria. B. G. Teubner, Leipzig (reprint of his Arte y grammatica mvy copiosa de la lengva aymara, Luís Zannetti, Roma, 1603).

Blahoslav, Jan
1857 Jana Blahoslawa Grammatika Česká dokonana 1. 1571, do níž wložen text grammatiky B. Optata z Telče, Petra Gzella z Prahy a W. Philomathesa z Jindřichowa Hradce podle wydání Normberského 1543. Z rukopisu bibliotheky Theresianske we Wídni wydali. I. Hradel a J. Jiraček.

Brerewood, Edward
1614 Enquiries touching the diversity of languages and religions, through the chiefe parts of the world. John Bill, London.

Bursill-Hall, Geoffrey L.
1963 Mediaeval grammatical theories. The Canadian Journal of Linguistics/ La Revue Canadienne de Linguistique, vol. 9, no. 1, Fall, pp. 40-54. Toronto.

Chomsky, Noam
1966   Cartesian linguistics; a chapter in the history of rationalist thought.
       Studies in Language [1]. Harper & Row, Publishers, New York and
       London.
Domingo de Santo Tomás
1560   Grammatica, o arte de la lengua general de los indios de los reynos del
       Peru. Francisco Fernandez de Cordoua, Valladolid (Edición facsimilar:
       Ediciones del Instituto de Historia de la Facultad de Letras en el IV
       Centenario de la Universidad Nacional Mayor de San Marcos, I. Lima,
       1961).
Ellis, Alexander John
1871   On early English pronunciation with especial reference to Shakspere
       and Chaucer. . . . Part III, Illustrations of the pronunciation of the
       XIVth and XVIth centuries. Early English Text Society, Extra Series,
       XIV. London.
García, Constantino
1960   Contribución a la historia de los conceptos gramaticales; la aportación
       del Brocense. Revista de Filología Española, anejo LXXI. Consejo
       Superior de Investigaciones Científicas, Patronato "Menéndez y Pela-
       yo," Instituto "Miguel de Cervantes." Madrid.
Gesner, Konrad
1555   Mithridates; de differentiis linguarum, tum veterum, tum quae hodie
       apud diversas nationes in toto orbe terrarum in usu sunt, Conradi
       Gesneri. . . observationes. Froschoverus, Tuguri.
Gilii, Filippo Salvadore
1780-84 Saggio di storia americana, o sia storia naturale, civile, e sacra
       de regni, delle provincie spagnuole di Terra-ferma nell' America
       Meridionale. Luigi Parego erede Salvioni, Roma. 4 vols.
Hanzeli, Victor Egon
1969   Missionary linguistics in New France; a study of seventeenth- and
       eighteenth-century descriptions of American Indian languages. Janua
       Linguarum, series maior, 29. Mouton, The Hague-Paris.
Jellinek, Max Hermann
1913-14 Geschichte der neuhochdeutschen Grammatik von den Anfängen
       bis auf Adelung. Germanische Bibliothek herausgegeben von Wilhem
       Streitberg, zweite Abteilung, Untersuchungen und Texte, siebenter
       Band, 1-2. Carl Winter's Universitätsbuchhandlung, Heidelberg. 2 vols.
Kukenheim, Louis
1932   Contributions à l'histoire de la grammaire italienne, espagnole et
       française à l'époque de la Renaissance. N. V. Noord-Hollandsche
       Uitgovers-maatschappij, Amsterdam.
1951   Contributions à l'histoire de la grammaire grecque, latine et hébraique
       à l'époque de la Renaissance. E. J. Brill, Leiden.
1962   Esquisse historique de la linguistique française et de ses rapports avec
       la linguistique générale. Leidse Romanistische Reeks van de Rijks-
       universiteit te Leiden deel VIII. Leiden.
Lakoff, Robin
1966   Pre-Cartesian linguistics (abstract). Linguistic Society of America,

Forty-first Annual Meeting, December 28-30, 1966, New York, New York. Meeting handbook, pp. 43-44. New York.

1969 Review: Grammaire générale et raisonée, ou La grammaire du Port-Royal. . . . Edited by Herbert H. Brekle. 2 vols. . . . Stuttgart-Bad Cannstadt: Friedrich Fromann Verlag, 1966. . . . Language, vol. 45, no. 2, June, pp. 343-364. Baltimore.

Lescarbot, Marc
1609 Histoire de la Novvelle France, contenant les navigations, découvertes & habitations faites par les François ès Indes Occidentales & Nouvelle France. . . en quoy est comprise l'histoire morale, naturele & géographique de la dite province. Iean Milot, Paris.

Lehnert, Martin
1936 Die Grammatik des englischen Sprachmeisters John Wallis (1616-1703). Sprache und Kultur der germanischen und romanischen Völker. A. Anglistische Reihe, Band XXI. Verlag Priebatsch's Buchhandlung, Breslau.

Mackie, John Duncan
1964 A history of Scotland. Pelican Books A 67. Penguin Books, Baltimore.

Marsden, William
1827 Bibliotheca Marsdeniana philologica et orientalis. A catalogue of books and manuscripts collected with a view to the general comparison of languages and to the study of oriental literature. Printed by J. L. Cox, London.

Megiser, Hieronymus
1592 Specimen XL diversarum atque inter se differentium linguarum et dialectorum; videlicet oratio dominica totidem linguis expressa. Frankfurt.

1603 Thesaurus polyglottus, vel dictionarium multilingue ex quadringentis circiter tam veteris quam novi (vel potius antiquis incogniti) orbis nationum linguis, dialectis, idiomatibus et idiotismis constans. Sumptibus auctoris, Francofurti ad Moenum.

Muñoz Manzano, Cipriano, Conde de la Viñaza
1892 Bibliografía española de lenguas indígenas de América. Est. Tipográfico "Sucesores de Rivadeneyra," Madrid.

Plessow, Max
1906 Geschichte der Fabeldichtung in England bis zu John Gay (1726). Nebst Neudruck von Bullokars "Fables of Aesop" 1585, "Booke at large" 1580, "Bref grammar for English" 1586, und "Pamphlet for grammar" 1586. Palaestra, Band LII. Berlin.

Rivet, Paul, and Créqui-Montfort, Georges de
1951-56 Bibliographie des langues aymará et kičua. Université de Paris, Travaux et Mémoires de l'Institut d'Ethnologie, LI. Paris. 4 vols.

Robins, Robert Henry
1951 Ancient & Mediaeval grammatical theory in Europe, with particular reference to modern linguistic doctrine. G. Bell & Sons Ltd., London.
1967 A short history of linguistics. Indiana Univeristy Studies in the History and Theory of Linguistics, no. [18]. Indiana University Press, Bloomington and London.

Rowe, John Howland
1964 Ethnography and ethnology in the sixteenth century. Kroeber Anthropological Society Papers, no. 30, Spring, pp. 1-19. Berkeley.
1965 The Renaissance foundations of anthropology. American Anthropologist, vol. 67, no. 1, February, pp. 1-20. Menasha, Wis.
Sarton, George
1955 The appreciation of ancient and Mediaeval science during the Renaissance (1450-1600). University of Pennsylvania Press, Philadelphia.
Sugg, Redding S., Jr.
1964 The mood of eighteenth-century English grammar. Philological Quarterly, vol. XLIII, no. 2, April, pp. 239-252. Iowa City.
Trabalza, Ciro
1963 Storia della grammatica italiana. Arnaldo Forni − Editore, Bologna (reprint of the first edition, Milano, 1908).
Vater, Johann Severin
1815 Litteratur der Grammatiken, Lexica und Wörtersammlungen aller Sprachen der Erde, nach alphabetischer Ordnung der Sprachen. . . . In der Nicolaischen Buchhandlung, Berlin (parallel text in German and Latin).

APPENDIX

FIRST PRINTED GRAMMARS (except ancient Greek and Latin)

A. Chronological List by Language

The language name in parenthesis indicates the language in which the grammar is written. Following the parenthesis is the author's name; see reference list (C) for details.

FIFTEENTH AND ₁SIXTEENTH CENTURIES

Spanish 1492 (Spanish) Lebrija
Arabic 1505 (Spanish) Acalá
Hebrew 1506 (Latin) Reuchlin
Italian 1516 (Italian) Fortunio
French 1521 (English) Barclay
Aramaic 1527 (Latin) Münster
Czech 1533 (Czech) Optat
Portuguese 1539 (Portuguese) Barros
Geez 1552 (Latin) Vittorio da Rieti
Tarascan 1558 (Spanish) Gilberti
Inca 1560 (Spanish) Domingo de Santo Tomás

Polish 1568 (Latin) Stator
Nahuatl 1571 (Spanish) Molina
German 1573 (Latin) Albrecht
Zapotec 1578 (Spanish) Córdova
Dutch 1584 (Dutch) Spieghel
Slovene 1584 (Latin) Bohorič
Old Church Slavonic 1586 (Bielo-Russian) Anonymous
English 1586 (English) Bullokar
Welsh 1592 (Latin) Rhys
Mixtec 1593 (Spanish) Antonio de los Reyes
Tupí 1595 (Portuguese) Anchieta

SEVENTEENTH CENTURY

Aymará 1603 (Spanish) Bertonio
Japanese 1604 (Portuguese) Rodrigues Girão
Croat 1604 (Latin) Kašić
Araucanian 1606 (Spanish) Valdivia
Millcayac 1607 (Spanish) Valdivia
Allentiac 1607 (Spanish) Valdivia
Tagalog 1610 (Spanish) Francisco de San José
Hungarian 1610 (Latin) Molnàr
Malay 1612 (Dutch) Ruyl
Turkish 1612 (Latin) Megiser
Timucua 1614 (Spanish) Pareja
Ilocano 1617 (Spanish) López
Chibcha 1619 (Spanish) Lugo
Modern Greek 1638 (Latin) Portius
Persian 1639 (Latin) Dieu
Guaraní 1640 (Spanish) Ruyz de Montoya
Kannada 1640 (Portuguese) Stephens
Mame 1644 (Spanish) Reynoso
Muchic 1644 (Spanish) Carrera
Armenian 1645 (Latin) Galani
Finnish 1649 (Latin) Petraeus

Vietnamese 1651 (Latin) Rhodes
Icelandic 1651 (Latin) Jónsson
Kongo 1659 (Latin) Brusciotto
Breton 1659 (French) Maunoir
Massachusett 1666 (English) Eliot
Danish 1688 (Latin) Pontoppidan
Georgian 1670 (Latin) Maggio
Irish 1677 (Latin) O'Molloy
Lusatian 1679 (Latin) Ticin
Cumanagoto 1680 (Spanish) Tauste
Tarahumar 1683 (Spanish) Guadalajara
Maya 1684 (Spanish) Gabriel de San Buenaventura
Anglo-Saxon 1689 (Latin) Hickes
Moeso-Gothic 1689 (Latin) Hickes
Swedish 1696 (Swedish) Tiällmann
Russian 1696 (Latin) Ludolf, Heinrich Wilhelm
Kimbundu 1697 (Portuguese) Dias
Amharic 1698 (Latin) Ludolf, Job
Cariri 1699 (Portuguese) Mamiani
Morocosí 1699 (Spanish) Anonymous Jesuit

B. Language List and Index (alphabetical by language)

Following the date is the author's name; see reference list (C) for details.

Allentiac 1607 Valdivia
Amharic 1698 Lùdolf
Anglo-Saxon 1689 Hickes
Arabic 1505 Alcalá
Aramaic 1527 Münster
Araucanian 1606 Valdivia
Armenian 1645 Galani
Aymará 1603 Bertonio
Breton 1659 Maunoir
Cariri (see Kariri)
Chaldaean (see Aramaic)

Chibcha 1619 Lugo
Croat 1604 Kašić
Cumanagoto 1680 Tauste
Czech 1533 Optat
Danish 1668 Pontoppidan
Dutch 1584 Spieghel
English 1586 Bullokar
Ethiopic (see Geez)
Finnish 1649 Petraeus
French 1521 Barclay
Geez 1548 Vittorio da Rieti

Georgian 1670 Maggio
German 1573 Albrecht
Greek (Modern) 1638 Portius
Guaraní 1640 Ruyz de Montoya
Hebrew 1506 Reuchlin
Hungarian 1610 Molnàr
Iberian (see Georgian)
Icelandic 1651 Jónsson
Ilocano 1617 López
Inca 1560 Domingo de Santo Tomás
Irish 1677 O'Molloy
Italian 1516 Fortunio
Japanese 1604 Rodrigues Girão
Kannada 1640 Stephens
Karirí 1699 Mamiani
Kimbundu 1697 Dias
Kongo 1659 Brusciotto
Lusatian 1679 Ticin
Magyar (see Hungarian)
Malay 1612 Ruyl
Mame 1644 Reynoso
Massachusett 1666 Eliot
Maya 1684 Gabriel de San Buenaventura
Millcayac 1607 Valdivia
Mixtec 1593 Antonio de los Reyes

Modern Greek (see Greek)
Moeso-Gothic 1689 Hickes
Morocosí 1699 Anonymous Jesuit
Muchic 1644 Carrera
Muysca (see Chibcha)
Nahuatl 1571 Molina
Old Church Slavonic 1586 Anonymous
Persian 1639 Dieu
Polish 1586 Stator
Portuguese 1539 Barros
Quichua (see Inca)
Russian 1696 Ludolf
Slavonic (see Old Church Slavonic)
Slovene 1584 Bohorič
Spanish 1492 Lebrija
Swedish 1696 Tiällmann
Tagalog 1610 Francisco de San José
Tarahumar 1683 Guadalajara
Tarascan 1558 Gilberti
Timucua 1614 Pareja
Tupí 1595 Anchieta
Turkish 1612 Megiser
Vietnamese 1651 Rhodes
Welsh 1592 Rhys
Zapotec 1578 Córdova

C. Reference List (alphabetical by author)

Albrecht, Lorenz
1573 Teutsch Grammatick oder Sprach-kunst. Michaël Manger, Avgustae Vindelicorum. (German; written in Latin in spite of its German title)

Alcalá, Pedro de
1505 Arte para ligeramēte saber la lēgua arauiga. Juan Varela de Salamanca, Granada. (Arabic)

Anchieta, José de
1595 Arte de grammatica da lingoa mais vsada na costa do Brasil. Antonio de Mariz, Coimbra. (Tupí)

Anonymous
1586 Boha bĺahaho bĺahodatiju a za prezbno ziteley Stolicy Welikaho Kniażstwa Litowskaho hradu Wilny, sija hramotika sĺowieńskaho jazyka z hazofilakij sĺawnaho hrada Ostroha wĺasnoje otczyny Jaśnie Wielmożnaho Kniażati i Pana Konstantina Konstantinowicza Kniażeti na Ostrohu, Pana na Dubnie, Wojewody Kijewkoho, Marszaĺka Zemli

Wołyńskoj i proczaya z szczodrobliwoje jeho Miłosti łaski wydana dla nauczenija i wyrozumienija Bożestwiennoho pisanija, a za pomoszczuju Christowoju na nesmertelnuju sławu narodu domu Jeho Kniażatowskoj miłosti wydrukowana w mestie Wilenskom, w roku od narożenija słowa i boha i spasa naszeho Juzusa Christa 1586 miesiaca Octiabra 8 dnia na pamiat predobnyja matere naszeje Pełahei a ot sotworenia swieta 7091. W drukarni domou Mamoniczów, Wilno. (Old Church Slavonic)

Anonymous Jesuit
1699 Arte y vocabulario de la lengua morocosi. (printer not given), Madrid. (Morocosí)

Antonio de los Reyes
1593 Arte en lengva mixteca. Pedro Balli, Mexico. (Mixtec)

Barclay, Alexander
1521 Here begynneth the introductory to wryte, and to pronounce French compyled by Alexander Barcley.... Robert Coplande, London. (French)

Barros, João de
1539 Grammatica da lingua portuguesa com os mandamientos da santa mádre igreja. Lisboa. (Portuguese)

Bertonio, Ludovico
1603 Arte y grammatica mvy copiosa de la lengva aymara. Luís Zannetti, Roma. (Aymará)

Bohorič, Adam
1584 Arcticae horae succisivae de Latino Carniolana literatura, unde Moshoviticae, Rutenicae, Polonicae, Boemicae et Lusatiae linguae cum Dalmatica et Croatica cognatio facile deprehenditur. Wittenberg. (Slovene)

Brusciotto, Giacinto
1659 Regulae quaedam pro difficillimi Congensium idiomatis faciliori captu ad grammaticae normam redactae. Typis Sacrae Congregationis de Propaganda Fide, Roma. (Kongo)

Bullokar, William
1586 Bref grammar for English. Edmund Bollifant, London. (English)

Carrera, Fernando de la
1644 Arte de la lengva yvnga de los valles del obispado de Truxillo del Peru, con vn confessionario, y todas las oraciones christianas, traducidas en la lengua, y otras cosas. Ioseph de Contreras, Lima. (Muchic)

Córdova, Juan de
1578 Arte en lengva zapoteca. Pedro Balli, Mexico. (Zapotec)

Dias, Pedro
1697 Arte da lingva de Angola. M. Deslandes, Lisboa. (Kimbundu)

Dieu, Lodowijk de
1639 Rudimenta linguae Persicae. Accedunt duo priores capita Geneseos, ex Persica translatione Jac. Tawasi. Ex officina Elzeviriorum, Lugdunum Batavorum. (Persian)

Domingo de Santo Tomás
1560 Grammatica o arte de la lengua general de los indios de los reynos del Peru. Francisco Fernandez de Cordoua, Valladolid. (Inca)

Eliot, John
1666 The Indian grammar begun; or, an essay to bring the Indian language into rules, for the help of such as desire to learn the same, for the furtherance of the Gospel among them. Marmaduke Johnson, Cambridge. (Massachusett)

Fortunio, Giovanni Francesco
1516 Regole grammaticali della volgar lingva. Bernardino Vercellese, Ancona. (Italian)

Francisco de San José
1610 Arte y reglas de la lengua tagale. Por Thomas Pinpin tagalo, en el Partido de Bataan. (Tagalog)

Gabriel de San Buenaventura
1684 Arte de la lengua maya. La viuda de Bernardo Calderón, Mexico. (Maya)

Galani, Clemente
1645 Historia Armenae nationis cum grammatica, logica et dictionario. Roma. (Armenian)

Gilberti, Maturino
1558 Arte de la lēgua de Michuacā. Iuan Pablos impressor, Mexico. (Tarascan)

Guadalajara, Tomás de
1683 Compendio del arte de la lengua de los Tarahumares, y Guazapares.... Diego Fernández de León, Puebla de los Angeles. (Tarahumar)

Hickes, George
1689 Institutiones grammaticae Anglo-Saxonicae, et Moeso-Gothicae. Grammatica Islandica Runolphi Jonae, Catalogus librorum septentrionalium. Accedit Edvardi Bernardi Etymologicon Britannicum. E Theatro Sheldoniano, typis Junianis, Oxoniae. (Anglo-Saxon and Moeso-Gothic)

Jónsson, Runólphar
1651 Recentissima antiquissimae linguae septentrionalis incunabula; id est grammaticae Islandicae rudimenta. Hafniae. (Icelandic)

Kašić, Bartol
1604 Institutionvm lingvae Illyricae libri dvo autore Bartholomaeo Cassio Curictensi Societatis Iesv. Editio prima. Apud Aloysium Zannettum, Romae. (Croat)

Lebrija, Elio Antonio
1492 La gramatica que nuevamente hizo el Maestro Antonio de Librixa sobre la lengua castellana. (printer not given), Salamanca. (Spanish)

López, Francisco
1627 Arte de la lengua iloca. En el Colegio i Vniversidad de S. Thomas de Aquino, por Thomas Pinpin, Manila. (Ilocano)

Ludolf, Heinrich Wilhelm
1696 Grammatica Russica, quae continet non tantum praecipua fundamenta Russicae linguae, verum etiam manuductionem quandam ad grammaticam Slavonicam. E Theatro Sheldoniano, Oxonii. (Russian)

Ludolf, Job
1698 Grammatica linguae Amharicae, quae vernacula est Habessinorum, in usum eorum qui cum antiqua hac et praeclara natione Christiana conversari volent. Apud J. D. Zunnerum, Francofurti ad Moenum. (Amharic)

Lugo, Bernardo de
1619 Gramatica de la lengva general del Nvevo Reyno, llamada Mosca. Bernardino de Guzman, Madrid. (Chibcha)

Maggio, Francesco Maria
1670 Syntagmatòn linguarum orientalium quae in Georgiae regionibus audiuntur. Liber primus, complectens Georgianae, seu Ibericae vulgaris linguae institutiones grammaticas. Liber secundus, complectens Arabum et Turcarum orthographiam ac Turcicae linguae institutiones. Romae. (Georgian)

Mamiani, Luigi Vincenzo
1699 Arte de grammatica da lingua brasilica da nação Kariri. Miguel Deslandes, Lisboa. (Karirí)

Maunoir, Julien
1659 Le sacré collège de Jésus, divisé en cinq classes, où l'on enseigne en langue armorique les leçons chrétiennes, avec les trois clefs pour y entrer, un dictionnaire, une grammaire et syntaxe en même langue. J. Hardouyn, Quimper-Corentin. 3 parts in 1 vol. (Breton)

Megiser, Hieronymus
1612 Institutionum linguae Turcicae libri quatuor, quorum I. continet partem isagoges grammaticae Turcicae priorem, de orthographia Turcarabica; II. vero isagoges grammaticae Turcicae partem posteriorem, de etymologia Turcorum; III. complectitur diversa linguae Turcicae exercitia. . . IV. dictionarium est Latino-turcicum et. . . Turcico-Latinum. Sumptibus authoris, Lipsiae. (Turkish)

Molina, Alonso de
1571 Arte de la lengua mexicana y castellana. Pedro Ocharte, Mexico. (Nahuatl)

Molnàr, Albert
1610 Novae grammaticae Ungaricae succincter methodo comprehensae et perspicuis exemplis illustratis libri duo. Impensis C. Biermanni, Hanoniae. (Hungarian)

Münster, Sebastian
1527 Chaldaica grammatica, antehac a nemine attentata, sed jam primum per Sebastianum Munsterum conscripta et aedita. Apud J. Frobenium, Basiliae. (Aramaic)

O'Molloy, Francis
1677 Grammatica Latino-hibernica compendiata. Ex typographia Sacrae Congregationis de Propaganda Fide, Roma. (Irish)

Optat, Beneš, and others
1533 Česká grammatika sedmerau stránku w sobe obsahující. W. Náměšti. (Czech)

Pareja, Francisco
1614 Arte y pronunciacion en lengua timvqvana y castellana. Ioan Ruyz, Mexico. (Timucua)

Petraeus, Eskil
1649 Linguae Finnicae brevis institutio. Aboae. (Finnish)

Pontoppidan, Erik Eriksen
1668 Grammatica danica. Typis C. Veringii, Hauniae. (Danish)

Portius, Simon
1638 Γραμματικὴ τῆς Ρωμαϊκῆς γλώσσας· Grammatica linguae Graecae vulgaris. Sumptibus Societatis Typographicae Librorum Officii Ecclesiastici, Parisiis. (Modern Greek)

Reuchlin, Johann
1506 De rudimentis Hebraicis. In aedibus Thomae Anshelmi, Phorcae. (Hebrew)

Reynoso, Diego de
1644 Arte y vocabulario en lengua mame. Francisco Robledo, Mexico. (Mame)

Rhodes, Alexandre de
1651 Linguae Annamiticae seu Tunchinensis brevis declaratio. Roma. (Vietnamese)

Rhys, John David
1592 Cambrobrytannicae Cymraecaeve linguae institutiones et rudimenta accurate, et (quantum fieri potuit) succincte et compendiose conscripta. T. Orwinus, Londini. (Welsh)

Rodrigues Girão, João
1604 Arte da lingua do Japão. No Collegio da Companhia de Jesus, Nangasaqui. (Japanese)

Ruyz de Montoya, Antonio
1640 Arte, y bocabvlario de la lengva gvarani. Juan Sánchez, Madrid. (Guaraní)

Ruyl, Albert Corneliszoon
1612 Spieghel van de Maleysche taal. . . . Amsterdam. (Malay).

Spieghel, Hendrick Laurenszoon, and others
1584 Twe-spraack van de Nederduydsche letterkunst. C. Plantin, Leiden. (Dutch)

Stator, Pierre
1568 Polonicae grammatices institutio. In eorum gratiam, qui eius linguae elegantiam cito et facile addiscere cupiunt. . . . Apud Mathiam Wirzbietam, typographium Regium, Cracoviae. (Polish)

Stephens, Thomas

1640 Arte da lingoa canarim, composta pelo padre Thomaz Esteuão da Companhia de Iesus & acrecentada pello padre Diogo Ribeiro de mesma Companhia. No Collegio de S. Ignacio da Companhia de Iesu, Rachol (Kannada)

Tauste, Francisco de

1680 Arte, y bocabvlario de la lengva de los indios chaymas, cvmanagotos, cores, parias, y otros diuersos de la provincia de Cumana, o Nveva Andalvcia. Bernardo de Villa-Diego, Madrid. (Cumanagoto)

Tiällmann, Nils

1696 Grammatica Suecana äller: en Svensk sprack- ock skrif-konst. Stockholm. (Swedish)

Ticin, Jakub Xaver

1679 Principia linguae Wendicae quam aliqui Wandalicam vocant. Typis Universitat: Carolo-Fernand: in Collegio Societ: Jesu ad S. Clementem, Pragae. (Lusatian)

Valdivia, Luís de

1606 Arte y gramatica, general de la lengva que corre en todo el reyno de Chile, con vn vocabulario, y confessionario. . . . Ivntamente con la doctrina christiana y cathecismo del Concilio de Lima en español, y dos traducciones del en la lengua de Chile. Francisco del Canto, Lima. (Araucanian)

1607 Arte y gramatica en dos lengvas de indios millcayac y allentiac de las ciudades de Mendoça y S. Iuan de la Frontera de la prouincia de Cuyo. Cō cathecismos, confessionarios, y dos breues vocabularios en ambas lenguas. Francisco del Canto, Lima. (in spite of the title, Millcayac only)

1607 Doctrina christiana y cathecismo en la lengua allentiac, que corre en la ciudad de S. Iuan de la Frontera, con vn confessionario, arte y bocabulario breues. Francisco del Canto, Lima (Allentiac)

Vittorio da Rieti, Mariano

1548 Chaldeae seu Aethiopicae linguae institutiones. . . . Item omnium Aethiopiae regum qui ab inundatio terrarum orbe usque ad nostra tempora imperarunt libellus. . . nuper ex Aethiopica translatus lingua. Roma. (Geez)

15. Humboldt's Description of the Javanese Verb

W. Keith Percival

Expositions of Humboldt's linguistic writings have concerned themselves exclusively with his theoretical papers and his treatise on the diversity of language structure.[1] The purpose of this paper is to focus attention on what is perhaps one of his less appreciated facets, namely his contribution to descriptive linguistics. To illustrate this aspect of his work I shall examine a morphological problem which Humboldt encountered in his study of Javanese. Let me recall the fact that the famous treatise on linguistic diversity was but the introduction to a three-volume study of the Old Javanese literary language and its position within the Malayo-Polynesian family of languages.[2]

Humboldt's aims in writing the work were complex. First of all he wished to refute the view, defended by a number of scholars at that time, that Old Javanese was related to Sanskrit in the same way as Pāli was, or in other words that Old Javanese was a linear descendant of Sanskrit with an admixture of local (i.e., Malayan) elements. Eduard Buschmann's foreword to the second volume made this aspect of the work clear (Humboldt 1838: III ff.), and one can also compare Humboldt's own discussion of the views of his predecessors (1838: 188-203).

It is clear, however, that the book was intended to do more than correct contemporary misconceptions about the genetic affiliations of Old Javanese. Humboldt also wished to characterize the structure of the Malayo-Polynesian languages in a general way, so that he could compare them typologically with Chinese and the languages of the Sanskritic family. This was in turn related to his more general purpose of exhibiting the interrelations between the linguistic and cultural development of the human species.

A description of Javanese was necessary, therefore, both to support his claim that the Old Javanese literary language was basically a Malayan, not a Sanskritic language, and to fill out his general characterization of the structure common to all Malayo-Polynesian languages. However, to describe Javanese adequately was no easy task in the thirties of the nineteenth

380

century. Humboldt meticulously consulted all available sources of information on the modern language.

These included a translation of the Holy Bible into modern Javanese by a German missionary, G. Bruckner, a grammatical sketch of modern Javanese together with a reader and word-list by another German missionary, J.F.C. Gericke, a Javanese word-list compiled by the British governor-general of Java, Sir Stamford Raffles, and a brief Javanese grammar by another Englishman, John Crawfurd. Humboldt also carried on a correspondence with a young Dutch scholar, Roorda van Eysinga, who had gone to Java and was studying the language on the spot. (Roorda van Eysinga was later to publish a grammar of Javanese, which Humboldt, however, did not live to see.)

For the old literary language, however, Humboldt performed the extraordinary feat of constructing the grammar himself on the basis of a text consisting of portions of an epic poem, the *Brata Yuddha*, which had been published by Sir Stamford Raffles. In addition to all this, as part of his more general project of characterizing the structure common to the Malayo-Polynesian languages, he examined the grammars of all related languages he could lay his hands on, in particular those of **Malay**, Tagalog (Philippines), and **Malagasy** (Madagascar). Humboldt emphasized (1838: 322) how especially helpful his knowledge of Tagalog was in analyzing Javanese.

Since he shared with many of his contemporaries the view that language relationship can be proved if a set of languages can be shown to possess the same grammatical structure, he felt that were he able to demonstrate that the grammatical structure of these languages (Javanese, Malay, Tagalog, and Malagasy) was basically identical, and to show what this basic structure was like, he would have achieved his twofold aim of vindicating his supposition as to the true nature of Old Javanese, and comparing the structure of Malay-Polynesian with those of Chinese and the Sanskritic languages.

However, although Humboldt's study of Javanese grammar was merely one link in a long chain of demonstration, it was none the less an essential link and one which he did not treat lightly. To show how conscientious his procedure was I shall examine a rather lengthy argument which he presented as part of his analysis of the Javanese verb.

The problem he faced was the following one. Many Javanese verbs appear to be represented by a pair of stems which differ from one another in the initial consonant.[3] Thus the Javanese verb "write" is represented by the pair of stems *nulis* and *tulis*. Humboldt found the most comprehensive description of this phenomenon in a grammatical sketch of Javanese published in 1831 by the German missionary, J. F. C. Gericke. Gericke showed that in certain cases the shift in the initial consonant is a device to derive substantives from verbs. The following are some of Gericke's examples, as quoted by Humboldt (1838: 88-89):

marêntah	"to order"	parêntah	"order"
miyos	"to be born"	wiyos	"birth"
neda	"to eat"	teda	"food"
nyenjata	"to shoot"	senjata	"gun"
nyatur	"to relate"	chatur	"story"
ngaranni	"to name"	haran	"name"
ngrasa	"to feel"	rasa	"feeling"
ngililanni	"to concede"	lila	"concession"

Thus for Gericke one of the functions of the shift was to derive a noun (e.g., *teda* "food") from a verb (*neda* "to eat"). The two sets of alternating consonants according to Gericke were as follows:

First set	Second set
m	w or p
n	t
ny	ch or s
ng	h
ngr	r
ngl	l

To make the ensuing discussion clearer I shall refer to forms with initial consonants from the first set as type A stems, and forms with initial consonants from the second set as type B stems. Thus in the case of the pair *neda* "eat" — *teda* "food" I shall call the former a type A stem, and the latter a type B stem.

Gericke, however, did not regard the difference between type A and type B stems as coinciding with the division of words into substantives and verbs. Type B stems, besides appearing in many cases as derived nouns, also occurred in the following forms:[4]

1. In passive forms.
2. In the imperative form.
3. In substantives derived by affixation.
4. In certain types of derived verbs.

Examples will make these facts clearer. Thus the type B stem *tingngalli* "see" occurs in the following forms:

1. In the passive form *dhipun-tingngalli* "seen".
2. In the imperative form; for example, in a sentence such as *sampêyan tingngalli* "Look!" (*sampêyan* "you").
3. In the derived substantive *tingngallan* "sight".
4. In the derived verb *tingngal-tinningngallan* "to look at one another".

Finally Gericke also observed that in some verbs the type A stem appeared preceded by the prefix *ha-* with no apparent change of meaning. Thus in addition to the form *marêntah* "to order" was the form *hamarêntah* with the same neaming.[5] Gericke called such forms lengthened forms of the verb.

To sum up, a fully conjugated verb, according to Gericke, reveals two types of stems: the type A stem, e.g., *nulis* "to write", and the type B stem, e.g., *tulis* appearing, for instance, in the passive *dhi-tulis,* and functioning as a derived substantive (*tulis* "piece of writing, letter"). All verbal and nominal derivatives formed by affixation contain the type B stem. A verb with a prefixed *ha-* is a lengthened form of the verb, or as Humboldt expressed it, a "fortuitous lengthening of the word".[6]

Having expounded Gericke's description in some detail Humboldt went on to present his own interpretation of the facts. But before doing so, he emphasized that he regarded Gericke's description as adequately reflecting contemporary Javanese usage, and that what he was about to say was in no way a contradiction of what Gericke had stated. For his own purpose in investigating these phenomena was a different one from that of his predecessor. Gericke had compiled the rules of Javanese to enable a reader so desirous to learn to speak and understand the language, whereas his own aim was to discover the deeper significance of the grammatical forms of Javanese, their original interrelations, and the process by which they came into being, often changing their character radically in so doing. This enterprise was fraught with uncertainty but could not be shrugged off, since it was the only way of discovering the structure of the language, and the nature of its relationship to other languages of the same family. But a prerequisite to any progress in this type of endeavor was strict reliance on the facts as revealed by those who have learned to speak the language. Their testimony must be followed without question.[7]

After stating his general aim, Humboldt then proceeded to reinterpret Gericke's description of Javanese verb morphology and in so doing completely altered Gericke's picture of the facts. The issue which Humboldt took up was precisely the relationship between type A and type B stems. Gericke, let us recall, had claimed that the type B stem was derived from the type A stem by a shift in the initial consonant.

It was on this initial consonant alternation which Humboldt focused attention. He once more posed the question as to which of the two sets of alternating consonants was the derived one, and unlike Gericke concluded that the first set was the derived set. He argued as follows. The initial consonants of the first set are sounds belonging to a single class, namely the class of nasals. The initial consonants of the second set, on the other hand, belong to no particular class. But the mere fact that the consonants of the first set share a common property indicates that they are derived, since the possession of a common feature presupposes a common cause, the operation of some special process. Conversely, the fact that the second set of sounds shares no property stamps it as original and nonderived, since it is precisely this state of affairs that characterizes the initial sounds of a language. That is to say, no language restricts the initial sounds of its non-derived words to one phonetic class. Any set of alternants whose initial sounds belong to only one class must therefore be derived, not original.[8]

Humboldt then showed that many words with initial consonants belonging to the second set were indeed original words, and more specifically original nouns, from which verbs were then formed at a later date. Thus the Sanskrit *viśesa* "power" was borrowed into Javanese and appears as the noun *wisesa* from which was formed the verb *misesa* "to have power", by the shift of *w* to *m*. Thus the historical facts corroborate what Humboldt had inferred on general grounds.

But he was not content to leave the matter there. Having shown which of the two sets of initials is the original one and which the derived one, he then proceeded to explain the consonant shift itself. His arguments involved two considerations: the articulatory nature of the shift in Javanese, and the conclusions that can be drawn from analogous consonant shifts in related languages. As to the first point, the shift itself replaces the initial consonant by its corresponding nasal. The comparative evidence is as follows: In Tagalog, Malagasy, and Malay, when a verbal prefix *man-* occurs in front of a stem beginning with a consonant, the latter is replaced by the corresponding nasal and the final *-n* of the prefix is dropped. Thus in Malay the stem *tolong* "help" appears after the prefix as *me-nolong.*

Humboldt then provided a step-by-step description of the shift.[9] He claimed that the resultant initial nasal of the stem in the Malay word *menolong,* for example, arose from the final *-n* of the prefix through loss of the original initial consonant of the stem, in this case *t-.* The final *-n* of the prefix remained unchanged before dental sounds but shifted in front of other sounds into the homorganic nasal (e.g., final *-n* becomes *-m* before initial *p-*), and then became the initial consonant of the verb stem. Schematically arranged a hypothetical stem such as *pata* might undergo the following changes:

Stage 1	man-pata
Stage 2	mam-pata
Stage 3	mam-ata
Stage 4	ma-mata

Humboldt then proposed that the same set of changes could be used to explain the Javanese facts, with the two minor differences that in Javanese the prefix has no initial *m-*, and that short forms exist without the vowel *a*. (Note that in the traditional orthography, which Humboldt used, an *h* was prefixed before an initial vowel, but was silent in the pronunciation, as Humboldt himself pointed out.) Thus in Javanese a hypothetical stem of the shape *pata* would have a double treatment:

	Longer Form	Shorter Form
Stage 1	han-pata	n-pata
Stage 2	ham-pata	m-pata
Stage 3	ham-ata	m-ata
Stage 4	ha-mata	mata

But once again Humboldt was not content merely to describe the two developments, but went further and posited that the shorter form was derived from the longer form by a process of vowel reduction. The evidence for this proposal was of two kinds. First, he noted that in Javanese a trisyllabic stem with an initial vowel often drops that vowel when suffixes are added to it. Thus the stem *hupama* "similarity" has the form *pama* before the possessive suffix in the word *pamane* "its similarity". Thus a process of vowel reduction must be posited for Javanese in any case. It is then merely a question of extending its scope to include the examples we are concerned with.

His second argument was of a more general nature. Similar vowel reductions occur in almost all languages, particularly if one takes dialects of the common people into consideration, and here he cited German *runter* and *rein* from *herunter* and *herein*. Finally, he quoted attested doublets, in Javanese, that is, long and short forms of the same word, e.g., *hamunduti* and *munduti* from *punduti* (no gloss provided), and listed examples from Javanese itself of nasal stems occurring with a prefix *ma-*, e.g., *ma-mukti* "to eat" (derived from *bukti* "food", cf. Sanskrit *bhukti*).

Humboldt's account of the facts was thus as follows. In Javanese, as in other related Malayan languages, stems were nominal in character (unlike the predominantly verbal roots of the Sanskritic family of languages). Verbs were formed from these nominal stems by the addition of the prefix *man-*, which entailed a series of sound changes in its own final consonant and the initial consonant of the accompanying stem. Thus verb forms were clearly marked as such by the appearance of a prefix and the associated alternations, and were thus distinguished from corresponding nominal forms. In Javanese an additional development took place. First, the initial *m-* of the verbal prefix disappeared, and then the vowel *a* of the prefix was also lost. This left only the final *n* of the prefix, the only physical manifestation of which was a set of alternations between the original initial consonants of the stems and the corresponding nasal continuants.

Thus in Humboldt's view the difference between a nominal and the corresponding verbal form in modern Javanese rests entirely on the consonant alternations, as Gericke described them. The modern speaker of Javanese is, however, unaware of the true significance of the alternations, taking them to be merely a device to distinguish nouns from verbs.[10] That is, Humboldt accepted Gericke's description of the facts as a true reflection of the native speaker's conscious intuition concerning them. Thus in emphasizing the importance of accepting the observations of linguists familiar with a particular language, he seems to have been recommending that these observations should be equated with the native speaker's knowledge of the language. There was perhaps also an implicit assumption that native speakers know very little more about their language than a linguist who writes an observationally accurate grammar adequate enough for the needs of those who want to learn the language. That is, it may be that Humboldt's view of the native speaker's knowledge of his own language was a rather restricted one.

In conclusion, certain general features of Humboldt's approach to description may be briefly pointed out. It seems clear that he had an understanding of the phonetic dimension of language. The notion of a class of sounds sharing a phonetic feature (in this case nasality) was a familiar one, as was the notion of a point of articulation. He also had definite, though unformulated notions about the distribution of phonetic features in base forms (stems).

In validating his inferences Humboldt aimed at explanations of as wide a generality as the facts warranted, and at no point did he disregard analogous facts from related languages or from languages in general. In this he differed from those descriptive linguists of the twentieth century who are inclined to suspect that an explanation is spurious if it appeals to facts outside the language under study.

In one other respect Humboldt's practice diverged from that of many present-day linguists. This has to do with his conviction that pure description is not a sufficient goal for the linguist. This means in practice that he constantly discussed diachronic phenomena while describing a language. This does not, however, mean that he confused description and history: he cited diachronic facts for their explanatory value. Thus Humboldt felt he had to establish the series of changes which culminate in a modern Javanese verb form in order to render such forms understandable, and such understanding was for him an indispensable goal of all linguistic work. But he did not claim that the derivation reflected conscious knowledge available to the native speaker.

Thus although Humboldt did not draw an explicit distinction between synchronic and diachronic aspects of language he leaned, at least in the case we are considering, toward the assumption that the complete set of shifts as he described them did not form part of the grammar of present-day Javanese, and that Gericke and other grammarians of the modern language were perfectly justified in describing them in a different way. I conclude, therefore, that the distinction between diachrony and synchrony, which was to loom so large in twentieth-century linguistic theory, was already implicit in Humboldt's work, and that for him synchronic grammar was equatable with that part of grammar of which the native speakers are consciously aware.

NOTES

1. For a bibliography of Humboldt criticism see Arens 1969: 763. Humboldt's significance as a theoretician of language has been discussed by Chomsky in a recent publication (1966: 19-31). It may be noted, however, that Chomsky's interpretation of Humboldt's theories has been challenged. See for example Zimmer 1968: 293-295. I am greatly indebted to Chomsky for directing my attention to Humboldt's work. I should also like to acknowledge much valuable stimulation from conversations with John Viertel.

2. Most of the quotations in this paper are from the second volume of the work, which appeared posthumously in 1838. For a recent description of Old Javanese see Teselkin 1963. A description of modern Javanese can be found in Kiliaan 1919.

3. The orthography which Humboldt used to transcribe Javanese forms has the following peculiarities: *dh* is the dental and *d* the retroflex stop, *ny* is the palatal nasal, and *ng* the velar nasal, *ngng* indicates a sequence consisting of a velar nasal followed by a velar stop, *y* is the palatal semi-vowel, and *j* and *ch* the voiced and voiceless palatal affricates respectively. Medial resonants often occur geminated but were not so pronounced.

4. I omit mention of the syntactic environments of the type B stems which Humboldt discussed at some length.

5. Gericke himself did not quote the form *hamarêntah*, but it is more suitable for purposes of exposition than the forms he cites which are all from stems with initial voiced stops, a category of stems whose behavior neither Gericke nor Humboldt were clear about.

6. The original phrase was "eine gleichgültige Verlängerung des Wortes", the implication being that the lengthening was without function or meaning. Humboldt believed this to be a very significant feature of modern Javanese for in a summary characterization of the language later in the book

he pointed out that certain grammatical features give Javanese the appearance of an inflectional language [den Schein, den flectirenden Sprachen näher zu stehn], but he continues: "Sie [die Javanische Sprache] entledigt sich dadurch der vielfachen, die Tag. Wörter beschwerenden Vorsylben, zerstört aber wieder durch eine gleichsam willkürliche Anhängung solcher verlängernden Laute diesen Eindruck ohne Nutzen, da diese Vorschläge der Bedeutung nichts hinzufügen" (Humboldt 1838: 321). The hidden assumptions here are that syllables or formatives which have no directly assignable meaning are a blemish on the language, and that what Gericke had called lengthened forms of the verb are indeed to be regarded as such from a synchronic point of view. Humboldt thus had very definite ideas about the ideal relationship between form and meaning, and it was against this ideal that he measured all the linguistic phenomena which he studied.

7. The original passage reads: "Es ist ganz etwas anderes, wie er [Gericke] es zur Absicht hatte, die Regeln einer Sprache zum Behuf der Anwendung beim Verstehen und Sprechen derselben darzulegen, und, wie ich es hier versuche, der wahren und inneren Bedeutung der grammatischen Formen und ihrem ursprünglichen Zusammenhang, dem Wege ihrer Entstehung, auf welchem sie sich oft wesentlich verändern, nachzuforschen. Man stösst bei einem solchen Unternehmen oft auf Punkte, wo nur der Vermuthung Raum bleibt, darf es aber darum nicht aufgeben, da man nur auf diese Weise die Analogie der Sprache und ihr Verhältniss zu den stammverwandten zu erkennen vermag. Die erste und nothwendigste Bedingung zum Gelingen eines solchen Versuches ist aber die genaueste Beachtung des factisch in der Sprache Vorhandenen; und dies kann man nur bei denen finden, welche die Sprache unter den Eingebornen, aus langer Uebung und eigenem Gebrauche kennen gelernt haben; ihrem Zeugniss muss man sich daher in allem Factischen ohne Widerrede unterwerfen" (1838: 91-92).

8. Humboldt expressed the matter thus: "Die Uebereinkunft der Laute deutet an, dass sie etwas Gemeinschaftliches an sich tragen, und weist dadurch auf eine gemeinschaftliche Ursach, eine künstliche Bildung hin, indess die zweite Reihe die Verschiedenheit der Consonanten an sich trägt, welche die Anfangsbuchstaben der Wörter einer Sprache überhaupt haben; in ihr scheint also der natürliche, ursprüngliche Zustand zu liegen" (1838: 97).

9. Humboldt described the shifts in the following way: "Im Tag., Mad., und eigentlich Mal. geht, wenn das Verbalpräfix *man* vor die Consonanten der zweiten Reihe tritt, jeder von diesen in den entsprechenden Nasenlaut über, oder dieser Nasenlaut entsteht vielmehr aus dem End -*n* des Präfixes, indem der ursprüngliche Consonant hinwegfällt; das End-*n* des Präf. wird also, vor Zahnlauten unverändert, vor anderen Lauten in den ihnen entsprechenden umgewandelt, zum Anfangsbuchstaben des Verbums. Denn in allen den genannten Sprachen gehört, wo diese Veränderung vorgeht, der Endnasenlaut des Präf, zur ersten Sylbe des Wortes, und trennt sich von der des Präfixes" (1838: 98-99).

10. After expounding his view that the consonant alternation was connected with and arose from prefixation, Humboldt then stated that he believed "dass dies aber jetzt nicht mehr im Bewusstsein des heutigen Volkes liegt, sondern dass dieses in dem veränderten Angangsbuchstaben gar keinen Zusammenhang mit irgend einem Präfix ahndet" (1838: 92). Once again it is clear that Humboldt considered the consonantal alternation with no overt prefixation as a *fundamental* characteristic of Javanese in contradistinction to other related languages. Thus in his brief characterization of Javanese he says: "Im Formenbau und in der grammatischen Fügung hat die Sprache ihre bestimmteste Eigenthümlichkeit in der Vernachlässigung der Verbalpräfixe und der durch ihre Abwerfung entstehenden Veränderung der Anfangsconsonanten" (1838: 321).

REFERENCES

Arens, Hans. 1969. Sprachwissenschaft: der Gang ihrer Entwicklung von der Antike bis zur Gegenwart. Zweite, durchgesehene und stark erweiterte Auflage. Freiburg & München: Karl Alber.

Chomsky, Noam. 1966. Cartesian linguistics: a chapter in the history of rationalist thought. New York & London: Harper & Row.

Gericke, J. F. C. 1831. Eerste Gronden der Javaansche Taal. Batavia.

Humboldt, Wilhelm Von. 1836. Ueber die Kawi-Sprache auf der Insel Java, nebst einer Einleitung über die Verschiedenheit des menschlichen Sprachbaues und ihren Einfluss auf die geistige Entwickelung des Menschengeschlechts. Erster Band. Berlin: Druckerei der Königlichen Akademie der Wissenschaften.

Humboldt, Wilhelm Von. 1838. Ueber die Kawi-Sprache auf der Insel Java. Zweiter Band. Berlin: Druckerei der Königlichen Akademie der Wissenschaften.

Kiliaan, H. N. 1919. Javaansche Spraakkunst. 'S-Gravenhage: Martinus Nijhoff.

Teselkin, A. S. 1963. Drevne-javanskij Jazyk (Kavi). Moskva: Izdateljstvo vostočnoj literatury.

Zimmer, Karl E. 1968. Review of Cartesian Linguistics, by Noam Chomsky. International Journal of American Linguistics 34: 290-303.

16. On Bonaparte and the Neogrammarians as Field Workers

Eric P. Hamp

Prince Louis-Lucien Bonaparte has left us an interesting legacy, and that is a sufficient reason for discussing him in the context of certain other related matters. It happens, too, that the collection of books which we have from him is also an enormously valuable one; and that aspect has its own interest, quite apart from considerations of material acquisitiveness and wealth. Before broaching our main topic it may be well to place the Prince and his books briefly in some perspective in relation to The Newberry Library and the conferences to which these papers owe a great deal.

Prince Louis-Lucien Bonaparte, a gentleman of some means residing in London, endowed with serious scholarly tastes, assembled over a large span of the nineteenth century a collection of books, pamphlets, offprints, and the like covering a broad substantive range of his linguistic and philological interests. By the time of his death, at the beginning of the last decade of that century, he was regularly purchasing and receiving from scholars a large proportion of the current publication on aspects of (largely) European languages that interested him. Some eleven years after his death, The Newberry Library in 1901 attracted considerable attention in the scholarly book market by acquiring the total collection as it then stood, a library numbering in excess of 15,000 volumes.

This linguistic collection comprises titles heavily centered on European languages and stretching back in time from the late nineteenth century to the Renaissance. Its particular strengths lie in retrospective dialectology and lexicographic source materials (i.e., it is strongly data-oriented), and these especially for many of the minor languages of Europe. The Prince's own active interest in Basque[1] guaranteed a remarkable and unique coverage (over 700 titles) of this language. The Celtic languages too (especially Scottish Gaelic, Welsh, Breton, and superlatively Manx) are represented to a high degree of quality and, in some cases, of proportionate quantity. The English books are strong in earlier British dialect materials, early English dictionaries, and in works relating to the study of English in England. In the Romance field the particular strength lies in dialect and earlier work, especially in provincial, ephemeral or out-of-print publications; the material on French and Italian dialects is vast. The Albanian materials[2] are really astonishingly rich. I have reported in some detail on these aspects at a conference on Linguistic Bibliography and Computer Technology held at The Newberry Library in 1966.

The total number of titles acquired in 1901 by The Newberry was not quite the complete collection held by the Prince at his death. A modest number of volumes was dispersed among the family, and no doubt some items vanished in unaccountable ways. But what we have is unquestionably the substantial collection, with very little skewing likely. The Newberry has since made further important acquisitions in these and parallel fields, thus enhancing the ambiance of the Bonaparte collection.

The collection has regrettably never been provided with a satisfactory classed catalogue. The *Attempt at a Catalogue . . .* by Victor Collins at the time of the sale is the only printed document we have. In 1955 plans were laid to produce a modern classed catalogue based on up-to-date linguistic knowledge, and a broad and carefully chosen team of experts labored over some years to produce a classification which now sadly lies in files, much of the material hand written and certainly not ready for print or machine processing. Rising costs have effectively put a stop to further progress on making such a classified account generally available. It is to be regretted that such a marvelous nucleus for a retrospective center for pre-1900 linguistics — the only one of its kind in the Western Hemisphere — lies at present so under-cultivated and little exploited. But this does not diminish the riches that the Prince so meticulously, tastefully, and learnedly assembled for us.

Bonaparte's Interests

If one opens the volume of the *Transactions of the Philological Society* (TPS) for 1882-84, one is struck by the numerous contributions by H. I. H. Prince Louis-Lucien Bonaparte (shown in the Members' list: 6, Norfolk Terrace, Bayswater, London W.).

At this time, while the Germans were engrossed in the nature of the reconstructed historical regularities recovered by the Junggrammatiker, and while Saussure was creating his imaginative abstract formulations of the symmetries in reconstructed sound structures (and Johannes Schmidt likewise in a farsighted way for morphological formations), Britain displayed its abiding interest in careful—though not merely practical—observation of the richly varied world that was constantly unfolding. It was only now that the detail of various smaller and obscure languages and dialects was becoming at all known to West Europeans. We were, if you will, in another phase of the knowledge opened by the Renaissance "voyages of discovery", though most of the voyages I have in mind in the present connection take us no farther than the reaches of the Doge's profitable vessels plying the serene waters that bound Europe as we know it.

For example, the President's (i.e., Alexander J. Ellis) Annual Address of 1882, printed in this volume of TPS, embodying as it did various reports submitted by the President and other members of the Society, included a Report on the Yaagan language of Tierra del Fuego (arranged from the papers of the Rev. Thomas Bridges) and a long Report (44-73) on South Andamanese (arranged from the papers of E. H. Man and Lieut. R. C. Temple). Symptomatic, too, of the incipient growth in dialect study is the report "On Dialect, Language, Orthoepy and Dr. G. Wenker's Speech Atlas" (20-32).

In some ways a perusal of the pages of the TPS of this period is reminiscent, in another medium and level of information, of IJAL. (J. A. H. Murray remarks (508): "It is noticeable, that no paper on any branch of Semitic or Oriental philology, and indeed none upon any extra-European language is to be found amongst the number [of the year's monthly meetings]".) In this connection, the work of H. Sweet is particularly pertinent; cf., especially, Spoken North Welsh in this volume of TPS (409-84), particularly the final pages:

> If my skech wer even mor imperfect than it is, I should stil feel myself partly justified in bringing it out, as a contribution to a hitherto totally neglected subject. If its errors lead any foneticaly traind Welshman to supersede it by such a ful and reliabl work as can only be done by a traind nativ, its most ambitious aims wil be fully acumplisht. Meanwhile it wil, I hope, be of sum use to general foneticians, as wel as Celtic specialists, and also to those who wish to lern to speak the language, which, on account of the wide divergence between the writn and spoken language, has hitherto been a practical impossibility for most foreiners. . . .

> I hope that as a specimen of the method of dealing with living languages, this wil be found to be an advance on my previous atempts. I think myself I hav made an advance in one respect, nl. in that of giving ful texts. This is no dout the most laborious and responsibl part of such an undertaking, and that which offers most pitfalls to any one dealing with a forein language, but, if done with reazonabl care, is of mor real value than any number of word-lists and paradigms, for it alone givs—or atempts to giv—the unsofisticated facts of the language.

I hav, of course, treated the language thruout as a living one, and hav givn the same prominence to the borrowd English as to the nativ element. The italicized words in the texts wil giv a good idea of the proportion of English words, which, after all, is surprizingly small, considering the long and intimate intercourse between the speakers of the two languages. Most of them, too, ar very thuroly naturalized, in meaning as wel as form, so that a patriotic Welshman has no mor reazon to be ashamed of them than an Englishman has of his French words. It is greatly to be wisht that educated Welshmen would cultivate the genuin spoken language insted of the artificial jargon of the newspapers, and reflect that the superiority of such a work as the *Bardd Cwsg* consists precisely in its style being founded (as shown by the numerous English words) on the every-day speech of the period. Welsh can no mor be made an exception to the inexorabl law of change than English or any other language: it is its change, its development, that proves it to be realy a living language; and a language that is prezervd only by writing is litl better than a ded language.

In this setting and company of dialectologist-phoneticians and naturalist-geographers we find the interests of the Prince in recording the diversity of European speech, particularly the out-of-the-way varieties, a fairly congenial fit. The volume of TPS in question gives us an excellent index to the Prince's interests:

Basque

The simple tenses in Modern Basque and old Basque, etc. (643-54);

Remarques sur certaines assertions de M. J. Vinson concernant la langue basque (Appendix VI, 4 pp.).

Typology

Initial mutations in the living Celtic, Basque, Sardinian, and Italian dialects (155-202);

Italian and Uralic possessive suffixes compared (485-91).

Exploration of the living dialects of Europe[3]

Words connected with the vine in Latin and the Neo-Latin dialects (251-311). This article is largely factual collectanea. It contains a rich bibliography (252-62), listing large numbers of books then in the Prince's own library, which should be checked against the Newberry's holdings.

Neo-Latin names for "artichoke" (41* - 45*, plus Appendix V of 3 pp.).

Names of European reptiles in the living Neo-Latin languages (312-54). These are stated to be collected from printed works, MSS., and the Prince's own field notes 1843-83. "For in my youth I was something of an herpetological amateur under the guidance of the late well-known zoologist Charles-Lucian Bonaparte, second Prince of Canino, and my eldest brother" (313). A footnote on the same page states that 1843, in Lucca, Louis-Lucien Bonaparte read a paper on the chemistry of the viper.

One cannot help thinking of the parallel of the herpetologist turned dialectologist in Bonaparte with the geologist turned anthropologist in Franz Boas. Important features differ; the quality of mind, level of excellence and performance, and range of intellectual power in the two men are greatly different. But there are striking similarities that are not accidental and which make their own contribution, of whatever size: Both were acute observers, and both were notably oblivious to the currents of historical reconstruction active all around them. Bonaparte had certain loves, such as the Basque; Boas had his attachment to the Kwakiutl, for whom he perhaps might have sacrificed some of his principles. Boas was a man of many parts, but a descriptivist; Bonaparte was a descriptive naturalist.

The Question of Field Work Accuracy

Now, if Bonaparte's interests were so strong in documentation, collection, and naturalist description, it would be interesting to know how accurate and trustworthy his materials were. Did he transmit his observations with precision? Was he perhaps just an unskilled, if well-meaning, amateur collecting antiquarian?

There is another question that it would be fruitful to link with the last: What were the standards of field work for the Neogrammarians in general? Obviously, it is never true that all individuals perform equally; and the present study could not hope to do more than probe one corner of such work. But the question has a particular interest beyond that of checking the accuracy of records that we might like to exploit; it has a bearing on the intellectual history of the time, particularly in light of more recent insistence on accuracy in field work. We know that the Neogrammarians were heavily interested in ancient languages, in early written remains, in the philology of ancient texts. They were, understandably, eager to approach as closely as possible the chronological and grammatical level of their reconstructions. This immediately raises the question—one with widely ramified and elaborately studied aspects—what credence are we to place in written records? The question applies, too, to scholars' field notes published in recent time. The present paper, I think, can make a point (not for the first time) on this question, in a new context.

There are cases where even the proverbial Neogrammarian could not restrict himself to dusty books and ancient stone fragments. Some languages, such as Lithuanian or Albanian, are attested so recently that there is no profit in restricting oneself to a limited corpus transmitted by chance in 1549 or 1555 (the latter, Albanian, book of Buzuku not known to the Neogrammarians), nor in eschewing modern spoken forms with all their troublesome variation. Moreover, the caricature of the Neogrammarian bookworm, oblivious to reality and STRUCTURE (or system!), popularized by earlier twentieth-century enthusiasts on method is simply not true to life. One might object that Otto Böhtlingk, whose *Über die Sprache der Jakuten* (St. Petersburg, 1851) constitutes a remarkable specimen of informant-based description for a preliterate exotic language, really antedates the Neogrammarians sensu stricto. It is also true that in the Irish field it took Finck, the typologist, and not Zeuss or Thurneysen, to write *Die Araner Mundart* (Marburg, 1899). Yet on the question of accurate phonetic observation of the syllabic prosodics in Lithuanian dialects it is salutary to read Leskien's remarks in the introduction to his and Brugmann's *Litauische Volkslieder und Märchen: aus dem preussischen und russischen Litauen* (Strassburg, 1882). And it would be hard to find a more forthright pronouncement on the principles of describing a language in its own terms without preconceptions than in the Foreword to the first edition (1895) of Thumb's Handbook of Modern Greek. The Neogrammarians were by no means oblivious to or scornful of field work and synchronic description.

If the Neogrammarians did indeed engage in what anthropologically oriented scholars are in the habit of calling "field work", we may fairly wonder how skillful they were, how well and precisely they performed, whether their principles in this domain matched the acuity they reached in comparing bodies of data. The present essay takes the opportunity to explore one multiple case.

In sum, the chapter seeks to throw light on Bonaparte as a scholar (i.e., preëminently a field worker, collector, and linguistic naturalist and geographer); to assay certain Neogrammarians as field or dialect phoneticians; to comment on problems of interpreting written records; and to present some fresh data on a highly interesting dialect.

The San Marzano Dialect

The isolated Albanian speaking enclaves of southern Italy have occupied me intermittently for some time, over two decades now. The village of San Marzano, in Provincia Tàranto, is the only Albanophone settlement left in Apulia; two centuries ago there were a dozen or more such villages in the Tàranto region. In point of fact, when I first learned of San Marzano I did not yet know whether the language still survived there.

The total publication on the dialect of San Marzano amounts to four items; this, however, represents a broader spread of treatment for this dialect than for any other single variety of Italo-Albanian, curiously enough. The relevant references are Bonaparte (1884, 1890); Hanusz (1889); Meyer (1891). These works are very unequal in certain respects: Bonaparte, the cosmopolitan gentleman, we know somewhat; Meyer, author of a famous historical Greek grammar, connoisseur of Modern Greek and Vlach, is the founder of systematic comparative study of Albanian within Indo-European, whose etymological dictionary of 1891 still stands (to our shame) as the sole such general tool; Hanusz, a young Pole of great promise, student of Lithuanian and Armenian who visited the Albanians of southern Italy and went on to Paris, where he suddenly and tragically died.[4] (See now also Hamp (1968), which discusses certain of the synchronic phonological rules of the San Marzano dialect).

Bonaparte (1884) surveys briefly (492-93) the general situation of Albanian in Italy, and adds a composite list of all the sounds said to be found in all known Albanian dialects. The forms given for San Marzano came from one P. De Vincentiis, an expert on Tàranto and on Tarentine dialect, who in turn got them from a native; these forms consist of a list of words, three brief phrases, and a short song (somewhat corrupt). Thus the work is really at third hand.

Bonaparte (1890) is a composite article, as the title suggests; the relevant portion for us is on pp. 341-51. It is a second edition of Bonaparte (1884), improved by Cosimo Santoro, a native of San Marzano, during a visit by the Prince to Tàranto and San Marzano. It repeats the essence of the earlier work, taking account of Hanusz (1889).

Hanusz' article (published posthumously) is a brief independent report based on a personal visit to San Marzano. Meyer's review includes forms he had gathered in passing on a brief visit; I have the impression that this is the only material Meyer gathered in this fashion at first hand in the Italian enclaves. Both these men were trained philologists and, so to speak, knew what they were looking for.

A good many years ago I collated all these materials, which overlap nicely; the result is shown in the respective four lists here appended. I also tabulated all the graphic correlations, taking care to recognize distinctions not on etymological grounds, but only so far as the writings justified a decision. From this inspection I evolved a biunique phonemic analysis of the sort then current, which still offers a useful connection with the orthographies. This is the basis of the transcription in the fifth column.

It is of interest now to reproduce my MS conclusions regarding the quality of our three field workers after I had made the analysis outlined above: "Bonaparte is second-hand, but his source was a native, a fact which partly redeems his performance; the improvement from 1884 to 1890 adds assurance. Hanusz is first-hand, and he was obviously a gifted and keen observer; though his transcription is crude by our standards. However, he apparently never read the proof before he died. I am inclined to put greatest trust in Hanusz. Meyer was apparently a mediocre phonetician. His vast etymological knowledge was both a help and a hindrance." That was as far as I could go at the time.

Later, in 1956, I was able to spend about three days in June in the area. I found the dialect still very much alive, in a sizable thriving village. I was able to check completely through the collated list, and to elicit a couple of hundred additional forms, mostly single words of predictable interest in relation to other dialects. This material was similarly analyzed phonemically. The relevant portion of the result is given in the sixth column.

San Marzano turns out to be highly interesting phonologically. At first hearing, the dialect sounds bizarre and quaint. I have heard only one Albanian dialect that strikes me as more unexpected, that of Mándres in northern Greece, which has migrated from an earlier Turkish and Bulgarian environment (see Hamp 1965). San Marzano has become acculturated to Pugliese in an odd and interesting way. It is the only Albanian dialect I know that has Italianate long consonants, which I write as geminates. On the other hand, except for some fairly simple phonetic mergers, it turns out on closer inspection to be remarkably retentive of many old distinctions. In fact, in generative terms the underlying forms are strikingly like the reconstructions; some late rules have simply been added.

In a general way, all proto-Tosk vowels are retained. All consonants except r^5 and original *h* that are not in pretonic syllables are doubled, when [+voc] follows. Then a final schwa is added to all forms which formerly ended in a consonant. Thus there are no final consonants and many geminates. A very Italianate Albanian!

The seventh column shows the minimum reconstructions that must be assumed, for ease in verifying the above rough and general statements.

One can see at a glance—what I never suspected beforehand—how misleading and etymological both Hanusz and Meyer are—and on the most characteristic aspects of the dialect! But note how generally correct Bonaparte is, underneath his clumsy orthography.

Let us now proceed to details and tabulate the important discrepancies and divergences in these lists.

There are numerous cases where Meyer is clearly inaccurate, or in error: 2 (he has the Italian word), 11 (detail of error unclear), 25 (appears to be Italian), 30 (he wrote what he etymologically expected), 86 (inconsistent on the initial palatal stop), 94 (failed to hear the long consonant), 101 (with his etymological bias, he misunderstood jessəšə), 153 and 154 (with imprecise consonantisms), 164 (failure to hear length again), 193 (fails to show stress), 225 (perhaps a miscopying?), 232, 295, 297 (no length), 299 (inaccurate consonantism)—these are mostly cases where no comparison with Bonaparte can be made.

Occasionally Meyer is valuable: 20, 115, 200.

Similarly, Hanusz, for all his merits, goes astray: 15, 87, 88, 90, 92, 93, 170, 223, 286 (all these omit final schwa); 63, 89, 286 (fail to show long consonant).

Both Meyer and Hanusz err in 39 (with etymological bias in the initial), 208 (each in different ways).

There are some cases where we can make no decision, since the word appears to have obsolesced in the meantime: 19, 27, 51, 56, 76, 83, 116, 163, 168, 224.

There are a few items of special note: 24 (all these are problematic to a degree), 32 (both Meyer and Bonaparte seem incompletely correct), 54 (the 1884 version looks more recognizable than the 1890), 68, 71, 222 (the difference in consonantism is real in the phonetics; I deal with that elsewhere), 167, 240, 306 (may have a basis in phonetics), 202 (opaque to me), 205 (an unclear vowel discrepancy both in Bonaparte and in the modern form collected by me), 255 (*št* is somewhat unclear throughout), 260 (simply a blunder of notation?), 307 (simply masks, by its poverty of related forms, the real interest of a word of this type; if I could elicit, so could Meyer).

We then find an understandably substantial number of inadequate forms in Bonaparte's list when set against the others and my own notes: 13 (*rr*), 17 (final schwa), 21 (vowel lacking), 22 (final schwa), 34 (but suggestive), 37 (initial nasal; the *k* is defensible), 38 (garble of "day" and "light"?), 41 (initial part), 57 (unclear), 58 (Italian), 60 (final schwa), 67 (sibilant), 69 (sibilant and missing vowel), 72 (long *k*), 73 (ditto), 74 (vocalism of *gruja* unclear), 80 (meaning?), 85 (consonants and final schwa), 126 (long sibilant), 135 (first vowel seems wrong), 142 (final schwa?), 146 (long *f*), 147 (this and the last lack final schwa), 159, 161, 179 (ditto), 182 (long *k*), 196 (native?), 254, 256, 257 (sibilant), 266 (consonants and lack of schwa), 278 (long *k* and final schwa), 284 (long *j*), 290 (long nasal), 292 (*dz* and schwa), 304 (*dz* puzzling), and 75 (with *d/t* confusion)—a total of 38 instances.

Against this we place the notable number of instances where Bonaparte's record is, when judged by control through the present-day dialect, better than both Meyer and Hanusz, or the sole and correct record in print: 3, 5, 6 (NB *l l*), 7 (NB schwa), 8, 9 (NB schwa and *tth*), 10 (NB accent), 11 (schwa), 18 (*kk*), 26 (schwa), 28 (*ll*), 31 (single *t* and schwa), 36, 45 (accent), 50 (schwa), 55, 61 (schwa), 66, 77 (*kk* and schwa), 80 (*l l*), 81 (*l l*), 84 (schwa and *tth*), 97, 99 (*tt*), 106 (single *l*), 108 (*tt*), 109 (schwa),

118, 120 (schwa), 125 (*vv*), 127, 133 (*-a*), 134, 139, 150 (*je*), 155 (schwa), 156 (schwa), 160 (*g* and *gg*), 171 (schwa), 174, 175, 176, 178, 180, (schwa), 183, 184, 188, 189, 190 (*tt*), 192, 194, 201 (*ss*), 207, 210 (*ddz*), 211 (*l l*), 217 (*kk*), 221 (f., actually), 226 (this lexeme is confirmed), 228 (NB *p*-and *tt*), 229 (*ll*), 230 (*zz*), 243 (*š, -r-*), 251 (*kkj*), 261 (*tt*), 267 (*ddž*), 270, 277 (spoken form of preterite), 280 (schwa), 291 (*šš*), 294 (*šš* and schwa), 301 (*ddz*), 306 (*tt*).—a total of 72 instances.

In these last instances the chief source of superiority lies in an absence of etymological expectation, which apparently prevented Meyer and Hanusz often from hearing what the dialect really said.

Finally, of course, Bonaparte's record reflects the feel of a native speaker.

NOTES

1. Note that his map of the Basque dialects still appears in the current (second) edition of *Les langues du monde*; and see especially the fine appreciation of his work by Luis Michelena, *Sobre el pasado de la lengua vasca*, San Sebastián, 1964, pp. 22-39.

2. For one rare and interesting specimen see my identification, *Annali I.O.N.* 3, 1961, 105-8.

3. Here we may note that Sweet's Spoken Portuguese (203-37) credits the Prince's On Portuguese Simple Sounds (1880-81) for suggestive ideas. Bonaparte adds a note on Portuguese vowels (404-8) contesting some of Sweet's statements; Sweet had not been entirely favorable on Bonaparte's phonetics.

4. When I returned north from my first trip to southern Italy, after the postwar poverty and lack of food there, I thought of Hanusz with melancholy piquancy as I lay with pneumonia in Bologna. I take this opportunity to record my lasting gratitude to my old friend Carlo Tagliavini, who spared no pains in securing me the most expert medical care in those difficult times.

5. This exception is neatly correlated with the fact that in what must have been the anterior (or parent) phonology (and in many conservative Albanian dialects) [r] and [r̄] (>SMarz. *r* and *rr*) are the only consonants distinguished mainly by length or duration.

REFERENCES

Böhtlingk, Otto. 1851. Über die Sprache der Jakuten. Grammatik text und Wörterbuch. (Reise in den äussersten Norden und Osten Sibiriens, ed. Dr. A. Th. v. Middendorff). 3 vols. St. Petersburg. [Reprinted Indiana University Publications, Uralic and Altaic Series, 35, (The Hague: Mouton, 1964).]

Bonaparte, Prince Louis-Lucien. 1880-81. On Portuguese simple sounds. Transactions of the Philological Society 23-41. London.

———. 1882-84. Albanian in Terra d'Otranto. Transactions of the Philological Society 492-501. London.

———. 1890. Albanian, Modern Greek, Gallo-Italic, Provencal, and Illyrian [i.e., Serbian] still in use (1889) as linguistic islands in the Neapolitan and Sicilian Provinces of Italy. Transactions of the Philological Society 335-364. (Eleven maps.)

Finck, F. N. 1899. Die Araner Mundart, Ein Beitrag zur Erforschung der Westirischen. Marburg. 2 vols.

Hamp, Eric P. 1965. The Albanian dialect of Màndres. Die Sprache 11: 137-154.

———. 1968. Acculturation as a late rule. Papers from the Fourth Annual Regional Meeting of the Chicago Linguistic Society 103-110.

Hanusz, J. 1889. L'albanais en Apulie. Mémoires de la Société Linguistique de Paris 6: 263-267.

Meyer, Gustav. 1890. Review of Bonaparte (1890). Zeitschrift fuer Romanische Philologie 15: 546-560.

Sweet, H. 1882-84a. Spoken North Welsh. Transactions of the Philological Society 409-84. London

———. 1882-84b. Spoken Portuguese. Transactions of the Philological Society 203-37. London.

Thumb. A. 1895. Handbuch der neugriechischen Volkssprache. Strassburg. (2nd ed., 1910). [Handbook of the Modern Greek Vernacular. Edinburgh, 1912.]

APPENDIX

Gloss	Bon. '84	Bon. '90	Hanusz
1. that		nə ja lemmi 'we release to them'	ajò (f.)
2. rain			
3. gold		arə (m.)	
4. loom			argalì
5. bone, fruit stone		aštə (m.)	
6. forehead		ballə (f.)	
7. white		bardə	bard
8. belly		barkə (m.)	
9. bean	baf	batthə, -a	bàθ
10. Virgin Mary God	bekkúmia ibekkúmia	bekkuámia ibekkuámi	bekùamja bekùami
11. you are doing		tə jessi bənnə 'may it be done'	jè te bèn
12. you must do			kà te bèše
13. son		(énbrəni) tə i bírriti (gen.)	
14. anus			
15. I buy			u bljèń
16. snow			
17. breeches	brek	brek (f.)	
18. (the) bread	búkka	buk, -a búkənə (acc.)	
19. beautiful		bukrə	bùkera (f. def.)
20. my brother			
21. powder, dust		burblə (m.)	

Meyer	Philological interpretation	In situ interpretation	Reconstructed Pre-form
aí (m.) ató 'they'	aí, ajó, ató (j-a)	aí, aj, ajó, ató	aí/ai, ajó, ató
acqua	ákua	—— (ši)	ši
	arə	arə, def. ari	ar, -i
	argalí	argalí, -u	argalí, -u
	aštə	aštə	ašt(ə)
	balə	ballə	balə
	bard(ə)	i-bardə	i-barðə
barku	barkə, -u	barkə, -u	bark, -u
baθɛ-tɛ	baθ(ə)	baθə, -tə (θθ?)	baθ(ə)
ebekuamia ibekuami	e-bekúamja i-bekúami	bekuámja —— (krišti)	bekuam-
bɛrɛ 'ben fatto'	bən(ə)	bənnə	bənə
	ka te bəše	ka tə bəšə	bəš
	i-bir(r)iti	(imə)birə	bir, def. -i gen. birit
biθa	biθa	biθə	biθ
	bleň	b ʌeňə	b ʌeň
bora	bora	borə	borə
brekɛ-tɛ	brek(ə)	brekə-tə	brek ?
bukɛ	buk(ə)	bukka (def.) bukkə (indef.)	bukə
bugrɛ	buK(ə)rə	—— (e-ndarə)	bukərə
im bulá	im-bula	imb-ulá 'my b.' it-ulá 'thy b.' ulázrə-tə(pl.)	vəlá vəlázrə
búrbulɛ	búrb(u)lə	búrbul-i (def.)	(Ital.)

Gloss	Bon. '84	Bon. '90	Hanusz
22. man		burr (m.)	
23. jacket		burrík (f.)	
24. lip	me bus	me buz budz, buz (f.)	me bùz 'fâché'
25. gave			
26. pear		dardə (f.)	dàrd-a
27. sheep, ram			
28. the ewe		dellə, dellja	
29. the pig			
30. the fox			
31. sea		detə (m.)	
32. bread, food		dəkrûmə, -a	
33. (we) two	di		dìa
34. that I know/knew		ti e dinjə 'tu lo sapevi'	tẹ dìna
35. yesterday			dìe
36. the sun		diélə (m.)	
37. help		dikə neve 'deliver us!' (plus dat.)	
38. day	drit -mir drit		
39. numerals -ties			tredjèt, katerdjèt pesdjèt, ǵaštdjet
40. the hand		dorə (f.)	
41. rose		drendafillə (f.)	
42. wood, firewood		dru, drutə (pl.)	

Meyer	Philological interpretation	In situ interpretation	Reconstructed Pre-form
	buɨ̄ buɨ̄k	burrə —— (ǯakketta)	buɨ̄ə
me buz buzɛ 'mouth'	buz	buzzə-tə	buzə
dava 'you gave'	dava	—— (pple. tənnə)	ðənə
	dard(ə)	dardə	darðə
dašɛ	daš(ə)	—— (mantúnn-i)	daš
délia	del(ə), delja	déʎe, déʎa	deʌe, deʌja
derku	derku	derkə, def. derku	derk, -u
derpra	derpra	terpra	ðeʌpra
	det(ə)	detə, def. deti	déet, -i
tɛkruomɛ	tə-krúam(ə)	tə kruámmi 'let's eat'	krua-
tɛ dia di	di, dia	di	di
	ti e diň(ə) tə-diňa	ti e diňňe u e diňňə	dinje di-ň
die	díe	dí(j)e	díe
dieli	diél(ə), -i	diél-i	diel + i
	diK(ə)	ndigəmə	ndih-
	d(r)it(ə)	ditta 'il giorno' dritta 'la luce'	dita drita
dietɛ tredietɛ, katrɛdietɛ	diét(ə)	tiéttə	ðiétə
dora	dor(ə), -a	dora	dorə
	drendafil(ə)	trəndafiʎʎa	trəndafiʌə
dru-tɛ	dru-tə	dru-tə	dru + tə

Gloss	Bon. '84	Bon. '90	Hanusz
43. I loved	denja	denja	dèɲa
44. he loved		denja	
45. we love	dukami	duákimi	dùgemi
46. I love	tua=dua	dúa	
47. wants	dó	do do ti 'you want'	dò
48. gun (portable)	duf	duf	
49. and		e	e
50. yes	énja	enjə	
51. angel		engljə (m.)	
52. the wind			
53. the barley	érbi	erbə, -i	
54. go	ets	eda	
55. the figs		ənblə (sweet)	
56. name		énbrənə énbrəni (def. nom?)	embr
57. silver		ərgjəndrə (m.)	
58. cheek		fattšə (f.)	
59. (the) fair		ferə (f.)	
60. flower		fiúr (m.)	
61. sleep (thou)	flî	flenjə 'to sleep' fli (impv.)	u fljeń 'I sleep'
62. l'aria			
63. garlic			fùdẹr
64. nose		fund (f.)	fund

Meyer	Philological interpretation	In situ interpretation	Reconstructed Pre-form
deńa	deňa	deňňə	denjə
deńɛ	deňə ?		
dugɛmɛ	dú(a)Kəmi	duámmi (active) dugəmi (mid.)	duamə duhəmi
	dúa	dúa	dua
do ndeńa 'vorrei'	do		do
	duf	dufə, def. duffi	duf, -i
	e	e	e
	eňa	eňňə	eňə ?
	englə	—— (aň ʒulíK̇Kə-tə)	əngʌə
era	era	era	era
erbi	erb(ə), -i	erbi	eʌb, -i
	ec ?	ecə	ec
t'ɛmblɛtɛ	əmblə	t-əmbʌ-a 'dolci' fiK̇ə-tə 'i fichi'	əmbʌ-
	embr(ə)	—— (nom-i)	embr(ə)
	ərgə́ndr(ə)	trigə́nd-i	(t)r(ə)gə́nd, -i
	fač̇(ə)	faK̇K̇a (def.)	faK̇(ə)a
	fer(ə)	fera (def.)	(Ital. ?)
	fjur	fjurə-tə	(Ital.)
	fli, fleň(ə)	fʌi, fʌeňňə	fʌi, fʌe-ň
frima	frima	frinə 'it blows'	frin (verb)
	fudər	fuddrə	huᵭrə
funda	fund, -a	funda (def.) fundə (indef.)	hundə

Gloss	Bon. '84	Bon. '90	Hanusz
65. that I might beat	funja	ka tə japə funjə 'che ti do mazzate'	
66. thorn, fishbone		glənbə (m.)	
67. finger		glistə (m.)	gljiˇst
68. tongue		glukə (f.)	gljùg
69. milk		gljumstə (m.)	
70. knee		glunjə (f.)	
71. raise (throw)	greg	gri 'rise! ' grigu 'rise up! ' grinə 'to rise (up)'	
72. the mouth		grik, -a	
73. the fork		grok, -a	
74. woman		grúə, gruja	
75. the grain	krúra	grurə, grurədə	
76. ass	kumáre	kumárə	
77. blood		gjakkə (m.)	
78. serpent		gjarprə (m.)	
79. 6			ǵaˇstdjèt
80. breast		gjellə (f.)	
81. the rooster		gjellə (m.)	
82. the middle		gjəmməsə (f.)	
83. relative	gyam	gjəndənə	

Meyer	Philological interpretation	In situ interpretation	Reconstructed Pre-form
	fuňa	fuňňe	huň-e
	gləmb(ə)	gʌambi (def.)	gʌamb, -i
glisti	gliš(t)(ə), -i	gʌišt-i	gʌišt, -i
glistra (pl.)	glištra	gʌištrə-tə	gʌištrə
gluga	gluK(ə), -a	gʌuga (def.) gʌuka [younger speaker]	gʌuhə
glúmestε	glum(e)st(ə) ?	gʌumməšti (def.)	gʌuməšt [sic]
	gluň(ə)	gʌuňňa (def.)	gʌunə (< pl.)
griku 'erhebe dich' (but M. says B's *g* is correct)	gri, griKu, grin(ə)	grigu	gri-, grih-u
grika	grik, -a	grikka (def.)	grikə
groka	grok, -a	grokka, furčinna	(Ital.)
	grúa, gruja	grúe	grúa
grurε	grura	grurə-tə	grurə
gumari gumaria 'l'asina'	gumar(ə), -i	—— (čuč-i m. -a. f.)	gumar, -i
	ǵak(ə)	ǵakku (def.)	ǵak, -u
	ǵarprə	—— (verpə kasaʎe)	ǵarprə
ǵaštε	ǵašt(ə)	ǵaštə	ǵaštə
	ǵel(ə)	ǵellə 'vita'	ǵelə
ǵeli	ǵel(ə), -i	ǵeʎi (def.)	ǵeʎ, -i
	ǵəməs(ə)	ǵəmməsə	ǵəməs(ə) [*í]
	ǵəndən(ə)	—— (kušərí)	ǵənd- [*í]

Gloss	Bon. '84	Bon. '90	Hanusz
84. all		gitthə	gìθ
85. ricotta		gidz (f.)	
86. the chest			
87. eat			uhãn̄
88. open!			hap
89. iron			hèkur
90. moon		thennə	hę̀n
91. I climbed			
92. enter!			hĩr
93. town		horə (f.)	hõr
94. bitter			
95. my	ime, imme imi (pl.)	immə (m. acc.) (f.)	ìmę̀ (f.)
96. was (v. also below)	isì	iх̌i	ix̌si, ix̌se
97. I give, you used to give		japə innə 'give us'*	ìpńe
98. thy		(énbrənə) itə (parraddzi) itə	
99. thy father	játta	jatti	
100. who is	se iete	tš̌ə jetə	
101. you must be to me	mi kadiessiei	ka-tə-jessesə	mę̌ kạ te jèsę̌š̌ jè 'art'

tə jessi bənnə
'may it be done'

*Ururi ïnna, Piana ə̃na
(p.352, 356) = *ə̃nna

Meyer	Philological interpretation	In situ interpretation	Reconstructed Pre-form
	ǵiθ(ə) (g?)	ǵiθθə (? ǵiθə pl.)	ǵiθ(ə)
	ǵiz (g?)	ǵizzə	ǵizə
giu	ǵiu (g?)	ǵíu	ǵi-u
	haň	haňňə	ha-ň
	hap	hapə	hap
	hekur	hekkur-i 'la zappa'	hekur, -i
hennɛ, hɛnne	hən(ə)	hənna (def.)	həna
hipa	hipa	hipə (1 sg. pres.)	hip
	hir	hirə	hir
	hor(ə)	—— (katúnd i-madə)	hor
idrɛ	idrə	e-iddrə	iðrə
imɛ (f.)	imə (f.)	ime mottrə 'my sister'	ime (unstressed)
	imə (m.)	imə nipə 'my nephew'	im
iši	iši	sg. 1. iňňə, 2.iňňe, 3. iši	injə, -e iš(+i)
	jap(ə), ipňe	japə	jap
	in(n)(ə)	—— (huá-mme, bié-mmi)	innə <*əm-nə
jatɛmɛ 'thy mother'	it(ə), jat		it
	jat-i, -a?	jatti 'suo padre'	j-at-i
		tatta 'il padre'	tata
	se/čə jet(ə)	čə jetə 'che cosa c'è? '	jet, jes-
		si jet ti 'come stai? '	
mɛ ka tɛ ješ	mə ka tə-jesəš(ə)	ka tə-jessəšə	
jam je istɛ jemi	jam, je ištə, jemi,	jamə, je, ištə, jemmi,	jam, je, ištə,
ini janɛ	ini, janə	inni, jannə	jemi, (j)ini, janə
íňa íňe isi íšeme	iň, -e, iši, išəm(ə),	iňňa, -e, iši	injə, -e, iš+i,
íšɛte isenɛ	išət(ə), išən(ə)	/išəmə, -ətə, -ənə	+m, +t, +n
u ka tɛ jamɛ. . .	ka tə-jam(ə)		
kleva kleve klevi	kleva, -e, -i, -əm(ə),	kʌevva, -e, -i, -əmə,	kʌe-va, -ve, -vi
klévɛme klévɛte	-ət(ə), -ən(ə)	-ətə, -ənə	
klévɛne			
	tə-jesi		tə-jesi

Gloss	Bon. '84	Bon. '90	Hanusz
102. no	jo	jo	
103. our		(tatta) inə	(gljùg) jònni
		(búkənə) jonnə	
		(tə tiratə) tə	
		tonnatə	
		tə tonna 'ours'	
104. you			ju
105. from		ka	
106. the horse	káli	kalə (m.)	
107. big stick			
108. good-day		mir dit	
		díttənə e mirə	
		dittə	
		pə dítnətə 'daily'	
109. I have	kom leu	kamə lən	ˋkàm e ljèn
	(u miswritten		'I have left it'
	for n?)		
110. the animal			
111. part of loom			kàš
112. 4			katerdjèt
113. village		katundə (m.)	
114. the staircase	kavaljería		
115. the ox			

Meyer	Philological interpretation	In situ interpretation	Reconstructed Pre-form
	jo	jo	jo
	in(ə) jon(ə) tə-tona-t(ə)		in(ə), jon(ə) t-ona-
ju	ju	ju	ju
	ka	ka	ka
kali	kal(ə), -i	kaʎə, kaʎʎi	kaʎ [sic], -i
kaloke̊	kaloke̊		
mirɛ ditɛ	mir(ə) dit(ə) ditan(ə)	dittə, pl. ditə	ditə, pl. dit
	pə ditnət(ə)	nga ditta 'daily' pə dittrətə 'per giorno'	nga dita ditrə-tə
kamɛ lɛnɛ 'I have left'	kam(ə) lən		
kamɛ ke ka kemi k̊ini kanɛ	kam(ə), ke, ka, kemi, kini, kan(ə)	kamə, ke, ka kemmi, kinni, kannə	kam, ke, ka kemi, kini, kanə
kińa kińa kis̊ɛ k̊is̊ɛme k̊is̊ɛte k̊is̊ɛnɛ	kiňa, -a(?), kis̊(ə), -əm(ə), -ət(ə), -ən(ə)	kiňňa, -e, kiši, -əmə,	kinja(?), -e kiš+i, +m, +t, +n~kin
u ka te kemɛ. . .	ka tə-kem(ə). . .		tə-kem
pata pate pati pátemɛ pátetɛ pátenɛ	pata, -e, -i, -əm(ə), -ət(ə), -ən(ə)	patta, -e, -i, -əmə, -ətə, -ənə	pata, -e, -i, -əm, -ət, -ən
kaš̆a kaš̆e-tɛ (pl.)	kaš̆-a -ə-ʈ(ə)	kaš̆ə 'giumenta' kaš̃še	kaš̆ <*kafš̆- kaš̆e
	kaš̆	—	
katɛr	katər	kattrə	katrə
	katund(ə)	katundi (def.) (tt?)	katund, -i
	kavalería ?	—— (škalla)	
kau	kau	k̊e, def. k̊eu	ka, -u, pl. k̊e

Gloss	Bon. '84	Bon. '90	Hanusz
116. evil		təkekia (nom. def.)	
117. lime		kerkjerə (m.)	
118. glass		kerkjə (m.)	
119. foot		kənbə (f.)	
120. the bell	kampára	kunborə, -a	kumbòr/kẹmbòr
121. the shirt		kumíš	
122. speak			u kušiloń kẹšilommi 'parlons'
123. thus		kəstú	
124. this			(me) kẹ̀t
125. I was, it was	klevui 'it was'	klevvi 'it was' kjoštə 'amen'	u kljèva, kljève 'it was'
126. church	klíša	kliša	kljiš
127. key		klittšə (m.)	
128. the penis			
129. sanctificetur		tə jessi kljottə enbrənə itə	
130. blow, coup			kopanè
131. il berretto			
132. the arms		kragə	
133. head		kríə (f.)	
134. worm		krinbə (m.)	
135. wine	krisí	krisí	
136. people, men	de kristéra	də krəštératə	greštèra

Meyer	Philological interpretation	In situ interpretation	Reconstructed Pre-form
	tə-keḱia (ə? accent?)	—— (dəmə)	(uncertain)
	kərḱer(ə)	krəḱḱerə	kə/ḱer
	ḱerḱ(ə) (surely ḱ-)	ḱerḱə, -i	ḱe/ḱ, -i
kɛmba	kəmb(ə), -a	kəmbə	kəmbə
	kumbor(ə)	kumborə	kəmborə
kɛmiša	kumiš, -a	kumišə (mm? ss?)	kəmišə
	kušiloň kušilomi	kušiloňňa (ll?) kušilommi	kašiló-ň
	kəštú	kəštú	kəštú
	kət	—— (me ḱi . . .)	kət(ə)
kleve 'it was'	kleva, -i ḱošt(ə)	k/evva etc.	(see above)
kliša	kliš, -a	k/iša (def.)	k/iša
	klič(ə)	k/ičči (def.)	k/ič, -i
klítšeka	kličeka	k/iččə kə 'scemo' (kan ǯárre 'penis')	
	klot(ə)	k/otə (tt?) tə tə k/ošši 'che ti benedica'	
	kopané	kopané~bottə	
kosulá	kosula	——	
krage-tɛ	kragə-tə	kragə, pl. -tə	krahə
krie	kríe	kría	kríe (-a ?)
	krimb(ə)	krimbə, pl. -tə	krimb, pl. -ə
	krisí	kr sí, -u (~verə)	krəsí (Apulian Gk.)
tɛ kristerɛ	tə-krəštéra	krəštérə, pl. tə-krəštéra	krəšter, pl. -a

Gloss	Bon. '84	Bon. '90	Hanusz
137. Christi			krĭšti
138. where	ku		ku
139. red		kukjə	
140. ring			
141. tu as penetré, du hast durchschaut			kundzędrò
142. (the) shoe(s)	kupúts	kupúts	
143. la caldaja			
144. who		kušJ	
145. cousin			
146. throat		kjaf (f.)	
147. the dog		kjen (m.)	
148. lamb		kjengrə (m.)	
149. coach		kjerrə	
150. the sky		kjelə	
151. the vagina			
152. 100			
153. snot			
154. the hoe			
155. high		jertə	

Meyer	Philological interpretation	In situ interpretation	Reconstructed Pre-form
kristi	krišti	krišti	krišt-i
	ku	ku	ku
	kuḱ(ə)	i-kuḱə, e-kuḱe	i-kuḱ, e-kuḱ +e (*e-kuḱe)
kunáze	kunaz(ə)	kunázzə	kunazə [sic]
kunzedroje	kunz dró-jə (?)	kunʒədró 'considera!'	(Ital.)
kupútse-te	kupúc(ə)-tə	kupúcə	kəpúc
kusía	kusía	kusía	
kuše	kuš(ə)	kušə	kuš
kušerí	kušərí	kušərí	kušərí
	ḱaf	ḱaffa (def.)	ḱafa
ḱeni	ḱen, -i	ḱenni (def.)	ḱen, -i
	ḱengrə	ḱenǵəri (def.), pl. ḱenǵəra	ḱenǵər-
	ḱeř(ə)		ḱeř(ə)
ḱieli	ḱel( ), -i	ḱeli (cf. dieli)	ḱ(i)él+i
ḱima "Eig. 'das Harr'" (since qime is a single hair, and lesh is 'hair', better to qij 'copulate')	ḱima	——(šahárre) ḱimmə-tə 'hairs'	ḱimə
ńe ḱinde	ńə ḱind(ə)	ńə ḱində	ḱind
ḱure	ḱuř(ə) ?	ḱurrə	ḱuř(ə)
l'amādia	lamadia	lamáǵǵa	
l'arte	lart(ə) ?	ʎartə 'sopra' jertu 'alto'	art Ital.

Gloss	Bon. '84	Bon. '90	Hanusz
156. leave	lenji 'I leave'	lenjə 'I leave' lən 'left'	ljèn 'left'
157. dimittere		lerə 'dimitte' lemmi 'dimittimus'	
158. the hairs	léšidi	leš̃sə (m.) (pl.) leštədə, leštə	
159. skin		ləkúr (f.)	
160. ugly		ligə nd-udə e lliggə 'in tentationem'	
161. tree		lis (m.)	
162. lean		lístəkə	
163. the testicles			
164. cow			
165. the grandfather			
166. but	ma	ma	
167. big		matə	mad
168. knife		mafiér (m.)	mafjèrja
169. fat		máimə	
170. to take you			tè̦ t'm̦àr ti
171. the cat		mattsə (m.)	
172. evening	brem	brəmmə, brənbə (f.)	mbrè̦m, mbrè̦mb
173. with	me	mə, me	me

Meyer	Philological interpretation	In situ interpretation	Reconstructed Pre-form
lenɛ	len(ə) 1.sg. lən(ə) pple.	ʌeňňə ʌənnə	ʌe-ň, ʌənə
	ler(ə) lemi	ʌer-e 'lasciala' ʌerə 'lascia!'	ʌer-
íes-tɛ	leš-tə, leš(ə)	ʌeš-tə	ʌeš, -tə
	ləkúr	ʌəkkúrə	əkúrə
	lig(ə)	i-ʌigə, e-ʌiggə	i-ʌig, e-ʌigə
	lis	ʌissi (def.)	ʌis, -i
	lístək(ə)	i-lístəkə ~i-hollə	i-holə
loke-tɛ	loke-tə	—	ʌoke
lopɛ	lop(ə)	ʌoppə	ʌopə
loši Eig. 'der Alte'	loši	imə ʌošə 'mio bisnonno'	ʌoš, -i
	ma		
	maT(ə)	i-madə, e-madde	i-mað, e-maðe
mafiéria	mafiér-ja	mafiérə (not used) hikkə	mahjér
	majm(ə)	i-majmə	i-majm(ə)
se tɛ marɛ ti	se/tə tə mar(ə) ?	tə tə márə mirə (impv.)	mar [sic] mir
matša	mač(ə), -a	macča (def.)	mača
mbrɛmba mirɛ mbrɛmbɛ	mbrəm(b)(ə), -a	brəmbə, -a brəmbrətə 'in the evenings'	mbrəm(b)ə mbrəmbrə-tə
me	me	me	me

Gloss	Bon. '84	Bon. '90	Hanusz
174. morning		menattə (f.)	
175. silk		mendãs̃sə (m.)	
176. noon		mezədittə (f.)	
177. mother	mma	jema, məmma	[ɱma] mḛma
178. medal		məralljə (f.)	
179. la tovaglia, tablecloth		məsál, -a	
180. good	mir	mirə	mir
181. the flesh	missi 'flesh'	mišt, 'flesh' mištədə	
182. beard		miekrə (f.)	
183. apple(-tree)		mollə (f.)	
184. don't		mosə	
185. my sister			
186. little piece			
187. the mule	múskia	muškə 'he-mule' muška 'she-mule'	
188. frog		nannaronkjə (f.)	
189. now	naní	naní	nanì
190. night		nattə (f.)	
191. in		ndə, nd(+V)	nd (gljùg)
192. beautiful		ndarə	
193. feel, hear			

Meyer	Philological interpretation	In situ interpretation	Reconstructed Pre-form
	menat(ə)	so-menáttə 'sta m.' menáttrətə 'in mornings'	(so-)menátə
	mendaš(ə)	məndašsi (def.)	mes(ə)dítə
	mezədit(ə)	mesədíttə	mes(ə)dítə
jatɛmɛ 'your mother'	jat- m(ə), j- ma	j-əma (mm ?)	j-əma
mɛma	məma	məmma	məma
	məraljə	məraΛə	Ital.
mɛsalla	məsal, -a	məsalla (def.)	məsala
mirɛ	mir(ə)	mirə	mirə
	mišt(ə)-tə	mištə	miš-tə
mjekrɛ	miékrə	miékkrə	miékrə
	mol(ə)	molla (def.)	mola
	mos(ə)	mosə	mos
imɛ motrɛ	motrə	mottrə	motrə
motsɛkɛ	mocək(ə)	mockə	mockə
	mušk(ə) muška	muškə muška (def.)	mušk muškə
	nanaronk̃(ə)	nannarrónkəla	
nani	naní	naní	naní
natɛ mirɛ nat	nat(ə)	nattrətə 'at night'	natrə-tə
ndɛ	ndə	ndə	ndə
	ndar(ə)	i-ndarə (*'distinto'?)	nda-
ndie 'senti'	ndíe	ndié ndiéňňə (1.sg. pres.)	ndié-ň

Gloss	Bon. '84	Bon. '90	Hanusz
194. to raise		ndzirə	
195. we		nə, nevé (dat.)	ne
196. water		neró	
197. 9			
198. each			ngà
199. not	ge	ngə	ngę̀
200. nephew			
201. the bride	rússia	nus, -i (m.)* nússie, -ia (f.) 'the betrothed'	nusja
202. the twine	nússi		
203. a little			ńaj
204. one			
205. man		njərí (m.)	
206. you know			ju nìgni
207. little		pagə	
208. I saw			peu
209. false	pansan	panzán	panzàn
210. paradise		párraddzi (def.)	
211. the mare	pélja	pellə, pellja	
212. the thought		pendzierin (acc.)	
213. 5			pesdjèt

*seems questionable.

Meyer	Philological interpretation	In situ interpretation	Reconstructed Pre-form
	nʒir(ə)	nʒir-e 'levalo!' nʒiérə (1 sg. pres.)	nʒiér [sic] nʒir-
ne	ne	ne	ne
	neró	újjə-tə	Apulian Gk. loan?
nεnde	nənd(ə)	nəndə	nóndə
	nga	nga	nga
ngε	ngə	ngə, nəngə (emphat.)	ngə, nóngə
nipε	nip(ə)	nipə	nip
	nusje, -ja	nusse, def. nussja	nuse, nusja
	?		
ńaj	ňaj	ňaj	ňai ?
ńε	ňə	ňə	ňə
	ňərí	aí ňorí 'uno quello' ató ňoríra 'tutti quelli'	ňerí (o!?)
	ju ňigni	sg.1. ňogə, 2. ňegə, 2 pl. ňigni	ňoh, ňeh, ňihni
	paK(ə)	pagə	pag
pava	pava pe u (?)	pavva, -e, -i etc. par (pple.)	pa-va etc. par
panzan	panzán	panʒánnə 'bugía'	
	páraʒi	parrázzi	paraz-i
pelia 'il giumento'	pel(ə), pelja	peʎe, peʎa	peʎe, peʎja
	penʒierin	pənʒiérə-tə (pl.)	Ital.
pesε	pes(ə)	pessə	pesə

Gloss	Bon. '84	Bon. '90	Hanusz
214. fish		pĕškə (m.)	
215. for	pe (pentsò pe 'think of')	pə (pər de 'on earth')	pę̇
216 think	pentsò	pəndzó	
217. apricot(-tree)		pərnakokkə	
218. before	perpona	pərpara	pęrpàra
219. the vagina			
219. pinches			
221. old man, old woman		plakkə (m., f.)	
222. il letame, dust		pləkə (f.)	
223. full			pljòt
224. the fair	potsára		
225. the priest			
226. let us return	pierrimi	piérrimi	prìremi
227. embers			
228. rich		pugattə	
229. the hen		pullə (f.)	
230. plant		rezzə (f.)	
231. toad		ruespə (m.)	
232. the dove			
233. the grapes	rrušă	rušə (f.)	

Meyer	Philological interpretation	In situ interpretation	Reconstructed Pre-form
	pešk(ə)	peškə (sg.=pl.) peškuti (gen. sg.)	pešk peškut
pɛ	pə	pə	pə(r)
	pənʒó	pənʒó	Ital.
	pərnakok(ə)	pərnakókkə-tə	
pɛrpara	pərpára	rpára	r(ə)pára
pitši	piči	[not elicited]	(piθ-i)
pítsɛkɛ	pícək(ə)	pícəkə (sg. indef.)	
	plak(ə)	m. pʌakə (pʌagə), pl. pʌakke~pʌeḱe f. pʌakkə, pl. pʌakke	pʌak pʌeḱ(+e) pʌakə
plegɛ-tɛ*	pleK(ə)-tə	pʌəga (def.) 'house dust'	pʌəha
	plot	e-pʌottə	e-pʌotə
	pocára	―	pocár-
prieti	prieti	pritti	priti (*ft)
priremi	priremi	piérrimi [sic]	piéř-
prušɛ	pruš(ə)	pruⱨⱨsi	pruš, -i
	bugat(ə) ?	i-pugáttə (gg?)	i-pəgátə
pulja	pul(ə), pulja	puʎʎə, def. puʎʎa	puʌe, puʌja
	rez(ə)	rrəzzə, pl. -a	řəzə
	ruesp(ə)	ruéspi (def.) [thought of as Ital.; = 'frog']	
ruka	ruka	rukka	
rušɛ	ruš(ə) (ř?)	rruš-tə	řus-tə

*"Bon. plɛkɛ ungenau,
da tosk. plĕhɛ entspricht."

Gloss	Bon. '84	Bon. '90	Hanusz
234. how much			
235. lenzuolo, bed-sheet		sandón (m.)	
236. that	se 'who' ke (obj. clause) ge 'what'	kə (obj. clause) tšə, sə	sè (obj. clause) čè̞ 'what', 'who' č̦ (plus V)
237. in order to			
238. as		si	
239. the eye(s)		si, -u, pl. sitə	
240. today		sodə	
241. 'vjerš'			sunèt
242. the hat		šárpəkə (m.)	
243. saints	šéndra	šendə, pl. šendədə šendidi (gen.) 'spirti'	
244. ladder		škal	
245. used to break			škandogše
246. belly			
247. I walked	skoda	škoda	škòda
248. (the) writing			tȩ škrùor
249. musket		škupette (f.)	
250. I see			ušòg
251. wife	skiókkje	šokkjə (f.)	šòkje
252. the husband		šokkjə (m.)	
253. lead		(mosənə) špirə 'don't lead us.'	

Meyer	Philological interpretation	In situ interpretation	Reconstructed Pre-form
sa	sa	sa	sa
sandón	sandón	sandonni (def.)	
se (obj. clause)	se, ǩə (?)	se	se
tše, se	čə	čə	čə
tše 'what'			
se tɛ	se tə	tə	(se) tə
	si	si	si
si-tɛ	si, -u, -t(ə)	si-tə pl.	si+tə
	soT(ə)	sotə	sot
	sunét	——	
šapoka	šápək-a ?	šarpə	šarpə(-kə)
sendi 'the saint'	šend(ə), -i pl. šendə-Tə gen. šendiTi	šendə pl. šendrə-tə	šend, pl. -rə šendit
	škal		
	škandogše ?	čaññə, -e, etc.	ča-ň
škefɛ	škef(ə)	——	
škoda	škoda	škoda	škoda
	tɪəǩúar	pple. škruátrə	skrua-
	škupete	škuppéttə	
	šog	šogə	šoh
šoke ešokia	šoke, e-šoka	ime šoǩke	soǩe
išoǩi	soǩ(ə), i-šoǩi	imə šoǩə	šoǩə
	špir(ə)	špir-e 'portalo via!' špíe 1.sg. pres.	špíe, špir-

Gloss	Bon. '84	Bon. '90	Hanusz
254. spiritus		spirti (gen.)	
255. 7			
256. the house	stipía	stipí, -a	štępìja
257. bed		stratə, -i	
258. button (of flowers) bud (of trees)		šunbə (m.)	
259. much		summə	
260. the plate		talurə (m.)	
261. the father		tattə, tatta inə 'our father' táttəsə (gen.)	
262. land		te, -u, de	tē
263. 8			
264. tooth		tənbə, -i	tęmb
265. son-in-law			tęndr
266. rope		tərgudz (f.)	
267. watch		tərloddžə (m.)	
268. thou	ti, mettí 'with you' ta (obj. of verb) te	ti, pərpara tə škoda	ti, tę (after prep.) te (obj. of verb) te pę tì
269. others		tə tiéravə (dat. pl.)	
270. debts		tə tíratə	
271. big		i ttrašə (m.) e ttrašə (f.)	

Meyer	Philological interpretation	In situ interpretation	Reconstructed Pre-form
	spirti ?	špirti	šprit-i
statɛ	štat(ə) ?	štattə	štatə
štepía	štəpí, -a	st pí	štəpí
	strat(ə), -i	štratə, štratti	štrat, -i
	šumb(ə)	sumbə, pl. -e	sumb(ə)
	sum(ə) ?	šummə	šumə
taĺúri	talúr(ə), -i	—— (pjatti)	taʎúr, -i
tata	tat(ə), -a / tatə s(ə)	tatta	tatə, -a / tatəsə
teu	te, -u	te-u	ðe, -u
tetɛ	tet(ə)	tettə	tetə
tembɛ-tɛ / timbalɛ-tɛ 'the molars'	təmb(ə), -i, -t / timbal -t	təmbə sg.=pl. / təmbállə-tə	ðəmb, -i, pl. -ə / ðəmbálə
	təndr	i-təndri (def.)	ðəndr-i
	tərKuz	trəkkúzə (zz?)	trəkúzə
	tərlož̌(ə)	tərlóž̌ž̌i (def.)	tərlož̌-i
ti; pɛrpara te (obj. of verb te)	ti / tə, te (+prep. ?) / tə (+verb)	ti, gen. tíuti / ti / tə	ti / ti, te / tə
	tə tiérav(ə) ?	tə tiérave	tiéra-ve
	tə tira-tə ?	tətírə sg. / tətíra pl.	ðatir- ?
	i-traš(ə) / e-traš(ə)	i-trašš̃ə / e-trašš̃ə	i-, e-traš̌.ə

Gloss	Bon. '84	Bon. '90	Hanusz
272. 3			tredjèt
273. the oats	trešíra	trašǝrǝ trǝšǝ́rǝdǝ (def.)	
274. young man		trimǝ (m.)	
275. the brain			
276. the ax			
277. I speak		ngǝ tǝ hava 'I didn't say	u hom
278. knife		thik, -a	hik / fik
279. I pretended	finja	thinja	θìńa
280. the fingernail		thonjǝ (f.)	
281. seat, bench			θròn
282. I	u	u	u
283. road		uddǝ (f.), udǝ	ūd
284. water		ujǝ (f.)	
285. the olives		ulinj (m.) 'olive tree', (f.) 'olive'	
286. vinegar			ùθuĩ
287. poor		vábbǝkǝ	
288. oil			
289. chin		vangarielǝ, -i	
290. baby, boy child, lad		vanjunǝ, -i	
291. low		i vašsu (m.) e vašsu (f.)	
292. girl		vadz (f.)	

Meyer	Philological interpretation	In situ interpretation	Reconstructed Pre-form
tre	tre	tre	tre
trešɛre 'biada'	trəšə́rə-Tə	trəšə́rə	trəšə́rə
	trim(ə)	trimə, def. trimmi	trim, -i
tru-tɛ	tru-t(ə)	tru-tə	tru, -tə
tsuppata	cupata	(cappúnni 'zappone')	supáta ?
θugeše 'was called'	hom, hava	homə, havva	θom, θa-
θa 'she said'	θa ?	havvi	θa
	θik h-?	hikkə, -a	θikə, -a
θińa	θiňa	hiňňə 'I was saying'	θinjə
θońa	θoňa	hoňňə, pl. -e	θoňə (<pl.)
	θron	fronə, def. fronni	θron, -i
	u	u	u
	ud(ə)	uddə	uðə
ujɛ	uj(ə)	ujjə	ujə
uliń-tɛ	uliň-tə	ulí~ulíňňə, pl. ulín-tə	ulí~uliňə (<pl.)
	úθul	úθθ(u)la (def.)	úθula
	vábək(ə)	i-vábbəgə	i-vábəg
valɛ	val(ə)	vaʎə, def. vartə	vaʎ, -tə
	vangariel(ə), -i	vangariélli (def.)	Ital.
	vaňun(ə), -i	vaňňunə, def. vaňňunni	Ital.
	vašu	vaššu	Ital.
vazɛ	vaz(ə)	vazzə, pl. -a	vazə { *vajzə / pl. vašazə[x]

Gloss	Bon. '84	Bon. 90	Hanusz
293. wine		verə	
294. ear		veš̃š̃ə (m.)	
295. alone			
296. come		tə vî 'may it come'	
297. thief			
298. little		vongljə	
299. I looked (at)			vrèta
300. 20			
301. black		zeddzə	
302. the heart	zímbra	zənbra	zè̦mbr, zè̦mbra
303. ti vorrei dare			
304. the fire		dziárr	
305. signore			
306. sir		zodərottə	
307. the birds			

Meyer	Philological interpretation	In situ interpretation	Reconstructed Pre-form
verε	ver(ə)	verə, def. vera	verə, -a
veš	veš(ə)	vešə, def. veš̃si	veš, -i
vetε vet	vet(ə)	vettə	vetə
	tə-vi	duá tə-viňə do tə-višə, -tə-vijji	tə-viň, viš, viji
viedεsarε	viedəsar(ə)	verb: 1 sg. pres. viédə pple. viéddrə	vieð vieðrə
	vonglə	i-vongʌə	i-vo(n)gʌə
vreda	vreTa	vreta, 1 sg. pres. vreňə	vreň, vre+ta
ńezét	ňəzét	—— (ditiéttə)	ňəzét
	zez(ə)	i-zezzə, e-zezzə	e-zezə
zεmbra	zəmbr, -a	zəmbra (def.) 'vorrei prenderti'	zəmbr-a
ti stε zεńa	zəňa (? sense?)	deňňa tə tə zəňňa 'vorrei prenderti'	zənja ?
ziaři	zjař, -i	zjarə, def. zjarri [sic]	zjar, pl. zjař( )
zodε	zoT(ə)	zotə, def. zotti	zot, -i
	zoTərot(ə)	zotəróttə	zotər(iaej)ótə
zoǵe-tε	zoǵə-t(ə)	zogə, def. zoggu, pl. zoǵe-tə [sic]	zog, -u, pl. zóǵ

17. Phonemics in the Nineteenth Century, 1876-1900

Rulon Wells

I. The Problem

The concept of language-structure is one on which we now begin to have historical perspective. It only flourished within recent decades; within the last twenty-five years it has undergone dramatic and important modifications. It still continues to serve as a major and fruitful concept.

It is, furthermore, a concept with kindred in other sciences: with Gestalt in psychology, with functionalism in anthropology, with "New Criticism" in literary criticism, and so on. The broader concept of which it is a version may fairly be called one of the key-concepts of recent social science.

One part of the general concept of language-structure has been applied with especial success; I mean phonemics. The reason why phonemics has been especially successful is that it is especially simple. Studies of the phonological subsystem of a language have an advantage in linguistics very roughly comparable to those by Galileo of falling bodies in physics, and by Mendel of unlinked dominant-recessive inheritance in genetics. So true has this been that much work with the structure-concept has consisted in simply trying to *carry over*, into other parts of linguistics, concepts and methods that have proved more or less workable in phonemics.

The comparison with Galileo and Mendel holds good as regards the chronological order. Simple laws of locomotion had been sought before Galileo, and of inheritance before Mendel. There was much that Galileo and Mendel never explained, but each of them hit on a subsystem of phenomena that he *could* explain, in abstraction from the rest of his total science. Likewise structuralism had been attempted before phonemics, most notably by Humboldt, but without success. The first real major successes in structural description were hypotheses that involved automatic alternation, complementary distribution, and morphophonemic pattern; and they will be

434

the focus of the present study. These successes were, at first, unaccompanied by methodological discussion. They were due to Brugmann, Saussure, Sievers, and others, in a cluster of discoveries in 1876-1880. Methodological discussion came from Kruszewski, Baudouin de Courtenay, and, some years later, Saussure and Meillet. Of all these men, Saussure is clearly outstanding in that he alone belongs to both groups. However, the theoretical work of Saussure as well as of Meillet falls later than the period of the present study, which is the last quarter of the nineteenth century (1876-1900).

Concepts, like animals, have a gestation period, but they differ in that they are conceived again and again before they are born. In fact the analogy is closer with something like starting a cold gasoline engine than with the life cycle which proceeds continuously and monotonically once it is commenced. Before the successful attempt which "takes", there are (all too often) preliminary sparks that don't take, that cause a brief sputter and then die. And sometimes an unsuccessful spark is worse than none at all; we sometimes find that we have to wait awhile, letting the engine stand, before it is worth while to make another try. At other times a spark even though unsuccessful helps to warm up the engine. Yet other sparks seem to make no difference one way or the other. All three kinds of sparks are found in the early history of phonemics.

I hope to write a larger history of the phoneme concept going as far back as 1791 (Kempelen) and as far forward as the mid-1930's; in the present study I sacrifice breadth to depth by focusing on a momentous transition. Phonemics had as its immediate background two main movements, phonetics and the comparative method. These two movements were intimately connected but had very different fortunes. Phonetics had fundamentally failed in the tasks it had set itself; the comparative method, on the other hand, reached new heights in the second edition (1897) of the first volume (Phonology) of Brugmann's *Comparative Indo-European Grammar*. The failure of phonetics led to a diagnosis of its mistakes; the success of comparative linguistics proved that in some way it was independent of phonetics. The precise relevance of phonetics to linguistics began to be re-evaluated; and the possibility and the necessity of a re-evaluation were proved at about the same time.

The reason why phonetics failed is what makes this topic pertinent to the history of the human sciences generally. One might argue that since language is a part of human life, the history of the science of language must be part of the history of the sciences of man. But there is no need to fall back on this abstract and a priori argument, when a very concrete one is at hand. Phonetics failed because it failed to observe *objectively*, and it failed to observe objectively because it failed to calibrate the observations of different observers. It needed a correcting formula like the "personal equation" of the astronomers. Only here the variation to be reckoned with is not from individual to individual, but from language-group to language-group. This is the cultural factor.

II. The State of Phonetics about 1876

A masterly presentation of the science is found in the *Phonetik* of F. Techmer (1880), a handsome specimen of the *Handbuch* genre, and a work which displays, if no outstanding originality, still a very wide, discerning, and acute erudition. Its subtitle, *Zur vergleichenden Physiologie der Stimme und Sprache*, shows its emphasis; Techmer's strength was in philosophy and in physiology, not in Indo-European linguistics. To learn of applications to historical linguistics and to the comparative method we must turn elsewhere, e.g., to Otto Jespersen's *Language* (1923) and *Linguistica* (1933). The next year Techmer founded the *Internationale Zeitschrift für allgemeine Sprachwissenschaft*, which ran until his death in 1889 and is a mine of information for the historian of linguistics.

The comparative method was applied first mainly to the Indo-European languages, as the unbalanced but not unfair book of Holger Pedersen shows, *Linguistic Science in the Nineteenth Century* (1931). As far as I know, all nineteenth-century advances in the comparative method and in the inductive generalizations which it yielded were made by workers in Indo-European languages, so that no distortion is introduced into our account by confining attention to this family.

(A distinction should be made between historical linguistics and comparative linguistics. Comparative linguistics is linguistics so far as it can be done by the comparative method when applied to cognate languages. The result of comparing two cognate languages is a language, ordinarily distinct from both of these, which may be regarded as a parent [or remoter ancestor] of them; either of them may be considered a later stage of it. But the study of earlier and later stages of the same language is historical linguistics. Consequently the task of comparative linguistics is something like the inverse of the task of historical linguistics; it is to advance the hypothesis, given such and such languages as data, that such and such a language could have given rise to all of these languages by the known processes and probabilities of historical linguistics. Thus the problem of comparative linguistics involves the problem of historical linguistics, and more besides.)

Now by 1876 phonetics had won recognition as the basis of comparative linguistics (cf. Jespersen *Linguistica* 4-5). However strange this might seem to us, it did not have this recognition from the outset. The history of the comparative method up to the present time may be divided into three stages: the literal, the phonetic, and the phonemic. In the literal phase, whose chief spokesman was Grimm, written language was regarded as primary; letters, therefore, were the elements of language, and "Buchstabenlehre" was the basis. In the second, phonetic phase, primacy was given to spoken language; at the same time a concomitant, though logically quite independent shift demanded a more rigorous accounting for changes than had been the practice. The first shift led to an interest in sounds; the second, to a minute interest in them. In the third phase spoken language was still primary, but a principle was discovered for being less minutely interested in sounds; this was the phonemic principle.

Now the passage from the first stage to the second required a battle; and a very important fact in the history of phonemics is that to the winners of the second stage the advance to the third stage looked like a mere relapse into the first. We have here a striking instance of a Hegelian triad, in which the negation of a negation is not a mere return to the original but an advance to something new in which what had gone before is absorbed and transcended. The first-stage talk about letters did have some point after all. "No wonder that the earlier linguists spoke in terms of 'letters'; the actual continuum of speech sound (*la parole*) was not what they meant, and they had no term for the abstraction of the socially determined features of this sound continuum" (Bloomfield 1927: 217). But to people whose minds were formed in the second stage, phonemics looked like a reintroduction of Grimm.

The comparative method in its second phase, then, was built on a certain conception of phonetics. History can give a nearly complete explanation of this conception, in the sense that it can exhibit the ideals of phonetics on the one hand and of comparative linguistics on the other as ideals generally shared by sciences of the day, and can justify failures of phonetics by showing that their avoidance would have required techniques that were not available to any science at the time. But there is one fact for which no historical explanation occurs to me; this is the failure of phonetics to take the "personal equation" seriously. I will return to this point.

III. The Theory of Gradual Phonetic Change

The connection between phonetics and comparative linguistics made perfect sense. Linguistics fully accepted the aim of explanation (as contrasted with sheer description). To explain a language then was to explain how it came to be what it is; that is, to explain the later by the earlier. And this involved sound-changes. But an explanation—any explanation—ought to be guided by the maxim of reasoning from the known to the unknown; in historical work this meant employing Lyell's principle of uniformitarianism, that only those basic processes should be invoked in our hypotheses which we can see to be now at work. These gradual processes will over a great period of time produce great effects. We should, therefore, have a minute knowledge of the possible processes of phonetic change.

Having reasoned this far, phoneticians made a very interesting further inference. To know the possible phonetic changes, we must know *all* the possible speech-sounds, that is, all those which the human voice is capable of producing and of employing in speech. Then, given any two sounds A and B, we can know that A can change directly into B if, and only if, A is extremely similar to B. And A can only change into B under two conditions: (i) if it can change directly into B, or (ii) if there exists a chain of possible speech-sounds A, C_1, . . . , C_n, B such that each one can change directly into the immediately following member of the chain. That is, the only possible indirect changes are those that can be wholly mediated by direct ones.

This very interesting inference is based, plainly, on a principle of continuity: sound changes must be gradual. Various exceptions had to be admitted; they do not concern us here, because it was held that in any case most sound change has this gradual character.

Notice the formal identity between this theory of sound-change and the theory of natural selection. To put the point in terms of logic, each theory assumes a similarity-relation which is non-transitive, but whose ancestral is transitive. The two theories differ only in the material side or nature of the similarity. In Darwinism the relation holds between a parent and its offspring; in sound-change, between two sounds. The cause of the relation is, in each case, quasi-teleological; in biological reproduction, each parent tries as it were to reproduce its own kind exactly, and each speaker making a certain sound tries to reproduce a certain ideal exactly, but in each case chance deviation enters in; in other words, exact replication is impossible, but close resemblance is possible. Parent and offspring will be indistinguishable in species, as judged by the fertility-test; model sound and replicated sound will be indistinguishable in species, by whichever of two tests they are judged: the test of articulation, and the test of auditory effect. But it is possible that A is indistinguishable from C_1, and C_1 from C_2, and . . . and C_{n-1} from C_n, and C_n from B, and yet that A is distinguishable from B. (Indeed, in the case of the just-noticeable-difference mentioned below, n = 1 : A is indistinguishable from C, and C from B, and yet A is distinguishable from B.) Distinguishability can emerge from indistinguishability.

In one further important respect the Darwinian model resembles the model for sound change. Darwin supposes that his minute variations are random, understanding this to entail that, if represented by the model of target-shooting (*stochastic* activity, to use the Greek word), the mean, or center of gravity, of the variations will coincide with the center of the target. And he supposes this first process, of random variation, to be followed by a second, selection, which divides the class of variants into two subclasses: those that are preserved or selected, and those that are rejected or destroyed. Inasmuch as the selection, unlike the variation, is not random, the selected subclass will have a different mean both from that of the other subclass and from that of the whole class, and it is this mean that will function as ideal or target in the next generation or reproductions. The analogue in the theory of sound change is stated by the ease-theory (stated as early as 1791, by Kempelen, according to Techmer 1880, 1.83): those variants that are easier to pronounce will be preserved, and those that are harder will be rejected. (It is not essential to suppose that a rejectable variant will actually be pronounced before it is rejected; the model describes variation and selection as two conceptually distinct steps, but does not require that they be chronologically separate. Thus the linguistic application of the theory differs materially from the genetic application, but not formally.)

Darwin's theory supposes two processes, then, of which the first depends on a relation (sameness of biological species between parent and offspring) which is not transitive though its ancestral is. He was not the first to call attention to such a relation, for Weber's study of just-noticeable-difference (on which see Techmer 1891: 1-92), developed into a psychophysics by Fechner, preceded him by a quarter of a century. The psychological work, however, was purely synchronic; Darwin's application was diachronic and was an instance of conforming to Lyell's uniformitarianism. Subsequently other applications of the formal model were noticed; Charles Peirce's discussion (1931-1935, 1: 209-10, 88-91) of the weights found by Flinders Petrie at Naucratis is notable; the process of selection is exquisitely clear, because weights for buyers tended to be excessive, and weights for sellers deficient. And the study of dialect-geography brought a linguistic application to light. Mutual intelligibility of dialects is not transitive, but its transitive ancestral defines what Bloomfield calls a language-community.

The foregoing account is my own reconstruction; I have not seen the formal identity between Darwinism and the theory of sound change stated so sharply, even by linguists writing on the topic "The influence of Darwinism on linguistics". Such a statement would have been anachronistic at the time when this topic was a favorite, for it makes use of two notions hardly exploited until around 1900, by Bertrand Russell and others: (1) the general notion of a pure or formal logic related to various applications as a pure mathematical theory is related to *its* applications, and (2) in particular, the pure logic of relations.

It was often said that sound-change is continuous. It would be more accurate to speak of *quasi*-continuity, by which I mean the property of a series that is discrete but with such small intervals between successive terms that they cannot be empirically observed.

What is of present importance is that this theory of sound change posed a certain task for phoneticians. They saw it as their task to describe every possible sound of human speech. With an organized inventory of all those sounds, each sound being adequately described, they could (in principle) answer every question of this form: Given sounds A and B, is there a series of direct changes that would lead from A to B? They thought that an affirmative answer to such a question was a necessary condition for explaining the change; as to whether it was also a sufficient condition, they appear to have been vague.

The phoneticians, then, supposed that they faced this task: to describe all speech-sounds. Only gradually did a very simple logically prior question dawn on them: What is a speech-sound? That is, only slowly did they realize that the seemingly obvious answer to this question won't do.

The question thus phrased looks like a request for a definition of the usual sort, but actually something is involved that definitions seldom do justice to. This is the question of identity-conditions. Under what conditions are sound A and sound B to be considered the same speech-sound?

One possible answer is that there is to be no qualitative difference between them whatever; they must differ, as in Leibniz's phrase, *solo numero*. If there is any qualitative difference between them, they are to be considered two speech-sounds, not one.

Another answer is that there is to be no *observable* qualitative difference between them. If we give this answer we must specify the means of observation. We might mean "observable by every adult with normal hearing", or "observable by every adult native speaker of the language in question with normal hearing" or "observable by any person who has been trained in such and such ways and has passed such and such tests", and so on. Or the observation might be made dependent on various instruments.

If we appeal to ears, or to instruments that take the place of ears, we describe the sound in terms of its effects. It is possible to describe a sound in quite different terms, namely its causes. The one description is acoustic (auditory), the other organic (articulatory). It then becomes a matter for investigation how far the auditory and the articulatory approach will agree. And this is a problem of identity-conditions. Let us call a sound described in articulatory terms an articulatory sound, and a sound described in auditory terms an auditory sound. If articulatory sound A and articulatory sound B are the same, by some specified criterion, then are auditory sound A and auditory sound B (respectively caused by the articulatory sounds) the same, by some specified criterion? This question was never *systematically* investigated, neither within our period nor later; but it came to be recognized that in some cases the answer is negative. For cases were found where two articulatory sounds that were indistinguishable by the methods of the day caused auditory sounds that were easily distinguishable. (This "alternating-sounds" phenomenon is discussed below, in connection with Boas.) Of course one can suppose that more precise observation could distinguish these articulatory sounds. Cases were also found of the converse phenomenon, where easily distinguishable articulatory sounds caused auditory sounds that were indistinguishable.

Now the important thing that began to be appreciated by the phoneticians, in our period, is that distinguishability of auditory sounds, as done by an unaided human being, depends (among other things) on that human being's native language. The first consequential recognition of this that I have come across is in Boas's paper of 1889. Before turning to Boas, though, it would be well to look at the second major source of phonemics, namely the attempt to explain phonetic changes in the Indo-European family. The leading representative of this approach is Baudouin de Courtenay.

IV. Baudouin de Courtenay

Jan Baudouin de Courtenay (1845-1929) (for biographical references see Jones 1957) has been hailed by Trubetzkoy (1933) as the first to clearly anticipate the phoneme-concept. Certainly he played an uncommonly large part in the development of it; he is particularly important as showing the transition from a diachronic and phonetic approach to a synchronic and phonemic one. Precisely the point of interest is that the two transitions, from diachronic to synchronic and from phonetic to phonemic, go hand in hand.

Baudouin de Courtenay's earliest major contribution to phonemics was a work which he published in Polish in 1894 and in German 1895. The title of his German version, *Versuch einer Theorie der phonetischen Alternationen*, gives the clue to his central concern. Expressed in present-day terms, his leading thought is that automatic alternations are the synchronic residue of the diachronic process called convergence. (An up-to-date statement is to be found in Hoeingswald 1960.)

Baudouin de Courtenay worked in the framework of the "neogrammarians", Brugmann (see V) and Osthoff, who published a sort of manifesto in 1878. He accepted their principle that a sound-law (*Lautgesetz*), when it operates at all, operates without exceptions, that is, is truly a law, and he addressed himself to the major puzzle of this theory, how it is that, if a sound-law is truly a law, it only operates for a particular language during a particular period. The puzzle was commonly acknowledged. These factors that work only for a limited time and group Baudouin de Courtenay "ethnologisch", in contrast with "allgemeinmenschlich" factors (46-7=173). Now if, for example, it is a sound-law that intervocalic *s* becomes *r*, how is it that this law operates in Latin at an early period but not at a later period, and never operates in Greek or in English at all? It doesn't take any knowledge of phonetics, but only a knowledge of scientific method, to see that the answer must lie somehow in a more precise statement of conditions. Perhaps observably different kinds of *s* should be distinguished. Or perhaps—this was Baudouin de Courtenay's idea—the difference lies not in the sounds themselves, so far as this is phonetically observable, but in something extrinsically attached to them—some quality or characteristic which, to use his term, is "psychical". We will see that Boas had the same idea.

The conjecture that, for example, observably different kinds of *s* should be distinguished gave no theoretical trouble, but it proved sterile. The supposed differences between early Latin and later Latin *s* were not in any way reflected in the available data (chiefly written records), so that to suppose them was to make this assumption probable. It was a way out, nothing more.

Actually, Baudouin de Courtenay's theory was subject to exactly this same difficulty. To suppose that early Latin and later Latin *s* are phonetically indistinguishable but psychically different is no better, as an explanation of their different evolution, than to suppose that their difference is phonetic; it is equally ad hoc. Replacing an intrinsic difference by an extrinsic difference does not help the theory, until independent grounds for supposing that sound A is somehow different from sound B can be given, other than the fact itself to be explained that A evolves differently from B.

It follows that, as a contribution to sound-law theory, Baudouin de Courtenay's suggestion was no advance. His conception of psychical difference opened up phonemics but didn't do what it was meant to do. He was thus in the position of Columbus.

As forerunners in his theory of alternances, Baudouin de Courtenay mentions Saussure (1879: 12) and especially Leskien (1884). He defines (1895: 7=1972: 151; 10=153; 12=154; 14=156) the term "morpheme" in a comprehensive way that includes roots, affixes, endings, etc., and speaks (10=153; 11=153-4; 13=155; 15=156) of morphemes as alternants, or in alternation, when they are (i) phonetically different, (ii) semantically related, and (iii) etymologically related. Some German examples of alternant morphemes are (11-12=154): (1) lŭs (*verlust*)~lôr (*verloren*) and (2) gįeb (*gehen*)~gap (*gab*). "But phonetic alternation of whole morphemes may be analyzed into alternations of individual phonemes, as the phonetic components of morphemes." Thus g$_i$eb~gap analyzes into g$_i$~g, e~a, and b~p.

This example clearly shows that Baudouin de Courtenay groups together two things that today are often separated. The German alternation g$_i$~g would be considered allophonic (the palatalized and non-palatalized g belonging to the same phoneme), whereas b~p would be considered morphophonemic, b and p being assigned to different phonemes. The history of this distinction, between phonemics and morphophonemics lies outside of our period; by way of a brief sketch let it be remarked that Sapir never makes it, that Bloomfield in his Menomini morphophonemics (1939) deliberately discards it for a certain purpose (see my "Automatic alternation", 1949: 113), and that Chomsky's transformational approach proposes to give up the distinction.

The definition of "morpheme" showed a diachronic viewpoint. Baudouin de Courtenay, like Gabelentz (see VI) at about the same time, intended to describe each language in its own terms, but by no means intended to ignore its history; he stresses (10=153) that *alternations* (within one language) are not to be confounded with *correspondences* from one language to another, and on the other hand he (2=147) criticizes the ancient Sanskrit grammarians for their non-historical approach.

Yet in another way Baudouin de Courtenay *is* synchronic. The usual statement that the *r* of *verlieren* changes to *s* in *verlust* is inaccurate, or fictive; really there is only a "nebeneinander" of the two forms (20=160).

Whether or not one distinguishes phonemic from morphophonemic alternations, the fact which underlies the distinction ought to be taken into account. This is the difference which is never exploited and one which is only exploited in some phonetic environments. German never exploits the contrast of palatalized and unpalatalized *g*; it does in some environments exploit the contrast of *b* and *p*, but not before pause. Baudouin de Courtenay didn't reckon with this fact; he defined a phoneme as the psychical equivalent of a sound, but didn't tell us when two sounds may have the same psychical equivalent, or when one sound may have more than one psychical equivalent. To use the terms stated earlier, he failed to indicate complete *identity* conditions for "phoneme".

Baudouin de Courtenay sets up a four-stage cycle of evolution: three stages of developing alternations, and one stage of extinguishing them. Stages I to III, in which an alternation exists, differ in the degree to which speakers are conscious of a unity between the alternants.

Recall his basic procedure: alternation of phonemes is *abstracted* or *derived* from alternation of morphemes. Hence (16) a statement such as "*p* alternates with *b*" is to be understood as elliptical for "*p* alternates with *b* in the pairs *gab~geben,...*". And thus the requirement of semantical and etymological connection is implicit in any statement of alternation. We are most conscious of an alternation when it has a grammatical function. Mere minimal contrast, e.g., of *t~p* in English, *hit~hip*, does not for Baudouin de Courtenay constitute an alternation.

His stage III resembles automatic morphophonemics, but is perhaps narrower in this respect, that every Stage III alternation has a grammatical function. I say "perhaps", because perhaps every morphophonemic alternation can be construed as having grammatical function—the notion is rather vague. In *geben~gap*, the alternation *e~a* doubtless has a grammatical function, but does *b~p*?

(The case of a morphophonemic alternation that is not automatic—what Bloomfield (1933: 101, n.9) calls morphological—is not dealt with.)

But under any way of understanding function such that not every automatic alternation has a grammatical function, those that do not would belong to Stage I or Stage II, and not to Stage III. And what we today would consider phonemic contrast overlaps his Stage I and Stage II; for we do not inquire whether a contrast is physiologically caused or is merely traditional.

The third surprising lack is his failure to connect meaning with "functional load" (in A. Martinet's sense) in any way. We acquire consciousness of an alternation when, owing to the extinction (convergence, Stage IV) of some other alternation, the hitherto automatic alternation becomes non-automatic. The classic case, Sarskrit *c~k*, was well known and had been successfully explained near the beginning of our period, 1878 (Holger Pedersen 1931: 280).

V. Contributions from Comparative Indo-European Linguistics

The Age of Brugmann was 1876-1900. One of the things that makes 1876 memorable is, that Karl Brugmann published his article on "*nasalis sonans*", i.e., on *n* and *m* functioning as syllabics. (Another is that Sievers published a phonetics textbook that superseded Brücke, and that in his article Brugmann refers to the book, Sievers being very close to the young Leipzig circle [cf. Pedersen 1931: 305]).

Brugmann's articles have several interesting aspects:

(1) The sounds in question had been noted years before by Rapp and by Brücke but had caused no particular interest. What caused interest was rather that they should occur in Proto-Indo-European, contrary to the then reigning theories of Schleicher, and in a way that spectacularly well explained some phenomena that were long-standing puzzles.

(2) The hypothesis is put forward as a *phonetic* hypothesis. Years later Meillet will disengage the phonetics of it from the remainder but not so Brugmann.

(3) However, the very phonetics of it helps to place it in an alternation: n (syllabic n) alternates with n (non-syllabic n) in some morphemes that are semantically and etymologically connected. At about the same time Sievers demonstrated (1878) a similar alternation involving $i{\sim}y$ and $u{\sim}v$. That there is a system of alternations, in Baudouin de Courtenay's sense, between six pairs of syllabic and non-syllabic alternants in PIE $i, u, n,$ $m, r,$ and l—was recognized within our period. (See for example Wackernagel 1896, 1.205 Section 182a, end of note. However, the full impact of this system was not seen, nor was the evidence for supposing it thoroughly marshaled, until 1943 by Edgerton.)

That the phonetic details were for certain purposes irrelevant was not generally recognized. For example, Wackernagel (1896: 203, Section 181d), argues that Sanskrit had the sequences *iya, uua* rather than *ia, ua* on the ground "dass die Halbvokale . . . die naturlichen Übergangslaute von *i* bezw. *u* zu folgendem anderem Vokal sind"—that is, on a principle of maximum continuity.

VI. Boas and Alternating Sounds

The main background for phonemics, in the period 1876-1900, was phonetics working in conjunction with comparative Indo-European linguistics. An account of phonetics has been given and some contributions both of theory (Baudouin de Courtenay) and of concrete practice (Brugmann, Sievers) to comparative linguistics have been described.

A quite different and largely independent approach confronts us in the work of Boas. (Kleinschmidt's work, besides falling outside of our period (1851), appears to be entirely isolated, one of those sparks that die out leaving no discernible trace either for better or for worse on the course of history.)

Bulletin 40 (Boas 1911) contains important contributions to phonemics (as well as to other parts of linguistic theory), but was written well in the twentieth century (submitted 1908). However, several of its points were made twenty years earlier, some of them more clearly, in "On alternating sounds" (Boas 1889).

The phenomenon of so-called alternating sounds was widely acknowledged. Max Müller (1865) had multiplied instances in his *Lectures on the Science of Language, Second Series,* Chapter 4 ("Phonetic change"). (Von der Gabelentz (1891: 201-3) also had a good collection.) Müller's theory was that the phenomenon is limited to primitive peoples who have not yet learned fixed phonetic habits. A more carefully thought out theory, but not essentially different, was advanced by Major Powell (1880: 12). On the basis of work by Washington Matthews (the army surgeon who also translated many Navaho chants) Powell says:

> In the Hidatsa there is a sound of such a character that the English student cannot decide to which of the sounds represented by *b, w,* or *m,* it is most nearly allied; and there is another which the student cannot distinguish from *o, n, r,* or *d*; such sounds are not differentiated as they are in English. They are synthetic; that is, they are made by the organs of speech in positions and with movements comprehending in part at least the positions and movements used in making the several sounds to which they seem to be allied. Such a synthetic sound will be heard by the student now as one, now as another sound, even from the same speaker.

Thus it is presented as an absolute fact that English *b, w,* and *m* are simple sounds, whereas Hidatsa has a composite sound that is (to put it crudely) one-third *b,* one-third *m,* and one-third *w.*

In 1885 the topic was taken up by Horatio Hale, an American ethnographer and philologist famed for his part in the Wilkes expedition of 1838-1842 to Oceania and Northwest America and for his Iroquois work. Hale cited Hidatsa, then gave examples from his Polynesian and Iroquoian work of the well-known fact that in many languages "there are elementary sounds of an indeterminate character, which seem to float between two, and sometimes even three or four, diverse articulations" (Hale 1885: 233).[2] Hale entertained three hypotheses: all speakers of such a language use the interchangeable sounds indifferently; some speakers prefer one of the sounds, others another; and

> that the difference of sound was not in the speaker's utterance, but in the ear of the listener; that the sound as spoken was an indistinct articulation, intermediate between the sounds represented by the two or more letters of each series, and that the hearer, unaccustomed to sounds of this peculiar character, involuntarily made distinctions where none really existed (234).

According to Hale, one or other of the first two hypotheses, sometimes both, had generally been adopted by students of such languages, himself included; the last theory would at first thought seem likely to be correct, and indeed had not occurred to him until forced on his attention during a stay at the home of Alexander Melville Bell (author of *Visible Speech*), when the two were joined on one occasion by a Mohawk, Chief George Johnson. Hale proposed that both Bell and himself record a list of words in Mohawk, Bell in the alphabet of his "Visible Speech", Hale in the method he usually followed. The two lists were left with Hale for study.

The result, writes Hale, was unexpected, and, as it seemed to him, instructive and valuable. The Iroquois languages do not distinguish *r* and *l*. All the missionaries, although differing widely in some other points of orthography, united in writing the sound in Mohawk with *r*. In the 21 occurrences of the sound in the list of words recorded by Bell and himself, Bell had used *l* nineteen times, *r* twice, whereas Hale had written *l* ten times, *r* ten times, and once repeated the word with both. "The conclusion appears inevitable that the sound which we heard was really neither *r* nor *l*, but an utterance midway between the two, and of such a character that to one listener it seemed an *r*, and to the other an *l*" (236).

Hale does not conclude that all such cases are due to a lack of clear perception in the listener. Very likely in some cases the pronunciation of different natives differs, or of one native varies. But his experience (elaborated with regard to other sounds and languages) proves that this is not always or perhaps usually the case. We must recognize the fact that there are elements, in some if not in all languages, which hold a middle place between two corresponding elements of some other language, and the sounds these medial elements represent may be as widely diverse as, according to our notions, *r* is from *l*, or *t* from *k*.

Hale observes that the first impulse of many persons will doubtless be to account for such phenomena by the fact that the languages are in the uncultivated or barbarous stage; but we know that the speakers of Sanskrit, Homeric Greek, and the Arabic of the Moallakat, although unlettered barbarians, discriminated sounds with an accuracy and a variety which their more civilized descendants have failed to preserve. Further, we discover that many barbarous communities today express delicate shades of pronunciation, which we can only with difficulty imitate (237). Hale further notes an interpretation of variant spellings in the English of Shakespeare's time as such a phenomenon of intermediate sounds (241).

The moral of the story, for Hale, has to do with accurate recording. Many languages reduced to writing of late years in America, Oceania, and Africa have undoubtedly suffered "a serious impoverishment in their phonology" because they were first written by foreigners accustomed only to the European mode of utterance. If Sanskrit had been first written by an Englishman, Frenchman, or German, it is doubtful if the lingual and dental distinction would have been preserved. Probably no one but a scholar familiar with the Semitic tongues, such as Dr. Riggs, would have distinguished and represented in Dakota the deep gutteral sonant resembling Arabic *ghain* and the strong gutteral surd resembling Arabic *kha*. There are still many unwritten languages for which alphabets will have to be provided, and it will be fortunate if this important duty is entrusted to scholars trained in the scientific study of language. Care may at least be taken that the settling of the alphabet not be entrusted to one person. The result of the experiment now recorded shows how essential it is, to determine the real distinctions in elementary sounds of a language, that its words be taken down by two or more persons, listening and writing simultaneously. Only in this way can one avoid the danger of confounding distinct sounds and of finding distinctions where none really exist.

For Hale the import of his finding was principally for work among yet unwritten languages. For Boas quite similar experiences were important as part of a quite general concern with human perception, stemming from his work in psychophysics, and were pertinent to a quite general conclusion as to the perception of sounds in any language, by speakers of any language, unwritten or European.[3]

Boas begins his paper by noting that experiments with English-speaking children have called attention to a phenomenon which has been somewhat misleadingly termed "sound-blindness". Despite the limitations of English orthography, in terms of which the experiments were conducted, they show very satisfactorily that "sounds are not perceived by the hearer in the way in which they have been pronounced by the speaker" (48). There follows discussion of the general nature of perception (to which I return shortly). Boas then introduced the field notes of philologists, not as itself the problem or concern, but as a source of

> far better material than that obtained in schools. . . . In this case men thoroughly trained in the science of phonology attempt to render by writing combinations of sounds to them without any meaning. The study of their misspellings cannot fail to be instructive. . . (51).[4]

The first phenomenon that strikes us, Boas notes, is that the nationality even of well-trained observers may readily be recognized. He then discusses some of his own experiences with Eskimo and languages of British Columbia.

The supposed fact, to which the conclusion of Boas's paper was addressed, as that of Hale, is that various languages, primitive ones, employ sounds that are composite of single sounds employed by more civilized languages. Boas's paper effectively made two notable contributions. First, it challenged the supposed fact:

> I think, from this evidence [philologists' field work], it is clear that all such misspellings are due to a wrong apperception, which is due to the phonetic system of our native language. For this reason I maintain that there is no such phenomenon as synthetic

or alternating sounds, and that their occurrence is in no way a sign of primitiveness of the speech in which they are said to occur (52).

Second, it offered a psychological explanation of how belief in this supposed fact arose.

Boas' general explanation, introduced with regard to experiments on perception of lengths of lines (49-50), is that "a new sensation is apperceived by means of similar sensations that form part of our knowledge" (50). And his explanation of the "alternating-sounds phenomenon" is simply that "alternating sounds are in reality alternating apperceptions of the same sound" (52). He notes in passing that sounds are not necessarily apperceived by means of one's own native language; the first language studied, or the language last studied, may bias the study of a language taken up afterwards. All such biases tend to induce classification of a sound which does not occur in the phonetic system one bears in mind, and is intermediate to several, alternately under those sounds which it resembles. A crucial test for the theory is that it must occur just as frequently that "various sounds [of language A] which resemble one known sound [of language B] are considered [by a native speaker of B who is not sufficiently familiar with A] the same although they are really different" (52). Boas reports such experiences in Haida, Kwakiutl, and Eskimo (cf. experiments reported 48-50, on which this conclusion appears also based).

For Boas, a second and better crucial test—one whose positive result he believes decisive—is that "individuals speaking one of these languages with 'alternating sounds' hear sounds of our language as alternating sounds" (53). So far as I have found, this is the first time in history that a fully relativistic viewpoint is applied to language.

To explain his general explanation, Boas offers this analogy (50):

> It is well known that many languages lack a term for green. If we show an individual speaking such a language a series of green worsteds, he will call part of them yellow, another part blue, the limit of both divisions being doubtful. Certain colors he will classify today as yellow, tomorrow as blue. He perceives green by means of yellow and blue.

This statement is most interesting. Two quite different cases are involved, and in finding the phonetic parallel Boas doesn't sufficiently distinguish them. All those worsteds are *the same color*, viz. green, but *different colors*, viz. different shades of green. Now in what I will call Case 1, one shade of green is consistently apperceived by the imagined observer as yellow, another shade is consistently apperceived as blue. In Case 2, one shade of green is inconsistently apperceived by the observer, now as green, now as blue. It would seem that in denying the alternating sounds doctrine, Boas means to deny the phonetic parallel to Case 1, and to admit only Case 2. And this would mean that "same sound" is the counterpart or parallel not to green but to some one shade of green; it would then be more like a modern allophone than like a phoneme. On the other hand, Boas remarks that in British Columbia Eskimo "the *n* is frequently pronounced the nose being closed. This gives rise to the alternating spelling *n* and *dn*." And he recognizes with full generality what we today would call free variation and allophony:

> Although we learn by practice to place our organs in certain positions, it will readily be understood that these positions will not be exactly the same every time we attempt to produce a certain sound, but will vary slightly. Preceding and succeeding sounds and many other circumstances will exert a certain influence upon the sound which we intend to produce (48).

But this is the phonetic Case 1, which elsewhere, as we have just seen, he seems to deny.

We must go back to the statement "the same sound is differently apperceived", and split it up into two. If "same sound" means a range of sounds as green is a range of shades, then Case 1 is possible but an appeal to apperception is needless. On the other hand, if "same sound" is understood as like a shade of green, then Case 1 is positively included, only Case 2 remains, and the explanation amounts to saying that the choice of apperceiving a sound this way or that is made at random. But is the only role of apperception to randomize?

It may be that Boas would claim no more than this. But if any additional role is assigned to apperception, I do not see any reason for saying that the two roles are performed by the same power.

In short, it appears that Boas's psychological explanation of "alternating sounds" has little, if any value. The color-analogy is not thought out to the point of distinguishing Case 1 from Case 2, and the conception of a randomizing power is not articulated. The positive and significant value of the paper lies, rather, in its vision that the old explanations won't do, and that they won't do because they assumed that an English (or other Western European) language-speaker's judgment of sounds was the true one. Boas did not go on to develop phonemics, or phonology, himself, but in this area as in others, his critical acumen and relativistic perspective cleared ground on which structural analysis could be built.

NOTES

1. This chapter was originally a paper submitted in April 1962 to a Conference on the History of Anthropology sponsored by the Social Science Research Council. It was also made available to participants in the Burg

Wartenstein Symposium on its History of Linguistics, 1964. Although the descriptive framework now seems old-fashioned in taking for granted a pre-Transformationalist conception of phonemics, I have not undertaken revision, because the main point would remain unaffected.

Edward Stankiewicz's splendid English translation of Baudouin de Courtenay makes it possible to cite his 1895 work by the English as well as by the original German pagination.

In Section VI, the long passage on Horatio Hale (including notes 2 and 3) is contributed by Dell Hymes, as is note 4. I am grateful to Hymes not only for thus enhancing my article, but even more for his boundless editorial wisdom and patience.

2. Hale was aware of Müller's discussion (1865, 2: 183-89), citing it (234, n.1). Müller likewise was aware of Hale's work, citing with great approval his views on the humanitarian significance of the European discovery of Sanskrit, and on language as the only feasible basis for classification of mankind (1899: 45, 51-52). On the second of these points, Müller first quotes the Director of the Bureau of Ethnology, John Wesley Powell (from *Science*, June 24, 1887), then "The very Nestor among ethnologists, Horatio Hale. . . "(61).

3. Hale's article is not cited by Boas, and had, so far as is known, no subsequent influence. (This fact is one reason, among others, for doubting the picture of the relationship between the two men painted by Gruber [1967]). Boas' article had obvious significance to his own intellectual development, and hence for the development of anthropology in the United States. Stocking (1968: 159) writes: "It is impossible to exaggerate the significance of this article for the history of anthropological thought. . . . Much of Boas' later work, and that of his students after him, can be viewed simply as the working out of implications present in this article".
[Hale's article came to attention early in 1970; I have supplied the present account of it—DHH.]

4. The experimental literature that Boas cites would seem to have been a nineteenth-century anticipation of later psycholinguistic research such as Brown and Hildum (1956). From another standpoint, Hale and Boas, can be seen as anticipating systematic analysis of phonic interference (Weinreich 1953, 1957).

REFERENCES

Baudouin de Courtenay, Jan. 1895. Versuch einer Theorie der phonetischen Alternationen. Strassburg.

———. 1972. A Baudouin de Courtenay Anthology. Translated and Edited with an Introduction by Edward Stankiewicz. Bloomington.

Bloomfield, Leonard. 1927. Recent work in general linguistics. Modern Philology 25: 211-230.

———. 1933. Language. New York.

———. 1939. Menomini morphophonemics. Travaux du cercle linguistique de Prague 8: 105-115.

Boas, Franz. 1889. On alternating sounds. American Anthropologist, o.s., 2:

47-53. [Reprinted in Selected papers from the American Anthropologist, 1888-1920, ed. Frederica de Laguna, 403-409. Evanston, Row, Peterson (later, New York, Harper and Row). Cited by original pagination, which the reprinting contains.]

———. 1911. Handbook of American Indian languages. (Bureau of American Ethnology, Bulletin 40, Part I). Washington, D.C.

Brown, Roger, and Hildum, D. C. 1956. Expectancy and the identification of syllables. Language 32: 411-419.

Brücke, E. W. R. von. 1856. Grundzüge der physiologie und Systematik der Sprachlaute für Linguisten und Taubstummenlehrer. Vienna.

Brugmann, K. 1876. Nasalis sonans in der indogermanischen Grundsprache. Curtius Studien 9: 287-338.

Brugmann, K., and Osthoff, H. 1878. Vorwort. Morphologische untersuchungen auf den Gebiete der indogermanischen Sprachen. Leipzig.

Brugmann, K., and Delbrück, B. 1897-1911. Grundriss der vergleichenden Grammatik der indogermanischen Sprachen. 2nd ed. Strassburg.

Cassirer, Ernst. 1945. Structuralism in modern linguistics. Word 1: 99-120.

Chomsky, Noam. 1964. The logical basis of linguistic theory. Proceedings of the Ninth International Congress of Linguists, ed. Horace G. Lunt, 914-978. The Hague.

Edgerton, Franklin. 1943. The Indo-European semivowels. Language 19: 83-124.

Gabelentz, George von der. 1891. Die Sprachwissenschaft. Leipzig. (2nd ed., 1901).

Gatschet, A. S. 1890. The Klamath Indians of Southwestern Oregon (Contributions to North American Ethnology, 2). 2 vols. Washington, D. C.

Gruber, Jacob W. 1967. Horatio Hale and the development of American anthropology. Proceedings of the American Philosophical Society 111: 5-37.

Hale, Horatio. 1885. On some doubtful or intermediate articulations: an experiment in phonetics. Journal of the Anthropological Institute, London (February), 233-243.

Hoenigswald, H. M. 1960. Language change and linguistic reconstruction. Chicago.

Jespersen, Otto. 1923. Language, its nature, origin and development. London and New York.

———. 1933. Linguistica. Collected papers in English, French and German. Copenhagen.

Jones, Daniel. 1957. The history and meaning of the term 'phoneme'. London.

Kempelen, Wolfgang von. 1791. Mechanismums der menschlichen Sprache nebst der Beschriebung seiner sprechenden Maschine. Vienna.

Kleinschmidt, Samuel. 1851. Grammatik der grönlandischen Sprache. Berlin.

Leskien, August. 1884. Der Ablaut der Wurzelsieben in Litauischen. Leipzig.

Martinet, Andre. 1955. Economie des changements phonétiques. Berne.

Matthews, Washington. 1877. Ethnography and philology of the Hidatsa Indians. (U. S. Geological and Geographical Survey, Miscellaneous Publications, 7). Washington, D. C.

Müller, Max. 1865. Lectures on the science of language. Second series. London.

———. 1890. Three lectures on the science of language and its place in general education. Chicago.

Pedersen, Holger. 1931. Linguistic science in the nineteenth century. Translated from the Danish by J. W. Spargo. Cambridge. [Reprinted as The discovery of language. Bloomington, Indiana University Press, 1962.]

Peirce, Charles Sanders. 1931-1935. Collected Papers of Charles Sanders Peirce. Ed. C. Hartshorne and P. Weiss. Cambridge, Harvard University Press. 6 vols.

Powell, John Wesley. 1880. Introduction to the study of Indian languages. Washington, D. C.

Riggs, Stephen R. 1893. Dakota grammar, texts and ethnography. (Contributions to North American Ethnology 9, 1-232). Washington, D. C.

Saussure, Ferdinand de. 1879. Mémoire sur le système primitif des voyelles dans les langues indo-européennes. Paris. [Appeared, 1878.]

Sievers, Eduard. 1876. Grundzüge der Lautphysiologie. Zur Einführung in das Studium der Lautlehre der indogermanischen Sprachen. Leipzig.

———. 1878. Zur Akzent- und Lautlehre der germanischen Sprachen. III. Zum vocalischen auslaut gesetz. Beitrage zur Geschichte der Deutschen Sprache und Literatur 5: 63-163.

Stocking, George W., Jr. 1968. Race, culture, and evolution. Essays in the history of anthropology. New York.

Techmer, F. 1880. Phonetik. Zur vergleichenden Physiologie der Stimme und Sprache. Leipzig.

Trubetzkoy, Nicolai. 1933. La phonologie actuelle. Journal de Psychologie 30: 227-246.

Wackernagel, Jacob. 1896. Altindische Grammatik. Göttingen.

Weinreich, Uriel. 1953. Languages in contact. (Linguistic Circle of New York, Publication 1.) New York. Revised edition, the Hague, 1964.

———. 1957. On the description of phonic interference. Word 13: 1-11.

Wells, Rulon S. 1949. Automatic alternation. Language 25: 99-116.

18. The Boas Plan for the Study of American Indian Languages

George W. Stocking, Jr.

I

That Franz Boas played a central role in the definition of twentieth-century American Indian linguistics, and that the *Handbook of American Indian Languages* (Boas 1911) represents in some respects a charter for that study, are of course commonplaces (Emeneau 1943: 35; Hymes 1964: 7-9). But the specific character of what Carl Voegelin called "The Boas Plan for the Presentation of American Indian Languages" (Voegelin 1952), and the intellectual, institutional, and interpersonal context in which the *Handbook* was produced are matters which bear some further investigation. Voegelin's own treatment of these issues was quite frankly a bit speculative and hypothetical, and based solely on the internal evidence of the *Handbook* itself. On this basis, he suggested the possibility that Boas himself "wrote the grammars which are editorially attributed to another anthropologist or anthropologists." Perhaps somewhat more seriously, he argued that

> if Boas were writing today, we might feel that it was no more natural and fitting to have him appear as the author of Tsimshian, Kwakiutl, and Chinook (based on his own field work), and as co-author of Dakota, than it was to have him appear as the author of *Structural Restatements of Maidu, Fox, Hupa, Tlingit and Haida* (based on the field notes gathered by Dixon, Jones, Michelson, Goddard, and Swanton) — in short, to regard Boas as the author of nine out of the ten sketches of Part I of the *Handbook* (Voegelin 1952: 440-441).

Voegelin went on to extrapolate from the twenty grammars ultimately published in the four volumes of the *Handbook* a rather detailed model of the "general plan of presentation" to which Boas referred in his *Introduction* (Boas 1911: vi). As will be evident in what follows, Voegelin's version of the Boas "master plan" seems to me to have a somewhat different and more highly structured character than Boas himself had in mind. Fortunately, however, these matters need not be approached solely in terms of internal analysis of published materials. Hopefully, scholars with more linguistic sophistication than I possess will also take advantage of the manuscript materials in the American Philosophical Society and the Smithsonian Archives of Anthropology to complete the historical examination which this paper presumes only to initiate.[1]

II

The *Handbook* was the major fruit of a linguistic connection with the Bureau of American Ethnology which can be traced almost to the beginning of Boas' career as anthropologist. In the fall of 1885 he wrote to the Bureau asking for a copy of John Wesley Powell's *Introduction to the Study of Indian Languages* (Powell 1880) as a guide to the analysis of Eskimo linguistic materials which were originally to have been included in the report subsequently published by the Bureau on his ethnographic work among the Eskimo of Baffinland (BAE: Boas letter of 10/3/85). The request itself suggests that at this point Boas was somewhat unsure of himself in linguistics, and other evidence indicates that he had no formal linguistic training and little systematic contact with the European tradition of comparative linguistics. True, sometime in this period he apparently met and subsequently did exchange at least one communication with Heymann Steinthal. But if Boas' later work gives this contact a special retrospective significance, it seems nonetheless to have been quite fleeting: Boas later "regretted never having attended" Steinthal's lectures (Jakobson 1944: 188; Harrington 1945: 98; APS: Steinthal to Boas, 9/15/1888). When it came to analyzing the Eskimo linguistic materials, Boas seems to have relied a good bit on the help of H. J. Rink, a Dane who had lived among them for some years, and who in fact was responsible for preparing the translations of Boas' Eskimo texts (BAE: Boas letters of 9/15/85, 10/3/85, 10/30/85, 5/13/87).

Starting then as an untrained novice, Boas achieved his linguistic competence during his first decade of general ethnographic work on the Northwest Coast, and there is every indication that he was largely self-taught. There is evidence that he may have referred to such works as Friedrich Müller's *Grundriss der Sprachwissenschaft* (APS: H. Hale to Boas, 4/30/88), and that he had a rather generalized familiarity with European philological traditions. He clearly read other European and American work on the languages that concerned him. Through his close relationship with Horatio Hale in his work for the British Association for the Advancement of Science he had fairly direct access to an American philological tradition going back to Gallatin. But the rather antagonistic tenor of his relationship to Hale suggests what other sources confirm: the major context of his "self-professionalization" was that of his own field work. It was in the process of recording myths and traditions from various Indian informants that he worked out his problems of orthography and developed his characteristic approach to the analysis of language (Jakobson 1944: 188; Lowie 1943: 183-184; Dell Hymes, personal communication; cf. Jacob Gruber 1967).[2]

Within a relatively short time, however, Boas had already drawn on this experience to offer a general critique of the traditional approach to "Alternating Sounds" which foreshadowed many of the characteristically relativist assumptions of his mature linguistic work (Boas 1889; cf. Stocking 1968a: 157-160). And from an early point he felt sure enough of his relative competence to offer Powell unsolicited reports on his research and discussions of linguistic problems in the Northwest area, as well as a proposal for a five-year program of research on the Salish languages (BAE: Boas to Powell, 8/8/88; Boas to H. Henshaw, 12/3/88). However, Boas was in fact able to get from the Bureau only piecemeal support for linguistic research supplementary to the general ethnographic work he was carrying on for the British Association (BAE: Boas to Powell, 12/22/88; Boas to Henshaw, 3/8/90). Furthermore, his letters in this period suggest that despite his interest in more intensive study of Salish, he was still working largely in terms of regional surveys, vocabulary lists, grammatical "notes", and problems of the classification of stocks (BAE: Boas to Henshaw, 1/24/89, 10/20/89, 3/8/90) – that is, that he operated largely within a Powellian framework, and was not yet in practice primarily concerned with the systematic and intensive study of grammatical structures.

This pattern seems to have begun to change with Boas' encounter in 1890 with Chinook. Although at first the problem was simply to determine its relation to Salish, Boas quickly became fascinated by the intricacies of the language for their own sake (BAE: Boas to Henshaw, 5/16/1890, 7/14/1890), and much of his linguistic effort of the 1890's was devoted to a study of the several branches of the Chinookan stock with a view to the "elucidation" of its structure (BAE: Boas to Powell, 1/18/93).

Unfortunately, however, Boas' relation to the Bureau was considerably attenuated (under rather acrimonious circumstances) in 1894, when he was pushed out of his job at the Field Museum as a result of a reorganization of Bureau personnel which sent William Holmes to Chicago. A year and a half later – apparently in part as compensation for this maltreatment – Boas was offered a permanent job in charge of the editorial work of the Bureau. Although he came close to taking it, he instead accepted the appointment which was to settle him permanently in New York City (APS: retrospective account by Boas, 1911; BAE: Boas to Powell, 6/19/95; Boas to W. J. McGee, 6/27/95, 1/26/96).

From 1896 on, however, Boas' relations to the Bureau were close (although not always amicable) throughout the period until the *Handbook* was published. Furthermore, it seems clear they were resumed in a somewhat different context than they had been disrupted. Later retrospective comments on his own early linguistic work suggest that it was from about this time that Boas regarded his largely autodidactic linguistic competence as having achieved an adequately professional level (Boas 1900: 708). And the Bureau, which in the late 1880's had thought him a bit of a pushy novice, now clearly recognized him as a, if not the, leading student of Indian languages. It is also from this time that one finds evidence of a continuous systematic attempt by Boas to train students who would carry on linguistic work at a thoroughly professional level. After 1899, when John Swanton went to South Dakota in an attempt to revise Sioux texts which had been collected for the Bureau by Rev. J. Owen Dorsey, students trained in Boas' linguistic seminar at Columbia were annually engaged in linguistic field work under Bureau auspices.

Finally, as far as Boas' linguistic orientation itself is concerned, one may regard his paper on the "Classification of the Languages of the North Pacific Coast" at the World's Fair Congress of Anthropology late in 1893 as marking the culmination of his early interest in classificatory problems. In its concluding paragraph he suggested the need for more intensive study of linguistic structures (Boas 1894: 346). And in fact his own work for the Bureau in the late 1890's focused largely on a continuing analysis of the material he had previously collected in Chinook and Tsimshian.

Exactly when the *Handbook* was conceived is not clear. At later points Boas mentioned the years 1895, 1897, and 1898, and suggested that it "had its inception in an attempt to prepare a revised edition of John Wesley Powell's *Introduction to the Study of Indian Languages*", which had gone out of print, and had also begun "to prove inadequate" (Boas 1911: v). In fact, however, as late as 1898 Boas asked for and received two copies of Powell's *Introduction* to give to his own field workers (BAE: Boas to McGee, 4/15/98, 4/21/98). On the other hand, a letter of the preceding year indicates that Powell had in mind some major linguistic project which Boas was to undertake (BAE: Boas to McGee, 4/12/97).

The first specific mention of the *Handbook*, however, occurs in the spring of 1901, when Boas wrote a letter to W. J. McGee, acting head of the Bureau, recalling that they had "been discussing now and again the desirability of publishing a handbook of North American Languages", and suggesting that his recently published sketch of Kwakiutl grammar in the *American Anthropologist* (Boas 1900) was prepared as a kind of model for the sort of treatments he had in mind. Boas felt that he had "trained now a sufficient number of young men to make it possible to take up work of this kind systematically", and that with the cooperation of the American Museum, Columbia, Harvard, and the University of California, it would be possible to do the necessary field work and bring the *Handbook* to completion within five or six years (APS: Boas to McGee, 4/4/01, 4/20/01; cf. 6/18/02). McGee and Powell responded favorably, and the following month Boas received an appointment as Honorary Philologist in the Bureau (APS: McGee to Boas, 4/5/01; 5/22/01; S. P. Langley to Boas, 5/23/01).

Although field work was carried out in the summers of 1901 and 1902, planning was still clearly in preliminary stages, and the whole proposal had to be renegotiated when McGee was forced out of the Bureau after Powell's death in 1902. Boas' personal relations with William Holmes, the new Bureau chief, were poor; and Boas' previous relations with McGee and the Bureau became something of an issue in the uproar surrounding McGee's departure. For a time, financial support for linguistic work was seriously curtailed (APS: Holmes to Boas, 1/6/03). By the end of 1903, however, revised and more detailed plans for the *Handbook* were finally approved, and Boas sent out invitations to the proposed collaborators (APS: Boas to Holmes, 3/5/03, 5/9/03, 11/2/03; Holmes to Boas, 11/25/03, 12/8/03).

III

In order to consider the problem of the *Handbook's* authorship, it will be helpful to examine its personnel in a more systematic way — and not only those whose names appeared in print as collaborators, but also those whose names might have and did not. In the first place, one notes the exclusion of both missionaries and old-line Bureau members. (For present purposes, the partial exceptions of Swanton, who *became* a member of the Bureau, and Goddard, who *had been* a missionary, are not really to the point). These omissions are hardly accidental, and have a good deal to do with defining both the intellectual context of the *Handbook* and the interaction patterns which define its authorship.

The historical significance of the *Handbook* tends to be distorted by our image of Powell and the Bureau as systematically involved in linguistic research. Although it is generally known that Powell's classification of American languages was lexical rather than morphological, the degree to which Boas' *Handbook* represented a radical departure in the study of Indian languages still tends perhaps to be obscured by the mountainous biblio-graphies, with numerous entries by missionary linguists, which went into the production of the Bureau's *Indian Linguistic Families of America North of Mexico* in 1891. Bureau members did *collect* considerable bodies of linguistic material, but prior to Boas' time they *published* relatively little in the way of extended grammatical analysis. And despite all this material, despite decades of speculation on the "incorporating" or "polysynthetic" character of American Indian languages, the amount of detailed and systematic study of specific Indian languages which would stand professional scrutiny – at least as far as Franz Boas and Edward Sapir were concerned – was virtually nil, and Boas' attitude toward these two important groups of nineteenth-century linguistic students reflected this estimate.[3] From 1896 on, a recurring part of Boas' activity for the Bureau was in effect to exercise a veto power on the entry of missionaries (and others) into what might be loosely called the "American Indian linguistics establishment". When missionaries wrote to the Bureau asking to consult unpublished manuscript materials or offering their own manuscripts for publication, the issue was as a matter of routine referred to Boas. Characteristically, Boas would suggest that the missionary had no knowledge of scientific philology, or that he should be restricted in effect to the published works of the Bureau, or – on one occasion – that while the missionary's work was better than some, it need not be published since Boas' own investigators were about to undertake work on the same tribe (BAE: Boas to McGee, 4/11/98; to Holmes 12/7/03, 11/23/04, 1/31/06, 7/14/06, 1/8/08: Holmes to Boas, 3/25/07, 1/15/08; APS: Holmes to Boas, 12/8/03; Holmes to Verwyst, 5/9/07; cf. Boas to A. Huntington, 1/30/06).

As far as the men of the Bureau are concerned, the most likely candidate was Albert Gatschet, an older scholar for whose abilities Boas had a fairly high regard. Gatschet's health was poor, and he in fact died before the *Handbook* was completed. Nevertheless, Boas proposed to McGee in 1900 that Gatschet should write a thirty-page sketch for each of the languages he had studied but not published so that the large body of material he had collected in the course of a long career would be usable by other investigators after his death (APS: Boas to McGee, 2/4/00; McGee to Boas, 3/1/00; cf. Boas to J. Dunn 11/7/07, and BAE: Boas to Holmes, 11/26/07, 12/5/07). The task was analogous to – although quantitatively much more difficult than – the job of preparing a sketch for the *Handbook* according to Boas' original conception, which envisioned a total of about fifty pages on each language, including texts (APS: Boas to Holmes, 3/5/03). Thus Boas' failure at any point even to mention the possibility of Gatschet's working on the *Handbook* may still signify something of a general attitude toward Bureau linguists, especially in the context of his derogatory remarks elsewhere on the competence of the older generation of American anthropologists, and the markedly evolutionary assumptions that pervade the grammar of the Klamath which Gatschet published in 1890 (APS: Boas to Z. Nuttall, 5/16/01; cf. below, p. 466).

The fate of the one Bureau man whom Boas did include in his plans is even more illuminating. Boas hoped to have J. N. B. Hewitt, a slightly eccentric part-Tuscarora Indian and long-time Bureau employee, do a sketch of Iroquois grammar. After several years of fruitless attempts through Holmes' mediation to get Hewitt to produce, Boas finally succeeded — after he himself had begun the study of Iroquois — in conferring directly with Hewitt to stay long enough in New York that he himself could "systematize spoke two Iroquois dialects fluently, had a good knowledge of the details of the language, and could "analyse each word", he had no "clear idea regarding the grammar of the whole language." Although Boas hoped that he might get Hewitt to stay long enough in New York that he himself could "systematize Hewitt's knowledge by questioning him", it was never possible to arrange this, and the proposed Iroquois sketch had to be abandoned (APS: Boas to Holmes, 5/9/03; Boas to Hewitt, 8/30/07; BAE: Boas to Holmes, 10/30/07, 1/27/08, 3/8/09, 8/1/09).[4]

Hewitt was not the only potential contributor who "washed out." Even among Boas' own students there was a fairly rigorous selection. As if to symbolize the growth of his own linguistic competence, Boas felt that his first doctoral student at Clark University, Alexander Francis Chamberlain, would prove inadequate to do a study of Kootenay, since he tended to get lost in detail, and "the essential points are liable to be obscured" (BAE: Boas to Holmes, 6/5/05, 6/3/08). Even after he was established at Columbia, Boas had several failures before he began to develop the group of promising young men whom he referred to in connection with his early plans for the *Handbook*. One, a Dr. Emil Seytler, seemed talented, but was rejected as irresponsible; a man named Henning proved to be a clerk and not a scientist (BAE: Boas to McGee, 1/26/96; 11/4/97; 11/25/97; 3/5/98). And even among the young men he later spoke of so favorably to McGee, there was one notable washout. Boas' earliest enumeration of the languages he planned to cover included two which were to be studied by H. H. St. Clair the second (APS: Boas to Holmes, 3/5/03). St. Clair in fact did field work during several summers, and two of the sketches in the second volume of the *Handbook* (Takelma and Coos) note a debt to field notes he collected. St. Clair's main work, however, was on the Shoshone, and at least in the beginning, Boas thought rather highly of his linguistic abilities (it was in fact St. Clair who carried out Boas' first attempt to use a phonograph as a field technique) (APS: Boas to Holmes, 5/9/03, 6/2/03). Unfortunately, however, St. Clair did not "feel the necessity of reporting regularly on the progress of his work", and Boas found this "failure to communicate with the home office . . . intolerable" (BAE: Boas to Holmes, 1/19/03, 2/13/03). Apparently over St. Clair's rather angry opposition, he was eliminated from the group of collaborators, and from American Indian linguistics as well (APS: Boas to St. Clair, 2/8/05).

In addition to those whom Boas eliminated, there was one who eliminated himself, and this, too, casts light on the nature of the group who finally collaborated. When the invitations to participate were sent out, Boas asked his first Columbia Ph.D., A. L. Kroeber, who had become Professor of Anthropology at the University of California, to write a sketch on the Yurok language (APS: Boas to Kroeber, 12/11/03). From the beginning, Kroeber was reluctant. He was not sure he had the time, he preferred to do Yuki, and he was concerned with what Boas would "do with the contributions" after he received them (APS: Kroeber to Boas, 12/27/03, 2/21/04, 3/27/04). When he did agree to participate, it was in a rather short, curt note which made painfully clear that it was an act of submission by a man whose assertion of his own scholarly individuality had not reached the point of permitting him to refuse his *guru* outright (APS: Kroeber to Boas, 3/27/04). After he sent in the Yuki manuscript, Kroeber balked at making additions Boas requested (APS: Kroeber to Boas, 5/21/06). When the publication of the *Handbook* was delayed for several years more, Kroeber suggested early in 1908 that he withdraw the Yuki on the grounds that he now felt that he had made mistakes in the phonetics, but could not spend the time required to do further field work. Instead, he offered Boas material he had already published on Yokuts, with the comment that he understood that Boas was "thoroughly editing all the contributions", and could "probably best get just what you want" by editing this (APS: Kroeber to Boas, 2/1/08). Boas returned the Yuki manuscript and rather curtly indicated that he preferred not to use the Yokuts (APS: Boas to Kroeber, 2/11/08).

None of the six early participants whose sketches saw publication showed any such recalcitrance as Kroeber. Four of them had been – or still were – doctoral students under Boas. Of these, three were still clearly in a dependent relation to him. Unlike St. Clair, they reported regularly from the field to the home office, and their letters make it clear that the psychic tone of the relationship was that of master and disciple. Edward Sapir was indeed for a time wont to close his letters "yours very respectfully" (APS: Sapir to Boas, 7/4/05). John Swanton on several occasions explicitly gave Boas permission to rework his manuscripts any way Boas wished (APS: Swanton to Boas, 2/2/05, 5/31/05, 11/27/07). Williams Jones' death in the Philippines before the final revision of his Fox manuscript gave Boas complete freedom to do the same.

In addition to these three, William Thalbitzer, a Danish scholar trained in the classical tradition of Indo-European philology, had published a volume on Eskimo phonetics which, in attitude if not in genesis, was at several points strikingly Boasian (Thalbitzer 1904: xii). Boas clearly chose him with this in mind, and Thalbitzer – still a bit unsure of his English – was more than anxious to have Boas' help and to give him what he wanted (APS: Thalbitzer to Boas, 2/13/07, 12/20/07, 6/1/08). Pliny Goddard, although in fact a onetime lay missionary, was even then taking his Ph.D. in linguistics at the University of California under Benjamin Ide Wheeler and in close association with A. L. Kroeber, who despite his recalcitrance was clearly Boasian in his basic approach to American Indian linguistics. Goddard was also anxious to please, and ended by formally thanking Boas for what he had done to improve his Hupa sketch (APS: Goddard to Boas, 10/20/08). Roland Dixon, who had first studied Maidu grammar as a doctoral student under Boas before he joined the Harvard faculty, was his own man in a way the other collaborators were not, but there was no fundamental difference in linguistic point of view. Paradoxically, Sapir, even though his Takelma sketch was in fact his doctoral dissertation, was by virtue of sheer linguistic brilliance the most independent of all. His is the one case where there is clear evidence of a partial reversal in the current of intellectual influence. Indeed, Boas asked Sapir to contribute a short essay on certain semantically significant phonetic peculiarities of Chinook to his own sketch of that language (APS: Boas to Sapir, 3/29/09, 3/31/09, 4/5/09).

Clearly then, the conditions of interaction were very favorable to Voegelin's interpretation of the authorship of the *Handbook*. Boas had rigorously winnowed and for the most part himself trained a group of still quite dependent young scholars whom he saw as "contributors" to a single, on-going enterprise he had single-handedly initiated: the establishment of American Indian linguistics on a scientific basis whose assumptions he was at no small pains to define. And one can indeed find passages in his correspondence which might be used to bolster Voegelin's interpretation. During the period of his most intense editorial work, in January 1908, Boas complained to William Holmes that "perhaps you do not appreciate the amount of labor involved in the final editing of all the sketches, some of which I have practically to rewrite entirely" (BAE: Boas to Holmes, 1/20/08; cf. 8/30/07, 3/8/09). However, other letters in the same period would seem to indicate that Boas was referring to St. Clair's Shoshone, which was never published; to his own Tsimshian; to the sketch of Sioux, on which his name appeared as co-author with Swanton; as well as perhaps Swanton's Tlingit, on which it did not (APS: Boas to Swanton, 1/13/08; to Laufer 3/11/08; BAE: Boas to Holmes, 1/27/08, 5/6/08, 6/3/08). As far as the rest are concerned, the correspondence would indicate that, however extensive Boas' editorial role, it was hardly that of author. He in effect specifically rejected the opportunity to do a "structural restatement" of Kroeber's Yokuts. The relatively minor additions to Jones' Fox manuscript he explicitly relegated to Truman Michelson, on the grounds that he himself had no time for them (BAE: Boas to Holmes, 8/9/09). Thalbitzer's Eskimo, despite the acknowledgement to Boas' "assistance in the revision and finishing", was the last sketch commissioned and arrived well along toward the completion of Boas' editorial work (APS: Thalbitzer to Boas, 6/1/08, 7/18/08). Its somewhat divergent character suggests that he did little to remodel it.[5] Dixon seems to have been quite willing to resist Boas' suggestions when he felt the evidence did not support them, as well as on his own initiative to add new material in the galley proofs (APS: Dixon to Boas, 3/2/09, 3/8/09). And with Goddard's Hupa, the suggestions Boas made for changes were offered as such, and were generally of a fairly specific character (APS: Boas to Goddard 11/23/07, 12/28/07; Goddard to Boas, 12/18/07, 10/20/08).

Indeed, it is the character of Boas' editorial work which provides the most important evidence on the problem of authorship. A good portion of his attention seems in fact to have been directed to such problems as the uniformity of systems of headings and indentation (BAE: Boas to collaborators, 7/16/04; Boas to Holmes, 1/8/08), and there is evidence to suggest that his plan of presentation was conditioned by aesthetic as well as strictly linguistic criteria. In only one instance did he feel that a sketch had "not conformed to the general plan of the book." The issue was not linguistic, however – Boas thought Sapir's Takelma was excellent. It was simply that it was too detailed and too long in its planned position, and would have either to be placed at the end or else published in a second volume (as in fact it was) (BAE: Boas to Holmes, 6/24/09).

As far as the substance of the various sketches was concerned, Boas' editing seems largely to have had to do with the addition of new material rather than with reworking the analyses themselves. The first manuscripts were turned in towards the end of 1904, but the project dragged on so long that the results of further research had often to be incorporated. Boas himself made a trip to the Carlisle Indian school and worked with Indian informants in New York in 1908, which apparently had a good deal to do with the reworking of the Sioux and Tsimshian (BAE: Boas to Holmes, 1/27/08, 2/12/08, 4/15/08). Even when the Kwakiutl was in galley proofs, he felt that he had to add considerable material in the light of his more recent deeper understanding of the language (BAE: Boas to Holmes, 6/24/09, 6/28/09, 8/1/09). In the same manner, he frequently asked collaborators to add examples to illustrate particular grammatical points, or to expand a portion of their argument. As far as one can judge from the correspondence, such restructuring as he proposed was of a fairly specific character: he suggested to Goddard a re-analysis of the Hupa verb and to Swanton a reclassification of Tlingit prefixes, and to both of them a tabular presentation of verbal forms, in order to point up a morphological relationship he felt existed between the two languages (APS: Boas to Goddard, 11/23/07, 12/28/07; to Swanton, 11/25/07, 12/26/07; cf. Boas 1911: 133, 190). On the whole, there seems to me no evidence (with perhaps the exception of Swanton's Tlingit) to sustain any attribution of authorship other than that indicated in the *Handbook's* table of contents.

IV

This conclusion of course depends in part on the answer to the second problem posed in the beginning of this paper: the purpose and nature of the Boas model itself. Voegelin suggested that Boas' "unflagging interest in linguistic structures" and his "masterful insistence on having linguistic structures so stated that they could be readily compared" was related to his tendency to explain language similarities in diffusional rather than genetic terms, and that the "Boas plan" was devised "in order to obtain the kind of cross-genetic comparability essential" to such explanation (Voegelin 1952: 439). Perhaps reflecting his own continuing interest in issues of typology and structure,[6] Voegelin's analysis of the "Boas plan" (under the headings of "sounds", "processes", and "meanings") seems to me to have given it a great deal more structural coherence than Boas intended. Thus Voegelin suggested in regard to "sounds" that one could make the various treatments of consonant sounds systematically "comparable" by rearranging them so that they read from left to right in the order of contact points in the mouth from front to back: b-d-g; p-t-k; p'-t'-k'. In this form Voegelin offered a "Generalized Model of Stops in American Indian Languages" as an example of how one could make Boas' "general plan explicit." Voegelin did note that Boas in fact accepted any arrangement a collaborator offered (1952: 443). What he did not note is that even Boas' own grammars differ in the order of arrangement of consonants (1911: 289, 429, 565). The point may seem trivial, but what is involved is in fact a rather important historical issue: was Boas a modern structuralist in historical disguise, or was he rather concerned with quite different issues, for which the arrangement of consonant sounds might not be at all critical, or in terms of which a less systematic arrangement might even seem more appropriate?

Turning to "processes", Voegelin suggested that what Boas usually called "grammatical processes" could be arranged in a continuum according to their association with problems of meaning. According to the resulting alphabetical typology, A to E stood for "non-semantic processes", and F to K for "grammatical processes" proper, the whole series reflecting the continuum of actual speech, with "sound replacement" at one end and "word order" at the other (1952: 445-450). There is undoubtedly a sense in which Boas was profoundly concerned with the continuum of actual speech; and for reasons which I shall discuss below, he did in fact subordinate and place at the end of each sketch the discussion of syntactical problems. Nevertheless, to my layman's eye Voegelin's typology bears only a tenuous derivative relationship to what actually appears on the printed pages of the *Handbook*. Most of what Voegelin called the first half of the continuum was simply the material treated in the separate sections called "phonetics". As for the "grammatical processes" proper, Voegelin seems to me to have obscured the issue by defining them rather vaguely in terms of the "representation" of the speech continuum. Boas himself defined grammatical processes in terms of their function of expressing the "relations" of the ideas expressed by "single" or "definite" "phonetic groups", and suggested that there were in fact only two such processes: "composition in a definite order, which may be combined with a mutual phonetic influence of the component elements upon one another, and inner modification of the phonetic groups themselves" (1911: 27). In fact the phenomena which were listed as grammatical processes in the various grammars are, at least terminologically, somewhat more differentiated. They include "affixation", "suffixation". "reduplication", "vocalic changes", "stem modification", "position", and "juxtaposition," and on one occasion, "incorporation". Taken as a whole, Boas' "grammatical processes" represent less a "continuum" than alternative ways for relating the elementary ideas of each single phonetic group, each present to varying degrees in the different languages of the world.

As "the next task in the Boas plan of presentation" Voegelin listed "meanings" — the determination of the "ideas expressed by grammatical processes", or synonymously, "grammatical categories." According to Voegelin, Boas' discussion of these was "a kind of promissory note" (reissued later by Sapir and Whorf) that "we would at last obtain reliable data on the various Weltanschauungen as reflected in the various native languages of primitive man in the New World, and thus attain an attested contrast to the Weltanschauung derived from European languages." It is in this context that Voegelin suggested that Boas' later collaborators became "relatively cool toward the idea of separate essays on grammatical categories, while Boas became more devoted" (1952: 450-451). Actually, even in Volume I the essays on "ideas expressed by grammatical categories" were very unevenly developed; nor were Boas' own treatments uniformly elaborate. For the most part these essays were simply brief summary statements of the most general themes of the grammatical analyses which followed them, and attenuation or absence is perhaps not so crucial as Voegelin suggested. But the important point is that they were less a promissory note than the embodiment of an analytic premise, and that it is this analytic premise, rather than any specific presentational structure, which underlies the Boas plan for American Indian linguistics. Quite diverse presentations could be and were found equally consistent with this premise. Indeed, in effect it required such diversity.

V

To understand why this should have been the case, it is necessary to consider in a bit more detail the context in which the *Handbook* was conceived. In the first place, it may help to look briefly at several American Indian grammars of the late nineteenth century. Matthew's Hidatsa (1877) and the Riggs-Dorsey Dakota (1893) were each structured in terms of the eight parts of speech we still learn today: Noun, Pronoun, Verb, Adverb, Adjective, Preposition, Conjunction, and Interjection. These were the basic categories; and while Gatschet's Klamath was from Boas' point of view much more satisfactory, it nevertheless contained statements which cast considerable light on what was implied in such categorization. In discussing inflection, Gatschet suggested that what was from an evolutionary point of view first the product of physical (i.e., phonetic) law and psychological principle was "finally subjected to rational logic . . . by which grammatical categories are established." Prior to this, what one found were merely *conventional* as opposed to *logical* principles. The existence of logical principles had to do with the degree of definition of the parts of speech, and from this point of view the Aryan languages were clearly at the top of the evolutionary scale (1890: I, 399).

Other late nineteenth-century sources suggest that "grammatical processes", too, could be viewed in evolutionary terms. Powell's *Introduction* (which Boas' *Handbook* was intended to replace), distinguished a series of "grammatical processes" not dissimilar from Boas'. But Powell saw them in evolutionary terms as solutions to the evolutionary problem created by the fact that ideas increased at a more rapid rate than the words which represented them. Grammatical processes were methods of expressing a large number of ideas with a small number of words. Under the general process of "combination", Powell listed four of these methods: juxtaposition, compounding, agglutination, and inflection. But these methods were also called "stages", and though Powell tended to regard even inflection as an inheritance from barbarism, he had no doubt that English was the highest language in the world because its grammatical processes were highly specialized (i.e., word derivation was accomplished by combination; syntax, by placement) and because the parts of speech were highly differentiated (1880: 55-58; 69-74).

It would be a mistake to imply that all nineteenth-century American thought on Indian languages was systematically structured along the lines I have suggested. What is involved is rather a matter of recurring themes and unstated assumptions. Furthermore, these could be integrated in various frameworks. Powell had insisted earlier that American Indian languages differed in degree but not in kind from Indo-European languages (1877: 104;

cf. Brinton 1890: 319). This was not, however, an argument against evolutionary ethnocentrism, but rather an implicit argument against another widely held nineteenth-century view of American languages: the suggestion, deriving from such men as Peter Duponceau, Wilhelm von Humboldt, Francis Lieber, and Heymann von Steinthal, that Indian languages differed fundamentally in type from other languages of the world — that they were "incorporative", or "polysynthetic", or "holophrastic" in character. Daniel G. Brinton, whose classification of American languages on morphological grounds appeared almost simultaneously with Powell's lexical classification in 1891, insisted on a distinction between these three processes (1890: 320-322). Brinton argued that American languages were polysynthetic in their method of word building, incorporative as regards the structure of their verbal forms (with the nominal and pronominal elements subordinated by incorporation into the verb stem), and holophrastic from the point of view of the psychic impulse which underlay the processes of polysynthesis and incorporation, the impulse "to express the whole proposition in one word" (1890: 359). Incorporation, however, was their distinguishing species characteristic, and Brinton was at great pains to explain away any apparent exceptions, and to argue that *all* American Indian languages were incorporative (1890: 307, 366-388). Powell was much more willing to allow for diversity of process, and in fact left "incorporation" out of his list — for which Brinton later rebuked him (1890: 358).

The issue here is not the differences between various individual exemplars of nineteenth-century linguistic thought. Some of them saw the origin of speech in the sentence, others in the word, some in the noun, some in the verb; some of them were highly ethnocentric, others relatively relativistic. The issue is rather the sort of assumptions that tend to run through them all, whether in a systematic, a random or even a self-contradictory way. Thus Brinton at times waxed ecstatic on the beauty of Indian tongues, and was inclined to argue on occasion that Aryan inflection was no nearer linguistic perfection than Algonkin incorporation (1890: 323). But he was equally capable of viewing his morphological types in evolutionary terms, of arguing that the higher languages separated the "material" from the "formal" elements; that incorporation was "vastly below the level of inflected speech"; that outside of incorporation, American languages had "no syntax, no inflections, nor declension of nouns and adjectives" (1890: 336, 342-343, 353). He even wrote an article hypothesizing the characteristics of paleolithic speech on the basis of American Indian languages. In it he argued that their present character suggested that paleolithic speech had neither tense, mode, nor person; that "what are called 'grammatical categories' were wholly absent in the primitive speech of man"; and that the process of incorporation was evidence of the "gradual" or evolutionary

"development of grammar". In the course of his argument, Brinton made a
large number of categorical statements about the empirical reality of
American Indian languages: that "abstract general terms" were "absent" or
"rare"; that their only distinction of gender was between animate and
inanimate; and that "a grammatical sex distinction, which is the prevailing
one in the grammars of the Aryan tongues, does not exist in any American
dialect known to me" (1890: 405, 406, 407).

VI

Boas' profound concern with certain of the issues posed by evolutionary linguists is evident as early as November, 1888, when he wrote his
essay "On Alternating Sounds." It is not certain whether he was already
familiar with Brinton's ideas on paleolithic speech, which were presented to
the American Philosophical Society during the same year. However, his
argument would suggest that he was: what Brinton had interpreted as traces
of the "vague", "fluctuating", and still tentative language of paleolithic man,
Boas saw as "alternating perceptions of one and the same sound" by an
observer whose own language had no equivalent (Boas 1889: 52; Brinton
1890: 397-399; cf. Stocking 1968a: 158-159). Indeed, the argument in Boas'
discussion of "Grammatical Categories" in the *Introduction* to the *Handbook*
is clearly built on the logic of his interpretation of alternating sounds
twenty-three years before. "Since the total range of personal experience
which language serves to express is infinitely varied, and its whole scope must
be expressed by a limited number of phonetic groups, it is obvious that an
extended classification of experiences must underlie all articulate speech" –
not as Powell had seemed to imply, evolved human speech, but human speech
in general. These classifications would be "in wider or narrower groups the
limits of which may be determined from a variety of points of view", which
"show very material differences in different languages, and do not conform
by any means to the same principles of classification." English offered a wide
variety of terms for water; Eskimo a wide variety of terms for snow. The
principle of "selection of such simple terms must to a certain extent depend
upon the chief interests of a people", and for this reason, "each language,
from the point of view of another language, may be arbitrary in its
classification." Every language "may be holophrastic from the point of view
of another", and "holophrasis can hardly be taken as a fundamental
characteristic of primitive languages" (Boas 1911: 24-27).
It was in this context that Boas offered the definition of grammatical
processes I have referred to already. He then went on to argue that the
"natural unit of expression was the sentence" and to suggest that our concept

of the word was entirely artificial, evident only as the outcome of analysis, and that "the same element may appear at one time as an independent noun, then again as part of a word, . . . which for this reason we are not inclined to consider as a complex of independent elements." After illustrating the point with references to the grammars of Reverends Riggs and Dorsey, Boas offered one of his characteristically indirect punch lines:

> It seemed important to discuss somewhat fully the concept of the word in its relation to the whole sentence, because in the morphological treatment of American languages this question plays an important role (1911: 27-33).

Turning then to the problem of "Stem and Affix", Boas went on to argue that the "separation of the ideas contained in a sentence into material contents and formal modifications is an arbitrary one, brought about, presumably, first of all, by the great variety of ideas which may be expressed in the same formal manner by the same pronominal and tense elements" — not, as Brinton and others would have had it, as the result of evolutionary progress. The method of treating material contents as the "subject-matter of lexicography" and formal elements as "the subject-matter of grammar" was simply the result of an ethnocentric Indo-European point of view. In American languages the distinction was often quite obscure and arbitrary, "owing to the fact that the number of elements which enter into formal compositions becomes very large" (1911: 33-35).

Boas then went on to discuss "grammatical categories" and to reject the notion that the Indo-European "system of categories" was present in every language. Indo-European languages classified nouns according to gender, plurality, and case, verbs according to person, tense, mood, and voice. Boas argued, on the one hand, that similar distinctions could be achieved by quite different means than we were accustomed to; and, on the other, that entirely different distinctions were possible, based on the tendency of each language "to select this or that aspect of the mental image" involved in a given idea as *necessary* to be expressed. If it was true, as Brinton had argued, that "true gender was on the whole rare" in American languages, this was because "the sex principle" was "merely one of a great many possible classifications" of nominal forms. Similarly, we said "the man is sick", whereas a Kwakiutl was in effect required to say "that invisible man lies sick on his back on the floor of the absent house", because the categories of visibility and nearness were obligatory in Kwakiutl (1911: 35-43).

Involved in all of this was of course the idea that there were underlying (although culturally conditioned) psychological differences between languages which were expressed in their vocabulary and their morphology. That these psychological differences might eventually be catalogued comparatively was indeed a promissory note. But the method of analysis that was predicated on their existence was not.

VII

The unifying leitmotif of Boas' correspondence relating to the *Handbook* is the word "analytical". The very first proposal to McGee suggests that the guiding idea embodied in the 1900 paper on Kwakiutl grammar was "to describe the language in an analytical way, giving the fundaments of the phonetics, grammatical processes, and grammatical categories" (APS: Boas to McGee, 4/4/01). Two years later, in restating the plan more elaborately to Holmes, Boas wrote that "my plan is to make the sketches strictly analytical, and it will be necessary to lay down definitely the fundamental points of view of analysis to be followed by all the collaborators" (APS: Boas to Holmes, 5/9/03). At a number of points, Boas offered qualifying or appositive statements which suggest what he meant by "purely analytical". Most importantly, an analytic treatment involved "a presentation of the essential traits of the grammar as they would naturally develop if an Eskimo, without any knowledge of any other language, should present the essential notions of his own grammar" (APS: Boas to Thalbitzer, 1/30/07). In other words, "grammatical categories" were to be derived internally from an analysis of the language itself rather than imposed from without. One must strive therefore "to keep out the point of view of Indo-European languages as thoroughly as possible", to formulate grammatical categories "without reference to the current classifications [of categories] of Indo-European languages, which have helped to obscure the fundamental traits of American languages for so long a time" (APS: Boas to J. Dunn, 11/7/07).

It is in this context that one must understand Boas' detailed instructions to collaborators in July, 1904. True, he enclosed a draft of his Kwakiutl sketch (and apparently of his general introduction as well), with the request that collaborators "adhere to a division into sections and paragraphs similar to the one here adopted." True, he offered his recent article on Chinook vocabulary as a model for the treatment of that section (BAE: Boas to collaborators, 7/16/04). But both the correspondence and the resulting grammars make it clear that the Kwakiutl headings were illustrative rather than obligatory. The crucial principle governing the sequence of topics was expressed in later letters to Hewitt and Thalbitzer:

> I have found it convenient in practically all the sketches to divide
> the subject-matter of morphology in such a way, that I have first

treated what might perhaps be called the etymological processes, or the elements which enter into composition in a word or sentence-word, without giving the syntactic relations involved in the subject-predicate of the sentence; that is to say, I have practically taken every morphological part that has nothing to do with syntax first, and all the syntactic elements (for instance, pronomial parts, etc.) after this portion has been settled (APS: Boas to Hewitt, 8/30/07; cf. Boas to Thalbitzer, 1/30/07).

Brinton and other evolutionists had treated syntax as an evolutionary development, and minimized its role in American languages. By arguing that the problem of relating the phonetic groupings which expressed various ideas could be and in fact was handled by various alternative processes which, given the character of American languages, were better regarded as matters of "etymology" (or word formation), and by relegating the treatment of traditional syntactical issues to a secondary position, Boas did two things. On the one hand, he emphasized the amount of "syntax" in Indian languages; on the other he in effect suggested that the traditional notion of syntax was in itself an ethnocentric concept.

VIII

Turning to the grammars themselves to see how Boas' instructions were carried out, one notes that the emphasis in each grammar was indeed on the etymological processes by which phonetic groups were related to each other and on the different sorts of ideas conveyed by classes of phonetic groups. Insofar as the traditional "parts of speech" were systematically treated, they appeared usually as sub-headings within a framework constructed on this basis — although in Goddard's Hupa one can still detect the old structure in terms of parts of speech. References to syntax were usually relegated to rather brief discussions at the end under the headings "syntactical particles", "syntactical relations", or "character of sentence". Beyond this, one is struck by the occasions in which the presentation or interpretation of the data seems implicitly to have been directed at undercutting particular generalizations about Indian languages or about primitive languages in general which I have suggested were current in nineteenth-century evolutionary linguistic thought: if Brinton argued that Indian languages had few conjunctions, then Boas noted the numerous conjunctions in Chinook (Boas 1911: 636; Brinton 1890: 344-345). On the other hand, one notes the infrequency of reference to "incorporation" as a grammatical process. It is almost as if the underlying theme of the book were the attempt to discuss American Indian languages without reference to the specific process which many nineteenth-century linguists had argued was their central structural principle.

Beyond these evident similarities of analytic approach, the striking thing about the grammars is their apparent diversity. Within the general framework I have suggested, the headings of analysis and the order of their presentation seem quite varied. But the present argument would in fact call for precisely this sort of diversity. If the goal was to describe each language in terms of its "inner form" and to derive its categories by a purely internal analysis, and if as Boas suggested to Kroeber the choice of languages had been guided by the desire to have "as many psychologically distinct types as possible" (APS: Boas to Kroeber, 4/4/04), then diversity of presentation was the logical result of consensus on the method of analysis. (It is perhaps in this context that we should understand the "interspersing" of "non-semantic processes among grammatical processes" which Voegelin suggested filled the sketches with "complex statements which crowd out simple patterns" [1952: 445].) Boas in fact made the basis of this general diversity quite explicit in his *Introduction:*

> Owing to the fundamental differences between different linguistic families, it has seemed advisable to develop the terminology of each independently of the others, and to seek for uniformity only in cases where it can be obtained without artificially stretching the definition of terms (1911: 82).

In the context of a critique of nineteenth-century assumptions, the insistence on the diversity and variety of Indian linguistic forms and processes was simply the obverse of the prevailing failure to mention incorporation.

In the light of the discussion to this point we may perhaps better understand certain "peculiarities of technical terminology" which Voegelin alleged appeared in "grammar after grammar of the first volume of the Handbook". Voegelin referred specifically to "composition" and to "coalescence". He suggested that "composition" was used "in a wide sense to summarize all linear morphemes which may appear in a word (as prefixes before stems, infixes within stems, and suffixes after stems) instead of in the usual narrow-sense use of 'composition' for compounding — for sequences of (generally) two stems serving as a base for affixation" (1952: 440). There is a passage in an article by Kroeber published at about this time which perhaps suggests why the *Handbook* should have used the term in the broad sense Voegelin described:

> It is thoroughly misleading to designate the same process respectively "composition" and "incorporation" according as one has in mind his own or other forms of speech. Some day philologists will approach their profession not with the assump-

tion that language must differ in kind or in being relatively better or worse, but with the assumption that the same fundamental processes run through them all, and with the realization that it is only by starting from the conception of their essential unity of type and method that their interesting and important diversities can be understood.

Kroeber was in fact inclined to define "incorporation" out of existence (Kroeber 1911: 583-584; cf. Kroeber 1909, 1910). His attempt to do so got him into a bit of a controversy with Edward Sapir (Sapir 1911). But Sapir's agreement on the underlying issue is quite evident, particularly in his own comments on the notion of "coalescence"

Voegelin suggested that "coalescence" was used in the *Handbook* as a "sort of chemical metaphor for alterations and contractions occuring when an affix is juxtaposed to a stem", and that Sapir, "evidently amused at this metaphor", "poked gentle fun" at it in his Takelma grammar (1952: 440). The quality of their reĺationship in this period makes it unlikely that Sapir would even indirectly poke fun at Boas in a doctoral dissertation Boas supervised. More to the point, however, is the fact that "coalescence" appears only incidentally in the *Handbook,* and then as rather more a common-sense than a technical term. What Sapir was talking about was an entirely different matter, and bears directly on the more general issue I am discussing. The passage quoted by Voegelin occurs in a general discussion of Takelma morphology, in which Sapir attacks the use of the terms "incorporation", "polysynthesis", and "agglutination" as "catch-words" to describe the general structure of American Indian languages, and of Takelma in particular.

> If we study the manner in which the stem unites in Takelma with derivative and grammatical elements to form the word, and the vocalic and consonantic changes that the stem itself undergoes from grammatical purposes, we shall hardly be able to find a tangible difference in general method, however much the details may vary, between Takelma and languages that have been dignified by the name "inflectional". It is generally said, in defining inflection, that languages of the inflectional as contrasted with those of the agglutinative type make use of words of indivisible psychic value, in which the stem and the various grammatical elements have entirely lost their single individualities, but have "chemically" (!) coalesced into a single form-unit; in other words, the word is not a mere mosaic of phonetic materials, of which each is the necessary symbol of some special concept (stem) or logical category (grammatical element) (Boas 1922: 52-53).

Although Sapir does not indicate this in so many words, the idea that inflected words coalesced chemically whereas agglutinated words were merely stuck together was simply a variant of the sort of thinking I have been discussing — in slightly different form, the notion goes back to Wilhelm von Humboldt. It was not at Boas, but at certain pervasive assumptions in nineteenth-century linguistics, that Sapir was poking fun.

Indeed, Sapir went on to argue in a manner quite consistent with Boas' general discussion of the "Characteristics of American Languages" (1911: 74-76) that from one point of view Takelma might be regarded as polysynthetic, from another, incorporative, from another, inflective, and that a "more objective, unhampered study of languages" — Boas would have said "analytic" — would "undoubtedly reveal a far wider prevalence than has been generally admitted of the inflectional type." The problem was that investigation had been sidetracked by taking "trivial characteristics" like sex gender and the presence of cases as "criteria of inflection", when in fact "inflection has reference to method, not to subject-matter" (Boas 1922: 54). It requires only a slight extension of Sapir's comment to get at the whole point of the Boas plan: grammatical categories had reference to method (or better process) and to cultural focus — not to any apriori ethnocentric or evolutionary notion of subject matter.

IX

If the discussion so far has perhaps clarified the central point of the Boas plan, there are still several matters relating to its genesis and significance which merit brief discussion: (a) Boas' attitude toward the problem of the classification of American languages; (b) his relation to the tradition of thinking on language and world view that is customarily traced back from Whorf and Sapir through Boas and sometimes Brinton to Wilhelm von Humboldt; and (c) his relation to the subsequent tradition of structural linguistics in America.

(a) In regard to the first of these, I have already noted Voegelin's suggestion that the purpose of the *Handbook* was to facilitate the "cross-genetic comparability" which was essential to "diffusional linguistics." While there is some basis for this interpretation, there are complexities that bear some comment. In the first decade or so of his linguistic work, Boas was by no means uninterested in genetic approaches to linguistic classification, and his early interest in the systematic study of structures in fact reflected his concern with genetic rather than diffusionary problems. After returning from the Northwest in 1888, he wrote Powell a letter in which he argued that, despite the number of borrowed words in Tlingit and Haida, their "grammatical structure" was "so much alike that they must be considered remote branches of the same stock" (BAE: Boas to Powell, 8/8/88). The same interest was still evident in his 1893 paper, where his advocacy of deeper study of structures was offered as a solution "in the present state of linguistic science" to the problem of defining the "generic connection" within each of the four groups of languages on the Northwest Coast (Boas 1894: 346). Various letters indicate that Boas thought of the *Handbook*, at least in its early stages, as a "morphological classification" of American languages, and that the languages were chosen in order to facilitate comparison of differing psychological types in a single broad geographical region (BAE: Boas to Holmes, 2/13/04: APS: Boas to Kroeber, 4/4/04). I have already noted his insistence that Goddard and Swanton point up a relationship he found between Tlingit and Athapaskan, which, along with his earlier suggestion of the kinship of Haida and Tlingit, in effect tied together the three major components of Sapir's Na-dene — a fact that is all the more interesting in the light of Boas' later attitude towards Sapir's genetic reconstructions (Boas 1911: 46; Sapir 1915; Boas 1920).

On the other hand, there is no doubt that there was a development in Boas' thought on these problems which reflects a tendency toward increasing skepticism also evident in other areas of his anthropological thought. From the beginning of his career, Boas had resisted "premature classification". When Kroeber and others were laboring in 1905 over a reformulation of Powell's scheme of American languages, Boas' response (although the issue at this point was simply one of nomenclature) reflected his deeply rooted conservatism on classificatory matters. After opposing the report Kroeber drafted, he indicated to F. W. Hodge that he would favor a simple statement that "among specialists who are working on linguistic stocks of America, the following names are at present in use, and therefore, for the time being, deserve recommendation", after which a list could be appended "made up by our California friends and other specialists" (APS: Boas to Hodge, 11/1/05). Perhaps more to the present point is the fact that Boas seems to have regarded an "analytic" treatment of language as essentially synchronic rather than diachronic. He suggested to Goddard that it made no difference that a substitute formulation which he had proposed lumped elements that differed in their origin. This was only to be expected in "any purely analytical treatment" in which elements that had become alike through the action of analogy or other causes would be part of a single grammatical category in the present (APS: Boas to Goddard, 12/28/07; cf. Boas 1911: 82). Furthermore, despite Boas' editing of the Tlingit and Athapaskan, the *Handbook* is on the whole notably lacking in any sort of systematic comparison of one language to another. In the end, the comparative analysis that was to have been its capstone was never attempted.

During the next decade, when Boas' students went far beyond him in arguing genetic relationships among American Indian languages, he responded with critical skepticism, and perhaps in reaction, considerably elaborated the diffusional arguments which were already present in the *Introduction* to the *Handbook* (Boas 1911: 47-53). Even in the *Handbook* itself, Boas was not willing to assume that the structural similarity of Tlingit, Haida, and Athapaskan was the result of common origin, despite the fact that he was at this point still inclined to minimize the possibility of a "radical modification of the morphological traits of a language through the influence of another language" (Boas 1911: 49). By 1920 his position on this issue had changed drastically, and he was inclined to believe that diffusion of morphological traits could "modify the fundamental structural characteristics" of a language, and specifically disavowed his suggestion in 1893 that the morphological similarities of certain Northwest languages were "a proof of relationship of the same order as that of languages belonging, for instance, to the Indo-European family" (Boas 1920: 367-368; cf. Boas 1917, 1929). If, as this evidence suggests, the extreme linguistic diffusionism associated with Boas is in fact to be understood in the context of his later disagreements with certain of his students, then it seems unlikely that the *Handbook* was specifically designed to meet the felt need of diffusionary linguistics for "structural similarities among languages, whether related or not," rather than for "cognates among morpheme lists" (Voegelin 1952: 439). On the contrary, it seems to have begun at least in part as an attempt to approach the problem of genetic relationship in morphological terms. But that goal was from the beginning subordinated to the goal of providing adequate "analytic" descriptions of the languages themselves, and by the time the *Introduction* was written in 1908, the whole problem of "the final classification of languages" was already postponed for an indefinite future time (Boas 1911 58, 82). Just as the possibility of deriving laws for the development of culture constantly receded behind the horizon of mounting empirical data of American cultures, so the possibility of a genetic classification of languages – even on morphological as opposed to lexical grounds – seems already to have begun to recede behind the empirical complexity of American Indian languages (cf. Kluckhohn and Prufer 1959: 24; Kroeber 1960: 656; Stocking 1973).

(b) The relation of the *Handbook* to the tradition associated with Wilhelm von Humboldt is also somewhat complicated. Boas later suggested that his greatest contribution to linguistics was to present each language in Steinthal's terms by analyzing it in relation to its own internal system rather than to categories imposed from without (Lowie 1943: 184). Steinthal was perhaps the leading European disciple of Humboldt, and this would seem to suggest a fairly clear lineage through Boas to Sapir and Whorf for the "promissory note" of a comparative study of languages and *Weltanschauungen* (cf. Brown 1967: 14-16; Hymes 1961a: 23).

On the other hand, there is evidence to suggest that Boas' psychological approach to language was at least in part a response to the experience of his own field work rather than simply an importation of a Germanic tradition. In a letter to the head of the Carnegie Institution in 1905, he suggested that:

> One of the remarkable features of American anthropology is the multiplicity of small linguistic families the origin of which is entirely obscure to us. The investigations made during the last ten years suggest that there may be larger unities in existence based rather on similarity of the psychological foundations of language than on phonetic similarity. This hypothesis is based on the observation that in several regions neighboring languages, although quite diverse in vocabulary, are similar in structure. The psychological significance of this phenomenon is still entirely obscure and would very probably be cleared up by a thorough study of those regions in which the greatest differentiation of language occurs (APS: Boas to Woodward, 1/13/05).

Furthermore, Humboldt's leading American disciple was Daniel Garrison Brinton, who cited Steinthal at length on the "incorporative" character of all American Indian languages, and who was upon occasion inclined toward a rather extreme racial determinism and evolutionary dogmatism (Brinton 1895). The point is that in the late nineteenth-century milieu, Humboldt's thinking had become linked with a melange of evolutionary and racial assumptions whose rejection was the cornerstone of Boas' own anthropology. More than any other single individual, it was in fact Brinton who was the target of the Boasian critique.

In this context, it is not surprising that Boas' comments in the *Handbook* on the relation of language and culture were not without elements of ambiguity and even of apparent contradiction. To begin with, Boas, in line with his general skepticism of artificial classifications, devoted the first ten pages of his *Introduction* to an argument that the independence of their historical development ruled out any correlation between race, language and culture, not only in the present, but even in an hypothesized primitive state (Boas 1911: 5-14). When it came to considering specifically the relation of "language and thought", he explicitly rejected as *not* "likely" any "direct relation between the culture of a tribe and the language they speak." On the contrary, if primitive men lacked certain grammatical forms, it was because their mode of life did not require them. If this mode changed, these forms would doubtless develop, since "under these conditions the language would be moulded rather by the cultural state" than vice versa (Boas 1911: 67).

At the same time, Boas went on to argue that linguistic processes offered an important insight into the processes of cultural determinism. Like linguistic categories, major cultural categories, values, and norms arose unconsciously. They differed only in that they were subsequently subject to secondary rationalization. This argument was an important link in Boas' critique of traditional racial assumptions (cf. Stocking 1968a: 222). However, it also provided a means for reintroducing indirectly a portion of the linguistic determinism he had previously rejected. If the occurence of "the most fundamental grammatical concepts in all languages" was proof of the essential psychological unity of man, it was also true that we think in words, and the words available to us could not but condition our thought. Thus it was an "open" question how far "linguistic expression" was secondary to the "customs of the people", and whether the latter "have not rather developed from the unconsciously developed terminology." Anticipating an argument his student Kroeber was to advance in 1909, Boas referred to kinship classes as an example. Coming then almost full circle, Boas concluded this section of the introduction by arguing that "the peculiar characteristics of languages are clearly reflected in the views and customs of the world" (Boas 1911: 67-73).

This argument is not intended to minimize the relation of Boas to the German tradition of Humboldt and Steinthal. His emphasis in the *Introduction* on "inner form" — which was a technical term for both men — is enough to suggest an important tie (Darnell 1967: 126). But the primary impact of Boas' thought was to support a thoroughgoing linguistic relativism, and to reject any form of linguistic determinism that might be used to bolster either racial determinism or an evolutionary hierarchy. To enlarge somewhat on a suggestion of Dell Hymes', it may be that it was, in a retrospective sense, necessary at this point in the lineage of Humboldtian thought to purge it of "Procrustean typological and evolutionary categories" (Hymes 1961a: 24). In the late nineteenth-century context, these had racialist implications which were clearly incompatible with the general thrust of modern anthropological thought. If the subsequent anthropological concern with linguistics and world view can legitimately be traced through Boas to Humboldt, there is nevertheless at this point a discontinuity some commentaries have perhaps passed over a bit too easily.[7]

(c) As far as Boas' relation to subsequent structural linguistics is concerned, it should be clear from what has gone before that Voegelin went too far in subsuming Boas within the framework of what came after him. There may be a sense in which it is useful to regard Boas as exemplifying "monolevel structuralizing" (Voegelin 1963). But insofar as the notion of structure implies (as it seems to me to do) "inferences from the internal relations of a system more than inferences from discrete pieces of reality", then it seems to me that Hymes was correct in suggesting that Boasian grammars "itemize", but "on the whole, they do not structure" (Hymes 1961b: 90; cf. Hockett 1954). Doubtless Boas was interested in "observed regularities, recurrences, and reduction of redundancies" (Voegelin 1963:

14), and his indication in 1908 that an "analytic" study of language was purely synchronic suggests an interesting parallel to Saussure. But it is also clear that he hesitated to carry the reduction to system too far. Indeed, his instructions to collaborators cautioned them against trying to make their analyses too tidy. Redundancies and inconsistencies would doubtless occur, since "in no language can be found a psychological system which is carried through logically" (BAE: Boas to collaborators, 7/16/04). As Hymes suggested, Boas is best seen as "clearing the way for, but not quite occupying the ground of, his structurally-minded successors" (Hymes 1961b: 90; cf. Hymes 1970 and Jakobson 1944: 195, and 1959).

Hymes advanced this interpretation in the context of arguing the consistency of Boas' approach to language with his approach to folklore. This consistency is in fact one of the most striking characteristics of Boas' anthropology as a whole. Thus his argument that classification of man according to race, according to language, and according to culture would not lead to the same results because each of these aspects of man had been differentially affected by historical processes is exactly parallel to his argument in regard to lexicon, phonology, and grammar as bases for the "Classification of Languages" (Boas 1911: 5-14; 44-58). And although there are aspects of his thought on culture that suggest the basis for an approach in terms of "system", his own orientation, in this area as in others, was anti-systematic (cf. Stocking 1973).

And for good reason. His whole anthropology was a reaction against the simple typological thinking and "premature" or "arbitrary classification" that he felt was characteristic of evolutionary thought about man. His criticism of racial "types" and cultural "stages" carried directly over into his thought on language, which was a conscious relativistic reaction to traditional evolutionary assumptions about so-called "primitive languages." Like the rest of Boas' anthropology, it shared with evolutionism the goal of elucidating development in time, but it did this by focussing in the first instance on processes observable in the present. It was – or attempted to be – rigorously empirical, and was above all concerned with the development of adequate methods of description.

Here we return to the title of the work itself. It was a *Handbook*; and whatever its later usage actually was, it was conceived, at least in part, as a guide to the study of Indian languages in the field. As Boas suggested to Holmes in 1903, "the principal point to be borne in mind is, on the one hand, to make a book which will show collectors how to proceed in recording Indian languages; and, on the other hand, to show by these ten examples what American languages really are (APS: Boas to Holmes, 5/9/03).

In realizing the goal of adequate description, Boas placed great emphasis on the collection of texts, the utility of which has been questioned by some later writers on the grounds that the process of their dictation led informants artificially to simplify their sentence structure (Voegelin: personal communication). Although it may seem tangential to introduce this issue at this late point, it in fact helps to place Boas' linguistic orientation – and indeed his whole anthropology – more firmly in context. On several occasions Boas wrote in defense of texts to the Bureau, which tended to regard their publication as uneconomic. No one, he suggested to Holmes, would advocate the study of the "antique civilizations" of the Turks or Russians without a thorough knowledge of the "literary documents in their languages." For the American Indian, practically no such literary material was available, and to make it available was a crucial task for anthropology.

> My own published work shows that I let this kind of work take precedence over practically everything else, since it is the foundation of all future researches. Without it a control of our results and deeper studies based on material collected by us will be all but impossible . . . . What would Indo-European philology be, if we had only grammars by one or two students and not the live material from which these grammars have been built up, which is, at the same time, the material on which the philosophic study of language must be based?

The point was nowhere clearer, suggested Boas, than in studies based on the "old missionary grammars", in which the characteristic features were so obscured that without new and ample texts our understanding would always be inadequate. "As we require a new point of view now, so future times will require new points of view, and for them the texts, and ample texts, must be available" (BAE: Boas to Holmes, 7/24/05; cf. APS: Boas to Holmes, 11/2/03). The passage is particularly revealing in that it suggests that despite his lack of training in European philology, Boas still tended to conceive linguistics (and indeed cultural anthropology) as the study of *written* documents. If these were lacking, then one provided them. But he was not unaware that the method of text recording involved certain distortions – his experimentation with phonographs makes this quite clear (BAE: Boas to Holmes, 11/3/06).

   More to the present point, however, is the transformation of traditional approaches that took place in the process of achieving a rather traditional goal. It is not merely that Boas was, "in cold and sober fact, the agent who . . . more than any other" focused "the attention of scholars on those unfamiliar languages that are the vehicles of the lowly and despised cultures of 'our primitive contemporaries.' " More than any other man, he transformed the negative evolutionary evaluation of these languages in the very process of defining the methods of their study. It is at this level of what modern

American linguists take *most* for granted that Boas was "the *guru,* the ancestor in learning, of all those in this country who work in descriptive linguistics." It is at this level of attitude, assumption, and method that the *Handbook* was "the 'manifesto' for this study" (Emeneau 1943: 35).

NOTES

1. Quite aside from limitations imposed by my lack of training in linguistics (cf. below, Some Comments on History as a Moral Discipline: "Transcending 'Textbook' Chronicles and Apologetics," chapter 21, this volume), I should note that this study is based largely on correspondence prior to the end of 1909—a period which includes the genesis and completion of the ten grammars in Volume I, as well as of Sapir's Takelma grammar in Volume II (although the latter was not published until 1922). I have profited from discussion and correspondence with Paul Friedrich, Dell Hymes, Joel Sherzer, and Carl Voegelin, and I would like to thank the American Philosophical Society and the National Anthropological Archives, Smithsonian Institution, for permission to quote from letters.

2. Since this paper was written in 1968, I have come across an article of Hale's treating the same problem Boas treated in his essay "On Alternating Sounds" (Hale 1884; cf. Boas 1889). In it, Hale recounts an experiment he performed by accident in 1882. He and Prof. Alexander Melville Bell were simultaneously recording the words of an Iroquois informant, and in a number of instances, Hale recorded as "r" a sound Bell recorded as "l". On this basis, as well as that of evidence from missionary vocabularies, Hale concluded that the general phenomenon of "intermediate articulation" lay not "in the speaker's utterance, but in the ear of the listener"—that "the sound as spoken was an indistinct articulation, . . .and that the hearer, unaccustomed to sounds of this peculiar character, involuntarily made distinctions where none really existed." The argument is somewhat Boasian, and one might use it to support Jacob Gruber's suggestion that Hale was an important source of the major ingredients of Boas' anthropology—although Gruber himself did not (Gruber 1967). Although it is certainly possible that Boas was familiar with Hale's article, I can find no reference to it in Hale's letters to Boas, and there is no overlap whatsoever between the data offered by Hale and that used by Boas. Furthermore, the differences between the articles are quite striking: in Hale's piece there is not the slightest trace of Boas' argument in psycho-physical terms, and in the end, Hale used alternating sounds as the basis of a rather strained argument about the process of differentiation within linguistic stocks. On the whole, I am still inclined to minimize Hale's influence on Boas, in this as in other matters.

3. Sapir 1917; cf., however, the comments of Carl Voegelin: "Boas' predecessors did their best work on constituents within a grammar rather than on comprehensive grammars, though some of the best examples, as

Dorsey's on Iowa-Oto person markers, remain in manuscript in the BAE archives" (personal communication). On the relation between Boas and the work of the Bureau, cf. Darnell 1969.

4. The Hewitt episode has interesting implications for Boas' methodological assumptions (cf. below, the idea that languages should be described as if a native were to define the categories of his own language). Apparently the critical variable was in fact formal training with Boas. William Jones, another part-Indian who spoke Fox fluently, had this, and did indeed become one of his collaborators on the *Handbook*.

5. Thalbitzer's sketch is suggestive as a kind of test case for the character of Boas' influence on the *Handbook*. Thalbitzer, who had been trained with Vilhelm Thomsen and Otto Jespersen, tried hard, out of a European tradition, to follow Boas' approach. The divergences of his presentation suggest that the others (who had all, save Goddard, studied with Boas) took much for granted that Thalbitzer labored with.

6. Quite aside from its relation to Voegelin's long run scholarly interests (cf. Voegelin 1955, 1963), the Boas Plan paper seems to have been written in the specific context of his work on two other key articles in which problems of descriptive models, structural restatements, typology, etc., were foremost in his mind—as evidenced by the fact that each of the three articles refers in footnotes to each of the other two (cf. Voegelin 1954, and Voegelin and Harris 1952).

7. This discontinuity would seem to be particularly relevant in evaluating the suggested role of Brinton in this lineage. In view of the fact that Brinton was the implicit critical target of so much of Boas' anthropological thought (whether in linguistics or in culture theory generally), and of the fact that the Humboldt tradition was more directly available to him through Steinthal—whom he clearly read if he did not study with—it seems to me unlikely that Boas was linked to Humboldt through Brinton in any positive way (cf. Hymes 1961, Darnell 1967, Brown 1967, and Stocking 1968b).

REFERENCES

APS American Philosophical Society. 1900-1909. Boas Papers, American Philosophical Society, Philadelphia.

BAE Bureau of American Ethnology. 1885-1909. Bureau of American Ethnology Correspondence, National Anthropological Archives, Smithsonian Institution, Washington, D. C.

Boas, Franz. 1889. On alternating sounds. American Anthropologist 2: 47-53.

———. 1894. Classification of the languages of the North Pacific Coast. Memoirs of the International Congress of Anthropology, 1893, ed. C. S. Wake, 339-346.

———. 1900. Sketch of the Kwakiutl language. American Anthropologist 2: 708-721.

———. 1904. The vocabulary of the Chinook language. American Anthropologist 6:118-147.

_____. 1911. Handbook of American Indian languages, Part I. (Bureau of American Ethnology, Bulletin 40.) Washington, D. C.

_____. 1917. Introduction. International Journal of American Linguistics 1: 1-8.

_____. 1920. Classification of American languages. American Anthropologist 22: 367-376.

_____. 1922. Handbook of American Indian languages, Part II. (Bureau of American Ethnology, Bulletin 40.) Washington, D. C.

_____. 1929. Classification of American Indian languages. Language 5: 1-7.

Brinton, D. G. 1890. Essays of an Americanist. Philadelphia.

_____. 1891. The American Race: a linguistic classification . . . New York.

_____. 1895. The aims of anthropology. Science 2: 241-252.

Brown, R. L. 1967. Wilhelm von Humboldt's conception of linguistic relativity. (Janua Linguarum, LXV) The Hague, Mouton.

Darnell, Regna. 1967. Daniel Garrison Brinton: an intellectual biography. Unpublished master's thesis. Department of Anthropology, University of Pennsylvania.

_____. 1969. The development of American anthropology 1870-1920: From the Bureau of American Ethnology to Franz Boas. Unpublished doctoral dissertation. Department of Anthropology, University of Pennsylvania.

Emeneau, Murray. 1943. Franz Boas as linguist. Memoirs of the American Anthropological Association 61: 35-38.

Gatschet, A. S. 1890. The Klamath Indians of South Western Oregon. 2 vols. Washington, D. C.

Gruber, J. W. 1967. Horatio Hale and the development of American anthropology. Proceedings of the American Philosophical Society 111: 5-37.

Hale, Horatio. 1884. On some doubtful or intermediate articulations. Journal of the Anthropological Institute 14: 233-243.

Harrington, J. P. 1945. Boas on the science of language. International Journal of American Linguistics 11: 97-99.

Hockett, C. F. 1954. Two models of grammatical description. Word 10: 210-234.

Hymes, Dell. 1961a. On typology of cognitive styles in language. Anthropological Linguistics 3(1): 22-54.

_____. 1961b. Review of Walter Goldschmidt, ed., The Anthropology of Franz Boas. Journal of American Folklore 74: 87-90.

_____. 1964. Language in culture and society. New York, Harper and Row.

_____. 1970. Linguistic method of ethnography. Method and theory in linguistics, ed. Paul L. Garvin, 249-325. The Hague-Paris, Mouton.

Jakobson, Roman. 1944. Franz Boas' approach to language. International Journal of American Linguistics 10: 188-195.

_____. 1959. Boas' view of grammatical meaning. The anthropology of Franz Boas, ed. Walter Goldschmidt, 139-145. San Francisco, Chandler.

Kluckhohn, C. and O. Prufer. 1959. Influences during the formative years. The Anthropology of Franz Boas, ed. Walter Goldschmidt, 4-28. San Francisco, Chandler.

Kroeber, A. L. 1909. Noun incorporation in American languages. Verhandlungen des XIV Internationalen Amerikanisten-Kongress (Vienna),
569-576.
_____. 1910. Noun composition in American languages. Anthropos 5:
204-218.
_____. 1911. Incorporation as a linguistic process. American Anthropologist
13: 577-584.
_____. 1960. Statistics, Indo-European, and taxonomy. Language 36: 1-21.
Lowie, R. H. 1943. The progress of science: Franz Boas, anthropologist.
Scientific Monthly 56: 184.
Matthews, W. 1877. Ethnography and philology of the Hidatsa Indians.
Washington, D. C.
Powell, J. W. 1877. Introduction to the study of Indian languages. 1st ed.
Washington, D. C.
_____. 1880. Introduction to the study of Indian languages. 2nd ed.
Washington D. C.
_____. 1891. Indian linguistic families of America north of Mexico. (Bureau
of American Ethnology, 7th Annual Report). Washington, D. C.
Riggs, S. R. 1893. Dakota grammar, texts and ethnography, ed. J. O. Dorsey.
Washington, D. C.
Sapir, Edward. 1911. The problem of noun incorporation in American
languages. American Anthropologist 13: 250-282.
_____. 1915. The Na-dene languages, a preliminary report. American Anthro-
pologist 17: 534-558.
_____. 1917. Linguistic publications of the Bureau of American Ethnology, a
general review. International Journal of American Linguistics 1: 76-81.
Stocking, G. W., Jr. 1968a. Race, culture, and evolution. New York, Free
Press.
_____. 1968b. Review of R. L. Brown 1967 (above). American
Anthropologist 70: 1039-1040..
_____. 1974. The Shaping of American Anthropology, 1883-1911: A Franz
Boas Reader. New York, Basic Books.
Thalbitzer, W. 1904. A phonetical study of the Eskimo language. Copen-
hagen.
Voegelin, C. F. 1952. The Boas plan for the presentation of American Indian
languages. Proceedings of the American Philosophical Society 96:
439-451.
_____. 1954. Inductively arrived at models for cross-genetic comparisons of
American Indian languages. University of California Publications in
Linguistics 10: 27-45. Berkeley and Los Angeles.
_____. 1955. On developing new typologies and revising old ones.
Southwestern Journal of Anthropology 11: 355-360.
Voegelin, C. F., and Z. Harris. 1952. Training in anthropological linguistics.
American Anthropologist 54: 322-327.
Voegelin, C. F., and F. M. 1963. On the history of structuralizing in 20th
century America. Anthropological Linguistics 5(1): 12-37.

V : COMPLEMENTARY PERSPECTIVES

19. The History of Science and the History of Linguistics

John C. Greene

I

As an academic discipline the history of science is a very recent phenomenon, much younger than the sciences it studies. Most of those sciences reach back into classical antiquity, but, although particular sciences have had their chroniclers from time to time throughout their history, it was not until the twentieth century that the history of science emerged as an organized field of study with a scholarly apparatus of professorial chairs, learned journals, historical museums, national and international organizations, and the like. The establishment of this field of study was the work of a generation of distinguished scholars, including George Sarton, Aldo Mieli, Lynn Thorndike, Pierre Brunet, Charles Singer, Alexandre Koyré, E. J. Dijksterhuis, and others, all of whom passed from the human scene within the last two decades. These men laid the foundations of the new discipline broad and deep, leaving to their pupils and emulators a rich legacy of ideas, publications, and institutions.

Building on those foundations the history of science has grown rapidly in the second half of the century, both in Europe and America. Whereas in 1950 there were only eight or ten American colleges and universities offering general courses in the history of science (as distinguished from historical courses offered by scientific departments for their own students), today there are more than one hundred institutions offering courses of this kind, and the number grows apace. On the graduate level, the number of universities offering doctoral programs has more than tripled in the last decade. A recent "Guide to Graduate Study and Research in the History of Science and Medicine" lists doctoral programs in the history of science at Brown, California (Berkeley and Los Angeles), Case Western Reserve, Chicago, Cornell, Harvard, Indiana, Johns Hopkins, Kansas, Oklahoma, Pennsylvania, Princeton, Washington, Wisconsin, and Yale.[1] In Britain lectureships or readerships in the history of science (often combined with philosophy of science) have been established at London, Cambridge, Oxford, Aberdeen, Leicester, Leeds, Belfast, and Hull, and the demand for qualified teachers in the history and philosophy of science throughout Great Britain and the Commonwealth has generated pressure for the establishment of new and larger graduate programs in these subjects. On the Continent, too, the new discipline has been growing, both in Communist and non-Communist countries.

The rise and spread of the history of science as an academic discipline in no way displaced the older tradition of historical scholarship within the particular sciences. Each science continued to include among its devotees persons interested in the history of their own science, sometimes to the extent of making that history their main field of research. Some of these scientist-historians were drawn into the history of science movement as members of history of science departments and active participants in history of science organizations. Others continued their historical researches independently. The result has been increasing interest among scientists in the history of their own sciences and increasing cooperation between historically oriented scientists and professional historians of science. Chemists seem always to have shown considerable interest in the history of chemistry, and this interest shows no sign of diminishing. Physicists have been less historically oriented, but there are evidences of a change of attitude here. A few years ago the American Institute of Physics established a Committee on the History and Philosophy of Science and asked the History of Science Society to appoint a liaison member. Since that time a Center for History and Philosophy of Physics has been established by the Institute, and its library has made rapid progress in collecting the papers of living and recently deceased physicists to provide resources for the study of the history of modern physics. In 1961 the American Physical Society, in conjunction with the American Philosophical Society, obtained National Science Foundation support for a three-year project of research, interviewing and manuscript hunting aimed at assembling sources for a history of the development of quantum physics. The materials collected by this project, deposited at the Library of the American Philosophical Society and the Library of the University of California at Berkeley, will be of inestimable value in establishing the record of a great revolution in scientific thought.

In other fields of science, too, there has been an encouraging growth of historical perspective, manifested in the organization of historical sections of scientific societies and in the holding of conferences designed to bring together scientists and historians of science. In the spring of 1962 the anthropologists, long notorious for lack of interest in the history of their own discipline, held a conference on the history of anthropology in New York, where they exchanged ideas and information with historians in an effort to lay the groundwork for studies of the historical development of anthropology. In the summer of 1963 a group of linguists interested in the history of linguistics assembled at Burg Wartenstein in Austria, inviting an historian of science and an anthropologist to join in their deliberations. Thomas Kuhn's *The Structure of Scientific Revolutions* served as a springboard for the discussion. A year later the microbiologists held a similar conference in Cleveland. In September, 1967, a group of geologists and historians interested in the history of geology convened at Rye Beach, New Hampshire, to discuss papers on the history of that science. This was followed in June, 1968, by a conference of biologists and historians and philosophers of biology.

From the foregoing narrative it should be plain that the growing interest among linguists in the history of their own field of study is part of a movement toward historical orientation in the sciences generally. The question at hand, therefore, is whether and to what extent linguists interested in the history of linguistics can benefit by association and exchange with professional historians of science. What can the linguist-historian-of-linguistics learn from historians of science?

The answer to this question will vary considerably depending upon the particular group of historians of science to whom it is addressed. One school of thought, represented in part by disciples of Otto Neugebauer, insists that the history of science, especially the history of exact science, has a long record of brilliant achievement antedating the establishment of this field of research as an academic discipline. They point to the writings of such men as Montucla, Delambre, Todhunter, Dreyer, Heiberg, Zeuthen, Kugler, Heath, Schiaparelli, and Nallino, arguing that these writings represent a solider kind of scholarship than the bio-bibliographical works of George Sarton, whose messianic preaching of the history of science as the harbinger of a new humanism that would bridge the gap between the sciences and the humanities did so much to arouse interest in the history of science in the United States. Adherents of this school are unsympathetic to demands for general synthesis and for the integration of the history of science with intellectual, social, economic, technological, and political history. As one of them writes: "... because of the limitation of our subject and because of its very nature, we can in the history of science, and particularly in the history of the exact sciences, achieve a level of understanding and control far beyond what ... a political historian in his right mind may dream of: in doing so we can supply the more general historian with good hard bricks with which he may ... strengthen his edifice." The advice of this school of historians of science to linguists interested in the history of linguistics would, presumably, be to emulate the example of such past scientist-historians as Dreyer and Heath rather than that of George Sarton or Henry Guerlac or Thomas Kuhn—in other words, to get busy making "good hard bricks" without worrying what professional historians of science may think of their activity.

A second school of historians of science, probably the dominant school in the Western world at the present time, look to Alexandre Koyré as their master. They are not unaware of the contributions of nineteenth-century scientist-historians to the history of science, but they find them lacking in proper historical perspective. The objective of these older historians of science, Thomas Kuhn (1968: 76-77) writes, was "to clarify and deepen an understanding of *contemporary* scientific methods or concepts by displaying their evolution rather than to understand the science of the past in its own terms." As for Neugebauer, Kuhn lumps him with Joseph Needham and Lynn Thorndike as scholars "whose indispensable contribution has been to establish and make accessible texts and traditions previously known only through myth," i.e., purveyors of bricks for the edifice of the history of science but not students of the internal evolution of scientific thought, which constitutes the core of the history of science for the Koyre school. George Sarton, says Kuhn, made an heroic effort to view the development of positive knowledge as a unified whole, but further study showed "that the sciences are not, in fact, all of a piece and that even the superhuman erudition required for general history of science could scarcely tailor their joint evolution to a coherent narrative." "Today," Kuhn adds, "as historians increasingly turn back to the detailed investigation of individual branches of science, they study fields which actually existed in the periods that concern them, and they do so with an awareness of the state of other sciences at the time." By immersing themselves in the intellectual world of the scientists of the past and by paying attention to their errors as well as to their insights these historians of science seek to exhibit the conceptual development of particular sciences and groups of sciences as an intellectual activity possessing its own internal dynamic and increasingly insulated from the common affairs of mankind by the growing complexity and sophistication of its theoretical structure. Understood in this way, the history of science has close connections with the history of philosophy, especially the history of the philosophy of science. Presumably it could also have fruitful intercourse with the history of linguistics at the level where the philosophy of language intersects with the philosophy of science and concepts of scientific method. One recalls, for example, the eighteenth-century idea of science as *une langue bien faite.* What counsel, then, might the linguist-historian-of-linguistics expect to receive from the Koyré school of historians of science? One suspects that the chief injunction would be to avoid carrying the linguistic concepts and controversies of the present day back into the past and to endeavor instead to understand the past in its own terms. It must be confessed, however, that this advice is easier to preach than to practice and that not all professional historians of science are above reproach in this regard.

A third group of historians of science, extremely vocal though not forming a school with an acknowledged master, condemn what they consider to be the unduly narrow and technical conception of the history of science which they find exhibited in Sarton's work and in that of both the Neugebauer and the Koyré schools. These critics assert that science is but one strand in the web of culture, influencing and influenced by such other strands as technology, economic life, educational practice, religion, politics, and government. The history of science should, therefore, display the institutional development of science, its national and regional peculiarities, its growing impact on human life and thought, its embodiment in particular individuals, societies, and elites, as well as the ways in which the evolution of scientific thought is shaped by economic, social, and cultural change. "The only object of study in the history of science is *Homo sapiens,*" writes A. Hunter Dupree, "and it is *Homo sapiens* in a social context that is the sole object of the historian's study of science. Hence all history of science . . . is social history. The scientists study the things; the historians study the scientist (1966: 869)." L. Pearce Williams insists that the historian of science must know the language of science but agrees with Dupree in lamenting the tendency toward creating separate departments of the history of science cut off from history departments, and the corresponding trend toward focusing on the technical aspects of the history of science. Williams would probably discourage linguists from studying the history of linguistics without acquiring a solid training in history first. Others of this school would not go so far as that, but would insist that the history of linguistics, at least in its non-technical aspects, is fair game for the historian with little or no linguistic training.

My own feeling is that the history of science is a vast and complex field that must be studied from many different points of view by scholars with widely different backgrounds and training. No sane person would deny that the technical development of the sciences is important or that technical training is prerequisite for successful study of these aspects. On the other hand, historians have long insisted that the past must be understood as much as possible in its own terms, and I think that scientists interested in the history of their own discipline are becoming increasingly aware of the dangers inherent in ignoring this maxim. The question to what extent the evolution of scientific thought is shaped by factors external to science itself— technological, social, religious, philosophical, and the like—is not a question to be answered for all sciences and all times by dogmatic pronouncements but rather one to be studied empirically with reference to particular developments in particular sciences, with all parties free to present evidence favoring their view of the matter. In any case, it will be hard to justify restricting the history of science to the study of the evolution of scientific theory and technique. Those who find these aspects of science of primary interest will have plenty to keep them busy. Meanwhile there will be others bent on studying science in its general social and cultural context. Finally, there will always be scholars concerned to integrate the findings of all these kinds of history of science into the general history of mankind.

All of these approaches have their place, and all should prove of interest and value in the study of the history of linguistics. Indeed, many of them are exemplified in the papers presented at this Newberry Library conference and in the earlier conference on the history of linguistics at Burg Wartenstein. These papers exhibit the history of linguistics as a going concern cultivated both by linguists whose primary interest lies elsewhere and by those who have made the history of linguistics their main area of research. As this field of study grows, it is natural and inevitable that the linguists who cultivate it will establish closer working relationships with professional historians of science, not for rigid prescriptions as to how the history of a science should be studied but rather for the stimulus that comes from the exchange of information, ideas, and points of view. Fortunately, there is a large and growing literature of the history of science (much of it in paperback) available to the linguist who seeks to acquaint himself with the field, and a growing disposition on the part of historians of science to expand the horizons of their discipline to include the social sciences and scholarly disciplines generally. The increasing number of papers on the history of the social sciences at the annual meetings of the History of Science Society is evidence of this trend. Nor should anyone suppose that the linguists will be the only ones to benefit from their contacts with historians of science. The benefit will be mutual, as would quickly be seen if a joint conference were held on some such topic as "Language Theory and Science in the Seventeenth and Eighteenth Centuries." The history of linguistics can and does flourish without the aid of professional historians of science, but there is much to be gained for all concerned by bringing this field of study within the broader purview of the history of science and learning.

II

Thus far I have been speaking in very general terms. In order to give a more specific idea of how the history of linguistics appears to a historian of science (one whose primary research interest is the history of evolutionary biology) I draw on my commentary on papers read at the Burg Wartenstein conference (Greene 1964).[2]

Let me begin by noting the presupposition that linguistics is a science. This assumption is a relatively recent one in the history of linguistics. At what period, I should like to know, did students of language, or a substantial part of them, begin to think of themselves as scientists or proto-scientists? May it not be that the relative slowness with which linguistic studies assumed a scientific aspect was due in large part to the humanistic image linguists had of themselves and their work? One's image of himself helps to determine his behavior, and it may be that the development of general theory, conscious methodology, and high level generalization in linguistics was retarded by the humanistic model of thought that prevailed in these studies until fairly recent times. Indeed, there seem to be strong survivals of that humanistic image in twentieth-century linguistics. At the same time, however, there is a strong tendency in our universities to divorce the study of literature from the study of linguistics, and this may have the effect of driving linguists further and further toward a scientific image of themselves.

Turning now to the historical development of the study of language, let me first observe that the periodization of this development seems to correspond rather closely to the periodization of the history of science in general: antiquity, the Middle Ages, the Renaissance, the "eighteenth century" extending from about 1660 to 1790, the "nineteenth century" extending to about 1880, and finally a revolutionary period passing over into the twentieth century. The main difference seems to be that, whereas physics and natural history achieved a stable conceptual framework in the seventeenth century, linguistics did not come to a focus on historically oriented comparative philology until the early nineteenth century. In this respect, however, it was not much behind geology, paleontology, embryology, and physical anthropology, all of which begin to find themselves in the early nineteenth century.

The development of the systematic study of language in classical antiquity presents an interesting analogy to the evolution of scientific anatomy in the same period. In both cases there was a general philosophical interest, formulated in different ways by different philosophical schools, and a practical interest, centering in the one case on the practice of the literary art and in the other on the practice of medicine. The study of anatomy was confined largely to the human body, except insofar as taboos on human dissection forced Galen and others to use other materials. The result was Galen's systematic description of human anatomy. In like manner, the study of language was confined to Greek and Latin and produced a systematic description of the sentence, "a descriptive taxonomy of language," as Robins (1964) has put it. There seems, however, to have been no attempt at a broader delineation of the field of linguistic studies comparable to Aristotle's delineation of the field of natural history in his biological writings. Language was too close to man, too much a part of his own culture, to be held at arm's length and circumscribed as a general field of study so early in the course of human development.

Diderichsen has described classical grammar as normative, static, and descriptive (see his chapter this volume). As in natural history, description went naturally with the static and normative approach to the subject matter. If language does not change, or changes only for the worse, there is little basis for a dynamic approach to the study of language. Yet there was some awareness that languages do change and hence a need for some model of linguistic change. The model adopted seems to have been that of decline from original perfection, degeneration from "the original accordance between words, concepts, and things", analogous to a very similar model that prevailed in natural history for many centuries.

In the Middle Ages, the study of language received an impetus analogous to that in other sciences from the establishment of universities and the translation of the works of Aristotle and other classical writers into Latin from Greek and Arabic texts. Yet, curiously enough, the Arabs seem to have contributed nothing to the study of language comparable to the additions and improvements they made in mathematics, astronomy, physics, medicine, and natural history. The culture-bound characteristic of language seems to have prevented Arabic scholars from taking an interest in the grammatical treatises of antiquity. It would be interesting to know, however, to what extent the Middle Eastern world had an indigenous linguistic science and whether any inkling of this science, if one existed, reached the Latin scholars in the West. It seems unlikely that the feverish activity of translation from Greek into Arabic into Latin was unaccompanied by any reflection on comparative grammar and philology in either East or West. But, so far as the record of the Symposium and Conference shows, the only new linguistic development of the Middle Ages was the rise of speculative grammar, designed to explain the rules of grammar with reference to Aristotelian categories of thought.

From the papers dealing with developments in the sixteenth and seventeenth centuries it seems clear that there was a genesis of comparative philology comparable to the genesis of comparative anatomy in the biological sciences in the same period. Linguistic study had hitherto concerned itself only with Greek and Latin, but the expansion of Europe and of the world of learning created an interest in comparison for its own sake. Anatomy, too, became comparative, but comparative anatomy remained purely descriptive whereas linguistic comparisons were definitely linked to the problem of origins and genealogical relationship. In this respect, linguistics was more like physical anthropology, with its strong interest in the origin of human races, than like zoology or botany, which were dominated by taxonomy. A main source of interest in comparative philology was the hope and expectation of proving something about the origins and connections of human races. National pride was another incentive; various scholars sought to show the antiquity and primacy of their own languages. And, as Metcalf has shown (see his chapter, this volume), comparative analysis drew not only on linguistic evidence but also on historical data taken from the Bible and profane history, just as it did in anthropology. The monogenist-polygenist controversy agitated both linguistics and physical anthropology, but apparently mono-genism was not a prerequisite for theological orthodoxy in linguistics as it tended to be in anthropology.

Under these circumstances linguists made important advances in comparative technique. Moreover, since linguistic comparison was oriented toward proof of affinity, there was necessarily some attention to the processes of change by which languages had diverged from common origins, as in the theory of *permutatio litterarum.* But, as Metcalf has indicated, the concept of change was not yet uniformitarian; the larger structures of language were not yet viewed as a necessary outcome of everyday processes of linguistic change. Finally, there seems to have been little effort to systematize the study of language, to define the relations of comparative grammar, etymology, phonetics, and the philosophy of language, or even to lay down rules for historical and comparative linguistics. Natural history achieved systematic form in the work of John Ray and Joseph Pitton de Tournefort, but the study of language defied systematization, possibly because it could not in its very nature be brought to a focus on descriptive taxonomy, except insofar as this had already been achieved in classical grammar.

In the absence of a successful effort to create a conceptual framework for linguistic research in the sixteenth and seventeenth centuries, the developments of that period are seen as extending without interruption into the eighteenth century, forming with it a long "pre-paradigm" period marked by: (a) accumulation of factual information, (b) improvement of comparative and descriptive technique, (c) high speculative interest in the nature, origin, and development of language, and (d) lack of paradigmatic achievements on the level of theory-combined-with-practice. By contrast to zoology and botany, both of which found a lawgiver in Linnaeus, the study of language seemed chaotic and disorganized, but there were other sciences in a similar condition. Physical anthropology was not as far advanced as linguistics by 1800. Comparative anatomy was not formalized until the time of Cuvier. Geology only began to find itself in the work of Werner and Hutton. Chemistry had a kind of paradigm (the phlogiston theory), but not a very powerful one. Meanwhile, linguistic studies were moving toward a decisive juncture.

Diderichsen has viewed the eighteenth century as a period of fusing established paradigms to form the model of linguistic study set forth by Turgot in the *Encyclopédie* and later applied with great success by Rasmus Rask in launching comparative philology on its brilliant nineteenth-century career. Gulya, on the other hand, has regarded the eighteenth century as one of preparatory development in which both the materials (vocabularies, etymological dictionaries, etc.) and the general methods and problems essential for a revolution in linguistics were brought together (see his chapter, this volume). He looks to Sajnovics and Gyarmathi for the paradigmatic achievements of the century rather than to Turgot or Adelung. Diderichsen has emphasized the gradual formation of a concept of comparative grammar, Gulya the accumulation of new information. Both have recognized methodological gains and particular achievements in techniques of comparison. On the whole, these two interpretations seem complementary rather than conflicting. Verburg has stressed the revolt against "mathematical rationality," which took two forms: (1) the probabilistic and analogical approach of Condillac and Beauzée, and (2) the "energetic" approach of Harris in England, Rousseau in France, and Herder in Germany (see his chapter, this volume). What is needed apparently, is detailed historical study of each of these developments (*grammaire raisonnée*, word-collecting, theories of the origin and development of language, etymology, comparative technique, philosophy of language) and of their interrelations. Was there a definite evolution of thought within the school of *grammaire raisonnée*? If so, what were its main stages? How did the essentially static point of view of the Port Royal school take on a dynamic aspect by association with the growing interest in the origin and development of language? What were the relationships between the word-collectors, the theorists of linguistic origins, the etymologists, and the practitioners of systematic comparison?

The relationships between linguistics and natural history in the eighteenth century also need further study. The influence of Linnaeus on linguists has been mentioned by several scholars, but the exact nature of his influence has not been made clear. On the whole, it seems that the taxonomic model of natural history was of very limited usefulness in linguistics. The number of languages, unlike the number of plant and animal species, was not so great as to make systematic description and classification of languages an absolute practical necessity. Languages were not objects of popular curiosity in the same way that plants and animals were, nor did they rank among the works of God whose structure and arrangement it was man's duty to study. Finally, and most important, the aspect of change and development was much more prominent in linguistic phenomena than in natural history. The idea of descent from common origins, which prevailed in natural history only after a long, hard intellectual struggle, was a natural starting point in the study of language, as it was in physical anthropology. It is significant in this connection that physical anthropology was more concerned with theories of the causes of variation than with classification, although relatively little progress was made in comprehending the processes of race formation before the advent of modern genetics.

The most fruitful interaction between natural history and linguistic studies in the eighteenth century took place in connection with theories of social evolution. About the middle of the century the idea began to take hold that human history, far from being a decline from a paradisaical state or golden age, was instead a slow progress from brutish beginnings. This idea sprang partly from the growing sense of improvement in science, technology, government, and society, but it also owed much to the development of comparative anatomy and the swelling literature concerning savage peoples, man-like apes, wild boys, and the like. Both Rousseau and Lord Monboddo were familiar with this literature and cited it in their speculations on human development. Both represented the first men as bereft of speech and language, the origins of which they found in man's intellectual capacity. It was this capacity that set man apart from other animals and destined him to evolve further and further away from his original nature while the animal species remained what they had always been. Similar ideas are to be found in Turgot's writings, especially in his lectures on human history at the Sorbonne. Thus, it seems that the idea of continual development, of a necessary evolution eventuating in genuine novelty, first took hold in humanistic studies dealing with phenomena such as language, where the aspect of mutability is more pronounced than in the realm of nature. It should be noted, however, that the same decade 1750-1760 that produced the anthropological speculations of Turgot and Rousseau also produced the speculations of Maupertuis, Buffon, and Kant concerning the history of nature.

We come now to the events of the very late eighteenth century and the early nineteenth century which all linguists seem to recognize as revolutionary, formative, and "paradigmatic" in the sense defined by Thomas Kuhn in his book *The Structure of Scientific Revolutions* (1962). This period was a revolutionary one in nearly all fields of science, and in politics and culture as well. In astronomy it produced the nebular hypotheses of Laplace and Herschel and the beginnings of systematic sidereal astronomy, in optics the revival of the wave theory of light, in electricity the discovery and study of current electricity, in the earth sciences the founding of paleontology and stratigraphic geology, in anthropology the rise of craniology, in chemistry the work of Lavoisier and Dalton, in botany of Jussieu and Candolle, in zoology of Lamarck and Cuvier, to say nothing of the American and French revolutions, the Industrial Revolution, and the Romantic revolt. Undoubtedly there was something in the social, intellectual, and spiritual condition of the time that fostered, even demanded, new ways of thinking. It would have been extraordinary if linguistic studies had remained unaffected.

In Kuhn's terms, the linguistic developments of this period can best be described as a transition from a pre-paradigm stage to a paradigmatic stage marked by the emergence of historically oriented comparative philology as the focus, one might almost say the sum and substance, of linguistic study. Diderichsen has argued that the essence of the comparative and historical method had been set forth in Turgot's article in the *Encyclopédie* a half century earlier, but since Turgot did not demonstrate the power of the method in actual research, he cannot be said to have founded the new discipline. Sir William Jones went much further than Turgot in the application of comparative techniques, but he, too, was a relatively isolated figure. Even Rasmus Rask's work might have proved less decisive than it was if it had not taken root in Germany, where the development of the German universities provided an ideal intellectual and institutional environment for scholarly research and where Wilhelm von Humboldt made it his business as Minister of Education to see that chairs of comparative philology were established in the Prussian universities and staffed with able linguists. Thus we find, not a single paradigmatic figure establishing a new field of science by the force of his insight and character, but rather the convergence of many lines of research and speculation in the work of several individuals, focusing on the well-defined and culturally important problem of the relationships of the European languages, and supported by a favorable intellectual and institutional context. The situation was analogous in some respects to that which attended the emergence of systematic natural history in the late seventeenth-century, but there was nothing in the latter development corresponding to the dramatic impact of the newly-discovered Sanskrit grammar of Pāṇini on the tradition of comparative philology at the very moment of its consolidation.

To a considerable extent the development of comparative philology in the mid-nineteenth century conforms to the pattern of research within a paradigm delineated by Kuhn. This period witnessed the discovery of a method of reconstructing the proto-language from which known languages have developed, the successful search for ways of explaining the apparent exceptions to sound laws, and the like. But just as there was a counter-paradigm associated with the name of Buffon in eighteenth-century natural history, so there was a counter-paradigm linked to the name of Wilhelm von Humboldt in nineteenth-century linguistics, a paradigm of typological linguistics stemming from certain ideas in the German philosophical tradition and reaching back beyond that to eighteenth-century conceptions of the genius of different languages. In general, however, German philosophy seems to have exerted less influence on linguistic studies than it did on the natural sciences. There seems to have been nothing in linguistics comparable to the natural scientists' infatuation with Natur-philosophie followed by a sharp reaction against it.

Here again the relationships between linguistics and the natural sciences are in need of closer investigation. In principle, comparative philology would seem to have been in a position to give a lead to biology by evolving models of change and genetic relationship that might have influenced biological speculation. According to Pedersen, however, linguists did not become preoccupied with processes of linguistic change until *after* the publication of Darwin's *Origin of Species.* Before that time linguists seem to have been satisfied with ideas of change analogous to those that prevailed in natural history ("linguistic decay," for example). Hoenigswald has indicated, however, that Schleicher worked out a theory of the survival of the fittest with respect to linguistic change before the publication of Darwin's *Origin of Species,* and Rulon Wells (1962) has described an interesting formal identity between certain nineteenth-century theories of phonetic change and the Darwinian theory of speciation by random variation and natural selection.

With respect to the situation in linguistics since about 1870, there seems to be general agreement that there have been revolutionary developments, though not of a kind that can be fitted into Kuhn's model of anomaly, crisis, and paradigm substitution. What has taken place is not a revolution within the framework of historically oriented comparative philology but rather a dramatic shift of interest and attention from diachronic to synchronic studies, similar to that which occurred in anthropology in the same period. The complaint of contemporary comparative philologists is not that their field has been revolutionized but rather that it has been abandoned or sadly neglected. The situation is much like that which prevailed in natural history in the mid-nineteenth century, when the traditional preoccupation with taxonomy was challenged by the development of a variety of new interests—embryology, paleontology, plant and animal physiology, and the like. These new developments had profound implications for taxonomy, but they did not constitute revolutions within the paradigm of taxonomic research. Men like Matthias Schleiden found taxonomy boring. Meanwhile Charles Darwin, seeking a solution to certain puzzles of geographic distribution of species he had encountered on the voyage of the *Beagle,* hit upon a theory that proved capable of unifying vast areas of biological research, taxonomic and otherwise. Twentieth-century linguistics would seem to be in its "pre-Darwinian" phase, burgeoning with new developments and exciting new ideas but lacking as yet a general hypothesis capable of unifying hitherto disconnected areas of research in the light of a profound theoretical insight. Efforts in this direction have not been lacking, however. Linguistics may yet have its Darwin.

NOTES

1. See Price (1967) and also the papers and comments by historians of science in several countries under the title "History of science as an academic discipline" in Crombie 1963: 757-794: Mays 1960; papers and comments on the teaching of the history of science by Dorothy Stimson, Henry Guerlac, et al., in Clagett 1959: 223-253; Butterfield 1959; Cohen 1955; and Sarton 1952.
2. The rest of the paper draws on the commentary that Professor Greene prepared at the Burg Wartenstein symposium (Greene 1964).

REFERENCES

Butterfield, Herbert. 1959. The history of science and the study of history. Harvard Library Bulletin 13: 329-347.
Clagett, Marshall (ed.). 1959. Critical problems in the history of science. Madison, University of Wisconsin Press.
Cohen, I. Bernard. 1955. Present status and needs of the history of science. Proceedings of the American Philosophical Society 99: 343-347.
Crombie, A. C. (ed.). 1963. Scientific change. Symposium on the history of science at the University of Oxford 9-15 July 1961. New York, Basic Books.
De Solla Price, Derek J. 1967. A guide to graduate study and research in the history of science and medicine. Isis 58: 385-395.
Dupree, A. Hunter. 1966. The history of American science—a field finds itself. American Historical Review 71: 863-874.
Greene, John C. 1964. Review of the symposium from the point of view of the history of science. Paper prepared during Burg Wartenstein symposium no. 25, "Revolution vs. continuity in the study of language", August 15-25, 1964. [The full paper was revised and distributed to participants by the Wenner-Gren Foundation for Anthropological Research shortly after the Symposium.]
Kuhn, Thomas S. 1962. The structure of scientific revolutions. (International Encyclopedia of Unified Science 2 [2]). Chicago, University of Chicago Press.
———. 1968. The history of science. International Encyclopedia of the Social Sciences 14: 74-83. New York, Macmillan and The Free Press.
Mays, W. 1960. History and philosophy of science in British Commonwealth universities. The British Journal for the Philosophy of Science 11: 192-211.
Robins, R. H. 1964. Some continuities and discontinuities in the history of linguistics. Paper prepared for Burg Wartenstein symposium no. 25,

"Revolution vs. continuity in the study of language", August 15-25, 1964.

Sarton, George. 1952. Horus: a guide to the history of science. Waltham, Massachusetts, Chronica Bontanica Co.

Wells, Rulon S. 1962. Phonemics in the nineteenth century, 1876-1900. Paper prepared for Conference on the History of Anthropology, April 13-14, 1962, Social Science Research Council. [The paper was made available to participants in the Burg Wartenstein symposium through the courtesy of Professor Wells.]

20. Notes on the Sociology of Knowledge and Linguistics

Kurt H. Wolff and Barrie Thorne

I

"Knowledge," in "sociology of knowledge," means something broader than, if not different from, the currently accepted connotation of the term. "Sociology of knowledge" is a translation of *"Wissenssoziologie"*; *"Wissen,"* however, is more comprehensive than "knowledge," which above all refers to scientific or positive knowledge, while the German word does not exclude other kinds; and *"Soziologie"* is not identical with "sociology" – its tradition, to put it briefly and cautiously, does not, at least, rule out "social philosophy." Efforts made in the name of the sociology of knowledge have in fact been less concerned with scientific knowledge than with ideologies, world views, conceptions, concepts, and categories of thought, and have been carried on less in an exclusively sociological perspective than in one grounded also in philosophy of history, epistemology, or philosophical anthropology. (The reader who wants an introduction to the sociology of knowledge should consult Mannheim 1931; Merton 1945; and for the United States only, Wolff 1967.) The sociology of knowledge thus is most comprehensively and systematically understood as the sociology of culture in its cognitive aspects—hence it includes both language and linguistics.

It follows that statements by the sociologist of knowledge—and also by the linguist—concerning the relations between linguistics and the sociology of knowledge are legitimate topics of analysis for the latter – and could also be such for the former. But we know of no treatment of either kind. If there indeed is none, this is a further topic for the sociologist of knowledge, though not for the linguist, because he, in contrast to the former, needs words to practice his craft on, while the sociologist of knowledge may also examine cases where words that on some identifiable ground could be expected, nevertheless have not been forthcoming. In other words, if there has been neither a sociological analysis of, for instance, the history of linguistics nor of the language of sociology, including the sociology of knowledge itself; that is, if the two disciplines are unacquainted with one another, even though their respective subject matters emerge as intimately related in the perspectives of each, if only each focuses on the other's subject matter, then we recognize that the task of seeking answers to the question why this should be so is a task for the sociology of knowledge.

Two promising avenues might be suggested. One is to analyze the references to language in writings by sociologists of knowledge, such as occur — to limit ourselves to American contributions — in Hinshaw (1943) (under the influence of Morris 1938), Wolff (1943), Mills (1939) (under the influence of Mead 1934, an influence which is generally widespread in the sociology of knowledge in the United States, cf., e.g., Child 1938, 1941, 1946; Berger and Luckmann 1966; or, in regard to a sociology of communication, in DeGré 1943, esp. p.86; Merton 1957, Part III; and Wolff 1959). The other is to investigate the institutional setting in which linguists and sociologists of knowledge work, beginning, perhaps, with the situation in joint sociology-anthropology departments (cf. Bennett and Wolff 1955, esp. pp.340-346).

More particularly, the sociology of knowledge can provide a framework for studying linguistics as a discipline that has, after all, been pursued within a variety of historical, social, and cultural contexts:

1. *Sociological Analysis of Orientations and Developments in the History of Linguistics.* The sociological analysis of the division between philology and anthropological linguistics, for example, can be analyzed in terms of the social, cultural, and institutional settings in which each field has developed and in terms of social characteristics of workers in each tradition. This can be carried beyond Malkiel's (1964) discussion of Romance linguistics and its mention of the impact of particular national cultures in fostering diverse lines of inquiry, with a resulting influence on "nomenclature, tone of phrasing, and slant of analysis" (p.681), as in the case of the influence of Central European scholarship during the critical growing years of Romance linguistics.

Reference to the social basis of ideas might also illuminate the history of the evolutionary approach to language within American anthropology. Hymes (1961) traces the origins of the modern linguistic themes of "equality, diversity, relativity" and the demise of an earlier evolutionary approach to language. This shift of emphasis might be related to the changing social and political structure in which the study of language was pursued, more particularly to the growth of a liberal and social-democratic outlook, which in turn can be traced to changes in society. Hymes suggests such a connection by pointing to the way Boas and his followers associated evolutionary modes of analysis with "the ethnocentric, the prejudiced, and implicitly, apologists for exploitation and oppression of non-Western peoples" (1966: 5), and by noting how Boas and others marshaled the equality-diversity-relativity theme in fighting Nazi racism (p.l). Other linguists have expressed quite different social and political perspectives in their work; thus, the discipline of linguistics began in Western culture with the study of the "form of language put forward as the norm of an elite justifying ideologically a political rule" (Hymes 1970: 339). These brief examples are merely suggestive of ways in which the changing social, cultural, and political context of linguistic studies has influenced the development of the discipline.

2. *Social Origins, Roles, and Other Characteristics of Individual Linguists*. The position of an individual in the social or class structure and his social and political interests have a bearing on his professional work. Turning again to the Boasian tradition of American linguistics, Hymes (1966: 5) notes the Germanic training and German Social-Democratic political outlook shared by Boas, Lowie, Radin, and Sapir. The social and political orientation of these leading figures is likely to be reflected in their general approach to linguistics. The sociological study of individual thinkers should include attention both to social origins and to the relation between the linguist's professional position and his other political and social roles. To illustrate the last point with reference to his professional role alone, one might investigate his world view as it can be inferred from his writing and compare this with views he expresses as elicited by other investigative techniques, for example, interview or questionnaire. One might also compare his professional role, as ascertained in this or in other ways, with other roles; one might go on to compare these findings with findings concerning roles of other professionals.

One might also try to locate linguists, and different types of linguists, according to Znaniecki's (1940) typology of "men of knowledge" and their respective "social circles." This typology includes: (1) those concerned with communicating "instrumental truths" or practical knowledge leading to manipulation and control of the external environment, such as magicians or technologists; (2) "ideologists" or apologists for a sect, class, occupation, or party; revolutionary spokesmen and party theorizers; (3) schoolmen or deductive theoreticians, concerned with the construction, development, systematization, and dissemination of theoretic truths; and (4) "explorers" or discoverers of new factual materials and the inductive organization of these empirical data. Use of Znaniecki's mode of analysis might provide better understanding of the position and functions of individual linguists and types of them within the social organization of the discipline.

3. *History of Linguistics in Relation to Linguistics*. A sociologically oriented history of linguistics is bound to differ from "textbook" versions, which are addressed to an "articulated body of problems, data and theory, and most often to the particular set of paradigms to which the scientific

community is committed at the time they are written" (Kuhn 1962: 135). A sociologically oriented history would attempt to understand linguistic ideas, whether accepted among modern linguists or not, in reference to the time and place in which they developed.

It is perhaps possible to range the various disciplines along a continuum from minimum to maximum relevance of the history of a discipline to its current state. It seems plausible to suggest, for example, that the history of physics is far less important for physics than is the history of literary criticism for literary criticism. What is the significance of its history to linguistics today? Perhaps it is more important than that of sociology to sociology, especially in its positivistic version, but less important than that of the history of art to the history of art. Another way of raising the question is to inquire into the social conditions of the chances of acquiring historically more relative and historically less relative knowledge bearing on different areas of intellectual endeavor. An answer to this question would allow more precise statements concerning the historicity, as against the systematicity, of various intellectual efforts, in this case linguistics.

If such suggestions were acted upon in concerted research efforts, both the sociology of knowledge and linguistics would change considerably and, we believe, gain in interest and relevance — and the former probably more than the latter.

II

Some problems germane to the foregoing considerations came up in discussions at this Conference. The first, suggested by Robins' and Malkiel's papers, concerns an approach focusing on theory as compared to one that is directed toward gathering data. The problem was discussed in historical perspective (notably by Greene) with reference to periods in which one or the other focus was in the forefront of linguistic endeavor. What should be emphasized, however, is that all ordinary thinking, not only scientific thinking, let alone thinking about linguistic problems, is characterized by both foci, which may alternate or concur. Not only can we not gather data without their being grounded in theory, whether we are aware of it or not, when we address ourselves to problems of linguistics — as was said in the discussions; but we cannot do so either in everyday life, if only because perception itself is also interpretive. What is of specific relevance to the historian of linguistics, however, is the systematic examination of a given work in linguistics or a given body of work (of an individual linguist, for instance) in respect to the distribution in it of foci on respectively theory and data-gathering. It may also be of use to the historian of linguistics that he try to explicate the theory on the basis of which he can justify the selection — both emphases and omissions — of the history of linguistics he is composing.

To analyze linguistic materials is to contribute to their intrinsic interpretation. Putting it loosely and glossing over serious epistemological questions, "intrinsic interpretation" refers to an interpretation which makes use of the interpretandum only, that is, which does not go outside of it in an effort to throw light on questions the interpretandum raises. In the course of the discussion, a number of such outside sources were mentioned, notably the biography and personality of the author of a given text or body of texts (cf. Hoenigswald on Schleicher, or Percival on Rask). Another source outside the published text came up when reference was made to unpublished materials written prior to and in preparation of the publication. It is clear that we would be in a better position to assess a text if we could inspect preparatory material, but it is probably as uncharacteristic of linguistics as one of us once found it to be of cultural anthropology to make such material publicly available (Wolff 1952); still, in many cases, this would serve to correct our interpretation of the text itself.

Among the extrinsic interpretations, there is the sociological interpretation (Mannheim 1926), that is, one which resorts, not primarily to the biography or personality of the author, but to his social situation, to the society and historical period in which he lived. Hoenigswald touches on such an interpretation when he refers developments in nineteenth-century linguistics to such factors as the function of the Napoleonic system in providing a center in Paris, where continental scholars learned oriental languages, and to the temporary decline of the English universities. However, in our perusal of the literature for preparing these notes, we have found relatively little attention given to attempts at sociological interpretation; yet we maintain that such a focus would benefit historical studies of linguistics.

How might one go about making a sociological analysis of this Newberry Library Conference itself? The first clue that may come to mind is to recognize that the participants have spoken and acted within a highly specific "world," precisely that of historians of linguistics, or within a number of "worlds," perhaps those of general linguistics, philology, history, cultural anthropology — possibly more. "World" is used here as Alfred Schutz did (see esp. Schutz 1945), in an application of basic thoughts of Husserl to the analysis of social life and the social sciences. One of the tasks which Schutz did not undertake and which is likely not to have been undertaken by anybody yet is the analysis of any one of the worlds just mentioned in its characteristic, that is, irreducible, nature, and thus its distinction from the world — or again perhaps worlds — of the sociologist. Only on such analysis and distinction would it seem possible to undertake the task of translating each of these worlds into any of the others, or to analyze the way in which different worlds may relate to each other (cf. Austerlitz's comments [in a memorandum distributed to participants] on how Friedrich Schlegel, the linguist, drew on the model of the natural sciences in elaborating his typological view of language). The description of a "world" is identical with its intrinsic interpretation, as this term has been referred to before; the only difference is that in the previous examples the interpretandum was a text or opus, whereas now it is the outlook of a particular profession, a typical approach, or way of being.

The world of the linguist, as that of other scholars, may well be changing in view of the critical situation in which our society finds itself. This situation, one of radical change, raises the issue of whether the goal of scholarly pursuit which has for quite some time been taken for granted, does not stand in need of being questioned. "Questioned" is to be taken literally: it means that we can neither continue unquestionably to take it for granted nor, equally without questioning, perhaps in an onslaught of panic, abandon it in favor of something else. Several answers have in fact been given — by Herbert Marcuse, Howard Zinn, and other scholars, and, among linguists, by Noam Chomsky and Dell Hymes, all of whom have tried more or less to combine scholarly pursuits with political activities. But do their answers have a theoretical foundation, such as is implied by the need for redefining the scholar's "world?"

The view of the "world" of linguistics as embodying a typical outlook or approach suggests a further point that has come up but could stand explication. Bursill-Hall (see his chapter, this volume) has called attention to the difference between medieval grammarians, who typically were also competent philosophers and logicians, and contemporary grammarians, who typically are not. It might be useful to construct types ("ideal types") of activities and competences that according to individuals or according to historical periods are connected or not connected. The concept of ideal type was developed above all by Max Weber (esp. 1904, 1911, 1911-13), but is well known from a considerable number of dichotomous types of societies constructed above all by cultural anthropologists — to name only one: Robert Redfield's folk-urban continuum. The purpose of the construction of such types is to increase the precision with which existing phenomena can be described in terms of the distance or nearness to the type constructed. It might be useful to construct such types in respect to approaches to the study of linguistics or in respect to linguists or periods of linguistic study, and the like; two of the components which might go into their construction would possibly be the previously mentioned emphasis on theorizing vs. data-gathering; or the evolutionary approach vs. a more synchronic emphasis on equality, diversity, and relativity (Hymes 1961); or the underplaying of race in non-linguistic correlates (in part for ideological reasons) vs. a view of language as racially determined. This, of course, is only illustrative.

A type such as data-gathering might fall under the more comprehensive rubric of methodological types. In the discussion on theory and data-gathering, Staal (see his chapter, this volume) added a third aspect of linguistic work, methodology — attention to how a linguist goes about theorizing or data-gathering. One might suggest a distinction between "method," in the sense of technique or instrumentality, and "methodology," under which both theorizing and data-gathering implementations would be subsumed.

REFERENCES

Bennett, John W., and Wolff, Kurt H. 1955. Toward communication between sociology and anthropology. In Thomas, William L., Jr. (ed.), Yearbook of anthropology 1955. New York, Wenner-Gren Foundation, 1955, pp. 329-351. Reprinted in Thomas, William L., Jr. (ed.), Current anthropology: a supplement to anthropology today, pp.329-351. Chicago, University of Chicago Press, 1956.

Berger, Peter L., and Luckmann, Thomas. 1966. The social construction of reality: a treatise in the sociology of knowledge. Garden City, N.Y., Doubleday, 1966. Pp.ix, 203

Child, Arthur. 1938. The problems of the sociology of knowledge: a critical and philosophical study. Berkeley, University of California (unpubl. Ph.D. diss.), 1938. Pp.v, 324.

_____. 1941. The theoretical possibility of the sociology of knowledge. Ethics 51: 392-418.

_____. 1946. On the theory of the categories. Philosophy and Phenomenological Research 7: 316-335.

Degré, Gerard. 1943. Society and ideology: an inquiry into the sociology of knowledge. New York, Columbia University Bookstore. Pp.iv, 114.

Hinshaw, Virgil G., Jr. 1943. The epistemological relevance of Mannheim's sociology of knowledge. Journal of Philosophy 40: 57-72.

Hymes, Dell. 1961. Functions of speech: an evolutionary approach. In Gruber, Fred C. (ed.), Anthropology and education, pp. 55-83. Philadelphia, University of Pennsylvania Press. [Bobbs-Merrill Reprint A-124.]

_____. (ed.) 1964. Language in culture and society. New York, Harper and Row. Pp.xxxvi, 764.

_____. 1966. Sociolinguistic determination of knowledge: notes on the history of its treatment in American anthropology. Sixth World Congress of Sociology, Evian. P.10 (mineo.).

_____. 1970. Linguistic aspects of comparative political research. In Holt, Robert T., and John E. Turner (eds.), The methodology of comparative research, pp.295-342. New York, The Free Press.

Kuhn, Thomas S. 1962. The structure of scientific revolutions. International Encyclopedia of Unified Science, Vol. 2, No. 2. Chicago, University of Chicago Press. Pp.xv, 172.

Malkiel, Yakov. 1964. Distinctive traits of romance linguistics. In Hymes 1964: 671-688.

Mannheim, Karl. 1926. The ideological and the sociological interpretation of intellectual phenomena. Wolff, Kurt H. (tr.). In Mannheim 1971: 116-131.

———. 1931. The sociology of knowledge. In Mannheim 1936: 237-280.

———. 1936. Ideology and utopia: an introduction to the sociology of knowledge (original publication in German in 1929). Tr. Wirth, Louis, and Edward Shils. New York, Harcourt, Brace. Pp.xxxi, 318. Reprinted Harvest Books, n.d., pp.xxx, 354.

———. 1971. From Karl Mannheim. Wolff, Kurt H. (ed. and intr.). New York, Oxford University Press. Pp.cxl, 393.

Mead, George Herbert. 1934. Mind, self and society from the standpoint of a social behaviorist. Morris, Charles W. (ed. and intr.). Chicago, University of Chicago Press. Pp.xxxviii, 401.

Merton, Robert K. 1945. Sociology of knowledge. In Gurvitch, Georges, and Wilbert E. Moore (eds.) Twentieth century sociology, pp.366-405. New York, Philosophical Library. Repr. in Merton 1949: 217-245, 386-391; in Merton 1957: 456-488.

———. 1949. Social theory and social structure. Glencoe, Ill., Free Press. Pp.423.

———. 1957. Social theory and social structure. Rev. and enl. ed. Glencoe, Ill., Free Press. Pp.xviii, 645.

Mills, C. Wright. 1939. Language, logic and culture. American Sociological Review 4: 670-680. Repr. in Mills 1963: 423-438.

———. 1963. Power, politics and people: the collected essays of C. Wright Mills. Horowitz, Irving Louis (ed.). New York, Oxford University Press. Pp.657.

Morris, Charles W. 1938. Foundations of the theory of signs. International Encyclopedia of Unified Science, Vol. I, No. 2. Chicago, University of Chicago Press. Pp.viii, 59.

Schutz, Alfred. 1945. On multiple realities. In Schutz 1962: 207-259.

———. 1962. Collected papers. I. The problem of social reality. Natanson, Maurice (ed. and intr.). The Hague, Nijhoff. Pp.xlvii, 361.

Weber, Max. 1904. Die Objektivität sozialwissenschaftlicher und sozialpolitischer Erkenntnis. In Weber, Gesammelte Aufsätze zur Wissenschaftslehre, pp.146-214. Tübingen, Mohr. Tr. as "Objectivity" in social science and social polity, in Weber, Max, On the methodology of the social sciences, pp.49-112. Shils, Edward, and Henry A. Finch (tr. and ed.). Glencoe, Ill., Free Press, 1949.

———. 1911. Debatte of Kantorowicz, Hermann, Rechtswissenschaft und Soziologie. In Verhandlungen des Ersten Deutschen Soziologentages, pp.323-330. esp. p.329. Tübingen, Mohr.

————. 1911-13. Wirtschaft und Gesellschaft. Winckelmann, Johannes (ed.). Köln-Berlin, Kiepenheuer & Witsch, 1956, esp. Ch.I, par.1. Tr. in Weber, The theory of social and economic organization. Henderson, A. M., and Talcott Parsons (trs.). New York, Oxford University Press, 1947, esp. pp.89 ff.

Wolff, Kurt H. 1943. The sociology of knowledge: emphasis on an empirical attitude. Philosophy of Science 10: 104-123.

————. 1952. The collection and organization of field materials: a research report. Ohio Journal of Science 52: 49-61, esp. p. 49 and n.2. Repr. in Adams, R. N., and J. J. Preiss (eds.), Human organization research: field relations and techniques. Homewood, Ill., Dorsey Press, 1960, pp.240-254, esp. p. 240 and n.2.

————. 1959. The sociology of knowledge and sociological theory. In Gross, Llewellyn (ed.), Symposium on sociological theory, pp.567-602. Evanston, Ill., Row, Peterson.

————. 1967. The sociology of knowledge in the United States of America. Current Sociology/La sociologie contemporaine, Vol. XV. No. 1. The Hague-Paris, Mouton. Pp.56.

Znaniecki, Florian. 1940. The social role of the man of knowledge. New York, Columbia University Press. Pp. 212.

21. Some Comments on History as a Moral Discipline: "Transcending 'Textbook' Chronicles and Apologetics"

George W. Stocking, Jr.

The part of my title in quotation marks paraphrases a passage in the original prospectus for the conference. It was assigned to me by the organizers, who wished me to draw on experience as a historian of anthropology to offer some kind of historiographical guidelines for a developing field of historical inquiry. That role seemed to me a bit presumptuous for a non-linguist, and I chose instead to try to explore a linguistic problem closely related to my anthropological interests. At this point, the title quoted above seems even more presumptuous, since the quality of the papers suggests that the historiography of linguistics is perhaps somewhat more advanced than that of anthropology. However, the organizers have not relented from their original plan, and finding it thus impossible to avoid presuming, I will enter wholeheartedly into the spirit of the title attributed to me, and offer a sermon on the one true path to historical truth. As in most sermons, little of what I say will be strikingly original. But it is the burden of my sermon that the special discipline of history is more a moral than a scientific one; and in inculcating any moral discipline, originality is perhaps less important than reiteration (cf. Stocking 1965a).

The text for today will be a passage from Professor Hoenigswald:

> Our feeling that scientific linguistics begins around 1800; in other words, that our understanding of the writings from that time on is immediate and direct and no longer in need of the historian's services—that feeling is only slightly less deceptive in the case of Schlegel and Bopp than it was in the case of Jones (Hoenigswald 1963: 3-4).

To "open" the text I would suggest that its phrasing can be read as implying several different views of the nature of scientific development which have in common an emphasis on *continuity* as opposed to *discontinuity*. Thus one can extract from the passage reference to a rather atemporal view in which at a certain point scientific linguistics "begins"—and henceforth everything is part of the same unbroken universe of discourse. In this framework, one may enter into direct debate with the figures of the past. Boas may have been "wrong" on a particular issue, but we can still confront his errors directly. Conversely, he may have been "right"—and though rectitude may have been obscured by intervening years, our renewed perception of it still has in a sense the character of direct discovery. At most it involves a brushing away of cobwebs and a slight reformulation of language.

In fact, of course, such a static viewpoint can be maintained only in relation to specific issues, since everyone knows that science progresses, and "progress" inevitably separates our universe of discourse from that of the past, at least in cumulative terms. From this point of view, we can extract a second model from our text, in which the directness of communication varies over time with the progress of science. We communicate with Bopp more directly than with Jones, and more directly still with Boas. Science and non-science, communication and self-deception are on two continua, science and communication rising together as their opposites fall toward the present.

Such an optimistic Whiggish view of course faces the problem of "dark ages"—periods in which the general progress was halted, as from a certain point of view the progress of linguistics was halted with Humboldt, only to have resumed with the early works of Chomsky. Still, for those in the present who have recovered the right path, communication with the Cartesian grammarians long dismissed as non-scientific is so direct and immediate that paraphrase and quotation may reduce explication almost to the vanishing point (cf. Chomsky 1966).

If all this sounds a bit simpleminded, I would suggest that much which linguists and other scientists *qua* historians write about their past rests implicitly on precisely the assumption that our communication with the past is "immediate and direct," or can be made so with a minimum reformulation of the language of texts. The most obvious example is the frequent search for "precursors" of a given point of view in the present. Now doubtless there are "precursors" for every present viewpoint; and much of the rhetoric of traditional conceptions of history in fact legitimizes an approach to the past in terms of continuity: " . . .plus c'est la même chose," "the seamless web," and the like. But it is the "doctrine" of this sermon that *discontinuity* in history is as important as *continuity*; that our perception of the past may not be immediate and direct even in the case of figures much closer to us in time than Bopp; that the problems of historical continuity and directness of perception are in fact among the most important points at issue in any historical inquiry, and should therefore never be assumed in advance; and finally, that from a heuristic point of view, one is perhaps better off assuming their opposites.

As "reasons" or "proofs" of this doctrine, I will offer only two: one by way of metahistorical elaboration, the other by way of illustrative example.

As for the former, let me begin by offering two primitive visual metaphors of the movement of the history of science. One of them (which I have already suggested) sees history in rather simple vertical linear terms, allowing of course for dark ages. The corresponding visual metaphor might be an arrow, or the graph of a bull market—but in each case the movement is linear and upward in a two-dimensional framework. The other representation is discontinuous and multidimensional, and in it synchrony is as important as diachrony. In these terms history can be viewed as a series of pie plates stacked somewhat irregularly one upon another. The irregularity is important, for the pie plates themselves have thickness in time—what we are in fact investigating as intellectual historians are "contexts of assumption" which exist through time in complex interrelation with each other. At this point, visual representation breaks down, but the pie-plate metaphor perhaps does serve to emphasize the element of discontinuity in history, the importance of synchronic or horizontal contextual analysis, and the somewhat problematic character of diachronic relationships. Futhermore, the opacity of pie plates may help to remind us of the problems inherent in historical perception from the top of the pile.

Now linguists are by no means unaware of similar ways of viewing historical phenomena. Hockett's well-known article on models of grammatical description in the twentieth-century lends itself to interpretation in these terms (Hockett 1954). And by now, many scholars outside the history of science are quite familiar with Thomas Kuhn's conception of the scientific "paradigm" (Kuhn 1962)—a more or less integrated world view based on shared assumptions about the nature of the scientist's universe and the questions which one may appropriately ask of it. In these terms, men with different scientific orientations will always in one way or another be talking past each other, even when the problem they are discussing is apparently the same. In these terms, each scientific (or linguistic) orientation is a kind of culture—or if one prefers, a language—and the starting point of historical understanding must be an attempt to analyze it in its own terms, which must be assumed to differ in various ways—many of them not immediately perceivable—from those of the contemporary scientific observer.

Regarding Kuhn's schema simply as a useful heuristic metaphor (and begging the question of whether linguistics is in Kuhn's terms a science, or whether all science in fact moves in terms of his model), let us turn now to the illustrative example. In the course of working on "the Boas plan" I came across another interpretation of Boas' linguistic work in the period of the *Handbook*. I refer to that advanced by Paul Postal (1964) in attacking a later characterization of Boas by both Carl and Florence Voegelin in 1963. According to Postal, the Voegelins maintained that Boas' views were "on all but a single crucial point, substantially those of certain modern conceptions of linguistic practice." Against this, Postal maintained that Boas was even more "modern" than the Voegelins pictured him, "being in fact a rough early version of the position now held by Halle, Chomsky, and others considering phonology from the point of view of generative grammar" (Postal 1964: 269).

Without going into the details of Postal's argument, I would simply note that it is based primarily on a reinterpretation of a single article by Boas on the Iroquois language which was the product of the work he undertook in connection with Hewitt's proposed sketch for the *Handbook*. By reformulating several of Boas' arguments, Postal attempted to show that "the Voegelins' claim that Boas' structuralizing was 'monolevel' is true only if one insists that a second level in phonology be the intermediate level of taxonomic phonemics" (271), and that Boasian phonology in fact "contained rules which can only be formalized as transformations" (273). Postal suggested that the Voegelins' claim that Boas was "pre-phonemic" tends to imply that the development of phonemics was "an improvement" in the history of linguistics (276). From Postal's point of view, of course, the Voegelins are associated with a recent "dark age" in that history, and to show that Emeneau's "ancestor in learning" of us all was *really* a kind of transformationist is quite important in legitimating the true succession of progressive historical development.

I do not feel sufficiently competent in linguistics to evaluate much of Postal's argument. Indeed there are portions of it that I could only read with difficulty. However, I would note that in arguing Boas' recognition of two levels of phonology, Postal was compelled to note that the distinction was "still rudimentary and implicit" (272) and inconsistently maintained. And I could not help feeling that through it all there ran a consistent current of anachronism.

But for present purposes, the point is simply that between Voegelin and Postal there is some difference in present orientation in linguistic theory, and that in this context two quite different views of Boas emerge. If this is not surprising, it does serve to confirm our "doctrine": even in the case of figures so close to us in time as Boas, we must reject the notion that our perception of the linguistic past is necessarily immediate or direct. It is all too easily obscured by the dust of grinding axes (and indeed this may be more true in the case of figures who, unlike Dionysius Thrax, are close enough still to "matter"). The important point, however, is that if the starting point of intellectual history must be to analyze each "paradigm"—or context of assumption—in its own terms, then the first task is clearly to get at the questions which *defined* that context, since it was *these questions* (and not the ones which agitate linguists today) to which the ideas of our historical subjects were *answers* (cf. R. G. Collingwood and J. R. Levenson, as discussed in Stocking 1965a). Posed in pungent colloquial language, the central question of intellectual history is *"what was bugging him?"* It follows that a central methodological problem is to sort out what is bugging *us* (which may indeed motivate our historical interest) from what was bugging *him*.

In this context, and continuing in the model of the Puritan sermon, let us turn to the "uses" or "applications" of our "doctrine"—that is, to the "services of the historian." To begin with, one might note that the approach to historical phenomena I am advocating is by no means wholly unfamiliar to linguists. Indeed, there is a sense in which all I am arguing is that the history of linguistics, like that of anthropology (Stocking 1965b: 144), must be approached much as practitioners of these disciplines approach the subject matter of their inquiry in the present. Pursuing this comparison a step further, I would suggest that just as linguists would certainly insist that the analysis of linguistic structures is only possible through methods requiring some training and discipline, so must we reject the notion that the understanding of historical contexts of assumption is an easy and common-sense sort of inquiry which any scholar can carry on in his spare time or his retirement. On the other hand, I suspect that historical phenomena are by nature sufficiently less systematic than linguistic phenomena that historical analysis will never be routinized in the way certain portions of linguistic analysis have been. But assuming all this is true what, exactly, are the services of the historian?

First I would suggest that they do not seem to me to be fruitfully formulated in terms of an "historical method" that is sharply distinguishable from scientific method, or from careful scholarship, or from rigorous thought in general. My own sense of the context of late nineteenth and early twentieth-century anthropology has its ultimate methodological basis in a content analysis of 500 articles in contemporary journals of social science which I carried on for my doctoral dissertation (Stocking 1960). But as originally conceived, there was nothing uniquely historical about the method of this analysis. On the contrary, it represented a rather self-conscious departure from traditional styles of intellectual history. Indeed, most of the more interesting methodological and conceptual orientations in recent historiography have come from outside of history itself, usually from the social sciences. As a result, I have been rather embarrassed on several occasions when some anthropologist friends were inclined to extrapolate from some of my efforts the existence of a "historical method" anthropologists must master if they were to write serious history. Once behind the barriers of language which may face any humanist scholar, and once beyond the periods when such skills as paleography are necessary, it seems to me that the "methods" of the old historical handbooks—internal and external criticism and all that—contain little that is really peculiar to history. Thus when a graduate student in anthropology once came to me for advice on historical method, there was little that I could offer beyond the suggestion that if he took a seminar with me, he might at the end feel he had learned something about the matter.

Implicit in that suggestion was the second aspect of the historian's services in the explication of contexts: experience. For it seems to me that the special competence of the historian is largely a matter of extended experience in the materials of a particular portion of the past. Once immersed, by whatever methods, in the sources of late nineteenth-century social science and the writings of Boas, certain things become much more readily evident: that the figure of Daniel Garrison Brinton is usually lurking somewhere in the background of Boas' theoretical and methodological concerns; and that Boas' anthropology was conditioned by evolutionism and racism in a way it is difficult for us to appreciate even in the context of our present image of Boas as arch anti-evolutionist. (We tend to see only the subsequent impact of his critique, whereas the crucial problem is the way Boas defined his questions in an evolutionary context.) But if this lived or relived experience of context requires much time and effort, it is nothing that in principle is unavailable to the non-historian.

I am inclined to argue—and here I return to the theme I suggested at the outset—that what is most characteristic of the historian (or of the historian as I conceive him ideally) is best described in terms of attitude, of a kind of moral posture that is ultimately premised on an act of faith. There are good philosophical grounds for rejecting this faith as self-delusory. But there seem to me good practical grounds for arguing that it is a necessary self-delusion, one indeed that we must cultivate assiduously.

The historical attitude involves not only the notion that in some sense the pie plates are "there," but also the belief that we can somehow overcome the distortion of intervening perspectives and see each context of assumption in its own terms. Immediately, we are confronted with various epistemological paradoxes. We can not afford to disregard subsequent perspectives completely, if only because it is their origins that are often the ultimate object of our historical study. And there is no doubt that the variety of our present preconceptions may often serve to illuminate facets of the past that would otherwise go unobserved. Futhermore, there is a sense in which our understanding of the past is only possible in terms of the perspectives and the knowledge of the present: it depends on the one hand on the objectification of the past which accompanies the passage of time, and on the other on the application to the past of the analytic categories of our present knowledge of human behavior. Most paradoxically of all, we are ultimately trying to achieve a knowledge of the past which transcends that which was possible to its actors, and which must transcend the terms in which they saw themselves.

Quite aside from these qualifications deriving from the paradoxical tensions between present and past inherent in historical understanding, the history of historical revisionism is enough to make us doubt the possibility that we may ever hope to "overcome the distortion of intervening perspectives." Nonetheless, this ideal seems to me essential to historical study even as that study calls into question its possibility. And the only way we can approach it is by a willing and self-conscious suspension, not only, as in the theater, of our "disbelief," but more importantly, of our "belief" as well—and particularly of those beliefs which relate most directly in the present to the subjects of our past investigation: in the present case, our beliefs about the true nature of linguistic method and theory.

Whatever the paradoxes it is entangled with, this suspension of belief seems to me a necessary methodological norm. For it we grant that commitment may sometimes illuminate, the fact that it frequently obfuscates is undeniable. Nor is this surprising. To seek the origin of our beliefs is quite a different thing than to seek to validate them. To apply the analytic categories of our present knowledge of human behavior to the issues of the past is quite a different thing than to impose on the past the preconceptions we hold on such issues in the present. To understand the past from the perspective of its consequent future is quite a different thing than to import that future into the past.

In each case, the difference, ultimately, seems to me one of attitude. The historical attitude incorporates the norm of disinterested and objective study which is common to all science. But it also goes a step further. It involves a respect for the element of uniqueness in each individual human phenomenon, for the integrity of the past—a willingness to see it in its own terms even as we attempt to transcend them. It is this attitude which underlies the tradition of "historicism," the concept of "*verstehen*," and the lengthy epistemological justifications of the independence of the *Geistes-wissenschaften*. It is not necessary to accept these justifications in order to adopt this attitude as a working tool. But it is necessary to become self-consciously aware of, and in a sense to suspend, the beliefs and commitments which tend to make respect and understanding impossible. It is this essentially moral posture that underlies the methodology of history.

Even at this point, however, we may still question whether there is anything unique about the historian's services. The historical attitude would in fact seem to differ little from the posture of the anthropological field worker, as exemplified in Franz Boas' approach to American Indian languages.

Furthermore, even if it might be argued that the historian has a certain attitudinal advantage stemming from his non-involvement in modern linguistics, from another point of view that same non-involvement can be a serious limitation in treating the history of linguistics. The historian will be much better able to treat broad questions concerning the relation of race and language, or of linguistic and evolutionary theory, or the origins and philosophy of language, than the technical issues which constitute much of the history of linguistics proper. It is not simply that I have trouble following Postal's argument. I also have difficulty reading the *Handbook of American Indian Languages*, or interpreting the field notes of Boas, or the field reports of Sapir—all of which made "The Boas Plan" a most difficult historical project for me, and still leave me dissatisfied with portions of the argument. Perhaps given time and effort enough I could solve these problems, but the point is rather that there is a real need for a kind of micro-historical study which can only be carried on by people with technical linguistic competence. A number of the papers of this symposium fall into precisely this category, and several of them seem to me of excellent quality. But until this sort of work is carried on more systematically, general histories of linguistics will continue to have a good bit the character of textbook chronicles.

On the other hand, there is in some of the symposium papers a certain narrowness of focus. One is tempted to suggest that if we are really to transcend chronicle there should be much more to the history of linguistics than the internal account of its technical development. There is, as I tried to indicate in my paper, another kind of micro-history which, where documentation exists, can also be extremely illuminating: the study of the interaction patterns of the men who form the community of linguistics in any given period or place. And at a somewhat broader level, there is the whole question of placing these interactions, the technical history of linguistics, and the broader issues of linguistic theory all within the most meaningful framework of social, cultural, and intellectual context, as Greene and Wolff have suggested in their papers. Perhaps for these tasks, the historian and the sociologist of knowledge might be of real help.

For better or worse, however, I suspect that the main burden of the history of linguistics will for some time to come be carried by linguists themselves. I have argued that in principle there is nothing to prevent them from carrying it. Nonetheless, the fact that I was asked to talk, and the topic given me, suggest that a problem may be felt still to exist. In this context, then, perhaps there is still justification for the "services of the historian." And a service is exactly what I have offered you: a sermon exhorting you to embrace and keep the faith.

REFERENCES

Chomsky, Noam. 1966. Cartesian linguistics: a chapter in the history of rationalist thought. New York, Harper and Row.

Hockett, C. F. 1954. Two models of grammatical description. Word 10: 210-234.

Hoenigswald, H. M. 1963. On the history of the comparative method. Anthropological Linguistics 5(1): 1-11.

Kuhn, Thomas. 1962. The structure of scientific revolutions. Chicago, University of Chicago Press.

Postal, P. M. 1964. Boas and the development of phonology: comments based on Iroquoian. International Journal of American Linguistics 30: 269-280.

Stocking, G. W., Jr. 1960. American social scientists and race theory: 1890-1915. Unpublished doctoral dissertation, University of Pennsylvania.

——. 1965a. On the limits of "presentism" and "historicism" in the historiography of the behavioral sciences. Journal of the History of the Behavioral Sciences 1: 211-218.

——. 1965b. "Cultural Darwinism" and "philosophical idealism" in E. B. Tylor: a special plea for historicism in the history of anthropology. Southwestern Journal of Anthropology 21: 130-147.

Voegelin, C. F. and F. M. 1963. On the history of structuralizing in 20th century America. Anthropological Linguistics 5(1): 12-37.